Lecture Notes in Computer Science 2455

Edited by G. Goos, J. Hartmanis, and J. van Leeuwen

T0217180

Springer
Berlin
Heidelberg
New York
Barcelona
Hong Kong
London
Milan
Paris
Tokyo

Kurt Bauknecht   A Min Tjoa
Gerald Quirchmayr (Eds.)

E-Commerce and Web Technologies

Third International Conference, EC-Web 2002
Aix-en-Provence, France, September 2-6, 2002
Proceedings

Springer

Series Editors

Gerhard Goos, Karlsruhe University, Germany
Juris Hartmanis, Cornell University, NY, USA
Jan van Leeuwen, Utrecht University, The Netherlands

Volume Editors

Kurt Bauknecht,
IFI, University of Zurich
Winterthurer Straße 190, 8057 Zürich, Switzerland
E-mail: baukn@ifi.unizh.ch

A Min Tjoa
Institute of Software Technology and Interactive Systems
Vienna University of Technology, Favoritenstraße 9-11/188
1040 Vienna, Austria
E-mail: tjoa@ifs.tuwien.ac.at

Gerald Quirchmayr
Institute of Computer Science and Business Informatics
University of Vienna, Liebiggasse 4, 1010 Vienna, Austria
E-mail: Gerald.Quirchmayr@univie.ac.at

Cataloging-in-Publication Data applied for

Die Deutsche Bibliothek - CIP-Einheitsaufnahme

E-commerce and web technologies : third international conference ;
proceedings / EC Web 2002, Aix-en-Provence, France, September 2 - 6,
2002. Kurt Bauknecht ... (ed.). - Berlin ; Heidelberg ; New York ; Barcelona ;
Hong Kong ; London ; Milan ; Paris ; Tokyo : Springer, 2002
   (Lecture notes in computer science ; Vol. 2455)
   ISBN 3-540-44137-9

CR Subject Classification (1998): C.2, K.4.4, H.4, H.3, K.6, J.1, J.4

ISSN 0302-9743
ISBN 3-540-44137-9 Springer-Verlag Berlin Heidelberg New York

Springer-Verlag Berlin Heidelberg New York
a member of BertelsmannSpringer Science+Business Media GmbH

http://www.springer.de

© Springer-Verlag Berlin Heidelberg 2002
Printed in Germany

Typesetting: Camera-ready by author, data conversion by PTP-Berlin, Stefan Sossna e. K.
Printed on acid-free paper   SPIN: 10871152   06/3142   5 4 3 2 1 0

Preface

The Third International Conference on E-commerce and Web Technology (EC-Web 2002) was held in conjunction with the DEXA 02 in Aix-en-Provence, France. This conference, first held in Greenwich, United Kingdom in 2000, is now in its third year and is very well established. As in the two previous years, it served as a forum bringing together researchers from academia and commercial developers from industry to discuss the current state of the art in E-commerce and web technology. Inspirations and new ideas emerged from intensive discussions during formal sessions and social events.

Keynote addresses, research presentations, and discussions during the conference helped to further develop the exchange of ideas among the researchers, developers, and practitioners who attended.

The conference attracted more than 100 submissions and each paper was reviewed by at least three program committee members. The program committee selected 40 papers for presentation and publication, a task which was not easy due to the high quality of the submitted papers.

We would like to express our thanks to our colleagues who helped to put together the technical program: the program committee members and external reviewers for their timely and rigorous reviews of the papers, and the organizing committee for their help in the administrative work and support. We owe special thanks to Gabriela Wagner and Maria Schweikert for always being available when their helping hand was needed.

Finally, we would like to thank all the authors who submitted papers, authors who presented papers, and the participants who together made this conference an intellectually stimulating event through their active contributions.

We had a successful conference and hope that you enjoyed the hospitality of Aix-en-Provence.

September 2002

A Min Tjoa (TU Wien, Austria)
Gerald Quirchmayr (Universität Wien, Austria
and University of South Australia)

Program Committee

General Chair
Kurt Bauknecht, University of Zurich, Switzerland

Program Chairs
Gerald Quirchmayr, University of South Australia
A Min Tjoa, Vienna University of Technology, Austria

Program Committee
Karl Aberer, EPFL Lausanne, Switzerland
Antonio Badia, University of Louisville, USA
Chaitan Baru, University of California San Diego, USA
Bharat Bhargava, Purdue University, USA
Anjali Bhargava, TRW, USA
Sourav Saha Bhowmick, Nanyang Technological University, Singapore
Martin Bichler, IBM T.J. Watson Research Center, USA
Walter Brenner, University of Essen, Germany
Stephane Bressan, National University of Singapore, Singapore
Wojciech Cellary, The Poznan University of Economics, Poland
Roger Clarke, The Australian National University, Australia
Asuman Dogac, Middle East Technical University, Turkey
Eduardo Fernandez, Florida Atlantic University, USA
Elena Ferrari, University of Milano, Italy
Farshad Fotouhi, Wayne State University, USA
Yongjian, Fu, University of Missouri-Rolla, USA
Chanan Glezer, Ben Gurion University, Beer Sheva, Israel
Rüdiger Grimm, Technical University Ilmenau, Germany
Kamalakar Karlapalem, HKUST, China
Hiroyuki Kitagawa, University of Tsukuba, Japan
Wolfgang Koenig, University of Frankfurt, Germany
Vijay Kumar, University of Missouri-Kansas City, USA
Karl Kurbel, Europe University Frankfurt (Oder), Germany
Winfried Lamersdorf, University of Hamburg, Germany
George Lausen, University of Freiburg, Germany
Alberto Leander, Federal University of Minas Gerais, Brazil
Juhnyoung Lee, IBM T. J. Watson Research Center, USA
Ronald M. Lee, Erasmus University, The Netherlands
Tan Kian Lee, National University of Singapore, Singapore
Qing Li, City University of Hong Kong, Chin
Ee Peng Lim, Nanyang Technological University, Singapore
Huan Liu, Arizona State University, USA
Heinrich C. Mayr, University of Klagenfurt, Austria
Michael Merz, Ponton GmbH, Germany

External Reviewers

Anya Sotiropoulou
George Lepouras
Thomi Pilioura
Torsten Priebe
Torsten Schlichting
Fredj Dridi
Holger Grabow
Markus Hütten
Natwar Modani
Biplav Srivastava
Manish Bhide
Fabien Petitcolas
Heiko Rossnagel
LIAU Chu Yee
Altigran Soares da Silva
Paulo Braz Golgher
Wagner Meira Junior
Edleno Silva de Moura
Radek Vigralek
L. Braubach
D. Fahrenholtz
A. Pokahr
C. Zirpins
Joan Fons
Silvia Abrahao
Yan Wang
Ruediger Zarnekow
Zoran Despotovic
Wojciech Wiza
Jarogniew Rykowski
Thomas Schlienger
Andreas Erat
Martin Steinert

Table of Contents

Security and Privacy I

Recommender Systems

Emerging Standards

Security and Privacy II

Business Models

E-payment

Position Paper

Enabling Virtual Enterprises: A Case for Multi-disciplinary Research

I.T. Hawryszkiewycz
Faculty of Information Technology
University of Technology, Sydney
igorh@it.uts.edu.au

Abstract: The paper begins by defining different kinds of virtual enterprises and the kinds of support needed to make them sustainable. The paper identifies three requirements must be satisfied. These are technology that supports interaction across distance, a favorable organizational culture and the desire to share knowledge. All must be present to result in sustainable virtual organizations. Thus participants in such organizations must be willing to share knowledge, be encouraged to do so by their work environment and have suitable services provided by technologies for this purpose. The paper concludes with some examples of research questions that need to be addressed.

1   Introduction

Virtual organization is a term that is frequently used by often not clearly defined. Too many this simply means working across distance. However, a more generic definition extends this to include the possibility of transient members that make up virtual communities. Furthermore any such definition must recognize the importance of social aspects of managing relationships [13] including criteria of developing trust and shared goals. Knowledge is another enabler. New knowledge is continually needed to develop improved products and services [14, 5] and the way business is done. Virtual organizations that provide such knowledge are more likely to be sustainable. In summary a successful virtual organization must somehow combine the three dimensions shown in Figure 1. This requires technologies that allow community relationships to evolve in ways that allow community members to gain benefit through the sharing and creation of knowledge.

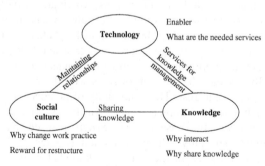

Fig. 1. The major Dimensions

K. Bauknecht, A M. Tjoa, G. Quirchmayr (Eds.): EC-Web 2002, LNCS 2455, pp. 1–6, 2002.

2   Community and Team Building

Virtual community means different things to different people. Sometimes people simply using the same repository like common file repository are termed as a community. Communities have been defined more specifically by Carrol (1998) and Mynatt (1998). The more specific ways include shared goals and multiple interaction styles. These can depend on community characteristics such as those shown in Figure 2. These are:

The length of relationship between participating members,
The degree of separation ranging from loosely to strongly coupled,
The degree of focus, that is, whether there is a specific objective to be met by the team.

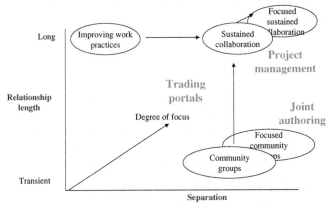

Fig. 2. Evolving organizations

Some examples in Figure 2 include trading portals, which are partially transient, joint authoring, which is more focused but often more transient and project management [2], which tends to extend over time. One distinguishing characteristic here can be community governance [10]. The governance on transient and widely separated community groups is usually minimal. In contrast governance in more focused groups is formalized, usually through the creation of roles with defined responsibilities and greater requirement placed on trust. The community of practice can include a variety of roles. In more elaborate environments, there can be owners, experts, novices or apprentices as well as a variety of users. Many writers also see shared terminologies [1, 4] to be important especially where interaction is intense. Research has also indicated interesting differences in the way new knowledge evolves. Results [17] indicate that loosely coupled teams often search finding than strongly coupled teams or that loose terminology can reduce collaboration in multi-disciplinary teams [4].

2.1 Virtual Project Teams

Research has also indicated the way focused teams evolve and place greater emphasis on process such as that shown in Figure 3, which illustrates the stages of team development [12] and what can be done face-to-face and across distance. Basically they suggest that trust building and goal formation often take place through face to face meetings whereas implementation of agreed goals can be done asynchronously.

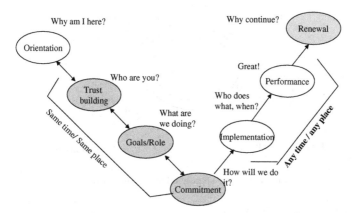

Fig. 3. Team dynamics

Project management groups [2] have more focus with shared goals and trust becoming important. Trust is an important component here. One interesting article [15] on trust is discusses identification of virtuous and virtual cycles. For example, loss of trust is often resolved through increasing the frequency of face-to-face meetings.

3   Knowledge Sharing

The next issue is what is needed to improve knowledge sharing and the services needed to support it. Nonaka sees knowledge sharing and creation following the process shown in Figure 4. These identify the kind of activities that are fundamental to knowledge management and identify needed services.

Nonaka's process includes four phases. The first phase is socialization where people bring together their experiences and share insights in an area. For example, this may be exchange of views of how a particular product was sold to clients. The next step, externalization, is where some of this captured expertise is interpreted into a form that can lead to some actions. In other words how to market the product in a customer's specific context to maximize the likelyhood of achieving a sale. The discussions now focus on identifying new ideas that are now externalized in familiar contexts to see their relevance to specific issues. This often requires the interpretation of new concepts in local terms requiring a clear terminology to articulate the ideas within new contexts. It also includes showing in explicit terms how a product could be used.

The ideas are then combined where necessary with existing information and then applied in practice during internalization. Any outcomes of any actions evaluated in further socialization and the cycle is repeated. Nonaka goes further and defines the environments under which knowledge sharing can effectively take place. He suggests that knowledge is only meaningful within a context and its environment.

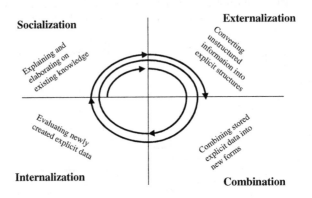

Fig. 4. Nonaka's knowledge creation process

3.1 Knowledge Sharing Services

The question then is what kind of services must be provided to encourage knowledge sharing, as for example the importance of a variety of services in teaching [9]. These they claim are required to give students the ability to do something. Strategies are also important here. There is for example a distinction between personalization and codification [7] found in business. Personalization is more likely to need services that encourage synchronous exchanges whereas codification calls for services such as filtering, classifying and the construction of databases.

4   Technologies

One view of technology is as a provider of services to support virtual communities. The variety of services includes:

Collaborative services including ways for community members to socialize and exchange messages and can include management services to organize communities..

Management services including registration and subscription services, setting up community roles and inviting people into the community and assignment of services to these members.

Discovery services including search engines, catalog systems. They include ways for learners to not only find relevant information but also to learn how to use this information in their environment.

Knowledge services including ways to capture and organize the body of knowledge and maintain knowledge maps and repositories based on some agreed metamodel structure. Knowledge services include the capture of experiences and interpreting them for inclusion in the body of knowledge.

The kind of services needed depend on the kind of virtual community. Simple bulletin boards form initial technologies. Application activities depend on the kind of application allowing the system to be used with a business purpose in mind. For example, in learning this may be self-assessment, group case analysis, or joint review of a document [9]. Trading services may include registration, searching, negotiation and others. Portals present a basis for combining a number of services to serve a virtual community.

4.1 Portal Structures

Figure 5 illustrates the portal structure at the highest level of abstraction. It has a body of knowledge, knowledge management services and a community of practice that uses the services in their business processes and adds to the body of knowledge.

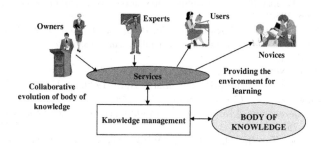

Fig. 5. The portal approach

4.2 Introducing Technologies

The last question to be addressed is how to introduce technologies to match the growth of virtual communities. It is not likely that participants will quickly adopt all services needed in a sustainable community. The chances of success are greater if services are introduced gradually continually as participant's experience grows. Generally the introduction can follow the steps [16] that start with socialization, followed by information exchange, then joint project work.

5   Summary

The paper described the main dimensions that make up successful virtual organizations. It suggested that a successful organization must balance social issues with technical design and facilitate knowledge sharing and creation. It developed a technical framework based on services for such organizations. Typical research directions that must be addressed are:

Processes that characterize different kinds of communities and the kinds of services
needed to improve knowledge sharing across these communities,

Overcoming social barriers to working with transient team members, or

How to progress early communities from socialization to more focused activities.

References

1. Boland, R.J. and Tenkasi, R.V. (1995): "Perspective Making and Perspective Taking in Communities of Knowing" in Fulk, J. and DeSanctis, G., (editors) (1995): *Focused Issue on Electronic Communication and Changing Organizational Forms, Organizational Science*, Vol. 6, No. 4, July-August, 1995.
2. Carmel, E. "Global Software Teams", Upper Saddle Hill, Prentice-Hall, 1999.
3. Carroll, J.M.. and Rosson, M.B. "Network Communities, Community Networks" CHI98 18-23 April.
4. Dougherty, D. (1992): "Interpretive Barriers to Successful Product Innovation in Large Firms", Organizational Science, Vol. 3. No. 2, May 1992, pp. 179-202.
5. Grant, R.M. (1996): "Prospering in Dynamically-competitive Environments: Organizational Capability as Knowledge Integration" *Organization Science*, Vol. 7, No. 4, July 1996, pp. 375-387.
6. Hansen, M.T. (1999): "The Search-Transfer Problem: The Role of Weak Ties in Sharing Knowledge across Organizational Sub-Units", *Administrative Science Quaterly*, 44 (1999), pp. 82-11.
7. Hansen, M.T., Nohria, N. and Tierney, T. (1999): "Whats your Strategy for Managing Knowledge" Harvard Business Review, March-April, 1999, pp. 106-116.
8. Hawryszkiewycz, I.T. (2000): "Knowledge Networks in Administrative Systems" *Working Conference on Advances in Electronic Government*, Zarazoga, Spain, February 2000, pp. 59-75.
9. Hiltz, R. and Turoff, M. (2002): "What makes learning networks effective?" Communications of the ACM, Vol. 45, No. 4, April, 2002, pp. 56-59.
10. Jones, C.T., Hesterly, W.S., and S.P. Borgatti (1997): A General Theory of Network Governance: Exchange Conditions and Social Mechanisms. *Academy of Management Review*, Vol. 22, No. 4, October, 1997, pp. 911-945.
11. Mynatt, E.D. Adler, A. Mizuko, I., O'Day, V.L. "Designing for Network Communities" CHI97 22-27 March, 1997..Nonaka, I. (1994): "A Dynamic Theory of Organizational Knowledge Creation" *Organization Science*, Vol. 5, No. 1, February 1994, pp. 14-37.
12. O'Hara-Devereaux, M., and Johansen, R. (1994): *GlobalWork: Bridging Distance, Culture and Time* Jossey-Bass Publishers, San Francisco.
13. Quresh, S. and Zigurs, I. (2001): "Paradoxes and Prerogatives in Global Virtual Collaboration" Communications of the ACM, Vol. 44, No. 12, December 2001, pp., 85-88.
14. Riggins, F.J. and Rhee , H-K. (1998): "Developing the Learning Network Using Extranets" *Proceedings of the Thirty-First Hawaiian Conference on Systems Sciences*, January 1998.
15. Sabherwal, R. (1999): "The Role of Trust in Outsourced IS Development Projects: Communications of the ACM, Vol. 42, No. 2., February, 1999, PP. 80-86.
16. Salmon, G. (2000): "E-Moderating: The Key to Teaching and Learning Online" Stylus Publishing, Sterling, VA.
17. Szulanski, G. (1996): "Exploring Internal stickiness: Impediments to the transfer of best practice within the firm", *Strategic Management Journal*, Vol. 17, Winter Special Issue, pp. 27-43.

Increasing Realized Revenue in a
Web Based Dutch Auction

Ravi Kothari[1]*, Mukesh Mohania[1], and Yahiko Kambayashi[2]

[1] IBM - India Research Laboratory
Block I - IIT Hauz Khas, New Delhi - 110016, India
{rkothari, mkmukesh}@in.ibm.com

[2] Department of Social Informatics
Kyoto University, Kyoto, Japan
yahiko@kuis.kyoto-u.ac.jp

Abstract. One variant of the Dutch auction roughly corresponds to a multi-unit, progressively ascending, uniform price, lowest winning bid, open auction. The overall revenue realized by the auctioneer in such an auction is given by $R = Q \times p_W$ where, Q is the number of units of the item being auctioned, and p_W is the lowest winning bid price at the end of the auction. R is only dependent on p_W (Q being fixed) and an interesting question is whether it is possible to increase R.

Proposed in this paper is a method for increasing p_W (and consequently R). Given that the maximum bid that a bidder places reflects his or her valuation, our method relies on increasing the valuation of those bidders whose valuations are in close proximity to the lowest winning bid price. We propose achieving this objective through the use of a coupon, which is introduced at an algorithmically determined time during the auction, and which, if introduced, assumes a non-decreasing face value. The coupon can be used by all participants — the price paid by participants with winning bids utilizing the coupon is discounted by the face value of the coupon at the end of the auction process. Assuming other things are equal, participants with bids at or near the lowest winning bid price during the auction are more likely to use the coupon and increase their bids by an amount in excess of their valuation (the excess being recovered through the use of the coupon) thereby creating additional competition and potentially increasing p_W.

We present an algorithm that determines, based on present auction dynamics, if a coupon should be introduced, the initial face value of it, and possible subsequent revisions of the coupon face value. We also present a simple example to illustrate the algorithmic steps and illustrate the increase in R that results as a consequence of the proposed methodology.

1   Introduction

One variant of the Dutch auction roughly corresponds to a multi-unit, progressively ascending, uniform price, lowest winning bid, open auction and is utilized

---

* On leave from the University of Cincinnati

K. Bauknecht, A M. Tjoa, G. Quirchmayr (Eds.): EC-Web 2002, LNCS 2455, pp. 7–16, 2002.
© Springer-Verlag Berlin Heidelberg 2002

by the popular auction site eBay^{TM}[1] amongst others [2, 3]. Typically, the *auctioneer* or the *seller* has multiple integral units (say, Q) of an item to be auctioned. A *bidder*, say identified by i, enters or revises his previous bid, so that his bid at some time t is for an integral number of units — say, $q_i(t)$, $1 \leq q_i(t) \leq Q$, at a price $p_i(t)$. The quantity-price tuple for a specific bidder is then $(q_i(t), p_i(t))$. Bidders continue to enter or revise bids through the *duration* of the auction. At the end of the auction, all *winning* bidders can purchase the quantity they bid for at the lowest *winning bid* price. The overall revenue realized by the auctioneer in such an auction is given by $R = Q \times p_W$ where, Q is the number of items, and p_W is the lowest winning bid price at the end of the auction.

For example, assume that $Q = 3$ and there are 4 bidders with the following quantity-price tuples at some point of time during the auction: $(1, p_1(t))$, $(2, p_2(t))$, $(1, p_3(t))$, and $(1, p_4(t))$ respectively. Assuming that $p_2(t) > p_4(t) > p_3(t) > p_1(t)$ and that the auction ends at time t, bidders 2 and 4 have the winning bids and each gets the quantity they bid on at the lowest winning bid price (in this case $p_4(t)$).

It is possible that there may not be enough units to fulfill the last winning bidders order. In that case, the bidder may or may not accept a partial order (lesser quantity than that entered in the bid). However, the price to all bidders is still influenced by this partial order. There may be alternate rules for such partial orders; however the specific rules as pertaining to these partial orders are known by all *a priori* and does not influence the main results of our paper.

The advantage of such a Dutch auction is that no buyer regrets another buyer having picked up the same item at a lower price and a sense of satisfaction and equality is experienced by all buyers. That satisfaction notwithstanding, the auctioneer would like to increase the overall revenue R generated from the sale of the item. In this paper, we propose a method for increasing R.

Clearly, R is only dependent on p_W (Q being fixed) and a method for increasing R must necessarily increase p_W. Of course, assuming that each bidder has a fixed valuation (amount that the bidder can afford to or is willing to pay for the item) and each bidder's final bids reflect their individual valuations, it is not possible to increase R (or p_W). Our method thus attempts to increase the valuations of bidders (without additional cost to them) so as to increase R through the use of a coupon. More specifically, we propose issuing a coupon, which is accessible to all, at an algorithmically determined point in the auction and whose face value is non-decreasing. The coupon discounts the actual price paid by a bidder using the coupon by the face value of the coupon. Since the probability of a bidder using a coupon is directly dependent on the proximity of his or her bid to the present lowest winning price, bidders whose bids are near the present lowest winning price are more likely to use the coupon and bid in excess of their valuation at no additional cost to them (the excess being recovered by the bidder from the coupon). Bidders with high valuations are less likely to use the coupon since they do not require additional increase in their bids to be winning bidders. The increase in valuations of bidders with valuations near the lowest winning bid price creates additional competition, raises p_W and increases

R. Of course, it is not always beneficial to introduce a coupon and we provide an algorithm for determining if and when a coupon should be introduced, the face value of the coupon and any possible revision to the face value of the coupon. Amongst other things, the algorithm relies on the auction dynamics such as the rate of bid increments and other factors.

We have laid out the rest of the paper as follows. In Section 2, we detail the specifics of the auction interface. In Section 3, we present the assumptions underlying the proposed methodology and provide a simplified example illustrating the benefits of the proposed methodology. A detailed description of the algorithm which is used to decide if and when to introduce the coupon, its face value and subsequent revisions to the face value appear in Section 4. In Section 5, we provide a realistic example and illustrate the algorithm in a step-by-step fashion. We conclude the paper with some discussion in Section 6.

2   The Auction Interface

In the Web based Dutch auction format considered in this paper, the user navigates to the *auction page* where a textual and/or pictorial description of the product along with other information appear. The entire bidding history of all bidders is visible either on this page or a page linked to the "auction page". A user can enter a new bid (price and quantity) or increase a prior bid after appropriate authentication.

A coupon, if and when offered, is displayed on the "auction page" (where it is accessible to *all* bidders) and is valid only for the duration of the auction. A bidder, on finding the coupon displayed on the "auction page" *acquires* the coupon by clicking on it. At the end of the auction, coupons acquired by winning bidders, are redeemed automatically by the seller by reducing the price paid per unit by an amount equal to the face value of the coupon. Coupons acquired by unsuccessful bidders automatically expire and have no value. The face value of the coupon is non-decreasing, i.e., it may be kept constant or increased but never decreased. A coupon acquired by a bidder *automatically* assumes the latest offered value (irrespective of the value when it was acquired) without any further action on the part of the bidder. The price paid by each winning bidder who have acquired a coupon is thus discounted by the same amount — that amount being the highest face value of the offered coupon.

3   Motivation and Assumptions Underlying the Proposed Algorithm

As stated before, our objective is to maximize the overall revenue, $R = Q \times p_W$, realized by the seller. Here, Q is the number of units and p_W is the lowest winning bid price at the end of the auction. Needless to say, we would like to increase R in a manner that is fair and transparent to *all* bidders.

Our method is based on, and motivated by the fact that (i) not all bidders will use (acquire) the coupon, (ii) bidders whose bid prices are at or near the highest bid price, are less likely to acquire the coupon as compared to those whose bid price is at or near the minimum winning bid price, and (iii) prompted by the coupon, some users may in fact increase their bid by an amount larger than the face value of the coupon and (iv) the effect of bid increases by bidders whose bids are near the minimum winning bid price is increased competition between the bidders. These four factors contribute to increasing the minimum winning bid price resulting in an increase in the total revenue realized by the seller.

3.1   A Simplified Example

A small (and highly simplified) example illustrates the observations outlined above. Assume that there are 2 units of an item and the bidders with the present highest bids (in this paragraph, we are dropping the time index for simplicity of notation) have quantity-price tuples as $(1, p_1)$ and $(1, p_2)$. Say, $p_1 > p_2$. Assuming that the auction ends, the total revenue realized by the seller is $R = p_2 + p_2$. Note that even bidder 1 gets the product at the *lowest winning bid* price. Now assume that a coupon whose face value is p_C is offered and bidder 2 (whose present bid is p_2), acquires the coupon and subsequently raises his bid to $(p_2 + p_C)$. Other bidders may also acquire the coupon but let us assume that bidder's 1 and 2 have the highest bids. The cost to bidder 2 if he or she wins is still p_2 so he or she is very likely to increase the bid. Bidder 1 already has the highest bid and possibly has no interest in increasing the bid. Assuming that these bidders remain the winning bidders at the close of the auction, the revenue realized by the seller is $R = ((p_2 + p_C) + (p_2 + p_C - p_C))$. The value within the first parentheses is the cost to bidder 1 and the value within the second parentheses is the cost to the second bidder (who used the coupon). The revenue has increased to $(2 \times p_2 + p_C)$ as compared to $(2 \times p_2)$!

There is the possibility that each bidder uses the coupon and only raises the bid by an amount equal to the face value of the coupon. In that case, there is no additional revenue that is realized by the seller. There is also a possibility that bidders acquire a coupon and raise their bids by an amount less than the face value of the coupon. In that case, there can be a net decline in revenue. For this reason, the face value of the coupon should typically be started small and gradually increased once the bids increases have been observed. However, in a probabilistic sense, we believe it is more likely that not every bidder will utilize the coupon[3] and it is more likely that bidders will increase their bids by at least the face value of the coupon. Indeed, it is likely that the so-called deal-effect (promotions positively affect sales) will result in bid increases which are larger than the face value of the coupon [4].

Whether or not a coupon is worth issuing at a given time t, and if so, the initial face value $p_C(t)$ of it and subsequent possible increases of the face value are done on the basis of the algorithm described in the next section. The algorithm is based on utilizing the present auction dynamics to compute the expected

---

[3] Not all store shoppers utilize store or manufacturers coupons either!

increase in the revenue and uses the computed value along with the expected cost of issuing the coupon to decide on issuing a coupon as well as revisions to its face value.

3.2   Related Work

Several auction formats, for example, the English auction – an open outcry ascending price auction or the traditional Dutch auction – a descending price auction or the Vickrey auction, have been intensely studied in the economics literature [3, 5] since Vickrey's seminar paper [6]. Even so, there is much lesser work related to multi-unit auctions [7]. To the best of our knowledge, the particular variant of the Dutch auction that we consider in this paper does not have any prior work with which comparisons can be made. In particular, lack of empirical or theoretical studies on the basis on which the expected revenue can be obtained as can be done for other auction formats [8], makes it difficult to accurately assess the impact of our proposed scheme. Nevertheless, the large and potentially global audience of a web based auction and given the large spread in valuations of such an audience, we believe the method we propose to have a significant effect on the revenue realized by the seller.

4   The Algorithm

The proposed algorithm is based on comparing the increments in bid prices over subsequent intervals of time. More specifically, we obtain a weighted average of the bid increments. The highest weight is assigned to the bid representing the lowest winning bid and the weights assigned to other bids decrease with increasing distance from the lowest winning bid. This results in the comparison of increments in subsequent periods of time to be more influenced by bids at or near the lowest winning bid price since it is these bids that determine the overall revenue that is realized. An increase in the weighted bid increments from one interval to the next implies that there is enough bidding activity left to increase the price without external stimulus. A decline in weighted bid increments from one time interval to the next indicates that external stimulus is required. Our algorithm uses this methodology in deciding when to introduce the coupon. In the following, we outline the algorithm in more detail.

Step 1: Find the minimum winning bid price at some point t during the auction, call it $\mu(t)$.

$$\left[\sum_{i=1}^{B} I(p_i(t) > \mu(t))q_i \right] \geq Q \tag{1}$$

where, B is the total number of bidders. $I(\cdot)$ is an indicator function that is 1 when its argument is true and 0 otherwise. Equation (1) is based on the actual bids received so far.

Step 2: Define a weight $w_i(t)$ with each bidder i,

$$w_i(t) = e^{-\lambda(|p_i(t)-\mu(t)+\alpha(t)|)} \tag{2}$$

Equation (2) defines a function centered at $(\mu(t) - \alpha(t))$. $\alpha(t)$ is used since bidders with a bid price lower than $\mu(t)$ are *not* the current winning bidders and will probably have greater interest in increasing their bids. λ is a chosen constant.

Further, let,

$$w_i(t) = \begin{cases} w_i(t) & \text{if } w_i(t) > w(t) \\ 0 & \text{otherwise} \end{cases} \tag{3}$$

where $w(t)$ is a chosen constant. Equation (3) thresholds the weights such that bidders with prices nearer $(\mu(t) - \alpha(t))$ influence the next step more.

Step 3: Define $\delta p_i(t)$ as the amount by which bidder i last increased his bid.

Step 4: Find the weighted average of bid increments, $\bar{\delta}(t)$, using,

$$\bar{\delta}(t) = \frac{\sum_{i=1}^{B} w_i(t)\, \delta p_i(t)}{\sum_{i=1}^{B} w_i(t)} \tag{4}$$

Step 5: If a coupon has *not* been issued thus far in this auction, then determine if it should be issued now. If a coupon has already been issued, then go to Step 6. If $\bar{\delta}(t) > \bar{\delta}(t-1)$, *do not* introduce the coupon and go to Step 1. If $\bar{\delta}(t) \leq \bar{\delta}(t-1)$, then we may introduce a coupon. To make it more robust, a weighted difference over time may be used as opposed to the simple difference of successive time intervals. The opportune moment for introducing a coupon is decided based on inspecting the rate of change of weighted average bid increments (i.e. $\bar{\delta}$'s).

Step 6: If a coupon has, or is being introduced, its face value can be determined as follows.

In the worst case, if everyone used the coupon and raised the bid, by say the smallest amount possible (say 1 cent), then the cost of issuing the coupon would be $Q \times p_C$ (ignoring the 1c since it is small). Assuming that the auction continues with the same dynamics, then we would like $Q \times p_C < Q \times \bar{\delta}(t)$. That is $p_C < \bar{\delta}(t)$ ensuring that the total revenue does not decrease (assuming of course, that $\bar{\delta}(t)$ persists). This would represent the most aggressive strategy with a risk of revenue decrease. On the more cautious side, one can make it a small fraction of $\bar{\delta}(t)$. The coupon value is thus related to the amount of risk that the auctioneer is willing to take. We suggest,

$$r(\bar{\delta}(t-1) - \bar{\delta}(t)) < a < \bar{\delta}(t) \tag{5}$$

where r can be chosen depending on the amount of risk that can be taken. Then,

$$p_C(t) = \begin{cases} a & \text{if } a > p_C(t-1) \\ p_C(t-1) & \text{otherwise} \end{cases} \tag{6}$$

Step 7: Repeat from Step 1 until end of auction.

5   A Realistic Example

In this section we illustrate the algorithm described in this paper based on some realistic data. Consider Table 1, showing the bid price and quantity for each bidder at some point during an ongoing auction.

Bidder Id.	Bid price (in $)	Quantity
1.	30.50	1
2.	30.07	1
3.	26.00	1
4.	25.01	1
5.	25.01	1
6.	25.00	1
7.	25.00	1
8.	24.50	1
9.	24.00	1
10.	24.00	1
11.	23.50	1
12.	22.50	1
13.	22.00	1
14.	15.51	1
15.	15.01	1
16.	14.00	1
17.	14.00	1
18.	13.51	2
19.	10.00	1
20.	6.50	1
21.	5.77	1
22.	5.00	1
23.	3.75	1
24.	3.50	1
25.	2.50	1

Table 1. The bids at time t. The total units of the item being auctioned, Q is 5.

The following steps correspond to the steps outlined in the algorithm.

Step 1: μ can be computed to be $25.01.

Step 2:   Find $w_i(t)$. The resultant values with $\lambda = 1$ and $\alpha = 5$ ordered from the highest to the lowest bidder are: 0.0000, 0.0000, 0.0025, 0.0067, 0.0067, 0.0068, 0.0068, 0.0112, 0.0185, 0.0185, 0.0305, 0.0829, 0.1367, 0.0111, 0.0067, 0.0025, 0.0025, 0.0015, 0.0000, 0.0000, 0.0000, 0.0000, 0.0000, 0.0000, 0.0000. Let $w(t)$ be 0.0026. The resultant $w_i(t)$ are thus, 0.0000, 0.0000, 0.0000, 0.0067, 0.0067, 0.0068, 0.0068, 0.0112, 0.0185, 0.0185, 0.0305, 0.0829, 0.1367, 0.0111, 0.0067, 0.0000, 0.0000, 0.0000, 0.0000, 0.0000, 0.0000, 0.0000, 0.0000, 0.0000, 0.0000, 0.0000.

Step 3: $\delta p_i(t)$ for the bidders whose $w_i(t) > 0$ in $ are, 0.6000 0.7000 0.6000 1.1000 0.7000 0.6000 0.5000 1.2500 0.9000 1.4000 0.9000 1.0000

Step 4: $\bar{\delta}(t)$ can be computed to be \$1.0716. Similarly, let $\bar{\delta}(t-1)$ be \$1.65.

Step 5: Since $\bar{\delta}(t-1) > \bar{\delta}(t)$ a coupon can be issued.

Step 6: Based on Equation (5), the value of the coupon is $r(\$1.65 - \$1.0716) < a < \$1.65$ or in other words, $r(\$0.5739) < a < \$1.65$. Assuming a value of $r = 0.5$, the coupon value is, $\$0.2869 < a < \$1.65$. A coupon of \$0.50 is issued.

Step 7: Repeat from Step 1 until the end of the auction.

For the sake of analysis, assume that the auction ended at time $(t + 1)$ and the state of the auction immediately preceding the end of the auction is as shown in Table 1. At time $(t + 1)$ the top five winning bids would be \$30.50, \$30.07, \$26.10, \$26.00, and \$25.71 (bidder #'s 1, 2, 7, 3, 5). This is assuming the $\delta p_i(t)$ as outlined in Step 3 above. The total revenue realized by the seller is $\$25.71 \times 5 = \$128.55$.

Assuming that the coupon is used by the four bidders whose bids at time t are \$25.01, and \$25.00. Let us say, that they increase their bids by $\delta p_i(t) + p_C$. Note that the end increase in cost to these four bidders is 0. The five winning bids are now, \$30.50, \$30.07, \$26.60, \$26.21, and \$26.11 (bidder #'s 1, 2, 4, 5, 7). Note that the bidder # 3 with a bid of \$26.00 is now not a winning bidder. The overall revenue to the seller is now $\$26.11 \times 5 = \$130.55$. Three of the winning bidders used the coupon — the cost of the coupon is \$1.50. The revenue factoring in the cost of the coupon is thus \$129.05 which is more than the previously realized revenue.

Note that even in this conservative analysis, where the increased competition resulting from the use of the coupon (it is likely that bidder # 3 may increase his bid) is not included, there is still an increase in the revenue to the seller. In a realistic scenario, the realized increase may be larger and is dependent on the actual increases in bids.

Obviously, the overall revenue realized by the seller depends on several factors such as future increases in bids as well as new bids. Therefore, it is not possible to accurately estimate the effect of the proposed methodology other than through actual implementation. Nevertheless, the example above does provide evidence as the efficacy of the method in increasing the revenue realized by the seller.

6   Discussion and Conclusion

In this paper, we presented a coupon based method for increasing the overall revenue realized in a Dutch auction. An algorithm for determining when a coupon should be introduced, the face value of the coupon as well as possible subsequent revisions in the face value was also presented. The introduction of the coupon is based on analyzing the weighted average of the bid increments over successive intervals of time. Since the overall revenue is determined by p_W, the weights decrease with increasing distance from the lowest winning bid price, i.e., bid prices at or near the lowest winning bid price influence the weighted average to a larger extent. A decline in the weighted average of the bid increments was proposed as the opportune moment for introducing the coupon.

Based on some realistic data we showed that an increase of revenue realized by the seller is likely when the proposed methodology is used within the context of a Dutch auction.

The variant of the Dutch auction that we considered here has the advantage that buyers feel more satisfied since all winning bidders purchase the item at the same price. To a small extent that satisfaction may be lost with the proposed method though we believe that such an effect, if present, would be small. If and when the proposed scheme is implemented in an actual auction, we recommend that a new name be used for the auction (for example, Coupon Based Dutch Auction) so as not to cause confusion with the traditional variant of the Dutch auction. In addition, the rules should clearly indicate, the possibility of a coupon being issued during the auction and the fact that the discount is available only to those who acquire the coupon. Additional details, including the fact that this variant may result in participants paying different prices, should also be clearly stated.

When all the rules and possibilities are clearly indicated, the proposed methodology allows competition to be restored when the bid increments start declining in an auction. Indeed, there is little difference between our proposal to use a coupon within an auction setting and the use of (store and manufacturer coupons) coupons commonly used in traditional brick-and-mortar establishments. In both situations, individuals benefit from utilizing the coupon.

Acknowledgements

Helpful discussion with M. Kumar and V. Jain are gratefully acknowledged.

References

1. http://www.ebay.com
2. R. Bapna, P. Goes, and A. Gupta, "A theoretical and empirical investigation of multi-item online auctions," *Information Technology and Management*, Vol. 1, pp. 1–23, 2000.
3. R. Bapna, P. Goes, and A. Gupta, "Compartive analysis of multi-item online auctions: evidence from the laboratory," *Decision Support Systems*, Vol. 32, pp. 135–153, 2001.
4. P. K. Kopalle, C. F. Mela, and L. Marsh, "The dynamic effect of discounting on sales: empirical analysis and normative pricing," *Marketing Science*, Vol. 18, No. 3, 1999.
5. P. Alsemgeest, C. Noussair, and M. Olson, "Experimental comparison of auction under single and multi-unit demand," *Economic Inquiry*, Vol. 36, pp. 87–98, 1998.
6. W. Vickrey, "Conter-speculation, auctions, and competetive sealed tenders," *Journal of Finance*, Vol. 41, pp. 8–37, 1961.

7. P. Milogram, "Auctions and bidding: a primer," *Journal of Economic Perspectives*, Vol. 3, pp. 3–22, 1989.
8. J.C. Cox, V. L. Smith, and J. M. Walker, "Expected revenue in discriminative and uniform price sealed-bid auctions," *Research in Experimental Economics*, Vol. 3, pp. 183–232, 1985.

Strategies and Behaviours of Agents in Multi-phased Negotiations

Samir Aknine

LIP6, Université Paris 6
8, rue du Capitaine Scott
75015 PARIS Cedex 15, France
Samir.Aknine@lip6.fr

Abstract. This paper presents new multi-agent negotiation models for electronic commerce. These models address M-N-P negotiation problems, i.e. negotiations between m buyers and n sellers for buying p dependent products or services. These products or services are not necessarily provided by the same seller. We propose two new negotiation protocols as well as algorithms describing the behaviors of seller and buyer agents.

1 Introduction

Electronic travel planning is a multi-facetted problem. Currently, many Internet sites propose flights, but it is rarely possible to plan a complete trip, including hotel and car reservations -or other services- at each step. Normally, a customer sends to each travel agency a query containing travel details: number of stops, preferred date, budget, type and quality of services. Then the system must provide a package deal containing all the services required. For instance, a query "Paris-Lyon-Marseille from the 1/6/2001 with two night stopover in a hotel in Lyon, and a car reservation for a week in Marseille, all for a budget of $1000" must provide a set of p products, i.e. train or airline tickets, hotel reservation and car hire contract. This task requires the resolution of several problems: determining the itinerary, looking for different available proposals, optimizing costs, satisfying the constraints and negotiating. Therefore, such a system is an ideal experimental field for research in Artificial Intelligence, in general, and multi-agent systems, in particular. Consequently, many systems have begun to address different aspects of this problem [2][3][5][8]. In our work, we are interested in e-commerce agents for M-N-P negotiations. This type of negotiation requires a special type of behavior, i.e. behavior to allow a combined negotiation between m buyers and n sellers concerning several products p having dependence constraints between them and which are not necessarily provided by the same seller. This kind of negotiation has rarely been studied in e-commerce, which is why it is necessary to propose several protocols to resolve the difficulties related to the constraints between the different negotiation processes concerning the p negotiable products.

This article is structured as follows. Section 2 analyzes related work on negotiation in e-commerce and, in particular, on negotiations with several sellers and buyers. Section 3 presents our negotiation models. The first part describes the two-phase protocol for combined negotiations and the second part the three-phase protocol for combined negotiations. Each of these phases has its own semantics and a level of penalty. The protocols are illustrated through our electronic travel application planning. Then, the negotiation algorithms adopted by each of the buyer and seller agents are presented. Section 4 concludes this work.

K. Bauknecht, A M. Tjoa, G. Quirchmayr (Eds.): EC-Web 2002, LNCS 2455, pp. 17–26, 2002.

2 Related Work

Most negotiation protocols for electronic commerce address the problem of negotiating one product at a time under only one dimension, usually the price. [6] consider that this choice is very simplistic and not realistic in the domain of electronic commerce. Their protocol is a modified version of auctions. But even with this improvement, an auction protocol still has drawbacks which restrict its use. The fact that the buyer is committed to conclude the transaction is problematic if it is still participating in other negotiations on other products having dependence constraints with the product bought. For simultaneous auctions, [7] presents an algorithm in order to guarantee that the agents send appropriate proposals for the different auctions in order to buy exactly the right number of products. It combines this with an algorithm determining when it is preferable to make a strong proposal in an auction that is closing, rather than to focus on other auctions. According to Sandholm et al. [9], when buyers wish to buy a combination of products, traditional auctions where only one product is sold at a time do not solve the problem, because the evaluation function of the products becomes strongly complex to compute. Participating simultaneously in several auctions leads to another problem: each buyer wants to wait until the end of each auction in order to maximize its income. Therefore, it is possible that no negotiation ends. One way to correct the undesirable purchases could be to allow the buyers to sell these products among themselves or else they could be allowed to retract, possibly facilitated by leveled commitment contracts with penalties [7]. The protocol proposed by Sandholm et al. consists of auctions in which buyers can send a global proposal on a combination of products. This allows them to express their wishes to buy complementary products [9].

However, an auction protocol still has limitations. This protocol leads always to earlier commitments of the sellers or the buyers even in combined negotiations. The fact that the last proposal wins and that the buyer or the seller is committed to conclude the transaction is problematic if it has not checked all the proposals. His decommitment on one or several products will involve a chain reaction of decommitments on others due to dependence relations between the products. In our work, we have introduced several negotiation phases in order to allow the buyer and the seller agents to check the proposals of the other agents before making commitments.

3 M-N-P Negotiation Models for Combined Negotiations

3.1 Negotiation Objects

In our application, the negotiation objects correspond to different travel components: travel by train or plane between the different stops, hotel reservations for each stop and car hire for each stop. The products have several characteristics (standard of hotel, car Park, ...). Some of them can be used to define the constraints: price, because the trip has to fall within a given budget; dates, because time intervals which are allocated to the journeys and to the stopovers must not overlap.

In *M-N-P* negotiation, there are several types of dependence relation between the products negotiated. According to these dependences, buyer and seller agents decide on which negotiation model to adopt. First, product dependences are identified using the queries sent by the users, then they are formalized. In the following we are not going to detail the different possible dependence relations but will just illustrate two because the aim of this article is to present our negotiation models.

For instance, we can distinguish two types of dependence between products: strong and weak. In the case of strong dependence, the purchase of one product is conditioned by all the other products. In this case, the user formulates a query in this form: "I want to go to Marseille for one day between 14/10 and 17/10, to stay in a hotel, for a maximum budget of $800". This query implies that the buyer agent that is associated to it must find, at the same time, a room available in a hotel for the specified time interval and train or plane ticket for the same date, with a total price within to the given limit. We cannot make any assumptions on the availability of the products sought. Furthermore, the sellers are free to apply the sale tactics and set up the negotiation margins they choose. The components of the trip are of variable importance for the user, so it is impossible to favor some elements over others (for instance, to look in priority for transport then look for the corresponding hotels).

In the case of weak dependence between products, there is a dependence relation between these products, but this relation can become an independence relation if all the constraints between the products cannot be satisfied. For instance, the user can formulate a query in the following form: "I want to go to spend a day in Marseille between 14/10 and 17/10 and stay in a hotel for a budget of $800 maximum, but if there are no rooms available, I will accept the plane ticket". This query implies that the buyer agent must try to find at the same time a room available in a hotel for the specified time interval and a train or plane ticket for the same date, with a total price within the given limit, but in the case of failure to satisfy all these conditions, the query can be satisfied by purchasing the airline ticket. Of course, first of all these queries are formalized in logical rules so that they can be analyzed by the agents at the next step. In the following, we will only present the negotiation models that the agents use to resolve the problem of M-N-P negotiation for purchasing p products having strong dependences between them. These models must be adjusted to address the problem of negotiating products with weak dependences.

3.2 Negotiation Protocol for Combined Negotiations

In this section, we will present two negotiation protocols that we propose to address the problem of concurrent M-N-P negotiations. In each of the two protocols, the buyer agent starts by negotiating for the p products that it wishes to buy from n sellers without having to inform them, initially, that they will participate in combined negotiations concerning the p products, i.e. that the buyer intends to buy p dependent products to form a package and that it needs each product of the package to conclude the transaction on the set of p products. The seller is informed about this later, i.e. at a certain stage of the negotiation. The first suggested protocol differs, precisely, from the second protocol in the choice of the stage at which the buyer agent informs the seller agent that it is carrying out several negotiations for purchasing p products. In the first protocol the buyer agent informs the seller agent earlier than in the second protocol that its product will serve to form a package. The interest for a buyer agent to delay this information is that the seller agent cannot use it to increase its prices.

The protocol proposed is an extension of the one we have presented in [1]. We proposed a multi-agent coordination model for task allocation based on the principle of pre-negotiation between agents. The aim being to provide a solution to several problems in current coordination protocols. (1) The length of negotiations that is long, due to the sequencing of negotiation processes, an agent can only negotiate with one other agent at a time. (2) The lack of efficiency in sequential negotiations: the agent is unaware of the proposals of the other agents when it is negotiating and therefore misses opportunities. This problem is more preoccupying in the case of combined negotiations, since having an agreement between the seller and buyer on one of the p products adds constraints on the other products. These constraints cannot necessarily be satisfied. In the case of failure in the negotiation on one product, this will necessarily lead to decommitment of the buyer agent for all the other products as we assume that the products are strongly dependent. (3) The decommitment possibility for agents, and the penalties that they must pay. In our model of combined negotiations, we have reconsidered the decommitment strategy with paying penalties, proposed by [8], since the value of the penalty depends on the stage at which the decommitment happens but also on the products for which the negotiations have already been totally or partially concluded.

In this protocol, we add a pre-negotiation phase that allows the buyer to check available proposals before proceeding to the transactions. Here, we have four phases: *Pre-Bidding, PreAssignment, DefinitiveBidding, DefinitiveAssignment.*

Nevertheless, as this model of combined negotiations is adapted for electronic commerce processes, we are not in cooperative negotiations as in [1]. It is therefore necessary to check the information provided to the sellers by the buyers. If a seller knows the dependences between its proposal and those of the other sellers on the $p-1$ other products of the combined negotiation, it can be encouraged to maximize its income at the expense of the buyer.

3.2.1 Negotiation Protocol Principle

- Pre-negotiation

In this phase, the buyer agent sends individual calls for proposals on each of the products to each of the seller agents that are likely to provide at least one of the p products. In response to each call for proposals sent by the buyer agent, the seller starts by sending a proposal for the product. At this point, the proposal does not commit it. Next, it can cancel its proposal without any penalties. This exchange of messages allows the buyer to be informed about the proposal of all the sellers concerning the p components of the travel package. If it observes that, for a given date, it receives an interesting proposal for a hotel room, it can decide that for other proposals for a room to be acceptable, they should contain this date.

- Definitive Negotiation

After pre-committing themselves, sellers are warned that they are part of a wider negotiation, i.e. a combined negotiation that implies purchasing p products at the same time and that they have now to commit themselves with the buyer to provide the product within the given deadlines, otherwise they will have to pay a penalty which is decided according to the consequences of this decommitment. Withdrawals set off a chain reaction when at least one of the sellers retracts.

3.2.2 Communication Primitives

The communication primitives used by seller and buyer agents during a negotiation to exchange information needed for the transactions are:

- Primitives of the Buyer Agent

The buyer uses the primitives *Cfp, Pre-Accept, Pre-Reject, Reject-and-new-Cfp, Def-Accept, Def-Reject* and *All-Reject*.
- *Cfp* "Call for Proposal" *(Buyer, Seller, Required Product):* the buyer sends this message to a seller to inform it that it wants to negotiate a product for which it gives the specifications. The buyer agent references only one product in a call for proposals in order to conceal initially the possible dependences between the products that it is looking for.
- *Pre-Accept (Buyer, Seller, Pre-Bid, Required Product):* with this message, the buyer informs the seller that its *"Pre-Bid"* proposal may be accepted and that it is included in a wider negotiation. In the *"Product"* field, it gives the characteristics of the product that it is looking for, thus giving this seller the possibility to improve its proposal. It is at this time that the seller agent knows that it is participating in a combined negotiation. The seller is not yet committed and can withdraw without paying a penalty. The strategy of delaying the announcement of a combined negotiation is important for the buyer agent because this lets the buyer know the value that the seller has defined for its product before it knew that the buyer had a strong need for this product in order to conclude the combined negotiation of the p products.
- *Pre-Reject (Buyer, Seller, Refused Pre-Bid, Accepted Pre-Bid):* the buyer uses this type of message to inform the seller that its *"Refused Pre-Bid"* proposal, is *Refused* and that another *"Accepted Pre-Bid"* proposal has been pre-accepted but that it cannot be accepted until it produces a better proposal than the one accepted.
- *All-Reject (Buyer, Seller, Refused Pre-Bid, Accepted Pre-Bid):* this message indicates for the seller that the buyer has not found any satisfactory proposals. It therefore rejects all the proposals and indicates the best *Refused* Pre-Bid to allow the sellers to improve their proposals.
- *Reject-and-new-Cfp (Buyer, Seller, Pre-Bid, new Cfp):* the buyer sends this message after having observed that the *Pre-Bid* that it had previously accepted is no longer compatible with the constraints of the other products. It therefore cancels its acceptance and sends a new more appropriate call for proposals.
- *Def-Accept (Buyer, Seller, Def-Bid):* the buyer has definitively accepted the proposal of the seller, and the negotiation is henceforth closed.
- *Def-Reject (Buyer, Seller, Pre-Bid):* with this message, the buyer definitively rejects the proposals of the seller and ends the negotiation.

- *Primitives of the Seller Agent*

The seller uses the following primitives: *Pre-Bid, Refuse, Def-Bid*.
- *Pre-Bid (Seller, Buyer, Cfp, Proposed Product):* the seller sends this message to the buyer to present a description of the product that it wants to sell. This description does not commit the seller for the moment.

- *Refuse (Seller, Buyer, Cfp):* with this message, the seller indicates that it is not able to meet the expressed conditions in the *Cfp* and that it therefore has no proposal to make.
- *Def-Bid (Buyer, Seller, Cfp, Product):* with this message, the seller confirms its proposal (possibly improved) and commits itself to providing it. A decommitment will be punished with a penalty which is computed by taking into account the fact that the seller already knew that the buyer is in a combined negotiation.

Let us now consider the algorithms applied by the agents. These algorithms are summarized in the graphs below. Remember that in our work, we are interested in the negotiation of *m* buyers, several sellers *n* for purchasing several products *p* which are not necessarily provided by the same seller and knowing full well that these *n* sellers can receive simultaneously other calls for proposals from other buyers and that these can influence their final decisions.

3.2.3 Agent Behaviors

In the following, we will simply describe the behaviors of each of the seller and buyer agents. It appears that due to the dependences between the products, the behaviors of the agents have to be more sophisticated than in classical negotiation to purchase a single product, several units of the same product [10][5][6], or several products with the same seller as is the case in [9].

- Behaviors of the Buyer Agent

The buyer has initially to fill a package of *p* different products having constraints between them. It knows *n* sellers that it contacts and tries to fill its package with their proposal. It therefore sends a *Cfp* to each seller that it considers likely to provide one or more required products. Initially, the sellers ignore the fact that their negotiation is part of a combined one, even if certain sellers may receive several *Cfp* on several products from the same buyer. The buyer is now in state 1 (cf. figure 1) and is waiting for the *Pre-Bids* of the sellers it has already contacted.

If among the answers of the sellers it finds at least *p Pre-Bids* which correspond to all the components of the package, it goes to state 2 in order to compute them. If all the sellers reply with a *Refuse*, the negotiation finishes with a failure.

But if the buyer receives *q Pre-Bids* which correspond to less than the number of *p* products, and *Refuse* messages for the others, it will attempt to modify its initial query with the intention of completing its package. In this case, it goes to state 5 where it sends another *Cfp* to the agents able to provide the products that are lacking. If it cannot, it sends a *Def-Reject* to all and closes the negotiation. Otherwise, it goes to state 6 in which it waits again for *Pre-Bids*. If, in state 6, it again receives *Refuse* messages for certain of the new *Cfp*, it goes back to state 5.

If it receives enough *Pre-Bids* to fill its package with the *p* products, it goes to state 2 and computes them. In this state, the buyer uses its strategy to analyze all the proposals received. With these *Pre-Bids*, it tries to build a global proposal which corresponds to its package, respecting the constraints imposed because of the dependences between the *p* products. If it succeeds, for each component of the package it sends a *Pre-Accept* to the seller that has made the best proposal, and *Pre-Rejects* to the others. It therefore sends *p*

Pre-Accepts and informs them that the negotiations are combined. Then it goes to state 3 in order to wait for the *Def-Bids*. If it does not succeed because the proposals are incompatible, it sends *q Pre-Accepts* to the proposals that it selects, *Pre-Rejects* to competing proposals for the same product and *All-Rejects* to the others. It then goes to state 7 in order to wait for *Pre-Bids* from the sellers which have received an *All-Reject* message.

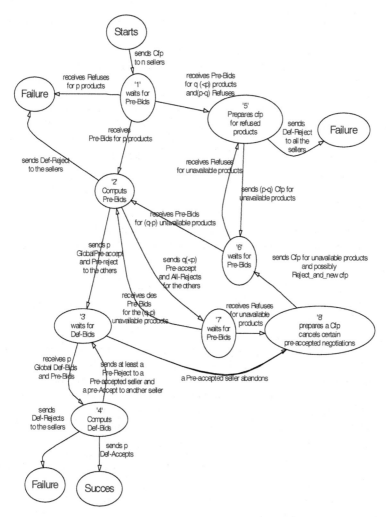

Fig. 1. Behaviors of a buyer agent in a two-phase combined negotiation process

In state 7, the buyer waits for the *Pre-Bids* that will allow it to complete its package. If it receives *Refuse* messages, it goes to state 8 in order to modify its package. Otherwise, if it receives enough *Pre-Bids* for its package, it goes back to state 2. In state 8, the buyer sends the *Cfp* again so that it obtains more interesting results. It can, for instance, relax its constraints in order to have sufficient choice and leave a bigger margin for the sellers. It can also completely modify certain components of the package. Therefore, certain *Pre-Bids* that have received a *Pre-Accept* answer may have to be cancelled. In this case, the buyer sends them a *Reject-and-new-Cfp* – as it does for those which have previously received a *Pre-Reject* – which means that the current package has been cancelled and that a new one has been opened. The buyer goes next to state 8 to wait for new *Pre-Bids*. In state 3, the buyer now waits for proposal that commit the seller. If a seller which has received a *Pre-Accept* withdraws – or does not reply after a certain time – the buyer goes back to state 8 in order to check if it must modify its offer or cancel certain *Pre-Accepts*. Otherwise, the buyer must receive p *Def-Bids* and eventually *Pre-Bids* from other sellers that want to improve their proposals. It computes these messages in state 4.

In this state, the buyer analyzes the *Def-Bids* and eventually the new *Pre-Bids*. If a *Pre-Bid* seems better than the *Def-Bid* corresponding to the same product, the buyer sends a *Pre-Accept* to its sender and a *Pre-Reject* to the seller which is no longer pre-accepted. Then it goes to state 3 where it waits for the *Def-Bid* of the new agent. When it receives a *Def-Bid* from each of the p pre-accepted agents, it sends them a *Def-Accept* in which it informs them that their proposals have definitively been accepted and that all negotiations concerning the p products are closed. The other sellers receive a *Def-Reject*. The negotiation finishes successfully.

- Behaviors of the Seller Agent

Symmetrically, the seller is initially waiting for a *Cfp* from the buyers. As soon as it receives a *Cfp* for purchasing a product, it analyzes it and goes to state 1 (cf. figure 2).

In this state, the seller prepares its *Pre-Bid*, or sends a message of the type *Refuse* if it considers that it is not able to meet the specified conditions. In this case, it goes to the initial state to wait for a new *Cfp'*, or a *Def-Reject* that will close the negotiation. If it considers itself able to satisfy the specifications, it sends its proposal in a *Pre-Bid* and goes to state 2 to wait for an answer.

In state 2, the seller waits for the buyer to react to its proposal. If it receives a *Pre-Reject* or an *All-Reject*, it returns to state 1 and tries to produce a better proposal. The negotiation ends if a *Def-Reject* is received. If it receives a *Pre-Accept*, it goes to state 3 and prepares a proposal that commits it after having received the information that the negotiations are combined. It is its last opportunity to withdraw without paying a penalty. It follows the negotiation, sends a *Def-Bid* and goes to state 4 to wait for an answer. In state 4, a *Def-Reject* closes the negotiation. Otherwise, a *Reject-and-new-Cfp* indicates to the seller that its proposal is no longer acceptable, so it goes to state 1, as it now has a new *Cfp* to analyze. If the agent receives a *Pre-Reject*, it also returns to state 1 in order to attempt to make a better proposal. Finally, if it receives a *Def-Accept*, the negotiation closes with the transaction.

In order to guarantee the convergence of the algorithm, it is possible to apply several strategies. In our case, we attribute a limited time to the negotiation. When the time for the pre-negotiation phase is up, the agents that wish to remain in the negotiation can only send *Def-Bids*. The buyer just sends p *Def-Accepts*, or *Def-Rejects*, to close the negotiation.

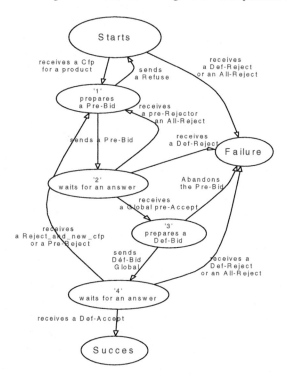

Fig. 2. Behaviors of a seller agent in a two-phase combined negotiation process

3.3 Extending the Protocol

In the two-phase protocol, sellers are informed that their proposal is part of a combined negotiation as soon as they receive the *Pre-Accept* from the buyer for their product, and they are then free to use this information in their strategy. For instance, an airline company can increase the price of its flights for a given date if it observes that the buyer is interested in this date. If the buyer negotiates other services for this date, it will certainly prefer to accept more costly proposals from the company than to reject them and risk not finding services available for another date. The aim of this extension (three-phase protocol) is to avoid this drawback for the buyer, unlike the two-phase protocol where the seller agent knew that it was part of a combined negotiation after sending a *Pre-Bid* but before committing itself with a *Def-Bid*. This protocol behaves so that the seller makes an initial commitment on the product, before knowing that it is participating in a combined negotiation. This commitment obliges it to provide the product that it has agreed to sell during the previous phase and to pay a local penalty, i.e. computed on the product, if it withdraws. When the seller is informed that the negotiation is on p products, it can make a stronger commitment than the previous one, i.e. a commitment that takes into account the fact that the buyer must have a package where all the p products are satisfied. This commitment allows it to renegotiate the *Def-Bid* that it has already sent and therefore to improve it. However, in this case it also agrees to pay a global penalty, i.e. a higher one because it is computed on the set of p negotiated products, if it withdraws, since its withdrawal would put into question other transactions, i.e. those on the *p-1* other products. It can also limit itself to the first weak commitment that it has accepted on the product. This negotiation protocol gives a better result regarding the quality of the solutions compared with the previous protocol. However the negotiation needs more time.

4 Conclusion

Currently, several multi-agent negotiation models for electronic commerce exist, but few of them address the problem of purchasing p different products not necessarily provided by the same seller. For this reason, we have proposed two new negotiation models to take this requirement into account efficiently. These models are based on two or three negotiation phases. The two protocols can check if the fact that a seller knows it is participating in a combined negotiation has a determining influence on its strategy. Each of the protocols is illustrated through an electronic application for travel planning. We have proposed negotiation algorithms applied by each buyer and seller agent. In current work, we are addressing some related problems: (1) the formalization of all dependence relations between products and the definition of negotiation protocols which correspond to them; (2) the computation of the penalties to be paid by each buyer and seller agent when using these protocols. These penalties are computed differently compared with a traditional M-N negotiation. In combined negotiations with several sellers, the decommitment for a product involves a chain reaction of decommitments on the other products due to dependence relations between the products; (3) we intend to compare the results of this model to another agent coalition formation model which we have proposed in previous work [4].

References

1. Aknine, S. "Issues in Cooperative Systems: Extending the Contract Net Protocol", Albus, J. (ed.), IEEE Joint Conference on Int. Systems, USA, September, 1998.
2. Anthony, P., Hall, W., Dang, V. Jennings, N.R. "Autonomous agents for participating in multiple on-line auctions", IJCAI, Workshop on E-Business, 2001.
3. Boutilier, C. and Hoos, H. "Bidding Languages for Combinatorial Auctions", IJCAI, 2001.
4. Caillou, P., Aknine, S., Pinson, S. "A Multi-Agent Method for Forming and Dynamic Restructuring of Pareto Optimal Coalitions", AAMAS, International Joint Conference on Autonomous Agents and MAS, ACM Press, Italy, 2002.
5. Morris, J., Ree, P., Maes, P. "Sardine: An Agent-facilitated Airline Ticket Bidding System", Agent, 2000.
6. Rocha, A.,P., Oliveira, E. "Adaptive multi-issue negotiation protocol for Electronic Commerce", PAAM, 2000.
7. Preist, C. Algorithm Design for Agents Which Participate in Multiple Simultaneous Auctions, HPL-2000-88, 2000.
8. Sandholm, T. and Lesser, V. "Issues in Automated Negotiation and Electronic Commerce : Extending the Contract Net Framework", ICMAS, San Fransisco, 1995.
9. Sandholm, T., Suri, S. "Improved Algorithms for Optimal Winner Determination in Combinatorial Auctions and Generalizations", AAAI, 2000.
10. Yokoo, M., Sakurai, Y., Matsubara, S. "Robust Multi-unit Auction Protocol against False-name Bids", IJCAI, 2001.

A New Approach to the Design of Electronic Exchanges

S. Kameshwaran* and Y. Narahari

eEnterprises Laboratory, Department of CSA,
Indian Institute of Science,
Bangalore-560012,
India
{kameshn, hari}@csa.iisc.ernet.in
http://lcm.csa.iisc.ernet.in

Abstract. Electronic Exchanges are double-sided marketplaces that allows multiple buyers to trade with multiple sellers, with aggregation of demand and supply across the bids to maximize the revenue in the market. In this paper, we propose a new design approach for an one-shot exchange that collects bids from buyers and sellers and clears the market at the end of the bidding period. The main principle of the approach is to decouple the allocation from pricing. It is well known that it is impossible for an exchange with voluntary participation to be efficient and budget-balanced. Budget-balance is a mandatory requirement for an exchange to operate in profit. Our approach is to allocate the trade to maximize the reported values of the agents. The pricing is posed as payoff determination problem that distributes the total payoff fairly to all agents with budget-balance imposed as a constraint. We devise an arbitration scheme by axiomatic approach to solve the payoff determination problem using the added-value concept of game theory.

1 Introduction

Markets play a central role in any economy and facilitate the exchange of information, goods, services, and payments. They are intended to create value for buyers, sellers, and for society at large. Markets have three main functions [1]:matching buyers to sellers; facilitating exchange of information, goods, services, and payments associated with a market transaction; and providing an institutional infrastructure. Internet-based E-markets leverage information technology to perform these functions with increased effectiveness and reduced transaction costs, leading to more efficient, friction-free markets. In this paper, our interest is in providing a new approach to the design of exchanges. Exchanges allows multiple buyers to trade with multiple sellers, with aggregation of demand and supply across the bids to maximize the revenue in the market. The approach is to decouple allocation from pricing. This is not a new approach as Vickrey

---

* This research is supported in part by IBM Research Fellowship awarded to the first author by IBM India Research Laboratory, New Delhi

K. Bauknecht, A M. Tjoa, G. Quirchmayr (Eds.): EC-Web 2002, LNCS 2455, pp. 27–36, 2002.

mechanisms essentially do the same. However, our objectives in the design are budget-balance and individual rationality rather than efficiency and incentive compatibility. Our approach is in the line with the constructive approach to mechanism design in [11], but our pricing scheme is different. We propose an arbitration scheme for pricing, based on an axiomatic approach that captures the intuitive relationships between the payoff and added-value concept of game theory.

2   Electronic Exchanges

Exchanges are double-sided marketplaces where both buyers and sellers submit bids for trading. We refer sellers' bids as *offers* if required to differentiate them from that of buyers. The exchanges differ in functionality with respect to timing of clearing, number of bid submissions, pricing, aggregation and the varieties of goods traded. In this paper, our interest is in designing one-shot exchanges, where buyers and sellers submit bids during the bidding period and the market is cleared at the end of the bidding interval. This is similar to *call markets* or *clearing house* [6] but the bids may have multiple attributes and can be combinatorial in nature.

2.1   Design Issues

The two core problems in an exchange are *allocation* and *pricing* [11]. In certain exchanges pricing determines the allocation. In call markets [6], the price at which there is a maximal match in supply and demand is used to clear the market. But there are exchanges that decouple allocation from pricing. For e.g., the Generalized Vickrey Auction (GVA) [13] allocates the goods that maximizes the reported bid values and pricing is done based on allocation. Our approach is to decouple allocation from pricing but with a different set of objectives than that of GVA. We call the allocation problem as the *trade determination problem* (TDP) and the pricing problem as the *payoff determination problem*. TDP determines the goods traded between every pair of buyers and sellers and the PDP prices the goods traded by determining the *payoff* (to be defined later) to individual agents.

3   Impossibility Result

Useful economic properties of an exchange include [11]:

- **Allocative-efficiency** (EFF): Trade should be executed to maximize the total increase in value over all agents.
- **Individual-rationality** (IR): No agent should pay more than its net increase in value for the items it trades.
- **Budget-balance** (BB): The total payments received by the exchange from agents should be at least the total payments made by the exchange to agents.

- **Incentive-compatibility** (IC): The equilibrium strategy for the agents is to reveal *truthful* information about their preferences in their bids.

The impossibility result of Myerson & Satterthwaite [10] demonstrates that no exchange can be EFF, BB and IR. This result holds with or without IC and for both dominant strategy and Bayesian-Nash equilibrium [11]. For impossibility results regarding the incompatibility of dominant strategies, EFF and BB refer [4][5].

3.1   Efficiency and Incentive Compatibility

Allocative-efficiency ensures that the allocation is Pareto-efficient and there are no resale of goods among the agents. In general, IC is not necessary for EFF, e.g. open-cry English auction. But for one-shot exchanges, IC is both necessary and sufficient for EFF. This can be easily seen as the one-shot exchanges obtain bids from agents only once and there is no other way to know the agents' preferences. The use of exchanges in electronic commerce for procurement and as intermediaries requires BB and IR as mandatory properties [11]. Without BB, the market-maker cannot operate the exchange in profit and without IR, agents cannot participate voluntarily. By the impossibility result we have to allocate goods inefficiently with BB and IR. So in our approach we relax EFF. The constructive approach to mechanism design developed in [11] adopt a similar approach, however the pricing problem is modeled as a mathematical programming problem to determine the pricing function that is in minimum *distance* from the VGA pricing and they investigate the use of different distance norms. We do not impose IC as a hard constraint for the following reasons:

- For the one-shot exchange, IC is desirable to implement EFF, but with BB and IR as hard constraints, EFF is not possible even with IC.
- IC is also important from the agents' perspective, as it avoids game-theoretic deliberation about other agents' strategies [13]. However, IC is useful only for private valued goods, as agents will not declare their true valuation to avoid winner's curse for common valued goods [12]. Use of exchanges in electronic commerce are mainly for procurement and brokerage which deal with correlated and common valued goods and hence IC will not help the agents much in the exchanges. It is to be noted here that GVA, in addition to being IC, avoids winner's curse. But unfortunately, GVA is not BB [11].
- IC very much depends on the allocation algorithm. The allocation problem for many exchanges are in general NP-hard and the IC that holds for optimal allocations generally breaks for approximate solutions [7]. We need to develop different IC mechanisms for different approximation schemes.
- The *revelation principle* [9] asserts that whatever that can be achieved by a non-incentive-compatible mechanism can be achieved by a IC direct mechanism. So we can indeed create a IC direct mechanism. However, it is not feasible in practice as the revelation principle makes unreasonable assumptions about the computational capabilities of the agents [11].

Thus we are interested in designing a BB and IR one-shot electronic exchanges. In the following sections we progressively describe the TDP and PDP.

4   Trade Determination Problem

TDP determines the goods traded between every buyer-seller pair such that the revenue in the market is maximized, by an allocation that maximizes the reported values (in the bids and offers) of the agents. This is desirable to avoid ex post claims from participants that an efficient trade was forfeited [11]. Such a revenue maximizing allocation need not be EFF and it is impossible to verify EFF if we do not have truth revelation from the agents. We model the TDP as a mathematical programming problem.

4.1   Notation

The following notation will be used for the rest of the paper. The notation is general enough to include combinatorial bids. Without loss of generality we will assume that an agent submits only one bid.

$\mathcal{B}$ \qquad Set of bids, $\{1, 2, \ldots, m, \ldots, M\}$

$\mathcal{S}$ \qquad Set of offers, $\{1, 2, \ldots, n, \ldots, N\}$

$\mathcal{G}$ \qquad Set of Goods $K \subseteq \mathcal{G}$

$WTP_m(K) \in \mathbb{R}_+ \setminus \{0\}$, *Willingness-to-Pay*: Maximum unit price a buyer m is willing to pay for K

$WTS_n(K) \in \mathbb{R}_+ \setminus \{0\}$, *Willingness-to-Sell*: Minimum unit price a seller n is willing to accept for K

$y_{mn}(K) \quad \in \mathbb{Z}_+$ Number of goods of K traded between agents m and n

TDP is the following mathematical programming problem:

$$R = \max \sum_{Feasible(m,n,K)} (WTP_m(K) - WTS_n(K))y_{mn}(K) \tag{1}$$

$$\text{subject to: } Feasible(y_{mn}(K))$$

where $Feasible(m, n, K)$ is the set of compatible bids with respect to the defined attributes and $WTP_m(K) \geq WTS_n(K)$. $Feasible(y_{mn}(K))$ is the set of feasible trades with respect to supply-demand constraints and aggregation constraints. TDP determines the optimal trade $y_{mn}^*(K)$ that maximizes the reported surplus and the maximum possible surplus out of all allocations is given by R in (1). This problem can be NP-hard depending on the set $Feasible(y_{mn}(K))$.

5   Payoff Determination Problem

The pricing problem in an exchange is to determine the payments made by the agents to the exchange and vice-versa after the exchange clears.

Definition 1 (Trade). *Trade of a buyer m is the $|\mathcal{G}|$ tuple $\alpha_m = (\alpha_m^1, \ldots, \alpha_m^{|\mathcal{G}|})$, where $\alpha_m^i = \sum_{K:i \in K} \sum_n y_{mn}(K)$. Similarly, trade of a seller n is the $|\mathcal{G}|$ tuple $\beta_n = (\beta_n^1, \ldots, \beta_n^{|\mathcal{G}|})$, where $\beta_n^i = \sum_{K:i \in K} \sum_m y_{mn}(K)$*

Definition 2 (Payment). *The payment $p_m(\alpha_m)$ to buyer m is the price paid by the buyer to the exchange if $p_m(\alpha_m) > 0$ and vice-versa if otherwise. The payment $q_n(\beta_n)$ to seller n is the price paid by the exchange to the seller if $q_n(\beta_n) > 0$ and vice-versa if otherwise.*

Definition 3 (Value of Trade). *The value $v_m(\alpha_m)$ is the monetary value of the trade α_m to buyer m and value $u_n(\beta_n)$ is the monetary value of the trade β_n to the seller n.*

The values of the trade are private information to the agents and will not be revealed unless the mechanism is IC. Agents will instead strategically reveal $\tilde{v}_m(\alpha_m)$ and $\tilde{u}_n(\beta_n)$ to the exchange in their bids and offers, respectively. With the revealed values, we implement IR as following constraints:

$$\tilde{v}_m(\alpha_m^*) - p_m(\alpha_m^*) \geq 0, \ \forall \text{ bids } m \tag{2}$$

$$q_n(\beta_n^*) - \tilde{u}_n(\beta_n^*) \geq 0, \ \forall \text{ offers } n \tag{3}$$

where α_m^* and β_n^* are allocated trades when the exchange clears. The above equations are satisfied at equality when the agents pay their quoted price. For BB, we require:

$$\sum_m p_m(\alpha_m^*) = \sum_n q_n(\beta_n^*) \tag{4}$$

The exchange operates at no profit with the above BB, but it can be assumed without loss of generality as the exchange can extract a fixed percentage of the payment to the agents as revenue.

Definition 4 (Payoff). *The payoff Δ_m to buyer m is $\tilde{v}_m(\alpha_m^*) - p_m(\alpha_m^*)$ and the payoff Θ_n to seller n is $q_n(\beta_n^*) - \tilde{u}_n(\beta_n^*)$.*

The payoff is the real utility to the agents *only* when the revealed values are the true values. With respect to payoffs, IR can be written as:

$$\Delta_m \geq 0 \ \forall \text{ bids } m \tag{5}$$

$$\Theta_n \geq 0, \ \forall \text{ offers } n \tag{6}$$

and BB as:

$$\sum_m \tilde{v}_m(\alpha_m^*) - \sum_n \tilde{u}_n(\beta_n^*) = \sum_m \Delta_m + \sum_n \Theta_n \tag{7}$$

It can be easily seen that $\sum_m \tilde{v}_m(\alpha_m^*) - \sum_n \tilde{u}_n(\beta_n^*) = R$, which is the maximized reported surplus given by TDP. The individual payoffs are distributed from this surplus. The exchanges are double-sided markets as both buyers and sellers submit bids. It is reasonable to assume that the exchange should be neutral to both the buyers and sellers in distributing the payoffs, so that it is attractive to both of them.

Definition 5 (Neutrality). *The exchange is neutral if* $\sum_m \Delta_m = \sum_n \Theta_n$.

There are infinite possible values for Δ_m and Θ_n that satisfy (7) and neutrality. For e.g. the mid-point pricing scheme that prices a trade between a buyer with bid value WTP_m, and a seller with offer value WTS_n, at the mid-point $(\frac{WTP_m + WTS_n}{2})$ satisfies the above conditions. The general approach is to determine the payoff through pricing, but we take the reverse approach i.e. price the agents based on the payoff.

Definition 6 (PDP). *The payoff determination problem (PDP) is to determine individual payoffs Δ_m to buyers and Θ_n to sellers such that (7) and neutrality are satisfied.*

The payoff determination and pricing are equivalent in the sense that one can be derived from the other. However, payoff determination approach handles certain critical issues that cannot be handled by pricing. In all market mechanisms different pricing schemes were only used to investigate IC and existence of dominant strategy equilibriums. These are sufficient if a single seller trades with a single buyer, like traditional auctions. Most of the research is focussed on how to carry over these properties of single-sided auctions to electronic exchanges with multiple buyers and multiple sellers (like GVA from Vickrey auctions). But the overlooked point is that electronic exchanges possibly allow trading multiple units of different goods based on multiple attributes with aggregation over supply and demand. A pricing scheme that achieves IC or dominant strategy equilibrium may not consider the *value* added by a bid in the current trade and hence may not *fairly* distribute the payoff to the bids.

Consider a multi-attribute procurement exchange with attributes like price, quantity, delivery time, post-sale service, warranty etc. Let there be a single seller who wants to procure some products with some desirable value for the above attributes. Bids are accepted from the buyers and let five bids be finally selected for trading that are compatible in all the attributes and also maximize the profit for the seller. Let us assume that we somehow calculated the total payoff to all the buyers as 100. How can we distribute this total payoff to individual buyers? One naive approach is to give a non-negative weight and a value to each attribute (where the weights sum up to unity) and to obtain a single numerical quantity that quantifies a bid, by the weighted average method. Then using these numerical quantities we can find the relative importance of each bid. However, it is not trivial to determine a weight and value to each attribute (some attributes like warranty, logistics are not easily quantifiable) that can convince all the agents as being *fair*. We will present an alternate approach to determine the relative importance of each bid using the concept of *added value*.

5.1 Added Value

The *added value* of a player in the game is the difference of the values of the game when the player is *in* in the game and when he is *out* of the game [2][3]. Added value measures what each player brings to the game. Added value concept is extensively used to design strategies for determining the payoff in a conflict situation [3]. In this paper, we use the added value concept for designing an arbitration scheme that determines the payoff to each agent, based on certain *fair* norms.

When neutrality is implemented as a hard constraint, we have $\sum_m \Delta_m = \sum_n \Theta_n = R/2$. We will consider only the case of distribution of payoff to buyers as roles of buyers and sellers are symmetric and the same line of arguments hold true for sellers. Let the TDP has determined the total payoff $X(= R/2)$ to buyers $1, 2, \ldots, M$ with final trade $\alpha_1, \alpha_2, \ldots, \alpha_M$, respectively. Let X_{-m} be the total payoff determined by TDP when bid m is removed. It is worth noting here our assumption that a buyer places only one bid.

Definition 7 (Added Value). *Added value of a buyer (bid) m, $V_m = X - X_{-m}$.*

The above definition assumes that the game is only among the buyers unlike the original definition in [3], which also includes the sellers. This is mandatory to implement neutrality.

Proposition 1. $V_m \geq 0$ *for buyer m.*

Proof. Let $V_m < 0$. Then $X_{-m} > X$, which contradicts the fact that R $(X = R/2)$ is the maximum surplus of all the possible trades.   □

We have implicitly assumed in the above proof that TDP is solved to optimality. If it is solved approximately, then it possible that $X_{-m} > X$. This assumption is equivalent to the unrestricted bargaining assumption of [2]

Proposition 2. *It need not always be true that $\sum_m V_m = X$.*

Proof. Consider a trade with total value X (to the buyers) and two buyers and one seller. Let the total trade $\alpha_1 + \alpha_2$ be aggregated and bought from the seller. If the seller is not interested to sell anything less than $\alpha_1 + \alpha_2$ then $V_1 = V_2 = X$.   □

Thus the added value is not the payoff to the agents. The added-value measure provides a partial, rather than a complete, answer to the question of how value is divided [2]. It is used to develop business strategies to determine the payoffs. We use the added value to devise an arbitration scheme that determines the payoff to all the buyers.

5.2   Arbitration Scheme

When the players in a conflict situation are unable to come to a conclusion, they will submit their conflict to an external arbiter who will resolve the conflict based on certain *fairness* criteria that convinces all players [8]. Let $V = (V_1, V_2, \ldots, V_M)$ be the added values of the buyers. We have to determine $x = (x_1, x_2, \ldots, x_M)$ where x_m is the *proportion* of the total payoff X to be granted to buyer m.

Definition 8 (Arbitration Scheme). *An arbitration scheme is a function which associates to each conflict situation $V \subseteq \mathbb{R}_+^M$ a unique $x \subseteq \mathbb{R}_+^M$ to the buyers.*

There clearly exists an infinity of such functions. We have to choose one that is *fair* to all the players. The *fairness* criteria are certain intuitive relationship that V_i and x_i should satisfy. We frame these fairness criteria as axioms and mathematically investigate the existence of such an arbitration scheme.

Axiomatic Approach. We take an axiomatic approach in determining the arbitration scheme by specifying a set of basic axioms that need to be satisfied.

Axiom 1. $x_m \geq 0$, *and* $x_m = 0$ *iff* $V_m = 0$.

This is quite obvious as the proportions have to be non-negative and a buyer who has not added any value should get zero payoff i.e. he pays his bid price. In [2], x_m can be zero even if $V_m > 0$.

Axiom 2. $V_m > V_k \Leftrightarrow x_m > x_k$ *and* $x_m = x_k$ *iff* $V_m = V_k$.

The buyer with a higher added value should get more payoff and buyers with equal added values should get equal payoffs.

Axiom 3. *For any given* V_i, V_j, V_l, V_m *with* $V_l \neq V_m$, $\frac{V_i - V_j}{V_m - V_l} = \frac{x_i - x_j}{x_m - x_l}$.

This axiom says that the rate of change of payment should be constant with respect to that of the added value. This avoids any unfair scheme that might favor buyers with either high added value or low added value.

Axiom 4. $\sum_m x_m = 1$.

This ensures BB ($\sum_m x_m \not> 1$) and the payoff distribution is Pareto-efficient ($\sum_m x_m \not< 1$).

Proposition 3. *The arbitration scheme with* $x_m = \frac{V_m}{\sum_m V_m}$ $\forall m$ *is the unique closed form function that satisfies all the four axioms.*

Proof. Axiom 3 means that x_m varies linearly with V_m and so we have $x_m = a_m V_m + b_m$ for some real a_m and b_m. Axiom 2 states that x_m is an increasing function and all x_m have to be the same so that they are equal at the same values of V_m. Hence we have $x_m = a V_m + b$ $\forall m$ with $a > 0$. Since $x_m = 0$ at zero added value by Axiom 1, it is a linear function of V_m i.e. $x_m = a V_m$. By Axiom 4,

$$\sum_m x_m = 1$$
$$\Rightarrow \sum_m a V_m = 1$$
$$\Rightarrow a = \frac{1}{\sum_m V_m}$$
$$\Rightarrow x_m = \frac{V_m}{\sum_m V_m}$$

$\square$

Proposition 4. *The above arbitration scheme is IR.*

Proof. The payoff to m, $\Delta_m = x_m X = (\frac{V_m}{\sum_m V_m}) X \geq 0.$ □

The above arbitration scheme being the unique closed form function that satisfies all the axioms is worth noting, because with the existence of multiple functions, each player will favor the one that gives him more payoff [8]. However, it requires $(N + M + 1)$ TDPs to be solved, which may demand additional computational requirements if the TDP is hard to solve.

5.3 Limitations

In this section we discuss some limitations of using the above arbitration scheme using simple example exchanges. We consider a homogeneous exchange with bid structure (*Quantity, Unit Price*). The bids are all-or-nothing bids, i.e. either entire *Quantity* is traded or none is traded.

Equal Added Values. We will show an example where buyers get equal added values which is not fair. Consider a single seller with offer (100, 1) and two buyers A and B with bids (75, 2) and (25, 1.5), respectively. The optimal trade is that seller sells 75 units to buyer A and 25 units to buyer B. One can easily see that $X = 87.5/2 = 43.75$. Without A there will be no trade as the supply and demand are not matched and similarly without B there will be no trade. Hence, $V_A = V_B = 43.75$, $x_A = x_B = 0.5$, and payoffs $\Delta_A = \Delta_B = 21.875$. The two buyers are getting the same payoff even though one is buying only one-third of the goods at a much lower price. By the added value concepts this is perfectly fine as both buyers have equal bargaining power since they need each other to get a positive payoff. However, its use in the arbitration scheme fails to be fair.

Zero Added Values. Consider an exchange with two sellers X and Y with offers (75, 1) and (25, 1), respectively. Let there be three buyers: A with bid (50, 2), B with (50, 2) and C with (50, 2). Here we have three optimal allocations: X and Y trade with A and B, or with A and C, or with B and C. Let us choose the first one. Then, $V_A = V_B = 0$ as $X_{-A} = X_{-B} = X$ by the alternate optimal solution. We will have added values of the buyers as zero for any optimal solution. Again, by the added value concept this is fine, as buyers will have nearly zero value when the supply is limited [3]. But it is not fair in our case as the buyers gets zero payoff. In fact we cannot even apply our arbitration scheme in this case.

The equal added values case arise due to the all-or-nothing structure of the bids. One can expect more such pathological cases when we go for more complex combinatorial bid structures. We have to use the arbitration scheme with additional constraints so that we avoid such unfair situations. The zero added values case is due to the presence of alternate optimal solutions. This can be avoided by using the arbitration scheme only on the winning bids. Thus, we may have to impose more constraints on an exchange depending on its structure while using the arbitration scheme to avoid *unfair* results.

6   Conclusion

We proposed a new approach to the design of exchanges by decoupling allocation from pricing. Allocation is the trade determination problem that maximizes the reported surplus of the agents. The general approach to the pricing problem is to achieve IC or dominant strategies. We proposed a different approach, an arbitration scheme that determines the payoff to an agent based on relative value of the bid in the market. The payoff achieves pricing that is budget-balanced and individually-rational for all the agents. The arbitration scheme is based on the added-value concept of game theory and developed using an axiomatic approach which captures the intuitive relationships between the added-value and the payoff. The arbitration scheme has some limitations but can be used with certain additional constraints, which depends on the type of exchange that is being designed. This is a first step towards determining pricing through payoffs and work remains to be done to consider the computational complexity and equilibrium strategies of the agents.

References

1. Bichler, M., Beam, C., Segev, A.: An electronic broker for business- to-business electronic commerce on the Internet. International Journal of Cooperative Information Systems 7 (1998) 315–341
2. Brandenburger, A., Stuart, H.: Value-Based Business Strategy. Jl. of Econ. & Mgmt. Strategy 5:1 (1996) 5–24
3. Brandenburger, A., Nalebuff, B. J.: Co-opetition. Currency Doubleday (1996)
4. Hurwicz, L.: On informationally decentralized systems, Decision and Organization, C. B. McGuire and R. Radner, Eds., North-Holland, Amsterdam (1972) 297–336
5. Ledyard, J. O.: Incentive Compatibility. Allocation, Information and Markets, The New Palgrave, W. W. Norton & Company, Ltd. New York (1989)
6. Friedman, D.: The Double Auction Market Institution: A Survey. In: Friedman, D., Rust, J. (eds): The Double Auction Market: Institutions, Theories and Evidence. Perseus Publishing, Cambridge, Massachusetts (1993) 3–26
7. Lehmann, D., O'Callaghan, L. I., Shoham, Y.: Truth Revelation in Rapid, Approximately Efficient Combinatorial Auctions (1999)
8. Luce, R. D., Raiffa, H.: Games and Decisions, Introduction and Critical Survey. Dover Publications, New York (1989)
9. Myerson, R. B.: Optimal Auction Design. Mathematics of Operation Research 6 (1981) 61–73
10. Myerson, R. B., Satterthwaite, M. A.: Efficient Mechanisms for Bilateral Trading. Journal of Economic Theory 28 (1983) 265–281
11. D. C. Parkes, J. Kalagnanam and Marta Eso. Achieving Budget-Balance with Vickrey-Based Payment Schemes in Combinatorial Exchanges. IBM Research Report RC 22218 W0110-065 (2001)
12. Wurman, P.R., Walsh, W.E., Wellman, M.P.: Flexible double auctions for electronic commerce: Theory and implementation. Decision Support Systems 24(1998) 17–27
13. Varian, R. H.: Economic Mechanism Design for Computerized Agents (2000)

Winner Determination Algorithms for Electronic Auctions: A Framework Design

Martin Bichler, Jayant Kalagnanam, Ho Soo Lee, and Juhnyoung Lee

IBM T. J. Watson Research Center
Yorktown Heights, NY 10598, USA
{bichler, jyl, leehs, jayant}@us.ibm.com
http://www.research.ibm.com

Abstract. During the past few years, auctions have become popular in conducting trade negotiations on the Internet. The design of new auctions and other negotiation protocols has become an important topic for both, industry and academia. Traditional auction mechanisms allow price-only negotiations for which the winner determination is a computationally simple task. However, the need for new auction mechanisms that allow complex bids such as bundle bids and multi-attribute bids has been raised in many situations. The winner determination in these auctions is a computationally hard problem. The computational complexity has been a significant hurdle for the widespread use of these advanced auction models. In this paper, we will outline the auction design space and classify resource allocation algorithms along multiple dimensions. Then, we will explain the design of an object framework providing an API to different types of winner determination algorithms. This framework enables application programmers to specify buyer preferences, allocation rules and supplier offerings in a declarative manner, and solve the allocation problems without having to re-implement the computationally complex algorithms.

1 Introduction

Auctions have become a fairly successful way of supporting or even automating negotiations on trading markets on the Internet. Examples of traditional auction mechanisms include the English, Dutch, First-Price Sealed-Bid, or Vickrey auction[1]. The competitive process of auctions serves to aggregate the scattered information about bidder's valuation and to dynamically set the prices and conditions of a deal. The typical auction process implemented by most auction platforms consists of the steps of bid submission, bid evaluation (in literature, winner determination and resource allocation are often used for bid evaluation; the three terms will be used interchangeably in this paper), and the calculation of settlement prices, followed by some feedback to the bidders in an iterative, or open-cry auction (see Figure 1). Auctions close either at a fixed point in time or after a certain closing criterion is met (e.g., a certain time elapsed).

K. Bauknecht, A M. Tjoa, G. Quirchmayr (Eds.): EC-Web 2002, LNCS 2455, pp. 37–46, 2002.
© Springer-Verlag Berlin Heidelberg 2002

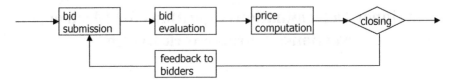

Fig. 1. Simplified auction process

A primary emphasis of auction research has been the various rules governing the auction process. The traditional literature mainly focuses on situations where participants negotiate only on price, with the quantity and quality of goods or services being fixed a priori (by the auctioneer). In these cases, the bid evaluation, i.e., the actual task of allocating (demand-side) bids to (sell-side) asks, is computationally simple and consists mainly of sorting bids by price.

During the past few years, however, a number of new auction formats that allow matching buyer's preferences with seller's offerings in a more general sense have been developed. These auctions allow complex bids such as bundle bids and multi-attribute bids and, therefore, allow the negotiation not only on price but also on quantity and qualitative attributes. A popular example of such advanced auction types is the combinatorial auction. It provides a useful negotiation mechanism when there are complementarities or substitutability among several products. In a procurement situation, for example, suppliers can often provide better overall prices if they are allowed to deliver not just one product type for the buyer (e.g., an office owner) but a bundle of product types that complement each other (e.g., computers, monitors and printers). Explicit consideration of these complementarities in combinatorial reverse auctions can lead to substantial cost saving for buying organizations. However, a major hurdle for the use of combinatorial auctions in practice has been that their winner determination is computationally hard. Many of the new auction mechanisms (e.g., multi-unit auctions, volume-discount auctions, and multi-attribute reverse auctions) require solving NP-hard optimization problems (see section 2.3).

The design and implementation of the appropriate decision analysis and optimization models requires skills in operations research as well as software engineering. In this paper we introduce an object framework with a generic API (Application Programming Interface) to winner determination algorithms. The software is intended as a standard solver component for electronic marketplaces and is currently in use with a large-scale procurement platform for the retail industry. This framework enables application programmers to specify buyer preferences, allocation rules and supplier offerings in a declarative manner, and solve the allocation problems without having to re-implement the computationally complex algorithms.

The design of new market mechanisms is a new and emerging field. Many new allocation algorithms have been developed during the past few years, and many new approaches can be expected in the near future. It is important to understand the design space for allocation algorithms, in order to design an easily extensible object framework. We introduce a multidimensional perspective of the auction design space that helps classify advanced resource allocation problems and improve the understanding of their requirements. The framework design can be used as a reference model for similar solver components of this type.

The rest of this paper is structured as follows: Section 2 explains the dimensions of the auction design space and classifies advanced auction formats by three dimensions. Also, typical allocation problems for the auction types are explained. Section 3 describes a number of auction design considerations including the representation of offers. In Section 4, the multidimensional winner determination package with its design objectives, object model, and implementation is described. Finally, in Section 5, the work is summarized and conclusions are drawn.

2   Allocation Algorithms for Multidimensional Auctions

In this section, we introduce and classify a number of advanced auction mechanisms and associated allocation algorithms for bid evaluation that have been developed over the past few years. We begin by outlining the overall design space for these allocation algorithms that later will be used to lay the foundation for the design of an object framework.

2.1   Design Space of Resource Allocation Algorithms

The problem of bid evaluation arises in many different applications, because it occurs in a variety of negotiation forms including bilateral bargaining, auctions and RFQ (Request For Quotes). Furthermore, auction protocols can be sealed-bid or open-cry, and the auctioneer can reveal various degrees of information about the current status. Also, the protocols can involve rules about who is allowed to bid, how the auction is closed, and what the minimum bid increment is. In addition, an auction can be chained with other negotiation protocols or conducted in multiple rounds, each involving a separate phase of bid evaluation and allocation. Problems similar to bid evaluation arise also in other applications. For example, in a catalog aggregation application where product and pricing data is automatically aggregated from multiple suppliers, buyers need to select one or more among the offerings. There is no negotiation involved in this application, but automated evaluation of various offerings is still a key functionality.

The design space for resource allocation algorithms is huge. The primary criteria for characterizing the allocation problems on electronic markets are:
- the number of participants, and
- the types of traded goods.

The *number of participants* heavily influences the design of an allocation algorithm. Micro-economists distinguish different market structures to categorize different negotiation situations (e.g., monopoly). Different types of negotiation protocols are analyzed in different settings ranging from bilateral bargaining to single-sided auctions and to double auctions. Likewise, the allocation problems change in different settings in terms of the number of participants:
- bilateral allocation problems,

- n-bilateral allocation problems (e.g., single-sided and double auctions), and
- multilateral allocation problems.

Bilateral allocation problems involve bargaining situations and bid evaluation with only two parties. N-bilateral allocation problems typically involve auction settings where there are two types of participants, i.e., buyers and sellers, but there can be more than one of them on each side of the bargaining table. In a reverse auction case, there is one buyer and multiple suppliers, whereas in a double auction, offers of multiple buyers and sellers have to be matched. Finally, multilateral negotiation situations involve more than two parties (e.g., negotiations for mergers and acquisitions including a selling organization, a buying organization and a bank).

An equally important criterion is the *type of traded goods* or services, and more specifically the way, how offers are described. Traditional micro-economic theory distinguishes between homogeneous and heterogeneous goods. For the actual design of a bid evaluation algorithm, one needs to consider more than homogenous goods. Earlier, we introduced combinatorial auctions and briefly mentioned other advanced auction mechanisms such as volume-discount auctions and multi-attribute reverse auctions. These advanced auctions formats can be categorized by several different dimensions of the goods in negotiation (as illustrated in Figure 2):

- the number of different items in negotiation (e.g., a single or multiple line items),
- the negotiable qualitative attributes (e.g., a single or multiple attributes), and
- the quantity for each item (e.g., a single or multiple units).

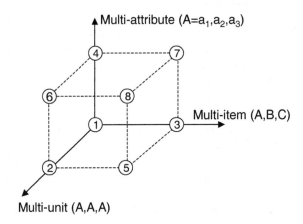

Fig. 2. Dimensions of a trade negotiation [2]

2.2 Multidimensional Auctions

These three dimensions of goods or services in a trade negotiation provide a way to characterize the relevant aspects of offers (i.e., bids and/or asks). Note that the offer type impacts the bid evaluation algorithm used. Figure 2 shows eight distinct types of offers:

- Offer type 1 describes single-item, price-only, single-unit offers. These offers are used in traditional auctions where all qualitative attributes and quantity are fixed *a priori*, and there is only one particular item in negotiation, e.g., the price for a rare piece of art. The economic behavior of these types of auctions has been extensively studied in game theory and experimental economics (see [1] for an overview).
- Offer type 2 describes single-item, price-only, multi-unit offers. Only one type of item is negotiated, and the quality is predefined. Examples include price-quantity offers in *multi-unit auctions* or offers describing supply-curves in a *volume-discount auction* (see next section).
- Offer type 3 is multi-item, price-only, fixed-quantity offers. An example is a bundle offer that comprises a number of items (a single unit for each) with a single price. Bundle offers are allocated by *combinatorial auctions*.
- Offer type 4 describes pure multi-attribute offers having a single item. These offers have only one type of one item up for negotiation and the quantity is fixed, i.e., suppliers can only provide the entire demanded quantity. These offers are often used in *multi-attribute reverse auctions* and in RFQs.
- Offer types 5 to 8 describe combinations of the dimensions. Offer type 5 contains multiple items where quantity is also negotiable. Offer type 6 describes fixed-quantity offers where qualitative attributes and quantity of goods are negotiable. Offer type 7 is multi-attribute, multi-item offers where the quantity is fixed. Finally, Offer type 8 describes pure multi-dimensional offers where all dimensions are negotiable.

In the next section, we will explain how these multidimensional offers can be evaluated in advanced auction mechanisms that allow complex offer types, such as multi-unit auctions, volume-discount auctions, combinatorial auctions or multi-attribute reverse auctions.

2.3 Allocation Problems in Multidimensional Auctions

Recently, there has been active research on *multi-unit auctions* in which bidders submit both the number of units of an item they wish to buy and how much they are willing to bid per unit. The first-price auction has two multi-unit generalizations which are used in practice – *discriminatory auctions* in which the bidders who bid the highest prices pay their bid, and *uniform-price auctions* in which all k successful bidders pay the $(k+1)$st bid price. The uniform price is set by the bid on the $(k+1)$st unit which is not a winning bid, because there are only k units on sale. Most on-line auctions are discriminatory auctions, where each bidder pays the bid price. If offers are divisible, i.e., the bidders are willing to accept a partial quantity for the same price, the winner determination becomes trivial and can be solved by sorting the offers by unit price. If, however, offers are indivisible, which is the usual case in multi-unit auctions, the auctioneer needs to solve a 0/1-Knapsack problem known to be NP-complete [3]:

$$\max \sum_i (n_i p_i) x_i \tag{1}$$

$$s.t. \sum_i n_i x_i \le K, \quad x_i \in \{0,1\} \tag{2}$$

In the above formulation a binary variable x_i is assigned to each offer, which indicates acceptance or rejection. p_i defines price and n_i the number of units in each bid. In practice, these problems are often solved using dynamic programming.

Volume-discount auctions are an interesting extension of multi-unit auctions. These auctions can be used in a procurement context where bidders are allowed to specify the price they charge for an item as a function of order quantity. Bids take the form of supply curves that specify the price to be charged per unit of item when the quantity of items being purchased lies within a particular quantity interval. The allocation algorithm described in [4] uses a mixed integer programming formulation to select the cost-minimizing set of bids.

Combinatorial auctions (also referred to as multi-item or bundle auctions) are an approach to achieving efficient allocations in situations where bidders are allowed to place bids on combinations of possibly heterogeneous goods or services [5, 6]. An example is a bid on a group of adjacent real estate properties. A combinatorial bid can win only if it is greater than the sum of the high bids in the auctions for the individual licenses. A winning bid on a shipping lane between two production plants is valuable to a transporter only if it also wins the lane in the opposite direction. The transporter must bid higher combinatorial for both than the sum of the high bids for the individual lanes.

Combinatorial auctions are also used in a procurement context where several goods or services that have complementarities among them are purchased together. In these situations, the auctioneer tries to find the combination of bids with the lowest cost. In other words, the winner determination problem for a combinatorial reverse auction is to select a winning set of bids such that the demand for each item is satisfied and, at the same time, the total cost of procurement is minimized. This problem can be formulated as a weighted set covering problem which is also known to be NP-hard. Set covering can also be solved by using integer programming techniques. Combinatorial forward auctions can be treated in a similar manner as a set packing problem [7].

Another interesting type of multidimensional auction is the *multi-attribute auction* [8] where bidders are allowed to submit multi-attribute bids and therefore negotiate not just on price but quantity and qualitative attributes. Typical multi-attribute auctions describe bids as a set of attribute-value pairs. An approach to handling multiple attributes is to convert qualitative attributes into price-equivalents by using a certain set of rules. Another approach is to define scoring functions for individual attributes and calculate the bid scores by aggregating attribute scores using a linear or non-linear utility function. These techniques have their origin in multi-attribute decision analysis [9]. More advanced settings considering multiple sourcing and indivisible bids also need to solve optimization problems.

All these advanced auction mechanisms provide bidders with increased flexibility and expressiveness in describing their offers. They promise higher market efficiency, because they allow for a more effective exchange of relevant market information. Most of these auctions already found successful applications in a variety of industries, and one can expect more developments in this field.

3 Design Considerations

A number of evaluation criteria are used to analyze auctions and other economic mechanisms [8, p. 73]. The auction process should converge to equilibrium, i.e., a solution, in which no agent wishes to change its bid. Of course, the speed of this convergence is important, too. A solution of an auction should be stable, so that no subset of agents could have done better by coming to an agreement outside the auction. Mechanism design theory also suggests that optimal auctions should be incentive-compatible; i.e., honest reporting of valuations is a Nash-equilibrium. These criteria are important for the design of the auction process. The key criterion for the winner determination is, however, whether the solution to an allocation is shows *allocative efficiency*. In other words, no rearrangement of resources could make someone better off without making someone else worse off.

In section 2.3 we have illustrated the complexities of determining efficient resource allocations. The major factor influencing this complexity is the bid representation. Bid representation has not been an issue in auction research until now. For example, offers in multi-attribute auctions are presented as sets of attribute-value pairs. A recent paper by Bichler, Kalagnanam and Lee [10] extends the notion of multi-attribute offers to *configurable offers*. The ECCO system presented in this paper allows the specification of multiple options for each attribute in an offer. The system defines for each attribute a set of possible values and their associated markup prices. Also, it allows the offers to include a set of logical rules on how to combine various attribute values (so called *configuration rules*), and how certain configurations impact the price (i.e. *discount rules*). The ECCO winner determination algorithm takes into account these rules along with buyer preferences and selects the best out of all possible configurations. In a similar way, logical bid languages have been defined for bundle offers, which allow for a *compact description* of a large number of explicit bundle bids [11]. Reeves et al. [12] use even the expressiveness of first-oder logic in representing complex offers. They presented an approach where offers in a negotiation are expressed as logic programs. More elaborate bid representation schemes enable higher expressiveness and flexibility in a negotiation at the expense of increased complexity of bid evaluation.

4 A Framework for Multidimensional Auction Markets

The Multidimensional Auction Platform (MAP) is a set of software modules for building multidimensional auction markets which has been developed at IBM T. J. Watson Research Center. MAP features several Java packages:

- Package *com.ibm.allocation* provides an object framework for resource allocation algorithms in electronic markets.
- Package *com.ibm.allocation.solvers* provides façade classes to various optimization packages such as IBM's OSL, or Ilog's CPLEX. These façade classes make it possible to seamlessly switch from one optimization package to another.

- Package *com.ibm.allocation.datasource* provides façade classes to different kinds of data sources. These façade classes make it possible to use algorithms with different data sources, e.g., databases or XML files, and different data schemas.
- Package *com.ibm.preference* provides Java classes for various preference elicitation methods useful in a multi-attribute negotiation [13, 14].

4.1 Design Objectives

In the following discussion, we will concentrate on the *allocation package* (com.ibm.allocation), which is the centrepiece of MAP. The allocation package is implemented as an object framework in the sense that it is a collection of cooperating objects that provide an integrated solution customizable by the developer. It is important to note that unlike a class library approach, the framework approach provides a bi-directional flow of control between an application and the framework [15]. This feature enables easy extension with customer specific code.

The primary design objective for the allocation framework relates to its reuse of various classes in solving different instances of allocation problems. The fundamental strategy used in designing the object framework involves identifying high-level abstraction of common problem classes. The main objectives in designing the framework are summarized as follows:

- The framework should provide an easy-to-use and declarative interface which hides the complexity of the underlying allocation algorithms.
- It should allow for rapid prototyping with maximal reuse of available problem representation and algorithms.
- It should be possible to switch between existing types of allocation algorithms with minimal effort, and adopt new allocation algorithms into the framework with little customisation.
- The basic data structures and algorithms should be reusable in different environments and applications, e.g., in electronic auction implementation, in stand-alone decision support tools for procurement, or in agent-based computer simulations.

4.2 Object Model

The object model of the allocation framework is illustrated in Figure 3. There are three core interfaces in the framework, *Offer*, *AllocationAlgorithm*, and *Solution*. These interfaces provide common denominators for various types of allocation algorithms possible. The *Offer* interface is implemented by many classes including *PriceOnlyOffer*, *PriceQuantityOffer*, *VolumeDiscountOffer*, *BundleOffer*, *MultiAttributeRequest*, and *MultiAttributeOffer*. Bundle offers assign a single price to a bundle of heterogeneous items. Volume-discount offers are used in volume-discount auctions as described in Section 2. Each *Offer* is submitted by an *Agent* and assigned to an *AllocationAlgorithm*. For each *Agent* or *AgentGroup*, an application programmer can define *AgentConstraints*, which defines minmum and maximum allocations per agent, or per agent and item. An implementation of *AllocationAlgorithm* can then allocate certain implementations of *Offer*, and return the result of this allocation in a *Solution*. For example, a *VolumeDiscountAllocation* assigns one or more responses of class *VolumeDis-coutOffer* to a *BundleOffer* which specifies the request.

Based on the number of participants, we distinguish three broad types of allocation algorithms, namely, *TwoPartyAllocation*, *SingleSidedAllocation* and *Clearing-HouseAllocation*. Examples of two-party situations are bilateral negotiations on price, or on multiple attributes, where only one buy-side offer and one sell-side offer are matched at a point in time. In addition, a set of classes implements the interface *ClearingHouseAllocation*. These classes allocate multiple buy-side and sell-side bids at a point in time. A typical application of such an algorithm can be found in financial call markets where bids and asks on price and quantity are collected over a specified interval of time, and then the market clears, i.e., the offers are allocated at a price that maximizes the turnover. Finally, an implementation of *SingleSidedAllocation* can be used when one or more responses need to be selected to satisfy a single request. Typi-cal applications of these algorithms are single-sided forward or reverse (i.e., procure-ment) auctions. In Section 2, we have discussed a number of such allocation problems.

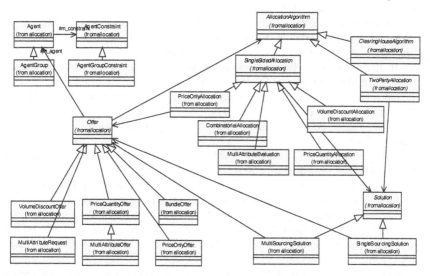

Fig. 3. Selected Class Hierarchies of the Allocation Package

5   Conclusions

Recently, there has been a significant shift in e-commerce from static forms of pricing to dynamic pricing [2]. Many new and versatile auction formats have been developed, which allow more flexibility in specifying demand and supply, and ultimately lead to more efficient outcomes. This trend has led to an increasing need for fast and efficient winner determination algorithms. Reusable implementations of these algorithms en-able businesses to easily deploy new negotiation protocols in their procurement proc-esses. In this paper, we have discussed the design space and the design objectives for such resource allocation algorithms. We have also described an extensible object framework which enables the reuse of the advanced allocation algorithms as a standard solver component in electronic markets. It provides a declarative interface and sheds developers from the complexities of a particular allocation algorithm. The framework has been developed at IBM T. J. Watson Research Center and is currently being used in a number of customer engagements.

References

1. E. Wolfstetter, "Auctions: An Introduction," *Journal of Economic Surveys*, vol. 10, pp. 367-420, 1996.
2. M. Bichler, J. Kalagnanam, K. K. Katircioglu, A. J. King, R. D. Lawrence, H. S. Lee, G. Y. Lin, and Y. Lu, "Applications of Flexible Pricing in Business-to-Business Electronic Commerce," *IBM Systems Journal*, 2002.
3. M. Eso, "Evaluation algorithms in auctions," IBM T.J. Watson Research Center, Yorktown Heights, Working Paper 2001.
4. A. Davenport and J. Kalagnanam, "Price Negotiations for Procurement of Direct Inputs," IMA "Hot Topics" Workshop: Mathematics of the Internet: E-Auction and Markets, Minneapolis, USA, Workshop Report December 3-5, 2000 2000.
5. M. H. Rothkopf and A. Pekec, "Computationally Manageable Combinatorial Auctions," presented at Maryland Auction Conference, Maryland, USA, 1998.
6. T. Sandholm, "Approaches to winner determination in combinatorial auctions," *Decision Support Systems*, vol. 28, pp. 165-176, 1999.
7. G. L. Nemhauser, A. H. G. Rinnooy Kan, and M. J. Todd, *Optimization*. Amsterdam: Elsevier, 1989.
8. M. Bichler, *The Future of eMarkets: Multi-Dimensional Market Mechanisms*. Cambridge, UK: Cambridge University Press, 2001.
9. D. L. Olson, *Decision Aids for Selection Problems*. New York, et al.: Springer, 1995.
10. M. Bichler, J. Kalagnanam, and H. S. Lee, "ECCO – Automated Evaluation of Configurable Offerings," IBM Research, Yorktown Heights, Research Report 2002.
11. C. Boutilier and H. H. Hoos, "Bidding Languages for Combinatorial Auctions," presented at 17th International Joint Conference on Artificial Intelligence (IJCAI) 2001, Washington, USA, 2001.
12. D. Reeves, B. Grosof, and M. Wellman, "Automated Negotiations from Declarative Contract Descriptions," presented at AAAI-2000 Workshop on Knowledge-Based Electronic Markets, Austin, TX, 2000.
13. M. Bichler, J. Lee, C. H. Kim, and H. S. Lee, "Design and Implementation of an Intelligent Decision Analysis System for E-Sourcing," presented at International Conference on Artificial Intelligence 2001, Las Vegas, NV, 2001.
14. V. S. Iyengar, J. Lee, and M. Campbell, "Q-Eval: Evaluating Multiple Attribute Items Using Queries," IBM Research, New York, Research Report 2001.
15. J. Sametinger, *Software Engineering with Reusable Components*. New York: Springer, 1997.

A Web-Based E-commerce Facilitator Intermediary for Small and Medium Enterprises: A B2B/B2C Hybrid Proposal

F.J. García, A.B. Gil, N. Moreno, and B. Curto

Departamento de Informática y Automática – Facultad de Ciencias
University of Salamanca
{fgarcia, abg, mmg}@usal.es, bcurto@abedul.usal.es

Abstract. The importance of intermediaries in electronic commerce and also in electronic marketplaces has long been recognised in specialised literature. In this paper, we propose a web-based intermediary for e-commerce, whose main goal is to facilitate the entry of small and medium enterprises into the virtual business arena, by allowing the formation of enterprise coalitions based on the role of this intermediary, which acts as a shopping-window for their products. The main characteristics of this intermediary for e-commerce are as follows. First of all, it offers a trading area, based on product catalogues (multi-vendor e-catalogues). Secondly, SMEs are represented by a software catalogue-designer tool that leaves the definition, publication and update of catalogues of products in the hands of these enterprises. From this point of view, the intermediary represents a B2B/B2C hybrid proposal instead of the typical B2B variety of these commerce intermediaries.

Keywords. Web-based intermediary; Electronic marketplace; B2B/B2C hybrid model; Multi-vendor catalogue; Catalogue-designer tool.

1 Introduction

The rapid growth of the Internet is stimulating an ever-increasing number of businesses that have found their development field in this Network. Electronic commerce and electronic marketplaces represent a new world of business that is full of potential benefits [13], but not free of barriers and problems [12].

The impediments are more important in small organizations or businesses, usually known as Small and Medium Enterprises (SME), where the amount of investment in technology solutions cannot be very large.

The entry of a SME into the virtual commerce scene is a winding road with not always a successful end, because this enterprise is usually an unknown one, faraway from its influence market context, and also it usually lacks the right technical and advertising methods to get known in Internet.

However, we think when several joined SMEs can make up a critical mass that makes them attractive for end-users. The most effective way to do this is through an e-commerce intermediary [6] that can serve as shopping-window for their [14].

K. Bauknecht, A M. Tjoa, G. Quirchmayr (Eds.): EC-Web 2002, LNCS 2455, pp. 47–56, 2002.
© Springer-Verlag Berlin Heidelberg 2002

An intermediary, also called a middleman or broker in the research literature in various fields, implies the entry of a new company into the value chain that connects buyers and suppliers, either as a provider of new and innovative services [3, 18], or as a competitor to existing intermediaries [8].

Electronic marketplaces require price setting, transaction processing and coordination, inventory management, immediacy, quality guarantees and monitoring [17]. With the appropriate motivation and profit opportunities, any industrial player, such as a buyer, a supplier or an IT vendor, can become a provider of an online market [4].

Bailey and Bakos [2] emphasize the need for intermediation in electronic marketplaces. They report that IT-mediated markets still need aggregator for one-stop shopping window, trust providers, information exchange facilitators and information filtering brokers.

However, the majority of the intermediaries appear in the B2B dimension of the electronic commerce. For this reason, we propose a web-based intermediary site to facilitate SMEs entrance in the virtual business area, but also to near them to the end-users. According to this, there are two dimensions in the proposed business model supported by the intermediary. The first one is a B2B (Business to Business) dimension, related to the communication between the SME and the intermediary. On the other hand, we have a B2C (Business to Client) dimension that succeeds in putting the end-users into contact with the products of the SME through the intermediary.

The result is a B2B/B2C hybrid model [9] whose main objective is to provide the SMEs with a uniform platform that implements the services needed for an e-commerce strategy development. This model is implemented now in an e-commerce architecture proposal, so-called e-CoUSAL [10].

This paper is devoted to describe this web-based e-commerce intermediary for SMEs. Thus, the remainder of the paper is organized as follows: Section 2 overviews the proposed e-commerce architecture. Section 3 examines the intermediary architecture. Section 4 defines the communicator element between the SMEs and the intermediary site: the catalogue of products. Section 5 describes the catalogue creation process supported by an authoring tool. Finally, Section 6 concludes the work.

2 An Overview of e-CoUSAL E-commerce Architecture

e-CoUSAL architecture is devoted to facilitate the entry of a business organisation, typically a SME, into the virtual commerce area. The main commercial policy is based on electronic catalogue (e-catalogue) shopping supported by two main agents, a web-base e-commerce intermediary and a visual catalogue-designer tool.

However, the overall architecture introduces more agents and more relationships among them. In Figure 1, the most representative entities, with the main communication flows, are shown.

As can be seen, there is a central element, the intermediary, which interconnects the different parts involved in a typical commerce environment, but with more dynamism compared to the traditional business forms.

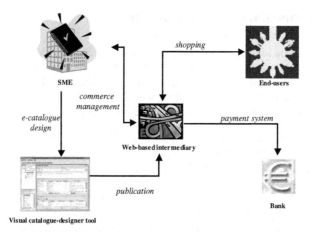

Fig. 1. General structure of the e-CoUSAL architecture

One of the most pursued premises is that the SME will become the main actor of its own virtual business proposal. In this approach it will be the responsible for the inclusion and the management of its own contents in the server, which allows the enterprise entrance into the e-commerce environment. The use of a specialised software-authoring tool to design its own catalogue of products permits the SME to be an active element within the commercial process.

The author tool allows the definition, publication and update of a product catalogue, and also the setting up of the intermediary architecture that allows end-users to have access to these products. However, for an efficient communication between the tool and the intermediary, and also for an automatic intermediary set up, the e-commerce intermediary has to arrange the restrictions for the e-catalogues to which the software tool is conformed. This is a different perspective because it is not necessary delegating these tasks to other service providers.

As far as the SME is concerned, the proposed model includes the facilities of shopping-window of its products in the server side, i.e., maintenance of statistics and other kinds of business information, a budget of the costs derived from the use of this environment, alerts and maintenance of historic information about its orders, and organisation of exhibitions, in order to show the features of the latest products available from the firm and so on.

The relationships between a SME and the e-commerce intermediary, through the catalogue-designer tool and also through the intermediary management services, represent the B2B dimension of this e-commerce model.

Moreover, the server has to provide the end-users with every typical service needed for navigating through the catalogue of products and for purchasing them, such as searching for a product in any published catalogue, shopping cart management, selling certificates, navigation help, and so on, and all these through a uniform and intuitive interface. These server's functionalities define the B2C dimension of this model.

The data interchange between the SME and the server, and their later automatic publication for final client's accessibility, is based on an XML (eXtensible Markup Language) [7] storage format that defines the structure of their catalogue ontologies.

3   The Intermediary Site Architecture

The intermediary is implemented using a Multi-Agent System (MAS) for e-commerce area. These agents are shown in Figure 2. We present the agent-based architecture in coarse granularity and high abstraction levels, because we are defining the architectural layer of the system. In other works thinner grained agents are presented [1, 21]. These approaches are not incompatible with ours.

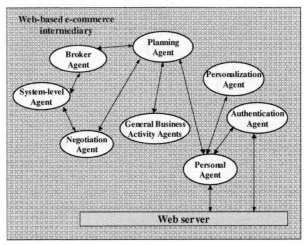

Fig. 2. Agent-based architecture for the e-CoUSAL

In the Figure 2 ovals represent agents and arrows represent communication between them or between external entities, as end-users.

The *broker agent* is in charge of receiving the e-catalogues from the SME, expressed in XML format, validating them, and storing the information in the proper internal database. The tool through the system-level agent sends these catalogues.

This agent should attend to every enterprise that belongs to the e-commerce site to publish and manage its e-catalogues.

This broker entity implements the communication protocol for data interchange between the enterprise and the e-commerce server, allowing the whole system to be built over a self-maintained platform, capable of configuring itself when changes are incorporated by the organisation, with a minimum interaction of the web master [10].

The *negotiation agent* receives the business components of each SME in the same way that the broker agent receives the e-catalogues. This property will allow not only that the SMEs are presented in the intermediary, but also they could personalize their business policies (discount, payments and so on) through these components. To support this facility the designer-tool should be improved to support this kind of business components.

The *general business activity agents* form a set of agents that manage the services of a typical e-commerce site: shopping-cart management, selling certificates and so on.

The *authentication agent* is a security agent type that is in charge of identifying the end-user to allow adapting its interfaces and shopping goods. Another type of security agent is the authorization agent that controls the access to sensitive information once identity has been verified.

The personal agent is responsible for customising the interaction with the user and the presentation and navigation of e-catalogues. It is implemented as an adaptive agent. This agent dialogs with the web server module to interact with the user and dynamically generates the hypertextual pages that represent the e-catalogues.

The intermediary offers to its end-users efficient access and shopping management for the different products that are published in the server. From an end-user perspective, the intermediary presents the specialised supermarket metaphor, where any client can find several related products from different suppliers.

Also, for an end-user the intermediary should be like another commercial site in Internet (it should present the same facilities and an easy and familiar interface), and the variety of the sources of the products has to be transparent for the end-user. For this reason, the personalizing capabilities of the site are very important.

The hypermedia pages that represent the e-catalogues are dynamically generating on the fly, getting the contents from the e-catalogues that were sent by the enterprises. However, to take out the information from the e-catalogues and introducing the data in the server database, there must be an ontology or meta-knowledge for e-catalogue definition that is shared between the server and the catalogue-designer tool.

A further work in the customisation area is the implementation of a *personalization agent* that will be in charge of acquiring and maintaining the end-users' profiles, which represent the system's hypotheses on the users' needs and can be used to tailor the layout of the hypermedia pages to each specific end-user. So this agent should learn from the visitors of the e-commerce site to infer the end-users' interests. From the visitor's viewpoint, the agent should help the user make sure that useful information is not overlooked. On the other hand, a personalized profile should be used to make the proper recommendations to the users [15], thus reducing their need to browse through pages.

Finally, the *planning agent* is due to the presence of heterogeneous problems to be faced and the fact that many tasks could be carried out at the same time suggest the design of the multi-agent architecture outlined above. This is a planner agent that controls the main data flows in the system, initialises and updates the user models during the interaction. In a few words, its responsibilities includes manage the e-catalogues database, accepting the orders of the e-commerce service agents, and in cooperation with the personalization agent giving to the personal agent the proper data to generate customised information pages handling the products and user databases.

4 The E-catalogue Format Definition

As we stated above, the e-catalogue is the chosen element by which the end-user views and interacts with the seller's information.

The decision of e-catalogues usage is based on the widely acceptance of these in web-based business. Also, while other applications can provide similar services, e-catalogues provide a range and effectiveness of service that exceeds the capability of any competing application, as physical or CD catalogues for example. The interactive possibilities of e-catalogues eliminate physical storage and makes continuous updating effective and efficient [5]. An e-catalogue can be defined as electronic representations of information about the products and/or services of an organisation [16].

Concretely, in the context of this work, we use the notion of multi-vendor electronic catalogues. These e-catalogues are an essential part of electronic procurement solutions. They integrate supplier information by merging data and performing some degree of semantic reconciliation. The data is then presented to end-users as a centralised access point to the products and services that can be purchased electronically. The web-server intermediary represents this centralisation in this research.

To the SMEs, the multi-vendor catalogue represents a way to infiltrate a wide variety of markets and exploit possible synergies with other selling parties. In addition, a catalogue integrator (the intermediary plays this role) bundles the offering with other features to make the aggregated catalogue more attractive (for example, the adaptive properties discussed in Section 3).

Ginsburg et al. [11] stand out three basic e-catalogue models. These models represent the most common ways that organisations choose today to use emerging technologies for e-commerce procurement. These models are: *Do-It-Yourself*; *Third-Party Integrator*; and *Real-Time Knowledge Discovery*.

The "Third-Party Integrator" approach is a typical B2B model, where the intermediary only manages the e-catalogue, and then rents access to parts of it. In this approach the buyers are not directly linked with the suppliers.

In the "Real-Time Knowledge Discovery" model the intermediary is the buyer firm too, but it relies on advanced software techniques to make a fine-combed search over Internet and locale suitable products and suppliers. The e-catalogues are created dynamically and subsequently allow access to supplier data in real time.

In our approach, the multi-vendor catalogue is based on the "Do-It-Yourself" approach, because in this model the intermediary takes the initiative to set up a catalogue, which comprises products from a controlled set of qualified SMEs. Besides, the communication between the intermediary and the SMEs is fixed, and it is made through an authoring tool, then this communication is not real-time as the model before.

XML is the basis to establish a communication protocol between the SME and the intermediary, allowing the whole system to be built over a self-maintained platform, capable of configuring itself when changes are incorporated by the SME, with a minimum interaction of the web master.

The intermediary stores the e-catalogues supplied by the SME, but it is the SME that determines what products will be shown, how these products will be organised and the visual format they will take. Also, in this approach, the SME always has the responsibility for managing the e-catalogue and its contents.

The intermediary self-maintenance capability is possible because the XML file with the catalogue data is a semantic entity (both the tool and the intermediary share the same format definition expressed in an XML definition file or schema; see Figure 3) that the intermediary can automatically validate and integrate it into its own database. After the information is stored in the intermediary side, the searching processes from the e-commerce site functionality could find the products of the e-catalogue, and show them in the dynamically generated web pages.

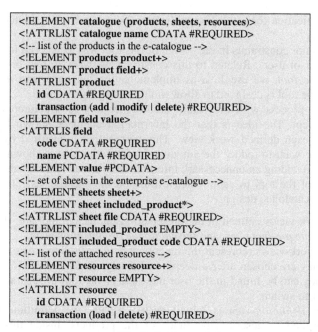

```
<!ELEMENT catalogue (products, sheets, resources)>
<!ATTRLIST catalogue name CDATA #REQUIRED>
<!-- list of the products in the e-catalogue -->
<!ELEMENT products product+>
<!ELEMENT product field+>
<!ATTRLIST product
    id CDATA #REQUIRED
    transaction (add | modify | delete) #REQUIRED>
<!ELEMENT field value>
<!ATTRLIS field
    code CDATA #REQUIRED
    name PCDATA #REQUIRED>
<!ELEMENT value #PCDATA>
<!-- set of sheets in the enterprise e-catalogue -->
<!ELEMENT sheets sheet+>
<!ELEMENT sheet included_product*>
<!ATTRLIST sheet file CDATA #REQUIRED>
<!ELEMENT included_product EMPTY>
<!ATTRLIST included_product code CDATA #REQUIRED>
<!-- list of the attached resources -->
<!ELEMENT resources resource+>
<!ELEMENT resource EMPTY>
<!ATTRLIST resource
    id CDATA #REQUIRED
    transaction (load | delete) #REQUIRED>
```

Fig. 3. Catalogue.dtd

In the next section we explain the process to create an e-catalogue with the visual catalogue-designer tool.

5 The E-catalogue Creation Process

Perhaps, one of the most innovative parts of this business model is the catalogue-designer tool that allows both e-catalogue creation and publication activities. This authoring tool is distributed to the every SME that belongs to the e-commerce platform.

The intermediary has to facilitate to the SMEs the contents creation, the update and the management of their products, and also a universal means for the supported e-catalogues. Then the majority of the transactions between the SMEs and the intermediary are made through this tool.

The SME develops the contents of the e-catalogue with the authoring tool, saving the catalogues in an XML-format file; the Figure 3 shows the DTD for the e-catalogues. The designer of the e-catalogue will be the person in charge of e-catalogue maintenance, which is done on local computers, and the resulting catalogue is subsequently sent to the intermediary server. The designer and the enterprise need not be worried about e-catalogue integration, because this is an automatic task on the intermediary side.

Using a tool such as a SME/intermediary interface facilitates the e-catalogue creation and publication processes, because the designer of them does not have to be a computer expert; he/she only needs to be familiar with basic office automation concepts, because all the knowledge concerning the saving format of the catalogues and the communication for catalogue publication aspects are encapsulated inside the tool functionality.

One of the major constraints in the design of this tool was to succeed in using it for a widely number of users. Related to this constraint we work in two directions: the *portability of the tool*, we use Java as implementation language, and *its language independence*, the tool is designed to allow multiple-language support.

The working process with the catalogue-designer tool is structured around the work-view concept. The idea is that the information could be shown by different angles, one for each defined work-view. This perspective is justified by two main reasons: first, we want to reduce the amount of information that is shown to the user of the tool, thus avoiding an unnecessary information overload. On the other hand, we want the users of the tool to centre their efforts on the specific task in the overall process of the e-catalogue design.

The main work-views defined in the presented visual design tool are: *the template definition view*, *the product view*, and *the catalogue organisation view*.

These three work-views represent the functional process used to create or design an e-catalogue. They are chosen after a deeper task analysis of the e-catalogue creation process, and they can be found in the user interface of the tool in separate tabs, thus making it easier to switch.

The *template definition view* is something like a data type definition mechanism that can be applied to describe the fields of the products. Inside this view two different elements are considered: the data template and the product template. The data template could be defined as the mechanism that allows us: first, to define the data format of one field for product description, and second, to help to the user to define the contents in a more effective way. Furthermore, a product template serves as a model for the later definition of the concrete products of the e-catalogues. A product template defines a set of fields that describes those products that will be defined using the product template, also this kind of template can be organised in a hierarchical way, inheriting field descriptions from its ascendants. The objective pursued is to group common characteristics to a set of products, reducing the efforts to define them.

The *product view* gathers all the functionality for concrete products. While the templates make the work easier, the products are the conceptual definition of each element that compounds the e-catalogue. This work-view is like a product-description repository that makes it possible to create new products, maintains existing ones, and so on. The products could be presented in this view in different ways: classified by product categories, classified by product templates or ordered by name.

The *catalogue organisation view* presents the grouping of the products in e-catalogues for their later publication in the server, and also their maintenance. The functionality associated with this view allows the inclusion of personalised security constraints to control what persons or what entities have access to the e-catalogue. When an e-catalogue is defined there is a separation between its conceptual definition and its visualization in the intermediary. This characteristic directs the e-catalogue composition process as can be seen in figures 4 and 5. An e-catalogue is organised by sections and subsections. Each section has sheets (Figure 4) where the products are located in a visual way (Figure 5).

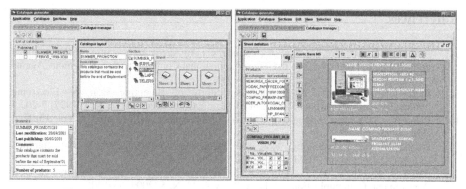

Fig. 4. Catalogue layout   **Fig. 5.** Catalogue sheet definition

6 Conclusions

In this paper a business model for e-commerce has been presented. The model is intended to facilitate the entry of small and medium enterprises into electronic commerce opportunities and into electronic marketplaces.

According to this, an intermediary appears as central element in the commerce architecture. The intermediary puts in contact this kind of enterprises with the end-users. In order to do that, the intermediary takes the initiative to set up a multi-vendor catalogue that comprises the products of the enterprises. Besides, the intermediary implements all the e-services for product purchasing. However, each SME is responsible for the creation, publication and maintenance of its e-catalogues. These tasks are performed by means of an authoring tool.

The working process to create an e-catalogue is supported by the designer tool through three different functional work-views: the template view, the product view, and the catalogue manager view. Also, a fourth non-functional view is presented, the repository view, which interrelates the other views.

The final result of this tool is an e-catalogue definition that is saved in an XML file that can be sent to the intermediary and automatically published in it.

The intermediary architecture is implemented by a multi-agent system that consists of a set of collaborative agents, where the adaptive characteristics are very important in interface, behaviour and navigation issues.

The overall business model presents a hybrid approximation of the two most widely used e-commerce models or dimensions: a B2B model among the SMEs and the intermediary, and a B2C model between the intermediary and the end-users.

As the final conclusion of this paper, we want to underline that one of the most interesting characteristics of the proposed model is the reduction on dependencies for the SMEs from third parties, allowing small enterprises to have a place in the global marketplace on Internet with a moderate investment.

References

[1]   Ardissono, L., Barbero, C., Goy, A., Petrone, G.: An Agent Architecture for Personalized Web Stores. In proceedings of the Third International Conference on Autonomous Agents – AGENTS'99. ACM. Pages 182-189. (1999).

[2]   Bailey, J. Bakos, Y.: An Exploratory Study of Emerging Role of Electronic Intermediaries. International Journal of Electronic Commerce, Vol. 1, N. 3 (1997) 7-20.

[3]   Bakos Y.: A Strategic Analysis of Electronic Marketplace. MIS Quarterly, Vol. 15, N. 4 (1991) 295-310.

[4]   Bakos, Y.: The Emerging Role of Electronic Marketplaces on the Internet. Communications of the ACM, Vol. 41, N. 8 (1998) 35-42.

[5]   Baron, J. P., Shaw, M. J., Bailey, A. D. Jr.: Web-based E-catalog Systems in B2B Procurement. Communications of the ACM, Vol. 43, N. 5 (2000) 93-100.

[6]   Bichler, M., Segev, A., Beam, C.: An Electronic Broker for Business-To-Business Electronic Commerce on the Internet. International Journal of Cooperative Information Systems, Vol. 7, N. 4 (1998) 315-330.

[7]   Bray, T., Paoli, J,. Sperberg-MacQueen, C. M.: Extensible Markup Language (XML) 1.0 (Second Edition). World Wide Web Consortium Recommendation October 2000. http://www.w3c.org/TR/2000/REC-xml-20001006. (2000).

[8]   Chircu, A. M., Kauffman, R. J.: Strategies for Internet Middlemen in the Intermediation / Disintermediation / Reintermediation Cycle. Electronic Markets – The International Journal of Electronic Commerce and Business Media, Vol. 9, N.2 (1999) 109-117.

[9]   García, F. J., Borrego, I., Hernández, M.J., Gil, A.: An E-Commerce Model for Small and Medium Enterprises. In Proceedings of ICEIS'2002, 2002 – The Fourth Conference on Enterprise Information Systems. M. Piattini, J. Filipe and J. Braz editors. (Ciudad Real, Spain, 3-6 April 2002). Vol. I, Pages 1035-1041. ICEIS Press. (2002).

[10]   García, F. J., Moreno, Mª N., Hernández, J. A.: e-CoUSAL: An E-Commerce Architecture for Small and Medium Enterprises. In Advances in Business Solutions. Catedral Publisher. (In press). (2002).

[11]   Ginsburg, M., Gebauer, J., Segev, A.: Multi-Vendor Electronic Catalogs to Support Procurement: Current Practice and Future Direction". In Proceedings of the Twelfth International Bled Electronic Commerce Conference. (1999).

[12]   Maes, P., Guttman, R. H., Moukas, A.: Agents that Buy and Sell. Communications of the ACM, Vol. 42, N. 3 (1999) 81-91.

[13]   Malone, T. W., Yates, J., Benjamin, R. I.: Electronic Markets and Electronic Hierarchies. Communications of the ACM, Vol. 30, N. 6 (1987) 484-497.

[14]   Marathe, M., Diwakar, H.: The Architecture of a One-Stop Web-Window Shop. SIGecom Exchanges, Newsletter of the ACM Special Interest Group on E-commerce, Vol. 2, N. 1 (2001) 11-18.

[15]   Pazzani, M. J., Billsus, D.: Adaptive Web Site Agents. In proceedings of the Third International Conference on Autonomous Agents – AGENTS'99. ACM. Pages 394-395. (1999).

[16]   Segev, A., Wan, D., Beam, C.: Designing Electronic Catalogs for Business Value: Results from the CommerceNet Pilot. CITM Working Paper WP-95-1005, Haas School of Business, University of California, Berkeley. (1995).

[17]   Spulber, D. F.: Market Microstructure and Intermediation. Journal of Economic Perspectives, Vol. 10, N. 3 (1996) 135-152.

Extended Decision Making in Tourism Information Systems

Franz Pühretmair[1], Hildegard Rumetshofer[1], and Erwin Schaumlechner[2]

[1]Institute for Applied Knowledge Processing (FAW)
Johannes Kepler University Linz, Austria
{fpuehretmair,hrumetshofer}@faw.uni-linz.ac.at

[2]Tiscover AG - Travel Information Systems
Softwarepark Hagenberg, Austria
erwin.schaumlechner@tiscover.com

Abstract. E-commerce initiatives show that tourism data is one of the most accessed data in the Web. The problem is that a high number of users is rather unexperienced in Web use. The handling of tourism information systems is often a complex and time consuming process for tourists. To satisfy the tourists expectations it is inevitable to support the tourist in travel planning and decision making. Most tourism information systems offer a variety of sharp query functionalities with some relaxation mechanisms but lack in providing vague results or alternatives. To meet the tourists interests and preferences this paper presents two methodological approaches to support the tourist. The first is the case-based reasoning approach, which gives tourists answers to "what is recommended" by deriving individual travel suggestions from previous cases stored in the knowledge base. The second is a visual approach through touristic maps, which give the tourist a good impression of "what is where" to decide which of the resulting objects is located best regarding the tourists needs and interests.

Keywords. Case-based reasoning (CBR), decision making in tourism, Geographic Information Systems (GIS), Scalable Vector Graphics (SVG), Tourism Information Systems (TIS)

1 Introduction

Tourism information and destination management systems can be considered as one line of business – besides the classical book and music shops - with increasing acceptance and success in the e-commerce area of the Internet. Sources like TIA (Travel Industry Association in Washington DC) [1] speak about 89 million people from a total of 101 million US Internet users, who use their Web-access for travel concerns. This would mean that about 45% of the US adult population uses the Web for travel, for leisure purposes on the one hand, but also covers such tasks like reservation of airline tickets, hotels and cars for business and purposes other than leisure.

K. Bauknecht, A. M. Tjoa, G. Quirchmayr (Eds.): EC-Web 2002, LNCS 2455, pp. 57–66, 2002.

European surveys indicate similar trends in West and Central Europe. But as additional results these studies also point out the typical behavior of the experienced power users and the not so experienced sometimes users, too – a mixture of try-and-error loops combined with a hunt for information over a variety of different Web-sites. Just to give an example potential online tourists search the Web-based information pool according to a German online survey from Ulysses Management [2] – a company with the focus on tourism oriented marketing research - mainly to use such different travel services like railway tickets, event search, airline tickets, last minute offers, rental cars, package deals and cruises, first of all to collect information, but also based on this information to buy the different offers.

The information that can be extracted from a large variety of such trend analysis and attitude surveys enforces some challenges in the development of Web-based systems from the Tourism Information System (TIS) developers and destination providers that can be summarized with the term "extended decision making support". Some of the methodological and functional answers to these challenges, especially these taken into consideration from Tiscover AG, a European oriented Tourism Information System developer and provider, will be presented in this paper, with the focus on the following topics:

- The number of Internet users interested in tourism services has grown from a small minority in 1996 to a majority in 2002. Service providers have therefore to take it for granted that many of their customers are not that experienced as the so-called power users. Support mechanisms for searching, deciding and buying are necessary.
- The bandwidth of Internet accounts used by unexperienced users should have enough potential nowadays to allow a particular amount of multimedia data. The use of the possibilities of this multimedia-enriched content is not only a nice-to-have but a definitive competitive advantage. Visual information eases the handling of information and the process of decision making.

To distinguish between advanced, but nonetheless broadly used methodologies and more sophisticated concepts in supporting the user in his decision making process, the following chapter discusses in few words the relevant mechanisms normally used in commercial systems. Based on this information two advanced approaches – case-based reasoning and visual touristic maps – will be discussed in their potential to enhance these functionalities. Both approaches will be described in the respective chapters 3 and 4 with an explicit focus on concrete projects. While the project related to the topic of case-based reasoning is in its definition and application modeling phase and therefore cannot provide concrete results at this point of time, the second project related to visual touristic maps will give some concrete details about realization and results. Finally the chapter 5 gives perspectives of the intended usefulness of these approaches to support tourists in their planning tasks.

2   Decision Making in State-of-the Art TIS

The development of efficient search functions is not an easy task in the field of information systems. As described in [3] this statement fits especially for the context of TIS, which differ from many other information systems in two special characteristics that are:

- TIS have to manage an extremely high amount of data, and - even worse - extremely heterogeneous data.
- Users are not able to specify the search criteria exactly enough to receive from the system what they have in mind.

The following paragraphs describe some of the mechanisms used in research [4] and in modern systems to find the most relevant information content corresponding to the tourist search input. The description follows a classification as visualized in Fig. 1.

These functions have mainly been developed and are in use in the Tiscover system from Tiscover AG – Travel Information Systems, the leading TIS in the German speaking market.

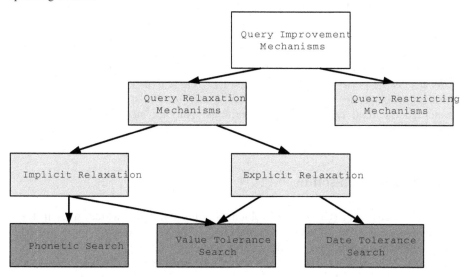

Fig. 1. Query Improvement Mechanisms

A general distinction can be done in dependance of the assistance that should be offered to the user. Sometimes the decision making process results in a failure because of too few or not any offers. To react to this situation a search with reduced search constraints is useful – the query relaxation. Another time the decision making process shows up to be complicated or not possible because of too many offered products. In this case a more strict search is necessary to reduce the search hits – the so-called query restricting.

As Fig. 1 indicates the main focus in current TIS concentrates on the relaxation of queries because a search without any result can provoke a frustrated user, and a frustrated user is a potential user who will leave the system.

If acceptable in the respective situation of decision making an implicit relaxation strategy will be preferable. Implicit means that the user supplies the search criteria but the system will decide "by itself" if the results are sufficient to make a decision or if the query must be relaxed.

The most common situation where such an implicit relaxation is often used is the phonetic search [3] – a situation where phonetic similarities must be detected if no direct hit can be accomplished. In the context of TIS such similarities are helpful when searching for regions, cities, or object names in general, and the exact phonetic representation of this name in the system is not known to the user. Another situation where implicit relaxation can be quite useful is a value based search i.e. when the search constraints include price limits and the system has price-related tolerance areas. In such a case, a search with no results can be relaxed to a new price limit, defined by the maximum tolerance value.

But system developers have to be careful when using implicit mechanisms. Sometimes such an automatic query relaxation can confuse the user. Another way to use the relaxation but not to perplex the user is explicit relaxation. This means that the customer must decide (i.e. with the help of a check box) by himself if he wants advanced search mechanisms. This is useful for some special value based searches, but is especially helpful when date based decisions are necessary. No implicit rule can clarify if tourists have a clear limit in their arrival and departure dates or offer just general planning milestones when using a TIS. But the tourist knows his restrictions, and he must decide if a relaxation is useful in his particular situation.

What must be clear when discussing the latter cases is that all the relaxation and restricting mechanisms have their limits, and these limits exist because they all base on normal database related search algorithms. Another step forward is desired anyhow, but this needs new topics.

3   Case-Based Reasoning

Case-Based reasoning (CBR) is a problem-solving paradigm, which gives in this case tourists answers to "What is recommended?". The key is to solve a new problem by remembering a previous similar situation and by reusing its information and knowledge [5]. This is different compared to traditional Artificial Intelligence approaches. Traditional techniques base on knowledge, which corresponds to a problem domain and solve appearing problems on first-principles or "from scratch". CBR allows to store gained knowledge in a pool of cases, the case-base, which serves as memory. Each available case represents a problem description and the description of its solution, which was yield in the past. As each time a new problem occurs, a new experience will be retained, CBR is an approach to incremental learning [5].

This procedure is very similar to real human acting. People often solve tasks by considering previous experiences and adapting them to new appearing problems. Consider a real travel agent: a tourist describes his preferences for making holidays in the coming winter season. The interests of this tourist can be well-known or be similar to another client of the agent. However, the agent accesses his knowledge full of similar cases and recommends travel destinations that he suggested already in past. If the client is not totally pleased, the agent can revise his proposed solution and extend his base of recommendations until the client will be satisfied.

The CBR model follows a four step process, which starts, after facing a new problem that is described as problem part of a new case [6].

- Retrieve previous cases, which are similar to the new one.
- Reuse most suitable or similar case as solution to the new problem.
- Revise the proposed solution by testing it in reality.
- Retain useful experience by updating the case-base with a new learned case or by modification of some existing cases.

The CBR process is often supported by general knowledge, knowledge being domain-dependent. This general knowledge can also be regarded as a set of rules additional to cases. So, general knowledge can be considered as decision making support engine to provide different searching mechanisms such as sharp query search or case-based search with respect to best matching practice.

As cases form the heart of CBR, their structure, content and organization determine strongly sufficiency and success of a case-based reasoning component. Additionally, the way of providing similarities among cases, supporting adaptation of cases gained from new experiences and deciding how many cases are stored in the case-base contribute as well [7]. As on the one hand, the CBR approach assumes that the represented world is regular and on the other hand that appearing problems recur [5], a case representing a tourist's travel needs and benefits can be modeled as a set of preferences such as period of time, budget, amount of travelers, kind of wanted activities or landscape [8].

The DIETORECS project [9] is an initiative of the European Union with its main objective to support tourists with travel recommendations. The approach that DIETORECS follows, is known as collaborative filtering and realized through case-based reasoning. Fig. 2 shows the architecture of DIETORECS.

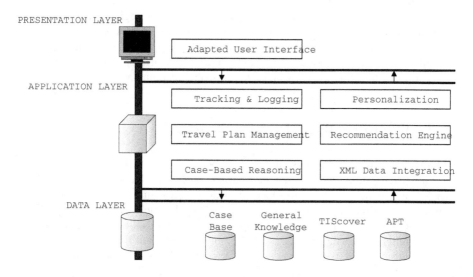

Fig. 2. DIETORECS Architecture

The DIETORECS system follows the traditional three-tier architecture divided into presentation, application and data level, whereby each of these tiers is responsible for supporting the recommendation process. The data is provided by tourist information providers such as Tiscover AG [10] and APT [11], having different operating systems. The integration of the heterogeneous data models is supported by an XML Data Integration Tool based on a Logical Data Model, which provides the ability to encourage meaningful destinations, accommodations or activities. The case-base contains user profiles gained by tracking and logging functionalities employed at each layer. The collected user profiles correspond to the mentioned cases. Therefore, DIETORECS will be able to increment the quality of given recommendations because the underlying CBR component learns from previous experiences.

Beside individual recommendations, DIETORECS supports the management of so-called "Travel Plans". A travel plan can be regarded as a set of items such as hotel, activity or destination that describe real travels and are collected individually by tourists. Each tourist manages his own travel plans in fact serving as example for new "official" travel plans, stored in the case-base but not being directly accessible by other users.

A travel plan is identified by a user-defined name such as "alpine skiing 2003". Its characteristics can be compared to common e-commerce shopping bags. The user collects interesting items, adds them to the bag or removes some uninteresting ones. Providing booking functionalities of items in a travel plan can be regarded as counterpart to convenient "buying" possibilities in normal shopping bags. However, there is one challenging difference concerning acceptable items for a single travel plan.

As one travel plan represents a concrete travel, the logical combination of hotels, destinations or activities, which are put into it, has to be considered and checked by the system. For instance, the user adds following items to the mentioned travel plan: "Innsbruck" as destination, "skiing slope of Innsbruck" as activity but "Hotel Sunshine located in Rome" as accommodation. In this case, neglecting a verification of distance among destination, activity and accommodation provokes   that the user will have to cover plenty of kilometers for reaching the skiing slope in Innsbruck from the selected hotel in Rome. It is up to DIETORECS to overcome such inadequacy and to support users with comprehensible recommendations.

4   Visual Location Based Decision Support

Touristic maps are visual representations of "What is where". They offer the tourist a visual representation of where specific touristic objects are located, how they can be reached, and which objects are located nearby. This information will be very important for tourists if their decision is steered by location of objects. E.g. If the tourist is looking for a hotel nearby an opera house, the visual representation will be more meaningful than the addresses of the objects. Touristic maps are an approach that starts from the user needs, very useful for visual decision making in TIS. Most TIS still have backlogs in using new visualization capabilities. They often offer simple static maps for information presentation or navigation aids which moreover mostly do not base on the same source and therefore do not have a unique look and feel.

The primary purpose of maps is to provide a spatial representation of the environment, or, in simpler terms, to help to locate or to describe a place. Maps are of great value for tourists decision making because they have the potential to represent large amount of information about area of interests within a single picture, compact and easy to read, exploiting the two dimensional capabilities of human vision.

Usual maps are a reproduction of the real world. Each point, each line and each object on the map is assigned to a themed layer, which is a categorization of objects. Each layer combines related objects like roads, buildings, vegetation or watercourses. To make them useable for tourist purpose, maps have to be extended with touristic information. To integrate tourism data the traditional layer model [12] with map layers like roads, buildings, vegetation, railways, watercourses, etc. must be enlarged with additional tourism layers like hotels, restaurants, sights, theaters, sport and leisure objects as well as further infrastructure layers (shown in Fig. 3).

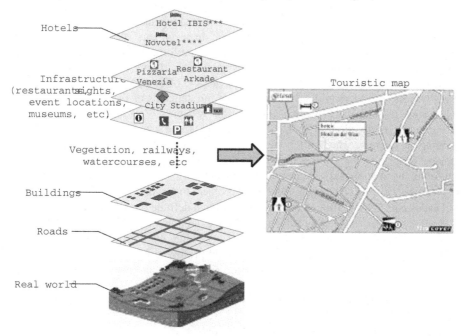

Fig. 3. Touristic map [13]

To build touristic maps, vector graphic shapes (e.g., points, multipoints, polylines or polygons [14]), textual information, and images must be integrated. In more detail geographic data has to be integrated with tourism data, which is described by:

- object symbols representing the type of the touristic object (e.g. hotel, sight, etc.),
- alphanumerical object descriptions (e.g., name of an object, category of a hotel),
- colors, e.g., to visualize the availability of hotels,
- links to the object homepage (e.g., a hotel's homepage) to enable further navigation and online booking for hotels.

To do the integration of tourism data and geographic data, each tourism object to be integrated in a touristic map must have a geographic representation (longitude and latitude) which describes the location of the object in geographic space.

To meet the tourists interests and therefore to support the decision-making process, the interests of the tourist must influence the map representation. This means that the information must be disseminated through an interactive session. The tourist needs the possibility to interact with the map, to select features to be displayed while ignoring unwanted data or to use the map as a starting point for further navigation. To offer the most up-to-date information (e.g. hotel availability) each request must lead to a new map generation. Changes in the geographic or touristic data must be immediately reflected on the next creation of the touristic map.

SVG (Scalable Vector Graphics) [15], the new recommended Web-standard for two-dimensional vector graphics, supports themed layers and the generation of user individual maps. Interactive touristic maps in SVG and their visualization of "What is where" give tourists the power for visual decision making and offer a variety of trend-setting functionalities like integration of vector shapes, textual alpha information and images. Furthermore the SVG standard offers high performance zooming and panning inside of graphics without reloading data, support of scripting languages and the use of XML-related technologies. Touristic maps in SVG offer a powerful, clear and user-friendly access to tourism data thus satisfying the demands of the users and offering substantial advantages for Tourism Information Systems.

Furthermore decision making in geographic scope can also be supported by geographic queries, which offer the tourist the possibility to locate what they are looking for [3]. To use the capacity of doing spatial analysis operations the support of the following spatial analysis operations are needed:

- Nearness search - to search for the nearest object to a given point,
- Distance search - to find objects located within a definite distance to a given point,
- Region search - to get objects located within a geographic region or map region.

The presented concept has been approved within the European Union funded XML-KM project [13] where a fully functional prototype for dynamically generated touristic maps in SVG has been developed. The implementation is based on a map server from ESRI [16], which has been extended to do the geographic search for touristic objects [3] by the use of the three introduced spatial operators. The map data is a vector data set in shapefile-format [16] from Tele Atlas [17]. The workflow to generate SVG maps can be summarized as follows:

- The tourist specifies the query via the user interface, whereby a query could be a geographic search, a zoom or other navigation events (e.g.: full extent, up, down, left, etc.).
- The query module queries the map server to get the map data and the matching touristic objects.
- Map and object data like object symbols, links to the object homepage and alphanumerical object description are integrated into the map and transformed into SVG.
- The availability of hotels is queried directly from the TIS and integrated by an XSL (eXtensible Stylesheet Language) transformation.

One of the most crucial tasks when integrating geographic data and tourism information into touristic maps is to keep maps simple and readable but to integrate all information expected by the tourist. This means, to support the decision making of tourists in an efficient way, it is very important not to overload the touristic map. In the XML-KM prototype we decided to limit the visualization of geographic and tourist layers to a customizable map scale range. E.g.: The hotel layer is only visible if the map scale of the touristic map is within 1:50 and 1:20000. This enables the creation of meaningful touristic maps and prevents from overloading maps.

Looking at a touristic map gives the tourist the knowledge of where things are, what they are, how they can be reached by means of roads or other transport, and what things are adjacent and nearby [14] to help them to find the most suitable location to stay or to visit.

5 Conclusion and Future Work

Modern TIS have the need to support the tourist in travel planning and decision making. The information presented must be readable, useful and valuable. Content, data quality and presentation must meet the tourist's needs and expectations.

The two approaches described in this paper offer tourists new trend-setting support in trip planning. The case-based reasoning approach offers a new level of personalization and customized travel recommendations. It helps the tourist to plan his travel by identifying similar cases. In simple terms, the recommendation application interacts with tourists, learns their preferences, and responds with highly targeted, personalized recommendations, which base on an underlying knowledge base. To avoid from difficulties in the initial phase of such a system, some search strategies are needed until the knowledge base has enough information to work similarity-based. Another challenge is the design of the user interface because recommendations based on mechanisms other than simple database search must be transparent to the user. As already mentioned before, Tiscover AG participates in the IST project DIETORECS [9] to implement a CBR based recommendation system and will evaluate it in real use. The project will run until the end of 2003, first detailed results can be expected by the end of 2002, when a first prototype will be in operation.

Touristic maps in SVG are a powerful, user-friendly and interactive access to tourism data with great benefits for tourists in decision making. The flexibility of the presented concepts and its implied technologies significantly improve the tourists decision making process and offer substantial advantages for TIS. The support of the decision making process through touristic maps is limited by the quality of maps and the completeness of the objects to be integrated.

Acknowledgement

This work has been partially funded by the European Union's Fifth RTD Framework Programme (under contracts DIETORECS IST-2000-29474 and XML-KM IST-1999-12030).

References

1. Homepage of TIA - Travel Industry Association of America, http://www.tia.org (2002)
2. Homepage of Web-Tourismus - Erfolg im Tourismus durch das Internet, Studien, Forschung, Trends und Fakten, http://www.web-tourismus.de (2002)
3. Palkoska, J., Pühretmair, F., Tjoa, A M., Wagner, R., Wöß W.: Advanced Query Mechanisms in Tourism Information Systems, Proceedings of the International Conference on Information and Communication Technologies in Tourism (ENTER 2002), pp. 438-447, Springer Verlag, Innsbruck, Austria (2002)
4. Ricci F., Blaas D., Mirzadeh N., Venturini A., Werthner H.: Intelligent Query Management for Travel Products Selection, Proceedings of the International Conference on Information and Communication Technologies in Tourism (ENTER 2002), pp. 438-447, Springer Verlag, Innsbruck, Austria (2002)
5. Leake, D., ed.: Case-Based reasoning: Experiences, Lessons, and Future Directions, Menlo Park: AAAI Press / MIT Press (1996)
6. Aamodt, A., Plaza, E.: Cased-Based Reasoning: Foundational Issues, Methodological Variations, and System Approaches, AI Communications, IOS Press, Vol. 7:1, pp. 39-59 (1994)
7. Bartsch-Spörl, B. Lenz, M., Hübner, A.: Case-Based Reasoning – Survey and Future Directions, http://citeseer.nj.nec.com/2536.html (1999)
8. Lenz, M.: Fallbasiertes Schließen für die Selektion von Reiseangeboten, Beiträge zum KI-94 Workshop "Angebotssysteme mit wissensbasierten Komponenten", FORWISS-Report FR-1994-004, pp. 8-13 (1994)
9. Homepage of the IST-2000-29474 DIETORECS project: Intelligent Recommendation for Tourist Destination Decision Making, http://dietorecs.itc.it/ (2002)
10. Homepage of Tiscover - The Travel Network, http://www.tiscover.com (2002)
11. Homepage of APT Trentino - Azienda per la Promozione Turistica del Trentino, http://www.trentino.to (2002)
12. Neumann, A., Winter, V: Vector-based Web Cartography: Enabler SVG, Carto.net - Cartographers on the net, http://www.carto.net/papers/svg/index_e.html (2001)
13. Homepage of the IST-1999-12030 XML-KM project: XML Knowledge Mediator, http://falbala.ibermatica.com/xmlkm/ (2002)
14. Zeiler, A.: Modelling Our World – The ESRI Guide to Geodatabase Design, ISBN 1-879102-62-5, ESRI Press (1999)
15. W3C – The World Wide Web Consortium: Scalable Vector Graphics (SVG) 1.0 Specification, Candidate Recommendation, http://www.w3.org/Graphics/SVG/ (2002)
16. Homepage of ESRI: GIS and mapping software, http://www.esri.com (2002)
17. Homepage of Tele Atlas - Intelligent Maps, http://www.teleatlas.com (2002)

Identifying Arbitrage Opportunities in e-Markets

John Debenham

University of Technology, Sydney

debenham@it.uts.edu.au

Abstract. A market is in equilibrium if there is no opportunity for arbitrage, ie: risk-free, or low-risk, profit. The majority of real markets are not in equilibrium. A project is investigating the market evolutionary process in a particular electronic market that has been constructed in an on-going collaborative research project between a university and a software house. The way in which actors (buyers, sellers and others) use the market will be influenced by the information available to them. In this experiment, data mining and filtering techniques are used to distil both individual signals drawn from the markets and signals from the Internet into meaningful advice for the actors. The goal of this experiment is first to learn how actors will use the advice available to them to identify arbitrage opportunities, and second how the market will evolve through entrepreneurial intervention. In this electronic market a multiagent process management system is used to manage all market transactions including those that drive the market evolutionary process.

1   Introduction

A three-year project commencing in 2002 at UTS is investigating the mechanisms required to support the evolution of eMarkets. The perturbation of market equilibrium through entrepreneurial action is the essence of market evolution. Entrepreneurship relies both on intuition and on information discovery. The term 'entrepreneur' is used here in its technical sense [1]. Market evolution is a deep issue, and so a more tractable goal has been adopted initially. The initial goal of this project is to identify arbitrage opportunities in the stock options market based solely on information that can be derived automatically from market data and newsfeeds such as those produced by Reuters. This initial goal has been chosen because the problem is well defined and does not involve intangible intuition to the degree necessary for market evolution. Even so, intricate machinery is required to support even a simplistic investigation of arbitrage opportunities. The systems developed may not even be successful in identifying opportunities of financial significance. They will however constitute a first iteration design of systems to support market evolution, and that is the rationale for this initial phase of the project.

The overall project aims to derive fundamental insight into how e-markets evolve. To achieve this it addresses the problem of identifying timely information for e-markets with their rapid, pervasive and massive flows of data. This information is distilled from individual signals in the markets themselves and from signals observed on the unreliable, information-overloaded Internet. Distributed, concurrent, time-constrained data mining methods are managed using intelligent business process management technology to extract timely, reliable information from this unreliable environment.

An electronic market has been constructed during 2001 in an on-going collaborative research project between a university and a software house. This

K. Bauknecht, A. M. Tjoa, G. Quirchmayr (Eds.): EC-Web 2002, LNCS 2455, pp. 67–76, 2002.

electronic market forms a subset of the system described here; it is called the *basic system*. The goal of this subset is to identify timely information for traders in an e-market. The traders are the buyers and sellers. This basic system does not address the question of market evolution. The basic system is constructed in two parts: the e-market and the actors' assistant. The e-market has been constructed by Bullant Australasia Pty Ltd—an Australian software house with a strong interest in business-to-business (B2B) e-business [www.bullant.com]. The e-market is part of their on-going research effort in this area. It has been constructed using Bullant's proprietary software development tools. The e-market was designed by the author. The actors' assistant is being constructed in the Faculty of Information Technology at the University of Technology, Sydney. It is funded by two Australian Research Council Grants; one awarded to the author, and one awarded to Dr Simeon Simoff.

One feature of the whole project is that every transaction is treated as a business process and is managed by a process management system. In other words, the process management system makes the whole thing work. The process management system is based on a robust multiagent architecture. The use of multiagent systems is justified first by the distributed nature of e-business, and second by the critical nature of the transactions involved. The environment may be unreliable due to the unreliability of the network and components in it, or due to the unreliability of players—for example, a seller may simply renege on a deal.

2   Arbitrage

The initial goal of the overall project is to identify arbitrage opportunities in the stock options market based solely on information that can be derived automatically from market data and newsfeeds. This initial goal was chosen because the problem is well defined and does not involve intangible intuition to the degree necessary for market evolution. *Arbitrage* is an opportunity for the purchase and sale of the same securities, commodities, or moneys in different markets to profit from unequal prices [Macquarie Dictionary]. For example, the practice of corporate asset-stripping— common-place in many countries— is typically associated with the identification of a low risk arbitrage opportunity. Arbitrage refers both to risk-free and to low-risk opportunities for such profit [2]. A market in which there is no opportunity for arbitrage is said to be in *equilibrium*. The majority of real markets, such as the capital markets, are not in equilibrium thus presenting the opportunity for transactions to take advantage of such risk-free, or low-risk, profits. Although the degree to which a market is not in equilibrium may be so small that profits from any attempted arbitrage activity will be eroded by transaction costs.

There are three different ways in which arbitrage opportunities may arise. First *pure arbitrage* in which there is an opportunity for *simultaneous* purchase and sale. In a single market these are rare. When opportunities do exist they can be expected to be short lived or to involve significant inherent risk. Second *delayed arbitrage* in which assets are switched from one investment to another and back again so increasing the original holding due to differing rates of return. Third *ex post arbitrage* in which bets are placed with two or more agents such that for some possible outcomes, at least, a profit will be returned, and under no circumstances will a loss be returned, with the exception, perhaps, of an unforeseen calamity. The initial goal of this project is to identify ex post arbitrage opportunities automatically.

Identifying opportunities for ex post arbitrage may require a considerable search and some calculation. The following example is adapted from Robert Nau's notes on Choice Theory [http://www.fuqua.duke.edu/faculty/alpha/rnau.htm]. This example illustrates the subtlety on ex post arbitrage and shows some of what has to be done to find it. Suppose that a Test is intended to indicate the presence of a substantial amount of Gold in a mining lease. Suppose that three engineers, A, B and C make the following statements. A: the chance of Gold is at least 0.4. B: If the Test is negative then there is less than 0.25 chance of Gold. C: Even if there is Gold the chance of the Test being negative is at least 0.5. On the basis of these statements, the observers A, B and C should be prepared to accept bets with the following odds:

Test Gold	Positive Yes	Positive No	Negative Yes	Negative No
Payoff to A	3	−2	3	−2
Payoff to B	0	0	−3	1
Payoff of C	−1	0	1	0

To see that there is an arbitrage opportunity here, multiply the payoff to observer B by two and observer C by three to obtain:

Payoff to A	3	−2	3	−2
Payoff to B × 2	0	0	−6	2
Payoff of C × 3	−3	0	3	0
Total	0	−2	0	0

So a bet of one dollar with A, two dollars with B and three with C has an ex post arbitrage opportunity in the event that the Test is positive and there is no Gold. If that event does not occur then nothing is lost. Further, if the probabilities of the four possible outcomes (taken from left to right as shown above) occurring are 0.2, 0.0, 0.2 and 0.6 then there is no arbitrage opportunity and the bets being offered are completely rational. The *degree* of an ex post arbitrage opportunity is the number of bets that have to be placed to establish a risk-free opportunity for profit. The source of arbitrage in this example is with the bets surrounding the existence of gold; it has nothing to do with the value, or potential value, of the gold itself.

An arbitrage opportunity differs from a "good bet". For example, if you choose to believe my advice that "shares in XYZ will go up because a takeover bid is about to be announced" then you may decide that purchasing shares in XYZ is a good bet. Arbitrage is more than that. In an arbitrage opportunity there should be "no apparent possibility of loss", as is shown in the Test/Gold example above.

Opportunities for ex post arbitrage may be found in the options and futures markets particularly when reliable information is present. However to find an option that appears to be a "good bet" is not to find an arbitrage opportunity, but may be the first step to an arbitrage opportunity. A second step is to look for other opportunities that provide "insurance" against loss in the first. The third step is to determine whether the size of bets on this collection of opportunities can be adjusted to create an arbitrage opportunity. In practice causality may be essential to establishing the opportunity. For example, "if the summer in Nauru is bad then the value of its coffee crop will fall". Inferences such as this provide a key that may lead to the identification of arbitrage opportunities in options for two or more different stocks whose value may be effected by this possible event. Data mining of newsfeeds and market data is used to identify these casual relationships as described in Section 5 below.

3   The E-market

The construction of experimental e-markets is an active area of research. For example, [3] describes work done at IBM's Institute for Advanced Commerce. The basic e-market is linked to the Sydney Stock Exchange and enables agents to 'trade' in options and futures in search of arbitrage opportunities without risking any funds. There are two functional components in the *basic e-market*: the e-exchange and a solution provider. The *solution provider* is 'minimal' and simply provides a conduit between buyer and seller through which long term contracts are negotiated. The *solution provider* in its present form does not give third-party support to the negotiation process.

An e-exchange is created for a fixed duration. An *e-exchange* is a virtual space in which a variety of market-type *activities* can take place at specified times. The time is determined by the e-exchange *clock*. Each activity is advertised on a notice *board* which shows the start and stop time for that activity as well as what the activity is and the *regulations* that apply to players who wish to participate in it. A human player works though a PC (or similar) by interacting with a *user agent* which communicates with a *proxy agent* or a solution provider situated in the e-market. The inter-agent communication is discussed in Sec 3. The user agents may be 'dumb', or 'smart' being programmed by the user to make decisions. Each activity has an *activity manager* that ensures that the regulations of that activity are complied with.

When an e-exchange is created, a specification is made of the e-exchange *rules*. These rules will state who is permitted to enter the e-exchange and the roles that they are permitted to play in the e-exchange. These rules are enforced by an *e-exchange manager*. For example, can any player create a sale activity (which could be some sort of auction), or, can any player enter the e-exchange by offering some service, such as advice on what to buy, or by offering 'package deals' of goods derived from different suppliers? A high-level view of the e-market is shown in Fig. 1.

The activities in the basic e-market are limited to opportunities to buy and sell goods. The regulations for this limited class of activities are called *market mechanisms* [4]. The subject of a negotiation is a *good*, buyers make *bids*, sellers make *asks*. Designing market mechanisms is an active area of research. For example, see optimal auctions [5]. One important feature of a mechanism is the 'optimal' strategy that a player should use, and whether that strategy is "truth revealing" [6].

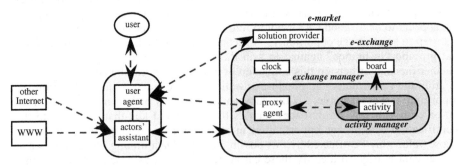

Fig. 1. High-level model of the e-market and user

4   Actor Classes

For some while there has been optimism in the role of agents in electronic commerce. "During this next-generation of agent-mediated electronic commerce,..... Agents will strategically form and reform coalitions to bid on contracts and leverage economies of scale...... It is in this third-generation of agent-mediated electronic commerce where companies will be at their most agile and markets will approach perfect efficiency." [7]. There is a wealth of material, developed principally by micro-economists, on the behaviour of rational economic agents. The value of that work in describing the behaviour of human agents is limited in part by the inability of humans to necessarily behave in an (economically) rational way, particularly when their (computational) resources are limited. That work provides a firm foundation for describing the behaviour of rational, intelligent software agents whose resource bounds are known, but more work has to be done [8]. Further, new market mechanisms that may be particularly well-suited to markets populated by software agents is now an established area of research [5] [4]. Most electronic business to date has centred on on-line exchanges in which a single issue, usually price, is negotiated through the application of traditional auction-based market mechanisms. Systems for multi-issue negotiation are also being developed [9], also IBM's Silkroad project [10]. The efficient management of multi-issue negotiation towards a possible solution when new issues may be introduced as the negotiation progresses remains a complex problem [11].

Given the optimism in the future of agents in electronic commerce and the body of theoretical work describing the behaviour of rational agents, it is perhaps surprising that the basic structure of the emerging e-business world is far from clear. The majority of Internet e-exchanges are floundering, and it appears that few will survive [12]. There are indications that exchanges may even charge a negative commission to gain business and so too market intelligence [12]. For example, the Knight Trading Group currently pays on-line brokers for their orders. The rationale for negative commissions is discussed in [13]. One reason for the recent failure of e-exchanges is that the process of competitive bidding to obtain the lowest possible price is not compatible with the development of buyer-seller relations. The preoccupation with a single issue, namely price, can overshadow other attributes such as quality, reliability, availability and customisation. A second reason for the failure Internet e-exchanges is that they deliver little benefit to the seller—few suppliers want to engage in a ruthless bidding war [13]. The future of electronic commerce must include the negotiation of complex transactions and the development of long-term relationships between buyer and seller as well as the e-exchanges. Support for these complex transactions and relationships is provided here by *solution providers*.

A considerable amount of work has been published on the comparative virtues of open market e-exchanges and solution providers that facilitate direct negotiation. For example, [14] argues that for privately informed traders the 'weak' trader types will systematically migrate from direct negotiations to competitive open markets. Also, for example, see [6] who compare the virtues of auctions and negotiation. Those results are derived in a supply/demand-bounded world into which signals may flow. These signals may be received by one or more of the agents in that world, and so may cause those agents to revise their valuation of the matter at hand.

5   Data Mining the Market Context

The identification of candidates for assembling an arbitrage package is made on the results of data mining the market context, consisting of newsfeeds and market data. E-markets reside on the Internet alongside the vast resources of the World Wide Web. In the experiments described here, the general knowledge available is restricted to that which can be gleaned from the e-markets themselves and that which can be extracted from the Internet in general—including the World Wide Web. The actors' assistant is a workbench that provides a suite of tools to *assist* a buyer or seller in the e-market. The actors' assistant does *not* attempt to replace buyers and sellers. For example, there is no attempt to automate 'speculation' in any sense. Web-mining tools assist the players in the market to make informed decisions. One of the issues in operating in an e-market place is coping with the rapidly-changing signals in it. These signals include: product and assortment attributes (if the site offers multiple products), promotions shown, visit attributes (sequences within the site, counts, click-streams) and business agent attributes. Combinations of these signals may be vital information to an actor. A new generation of data analysis and supporting techniques—collectively labelled as *data mining* methods—are now applied to stock market analysis, predictions and other financial and market analysis applications [15]. The application of data mining methods in e-business to date has predominantly been within the B2C framework, where data is mined at an on-line business site, resulting in the derivation of various behavioural metrics of site visitors and customers.

The estimation of the significance of a signal to a matter at hand is complicated by the fact that one person may place more faith in the relevance of a particular signal than others. So this estimation can only be performed on a personal basis. This work does *not*, for example, attempt to use a signal to predict whether the US dollar will rise against the UK pound. What it *does* attempt to do is to predict the value that an actor will place on a signal [16]. So the feedback here is provided by the user in the form of a rating of the material used. A five point scale runs from 'totally useless' to 'very useful'. Having identified the signals that a user has faith in, "classical" data mining methods [17] are then applied to combine these signals into succinct advice again using a five point scale. This feedback is used to 'tweak' the weights in Bayesian networks and as feedback to neural networks [18]. Bayesian networks are preferred when some confidence can be placed in a set of initial values for the weights. The system is able to raise an alarm automatically and quickly when a pre-specified compound event occurs such as: four members of the board of our principal supplier "Good Co" have resigned, the share price has dropped unexpectedly and there are rumours that our previous supplier "Bad Co" is taking over "Good Co".

The actors' assistant integrates two different approaches in data mining — the data driven and the hypothesis-driven approach. In the data-driven approach the assistant is just "absorbing" the information discovered by the scanners. It only specifies broad parameters to constrain the material scanned. For example, in the text analysis of the news files a text miner observes the frequencies of word occurrences and co-occurrences that appear to be relevant to a keyword such as 'steel prices'. The result of this process is an initial representative vocabulary for that news file. In the hypothesis-driven approach, the actors' assistant specifies precisely what it is looking for, for example, it formulates a hypothesis that a fall in the price of steel is likely within a month. The combination of data-driven and hypothesis driven approaches aims to provide a mechanism for meeting tight time constraints. Managing and synchronising the actors' assistant is handled by process management plans in the user agents. For example, a request is made for the best information on the Sydney Steel Co to be delivered by 4.00pm. This request triggers a business process. Things can go wrong with this process, for example a server may be down, in which case the process management plans activate less-preferred but nevertheless useful ways of obtaining the required information by the required time.

6   Process Management

Fig 1. may give the false impression that all the process management system does is to support communication between the user agents and their corresponding proxy agents. All transactions are managed as business processes, including a simple 'buy order', and a complex request for information placed with an actor's assistant. Building e-business process management systems is business process reengineering on a massive scale, it often named *industry process reengineering* [19]. This can lead to considerable problems unless there is an agreed basis for transacting business. The majority of market transactions are constrained by time ("I need it before Tuesday"), or more complex constraints ("I only need the engine if I also have a chassis and as long as the total cost is less than..). The majority of transactions are *critical* in that they must be dealt with and can't be forgotten or mislaid. Or at least it is an awful nuisance if they are. So this means that a system for managing them is required that can handle complex constraints and that attempts to prevent process failure.

E-market processes will typically be *goal-directed* in the sense that it may be known *what* goals have to be achieved, but not necessarily *how* to achieve those goals today. A goal-directed process may be modelled as a (possibly conditional) sequence of goals. Alternatively a process may be *emergent* in the sense that the person who triggers the process may not have any particular goal in mind and may be on a 'fishing expedition' [20]. There has been little work on the management of emergent processes [21]. There a multiagent process management system is described that is based on a three-layer, BDI, hybrid architecture. That system 'works with' the user as emergent processes unfold. It also manages goal-directed processes in a fairly conventional way using single-entry quadruple-exit plans that give almost-failure-proof operation. Those plans can represent constraints of the type referred to above, and so it is a candidate for managing the operation of the system described in Sec. 2.

Multiagent technology is an attractive basis for industry process re-engineering [22] [23]. A multiagent system consists of autonomous components that negotiate with one another. The scalability issue of industry process reengineering is "solved"—in theory—by establishing a common understanding for inter-agent communication and interaction. Standard XML-based ontologies will enable data to be communicated freely [24] but much work has yet to be done on standards for communicating expertise [25]. Results in ontological analysis and engineering [26] [25] is a potential source for formal communication languages which supports information exchange between the actors in an e-market place. Systems such as CommerceNet's Eco [www.commerce.net] and Rosettanet [www.rosettanet.org] are attempting to establish common languages and frameworks for business transactions and negotiations. Specifying an agent interaction protocol is complex as it in effect specifies the common understanding of the basis on which the whole system will operate.

A variety of architectures have been described for autonomous agents. A fundamental distinction is the extent to which an architecture exhibits deliberative (feed forward, planning) reasoning and reactive (feed back) reasoning. If an agent architecture combines these two forms of reasoning it is a *hybrid architecture*. One well reported class of hybrid architectures is the three-layer, BDI agent architectures. One member of this class is the INTERRAP architecture [27], which has its origins in the work of [28]. A multiagent system to manage "goal-driven" processes is described in [21]. In that system each human user is assisted by an agent which is based on a generic three-layer, BDI hybrid agent architecture similar to the INTERRAP architecture. That system has been extended to support emergent processes and so to support and the full range of industry processes. That conceptual architecture is adapted slightly for use here; see Fig 2(a). Each agent receives messages from other agents (and, if it is a personal agent, from its user) in its message area. The world beliefs are derived from reading messages, observing the e-market and from the World Wide Web (as accessed by an actor's assistant).

Deliberative reasoning is effected by the non-deterministic procedure: "on the basis of current *beliefs*—identify the current *options*, on the basis of current options and existing commitments—select the current commitments (called the agent's *goals* or *desires*), for each newly-committed goal choose a *plan* for that goal, from the selected plans choose a consistent set of things to do next (called the agent's *intentions*)". A *plan* for a goal is a conditional sequence of sub-goals that may include iterative or recursive structures. If the current options do not include a current commitment then that commitment is dropped. In outline, the reactive reasoning mechanism employs triggers that observe the agent's beliefs and are 'hot wired' back to the procedural intentions. If those triggers fire then they take precedence over the agent's deliberative reasoning. The environment is intrinsically unreliable. In particular plans can not necessarily be relied upon to achieve their goal. So at the end of every plan there is a *success condition* which tests whether that plan's goal has been achieved; see Fig 2(b). That success condition is itself a procedure which can succeed (✓), fail (✗) or be aborted (**A**). So this leads to each plan having four possible exits: success (✓), failure (✗), aborted (**A**) and unknown (**?**). In practice these four exists do not necessarily have to lead to different sub-goals, and so the growth in the size of plan with depth is not quite as bad as could be expected.

KQML (Knowledge Query and Manipulation Language) is used for inter-agent communication [29]. Each process agent has a *message area*. If agent A wishes to tell something to agent B then it does so by posting a message to agent B's message area. Each agent has a *message manager* whose role is to look after that agent's message area. Each message contains an instruction for the message manager.

7   Conclusion

The first step in an investigation of the mechanics of e-Market evolution is to assemble machinery to identify arbitrage opportunities. This is done using a 'toy' e-Market that is hooked onto the Sydney Stock Exchange. Arbitrage opportunities are identified on the basis of intelligence derived from newsfeeds and from market data using data mining bots. The form of arbitrage considered here is opportunities triggered by this intelligence [*] rather than strictly based on derivatives [*]. The whole experiment operates using a powerful multiagent process management system that treats every transaction as a business process. The use of a powerful business process management system to drive all the electronic market transactions unifies the whole market operation. The development of computational models of arbitrage identification, deploying those models in the e-market place, and including them as part of the building blocks for investigating e-market evolution provides a practical instrument for continued research and development in electronic markets.

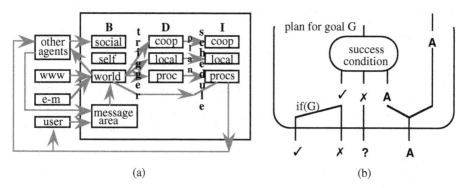

(a)   (b)

Fig 2. (a) conceptual architecture, (b) the four plan exits

References

[1]   Israel M. Kirzner Entrepreneurial Discovery and the Competitive Market Process: An Austrian Approach" Journal of Economic Literature XXXV (March) 1997 60-85.

[2]   Bjork, Tomas.   Arbitrage Theory in Continuous Time.   Oxford University Press (1999)

[3]   Kumar, M. & Feldman, S.I.   Business Negotiations on the Internet.   Proceedings INET'98 Internet Summit, Geneva, July 21-24, 1998.

[4]   Bichler, M.   The Future of E-Commerce: Multi-Dimensional Market Mechanisms. Cambridge University Press (2001).

[5]   Milgrom, P.   Auction Theory for Privatization.   Cambridge Univ Press (2001).

[6]   Bulow, J. & Klemperer, P.   Auctions Versus Negotiations.   American Economic Review, 1996.

[7]   R. Guttman, A. Moukas, and P. Maes.   Agent-mediated Electronic Commerce: A Survey.   Knowledge Engineering Review, June 1998.

[8]   Moshe Tennenholtz.   Electronic Commerce: From Economic and Game-Theoretic Models to Working Protocols.   Invited paper.   Proceedings Sixteenth International Joint Conference on Artificial Intelligence, IJCAI'99, Stockholm, Sweden.

[9]   Sandholm, T.   Agents in Electronic Commerce: Component Technologies for Automated Negotiation and Coalition Formation. Autonomous Agents and Multi-Agent Systems, 3(1), 73-96.

[10]   Ströbel, M.   Design of Roles and Protocols for Electronic Negotiations.   Electronic Commerce Research Journal, Special Issue on Market Design 2001.

[11]   Peyman   Faratin.   Automated   Service   Negotiation   Between   Autonomous Computational Agents.   PhD dissertation, University of London (Dec 2000).

[12]   R. Wise & D. Morrison.   Beyond the Exchange; The Future of B2B.   Harvard Business review Nov-Dec 2000, pp86-96.

[13]   Kaplan, Steven and Sawhney, Mohanbir.   E-Hubs: The New B2B Marketplace. Harvard Business Review 78 May-June 2000   97-103.

[14]   Neeman, Z. & Vulkan, N.   Markets Versus Negotiations.   The Hebrew University of Jerusalem Discussion Paper 239.   (February 2001).

[15]   B. Kovalerchuk & E. Vityaev. Data Mining in Finance: Advances in Relational and Hybrid Methods. Kluwer, 2000.

[16]   J. Han, L.V.S. Lakshmanan & R.T. Ng. Constraint-based multidimensional data mining. IEEE Computer, 8, 46-50, 1999.

[17]   Han, J. & Kamber, M. Data Mining: Concepts and Techniques. Morgan Kaufmann (2000).

[18]   Chen, Z. Computational Intelligence for Decision Support. CRC Press, Boca Raton, 2000.

[19]   Feldman, S. Technology Trends and Drivers and a Vision of the Future of e-business. Proceedings 4th International Enterprise Distributed Object Computing Conference, September 25-28, 2000, Makuhari, Japan.

[20]   Fischer, L. (Ed). Workflow Handbook 2001. Future Strategies, 2000.

[21]   Debenham, J.K.. Supporting knowledge-driven processes in a multiagent process management system. Proceedings Twentieth International Conference on Knowledge Based Systems and Applied Artificial Intelligence, ES'2000: Research and Development in Intelligent Systems XVII, Cambridge UK, December 2000, pp273-286.

[22]   Jain, A.K., Aparicio, M. and Singh, M.P. "Agents for Process Coherence in Virtual Enterprises" in Communications of the ACM, Volume 42, No 3, March 1999, pp62—69.

[23]   Jennings, N.R., Faratin, P., Norman, T.J., O'Brien, P. & Odgers, B. Autonomous Agents for Business Process Management. Int. Journal of Applied Artificial Intelligence 14 (2) 145—189, 2000.

[24]   Robert Skinstad, R. "Business process integration through XML". In proceedings XML Europe 2000, Paris, 12-16 June 2000.

[25]   Guarino N., Masolo C., and Vetere G., OntoSeek: Content-Based Access to the Web, IEEE Intelligent Systems 14(3), May/June 1999, pp. 70-80

[26]   Uschold, M. and Gruninger, M.: 1996, Ontologies: principles, methods and applications. Knowledge Engineering Review, 11(2), 1996.

[27]   Müller, J.P. "The Design of Intelligent Agents" Springer-Verlag, 1996.

[28]   Rao, A.S. and Georgeff, M.P. "BDI Agents: From Theory to Practice", in proceedings First International Conference on Multi-Agent Systems (ICMAS-95), San Francisco, USA, pp 312—319.

[29]   Finin, F. Labrou, Y., and Mayfield, J. "KQML as an agent communication language." In Jeff Bradshaw (Ed.) Software Agents. MIT Press (1997).

[30]   Reverre, S. "The Complete Arbitrage Deskbook." McGraw-Hill, 2001.

[31]   Hull, JC. "Options, Futures, and Other Derivatives." Prentice-Hall, 2000.

An Architecture for Building User-Driven Web Tasks via Web Services

Jin Lu and Lihui Chen

School of Electrical and Electronic Engineering
Nanyang Technology University
Singapore
{ps142778877, elhchen}@ntu.edu.sg

Abstract. With the rapid development of web services technology, the Internet becomes a giant programming interface and users can access and use the information via such an interface [1]. And the need on facilities for end users to achieve web task automation becomes more significant as the number of web services and online users increases. In this paper, we describe the proposed architecture of such an end-user builder called WTABuilder in a web services setting. WTABuilder makes use of the existing Web Service Oriented Architecture as the infrastructure [2]. Our WTABuilder architecture is designed for end-users to build complex web service-based tasks and to perform the tasks automatically. This paper gives a description of the infrastructure in place and briefly explains each component involved. The preliminary design of major components in the proposed architecture is presented.

1 Introduction

1.1 Automation Demand in Web Tasks

In order to show that the current web tasks are lack of automation, let's look at a specific scenario. A typical web task we shall consider is that a user who wants to buy a book from online book stores. We can assume the online book stores have already provided the web service components for checking book price, placing orders and online payment, even a client stub such as a servlet for the web service component that enables end user access the component from a web browser. The user visits each online book store to check whether the book is available. Then he retrieves their prices and makes a comparison. If the book price is within his budget he will place the order. He wished to automate this task so that he has more free time for other tasks. What are the issues and problems that must be resolved before such automation can be achieved?

- *Problem of Direct Interaction*

K. Bauknecht, A M. Tjoa, G. Quirchmayr (Eds.): EC-Web 2002, LNCS 2455, pp. 77–86, 2002.

To use a web service, a user has to navigate web pages, fill in forms and click on buttons. These web sites reply on the user being physically present and interacting with the web pages, via the browser. The user must interact directly with the web site to use the service as there are no other access methods available.

For automation to be possible there must be an alternation way of using these services. This alternative should be a standard, programmatic method of access so that direct request for services can be replaced by some form of automatic request.

- *Problem of Integration*

Web services on different web sites generally require different inputs and generate different outputs. Even services of the same type, e.g. book-order services, can differ in these two aspects. These differing web services may all be used in the same web task. Furthermore, in each web task, there are normally temporal constraints where one web service must be completed before another may begin.

For automation, some sort of common standards need to be established such that the differing services can be integrated together to form a single task.

1.2   Enabling Technology: Web Services

Web Services are loosely coupled reusable software components that semantically encapsulate discrete functionality and are distributed and programmatically accessible over standard Internet protocols [3].

Web Services are based on existing Internet protocols. First there was HTTP; with this communication protocol it is possible to send information from one point on the Internet to another point. The information that is sent over the wire can be structured by using XML. The XML protocol defines the format and the semantics of the information. XML is a basic foundation for the later layers. SOAP is a protocol that defines how to invoke function calls from objects that live in different environments [4]. HTTP, XML, and SOAP can be seen as the core layers for Web Services. These layers define how Web Services have to interact with each other. The protocol WSDL describes how to communicate with a Web Service [5]. In the WSDL definition, different types of communication (bindings) are allowed. And UDDI is a central market place where the business entity can publish their web services, and other parties can find it and use it [6]. The complete protocol stack is detailed in Fig. 1 [7].

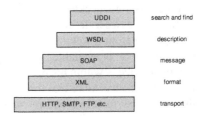

Fig. 1. Web Service Protocol Stack

For web service to become a reality there must be common architectures and open Internet standards to support it. The Service-Oriented Architecture (SOA) is a conceptual architecture for implementing the web service.

Regardless of the implementation, SOA is comprised of three participants and three fundamental operations as illustrated in Fig. 2 [8].

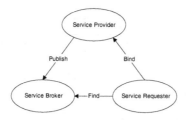

Fig. 2. Service-Oriented Architecture

Our proposed WTABuilder is based on the Service-Oriented Architecture infrastructure. In the later section of this paper, the architecture of the WTABuilder will be introduced.

2   Architecture of the WTABuilder

In order to understand the WTABuilder architecture, here we will analysis it in the architectural view.

Fig. 3 shows the architecture of the WTABuilder. It defines the set of components that can be incorporated into the WTABuilder system. The WTABuilder Architecture is based on the SOA described in Fig. 2.

The role of each part of the architecture is as follows:

Front-End: Web Service Discovery and Task Composer

• UDDI Search Engine
The UDDI search engine is used to browse the information about Businesses, Business Services, Binding Templates, tModels and their associated information in the UDDI Registry. The search engine returns the web service description (WSDL) to the user.

• Task Composer
It's a visual design-time tool for creating the workflow of a web task.
Back-End: Web Task Automation Server

It's a runtime component that executes and manages the workflow of a web task created in Task Composer.

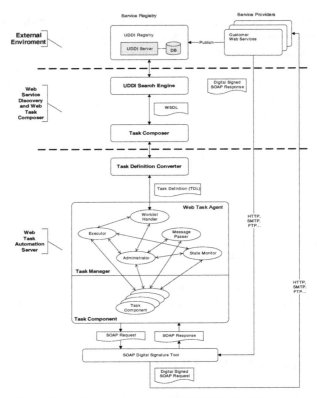

Fig. 3. Major Components in the WTABuilder Architecture

• Task Definition Converter

The Task Definition Converter is a tool to convert the user task created using the Task Composer to the Task Definition. The Task Definition Converter has two main responsibilities: firstly, to support users in the creation of Task Definition and secondly to check the validity of the Task Definition created.

• Task Definition and TDL

The Task Definition Converter translates a user tasks from the real world into a formal, computer processable Task Definition. The Task Definition must contain all necessary information about the task to enable it to be interpreted by the Task Manager.The task definition is modeled using Task Definition Language (TDL). TDL is an XML-based high level description language for the web service compositions.

• *Web Task Agent*

Once the Task Definition has been constructed, the execution will be done by the Web Task Agent. This Web Task Agent is a program that can understand the semantics of the TDL such that it can be interpret all Task Definitions accordingly and invoke the web service components as defined by user. The Web Task Agent is consisting of two parts: Task Manager and Task Component

The Task Manager's role is to support users in the management of their tasks. This includes support for activation of tasks, control of the active tasks, abrupt termination of the active tasks and the exception handling. The Task Manger is also responsible for interpreting the Task Definition.

The Task Component contains a set of component each one of them is responsible for a specific task, such as send a credit-checking request or notifies the user to take certain action.

- *SOAP Digital Signature Tool*

The goal of the SOAP Digital Signature Module is to provide a simple and elegant solution for incorporating digital signatures in a SOAP RPC call. Digital signature uses public key cryptography, which calls for infrastructure to manage keys and certificates.

External Environment: UDDI Registry and the Web Service Provider

- *UDDI Registry*

The UDDI Registry is a web service registry for business user or customer to register and discover web services.

- *Service Provider*

The service providers deploy and publish their web services by registering them with the UDDI Registry.

3 Properties of the Major Components

3.1 Web Service Discovery: UDDI Search Engine

The core information model used by the UDDI registries is defined in an XML schema. The UDDI XML schema defines four core types of information that provide the kinds of information that a technical person would need to know in order to use a web service. These are: business information; service information, binding information; and information about specifications for services.

Like the normal internet search engine, the UDDI search engine interface allows the user to select different search criteria. The search criteria are the elements in the UDDI data structure, including:

- Business
- tModel
- Service
- Binding

Any of a number of keys from these criteria can be AND'ed together to make the search more specific.

3.2 Task Definition and Task Definition Language (TDL)

The user task of web services is easy to be understood for human beings. However, in order to automate the task using computer software, we shall translate it from real world to a formal, computer processable task model. In our proposed architecture, we define a Task Definition Language (TDL) to model the user task.

The Task Definition Language is an XML-based high level description language for the web service compositions. It can be used to define the structure and relationships among a set of components which constitutes a task that can be automated.

A Task Definition must contain sufficient information such that is can be used by the Web Task Automation Server to perform the task. The information is defined using the TDL. It includes the following:

1. The basic operations that should be performed in a web task.
- Set of web service components that provide the required services for the operation
- Task components that perform the operation
- Mathematical of logical functions bound with the operation

2. A flow control for the various basic operations.
- Sequence operations
- Synchronize operation
- Choose an operation to perform based on certain condition

3. A life cycle management for a user task.
- Start a new process
- Suspend a running process
- Resume a suspended process
- Terminate a running process

4. An exception handling for a user task
- Process that should be performed if an exception occurs

3.3 Web Task Automation Server

The Web Task Automation Server is a cooperative multi-agent system in which multiple processing entities cooperate in order to accomplish the web tasks. The core part of the Web Task Automation Server is the Web Task Agent. It is consisting of a Task Manager and several Task Components that work together to carry out a web task. The task Manager is responsible for the planning of the actions in the multi-agent system. Typically the it provides facilities to handle:
- Interpretation of the process definition

- Control of the process instances - creation, activation, suspension and termination
- Navigation between process activities, which may involve sequential or parallel operations
- Scheduling, interpretation of the relevant data
- Sign-on and sign-off of specific participants
- Maintenance of the process flow control data and process flow relevant data, passing the data to/from applications or users
- An interface to invoke the task components and link the process relevant data
- Supervisory actions for control, administration and audit purposes

Base on the facilities that should be handled, the Task Manager is consisting of a collection of agents. The currently available components of our implemented system are:

- *Worklist Handler*

The Worklist Handler receives the current task definition from the Interface Layer. A task definition consists of a number of single actions that must be processed sequentially or parallel. The Worklist Handler must analysis the task definition and determines when specific actions are to be made available for execution.

- *Executor*

The Executor receives information from the Worklist Handler and executes the next outstanding action.

- *State Monitor*

The State Monitor coordinates with the Executor and monitors the state of each executing process. The State Monitor returns the status of each process to the Administrator.

- *Message Passer*

To facility the communication between agents, a component called Message Passer is used. It knows the physical address of any other agents in the system, as an address server. When an agent wants to communicate with others, for example, send or require message from others, it may submit a query to the Message Passer with necessary information. The Message Passer will handle the query and return required information to the agent.

- *Administrator*

The Administrator coordinates with the other Control Agents and keeps a record of all the process. It's also responsible for the lifecycle control of the task component. It may suspend, resume, or terminate its execution.

The internal components pass information to one another during runtime processing by way of XML input and output DOMs (Document Object Models, used here to mean the in-memory object that represents the content and structure of an XML document). The XML output for one component is often the XML input for another component; however, components don't actually pass these XML documents as disk files, but rather pass "in memory" DOM images of the files. This is an important distinction, as these DOMs can be destroyed, changed, and recreated during processing to achieve the data integration goals without ever being written to disk or actually changing any disk files. Once an XML document's DOM is loaded into memory, it can be manipulated by the various mapping, transformation, and transfer features.

The method for message passing between agents is to use a system database. The database provides all agents within the system with a common work area in which they can exchange information, data and knowledge. An agent may initiate a communication by writing an information item to the database. Then the data is available for all other agents of the system. The agent can at any time access the database to determine whether its required information has arrived. If yes, it can read this information.

However, considering the security issue, in practice an agent are not allowed to directly communicate with the database. Instead, it will use the Message Passer to extract the required information from the database. The mechanism is shown in Fig. 4.

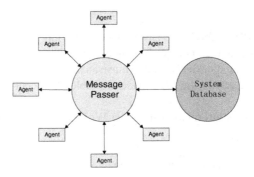

Fig. 4. Message Passing Mechanism

There is no public areas exist within the database. The database provides different regions to which individual agents are assigned. In this case, an agent only needs to observe those regions to which it is assigned instead of search through a large amount of information. An agent must firstly register with the Administrator to receive an access authorization to a specific region. When it required information, it submits a query to the Message Passer together with its agent ID. The Message Passer will use the agent ID to determine its access authorization and access region. Unauthorized access will be blocked.

In our proposed architecture, the Web Task Automaton Server will use the following types of data:

• *Task definition data*

The task definition data is all necessary information about the user task to enable it to be executed by the Task Manager. This includes information about the task starting and completion conditions, constituent activities and rules for navigating between them, user tasks to be undertaken, etc.

• *Web service description data*

The web service description data contains the technical data about a web service component, for example, the access point and protocol, data type of the input and output parameter, etc. And it also includes some general information about a web service, such as the details about the company providing the web service and its contact number.

• *Task control data*

The task control data is managed by the Task Manager. Such data is internal to the Task Manager and is not normally accessible to applications. For example, it represents the dynamic state of the system and its process instances.

• *Task relevant data*

The task relevant data contains the log information of the system, such as the exception of a process, or a message transfer failure.

• *Task application data*

The task application data is a run-time data and is generated by the task components. It includes the outputted data of a task component and the retrieved data from the web service component.

4   Conclusion and Future Work

In this paper we proposed the WTABuilder architecture for Building End-User Driven Web Tasks via Web Services that solve the directly interaction and integration problems and make the web service more accessible to end user even a non-programmer. The architecture solves the web task automation problem by letting users browse and assemble the web service components to form a complex user task. The definition of the task can be represented by an XML document. Then the Web Task Automation Server will use the document and perform the task on the user's behalf. The major components of the architecture are the UDDI Search Engine, Task Definition Language and the Web Task Automation Server. The main characteristics of the builder include:

• The UDDI Search Engine allows user to browse the available web services according to his region of interest. Multiple search criteria can be AND'ed or OR'ed together to make the search more specific.
• The TDL imposes a standard way of defining the web tasks in a structured XML document. Such a standard allows a program such as the Task Manager to automatically invoke the programs and web services.
• The Web Service Automation Server is based on a multi-agent architecture. It's consisting of a Task Manager and several Task Components. The Task Manager serves as a workflow engine. It analyzes the Task Definition and invokes the Task Component to perform the user-defined web task. In the mean time, it will monitor the status of each component and handle the exception accordingly.

The benefits of our proposed architecture described above provides sufficient reasons for continue development in this area. As for future work, we would like to recommend considering the following directions:

1. Refinement of the Task Definition Language: such as adding more elements and attributes, in order to let user build more complicate task model.

2. Optimization of the UDDI Search Engine: As the web services become dominate in the internet, the amount of web services will increase significantly. At present, the UDDI Search Engine only returns the web services that can be found in the UDDI Registry, and without any sorting. But later since a simple search can result in millions of search results, certain algorithm should be provided to sort the result. For example, a tModel can be referenced by many businessEntity. Therefore a "businessEntity" search result can be sorted by the appeared frequency in the UDDI Registry of its tModel.

References

1. Enrique Castro-Leon, *A perspective on Web Services,* WebServices.org, February 18 2002, http://www.webservices.org/index.php/article/articleview/113/1/3/
2. Dave Fisco, *Web Services architecture debuts,* IBM Developer Works, September 2000, http://www-106.ibm.com/developerworks/webservices/library/w-int.html?dwzone=webservices
3. Brent Sleeper, *Defining Web Services,* the Stencil Group, June 2001, http://www.stencilgroup.com/ideas_scope_200106wsdefined.html
4. W3C Note, *Simple Object Access Protocol (SOAP) 1.1,* World Wide Web Consortium, 08 May 2000, http://www.w3.org/TR/SOAP/
5. W3C Note, *Web Services Description Language (WSDL) 1.1* World Wide Web Consortium, 15 March 2001, http://www.w3.org/TR/wsdl
6. UDDI.org, Commerce UDDI resources, http://www.uddi.org
7. Dan Gisolfi, *Web services architect,* IBM Developer Works, April 2001, http://www-106.ibm.com/developerworks/webservices/library/ws-arc1/?dwzone=webservices
8. James Snell, *Web services insider,* IBM Developer Works, April 2001, http://www-106.ibm.com/developerworks/webservices/library/ws-ref1.html?dwzone=webservices

Efficient XML Data Management: An Analysis

Ullas Nambiar[1], Zoé Lacroix[1], Stéphane Bressan[2], Mong Li Lee[2], and
Ying Guang Li[2]

[1] Arizona State University
{mallu,zoe.lacroix}@asu.edu
[2] National University of Singapore
{steph,leeml,liyg}@comp.nus.edu.sg

Abstract. With XML rapidly gaining popularity as the standard for
data exchange on the World Wide Web, a variety of XML management
systems (XMLMS) are becoming available. The choice of an XMLMS is
made difficult by the significant difference in the expressive power of the
queries and the performance shown by these XMLMS. Most XMLMS are
legacy systems (mostly relational) extended to load, query, and publish
data in XML format. A few are native XMLMS and capture all the characteristics of XML data representation. This paper looks at expressive
power and efficiency of various XMLMS. The performance analysis relies
on the testbed provided by XOO7, a benchmark derived from OO7 to
capture both data and document characteristics of XML. We present efficiency results for two native XMLMS, an XML-enabled semi-structured
data management system and an XML-enabled RDBMS, which emphasize the need for a delicate balance between the data-centric and
document-centric aspects of XML query processing.

1 Introduction

The *eXtended Markup Language* (XML) is designed as the standard for information interchange on the Web. XML is a subset of SGML (Standardized General Markup Language) designed to provide structure to textual documents and
augments HTML (Hyper Text Markup Language) by allowing data to carry
its meaning and not just presentation details. XML's development was not fur-
thered directly by the mainstream database community, yet database researchers
actively participated in developing technology for XML, particularly query languages. This led to the development of query languages such as XML-QL [18],
LOREL [3] and XQL [27]. These languages designed by the database community
are biased toward the data-centric view of XML that requires data to be fully
structured. But XML was developed primarily as a document markup language
that would be more powerful than HTML yet less complex than SGML and does
not require the content to adhere to structural rules. The document characteristics of XML representation not only relies on the data representation expressed
through markups but also on the ordering of the document components within
the file. This leads us to question whether the query languages designed by

K. Bauknecht, A M. Tjoa, G. Quirchmayr (Eds.): EC-Web 2002, LNCS 2455, pp. 87–98, 2002.
© Springer-Verlag Berlin Heidelberg 2002

the database community and the data management systems that use these languages to manipulate XML data, capture the whole essence and power of XML. In essence, these languages and systems have a data-centric view of XML, and merely use XML to publish the data. On the other hand many systems use implementations of XPath [14], a language designed to identify parts of XML documents, to query XML data. Such systems then subscribe to the document-centric view of the XML. Thus the initial use of XML has been largely polarized with a large number of users (coming from the database community) developing systems for the data-centric characteristics of XML, while many others in areas like Bio-informatics research, Medical Systems and Geographical Information Systems (GIS) use XML for its ability to manipulate documents. Recently the World Wide Web Consortium (W3C) published XQuery [12] as a candidate for a standard query language for XML, combining both the data and document centric characteristics of XML.

In this paper, we study XML management systems (XMLMS) by addressing the issues of data representation and storage, and XML query functionalities and processing efficiency. We first analyse the design of XMLMS and identify XML characteristics and XML query capabilities and their corresponding consequences on the performance. In the second part of the paper, we run experiments to coroborate our analysis. We use XOO7 [26,9], a benchmark for XML databases, to compare the current XML data management systems. The systems we compare are : LORE [3], Kweelt [28], XENA [31] and an XPath [14] implementation[1].

Section 2 explores XML in terms of its known representations and describes four XMLMS that use these representations. . We also investigate how XML data affects processing efficiency of database systems. We briefly introduce XOO7, the benchmark we use in Section 3. In Section 4 we analyze the results from the performance study of the four XML data management systems we chose against the benchmark queries, and conclude in Section 5 by highlighting our contributions and the possible extensions of this work.

2   Representational Diversity and Processing Efficiency of XML

XML was designed to overcome the shortcomings of its two predecessors, SGML and HTML. SGML is complex, in particular for simple applications such as publishing on the web. The principle drawback of SGML is its strict adherence to marked-up structure of the documents. On the other hand, HTML designed at CERN as a watered down version of SGML, provides a common set of tags for display. So parsers can be incorporated into Web Browsers which made HTML the first language of the World Wide Web. But this *flexibility in usage of its syntax* that made HTML popular also makes it a bad candidate for exchanging

---

[1] The developers of the commercial product dismissed our request to use actual name of the product.

data over the Web. HTML allows multiple interpretations of the same data and makes it impossible to add semantics to the data published in HTML. In contrast, XML is a very versatile yet easy to use markup language, that has the extensibility of SGML but remains as simple as HTML.

2.1 Data-Centric versus Document-Centric View of XML

The initial attempts at developing tools for storage of XML content were biased by the legacy of the researchers who worked on providing the solutions. Solutions developed by the database community focused at using XML as *yet another data format* and the use of relational and sometimes object-relational data processing tools. While this use of XML is acceptable, it raises the question of harnessing the full power of XML. XML is inherently semi-structured. Although, like SGML, XML documents can use a DTD to derive their structure, DTDs are not a must for all XML documents. Thus XML documents can take any structure. On the other hand, relational and object-relational data models have a fixed pre-defined structure. We can represent totally structured data using XML in combination with DTDs or XML Schema specifications [20,30,5], which we term as *data-centric* characteristic or format of XML. The documents subscribing to the data-centric view of XML will be highly structured. Similar to traditional (relational) databases, the order of sibling elements is unimportant in such documents. On the other hand, *document-centric* XML content is highly unstructured, and both the implicit and explicit order of elements is important in such documents. The implicit order is carried by the order of the elements (as siblings in a tree-like representation) within the file, whereas an explict order would be expressed by an attribute or a tag in the document. Although it is easy to express the explicit order in relational databases, capturing the implicit order while converting a document-centric XML document into relational database proves to be a problem. Besides the implicit order, XML documents differ from a relational representation by allowing deep nesting and hyper-linked components. Implicit order, nesting and hyperlinks can always be represented in tables but with costly transformations in terms of time and space.

2.2 XML Processing Efficiency

Query languages designed to operate using the data-centric view cannot exploit the implicit order present in XML. But relational systems can efficiently process most data-centric queries. XML management systems that focus on a data-centric representation are less expressive but should be able to give good performance. On the other hand, systems using query languages that exploit document characteristics of XML have greater expressive power but are likely to be less efficient.

An adequate XML query language should definitely provide support for issuing all XML queries including: (1) Relational queries, (2) Document queries, and (3) Navigational queries. We classify XML queries that have expressive power similar to Datalog [15] and [19] for relational model as *Relational queries*. Queries that use the implicit and explicit order of elements in an XML document, as well as textual functionalities are classified as *Document queries* while the queries that require traversal of XML document structure using references/links as supported by XLink/XPointer specification [17] and [16] are *Navigational queries*. A detailed classification of essential XML query characteristics is given by [26].

The ability to express and process document and navigational queries in addition to the traditional relational queries affect significantly the performance. A totally unordered XML data will require least processing time. The simple explanation is the similarity of such data with relational data and hence the ability to use optimized approaches from relational database community to process such data. In contrast, fully ordered data, requires the preservation of the structure of XML document for processing any query. Existing approaches at processing queries over fully ordered data require loading the entire document into main memory and creating a tree structure of the document. Similar analysis can be made for nested or hyperlinked documents versus flat data.

2.3   XML Management Systems

From the above discussion we divide current XML management systems into *XML-Enabled* and *Native XML databases*. XML-Enabled databases (usually relational) contain extensions (either model- or template-driven) for transferring data between XML documents and themselves and are generally designed to store and retrieve data-centric documents. For a detailed classification of XML management products refer to [8]. An example of a native XMLMS is Kweelt [28], a proposed implementation of Quilt [13]. Kweelt stores data in flat files and hence favours the document-centric nature of XML. LORE [3] is not exactly native but it is a semi-structured data management system later revised to handle XML documents [23]. The main difficulty of the conversion was indeed tackling the implicit order. Most of the existing XML data management systems are XML-enabled and built on top of relational or object-relational systems. They are used to publish data in XML and allow XML queries to be translated into SQL statements. We use XENA [31], designed at the National University of Singapore as an XML-enabled data management system. It stores the XML data into tables automatically according to the XML schema. XENA then retrieves data from tables by converting an XPath query into several SQL queries automatically, using the XML schema.

Our decision of choosing the above mentioned XML data management systems was primarily motivated by the easy availability of their source code and the detailed documentation about their implementations.

3   XML Database Benchmarks

Semistructured data models and query languages have been studied widely in [1] and [10]. In [22] several storage strategies and mapping schemes for XML data using a relational database are explored. Domain-specific database benchmarks for OLTP (TPC-C), decision support (TPC-H, TPC-R, APB-1), information retrieval, spatial data management (Sequoia) etc. are available [25]. XOO7 [26] and [9], XMach-1 [6] and XMark [29] are the three benchmarks currently available that test XMLMS for their query processing abilities.

Table 1. Comparing Benchmarks over XML system characteristics

System Characteristics	XMach-1	XMark	XOO7
Selection Queries	√	√	√
Projection Queries	√	√	√
Reduction: Remove a selected element	√	√	√
Restructuring: Reorder sub elements	√	√	√
Construction: Output new structure	√	√	√
Remote Execution: Data and Evaluator on different machines			
Preserve Implicit Order			√
Exploit Schema	√	√	√
Schemaless Document Manipulations			√
XLink and XPointer Manipulations			
Streaming Data Processing: Schema generation on the fly			
Transaction Processing			
Text Search	√	√	√
View Processing			
Stored Procedures and Triggers			
User Defined Functions		√	√
Aggregate Manipulations			√
Update Element/Database			
Delete Element/Database	√		
Append Data	√		
Extract results based on Similarity Criterion			
Navigational Queries			√

XOO7 design attempts to harness the similarities in data models of XML and object-oriented approaches. Although XML attempts to provide a framework for handling semistructured data, it encompasses most of the modeling features of complex object models [2] and [4]. There are straightforward correspondences between the object-oriented schemas and instances and XML DTDs and data. XOO7 is an adaptation of the OO7 Benchmark [11] for object-oriented database systems. XOO7 provides 18 query challenges. The current implementation of XOO7 tests XML management systems which store their data locally. For a detailed description of XOO7 refer to [26].

XMach-1 tests multi-user features provided by the systems. The benchmark is modeled for a web application using XML data. It evaluates standard and non-standard linguistic features such as insertion, deletion, querying URL and aggregate operations. Although the proposed workload and queries are interesting, the benchmark has not been applied and no results have been published yet. XMark developed under the XML benchmark project at CWI, is a benchmark proposed for XML data stores. The benchmark consists of an application scenario which models an Internet auction site and 20 XQuery challenges designed to cover the essentials of XML query processing. These queries have been evaluated on an internal research prototype, Monet XML, to give a first baseline.

Table 1 compares the expressive power of queries from XOO7, XMark and XMach-1. As can be seen XOO7 is the most comprehensive benchmark in terms of XML functionalities covered. Both XMark and XMach-1 focus on a data-centric usage of XML. All three benchmarks provide queries to test relational model characteristics like selection, projection and reduction. Properties like transaction processing, view manipulation, aggregation and update, are not yet tested by any of the benchmarks. XMach-1 covers delete and insert operations, although the semantics of such operations are yet to be clearly defined under XML query model. In [26] detailed information about the data and schema used by these benchmarks is provided.

We choose to use XOO7 to analyze the performance of chosen XML data management systems. Our decision is motivated by the fact that XOO7 is a comprehensive benchmark as can be seen from Table 1 and also empirical evaluations show the ability of the XOO7 queries to distinguish all the desired functionalities supported by an XML database [9]. In the absence of queries exploiting the document-centric features, XMark and XMach-1 may not be able to clearly distinguish XML-enabled systems from Native XML management systems.

4   Empirical Study and Analysis of XML Databases

In this section we present results of experiments conducted to study the expressive power and processing efficiency of the four data management systems: LORE, Kweelt, XENA and a commercial implementation of XPath, which we call DOM-XPath. We compare the systems in terms of their response times for relational, document and navigational queries taken from the XOO7 benchmark [26]. The experiments are run on a 333 Mhz system running SunOS 5.7 with 256 MB RAM.

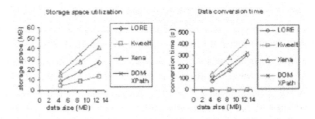

Fig. 1. Space Utilization and Data Conversion Time

4.1   Data Conversion: Time and Space Requirements

We recorded the time and space utilized by the XMLMS for converting the datasets provided as part of XOO7 to their proprietary format. The space utilization is measured in terms of secondary storage space used by each system for the various databases in the benchmark. Figure 1 compares the space and time requirements of the various XML data management systems we test. We use datasets of three sizes: small, medium and large for our tests. Small dataset is of size 4.2MB, medium of size 8.4MB and large has size 12.8 MB. The datasets are designed using the schema provided in XOO7 [9].

Kweelt queries the ASCII file directly and does not need to convert the XML data into another format. So the storage space it needs is the same as the size of the XML data. XENA stores XML data in MySQL tables. Although the conversion from XML format to relational tables ends up removing the redundant tags around the XML data, XENA ends up generating a number of relational tables to represent the XML data. In fact XENA creates two groups of tables. One group is based on the XML schema with one table per entity; the other group is for the management of these tables. Hence XENA requires almost double the space used by actual XML data after conversion. LORE creates Dataguides [24] for the datasets to help in efficient query processing. Dataguides are a concise and accurate summary of all paths in the database that start from the root. Hence LORE requires almost three times the space of the actual XML data, as can be seen from Figure 1. The commercial implementation of XPath, DOM-XPath, also creates three binary files for an XML dataset. One of the files is a proprietary database that preserves the native XML structure by storing the entire document tree of the dataset thereby occupying much larger space than the XML dataset.

Not surprisingly, Kweelt, is most efficient compared to other systems in terms of space usage. Since Kweelt processes directly raw XML data, it requires no time for data conversion. As expected, XENA, an XML-enabled database system requires the most amount of time to convert from the XML model to a relational model. LORE requires time for generating Dataguides and we assume the XPath implementation is also generating indexes, task that requires time.

4.2   Response Time Analysis

We divide the XOO7 queries into three groups: Relational queries, Navigational queries and Document queries. Table 2 depicts the proposed classifcation of XOO7 queries. In the following, we will illustrate the performance of the various systems for the representative queries in each group.

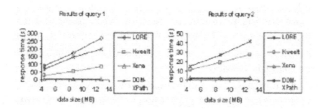

Fig. 2. Response time for Q1 and Q2 (relational queries)

Table 2. XOO7 benchmark queries

ID	Description
	Relational Queries
Q1	Randomly generate 5 numbers in the range of AtomicPart's MYID. Return AtomicPart according to the 5 numbers.
Q2	Randomly generate 5 titles for Documents then return the first paragraph of Document with the titles.
Q3	Select 5% of AtomicParts via later buildDate (in a certain period).
Q5	Join AtomicParts and Documents on AtomicParts docId and Documents MyID.
Q7	Randomly generate two phrases among all phrases in Documents. Return the documents with both the phrases.
Q8	Repeat query 1 but replace duplicate elements using their IDREF.
Q13	For each BaseAssembly count the number of documents.
Q14	Sort CompositePart in descending order where buildDate is within a year from current date.
Q16	Return all BaseAssembly of type "type008" without any child nodes.
	Navigational Queries
Q4	Find the Compositepart if it is later than BaseAssembly it is using.
Q6	Select all BaseAssemblies from an XML database having same "type" attribute as the BaseAssemblies in another database but with later buildDate.
Q9	Select all AtomicParts with corresponding CompositeParts as their sub-elements.
Q10	Select all ComplexAssemblies with type "type008".
Q15	Find BaseAssembly of not type "type008".
Q17	Return all Connection elements with length greater than Avg(length) within the same composite part without child nodes.
Q18	For CompositePart of type "type08", give 'Result' containing ID of CompositePart and Document.
Q19	Select all of the CompositePart, Document and AtomicPart.
	Document Queries
Q11	Among the first 5 Connections of each CompositePart, select those with length greater than "len".
Q12	For each CompositePart, select the first 5 Connections with length greater than "len".
Q20	Select the last connection of each CompositePart.
Q21	Select the AtomicPart of the third connection in each CompositePart.
Q22	Select the AtomicPart whose MyID is smaller than its sibling's and it occurs before that sibling.
Q23	Select all Documents after the Document with MyID = 25.

Figure 2 compares the performance of the four XMLMS for two relational queries in the XOO7 benchmark. Query $Q1$ tests simple selection processing efficiency while query $Q2$ uses selection having string comparison. XENA gives the best performance in both queries because it leverages the power of its backend relational database. LORE gives interesting results: it is efficient for query $Q2$ as we expected whereas has poor response for $Q1$, and has most response time for $Q1$. The default data type in LORE is string, hence string comparison is very fast, but comparisons on other types require frequent type casting and drop its performance. Both Kweelt and DOM-XPath are implemented based on DOM, but Kweelt always gives a better performance than DOM-XPath (This is also the case for the navigational and document queries). There are two possible reasons. First, they may be using different parsers. Second, DOM-XPath, being a commercial product, is required to handle additional issues like admission control, which may introduce some additional workload. Kweelt, being a research prototype, concentrates on optimized query processing only.

Overall for the relational queries, the two native XMLMS, Kweelt and DOM-XPath, give relatively poorer performance than the two XML-enabled systems. LORE does not perform well when data type coercion is required. XENA leverages the query processing power of the relational database engine and yields the best performance. Kweelt and DOM-XPath always need to follow a particular path to check whether an element or an attribute satisfies certain conditions, thus more processing is needed.

In Figure 3 we compare the performance of the XMLMS for two representative navigational queries, $Q4$ and $Q15$. Query Q4 tests the parent-child relations in XML data, while query $Q15$ measures the ability to preserve the structure of original XML data i.e. preserving the paths and the sibling orders as those in the

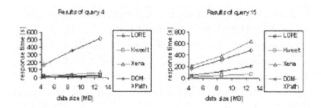

Fig. 3. Response time for Q4 and Q15 (navigational queries)

original XML document. LORE shows the worst performance. XENA is much faster than LORE in query $Q4$ but slower for $Q15$. To keep the parent-child relations, XENA saves the parent index for each element. The indices on the path fields are built automatically. The response time of XENA increases almost 10 times from query $Q4$ to query $Q15$. Unfortunately, we could not ascertain how LORE maintains the response time to be almost a constant for the both the queries. Kweelt and DOM-XPath store the XML data in the original form, therefore they perform relatively better.

In general, the two XML-enabled systems show poor performance for navigational queries. The primary reason is they change the structure of the XML data to proprietary formats, so they need additional time to reconstruct the original XML data. The two native XML management systems store the XML data in the original form, hence they simply return the elements satisfying the conditions following the original structure.

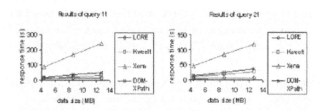

Fig. 4. Response time for Q11 and Q21 (document queries)

Figure 4 gives a performance comparison for two document queries in the XOO7 benchmark. Query $Q11$ tests whether elements in a certain range satisfy given conditions while query $Q21$ selects elements with a particular order. The implicit order is required to answer both the queries. XENA gives the worst performance for both queries. The results given by XENA strengthen our belief that it is difficult to preserve the implicit order of elements in a relational database. LORE performs the best in the two document queries because it makes use of DataGuide to record the orders of elements. Kweelt and DOM-XPath perform relatively better than XENA. They simply check the element orders based on the knowledge from the DOM tree. We did not care about the attribute order as it is not required by the W3C working group.

From the experiments with the XOO7 benchmark, we can see that the basic XML-enabled management systems are inadequate to perform navigational queries and document queries, but they can be improved by introducing some techniques, like DataGuide, to record the original structure of the XML data. The native XML implementations prove to be more efficient for navigational queries and document queries. New techniques for representing and extracting relational data in native XMLMS such as storing meta information about tuple structure, creating relational style indexes or incorporating a small relational optimizer would help improve the performance for relational queries.

5   Conclusion and Future Work

To evaluate the underlying XML technologies (e.g. XPath, XPointer, XQuery, etc.) and efficiency of an XMLMS using them, a benchmark becomes inevitable. In this paper, we identify current XML representations and analyze their effect on the performance of the systems. Then we corroborate our study by running experiments with XOO7. Our results confirm that XML-enabled relational database systems which use the data-centric view of XML process more efficiently the queries that only manipulate data and do not use the implicit order or the hyperlinks in documents. On the other hand, native XMLMS designed to handle raw XML data and documents are efficient in processing document or navigational queries whereas they show poor performance for relational queries. Currently no system seems to offer a needed balance between the data-centric and document-centric approaches. The choice of an XMLMS then depends on the type of data that needs to be stored and the type of queries that will be expressed. A user with data centric needs will favor an XML-enabled DMS whereas one wishing to store and manipulate documents will chose a native XMLMS.

Acknowledgements. We thank the XENA project team for providing us with the source code and valuable comments in setting up XENA.

References

1. S. Abiteboul. Querying semi-structured data. In *Proc. of Intl. Conf. on Database Theory*, pages 1–18, Delphi, Greece, January 1997. LNCS 1186, Springer Verlag.
2. S. Abiteboul and S. Grumbach. COL: A Logic-Based Language for Complex Objects. *EDBT*, pages 271–293, 1988.
3. S. Abiteboul, D. Quass, J. McHugh, J. Widom, and J.L. Wiener. The Lorel Query Language for Semistructured Data. *Journal on Digital Libraries*, 1997.
4. S. Abiteboul and M. Scholl. From Simple to Sophistic Languages for Complex Objects. *Data Engineering Bulletin*, 11(3):15–22, 1988.
5. P. Biron and A. Malhotra. *XML Schema Part 2: Datatypes.* W3C, 2001. Recommendation – available at http://www.w3.org/TR/2001/REC-xmlschema-2-20010502.

6. T. Bohme and E. Rahm. XMach-1: A Benchmark for XML Data Management, 2000. Available at http://dbs.uni-leipzig.de/projekte/XML/XmlBenchmarking.html.

7. A. Bonifati and S. Ceri. Comparative analysis of five xml query languages. *SIG-MOD Record*, 29(1):68–79, 2000.

8. R. Bourett. Xml database products, May 2001. available at http://www.rpbourret.com/xml/XMLDatabaseProds.htm/.

9. S. Bressan, G. Dobbie, Z. Lacroix, M. L. Lee, Y. G. Li, U. Nambiar, and B. Wadhwa. XOO7: Applying OO7 Benchmark to XML Query Processing Tools. *Proceedings of CIKM. Atlanta.*, November 2001.

10. P. Buneman. Semistructured Data. In *Proc. ACM Symp. on Principles of Database Systems*, Tucson, 1997.

11. M.J. Carey, D.J. DeWitt, and J.F. Naughton. The OO7 benchmark. *ACM SIG-MOD Conference*, pages 12–21, 1993.

12. D. Chamberlin, D. Florescu, J. Robie, J.Siméon, and M. Stefaescu. *XQuery: A Query Language for XML*. W3C, 2000. Available at http://www.w3.org/TR/xmlquery.

13. D. Chamberlin, J. Robie, and D. Florescu. Quilt: An XML Query Language for Heterogeneous Data Sources. In *Proceedings of the Workshop WebDB (in conjunction with ACM SIGMOD)*, Dallas, TX, 2000.

14. J. Clark and S. DeRose. *XML Path Language (XPath)*. W3C, 1999. Available at http://www.w3.org/TR/xpath.

15. C. J. Date. *An Introduction to Database Systems*. Addison-Wesley, 1995.

16. S. DeRose, R. Daniel, and E. Maler. *XML Pointer Language (XPointer)*. W3C, 1999. Available at http://www.w3.org/TR/WD-xptr.

17. S. DeRose, E. Maler, D. Orchard, and B. Trafford. *XML Linking Language (XLink)*. W3C, 2000. Available at http://www.w3.org/TR/xlink.

18. A. Deutsch, M. Fernandez, D. Florescu, A. Levy, and D. Suciu. XML-QL: a query language for XML. Available at http://www.w3.org/TR/NOTE-xml-ql/, 1998.

19. R. Elmasri and S. B. Navathe. *Fundamentals of Database Systems*. Addison-Wesley, 1998.

20. D. Fallside. *XML Schema Part 0: Primer*. W3C, 2001. Recommendation – available at http://www.w3.org/TR/2001/REC-xmlschema-0-20010502/.

21. P. Fankhauser, M. Marchiori, and J. Robie. *XML Query Requirements*. W3C, 2000. Available at http://www.w3.org/TR/xmlquery-req.

22. D. Florescu and D. Kossman. A Performance Evaluation of Alternative Mapping Schemes for Storing XML Data in a Relational Database, May 1999. Report 3680 INRIA, France.

23. R. Goldman, J. McHugh, and J. Widom. From Semistructured Data to XML: Migrating the Lore Data Model and Query Language. In *ACM SIGMOD Workshop on the Web and Databases (WebDB'99)*, 1999.

24. R. Goldman and J. Widom. DataGuides: Enabling Query Formulation and Optimization in Semistructured Databases. In *Proc. of Intl. Conf. on Very Large Data Bases*, Delphi, Greece, August 1997.

25. J. Gray. *The Benchmark Handbook: For Database and Transaction Processing Systems*. Morgan Kaufmann, 2nd edition, 1993.

26. U. Nambiar, Z. Lacroix, S. Bressan, M. L. Lee, and Y. G. Li. Benchmarking XML Management Systems: The XOO7 Way. *Proceedings of IIWAS, Linz, Austria.*, September 2001.

27. J. Robie, J. Lapp, and D. Schach. XML Query Language (XQL). In *Proc. of the Query Languages workshop*, Cambridge, MA, December 1998. Available at http://www.w3.org/TandS/QL/QL98/pp/xql.html.
28. A. Sahuguet. KWEELT : More than just "yet another framework to query XML!". *Sigmod Demo*, 2001.
29. A. R. Schmidt, F. Waas, M. L. Kerste, D. Florescu, I. Manolescu, M. J. Carey, and R. Busse. The XML Benchmark Project. Technical Report INS-R0103, April 2001.
30. H. Thompson, D. Beech, M. Maloney, and N. Mendelsohn. *XML Schema Part 1: Structures*. W3C, 2001. Recommendation – available at http://www.w3.org/TR/2001/REC-xmlschema-1-20010502/.
31. Y. Wang and K. Tan. A Scalable XML Access Control System. *10th World Wide Web Conference*, May 2001.

Commercial Tools for the Development of Personalized Web Applications: A Survey

Andrea Maurino[1] and Piero Fraternali[1]

Politecnico di Milano, via Ponzio 34/5
20133 Milano, Italy
{maurino,fraterna}@elet.polimi.it

Abstract. In this paper we examine the state-of-the-practice of development tools for delivering personalized Web sites, i.e Web-oriented applications that collect, elaborate and use information about the site's users to better fulfill their mission. Personalization is at the same time one of the crucial success factors of B2C applications and one of the most significant cost factors in Web application development. In this paper, we classify the dimensions of personalized Web site development, review and classify 50 tools claiming to support such development, and motivate our conclusions on the need of a different approach to the personalization design and a novel generation of personalization tools.

1 Introduction

In the area of Web application development, personalization is the *process* of gathering and storing information about the visitors of a Web site, analyzing the stored information, and, based on such analysis, delivering to each visitor the right information in the right way with the appropriate access rights Personalization was not born with Web site development, but there are reported antecedents in other software fields, namely adaptive hypermedia [3], user modelling [9] and computer-based training systems [8]. In recent years, a different approach to the design and development of Web applications has emerged: Web conceptual modelling. Works in this field [4], [5], [14], propose that the design of a Web application is obtained by addressing three different models: content, hypertext and presentation. The data model is generally devoted to the description of the data content of the site; the navigation model describes the hypertext of the application, and the presentation model deals with the description of the graphical representation of pages. The designer can use one of these approaches to create even personalized Web applications; but there are very few explicit conceptual primitives supporting the modelling and designing of personalization requirements.

With the advent of B2C e-commerce applications, personalization has assumed an enormous industrial impact, which has caused the appearance of a menagerie of commercial products, claiming support to the personalization process. In fact, as shown by several industrial experiences [12], personalizing a Web site is a key

K. Bauknecht, A M. Tjoa, G. Quirchmayr (Eds.): EC-Web 2002, LNCS 2455, pp. 99–108, 2002.
© Springer-Verlag Berlin Heidelberg 2002

ingredient of the success of B2C Internet applications, because it makes information browsing more effective by addressing to each individual user a narrower but more focused range of contents, which is a prime factor for improving customers' fidelization.

The goal of this survey is to review the tools available for building personalized Web applications, classifying them into categories that might help the designer to choose the right tool for his needs. Fifty tools have been considered, and for each product the available documentation has been used to assess its features. As resulting from the comparative review, in the e-commerce application domain a number of tools exist, which support the entire life cycle of the development of tailored Web applications and offer a high degree of automation. In other application domains, vertical solutions are not available, and a lot of manual coding is needed to achieve good quality personalization effects.

The paper is organized as follows. Section 2 gives the dimensions of the personalization process. Section 3 describes a categorization of reviewed tools and the following section 4 shows the most important results of our survey. In appendix we indicate the URL of all reviewed tools

2   Dimensions of Web Site Personalization

The personalization process is characterized by three methodological steps: data acquisition, elaboration and use. The acquisition phase is the collection of users' data, the elaboration phase is the analysis of users' profile data, and the use phase is the creation of the personalized Web application.

2.1   Collection of User Data

Three different approaches can be identified for the acquisition of information about the users of Web applications.

- *Explicit acquisition.* The easiest way to acquire data about users is to ask them directly. The advantages of explicit acquisition are the possibility to collect detailed information about users (e.g., their age, gender, job etc) and to ascertain their interests in a given domain (e.g., musical preferences). On the negative side, since data are inserted directly by the user, there is no possibility to verify their correctness. Besides casual errors, privacy concerns and the fear of being exposed to undesired marketing actions are common reasons for the occurrence of false data in the explicit acquisition process.
- *Implicit acquisition.* An alternative data source about users is their navigation behavior within Web applications. By studying the sequence of pages visited by users (known as clickstream) it is possible to discover what sections of a Web site the user is particularly interested in. The advantages of this approach are the simplicity in the acquisition of data, the ignorance of

users that their navigation is registered (consequently the level of confidence of data improves). The main disadvantage is that the information content of clickstream is quite poor. Consequently user profile analysis becomes more complex because algorithms work on very raw information. Moreover the amount of data to store and analyze is normally very large

- *Third part acquisition.* Another way to obtain data about users is to acquire information from other data sources like company databases, third party archives and so on. In this case, the user has no direct role in the acquisition of information, because the supply of users' data occurs in a different moment with respect to their acquisition.

2.2   Analysis of User Profile

The second phase of the personalization process is the analysis of raw user data. The result of this phase is a set of structured data or rules usable to build a tailored Web application. A number of techniques can be used, which fall in one of the following four categories:

- *Event Condition Action rules.* ECA rules [15] allow defining an action when an event occurs if a given condition is true. A typical application of the ECA rules is the following: when a user logs into the Web application (event) if it is his/her first time (condition) then a set of predefined items with special discounts must be shown by the Web application (action). ECA rules are very useful when the designer wants to create different sections of Web site for different users' group.
- *Collaborative filtering.* These techniques [7], are very popular for defining personalized Web applications (for instance they are used in www.amazon.com [11]). It collects the visitor's opinions on a set of objects, using ratings provided explicitly by the users or implicitly computed, to form peer groups. Then it uses such information about peer groups to predict a particular user's interest. For instance in a e-catalog a set of users buy Tolkien's books and Stephen King's ones: if a new user buys Tolkien's "Lord of the Rings" probably s/he could be interested in a Stephen King's book. The main advantage of collaborative filtering is that the Web application discovers at run time groups of interest and so it captures users' behaviors in a dynamic way. The main disadvantage is that collaborative filtering need an elevated number of users before to supply accurate recommendations.
- *Neural nets.* Neural network[2] is a network of several simple processors ("units"), each possibly having a small amount of local memory. The units are connected by communication channels ("connections"), which usually carry numeric (as opposed to symbolic) data, encoded by various means. The units operate only on their local data and on the inputs they receive via connections. The restriction to local operations is often relaxed during training. Most neural networks have some sort of "training" rule whereby the weights of connections are adjusted on the basis of data. In other words, neural networks "learn" from examples (as children learn to recognize dogs

from examples of dogs) and exhibit some capability for generalization beyond the training data. For personalization purposes, neural networks learn about the user's behavior and they can try to predict the user's interest after a learning phase, where someone must provide the neural networks with examples of personalization.

- *Proprietary technologies.* The last category contains all those technologies developed by companies as evolution of well-known algorithms as Bayesian's net (Autonomy), OLAP and data-mining (Broadbased, Elity System) or predictive models (Cl!xSmart).

2.3   Creation of Personalized Web Applications

The last phase in the personalization process is the use of structured data computed by the analysis phase to personalize the Web application. We use the three conceptual layers shown in the introduction to describe the possible personalization of a Web application.

- *Content.* Personalize data content means that each user sees a different content. The typical example of personalized content is the definition of the price of an article based on the user profile data.
- *Navigation.* Navigation describes primitives by which users browse the content of Web application. Two main elements characterize navigation: links and access collections. A link is the way in which it is possible to move from one page to another one. A link can move the focus to an item semantically related to the previous page or to an unrelated page of the application (for instance, users can see an article and its photos or move from an article to the home page). An access collection is a group of objects having some semantic relationships, which is used to provide a meaningful access path to the site content (for instance the collection of fantasy books in a e-catalog). Personalize navigation means to add, remove links, create a new collection or modify an existing one for a given user. A typical example of link addition is cross-selling (see www.amazon.com), i.e., the addition in a product page of links pointing to related items deemed potentially interesting for the customer. Sometimes, the modification of navigation can be used to hide a part of Web application, so that two different users see different hypertexts based on the same content.
- *Presentation.* Presentation defines the graphical resources of the pages and their layout.

3   Commercial Tools for the Development of Personalized Web Applications

Personalized Web application development is the subject of a large number of commercial products: from the analysis of fifty tools, two different approaches emerge, which represent two different solutions for the design of personalized

Web applications. The identified approaches are: *End-to-end tools* and *Combination of dedicated tools*.

The first approach is represented by a number of tools covering all the phases of the personalization process. The second approach allows the creation of personalized Web applications by using several tools (typically one for each of the phases of the personalization process). Tools falling in this latter category are sub-dived in three sub-classes according to the phase of the personalization process they serve.

3.1   End-to-End Tools

Tools of this class allow the designer to create a Web application using a one-stop solution. Tools of this class can be further sub-divided in two categories: vertical solutions, representing tools devoted to a specific application domain, and general-purpose solutions, which include tools able to design a general purpose personalized Web application.

End-to-end vertical tools. Vertical tools supply a complete solution for the development of personalized Web applications, but limited to a specific application domain. For instance Engage's Customer Retention Suite and Ilux2000 are specialized in the Web promotion area. They acquire and analyze users' data to create user profile and add the best promotion according to the user's preferences and behavior. All the phases of this particular application domain are fully covered with a high level of automation.

Broadvision's One-To-One and ATG's dynamo offer partially instantiated applications for multiple vertical domains. For example, BroadVision includes a set of application frameworks for such vertical domains as e-commerce, finance, procurement, and retail commerce, which help the designer in the creation of personalization process. The strong point of these tools is the capability of integration with other tools, specialized for specific tasks (for instance Macromedia's LikeMind or Dreamwaver).

End-to-end general-purpose tools. This category includes tools able to create a generic personalized Web application. Two of the most representative tools of this category are Macromedia's Spectra and Divine Open Market; both products have a very simple conceptual model-driven approach to the design of Web applications. OpenMarket describes objects of the real world in terms of asset types (examples of asset types are articles, images, product info and so on). It is possible to group a set of assets (of the same type) into a collection. The assets are inserted into Templates, which control the look and feel of pages. Segment is an asset type defined by the Personalization Centre tool and the designer creates Segments to place site visitors into dedicated target groups. The Personalization Centre tool then associates rules to segments, to refine the relevancy of displayed assets to user of a given segment. The Personalization Centre includes a Java-based active rule engine, which enables quick parsing of XML based personalization rules. Open Market may exploit collaborative filtering, by interoperating with third part tools such as LikeMinds or NetPerceptions.

Macromedia's Spectra is a more programming-oriented tool. The Spectra designer creates ObjectContainers, which are an object-model data structures representing the building blocks of every application. These objects may be connected to various services, for instance a database, by using a set of API. Then the designer creates the Macromedia's Spectra site layout model, which represents the navigation design of the Web site. A Spectra site consists of sections, which map to the site's top-level navigation links. A section consists of pages and each page is filled with an ObjectContainer. The designer defines the content objects, the publishing rules for all containers, and uses predefined publishing rules, but s/he can also write custom rules. Spectra supports the personalization process described in section 2. On the negative side Spectra, has less automatic support, because a good deal of code must be hand-written by the designer.

3.2   Combination of Dedicated Tools

In alternative to the end-to-end approach, the tool market offers a wide selection of products Specialized in one phase of the personalization process: it is possible to select one tool for data acquisition, one for recommendation, and one for the development of personalized Web pages. In this software architecture the designer must connect the output of the various tools, to obtain a homogenous application. In the next sections, we briefly review the tools covering each different phase of the personalization process.

Implicit data acquisition tools The products of this category are specialized in the acquisition of user's navigational behavior. Typically these tools analyze the log file of the Web server and offer the designer a number of statistics. Many log analyzers are available on the market , but no one offers a way to interoperate with external tools. Conversely, they supply a wide range of statistics, for example, they aggregate access data by user agent, geographical location, and so on.

Recommendation engines This category includes tools that analyze users' profile data to compute recommendations to use in the development of personalized Web applications. The tools of this category typically load data from data sources using various technologies (like JDBC-compliant data sources or XML files, see, for instance, BlackPearl, and BlazeSoft) and analyze them as described in section 2.2. Most tools use ECA rules for computing recommendations, like, for instance, Elity's Leadstream and Ilog's Jrules. Manna's Frontmind uses wizards to help the designer in the definition of rules. Another popular technology in this category is collaborative filtering; tools like Gustos, NetPerceptions, Yourcompass and Yo!box use it in order to define cross selling recommendation. Some tools like E.piphany'a E.5 system and Manna's FrontMind use multiple technologies for example they use ECA rules and collaborative filtering. A few tools

(Trivida, Magnify, Cl!xSmart) have developed proprietary technologies, based on Bayesan nets or other predictive models.

Independently from the kind of technology adopted, recommendations are integrated to the Web applications using different technical solutions. Yo!box uses owner tag embedded into the application. Gustos integrates its result within dynamic page templates via API. Ilog uses Enterprise Java Beans to obtain the same result. Finally Macromedia's LikeMind could be directly integrated with Boradvision One-To-One, a end-to-end vertical solution tool

Web application development tools These tools (Microsoft's FrontPage, Macromedia's Dreamweaver, Oracle Web Designer etc.) are devoted to the design and implementation of Web applications, not necessarily personalized ones. The designer must integrate personalization features, e.g., recommendations, into the work process of these tools manually. Thus he must create the form to acquire implicit data, store users data, analyze them and modify the Web application according to the output of such analysis. From more details, [6] includes a broad survey of Web application development tools.

4   Evaluation

From the analysis of the previous categories of tools and approaches (summarized in table 1), it is possible to underline a number of aspects and to point out some future research directions.

Table 1. Synopsis reviewed tools. Legend: Cat A= end-to-end vertical solution, Cat B = general-purpose tools. Cat C = data acquisition tools, Cat D = recommendation engine tools, Cat E = tools for Web development. Data acq.=Data acquisition; Ela.= Elaboration, Appl.= Application of recommendation

	Cat A	Cat B	Cat C	Cat D	Cat E
Phases covered	Data acq. Ela., Appl.	Data acq. Ela., App.	Data acq.	Ela.	Appl.
Automatic support	Medium-High	Low-High	High	High	Low-high
Integration other tools	Medium	Medium	None	Medium-high	Low
Num. of reviewed tools	14	2	7	24	See [6]

Our survey shows that if the designer wants to build a Web application falling in a specific application domain for which a vertical end-to-end tool is available, this solution is the most convenient. Vertical tools offer a good level of automation and cover the entire personalization process, thanks to their hard-coded model of the application domain. On the negative side, vertical tools are rigid, in the sense that if the designer needs to add features not included in the application model, he must add them manually. This reduces the reusability of the code generated by tools of this category, and makes the customization of these tools expensive. Collaborative Web applications, added value services, community Web sites represent application domains not covered by existing vertical end-to-end tools. In collaborative Web applications, users work, in a cooperating way, to achieve some common goal. Examples of this application domain are Web applications for concurrent programming like www.mozilla.org. In this domain, personalization, in the sense defined in the introduction of this paper, is mandatory because users interact with one another according to a well-define process, and must receive the right information at the right time and with the adequate access right. Service-oriented Web applications offer special-purpose services, e.g. sending e-mail or SMS. In these Web applications, users must see different information (for example users must see their own private contacts list). End-to-end general-purpose tools have an application-independent model, which allows the designer to create a general-purpose Web application, but this model is often too simple. All the reviewed tools describe a Web application as a tree of pages, including a set of object containers (like OpenMarket's asset types or Spectra's ObjectContainers). These objects are then personalized to create a tailored application. This model does not describe how the objects containers are interconnected (within the same page or across two different pages) to yield complex navigation mechanisms. Moreover, there is no a high level description of the content of the application, and of how to bind content elements to data containers.

An important drawback of both end-to-end tools and combinations of dedicated tools is the absence of a high-level, declarative, and orthogonal language for expressing the personalization policies of an application. As a consequence the personalization of content, navigation and presentation of a Web site and the access control are managed as separated tasks instead of consider them as part of a unique policy. The lack of a technology-independent centralized view of the personalization policy may create, for example, inconsistency problems and errors. The former occurs when two different personalization actions are applied for the same user at the same time and yield conflictual results. For instance, in an e-catalog application one personalization action may give a discount of 10% if a user buys for the first time, while another one may apply a discount of 15% if a user buys more then 10 articles. The problem arises when a user buys 11 articles in his first purchase; it is not clear how to reconcile the two applicable actions to get a global policy. Errors occur when, for instance, a personalization action is never executed because the user associated to it cannot access the page on which the personalization action is applied. A formal and declarative description of personalization policies could solve these issues, because personalization rules could be analyzed to verify properties like reachability (e.g. all personalization actions are executed at least one time for every user), and absence of interference. High level, declarative specifications of personalization rules could then be mapped to low-level implementation primitives, on top of the selected personalization technology).

Another missing feature affects the design environment. No end-to-end general-purpose tool allows the designer to view the design of the application according to the rules relevant to a particular user or group. This functionality could be very useful to evaluate the result of personalization policies before the application is deployed and to perform what-if analysis during the construction of personalization rules. A few recommendation tools offer a less powerful functionality, as they show the list of ECA rules applicable to a selected user; however, they cannot simulate the result of their recommendation applied to the Web application seen by the specific user, nor support what-if analysis.

Another design problem emerged in the survey is the frequent case in which different ways are available to obtain the same personalization effect; for example, a designer may prevent a student to see the grades of other students in several ways: by removing the link to the page containing the grades from all pages accessible by students (personalized navigation), by using an access control list (access control), by showing an error message instead of the grades list (personalized layout). This creates potential usability problems resulting in users' disorientation. These problems could be alleviated by defining and enforcing "personalization design patterns" [13]

A specific problem affects the combination of dedicated tools: there is no universally accepted standard governing the exchange of intermediate results among the component tools, and thus the portfolio of chosen tools could constraint future evolutions. Moreover the designer must develop a lot of code manually to integrate the result of recommendation engine and the Web application development tool. As result of this lack of standard and automatic software integrator the designer will face problems of bugs, integration, maintenance and so on.

As a side comment, we also noticed that very few tools address privacy issues, In the next years this problem will become very important for personalized Web applications[10].

It is our opinion that the weak aspects underlined before open the way to interesting research issues. In the research community, there have been several projects proposing models and tools to design Web applications [4],[1], [14], but only a few of these proposals have integrated a personalization methodology into their Web application development framework. Innovative conceptual models for Web applications, with personalization features, rigorous methodologies for the construction of personalized Web sites, and novel tools for the development of personalized Web applications are a very promising research direction.

References

1. L. Ardossono, A. Goy, Dynamic generation of adaptive web catalogs, Springer LNCS 1892, 2000: 5-16
2. Bishop. Neural networks for pattern recognition, Oxford England Oxford university press. 1996
3. P. Brusilovsky: Adaptive Hypermedia in User Modeling and User-Adapted Interaction 11: 87-210, 2001.
4. S. Ceri, P. Fraternali, A. Bongio: Web Modeling Language (WebML): a modeling language for designing Web sites. Computer Networks 33,1-6: 137-157, 2000

5. O. De Troyer, C. Leune: WSDM: A User Centered Design Method for Web Sites. Computer Networks 30,1-7: 85-94,1998
6. P. Fraternali, Tools and Approaches for developing data-intensive Web applications: a survey, ACM Computing surveys, Vol31, n 3 1999, 227-263
7. D. Goldberg, D. Nichols, B. M. Oki and D.Terry, Using collaborative filtering to weave an information tapestry, Communication of ACM, 35(12) 1992, pp 66-70
8. J. Kay: Learner Control in User Modeling and User-Adapted Interaction 11: 111-127, 2001.
9. A. Kobsa: Generic User Modeling Systems in User Modeling and User-Adapted Interaction 11, 2001
10. The Personalization and Privacy Survey, www.personalization.org, 2000
11. D. Pescovitz, Accounting for taste, scientific American (6) 2000
12. D. Peppers, M. Rogers, B.Dorf: The One to One Fieldbook : The Complete Toolkit for Implementing a 1 To 1 Marketing Program, Bantam Books, 1999
13. G.Rossi, D.Schwabe, R.Guimaraes. Designing personalized web applications, in proceeding of 10 www Conference Hong Kong China 2000
14. D. Schwabe, G. Rossi, An Object Oriented Approach to Web-Based Application Design, Theory and Practice of Object Systems 4(4), 1998. Wiley & Sons
15. J. Widom, S.Ceri, Active Database Systems: Triggers and Rules For Advanced Database Processing. Morgan Kaufmann 1996,

Appendix

End-to-end vertical tools ATG Dynamo: www.atg.com; *Autonomy Content Server*: www.autonomy.co.uk; *Broadbase*: www.broadbase.com; *Broad Vision One-to-One:* www.broadvision.com; *SelectCast*: www.ehnc.com; *Engage*: www.engage.com; *iLux2000:* www.ilux.com; *ePower:* www.pivotal.com; *NovuWeb Genius:* www.novuWeb.com;*StoryServer*: www.vignette.com; *Responsys Interact*: www.responsys.com;*Annuncio*: www.annuncio.com; *E-Merchandising*: www.bluemartini.com; *Birghtware*: www.brightware.com

End-to-end general-purpose tools: *Spectra*: www.allaire.com; *Open Market*: www.openmarket.com

Data acquisition tools *Deepmatrix*: www.deepmetrix.com; *Mach5*: www.mach5.com; *NetTracker*: www.sane.com; *Starfire*: www.elipva.com; *Web-Suxess*: www.exody.net; *Weblog*: www.monocle-solutions.com; *Swamill*: www.flowerfire.com

Recommendation engine *BlackPearl*: www.BlackPearl.com; *Advisor builder*: www.blazesoft.com; *Cl!xSmart*: www.Changingworlds.com; *Elity*: www.elity.com; *E.piphany*: www.epiphany.com; *Corauve*: www.corauve.com; *Gustos*: www.gustos.com; *ILOG*: www.ilog.com; *Likemind*: www.macromedia.com *IntelliWeb*: www.micromass.com; *FrontMind*: www.mannainc.com; *Blazesoft*: www.blazesoft.com; *Net Perceptions*: www.netperceptions.com; *Angara*: www.angara.com *Magnify*: www.magnify.com; *Affinium interact*: www.unica.com; *Open Sesame*: www.opensesame.com; *ResponseLogic*: www.responselogic.com; *Tian*: www.tiansoft.com; *TriVida*: www.trivida.com; *Yo!Box* : www.yo.com; *Your Compass*: www.yourcompass.com; *Personalogy*: www.personalogy.com; *Active Profile*: www.infomentum.com/activeprofile/

An Agent-Based Hierarchical Clustering Approach for E-commerce Environments

F. Buccafurri, D. Rosaci, G.M.L. Sarnè, and D. Ursino

DIMET – Università "Mediterranea" di Reggio Calabria
Via Graziella, Località Feo di Vito, 89060 Reggio Calabria, Italy
{bucca,rosaci,sarne,ursino}@ing.unirc.it

Abstract. In this paper we propose an agent-based hierarchical clustering technique operating on both user profiles and e-commerce sites. We show, by designing a number of appealing applications, how exploitation of such hierarchies can really benefit both customers and vendors in their activity. As a support for the customer, we provide a categorization of sites of interest as she/he perceives them, and also dynamic e-commerce portal personalization. As a support for the vendor, we design a categorization of customers directly supporting knowledge discovery on customer behavior.

1 Introduction

E-commerce is one of the most evident case in the Web in which the necessity of an adequate support to human activities strongly arises, mainly because of the large and various universe of information both clients and vendors have to deal with. Differently from traditional commerce, the direct contact between customer and vendor is completely missing. Moreover, e-commerce sites are often stores with a large offer and a great number of customers visiting them at each time; their location in the Web is often not easily detectable by a given customer and, sometimes, it is even unknown. In this virtual scenario, as in real life, customers desire some kind of guide, for both easily reaching suitable e-commerce sites and having a support in their choices. Symmetrically, vendors would like to *see* their customers, their preferences and expectation, in order to catch new customers and better satisfy the current ones. Unfortunately, the risk that customers get lost in front the offers and vendors do not have a good perception of real customer requirements, actually occurs. In order to reduce this risk, e-commerce sites (possibly appearing in specialized e-commerce portals) should be presented to customers by a clear categorization, hopefully close to her/his expectation. On the other hand, vendors should have a perception of their client categorization differentiating them on the basis of hits and purchases. For reaching the above goal since classes (representing categories) are not *a priori* known, clustering activity appears needed [4]. In particular, hierarchical clustering is very suitable for our purpose, since it allows us to carry out the categorization activity at different abstraction levels.

K. Bauknecht, A M. Tjoa, G. Quirchmayr (Eds.): EC-Web 2002, LNCS 2455, pp. 109–118, 2002.

In this paper we propose an approach for constructing a cluster hierarchy for an e-commerce environment. The first step we face consists of the definition of a conceptual model, that we call B-SDR network, capable of representing both customer profiles and e-commerce sites. Such a model merges the capability of representing the structure and the semantics of a reality of interest (which is typical of models representing information sources but is not handled by models managing user profiles) with the capability of representing the perception the user has of such a reality (which is common in user modeling but not supported by data source models). Thus, a B-SDR network embeds both knowledge coming from the structure and the semantics of e-commerce sites and knowledge coming from the user behavior in accessing such sites. As a consequence, the same model may be exploited by following a dual approach. If we fix a user and construct a B-SDR network for each e-commerce site she/he visits, then we obtain a representation of the perception such a user has of the visited e-shops. On the other hand, if we fix an e-commerce site and construct a B-SDR network for each client visiting it, then we obtain a collection of different views of the e-shop from the perspective of users; each point of view actually provides us with information about client preferences. For implementing the above task we provide, from the side of the customer, a B-SDR agent for each visited site, and, from the side of the vendor, a B-SDR agent for each visiting client. Hierarchical clustering is now applied to such collections of agents, in order to obtain multi-level categories of e-commerce sites, from a side, and multi-level categories of customers, from the other side. A B-SDR network is also associated with each cluster for representing it. In case of customer categorization carried out by vendors, such a B-SDR network represents a sort of profile of a class of homogeneous customers. This symmetrically happens for clusters of sites. Moreover, B-SDR customer profiles maintain a number of information allowing us to directly support data mining activities, such as discovering of association rules monitoring the behavior of the client in the site. As a further application of our approach, we have designed the construction of customized e-commerce portals which suitably adapt their site categorization to the customer expectation. We observe that our approach necessarily deals with problems arising in the context of heterogeneous environment[2,3], like the detection of inter-source properties. Furthermore, our model permits to represent also the user perception of concepts. It is worth pointing out that approaches detecting user behavior, like [8,9], do not deal with inter-source properties.

2   The B-SDR Agent Model

As previously pointed out, a B-SDR agent is relative to a customer c and an e-commerce site s; it monitors the behavior of c on visiting s. The collected information, allowing to define how the content of s is perceived by c, is stored in its ontology; this is represented by means of the B-SDR network conceptual model which appears well suited in this application context because it is capable of representing not only the information content of e-commerce sites (possibly heterogeneous in their structure, semantics and formats) but also the perception that customers have of them.

Let us define the B-SDR network. Consider a *universe* $\mathcal{U}$ of information sources, each encoding information both at *extensional* and *intensional* levels. The basic elements of the extensional level are *instances* whereas, at the intensional level, we deal with *concepts*. We denote by I the set of instances relative to all concepts of $\mathcal{U}$ and by C the set of such concepts. We assume that each concept $a \in C$ has a name denoted by *name(a)*. In its most general version, the B-SDR network is defined for a given user u and a given set of concepts in C. Given a subset of concepts $N \subseteq C$ and a user u, a *B-SDR network* (for u on N) is a rooted labeled direct graph $B\_Net(N, u) = \langle N, A \rangle$, where N denotes the set of nodes and $A \subseteq N \times N$ is the set of arcs. We denote by I_N the set of instances appearing in the concepts of N. Informally, N represents the set of concepts of interest for u. Since a B-SDR network node represents a concept of the corresponding information source, and vice versa, in the following we use the terms B-SDR network node and concept interchangeably. Arcs encode semantic relationships between concepts. Their labels define a number of properties associated with relationships of $BNet(N, u)$, containing also the dependency of the model on the user u. More precisely, a label $\langle d_{st}, r_{st}, h_{st}, succ_{st} \rangle$ is associated with an arc (s, t), where both d_{st} and r_{st} belong to the real interval $[0, 1]$ and h_{st} and $succ_{st}$ are non negative integer numbers. The four *label coefficients* introduced above encode different properties and their definition, which we next provide, clarifies why our graph is directed. In particular: (1) d_{st} is the *(semantic) independence coefficient*. It is inversely related to the contribution given by the concept t in characterizing the concept s. As an example, in an E/R scheme, for an attribute t of an entity s, d_{st} will be smaller than $d_{ss'}$, where s' is another entity related to s by a relationship. Analogously, in an XML document, a pair (s, t), where s is an element and t is one of its sub-elements, has an independence coefficient d_{st} smaller than $d_{ss'}$, where s' is another element which s refers to through an *IDREF* attribute. (2) r_{st} is the *(semantic) relevance coefficient*, indicating the fraction of instances of the concept s whose complete definition requires at least one instance of the concept t. (3) h_{st} is the *hit coefficient*, counting the number of contacts which the user u carries out on t coming from s. (4) $succ_{st}$ is the *success coefficient*, denoting the number of purchases of an instance of t the user u has concluded coming from s (i.e., coming from some instance of s).

Similarly to the relationship between concepts, also the membership of instances to concepts is weighed by labeling. In particular, we associate a label $\langle h_{st}, succ_{st} \rangle$ with each pair (s, t) such that s is a node of the graph and t is an instance relative to s; in this case h_{st}, called *hit coefficient*, and $succ_{st}$, called *success coefficient*, are defined in an obvious way, coherently with the corresponding coefficients presented above. It is worth observing that the independence and relevance coefficients have been conceived for describing "structural" and "semantic" properties of concepts and relationships of interest for the user, whereas hit and success coefficients model her/his behavior on accessing concepts and instances of her/his interest. Thus, they represent a crucial component of the model, making it suitable for constructing the B-SDR agent. Although hit and success coefficients are related to user behavior, they need to be elaborated in order to become really interpretable. To this aim, we define two functions θ, ρ defined only on arcs (s, t) of $B\_Net(N, u)$ and on pairs concept-instance (s, t) such that t is an instance of s. The function θ, computed on a given pair (s, t), exploits hit and success coefficients of (s, t) for giving a measure of the "interest" the user u has for t when she/he accesses t through s. In particular: $\theta(s, t) = h_{st} + q \times succ_{st}$, where q (a real number greater than or equal to 1) is a given coefficient modulating the importance of purchases w.r.t. the number of hits. The function ρ, computed on a given pair (s, t), represents the preference the user u gives to t w.r.t. all the other concepts reachable in just one step coming from s, in case t is a concept, or all the other instances of s, in case t is an instance. The preference is computed as a fraction of the overall interest. More precisely, ρ is defined as $\rho(s, t) = \dfrac{\theta(s,t)}{\sum_{t' \in A(s)} \theta(s,t')}$, where $A(s)$ is *(i)* the set of nodes reachable in just one step coming from s, or s itself, if t is a concept; *(ii)* the set of instances relative to s, if t is an instance [1] Whenever it is not necessary to represent and handle information regarding instances and user behavior, thus reducing our interest to information typically stored and managed by a classical conceptual model, we can exploit a reduced version of the B-SDR network model, called SDR network [7]. A B-SDR agent associated with a customer c and an e-commerce site s operates as follows: it keeps in its ontology[2] both the content of s and the behavior of c on accessing it. In order to store in its ontology the information about the content of s, the B-SDR agent must translate s from the original data representation format to the SDR network; translation rules from various formats (such as XML, OEM, E/R) to SDR network have been already defined and can be found in [7]. Behavior information can be determined by monitoring what products of s are examined and, possibly, purchased by c[3]. In particular, for each access (resp., purchase) that c carries out on an instance t' of the concept t, coming from an instance of the concept s, h_{st} and $h_{tt'}$ (resp., $succ_{st}$ and $succ_{tt'}$) are increased by 1.

3   Constructing the Agent Cluster Hierarchy

In this section we illustrate our approach for constructing the hierarchy of B-SDR agent clusters. First we describe the model we exploit for representing the cluster hierarchy and then we illustrate the approach in detail.

3.1   Modeling the Agent Cluster Hierarchy

Each cluster of the hierarchy represents a group of B-SDR agents having similar B-SDR networks (i.e., similar ontologies). Agent clusters can be classified as basic and derived. A *basic cluster* is constructed by directly grouping B-SDR agents;

---

[1] Recall that, due to the features of the B-SDR network model, also t is an instance of s.

[2] Recall that the ontology of a B-SDR agent is a B-SDR network.

[3] In this application context a product can be seen as an instance of a concept.

vice versa, a *derived cluster* is obtained by grouping previously constructed clusters. Each cluster Cl is represented by a B-SDR network. The cluster hierarchy consists of several levels so that each cluster belongs to one level; each cluster of level $n \neq 0$ is obtained by grouping some of the clusters of level $n - 1$[4]. Clusters of level 0 are obtained by directly grouping the B-SDR networks of the input agents. Each basic cluster Cl_b is characterized by: *(i)* its identifier; *(ii)* its B-SDR network; *(iii)* the set of B-SDR agents having similar B-SDR networks and which Cl_b has been derived from (hereafter called *source B-SDR agents*); *(iv)* a level index. Each derived cluster Cl_d is characterized by: *(i)* its identifier; *(ii)* its B-SDR network; *(iii)* the set of identifiers of those clusters whose B-SDR networks originated the B-SDR network of Cl_d (hereafter called *source identifiers* and *source clusters*, resp); *(iv)* a level index.

Given a cluster Cl, we define the *source B-SDR network* of Cl as *(i)* the B-SDR networks associated with its source B-SDR agents, if Cl is basic; *(ii)* the B-SDR networks associated with its source clusters, if Cl is derived.

3.2   Description of the Approach

The proposed approach for constructing an agent cluster hierarchy receives a set *AgSet* of B-SDR agents. It behaves as follows: first it derives semantic similarities possibly existing among concepts represented into the B-SDR networks associated with the agents into consideration; derived similarities are, then, stored into a specific dictionary. After this, it groups the involved B-SDR networks into clusters.

In order to carry out such a task, it uses a matrix M_{Cl} such that $M_{Cl}[i, j]$ stores a coefficient representing the similarity degree between the B-SDR networks B_i and B_j. In particular, in order to obtain $M_{Cl}[i, j]$, it takes into account both the strength of *similarities among the concepts* represented in B_i and B_j and the *similarity among the behaviors* registered in B_i and B_j. The general idea is that the stronger both concept and behavior similarities are, the higher the overall similarity degree between B_i and B_j and, therefore, $M_{Cl}[i, j]$, will be.

The similarity among concepts of B_i and B_j can be determined with the support of the Synonymy Dictionary SD. In particular, it is obtained by defining a maximum weight matching [6], on a bipartite graph whose nodes are associated with concepts stored in B_i and B_j and whose arcs are labeled with the similarity degrees among concepts of B_i and B_j, as stored in SD. The inputs are: *(i)* two sets of nodes $P = \{p_1, \ldots, p_n\}$ and $Q = \{q_1, \ldots, q_m\}$, *(ii)* a set of triplets SP of the form $\langle p_i, q_j, f_{ij} \rangle$, where, for each $p_i \in P$ and $q_j \in Q$, $0 \leq f_{ij} \leq 1$ and *(iii)* a coefficient w. The output is a value in the real interval $[0, 1]$. Let $BG = (P \cup Q, A)$ be a bipartite weighed graph, where A is the set of weighed edges $\{(p_i, q_j, f_{ij}) \mid f_{ij} > 0\}$. The maximum weight matching for BG is a set $A' \subseteq A$ of edges such that, for each node $x \in P \cup Q$, there is at most one edge of A' incident onto x and $\phi(A') = \sum_{(p_i, q_j, f_{ij}) \in A'} f_{ij}$ is maximum. The corresponding objective function is:

---

[4] Actually, in our architecture, clusters of level n can be obtained by grouping the agents of some of the clusters of any level $l \leq n - 1$ (see below).

$$Matching(P, Q, SP, w) = \left(1 - w\frac{|P|+|Q|-2|A'|}{|P|+|Q|}\right)\frac{\phi(A')}{|A'|}$$

where the factor $\frac{1}{|A'|}$ is used to normalize $\phi(A')$ whereas the other one is used to take into account unmatched nodes. Indeed, $2|A'|$ indicates the number of matched nodes, $\frac{|P|+|Q|-2|A'|}{|P|+|Q|}$ denotes the proportion of unmatched nodes, w is a coefficient used to weigh the role of unmatched nodes in the objective function. $Matching(P, Q, SP, w)$ is set to 0 if $A' = \emptyset$.

The similarity among behaviours of two B-SDR networks B_1 and B_2 is carried out by defining the set APS of pairs of arcs $[A_{1_i}, A_{2_i}]$ such that A_{1_i} belongs to B_1, A_{2_i} belongs to B_2 and there exists in SD a synonymy between the source node s_{1_i} (resp., the target node t_{1_i}) of A_{1_i} and the source node s_{2_i} (resp., the target node t_{2_i}) of A_{2_i}. If we represent APS as:

$$APS = \{[A_{1_1}, A_{2_1}], \ldots, [A_{1_i}, A_{2_i}], \ldots, [A_{1_n}, A_{2_n}]\} =$$
$$= \{[(s_{1_1}, t_{1_1}), (s_{2_1}, t_{2_1})], \ldots, [(s_{1_i}, t_{1_i}), (s_{2_i}, t_{2_i})], \ldots, [(s_{1_n}, t_{1_n}), (s_{2_n}, t_{2_n})]\}$$

the behavior similarity can be defined as $b_{B_1 B_2} = \frac{\sum_{i=1}^{n} 1 - |\rho(s_{1_i}, t_{1_i}) - \rho(s_{2_i}, t_{2_i})|}{|APS|}$.

This formula implements the policy described previously, i.e., given two B-SDR networks B_1 and B_2, the closer the preferences relative to synonym concepts they represent are, the stronger the similarity of their behavior is. The coefficient α is used to define the weight of concept and behavior similarities in the computation of the overall similarity of B_i and B_j. Generally $\alpha = 0.5$, i.e., concept and behavior similarities have the same importance in the computation of the overall similarity. However, there could exist some cases which do not require the exploitation of behavior information; in these cases α is set equal to 1.

After $M_{Cl[i,j]}$ has been defined, cluster construction is obtained by executing any clustering algorithm (e.g., PAM based on the k-medoids method [5]).

The B-SDR networks relative to each cluster are then integrated for obtaining a global B-SDR network; this is eventually abstracted for producing the B-SDR network of the cluster. Once all clusters of the lowest level have been obtained, semantic similarities possibly existing among concepts represented into their B-SDR networks are derived and suitably stored. After this, the B-SDR networks relative to these clusters are grouped in more abstract clusters and integrated; the global B-SDR networks thus produced are abstracted, in their turn, for obtaining the B-SDR networks relative to these more abstract clusters. These steps are iterated until to only one global cluster, representing all B-SDR agents into consideration, is obtained. When this happens, further abstraction steps can be applied on its corresponding B-SDR network.

The interested reader can find further details about this approach in [1].

4   Customer Categorization of E-commerce Sites

As already pointed out, it is clear that the overwhelming amount and the great variety of offers, possibly interesting for a customer require new approaches for organizing them. Moreover, we have observed that information has both an objective and a subjective component and that the same site can be perceived under different points of view by different visitors; as a consequence, the exploitation of an approach for organizing e-commerce sites which clusters them on the basis of how the information stored therein is perceived by the visitors appears particularly suited.

In this section we show how the exploitation of B-SDR agents allows to successfully support a customer by providing a categorization of e-commerce sites of her/his interest on the basis of the perception she/he has of them. Let c be a customer. The categorization of e-commerce sites of interest for c can be obtained by *(i)* associating a B-SDR agent with each visited e-commerce site so that the agent ontology represents the content of the site as it is perceived by c; *(ii)* organizing the B-SDR agents thus obtained into a cluster hierarchy; the construction and the maintenance of the cluster hierarchy is carried out by an agent which we call *hierarchy agent*. We have already described how a B-SDR agent is capable of monitoring the behavior of a customer c on accessing an e-commerce site s. Here we illustrate how the *hierarchy agent* operates. A number of problems has to be solved in order to maintain in a feasible way the cluster hierarchy: *(i)* The number of basic clusters and, more in general, the number of B-SDR agents cannot grow indefinitely. Thus, some mechanism for limiting the number of B-SDR agents taking part to the cluster hierarchy must be designed. *(ii)* The perception a customer has of the site can change over time; if this happens it could be necessary to move the corresponding B-SDR agent from a basic cluster to another one appearing to be closer to the new perception. In this sense, the cluster hierarchy must be dynamic and it requires a continuous checking. But thinking to a *redo* operation at each new access does not lead to a feasible approach: some less naive strategy guaranteeing, at each time, an acceptable correctness of the site classification, is necessary. *(iii)* Once clustering has been done, and a new site is taken into account, it may happen that such a site cannot be classified into any current basic cluster. What we have to do with such new entry sites? Discard or keep them? In the latter case, how to handle such sites?

We describe now how the hierarchy agent solves these problems. In the following we call ACH the agent cluster hierarchy. The hierarchy agent uses an *agent buffer* B maintaining a certain number of B-SDR agents. This buffer implements also an index on basic clusters of ACH in such a way that each B-SDR agent of the buffer points to the basic cluster which it belongs to. There is an extra cluster, named *Parking cluster* (hereafter called P). P collects all currently unclassified B-SDR agents (see below). The hierarchy agent performs the following three activities: (1) new entry, (2) check clusters and (3) check consistency. The task (1) manages the entry of a new B-SDR agent. The task (2) verifies the current categorization of each B-SDR agent of the buffer B. If a B-SDR agent, say a, appears to be no longer correctly clustered, it is necessary to move it from the current cluster to a different and more suitable one, or to P, in case no cluster appears adequate. Each transfer of a B-SDR agent from a cluster to another one moves away the hierarchy from a state of consistence between its clusters and the B-SDR agents currently present in the agent buffer. Such an inconsistency may be tolerated until to a certain measurable degree. Up to such a threshold, it is necessary to redo the cluster hierarchy construction taking as input all clusters occurring in B; this is carried out by applying the algorithm shown in Section 3. The check of the consistence degree and the re-clustering management is the subject of the task (3). Next we describe the three tasks in more detail:

- **(1) New entry.** The agent uses a variable V counting the number of B-SDR agents discarded from the buffer in order to insert new entries. Let S be the B-SDR agent to enter. If B is full, then a victim B-SDR agent is selected according to a *Least Recently Used* strategy. Let T be such a victim. T is discarded from B and the victim counter is updated to be $V = V + 1$. In case B is not full or after having discarded the victim B-SDR agent, S is inserted in B and classified into the best basic cluster (according to the B-SDR network similarity metrics defined in Section 3.2) using a suitable thresholding. If its classification is not possible, S is inserted in the P cluster.
- **(2) Check Clusters.** The hierarchy agent uses a variable M counting the number of B-SDR agents moved from a cluster to another one. For each B-SDR agent a appearing in the buffer, *Check Clusters* periodically verifies if the ontology of a is similar enough to the B-SDR network of the cluster which a belongs to. In the negative case, a is moved to the cluster with the highest similarity, if the corresponding similarity degree is beyond the threshold; otherwise, it is transferred to the parking cluster. Moreover, the variable M is updated to be $M = M + 1$.
- **(3) Check Consistency.** The agent periodically checks the value $V + M$; this gives a measure of the inconsistency degree since it counts how many times an agent ontology is dropped out from some cluster without updating the cluster hierarchy. If $V + M$ is up to a suitable threshold, representing the maximum tolerated degree of inconsistency, then V and M are set to 0, the current cluster hierarchy is deleted and a new one is constructed by applying, on the agents of the buffer B, the algorithm described in Section 3. After this operation, P will be empty.

5   Vendor Categorization of Customers

In this section we show how our approach may be profitably used for supporting vendors in their activity of market trend analysis and customer satisfaction. As it can be easily understood, this is a key issue in every commerce context and, thus, also in the field of electronic commerce.

Also for this application we use B-SDR agents and a hierarchical clustering of B-SDR agents, but the difference here is that we provide a B-SDR agent for each customer visiting the site and, thus, categories we build by hierarchical clustering represent collections of customers, grouped according to the perception they have of the site. With each cluster, a B-SDR network representing a sort of generic user profile valid for all customers belonging to the cluster, is associated. Also for this application we adopt a hierarchical clustering and, thus, customer categories we obtain are organized in an abstraction hierarchy directly supporting analysis at different abstraction levels. A hierarchy agent, located in the e-commerce site, builds the hierarchy and maintains it, by using the same approach described in Section 5. Among all possible exploitations of a similar customer categorization, we have designed a data mining activity directly supported by B-SDR networks associated with clusters. Consider a cluster of the hierarchy and its B-SDR network, say B, and let s be a node of B; s is a concept which, concretely, represents a product typology. By $Adj(s)$ we denote concepts adjacent to s in B; these represent concepts (i.e., product typologies) semantically related to s. In order to implement marketing strategies, it would be useful discovering whether accesses of the customer to the concept s make her/him want to purchase some products whose typology is one among those of $Adj(S)$. In other words, we want to discover association rules of the type: $acc(s) \rightarrow purch(t)$, where $t \in Adj(s)$ and $purch(t)$ denotes a purchase of some product whose typology is t. Interestingly enough, labels of the B-SDR network allow us to evaluate *confidence* and *support* of the above association rules, for each concept s belonging to the net. If, for a concept s, we denote by $Adj^{-1}(s)$ the set of concepts $\bar{s}$ of B such that $s \in Adj(\bar{s})$, we obtain $confidence(acc(s) \rightarrow purch(t)) = \dfrac{succ_{st}}{\sum_{\bar{s} \in Adj^{-1}(s)} succ_{\bar{s}t}}$ and

$$support(acc(s) \rightarrow purch(t)) = \frac{\sum_{\bar{s} \in Adj^{-1}(s)} h_{\bar{s}s} + \sum_{\bar{s} \in Adj^{-1}(t), \bar{s} \neq s} succ_{\bar{s}s}}{\sum_{\bar{s} \in Adj^{-1}(s)} h_{\bar{s}s} + \sum_{\bar{t} \in Adj(s)} \sum_{\bar{s} \in Adj^{-1}(\bar{t}), \bar{s} \neq s} succ_{\bar{s}\bar{t}}}$$

Explanation of the above formulas directly derives from the definition of confidence and support and from the semantics of the coefficients h_{st} and $succ_{st}$ associated with an arc (s, t) of a B-SDR network (see Section 2). The database on which we evaluate confidence and support for an association rule $acc(s) \rightarrow purch(t)$ is a (virtual) database recording all access to s plus all purchases of products of type $\bar{t}$, for each $\bar{t} \in Adj(s)$, coming from B-SDR network nodes $\bar{s}$ such that $\bar{s}$ belongs to $Adj^{-1}(t)$ and $\bar{s} \neq s$.

6 Customized E-commerce Portals

A cluster hierarchy representing a customer categorization of e-commerce sites of her/his interests can be exploited for implementing a challenging application to e-commerce portals. These generally provide the customer with a set of categories helping her/him in choosing the sites of interest. Our goal is more ambitious: we want a portal front-end adapting to the customer preferences, showing different organization of categories for different customers. The customized front-end is built dynamically, on the basis of the cluster hierarchy of the customer contacting the site. This application needs a new agent, called *pc-agent*, for each customer, and a new agent, called *ps-agent*, for each portal; such agents support the negotiation protocol. Moreover, it is necessary to construct a B-SDR network for each site handled by the portal. The exploitation consists of classifying the sites of the portal in the most suitable way w.r.t. the customer profile. It behaves as follows: the pc-agent, with the support of a hierarchy agent, maintains a cluster hierarchy representing the customer categorization of information sources of her/his interest. After the connection has been established, the pc-agent and the ps-agent negotiate the cooperation. In particular the ps-agent asks to the pc-agent if its customer wants to send her/his cluster hierarchy (or simply its public part) in order to obtain a customized portal front-end. Clearly, such a decision may be obtained on the fly or could be previously set as default from the customer. If the pc-agent refuses the cooperation, the negotiation halts, and the navigation proceeds in a standard mode. Otherwise, the pc-agent sends the cluster hierarchy and tries to classify its sites into the basic clusters of the hierarchy. This is done by first computing the similarities between the B-SDR networks of the site and the B-SDR networks of the basic clusters and, then, using a suitable thresholding. For some sites of the portal the threshold value might not be reached. These sites are collected in a *dummy* basic cluster and this is inserted as a child node of the root. At this point, the sites of the portal are categorized according to the cluster hierarchy of the customer, representing her/his profile; therefore, the customized organization of the portal sites is completed, and a portal front-end reflecting it can be presented to the customer. The front-end is, therefore, organized in such a way that the customer is provided with a hierarchy of site categories reflecting the structure of the customer cluster hierarchy modulo the presence of the dummy category.

References

1. F. Buccafurri, D. Rosaci, G.M.L. Sarnè, and D. Ursino. Exploiting Hierarchical Clustering for E-Commerce Environments. Manuscript. Available from the Authors.
2. S. Castano, V. De Antonellis, and S. De Capitani di Vimercati. Global viewing of heterogeneous data sources. *Transactions on Data and Knowledge Engineering*, 13(2), 2001.
3. A. Doan, P. Domingos, and A. Halevy. Reconciling schemas of disparate data sources: A machine-learning approach. In *Proc. of International Conference on Management of Data (SIGMOD 2001)*, Santa Barbara, CA, 2001. ACM Press.
4. U. Fayyad, G. Piatetsky-Shapiro, P. Smyth, and R. Uthurusamy. *Advances in Knowledge Discovery and Data Mining*. The AAAI - The MIT press, Cambridge, MA, 1996.
5. A.K. Jain and R.C. Dubes. *Algorithms for Clustering Data*. Prentice Hall, Englewood Cliffs, 1988.
6. J. Madhavan, P.A. Bernstein, and E. Rahm. Generic schema matching with cupid. In *Proc. of International Conference on Very Large Data Bases (VLDB 2001)*, pages 49–58, Roma, Italy, 2001. Morgan Kaufmann.
7. L. Palopoli, G. Terracina, and D. Ursino. A graph-based approach for extracting terminological properties of elements of XML documents. In *Proc. of International Conference on Data Engineering (ICDE 2001)*, pages 330–337, Heidelberg, Germany, 2001. IEEE Computer Society.
8. J.S. Park and R.S. Sandhu. Secure cookies on the web. *IEEE Internet Computing*, 4(4):36–44, 2000.
9. G. Somlo and A. E. Howe. Incremental clustering for profile maintenance in information gathering web agents. In *Proc. of International Conference on Autonomous Agents 2001*, pages 262–269, Montreal, Canada, 2001. ACM Press.

A Multi-agent Approach to SACReD Transactions for E-commerce Applications

M. Younas, N.H. Shah, and K.-M. Chao

Data and Knowledge Engineering Research Group (DKERG)
School of Mathematical and Information Sciences, Coventry University, UK
{M.Younas,N.Shah,K.Chao}@Coventry.ac.uk

Abstract. E-commerce systems provide Web users with different facilities such as online banking, online (window) shopping, and online auctions. However, behind the provision of these facilities are certain requirements posed by the e-commerce applications including: data consistency, concurrency, dynamic behaviour, fault tolerance and high availability. Our research identifies that traditional ACID and agent transaction models are inadequate. We propose a new approach that enforces novel transaction correctness criteria, called SACReD (Semantic Atomicity, Consistency, Resiliency, and Durability) using a new multi-agent model. Initial evaluation shows that the new approach potentially meets the aforementioned requirements of e-commerce applications.

1 Introduction

E-Commerce has enormously increased with introduction of the Web. However, this new business paradigm is characterised by a number of requirements such as data consistency, dynamically scoped applications, interaction and negotiation between different businesses, service availability and fault tolerance. These characteristics introduce complexities that cannot be handled using a single mechanism. Classical ACID (atomic, consistent isolated, durable) transactions are widely used to provide e-commerce applications with correctness and consistency features [1, 8, 12]. However, these are inappropriate for e-commerce due to their strict isolation and atomic policy. We propose a new approach that enforces SACReD correctness criteria (previously proposed in [12, 13]) using a new meta-plan scheme of multi-agents [6, 11].

Section 2 describes the transaction models for e-commerce applications, and establishes motivation for the new approach. In Section 3, a new meta-plan scheme of multi-agents is proposed. Section 4 presents the proposed approach. Section 5 discusses related work and concludes the paper.

2 Transaction Models for E-commerce Applications

This section describes the nature of e-commerce transactions through an example application of a Web booking system for the Football World Cup 2002 (in Korea and Japan), which integrates systems for flight, accommodation, transport, and match tickets. A football fan may use such a system to buy a match ticket, book a flight, reserve accommodation and arrange transport at the match's venue. This application

---

K. Bauknecht, A M. Tjoa, G. Quirchmayr (Eds.): EC-Web 2002, LNCS 2455, pp. 119–128, 2002.

requires that: (i) it must be scoped *dynamically* so that it can navigate arbitrary information sources (e.g., search for cheap hotels) (ii) it must maintain **consistency** of the target data sources (e.g., airline data source) (iii) component systems may need to form a (temporary) partnership so that they can **interact** and **negotiate** in providing requested services (iv) the system must show **resilience** to failures such as communication or component systems failures, or unavailability of requested services.

In order to provide football fan with requested services, the Web booking system must complete all the specified tasks including: buy a match ticket, book a flight, reserve accommodation, and arrange transportation. However, if any of the tasks cannot complete, then the remaining (completed or uncompleted) tasks must be cancelled, as partial arrangements will not be acceptable to football fan. To guarantee this all-or-nothing condition, such applications must adhere to certain criteria. The most common criteria are called the ACID (atomicity, consistency, isolation, durability) correctness criteria. Majority of current Web transaction approaches, e.g. [1, 3, 7, 8], are based upon ACID correctness criteria. ACID follow a strict isolation policy such that intermediate results of an active transaction are not exposed to others. ACID criteria do not therefore support dynamic e-commerce applications that require interaction and negotiation between them. This is because, interaction and negotiation demand exchange of intermediate data between transactions [10]. Further, current ACID approaches are also not failure resilient in that there is no support to execute alternative transactions so as to save the whole transaction from failures. Despite these limitations, ACID criteria are useful in ensuring data consistency and durability.

The limitations of ACID criteria motivated the need for transaction models to enforce new correctness criteria. The transaction mechanism proposed here enforces novel correctness criteria called SACReD (*semantic atomicity, consistency, resiliency, and durability*) (proposed in [12, 13]). SACReD relax the isolation and atomicity policy of ACID criteria, and add a new resilience property as described below.

- **Semantic atomicity** allows that each subtransaction can unilaterally commit. For example, a component transaction can commit as soon as it books a flight. However, a transaction can commit only when all of its subtransactions have committed. Otherwise transaction must abort, in which case the effects of any committed subtransaction must undone by executing a compensating transaction.
- **Consistency** requires that a component database must be consistent before and after executing a transaction.
- **Durability** requires that effects of a committed transaction must be made permanent in the respective databases.
- **Resiliency** is defined by associating alternative transactions with subtransactions. This property enhances fault tolerance and service availability. Thus, if a car is not available then football fan can be provided with a taxi.

We enhance the capability of SACReD transactions through a meta-plan of agents BDI (**B**eliefs, **D**esires and **I**ntentions) model, thus establishing a new approach, called multi-agent SACReD transaction model (see Section 4). Agents have the potential to execute transactions dynamically such that they can navigate arbitrary information sources. The social characteristics of agents also correspond to coordinating transactions among participating organisations. Further, agents can support negotiation between different applications, exchange data and programs to perform various business activities [2].

3   The Proposed Meta-plan in Multi-agents BDI Model

Agents BDI model is a potential tool for modelling the behaviours of transactions with non-deterministic features [9] such as navigation of arbitrary information sources. This section first describes the traditional BDI model and establishes its limitations towards managing e-commerce transactions. It then describes the proposed meta-plan in BDI model that addresses the issues of traditional BDI model. The meta-plan is then applied to SACReD transactions in the subsequent sections.

3.1   Overview of the Traditional BDI Model

Agents are autonomous entities, which can be used to automate a number of activities in e-commerce applications. Agents can also be used to mediate between customers and the service providers (football fan and a travel agent), to exchange data, and to exchange programs to perform various business activities. Agents are therefore characterised by a set of **B**eliefs, **D**esires and **I**ntentions, or BDI as an acronym [2]. The BDI is a procedural reasoning model, which is driven by goals (e.g., making match arrangements). It is an effective reasoning mechanism for applications that need to contend with uncertain and dynamic environments such as the Web. The basic elements of the BDI model are explained in Table 1.

Traditional BDI model is useful for the e-commerce applications with the provision of semantic representation and reasoning mechanism. In addition, BDI model supports multiple planning-mechanism, so as to provide different types of services thus increasing service availability in the case of failures. However, certain limitations are associated with the traditional BDI model when applied to e-commerce transactions. Consider a plan (i.e., obtaining a cheapest flight ticket) that include actions of (a) collecting information from various airlines, (b) selecting cheapest flight (c) conducting transaction to buy a ticket. In this plan, if actions a, b are completed but c fails then the whole plan (i.e., actions a, b, and c) must be redone using the traditional BDI. Consequently, information from various airlines needs to be re-collected so as to buy a cheapest flight ticket. However, redoing the whole plan is time as well resource consuming, especially, in the Web environment, where communication links and component systems (e.g., Web servers) are heavily loaded. In addition, traditional BDI agents may have difficulty in obtaining the optimised solution since it is a partially planning reasoning system [5]. Thus sub-optimised plans may be selected due to the change of environment. For example, a cheaper flight may be available, but the agent may not be willing to change since a transaction has been carried out with the other travel agent.

These limitations negate the feasibility of traditional BDI model in managing e-commerce transactions. We therefore propose a new approach, by introducing a meta-plan in the BDI model. We believe that the new approach can potentially overcome the aforementioned limitations when applied to e-commerce transactions.

Table 1. Elements of Multi-agents BDI Model

Element	Description
Belief	represent states of the world that includes external and internal states. For example flights, rental car, etc.
Desires	represent the global goals that the system desires to achieve. For example, the *desire* of the Football Cup application is to make match arrangement for a football fan.
Intention	represent the current chosen course of actions to achieve the selected desire after deliberation. For example booking a flight via British Airline or Japanese Airline.
Plans	means of fulfilling intentions. A plan consists of a number of actions to be executed. For example, in Football World Cup application *one possible plan is to obtain the cheapest flight ticket that enables the football fan to reach the match venue well in time.* Possible actions for this plan include: (a) collecting information from various airlines, (b) selecting cheapest flight (c) conducting the transaction to buy the ticket. Further, to achieve the selected intention, the plan may include other sub-goals that correspond to other intentions (e.g., booking accommodation at the hotel or at a guest-house). Once the plan is triggered, it will carry out the actions (e.g. committing transactions) until the global goal or its intention is achieved. The execution of the plan may stop if there is an action failure.

3.2   The Meta-plan in the BDI Model

In this section we propose a meta-plan in the BDI model so as to deal with efficient recovery of plan failure by avoiding re-execution of unanticipated actions (e.g., recollecting airline information). Meta-plan is defined as a containment of information about all the possible plans to achieve top-level goal (e.g., to make match arrangement). In the meta-plan, a decision tree is constructed such that different paths within the tree correspond to the possible plans devised to achieve the goal. The meta-plan is built upon the assumptions that the goals can be achieved and the plan will not fail. The criteria for selecting plans are based on their utility and their feasibility (e.g., availability of cheapest flight ticket). The selected plans will be ordered according to their utility so as to reduce the need of regenerating the Applicable Plan List (APL). APL contains a list of feasible plans. We therefore believe that meta-plan will reduce great amount of time and computation in event of action failures. The meta-plan requires the availability of (more or less) complete information for the decision nodes prior to its execution. Thus the meta-plan model can effectively be used in the e-commerce transactions. This is attributed to the practicability of assembling the required information from other related agents-web information systems (e.g., airline booking system), before making any decision (Note that other problem domains require further investigations).

The new algorithms include a meta-plan that will produce a set of applicable plans with highest utilities to achieve the goal that is represented in one thread. The BDI model is in the other thread to carry out the actions and reflect the change on internal states. If there is any failure occurred, the exception handling section will inform the meta-plan for re-assessing. Since they have shared states, the meta-plan will be aware of the state of actions.

The following describes the notations related to utility calculation and plan selections in the proposed meta-plan BDI model.

$f : x \rightarrow y$; f is a function that maps x to y

$u = Utility(y)$; *Utility* is a utility function and u is a utility

e ;a set of actions

P ;a set of plan and p is a plan in the P

$u = MAX_u(U)$; u is the highest utility in set U and *MAX* is a function that retrieves the maximum utility in the set u.

Feasible $P = Option(B, I) = MAX_p(u) \wedge (Pre\text{-}Condition) \wedge Goal$

This represents that the plan has highest utility. The pre-condition for carrying out the plan must be true, and it contributes to achieve the goal.

$Filter(P \wedge \neg p)$;filtering out options apart from the selected plan p.

$$P_u = \frac{\sum\limits_{i:1 \rightarrow N} x_i}{N}$$
;if all sub-plans in the P_u must be carried out in order to achieve the intention, the utility is derived from the average of the sum of the all sub-plans. $p_u = MAX_u(P_u)$, if any plan in the plan set P is carried out, the intention can be fulfilled. The plan p with highest utility will be selected. The above can be applicable to the Intention I.

Failed is a function which applies to actions, plans and intents. *Failed(e)* represents that action e has failed. *Failed(e)* $\rightarrow$ *Failed(p)* iff there is no alternative action available to p and *empty(e)* is true. *Failed(P)* $\rightarrow$ *Failed(i)* iff there is no alternative plan available to achieve Intention i and *empty(P)* is true. BDI will attempt the intention until no other plans can possibly fulfil the goal (goal succeeds, or is not achievable). *Succeeded* is a function that could apply to actions, plans and goals. *Succeeded(e)* represents action e has succeeded. *Succeeded(e)* $\rightarrow$ *Succeeded(p)*; all selected actions e in the plan p have succeeded. *Succeeded(p)* $\rightarrow$ *Succeeded(i)*; all selected plans in the Intention i have succeeded.

Meta-plan produces a list of applicable plans to achieve a goal. When an agent is activated, complete information will be gathered to form a belief possible world in order to populate the meta-plan with information prior to the actions undertaking. The resulting utilities of these beliefs will take users' preference into account after information has been normalised. Each node in the possible decision tree is associated with a set of utilities for decision-making. So optimal solution can be obtained via meta-plan, which maintains available options for agent to achieve a goal. The plans and actions can be carried out accordingly. If a failure occurs in the plan then it will be marked as a failed plan. Failures trigger agent to reconsider its current failed intention, and perform alternative one (if there is one available). Interesting characteristic of BDI is that it will pursue its top-level goal (e.g., making match arrangement) until it succeeds or believes that the goal is unachievable. In the latter case, agent needs to devise recovery plans for undoing the completed sub-goals (e.g., cancelling hotel reservation). Through the recovery plans other agents can be informed so that they can handle their completed sub-goals, as appropriate.

4   A Multi-agent SACReD Transaction Model

We use the Football World Cup example to illustrate the proposed model. In the World Cup example, user specifies her preferences and desire for a Web booking system, which is (assumed to be) implemented at a particular travel agency. The system devises a meta-plan based on the user's preferences and desire. The meta-plan comprises different possible solutions (or plans) that can fulfil the user request (i.e., making match arrangement). In each plan, agents process user's request by setting a top-level goal and different sub-goals. For example, buying a match ticket is a top-level goal for the agents. Agents must therefore achieve the top-level goal by getting a match ticket. If the match ticket is not available, then it is unnecessary to book a flight, accommodation, or rent a car, which are considered as sub-goals of the agents.

In order to maintain the application correctness agents must process all the actions (of a particular plan) in a consistent way. That is, either all of the sub-goals and the top-level goals are achieved so as to fulfil the user's request, or none of them is achieved, as partial services are not acceptable to the football fan. We see that the execution correctness of the World Cup application can be achieved if agents process each action (of a particular plan) by executing a component transaction for it. Thus each of the individual actions (e.g., buying a match ticket) of a particular plan can be modelled as a component transaction. The main requirement for the component transactions is that they must adhere to the SACReD correctness criteria, presented in the preceding section. That is, all of the component transactions (performing different actions of the plan) must either complete successfully, or if any of them is unable to complete then the completed ones must be cancelled. This all-or-nothing characteristic will provide them with *semantic atomicity* property. Similarly, each of the individual component transaction must maintain *consistency* of information source (e.g., airline system, etc.). Further, it is required that the affects of successfully completed transactions must be made persistent in persistent storages so as to meet the requirement of *durability* property. That is, if a transaction books a flight, then the modified information, about flight seats, must be made persistent in the airline data source so as to survive failures. Finally, the *resiliency* requirement is that component transactions must replace failed transactions in a particular plan so as to take an alternate action. For example, if a room at a hotel is not available then it can be booked at a guest-house.

4.1   Commit Actions of Transactions

The meta-plan contains all information required to achieve a goal, i.e., to make a match arrangements. Once the plan is initiated by the system, agents start gathering relevant information for achievement of goals defined in a meta-plan. Agents use information of the meta-plan so as to generate an appropriate Applicable Plan List (APL). APL is comprised of different possible plans, which are devised to meet the user requirements. Plans are classified as high utility plans and low utility plans.

Figure 1 diagrammatically represents the information (of a meta-plan) that pertains to the World Cup application.

In Figure 1, circles and rectangles represent goals and sub-plans respectively. In the example, the meta-plan will construct a tree with all possible plans (in the APL) to achieve the goal. We represent some possible plans of the APL as follow: Plan1 = {MT-FB-HB-CB}, Plan2 = {MT-FB-HB-TB}, Plan3 = {MT-FB-GB-CB}. In addition, other plans are also possible. For example, if the football fan prefers a cheapest package, then the plan will be {MT-FB-GB-TB}. Plan1 is considered as the high utility plan where plans-2,3 are the considered as low-utility plans. This is because, user prefers the services specified in the plan1. However, if plan1 fails to achieve the specified goals then the system will pick another plan from the APL. Thus, the user can be provided with alternative services described in the alternative plans. It is to be noticed that all the actions in different plans are executed as component transactions. For example, to process plan1, four component transactions are executed, so that they can book: a match ticket, a flight, a hotel and a car. Once the component transactions perform the specified tasks they are unilaterally committed. They are not required to wait for the completion of other component transactions. This unilateral commit is allowed under the SACReD criteria. Once all the component transactions are committed according to the SACReD criteria, the goal of the plan is achieved. That is, the World Cup application is successfully executed making match arrangement for the football fan. Note that the classical atomicity and isolation policy (of ACID criteria) does not allow the unilateral commit of component transactions. Under ACID criteria, component transactions have to wait for each other completion. However, this requirement cannot be employed in e-commerce applications, where information sources belong to autonomous organisations that may not allow their transactions to wait for the completion of others [13].

If any of the component transaction fails to complete its specified task, then it is aborted. In this case, an alternative plan is executed so as to perform another task. For example, plan2 can be executed. Note that completed component transactions of the failed plan1 are not required to be re-executed. But only, failed component transactions are replaced with alternative ones. For example, if a component transaction of plan1 fails to book a hotel, then the alternative component transaction is executed to book a guest-house in plan2. This is an interesting characteristic of our approach that allows transactions of alternative plan to execute in the case of failures. Existing approaches [1, 2] fall short of this feature and they do not have any support for alternative transactions. Once the component transaction completes alternate tasks, then it is committed, and the goal of the plan is achieved. However, if none of the alternative transactions is completed, then completed transactions are compensated according to the SACReD criteria. In this case, the goal of the plan cannot be achieved, and thus match arrangements cannot be made.

Furthermore, different e-commerce applications (employed by various organisations) are dynamically coordinated with their activities in order to meet the user's requirements. Using agents to model e-commerce transactions is an effective means since agents can coordinate with each other to dynamically form a team for serving the purpose. Prior to formation of the team, a number of interactions and negotiations are required to ensure that participating agents are aware of the mutual benefits that lead them to bind to their commitments. Consequently, the social and autonomous characteristics of agents enable the proposed agents to support the transaction management of E-Commerce applications with properties of de-centralised control, flexible teamwork, and reliable services.

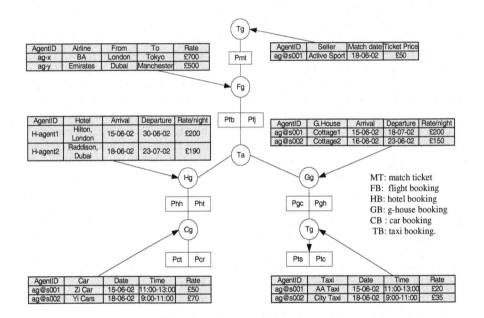

Fig. 1. The meta-plan populated with information

4.2 Failures and Recovery

Having described the commit process, we now illustrate the recovery mechanism that deals with the situation when transactions suffer from failures such as component system failures, communication failures, or unavailability of the requested services. We believe that our proposed model will provide efficient transaction recovery from failures thus increasing the service availability and avoiding re-execution of unanticipated actions.

Consider a plan {MT-FB-HB-TB} that books match ticket, flight, hotel, and a car. The plan contains several component transactions so as to perform these tasks. Further each component transaction contains several actions, for example, (a) collecting information from various airlines, (b) select appropriate flight (c) and then buy the ticket. In this situation, if actions a, b are completed but c fails then using our model, the completed actions a, b, are not required to be redone. But only the failed action can be replaced or re-executed so as to buy a flight ticket. We avoid redoing of completed actions by storing the necessary information in a meta-plan. Consequently, information from various airlines needs not to be re-collected so as to buy a flight ticket. Thus our proposed model provides an efficient recovery. Redoing the whole plan would otherwise result in time and resource consumption, especially, in the Web environment, where communication links and the component systems (e.g., Web servers) are heavily loaded. However, using the traditional BDI (as in [2] and [9]) all the actions of the plan needs to be redone in the case of failures.

5 Related Work and Conclusions

We discussed several issues of e-commerce applications that are not well addressed by current approaches, majority of which are based on the ACID criteria [1, 8, 7 3]. The effectiveness of these solutions is limited by the strict isolated and atomic policy that does not allow cooperation between different applications. These solutions are found to be inappropriate for current e-commerce applications. Alternative to ACID criteria is the flexible transaction model proposed for multidatabases [14]. This approach is interesting but it does not take into account Web and agent technologies.

Recently agent transaction models are introduced for e-commerce applications [2, 4, 11]. The approach in [4] uses Multi-agents to model dynamic Web transactions. It introduces a scripting language, called Multi-Agent Processing Language (MAPL), which is intended to simplify the execution and interaction of agents. However, [4] does not specify any correctness criteria as to whether transactions will follow ACID criteria or not. Similarly, [2] also contributes to agent-based transactions. It applies traditional agents BDI approach to model cooperative transactions in e-commerce applications. However, there are issues associated with traditional BDI model, as described earlier. Specifically when failures occur, then the entire plan needs to be re-executed which results in time and resource consumption. Further, appropriate transaction correctness criteria are also missing in [2].

In this paper we presented a transaction model based on novel correctness criteria, the SACReD criteria. Also proposed is a new meta-plan in the multi-agents BDI model. This has therefore established a new approach, called multi-agent SACReD transaction model that improves upon the current approaches. The proposed model has been partially implemented. A further implementation is required in order to see its complete effectiveness in e-commerce applications. Initial evaluation shows the following contributions of the proposed model:

- Efficient transaction recovery is provided thus increasing resiliency and service availability and avoiding re-execution of unanticipated actions. This is achieved through executing alternative plans of actions in e-commerce applications. Support for alternative plans provides services of different choice (e.g., cheaper flights).
- Correctness and consistency of applications and information sources are maintained. For example, in case of successful execution of World Cup applications, respective data (e.g., airline seats) are modified to a new consistent state. In case of failures these data are brought to a previous consistent state.
- Transactions can dynamically be executed thus allowing them to navigate arbitrary information sources. Thus a business partnership can be created dynamically and maintained only for the required duration such as a single World Cup transaction.

In addition to the above contributions this approach has also limitations. The introduction of agent technology to transaction management could increase overhead of design time, since agent is a complex technology without appropriate case tools to support its design and implementation. Even though the agents can work with others dynamically, they can only operate in a pre-defined agreed framework such as common co-ordination protocols, communication languages, and architectures. In other words, different E-Commerce applications implemented in different frameworks may not be able to communicate. This may hinder its adoption in an open and global E-Commerce era. However, we believe that the proposed approach has wider scope for further research. These issues need to be addressed by a wider research community and industry.

References

1.   D. Billard: Transactional Services for the Internet. Proc. of International Workshop on the Web and Database (WebDB'98), Valencia, Spain,1998.
2.   Q. Chen, U. Dayal: Multi-agent Cooperative Transactions for E-Commerce. Conference on Cooperative Information Systems, 2000.
3.   S.A. Ehikioya, K. Barker: A Formal Specification Strategy for Electronic Commerce. Proceeding of the International Database Engineering and Application Symposium (IDEAS), Montreal, Canada, August, 1997
4.   S.A. Ehikioya: An Agent-based System for Distributed Transactions: A Model for Internet-based Transactions. IEEE Canadian Conference on Electrical and Computer Engineering, Edmonton, Alberta, Canada, May, 1999
5.   M.J. Hubber: JAM Agents in a Nutshell. Intelligent Reasoning Systems Oceanside, California, 2001
6.   N. R. Jennings: On Agent-Based Software Engineering. Artificial Intelligence, Vol. 117, No 2, 2000, pp. 277-296.
7.   J. Lyon, K. Evans, J. Klein: Transaction Internet Protocol: Version 3.0. Internet-Draft, April 1998 (http://www.ietf.org/ids.by.wg/tip.html)
8.   M.C. Little, S.K. Shrivastava: Java Transactions for the Internet. Proc. of 4th Conf. on Object-Oriented Technologies and Systems (COOTS) April, 1998
9.   S. Rao A., and M. P. Georgeff: BDI Agents: from Theory to Practice. Proceedings of 1st International Conference on Multiple Agent System, San Francisco, California, 1995
10.   Shalom D. Tsur: Are Web Services the Next Revolution in E-Commerce? Proc. of the 27th VLDB Conference, Rome, Italy, 2001
11.   H. Schuldt, A. Popovici: Transactions and Electronic Commerce. 8th Int. Workshop on Foundations of Models and Languages for Data and Objects: Transactions and Database Dynamics, Springer LNCS No. 1773, 1999.
12.   M. Younas, B. Eagelstone, R. Holton: A Review of Multidatabase Transactions on the Web: From the ACID to the SACReD. Proceeding of British National Conference on Databases (BNCOD), Exeter, UK, 2000, Springer, LNCS, 2000
13.   M. Younas, B. Eagelstone, R. Holton: A Formal Treatment of a SACReD Protocol for Multidatabase Web Transactions. Proc. of 11th Int. Conf., DEXA 2000, Greenwich, London, 2000, Springer, LNCS, 2000.
14.   A. Zhang, M. Nodine, B. Bhargava: Global Scheduling for Flexible Transactions in Heterogeneous Distributed Database Systems. IEEE TKDE 13(3), 2001, 439-450

A Parallel Dispatch Model with Secure and Robust Routes for Mobile Agents

Yan Wang, Kian-Lee Tan, and Xiaolin Pang

Department of Computer Science
National University of Singapore
3 Science Drive 2, Singapore 117543
{ywang, tankl, pangxiao}@comp.nus.edu.sg

Abstract. For mobile agents to be widely accepted in a distributed environment like the Internet, performance and security issues on their use have to be addressed. In this paper, we first present a parallel dispatch model with secure dispatch route structures. This model facilitates efficient dispatching of agents in a hierarchical manner, and ensures route security by exposing minimal route information to hosts. To further enhance route robustness, we also propose a mechanism with substitute routes that can bypass temporarily unreachable hosts, dispatch agents to substitute hosts before attempting the failed hosts again. Finally, a model for distributing the load of decrypting substitute routes is presented. We also present results of both analytical and empirical studies to evaluate different models.

1 Introduction

For mobile agent technologies to be accepted, performance and security issues on their use have to be addressed. First, deploying a large number of agents may cause significant overhead when dispatching them. Efficient dispatch methods are desirable. Second, when a mobile agent arrives at a host for execution, the code and data will be exposed to the host and the resources at the host may also be exposed to the mobile agent. Thus, security mechanisms should be set up to protect mobile agents from malicious hosts and vise versa. Particularly in EC environments, since a lot of e-shops selling the same product should be visited to respond to a customer's request, and they are competitive, it is important to protect the routes of a mobile agent if it should visit a list of hosts (e-shops) or if it should dispatch some mobile agents to other hosts. If a malicious host knows the route information, it may tamper with it so that its competitors that may offer better prices or services will not be visited.

In this paper, we first present a binary dispatch model that can hierarchically and efficiently dispatch n mobile agents in parallel with a complexity of $O(log_2n)$. Based on it, we present a secure dispatch route structure where the agent at a dispatch layer only exposes the addresses of its child host to the current host. Thus, we preserve the efficiency of the binary dispatch model while ensuring route security. In addition, we propose a mechanism with encrypted substitute routes to facilitate robustness without sacrificing security and efficiency. It can bypass temporarily unreachable hosts by dispatching agents to substitute hosts, and try failed hosts again at the end of the whole

K. Bauknecht, A M. Tjoa, G. Quirchmayr (Eds.): EC-Web 2002, LNCS 2455, pp. 129–138, 2002.
© Springer-Verlag Berlin Heidelberg 2002

dispatch process. Finally, a model for distributing the load of decrypting substitute routes is presented.

In this paper, we employ well-known public-key encryption algorithm and signature scheme [1, 2]. In the following, we assume that there exists a secure environment including the generation, certification and distribution of public keys and each host can know the authentic public keys of other hosts.

2 Basic Binary Dispatch Model and Its Secure Route Structure

In this paper, we assume a *master agent* A_0 running at home host H_0 is responsible for dispatching other agents. We call an agent a *Worker Agent* (WA) if its sole responsibility is to perform simple tasks, e.g., accessing local data on a host. If a WA also dispatches other agents besides its local data-accessing task, it is called a *Primary Worker Agent* (PWA) [3].

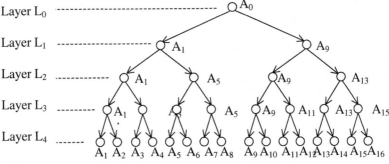

Fig. 1. Dispatch tree with 16 WAs

Here, we briefly introduce the basic binary dispatch model. As shown in the *dispatch tree* in Fig. 1, master agent A_0 has to dispatch 16 agents to 16 hosts (e.g. agent A_i to host H_i). Now, 16 mobile agents can be divided into 2 groups led by two PWAs, say A_1 and A_9. After A_1 is dispatched to H_1 it will dispatch A_5 and distribute 4 members to it. After that A_1 will transit to the same layer (i.e., L_2) as A_5, which is called a *virtual dispatch* costing no time. Now A_1 has 4 members only. Following the same process, A_1 dispatches A_3 and A_2 successively. Meanwhile, A_0 dispatches A_9 to H_9 to activate all agents in another branch in parallel. At last, A_1 becomes a WA and starts its local data-accessing task at H_1. As a whole, the model benefits from the parallel dispatches by different PWAs at different hosts. When there are $n=2^h$ mobile agents and T is the average time for dispatching a mobile agent, $(h+1)T$ will be the time for dispatching n mobile agents. So, the dispatch complexity will be $O(log_2n)$.

To ensure route security, we applied cryptographic technique to binary dispatch model. A basic definition of route structure is as follows:

(1) For a PWA at current host CH, r(CH)=P_{CH}[isPWA, ip(RH), r_L(CH),

   r_R(CH), S_{H0}(isPWA, ip(PH), ip(CH), ip(RH), r_L(CH), r_R(CH), t)]   (I)

(2) For a WA at current host CH, r(CH)=P_{CH}[isWA, ip(H_0), S_{H0}(isWA,

   ip(PH), ip(CH), ip(H_0), t)]

   where

- r(CH) denotes the route at the current host, CH, where the agent should reside;
- isPWA or isWA is the token showing the current state of the agent;
- ip(H) denotes the IP address of host H; RH denotes the right child host of current host; PH denotes the parent host of current host;
- $r_L(CH)$ and $r_R(CH)$ denote the encrypted route for the left and right children respectively;
- $P_{CH}[M]$ denotes the message M is encrypted by the public key P_{CH} of the current host CH; $S_{H0}(D)$ denotes the signature signed on document D by host H_0 using its secret key S_{H0};
- and t is the timestamp at which the route is generated. t is unique for all routes within a dispatch tree.

Starting the binary dispatch process with secure routes, the agent A_0 dispatches two PWAs to different hosts, each being encapsulated with an encrypted route for future dispatch tasks. When an agent has successfully arrived current host CH, the carried route r(CH) can be decrypted with the secret key of CH so that the agent can know:

(1) it is a PWA or a WA. It is used to determine the next task of the agent;
(2) the signature signed at host H_0: S_{H0}(isPWA, ip(PH), ip(CH), ip(RH), $r_L(CH)$, $r_R(CH)$, t) for a PWA, or S_{H0}(isWA, ip(PH), ip(CH), ip(H0), t) for a WA.

If it is a PWA, it will also know

(1) the address ip(RH) of the right child host RH;
(2) the encrypted route $r_R(CH)$ for its right child agent, which can only be decrypted by the right child host
(3) the encrypted route $r_L(CH)$ for the left dispatch (virtual dispatch).

If it is a WA, it will know the address of H_0, ip(H_0), the home host where A_0 is residing. With this address, the WA can send its result to A_0.

Clearly, in this model, at any layer, only the address of the right child host is exposed to current host so that the right dispatch can be performed. For a PWA, if it has $m=2^k$ members altogether, only k addresses are exposed to the host.

For any route, since all information included in the route appears in the signature, any tamper attack will not success. Also the wrong dispatch attack and replay attack can be found by the destination host. Meanwhile, with nested structure, the dispatch skip attack will not success. More discussions on security threats can be found in [4].

3   Robustness Enhanced Extension

So far we have presented a security enhanced dispatch model for mobile agents. However, each PWA only knows the right child host RH where its right child agent is to be dispatched at a certain layer. As such, should the right host be unreachable, the right dispatch branch cannot be deployed and all the members grouped in this agent will thereby not be activated.

In [5] Li proposed a robust model for serial migration of agents and the route robustness is enhanced by dividing a route, say {ip(H_1), ip(H_2), ..., ip(H_n)}, into two parts, say {ip(H_1), ..., ip(H_i)} and {ip(H_{i+1}), ..., ip(H_n)}. They are distributed to two agents A_1 and A_2 respectively. A_1 and A_2 are in partner relationship. Each agent residing at any host en route knows the addresses of the next destination and an alternative host. But the latter is encrypted by the public key of its partner agent. In case the migration cannot be performed, the encrypted address will be sent to the partner agent for decrypting. With its assistance, the agent can continue its migration.

The problem of Li's model is that since both A_1 and A_2 are dynamically migrating, when one needs the other's assistance, locating each other will be costly for both time and system resources. Meanwhile, the model is serial so it is not efficient. But the idea using the mutual assistance of two agents to enhance the robustness is good and can be easily used in our model, where the two first PWAs in the left and right branches can do it better.

To provide one substitute route, the route structure (I) can be extended as follows:

(1) For a PWA at current host CH, $r(CH)=P_{CH}[isPWA, ip(RH), r_L(CH),$
$r_R(CH), r_R'(CH), S_{H0}(isPWA, ip(PH), ip(CH), ip(RH), r_L(CH), r_R(CH),$
$r_R'(CH), t)],$
where $r_R'(CH)=P_{APWA}[ip(SH), r(SH), S_{H0}(ip(SH), r(SH), t)]$ is the sub-   (II)
stitute route for the right branch of host CH, SH is the substitute host.

(2) For a WA at CH, $r(CH)=P_{CH}[isWA, ip(PH), ip(H_0), S_{H0}(isWA, ip(PH),$
$ip(CH), ip(H_0), t)]$

$r_R'(CH)$ is encrypted by the public key of the first PWA in another branch of the whole dispatch tree, which here is termed as *Assistant PWA* (APWA). For example, in Fig. 1, A_1 is the first PWA in left branch so it is the APWA for the right branch following A_9. A_9 is the APWA for the left branch following A_1.

Now suppose A_1 is the first PWA in the left dispatch sub-tree. A_m is the right one. If the current host CH is the descendant of A_1, then $r_R'(CH)$ is encrypted by the public key of A_m, say P_{Am}. Otherwise, if CH is in the right dispatch sub-tree from the root node, $r_R'(CH)$ is encrypted by P_{A1}. If the dispatch failure occurs when A_{CH} is dispatching A_{RH} to right host RH, and A_{CH} is in the left sub-tree, A_{CH} should report it to A_m attaching the substitute route $r_R'(CH)$.

$$msg=P_{Hm}[ip(CH), ip(RH), r_R'(CH), S_{CH}(ip(CH), ip(RH), r_R'(CH), t_1)] \qquad (1)$$

where t_1 is the time when msg (1) is generated.

When A_m gets such a message, it will

Step 1: Detect whether RH is unreachable. If it is true, then go to step 2, otherwise go to step 3

Step 2: A_m will decrypt $r_R'(CH)$, $r=S_{Hm}[r_R'(CH)]=[ip(SH), r(SH), S_{H0}(ip(SH), r(SH),$
$t)]$, and send r to A_{CH} through a message
$$msg=P_{CH}[ip(SH), r(SH), S_{H0}(ip(SH), r(SH), t), S_{Hm}(ip(SH), r(SH),$$
$$S_{H0}(ip(SH), r(SH), t), t_2)] \qquad (2)$$
Stop.

Step 3: If RH is in the correct state, A_m will tell A_{CH} about it and record the request in a database. Stop.

In msg (2), the second signature is generated by H_m and t_2 is the corresponding timestamp; SH is the substitute host.

In this way by route structure (II), a PWA will have a substitute route for the dispatch of its right child agent. Once the original dispatch is not successful, with the assistance of its APWA, it can have another destination to dispatch.

What we should address is that the substitute host is originally included in the members for the right dispatch branch. Taking the dispatch tree in Fig. 2 as an example, if the dispatch failure occurs when A_1 at host H_1 is dispatching A_{17} to H_{17}, A_1 can get a substitute route with the assistance PWA A_{33} at H_{33}. To generate the substitute route, choosing H_{18} to be the substitute host is better. By exchanging the positions of H_{17} and H_{18} as shown in Fig. 2(b), though H_{18} becomes the root of the branch with H_{17} to H_{32}, most sub-branches under H_{18} is kept unchanged. This is very important and can reduce the complexity to generate a new substitute route.

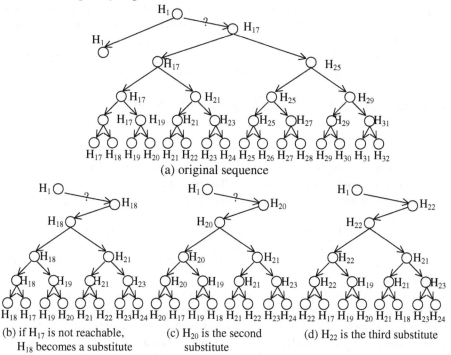

(a) original sequence

(b) if H_{17} is not reachable, H_{18} becomes a substitute

(c) H_{20} is the second substitute

(d) H_{22} is the third substitute

Fig. 2. Examples of substitute routes

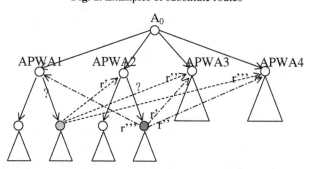

Fig. 3. A model with 4 branches and 3 substitute routes

Following the same idea, the second and the third substitute routes can be generated as shown in Fig. 2(c) and 2(d), where H_{20} can be the second substitute and H_{22} can be the 3rd one. An originally unreachable host should be put to be a leaf node so that the failure of the second dispatch attempt can be made without increasing more load of the APWA for route decryption.

As shown in Fig. 3, when there exist 3 substitute routes, 4 APWAs can be considered to partition the burden for decrypting substitute routes. In each branch following an APWA, the dispatch is performed in binary way. Each substitute route is encrypted by public keys of hosts where different APWAs reside. For instance, when a dispatch failure occurs in the first branch, the first substitute route is sent to APWA2 for decryption. The second substitute route will be sent to APWA3. Likewise the 3rd substitute route can only be decrypted by APWA4. Similarly, the first substitute route in the branch of APWA2 should be sent to APWA3 for decryption and so on. In this way, the burdens of decryption for APWAs are partitioned. The whole dispatch efficiency is not significantly decreased while the robustness is enhanced.

4   Complexity Analysis and Experimental Study

4.1   Complexity Analysis

In this section we compare our model with two existing secure models.

Westhoff's model in [6] adopted a fully serial migration providing secure route structure without any robustness mechanism. Suppose the visited hosts are H_1, H_2, ..., H_n, the route is:

$$r(H_i)=P_{Hi}[ip(H_{i+1}), r(H_{i+1}), S_{H0}(ip(H_i), ip(H_{i+1}), r(H_{i+1}), t)] \ (1 \leq i < n)$$
$$r(H_n)=P_{Hn}[EoR, S_{H0}(ip(H_{n-1}), ip(H_n), t] \tag{i}$$

where S_{H0} is the secret key of home host H_0 and EoR is the token meaning the end of the route.

Obviously the migration complexity is $O(n)$ if there are n hosts to be visited.

Li's model [5] mentioned in Section 3 ensures both security and robustness. In Li's model, as the addresses of n hosts are distributed to two agents, say {$ip(H_1)$, ..., $ip(H_m)$} and {$ip(H_{m+1})$, ..., $ip(H_n)$}, the nested route structure is:

$$r(H_i)=P_{Hi}[ip(H_{i+1}), r(H_{i+1}), r(H_i)', S_{H0}(ip(H_{i+1}), r(H_{i+1}), r(H_i)', t)] \tag{ii}$$

where $r(H_i)'=P_{AA}[ip(H_{i+2}), r(H_{i+2}), r(H_{i+2})', S_{H0}(ip(H_{i+1}), r(H_{i+2}), r(H_{i+2})', t)]$ is the substitute route where H_{i+2} is the new destination if H_{i+1} is not reachable. P_{AA} is the public key of the assistant agent.

The whole migration time can be theoretically half of the first model. However the time complexity is $O(n)$.

Theorem 1: Disregarding the time spent on local data access, the time complexity of migration of Westhoff's model and Li's model for visiting n hosts is $O(n)$.

In comparison, in our model the dispatch efficiency is greatly improved.

Theorem 2: If n $(n \geq 2)$ WAs are dispatched by binary dispatch model, $h=log_2 n$ $(h \geq 1)$ is an integer and the height of the dispatch tree, t is the time for dispatching a PWA or a WA, then the total dispatch time for n WAs is $T=(h+1)t$ and the time complexity is $O(log_2 n)$.

With regard to the complexity for generating routes, three models have different performances. Based on nested secure structure, which helps to prevent route tampering or deleting attacks and detects them as early as possible, assuming that the time to encrypt a route of arbitrary-length is a constant, the complexity for generating routes can be analyzed as follows.

Theorem 3: The time complexity for generating routes of Westhoff's model is $O(n)$.

For Westhoff's model, the route with n addresses can be generated after the route with n-1 addresses has been generated. So, the complexity is $T(n)=O(n)$ where $T(n)=T(n$-$1)+C$ and $T(1)=C$. C is a constant and the time of encrypting a route.

Theorem 4: The time complexity for generating a route with 1 substitute route of Li's model is $O(n)$.

In Li's model, suppose the hosts in predefined sequence are $\{H_1, \ldots, H_i, H_{i+1}, H_{i+2}, \ldots, H_n\}$, if host H_{i+1} is not reachable, H_{i+2} will become the next destination from H_i and H_{i+1} will never be visited for this journey. Consequently, from route structure (ii), when generating $r(H_i)$, both $r(H_{i+1})$ and $r(H_i)'$ should be generated first. $r(H_i)'=P_{AA}[ip(H_{i+2}), r(H_{i+2}), r(H_{i+2})', S_{H0}(ip(H_{i+1}), r(H_{i+2}), r(H_{i+2})', t)]$, it is a substitute route with the addresses of $H_{i+2}, H_{i+3}, \ldots, H_n$ in sequence. Note $r(H_{i+1})=P_{Hi+1}[ip(H_{i+2}), r(H_{i+2}), r(H_{i+2})', S_{H0}(ip(H_{i+1}), r(H_{i+2}), r(H_{i+2})', t)]$. The difference of two routes is that they are encrypted by different public keys. Therefore when generating $r(H_i)'$, $r(H_{i+2})$ and $r(H_{i+2})'$ exist already and the cost for generating $r(H_i)'$ is constant C only. Hereby the route generation complexity is $T(n)=T(n$-$1)+2C$ and $T(1)=C$. And $T(n)$ is $O(n)$. Likewise, the time complexity for generating 3 substitute routes is the same where $T(n)=T(n$-$1)+4C$.

However, if a failed host is used for a second attempt in Li's model, the complexity for generating routes will become extremely bad since the sequence of hosts in a substitute route has been changed and the route should be generated and encrypted again.

If host H_{i+1} is not reachable from H_i, when H_{i+1} is put as the last destination for the second attempt, the sequence of hosts in the substitute route will be $\{H_{i+2}, H_{i+3}, \ldots, H_n, H_{i+1}\}$. In such a case, when a migration route includes 1 substitute route, the time complexity will be $T(n)=2T(n$-$1)+C$ and $T(n)$ is $O(2^n)$. Likewise, when there are 3 substitute routes, the time complexity will be $T(n)=4T(n$-$1)+C$ and $T(n)$ is $O(4^n)$.

Theorem 5: The time complexity for generating routes with 1 or 3 substitute routes of Li's model making the 2nd attempt to the failed hosts are $O(2^n)$ and $O(4^n)$ respectively.

Theorem 6: In the secure binary dispatch model, the complexity for generating routes without substitute route is $O(n)$.

For our model, the complexity for generating routes without substitute route is $O(n)$, where

$$\begin{cases} T(n)=2T(n/2) \ (n=2^k) \ //2 \text{ routes are generated for left branch and right branch, each} \\ \qquad\qquad\qquad\qquad \text{has } n/2 \text{ addresses} \\ T(i)=2T(i/2)+C \ (i=2^h, \ 2^{k-1}\leq i \leq 2) \ // \text{ if } r(CH) \text{ has } i \text{ addresses, each of its } r_L \text{ and } r_R \\ \qquad\qquad\qquad\qquad \text{has } i/2 \text{ addresses} \\ T(1)=C \end{cases}$$

Theorem 7: In the robust binary dispatch model, the complexity for generating routes with 1 or 3 substitute route is $O(nlog_2n)$.

When generating the first substitute route for a branch, only a few steps should be taken in the left sub-branch of this branch. Considering the case in Fig. 2(b), when H_{17} and H_{18} are exchanged, the branches with the root of H_{19}, H_{21} and H_{25} are all not changed. The number of the steps is the height h of the sub-branch. And hereby $T(n)$ is $O(nlog_2n)$, where $T(n)=2T(n/2)+C$, $T(i) \leq 2T(i/2)+(h+1)C$ $(n=2^k, \ i=2^{h+1}, \ 2^{k-1}\leq i \leq 2)$ and $T(1)=C$.

Similarly, the step numbers for generating the second substitute route and the third one are all *(2h-1)*. The time complexity for generating a route with 3 substitute routes and 4 branches is $O(nlog_2 n)$, where $T(n)=4T(n/4)+C$, and $T(i) \leq 2T(i/2)+(5h-1)C$ ($n=2^k$, $i=2^{h+1}$, $2 \leq i \leq 2^{k-2}$) and $T(1)=C$.

4.2 Experiments

In Section 4.1, for simplicity, the analysis is based on the assumption that the encryption time of a message of any length is a constant. To further study the performance of the different models, we conducted 3 experiments on a cluster of PCs connected to a LAN with 100Mbytes/s network cards PCs running Window NT, JDK [7], IBM Aglets 1.0.3 [8]. For route generations, experiments are based on a PC of Pentium III 700 MHz CPU and 128 Mbytes RAM. For serial migration and binary dispatch, the experiment is put on a cluster of PCs. Each PC has a Pentium 200MMX CPU and 64 Mbytes RAM. All programs run on the top of the Tahiti servers from the ASDK [8, 9] and JDK from Sun Microsystems [7].

Note that all encrypted routes adopt nested structure. To encrypt a route, we use the RSA algorithm [2] with the key length of 1024 bit. Hash function MD5 is used to generate a hash value with fixed-length of 128 bytes.

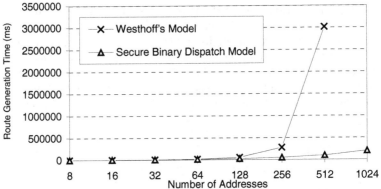

Fig. 4 Route generation time for Westhoff's model and binary dispatch model

In experiment 1, we first compare the route generation time of Westhoff's model and our secure binary dispatch model. All results are shown in Fig. 4. When the number of addresses is fewer than 128, the 2 models deliver similar performances. When the number becomes 256 or more, the binary dispatch model begins to outperform the serial model.

For Westhoff's model, each time after encryption, the route's length is increased at least with a length of an IP address and a signature. For example, when there are 512 addresses, the Westhoff's model performs 512 encryptions. As we measure, it uses 284 seconds to complete the first 256 encryptions and 2731 more seconds for the last 256 encryptions. The total time is 3015 seconds. For the binary dispatch model, it completes all encryptions in 101 seconds, and takes 37 seconds for 512 leaf nodes. But when generating the route with 1024 addresses, the program of the Westhoff's model ran out of memory after the 771th address is added where the heap size is set up to 1200 Mbytes and it has reached the maximum.

In experiment 2, we compare the generation time for routes with one substitute route. For Li's model, we implemented the case of skipping a failed host. The results shown in Fig. 5 illustrates that though time complexities of the two models analyzed in Section 4.1 are different (i.e. $O(n)$ vs. $O(nlog_2n)$), their performances are very close to each other when the number of addresses is not greater than 256. But when the there are 512 addresses or more, the binary dispatch model begins to outperform.

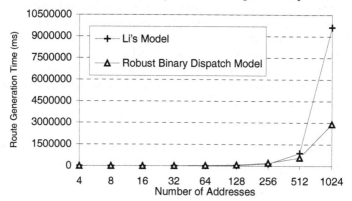

Fig. 5 Comparison of the time for generating a route
with 1 substitute route

In experiment 3, we tested up to 64 hosts to compare the migration/dispatch time of different models ignoring any robustness mechanism. In the implementation, a mobile agent will not access any local data so that the measured time is used for migration or dispatch only. The results are shown in Fig. 6.

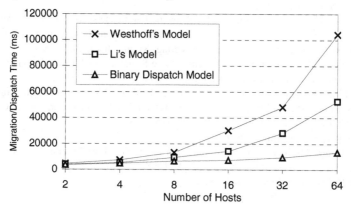

Fig. 6 Comparison of migration/dispatch time

When the number of visited hosts is no more than 8, the performance differences are not significant. With the increase of the number of hosts, the migration time of any serial migration model increases very fast. In comparison, the dispatch time for binary dispatch model increases fairly slowly. When having 64 hosts, the binary dispatch model can get 74.9% and 87.3% savings respectively in comparison to Li's model and Westhoff's model.

5 Conclusions

In this paper we have proposed a binary dispatch model of mobile agents with secure routes and robustness mechanisms. It utilizes the automation and autonomy of mobile agents and the corresponding code is simple. Besides the high efficiency from binary dispatch, the secure mechanism provides the capability to protect mobile agents from malicious hosts. Meanwhile, the robustness mechanism enables the fault-tolerance without any loss on security. Additionally, for practical applications, mobile agents having tasks of the same type and having physically close destinations can be put in the same group encapsulated with pre-encrypted route structures.

Acknowledgement. This work is supported by the NSTB/MOE funded project on Strategic Program on Computer Security (R-252-000-015-112/303).

References

1. Wayner P., Digital Copyright Protection, SP Professional, Boston, USA (1997)
2. Rivest R.L., Shamir A., Adleman L., A Method for Obtaining Digital Signatures and Public-key Cryptosystems, Communications of the ACM (1978)
3. Wang Y., Dispatching Multiple Mobile Agents in Parallel for Visiting E-Shops, Proc. of 3rd International Conference on Mobile Data Management (MDM2002), IEEE Computer Society Press, Singapore 2002 (61-68)
4. Wang Y. and Tan K. L., A Secure Model for the Parallel Dispatch of Mobile Agents, Proc. of Third International Conference on Information and Communications Security (ICICS2001), LNCS Vol. 2229, Springer-Verlag, Xi'an, China, 2001 (386-397)
5. Li T., Seng C.K. and Lam K.Y., A Secure Route Structure for Information Gathering, 2000 Pacific Rim International Conference on AI, 2000
6. Westhoff D., Schneider M., Unger C. and Kenderali F., Methods for Protecting a Mobile Agent's Route, Proceedings of the Second International Information Security Workshop (ISW'99), LNCS 1729, Springer Verlag, 1999 (57-71)
7. URL: http://java.sun.com/products/
8. Lange D., and Oshima M. Programming and Deploying Java Mobile Agents with Aglets, Addison-Wesley Press, Massachusetts, USA (1998)
9. URL: http://www.trl.ibm.co.jp/aglets/

An Agent-Based Framework for Monitoring Service Contracts

Helmut Kneer[1], Henrik Stormer[1], Harald Häuschen[1], and Burkhard Stiller[2]

[1] Department of Information Technology, IFI, University of Zurich, Switzerland
{kneer, stormer, haeusche}@ifi.unizh.ch
[2] University of Federal Armed Forces Munich, IIS, Germany and ETH Zürich, TIK, Switzerland
stiller@tik.ee.ethz.ch

Abstract. Within the past few years, the variety of real-time multimedia streaming services on the Internet has grown steadily. Performance of streaming services is very sensitive to traffic congestion and results very often in poor service quality on today's best effort Internet. Reasons include the lack of any traffic prioritization mechanisms on the network level and its dependence on the cooperation of several Internet Service Providers and their reliable transmission of data packets. Therefore, service differentiation and its reliable delivery must be enforced on a business level through the introduction of service contracts between service providers and their customers. However, compliance with such service contracts is the crucial point that decides about successful improvement of the service delivery process. For that reason, an agent-based monitoring framework has been developed and introduced enabling the use of mobile agents to monitor compliance with contractual agreements between service providers and service customers. This framework describes the setup and the functionality of different kinds of mobile agents that allow monitoring of service contracts across domains of multiple service providers.

1 Introduction

The recent development on the E-Commerce services market shows an upcoming demand for streaming technology in form of video-conferencing, video-, audio-, or news-on-demand applications. Besides the time and resources that long and expensive downloads entail, streaming technology offers a cheap solution to widely broadcast real-time data making high demands on systems and networks. Streaming means that continuous data is cut into single units (packets) and subsequently sent from sender to receiver. The sequence of single packets is called stream [19].

The global Internet is considered a network of networks where the networks or domains of several Internet Service Providers (ISP) are interconnected with each other to span a network around the globe. Communication within such a network requires a standardized protocol, the Internet protocol [17], [5] allowing different domains to exchange data. In order to achieve global connectivity for every single host on the Internet, every autonomous domain needs to route data within its scope (intra-domain routing) but also between other neighboring domains (inter-domain routing).

Fig. 1 shows a general network model of a streaming scenario where end-customers receive data (e.g., streamed video data) from Content Service Providers

K. Bauknecht, A M. Tjoa, G. Quirchmayr (Eds.): EC-Web 2002, LNCS 2455, pp. 139–151, 2002.
© Springer-Verlag Berlin Heidelberg 2002

(CSP) via several interconnected ISP networks [13]. The network model shows the integration of several business entities into the process of service provisioning. It is not only the cooperation of these entities that influences the service delivery but also the reliable transport service and other value-added services [12] provided by ISPs.

Unfortunately, current Internet technology is based on a packet-switched network where forwarding of data packets relies on a best effort service without any service guarantees and service prioritization mechanisms. Reliable and fast routing of data through the different networks underlies strict performance restrictions as far as data throughput, packet delay, loss and error rate among others are concerned.

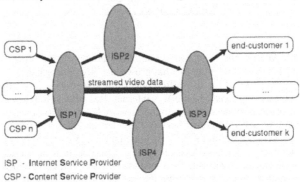

Fig. 1. General network model in a multi-provider environment

In order to offer and receive satisfying real-time Internet services, an efficient and economic resource management on the part of the service providers (CSPs and ISPs) is most urgently required. We claim that the introduction and monitoring of service contracts between service providers and service customers is one way to improve streaming real-time service provisioning. The usage of mobile agents for monitoring purposes provides the opportunity to control compliance with the guaranteed service levels across ISP domains. The agent-based monitoring framework describes the tasks of monitoring agents and their cooperation in order to identify malfunctioning service providers that cause service shortcomings or service failure.

The paper is structured as follows. The next section provides technical background for the usage of service contracts and mobile agents for monitoring purposes before section 3 introduces a contracting protocol for the service level negotiation. Section 4 describes the agent-based monitoring framework with the setup of agents and monitoring tasks. Section 5 describes implementation issues for the framework and demonstrates a practical example of how the agent-based framework could be applied in a real world scenario. Finally, section 6 summarizes the paper, draws conclusions, and gives an outlook on future work.

2   Technical Background

This section provides scientific background for the understanding of service contracts in form of Service Level Agreements (SLA) and Operational Level Agreements (OLA) and the usage of mobile agents for monitoring purposes.

2.1   SLAs and OLAs for Streaming Internet Services

While the demand for high-bandwidth multimedia E-Commerce services (e.g. streaming Internet services) is increasing steadily, the expectations for the service quality is growing in just the same measure. This means for a big E-Commerce services market that service provisioning on today's Internet is very exacting and challenging for service providers in order to meet all the requirements as far as the Quality of Service (QoS) is concerned. These QoS expectations will drive service customers more and more to negotiate service parameters with their service providers.

The concept of Service Level Agreements is fairly well understood and widely used, especially for the Service Level Management (SLM) within an enterprise [16]. A SLA defines a contract between a service provider and its customer, which are considered in a broad sense [7]. While its dedicated content may vary according to the service being offered, the general service description and additional parameters are required. Those include the customer and provider identification, a service definition, service monitoring and control information, pricing-, charging-, and business-related information as well as legal agreements [10]. SLAs for the Swiss market offered by UUNET guarantee 100% network and service availability, network latency, and outage reporting or they guarantee Virtual Private Network security [20].

Transferring the concept of SLAs and contractual agreements onto our network model of Fig. 1, we can distinguish two layers for applying the concept. The top layer entails a contractual agreement between the CSP and the end-customer while the bottom layer combines contracts among the ISPs for the data transport service. The bottom layer agreements are underpinning contracts and support the top layer to operate and fulfill the service between CSP and end-customer. Hence, they are called Operational Level Agreements. Negotiating service parameters (e.g., delay, error rate, jitter) and stipulating service contracts will help service providers to manage their network resources efficiently and economically and will improve customer satisfaction for QoS-based end-to-end service provisioning.

The Differentiated Services Internet (DiffServ) Architecture [1] uses SLAs to describe a "service contract ... that specifies the forwarding service a customer should receive". The detailed technical parameter specification is part of a second container, which, in case of DiffServ, is termed Service Level Specification (SLS). It mainly includes those parameter specifications, which cover values and traffic data within a dedicated DiffServ domain. The Traffic Conditioning Specification (TCS) forms an inherent part of a SLS and defines the detailed classifier rules and traffic profile values [7]. Therefore, a SLS can be considered a DiffServ OLA.

2.2   Mobile Agents for Inter-Domain Monitoring

The term 'agent' is used by a number of different research communities, for instance within the fields of artificial intelligence (intelligent agents) [15] or software engineering and distributed systems (software agents) [21]. The Object Management Group (OMG) defines a software agent as "a computer program that acts autonomously on behalf of a person or organization" [4]. Additionally, agents are often characterized using the following properties:

☐ proactive (support of the user's work)
☐ adaptive (learning the user's preferences or the ability to work on different platforms)

☐ autonomous (not communicating with its creator)
☐ intelligent (making 'intelligent' decisions [6])
☐ mobile (can actively migrate within networks to different systems and move directly to the local resources, like databases or application servers).

Most of the agents introduced in this paper are mobile. Therefore, each system needs to install a so-called 'agent-place' to create, delete and execute agents. Then, agents can migrate from system to system and perform their tasks locally.

2.3   Motivation for Using Mobile Agents

Monitoring of SLAs/OLAs is indispensable for an E-Commerce scenario where the end-customer pays money for guaranteed service provisioning and where the process of service delivery is dependent on several independent service providers (CSP and ISPs). The question to be discussed is why to use mobile agents for performing monitoring tasks.

Lange and Oshima give seven reasons why to use mobile agents [14], which can be favorably applied for the given example of a network model as illustrated in Fig. 1. For example, there is the reduced network load if agents can process and evaluate monitoring data locally instead of being transmitted over the network. The use of mobile agents can also overcome network latency, especially in case of real-time applications like streaming Internet services where quick actions are required in case of service failure or shortcomings. Furthermore, mobile agents can adapt dynamically to changing environments and execute asynchronously and autonomously since they do not require a continuously open connection to a fixed network. And finally, mobile agents can encapsulate protocols by wrapping monitoring information and communicating it based on proprietary protocols.

Lange and Oshima have also defined some applications that benefit from using mobile agents. Included is "monitoring and notification", where the main advantages are the asynchronous nature of the monitoring agents as well as the ability to monitor any given information source without being dependent on the system the information originates from. Providing an agent-place within the service providers' networks allows the agents to have access to monitoring data in a controlled fashion.

3   Service Level Negotiation

This section introduces one approach how to integrate SLAs/OLAs into the network model of Fig. 1. Several bilateral contracts in form of SLAs and OLAs are required between the entities to enable a combined real-time streaming service between CSP and end-customer. The contracts are negotiated in a contracting process prior to the actual service delivery process. Therefore, a contracting protocol based on the exchange of XML documents was developed to implement the different steps of the contracting process (see also [10]). The single steps of the contracting protocol are illustrated in Fig. 2, which shows a simplified network structure compared to Fig. 1 with only one CSP, a single end-customer, two ISPs and a Service Broker (SB) embedded into the network model.

2.,3.,4. Operational Level Requirements (OLR)

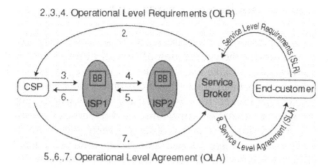

5.,6.,7. Operational Level Agreement (OLA)

Fig. 2. Contracting Protocol with a Service Broker to stipulate service contracts

The SB works as a negotiator between end-customer and CSP. It represents the point of contact for end-customers if they want to request and negotiate a service with certain QoS requirements. The SB can be an independent business entity but it is also possible that an ISP for example inherits that role.

In a first step, the end-customer as the receiver of the service (e.g., a video stream) defines Service Level Requirements (SLR) as the service parameters that define the QoS. After checking its own resources, the SB transforms the SLR into Operational Level Requirements (OLR), a technical translation of the informal SLR. The SB requests the OLR from the CSP (step 2), who checks its own resources before forwarding the request to ISP1 (step 3). ISP1 checks its resources with the help of a network manager (in Fig. 2, this role is taken by a Bandwidth Broker (BB)) and if resources available forwards it on to ISP2 (step 4). This process continues until the OLR reaches the last ISP in line that could deliver the service to the SB (in Fig. 2, this is ISP2). Only if the last ISP in line agrees to the OLR, the reverse process of creating OLAs can be initiated. ISP2 signs the OLR to make an OLA out of it before returning it to ISP1 (step 5). This reverse process continues until the SB receives an OLA from the CSP (step 7). Only now, the SB can react to the end-customer's SLR with a signed SLA and the guarantee that the service will be delivered according to the pre-defined service parameters.

If an ISP cannot meet the specifications of the OLR, it rejects the OLR and either an alternative route needs to be found or the SLR needs to be redefined by the end-customer to fit the service conditions of all the ISPs [11]. Notice, that no OLA is required between ISP2 and the SB, since physical interconnection between the two entities must already exist on a network level and also, ISP2 is the last ISP in line to agree to the OLR originally requested by the SB.

The SB collects (flexible and temporally limited) service offers from CSPs and service requests from end-customers and tries to match them in an optimal way. The SB could even request resources from a CSP for a service that it is going to sell to end-customers in the future. Service requests can eventually be reformulated and resubmitted to the customer in case of major changes in price or QoS. In case several end-customers in a certain neighborhood request the same service (e.g., 100 m Olympic final) with slightly different QoS parameters, the SB can gather single requests in compound OLAs with the service providers. SLAs represent digital goods that can be traded on a marketplace [10].

4   Agent-Based Monitoring Framework

As illustrated in the previous section, the set up of several bilateral contracts in form of SLA/OLAs coordinates the cooperation of several business entities to provision a real-time streaming service to the end-customer. It involves every business entity and ties them to an official document that service customers can rely on if problems occur. Especially the service broker tries to represent a trustworthy entity to its end-customers. In order to maintain trustability and legitimacy of SLAs/OLAs, the existence of a monitoring system to observe compliance with the contracts is indispensable. Therefore, an agent-based monitoring framework has been developed to realize inter-domain monitoring across autonomous ISP domains.

4.1   Setup of the Monitoring Agents

The setup of the agents within the network of the different service providers and the service broker follows a four-step agent setup protocol, as illustrated in Fig. 3. The protocol is independent from the contracting protocol where the SLA/OLAs are negotiated. The negotiation of service contracts can be performed for an immediate service or service reservations can be made in advance where the end-customer reserves a service that will be delivered in the future (e.g., watching an Olympic hurdle race at some point in the future). If the service is provided immediately, the agent setup protocol is executed following the successful termination of the contracting protocol. In case the service is delivered in the future, the agent setup is triggered accordingly by the service broker at a reasonable time before the service.

Within the monitoring framework, we distinguish three different kinds of monitoring agents at different locations. There is a SB-agent, a CSP-agent, and possibly several ISP-agents with the following functionalities:

SB-agent:
- Monitoring of network communication and traffic parameters by collecting monitoring data delivered from the monitoring devices according to the specified filter
- Supervision of overall service provisioning
- Notification and taking steps in case of service failure or shortcomings
- Resides at the service broker

CSP-agent:
- Monitoring of network communication and traffic parameters by collecting monitoring data delivered from the monitoring devices according to the specified filter
- Eventually, monitoring of system components and hardware devices that are responsible for transmitting the content (e.g., CPU, operating system, memory, etc.)
- Eventually, real-time evaluation of collected data
- Resides at the CSP

ISP-agent:
- Monitoring of network communication and traffic parameters by collecting monitoring data delivered from the monitoring devices according to the specified filter
- Eventually, real-time evaluation of collected data
- Resides at the ISP

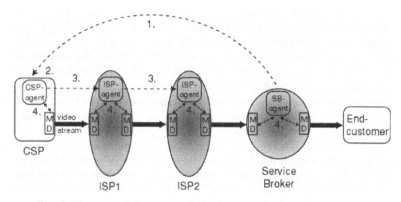

Fig. 3. The setup of the agents within the network of service providers

The sequence of steps to setup and place the different agents within the monitoring framework can be executed as follows:

1. In time, before the service is to be monitored, the service broker triggers the setup of the agents by creating the SB-agent. The SB-agent creates a CSP-agent that migrates to the CSP's agent platform.
2. The CSP-agent creates an ISP-agent. The CSP-agent provides the ISP-agent with the necessary information about location of ISP1 in order for the ISP-agent to migrate there.
3. The created ISP-agent migrates to ISP1. Having arrived there at ISP1's agent platform, the ISP-agent generates a copy of itself (also referred to as clone) which becomes the future ISP-agent of ISP2. Similarly to step 2, the clone receives the necessary information about ISP2 and migrates there. This procedure of "copying and migration" repeats until all the ISPs along the communication path that contribute to the service provisioning process have their ISP-agents. Information about the neighboring ISPs had been exchanged and stipulated by the bandwidth brokers (BB) in the previously executed contracting protocol.
4. The final step is to connect the ISP-agents as well as CSP- and SB-agent with the local monitoring devices (MD) through services and interfaces provided by the respective agent platform. Such monitoring devices could be agents as described in [8] or commercial monitoring tools provided for example by NeTraMet [2], Netflow [3], or IUM [9]. As illustrated in Fig. 3, we assume that monitoring devices consists of two devices that monitor both incoming and outgoing traffic at the ingress and egress routers of the ISP network. This has the advantage that all incoming traffic from a particular neighboring ISP can be monitored at the ingress router and compared with the outgoing traffic through the egress router. However, another option could be to place the monitoring devices at different and distributed locations within the network where traffic is reduced and monitoring can be performed more specifically.

After the agents have migrated to the different platforms and the connection is setup to the local monitoring devices, monitoring can be performed during service provisioning according to the QoS specification as stipulated in the SLA/OLAs. After the service has been finished and no monitoring is required anymore, the agents will be deleted.

The CSP-agent and the ISP-agents are local agents that are autonomous but work on behalf of the service broker. That means there is a fixed correlation between the broker agent and CSP/ISP-agents. However, other service brokers also have their broker-agents, which also generate their own CSP/ISP-agents that migrate to CSP/ISP networks accordingly. The monitoring devices are installed locally within the networks and systems of SB/CSP/ISPs and their task is it to provide the SB/CSP/ISP-agents with the relevant monitoring data after successful connection. That means the local monitoring devices provide several local agents with monitoring data. Monitoring devices scan the IP traffic by simply filtering out the information that is relevant to the corresponding agent. The filter is communicated to the monitoring devices during the connection process with the SB/CSP/ISP-agent. Filter functions are provided through specifications on the part of the local agent platform (see Section 5).

The service broker as an intermediary between CSP and end-customer might cause a bundling of several single requests of end-customers to one compound request to the CSP. In such a case, one pair of monitoring devices does not have to monitor several single services but just the one bundled service. Still, the service specifications for the bundle of single services have to be correct and monitored accordingly. After receiving the bundle of data, it is the task of the service broker to provide the different end-customers with the corresponding data. For that case, the service broker has its own monitoring devices to monitor incoming traffic (in form of a bundle) and also traffic that goes to every single end-customer (end-customer oriented monitoring).

4.2   Monitoring the Service Performance

Monitoring in general is applied in different areas (e.g., workflow applications, banking systems, web content) where monitoring is performed in form of data logging and reporting and simply serves for documentation purposes. However, within the agent-based monitoring framework, monitoring data is collected by SB/CSP/ISP-agents in order to evaluate the service delivery process, and as a consequence to take steps in case of service failure or shortcomings as defined in the SLA/OLAs. Monitoring can be subdivided into **static monitoring** and **dynamic monitoring**. Static monitoring implies a service evaluation after the service is performed, while dynamic monitoring foresees an examination of collected monitoring data 'on-the-fly' while the service delivery process is being executed. This is of prime importance if the corresponding service provider can be notified already as a preventive measure in case of service shortcomings and thus eventually avoid a complete service failure.

The MDs scan IP traffic by filtering relevant data for the corresponding agent and service with respect to service parameters such as delay, bandwidth, packet loss, etc. With static monitoring, an evaluation of the monitoring data is performed by the SB after the service delivery and after the CSP/ISP-agents have migrated back to the SB with the monitoring data attached. Eventually, the CSP/ISP-agents undertake a pre-evaluation of the results in order to reduce the amount of data before migrating back to the SB. With dynamic monitoring, evaluation of monitoring data is performed constantly by all the monitoring agents and therefore, the CSP/ISP-agents maintain a communication path to the SB-agent and exchange 'on-the-fly' evaluated monitoring data concerning the service level. In case of service shortcomings, the local BB can additionally be notified (preventive measure to avoid service failure). That means a communication path between the CSP/ISP-agents and the SB-agent exists for exchanging monitoring information.

With static monitoring, consequences in case of non-compliance with the service contract can be taken after the evaluation of all monitoring data. With dynamic monitoring, steps in case of service failures can be taken immediately when discovered. This could result in an exchange of a malfunctioning ISP 'on-the-fly' during service delivery. An overview of differences between static and dynamic monitoring is given in the following table.

	Static monitoring	Dynamic monitoring
Functionality	Evaluation of monitoring data is performed by the SB after the service delivery	Evaluation of monitoring data is performed by all monitoring agents during service delivery
Communication	There exists no communication among the SB, CSP, and ISPs	A communication path between the CSP/ISP-agents and SB-agent exists
Type	Reactive monitoring	Preventive monitoring
Consequences	Delayed consequences after evaluation of monitoring data	Immediate consequences possible

5   Implementation and Example

The agent-based monitoring framework is designed with one standardized agent platform. The platform is installed at the SB, CSP, and ISPs and provides a minimal set of standardized functions as described in the following. Any extension of monitoring functionality is achieved by extending the corresponding agent's functionality. This keeps the agent platform simple and small, supports a quick diffusion of the platform and guarantees a better reliability. The agent platform consists of three areas: In/Out Area, Working Area and MD Connection Area (see also Fig. 4).

As described in section 4.1, agents migrate from SB to CSP and on to different ISPs. For security reasons, the agents' source code will be encrypted and digitally signed by the SB before they migrate. Therefore it is impossible to change or to forge the agent while it is transferred from one provider to the other. After arriving in the In/Out Area the system decrypts the agent, checks its integrity, and verifies the authorization. The authorization is verified with the aid of a digital signature. After the agent's successful authorization, it can proceed to the Working Area. In the Working Area the agent can execute all implemented functions and communicate with the MDs with the aid of an interface provided by the MD Connection Area. The MD Connection Area is different for every provider because not all the MDs are standardized and the framework is MD-independent. Therefore, we do not describe this area in more detail at this point.

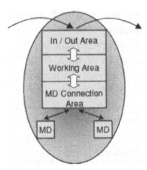

Fig. 4. The agent platform

5.1   In/Out Area

The In/Out Area performs the following security checks on the mobile agents. The checks are implemented with standard security functions like public key encryption, message authentication code and digital signature [18].

☐ Decryption of agents and information
☐ Integrity check
☐ Verification of Authorization
☐ Encryption and transfer to the next platform

5.2   Working Area

The Working Area serves to execute agents and to provide access to the MDs through the MD Connection Area. The agents are executed independently from each other and the area guaranties that an agent cannot change other agents and can only use the allocated resources. The Working Area must support the following functions:

☐ **OpenMD**: This function opens a connection to the MD (of either the ingress or egress router) and allows to monitor incoming or outgoing traffic related to the corresponding SLA/OLA.
☐ **RegisterFilter**: The agent can define an unlimited number of filters and use them for monitoring a stream (specified by source and destination address). To create such a filter for a certain stream the agent can define the following parameters among other things:

  ☐ *size*: This parameter defines the size of the captured data.
  ☐ *number*: This parameter defines how often a filter is executed.
  ☐ *interval*: The interval defines the delay between two filter accesses.

  RegisterFilter(size=500, number=10, interval=2) means this filter is executed 10 times every two minutes where 500 bytes are sent to the agent.

☐ **StartFilter**: With help of this function the agent can start a monitoring process with a specific filter. The function requires a reference to an already defined filter in order to open connection to a MD.
☐ **StopFilter**: The monitoring with a specific filter will be stopped. The function requires a reference to an already activated filter.

☐ **RegisterEvent**: This function allows to define an event (e.g., MD failure). An event allows to start or stop a filter when a specific event occurs. The function requires an event, a reference to an already defined filter and open connection to a MD. The agent can define an unlimited number of events.

☐ **StartEvent**: This function activates an already registered event. After the event occurs the agent will be notified and monitoring with the specific filter will be started or stopped.

☐ **StopEvent**: This function deactivates an already activated event.

☐ **DeleteFilter**: An already defined filter will be deleted.

☐ **DeleteEvent**: An already defined event will be deleted.

All the filters and events are stored in a database. After the agent is deleted all the filters and events will be automatically deleted, too.

5.3 Practical Example

This practical example illustrates the applicability of the agent-based monitoring framework. Given a scenario with an end-customer connected to a CSP where the connecting path is routed across ISP1, ISP2, and a service broker (see Fig. 5). The end-customer requests a video stream from 09 to 11 pm with specific information about some QoS parameters such as error rate, delay time, jitter, etc. These parameters are negotiated between the end-customer, the service broker, and the service providers and subsequently stipulated within one SLA and three OLAs (see Fig. 5).

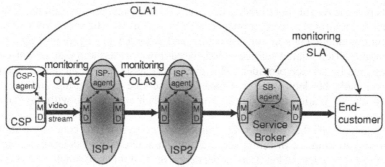

Fig. 5. Setup of the different agents to monitor the SLA/OLAs

Before the service provisioning process is executed, the service broker initiates the setup of the different monitoring agents for monitoring compliance with the contracts. Therefore, a SB-agent is created and positioned in the working area of the service broker. The SB-agent creates a CSP-agent that migrates to the CSP's working area. Afterwards, the CSP-agent creates an ISP-agent that migrates to ISP1. Finally, the ISP-agent of ISP1 generates a clone of itself that migrates to ISP2. Now, the different agents open connections with the corresponding local monitoring devices (MD) as described in section 5. By specifying filters, the agents can request from their MDs the kind of information they are interested in. By the time service provisioning starts, the agents are ready to perform their monitoring task.

Since streaming is very sensitive to the transmission of subsequent data packets, we choose delay as one QoS parameter to be monitored within this example. Therefore, the ISP-agents open a connection to their ingress and egress MDs and collect monitoring information about incoming and outgoing packets as defined in the monitoring filter. Depending on the filter specification monitoring can be performed permanently during the entire service duration or just temporarily within defined time intervals. The duration of the monitoring should be defined within the SLA/OLAs as well as the sanctions in case of service failure or service shortcomings. If equipped with the right functionality, the ISP-agents could calculate the delay time for the monitored data packets and pre-select and store only the kind of data that is not in compliance with the OLA. This information can be used by the service broker to take measures against the malfunctioned ISP.

If service shortcomings or service failure is noticed by ISP-agent of ISP1 and static monitoring is performed, sanctions are executed by the SB-agent after the service is finished. Possible sanctions could include a surcharge for the malfunctioned service provider. If dynamic monitoring is performed, steps can be taken during service provisioning such that the network manager of the corresponding ISP is notified about the shortcomings. If the situation is not improved, further steps could include for example the replacement of an ISP by choosing a new route with a different ISP.

6   Summary, Conclusions, and Future Work

This paper has presented an agent-based framework for monitoring service contracts. Agents provide useful functionality that was taken advantage of within the framework in order to monitor service compliance with SLAs/OLAs. The framework is based on assumptions about network infrastructure and resource management (e.g., resource reservation, differentiated services, QoS-based transport service) that are currently not fully applied by service providers. However, these assumptions are advantageous and will eventually be deployed for a QoS-based service provisioning and provide the basis for the stipulation of service contracts and their compliance with the real service delivery.

Advantages of the monitoring framework comprise its generic usability for monitoring all kinds of different services and parameters (e.g., delay time, error rate, correct order of data packets), its dependence on a number of small and cooperative agents, and its customer-friendliness due to monitoring based on customer requirements. Furthermore, monitoring was classified into static and dynamic monitoring such that static monitoring evaluates monitoring data after the service delivery while dynamic monitoring offers possibilities to evaluate monitoring data 'on-the-fly' during the service performance.

Future work in this area will deal with the detailed specification of different interfaces for special filter functions that establish communications between the monitoring agents and the local monitoring devices (MD). Most importantly, the developed and presented approach is based on a standardized format for service contracts and, therefore, future attempts have to address the definition of special SLAs and OLAs that allow automated monitoring activities based on the content of service contracts.

References

[1]   S. Blake, D. Black, M. Carlson, E. Davies, Z. Wang, and W. Weiss: *An Architecture for Differentiated Services;* IETF, Request for Comments RFC 2475, December 1998.

[2]   N. Brownlee: *NeTraMet (Network Traffic Meter);* http://www2.auckland.ac.nz/net/Accounting/ntm.Release.note.html, February 2001.

[3]   Cisco: *IOS Netflow;* http://www.cisco.com/warp/public/732/Tech/netflow/, February 2002.

[4]   Crystaliz, Inc., General Magic, Inc., GMD Focus, IBM Corp.: *Mobile Agent Facility Specification;* Technical Report, Object Management Group (OMG), 1997.

[5]   S. Deering, R. Hinden: *Internet Protocol, Version 6 (IPv6) - Specification;* IETF, Request for Comments RFC 2460, December 1998.

[6]   J. Ferber: *Multi-Agent Systems: An Introduction to Artificial Intelligence;* Addison Wesley Publishing Company, 1999.

[7]   D. Grossman: *New Terminology and Clarifications for Diffserv;* Internet Draft, draft-ietf-diffserv-new-terms-08.txt, January 2002.

[8]   M. Günter, T. Braun: *Internet Service Delivery Control with Mobile Code;* IFIP Conference on Intelligence in Networks (SmartNet 2000), Vienna, Austria, September 18-22, 2000.

[9]   Hewlett-Packard: *IUM (Internet Usage Manager);* http://www.hp.com/communications/usage/ium/index.html, February 2002.

[10]   H. Kneer, H. Häuschen, K. Bauknecht: *Tradable Service Level Agreements to Manage Network Resources for Streaming Internet Services;* 10th European Conference on Information Systems (ECIS 2002), Gdansk, Poland, June 6-8, 2002.

[11]   H. Kneer, R. Marfurt: *Contracting Protocol for Managing Quality of Service in a Multi-Provider Environment;* Submitted to IADIS International Conference WWW/Internet, Lisbon, Portugal, 2002.

[12]   H. Kneer, U. Zurfluh, B. Stiller: *A Model for Value-added Internet Service Provisioning;* First IFIP Conference on E-Commerce, E-Business, and E-Government, Zurich, Switzerland, October 3-5, 2001.

[13]   H. Kneer, U. Zurfluh, G. Dermler, and B. Stiller: *A Business Model for Charging and Accounting of Internet Services;* International Conference on Electronic Commerce and Web Technologies (EC-Web 2000), Greenwich, U.K., September 4-6, 2000.

[14]   D.B. Lange, M. Oshima: *Seven Good Reasons for Mobile Agents;* Communications of the ACM, Vol. 42, No. 3, pages 88-89, March 1999.

[15]   R. Murch, T. Johnson: *Intelligent Software Agents;* Prentice Hall, 1999.

[16]   J. Niessen, P. Oldenburg: *Service Level Management - Customer Focused;* The Stationary Office, Central Computer and Telecommunications Agency (CCTA), 1997.

[17]   J. Postel (Edt.): *Internet Protocol;* IETF, Request for Comments RFC 791, September 1981.

[18]   B. Schneier: *Applied Cryptography;* Wiley, 1995.

[19]   R. Steinmetz: *Multimedia-Technologie: Grundlagen, Komponenten und Systeme;* 2nd edition, Springer, 1999.

[20]   UUNET: *Service Level Agreements;* http://www.uu.net/terms/sla/, February 2002.

[21]   M.J. Wooldridge, N.R. Jennings: *Software engineering with agents: pitfalls and pratfalls;* IEEE Internet Computing, pages 20-27, May/June 1999.

Constraint Search for Comparing Multiple-Incentive Merchandises

Masayuki Kozawa, Mizuho Iwaihara, and Yahiko Kambayashi

Department of Social Informatics, Kyoto University,
Sakyo-Ku, Kyoto, 606-8501 Japan
{kozawa, iwaihara, yahiko}@db.soc.i.kyoto-u.ac.jp

Abstract. This paper discusses about electronic commerce trading merchandises having multiple and various incentives. Incentives here mean sellers' conditions for promoting certain types of merchandises. Typical examples of incentives are discounts on not-popular items. Buyers need to compare not only prices and contents but also incentives, and know reasons why one product is expensive than others. In this paper, we introduce a framework to support selections of multiple-incentive merchandises, by representing incentives using constraints, and offering constraint search mechanism to examine and compare those incentives. A typical example of multiple-incentive merchandises is airline tickets, where various prices are supplied according to restrictions. We show how complex incentives of airline tickets can be represented as constraints and can be queried using dynamic constraint databases.

1   Introduction

Electronic commerce has been rapidly growing in volume and diversity. One important area of E-commerce research is to develop advanced models for matchmaking vendors and buyers. Matchmaking can be arranged in various ways, including online catalogs, auction, one-to-one negotiation, and agent-based negotiation[10]. Comparing merchandises according to price and conditions is a fundamental task for buyers in every matchmaking scheme. Buyers in the real world often compare products not only by prices but also by various conditions associated with the products. Such conditions include discounts, usages, delivery, return policy, and so on. In current E-commerce marketplaces and XML libraries, vendors need to describe these complex product conditions in the form of a natural language. In this situation, it is hard to provide intelligent system support for matchmaking. Electronic contract is another area requiring formal support.

In the research field of E-commerce, several approaches have been proposed for advanced matchmaking. RuleML[2][3] is a standardization project aiming at providing XML interfaces for rules and formulae as a part of Semantic Web. RuleML incorporates research results on business rules from [4] and IBM Common Rules[5]. EContracts[8] provides a formal model for machine-interactive and analyzable E-commerce information, and provides Commerce Automata

K. Bauknecht, A M. Tjoa, G. Quirchmayr (Eds.): EC-Web 2002, LNCS 2455, pp. 152–161, 2002.
© Springer-Verlag Berlin Heidelberg 2002

for matchmaking buyer and vender conditions. In the study of multi attribute auctions[1], multidimensional vectors are used in buyer's scoring function to compare goods. The schalar product of the vectors and the buyer's weight vetors is the target variable. However, it is a problem how to find a proper weight vector, and attributes having set-values cannot be linearly ranked. Moreover, it is not confirmed that even the highest scored item satisfies the condition the buyer wishes.

One of the authors has proposed the Dynamic Constraint Algebra (DCA) [6][7] for processing E-commerce constraints. The DCA is a database query language based on constraint databases[9]. One of the unique points of the DCA is that it provides a framework for manipulating and querying commerce constraints. The DCA offers relational algebra-style operations, while they have significantly more expressive power than the classical relational algebra. This database query language approach enables flexible composition of various matchmaking styles, such as constraint search by one buyer on multiple goods, or one-to-one contract negotiations.

In this paper, we investigate a formal model for merchandises having multiple incentives. Incentives here mean conditions attached to a class of merchandises for inducing customers to a certain subclass of merchandises. Incentives are used in various market sectors; typical examples are special discount price for promoting new goods, and weekday discount of theme parks to attract guests on weekdays. Incentives may also be used to reduce cancel or change of tickets by offering cheaper tickets in exchange for larger penalties for cancel or change. Multiple incentives may be applied to goods offering seemingly the same service, resulting in complex price structures. These incentives are designed according to vendors' intentions to maximize sales and/or profits. Buyers need to carefully examine available incentive options and choose optimal combinations. However, this is not a trivial task because incentives are vender-oriented and generally do not correspond with buyers' motivations, and the structure of incentives varies from vendor to vendor.

It is important to provide a querying mechanism for buyers to compare various incentives offered by vendors and to find goods matching buyers' constraints. In this paper, we propose a model for formally representing incentives. We classify them into several categories, and discuss queries utilizing the DCA for comparing and testing useful properties of incentive rules. We take up the case of airline tickets to study incentive modeling. Airline tickets are a typical example of merchandises having complex combinations of incentives, such as advance purchase, minimum stay, stop over and so on. One airline vendor sells tickets of various restrictions at varying or identical price. We categorize incentive rules of airline tickets according to our model, and derive a constraint database storing those rules. Current E-commerce sites for airline tickets describe incentive rules in text, or check rules through program codes. In this situation, buyers need to carefully read the text to figure out reasons why one ticket is cheaper than others, or try many cases on the web page to obtain satisfying ones. On the other hand, our approach separates constraints from checking programs, and allows finding tickets and associating constraints by a single query. By this way, a great potion of buyers' tasks can be automated.

This paper is organized as follows. In Section 2, we introduce the dynamic constraint algebra which we use for our underlying formalism. In Section 3, we describe incentive rules and give a classification of these rules. We take an example of airline tickets and show DCA queries for comparing tickets in Sections 4 and 5. Section 6 concludes this paper.

2   Dynamic Constraint Algebra

In this section, we describe the Dynamic Constraint Algebra (DCA)[6][7] as our underlying formalism for modeling incentives and other business rules. Constraint databases[9] have been studied as a powerful approach for extending querying power of databases from the traditional relational database model. The key idea of constraint databases is that instead of storing a collection of tuples as data representing the real world, constraint databases store collections of *constraints*. Constraints are logical formulae having truth values for a given (ordinary) tuple. The facts a constraint database represents is the set of tuples satisfying one of the constraints. By this way, constraint databases truly extend the expressive power of relational databases. Constraint representation of data also allows flexible logical operations on constraints, while deductive databases have restrictions on evaluation manner of horn clauses. Constraint databases are suitable for E-commerce applications, since business rules can be directly represented as database objects and those rules can be queried by a declarative query language.

In the following, in stead of giving full formal definitions, we describe the DCA to be concise sufficient for later discussion. A (constraint) tuple $[a_1, \ldots, a_k]/\phi$ consists of values $a_1, \ldots, a_k$ and constraint ϕ. The values are either constants or variables. Any class of constraints can be used for ϕ if the satisfiability problem is decidable in the class. We particularly choose the class of equivalence constraints such that equalities of the form like $x =$ "USD 120" or $x = y$ are connected by logical operations $\wedge$ (AND), $\vee$ (OR), $\neg$ (NOT), $\rightarrow$ (IMPLICATION). An example of constraint relations is shown in Table 1. The class of equivalence constraints can represent Boolean combinations of possible constants, which are frequent in selling and buying constraints.

In addition to the general framework of constraint databases, our approach of the DCA has the following unique features:

– We do not suppose a predefined set of variables which appear in constraint relations. This is based on the observation that business rules of E-commerce have different formulations among products and vendors, so it is difficult to define a fixed schema/signature of variables.
– First-order queries on constraints can be formulated by Boolean operations of constraints and by quantifications over variables. We need to specify argument variables, although we do not assume the existence of a predefined variable schema. To support querying on such schema-free constraints, we

Table 1. Constraint Relation

pid	Item	Model	Price	Buy	Condition
p0	MPU	m_1	p_1	b_1	$(m_1 = 500 \vee m_1 = 750) \wedge (m_1 = 500 \rightarrow p_1 = 249) \wedge (m_1 = 750 \rightarrow p_1 = 399)$
p0	RDRAM	m_2	p_2	b_2	$m_2 = 128\text{MB} \vee m_2 = 256\text{MB}$
p0	SDRAM	128MB	100	b_3	T
p0	Fan	Twin	60	b_4	$m_1 = 750$
p0	Fan	Single	p_3	b_5	$(b_1 = 1 \rightarrow p_3 = 30) \wedge (b_1 = 0 \rightarrow p_3 = 40)$

have introduced *dynamic constraint operations* to quantify variables without explicitly specifying them.

In the following, we describe the operations of the DCA. The standard operations of the traditional relational algebra can be extended to the constraint database version.

- **Union, Difference, Cartesian Product:** For constraint relations r and s, the union, difference and Cartesian product are denoted as $r \cup s$, $r - s$, and $r \times s$, respectively. Boolean operations on constraints are associated to those set operations. For $r \times s$, one tuple of r and one tuple of s are joined and AND of their constraints becomes result.
- **Selection, Projection, Substitution:** For a constraint relation r, $\sigma_F(r)$ gives the selection of r by the condition formula F, where each tuple's constraint is combined with F by AND, and the tuple will be in the result if the new constraint is satisfiable. The projection $\pi_A(r)$ is similar to the traditional projection. The substitution $S_\theta(r)$ gives the constraint relation such that θ is a mapping from variables to constants, and each variable v in r is replaced by $\theta(v)$, and the new tuples whose constraints are satisfiable will be in the result.

The following three operations are dynamic constraint operations, and they are unique to the DCA. The Boolean operation gives universal or existential quantification over all the variables of each tuple's constraint. The cardinality and dependency operations are specialized on the class of equivalence constraints, where number of satisfying constants for a certain variable is examined.

- **Boolean:** The Boolean operation has two forms: B_T and B_M. $B_T(r)$ returns tuples whose constraints are true, while $B_M(r)$ returns tuples whose constraints are unsatisfiable, i.e., there exists a constant assignment which makes the constraint false.
- **Cardinality:** The cardinality operation $C_{|A|\alpha k}$ finds tuples satisfying the cardinality predicate $|A|\alpha k$ where A is an attribute, $|A|$ is the number of constants such that the tuple's constraint is satisfiable if the constant is assigned to A, α is a comparison operation in $\{<, =, >\}$, and k is a non-negative number where k can be the infinity symbol ∞.

- **Dependency:** The dependency operation has two forms: $D_{cv(A)\beta Dep}$ and $D_{x\beta Dep}$. Here, Dep is the set of variables such that a tuple's constraint is dependent on. For each tuple, Dep is calculated and the predicate $cv(A)\beta Dep$ or $x\beta Dep$ is evaluated. Symbol $cv(A)$ is a variable on attribute A, if the value for A is actually a variable; otherwise the predicate is evaluated as true. Symbol x is a variable; this form is used for directly specifying a variable. Symbol β is a membership operator in $\{\in, \notin\}$. Dependency operation can be used to find tuples satisfying a given dependency relationship between variables and constraints.

Adopting constraint databases has drawback of increased complexities in query evaluation. Testing satisfiabilities of equivalence constraints is NP-complete. However, in practical situations we have to pay attentions on what subclasses of constraints we are actually dealing with. We could find a number of polynomial-time solvable constraint subclasses. Constraints of airline tickets we are modeling in this paper also have efficient algorithms.

3   E-commerce of Multiple-Incentive Merchandises

3.1   Incentive

Incentive rules can be regarded as a classification of goods according to various aspects of added values of the goods. Vendors design incentive rules to guide or attract buyers to a specific class of goods. In the following, we give a classification of incentive rules.

Selection Rule: This is a rule offering choices of goods to buyers, and optionally gives pricing to each type. In the example of airline tickets, days of the week, terms, flight names and others can be selection parameters. It is usual that prices are different according to choices. There are selections that offer low prices in exchange for restricted conditions such as valid only on weekdays.

Combination Rule: This is a subclass of selection rules. It describes permitted combinations of goods.

Penalty Rule: This is a rule on penalties or forfeits applied when a buyer changes the contents of a contract. It is considered as a subclass of selection rules. One example is charges for cancellation and change of reservation of airline, hotel, and rent-a-car. Some merchandises have lower price but higher penalty than others.

Qualification Rule: This rule describes conditions which a buyer should fulfill upon his/her purchase of goods. Examples are child/senior discount, and restriction of selling liquor to nonage. The seller checks whether the buyer fulfills qualification or the buyer declares voluntarily. Qualification rules do not provide choices to buyers.

Exception Rule: This rule describes exceptional conditions applied only to a limited subclass of goods beside the main classification. Examples of exception rules are such as prize, discount by coupons or promotion codes, bargain sale, exception of handling charges for a specific item and so on. It generally comes from the sales promotion strategy of sellers.

Besides the above classification, it is important to provide a scheme to compare constraints representing rules for various purposes. For example, a buyer wants to know which ticket is more (less) restrictive than others, or which option is more valuable (besides the price) than others. We define two types of comparison: *total-order comparison* and *partial-order comparison*. We assume that a total order $\leq_v$ is defined on the values for a variable v.

Total-order comparison. Suppose that constraints r_1 and r_2 have unique satisfying constants c_1 and c_2, respectively. Then we define that $r_1 \leq_v r_2$ holds iff $c_1 \leq_v c_2$ holds.

Partial-order comparison. Suppose that for $i = [1, 2]$, C_i is the set of constants such that r_i is satisfiable if a constant in C_i is assigned to v. Then, $r_1 \subseteq_v r_2$ holds iff $C_1 \subseteq C_2$ holds.

In general, constraints have multiple satisfying constants on a variable, and in this case total-order comparison is undefined. It is possible to define more varieties of comparisons by combining total order and set containment, but it is beyond the scope of this paper.

Based on the meaning of variables, we can assign interpretations of total- and partial-order comparisons. For example, a ticket selection rule r_1 can be said as more restrictive than another rule r_2 if $r_1 \subseteq_{v_d} r_2$ holds in partial-order comparison on variable v_d, where we assume that v_d represents valid days of tickets.

4   Modeling Incentive Rules of Airline Tickets

We take the case of airline tickets sales as an example of multiple incentives, because airline tickets are already treated on actual e-commerce sites and also have various instances of incentives such as selection rules, penalty rules, and qualification rules, resulting in a complex price system. Examples of selection rules are early purchase discount and weekday discount. On the other hand, occasional discount offers based on sellers' business strategy are also presented and they work as exception rules. How restrictive or how valuable those rules are affects their price. Buyers have to examine whether those rules match their constraints and requirements. However, this task is costly for the buyers because they have to read long lines of texts.

In the current ticket selling sites, the following sequence of processes is typical for reservation.

1. A buyer specifies the date of his/her departure, origin and destination.
2. A list of tickets sorted by price is displayed.
3. He/she reads and compares rules described in a natural language and choose one to purchase.

At step 2., more than dozens of tickets can be listed and it is not easy to compare how the rules differ. Our approach has the following steps: replace these rules to constraints, query and compare them logically, and support buyers to choose optimum tickets.

4.1   Example of Ticket Rules

We have collected ticket data of round trip between Los Angeles and New York from Travelocity.com[1], which is a popular sale-by-subscription site. We transformed those data to constraint relations. We describe the process in the following.

As described in the previous section, various incentive rules are used in airline tickets, so that a large number of different tickets exist. For example, there are about 80 types of tickets between LA and NY. It is necessary to provide a tool to assist buyers to find out reasons why one ticket has lower price than others.

The rules attached to the tickets can be classified into rules on describing when the ticket is valid (corresponding to selection rule), rules on the procedure of purchase, change or cancellation (penalty rule), rules on surcharge or discount (exception rule), and rules on combining routes (combination rule). The factors that mainly affect the prices are rules on valid terms and procedures.

4.2   Constraint Representation

The rules of the tickets were transformed to dynamic constraints in the way described as follows:

- Tickets are gathered up by each airline company and differences within one company are expressed in constraint formulae as selection rules.
- Fundamental information which appears in almost all tickets such as price was made into attributes, and other individual conditions were expressed as a part of constraint formulae.

The attribute list of the constructed constraint relation is shown in Table 2. T and P in the column Type, mean total-order comparison and partial-order comparison, respectively. A part of the constraint relation is shown in Table 3.

5   Queries for Searching and Comparing Ticket Rules

5.1   Matchmaking

When buyers are going to search and compare tickets, they will provide their requests and wishes. We may represent them in a constraint relation. The relation should represent where and when to go to the destination (correspond to attribute AD, AW, AT, LT), the range of price (PR), when to purchase ("just

---

[1] http://www.travelocity.com/

Table 2. The Attributes of Constraint Relations for Airline Tickets

Attribute Name		Description	Type
Airline	AL	Name of Airline Vendor	—
Price	PR	Price of Ticket	T
Advance Purchase	AP	There are restrictions such as "Buyers must purchase the ticket before 14 days of the departure." This is a selection rule.	T
Ticket Issue by	TI	There are restrictions such as "This ticket must be purchased by 2001/11/10." This is a selection rule.	T
Available Date	AD	Restricts the date of departure	P
Available Day of the Week	AW	There are restrictions like "Only available on Tue, Wed, Thu." This is a selection rule.	P
Available Time	AT		P
Latest Travel	LT		T
Minimum Stay	MS	There are restrictions such as "Return travel is valid on 1st Sun."	T
Latest Return	LR		T
Reroute	RR	There are restrictions such as "Passenger can change when to travel but cannot change where to go." This is a penalty rule.	P
Change Charge	CC	Penalty for changing ticketed reservation. This is a penalty rule.	T
Co-Terminals	CT		P
Stop Over	SO		T

now", "later" etc. correspond to MS), when to return(MS, LR), and the possibility of changes(CC). The relation can be regarded as selection rules of the buyers. They need not tell all of their requirements and can leave some of them unspecified.

An example of a buyer's requests is shown in Table 4. Buyers can express complex requests such as "in the case of A, request B and C, but in the case of D, request E or F". Matchmaking rules of sellers and buyers' wishes can be done by a join operation (equivalent to Cartesian product and selection). Selection operation also finds tuples – in this case, tickets – such that satisfy specified conditions. Substitution operations can be used as decision on available options.

As an example, we take the join of FlightList (Table 3) and Wish (Table 4). by the query $P = \sigma_{PR=Price}\sigma_{AD=Date}(\text{FlightList} \times \text{Wish})$, to matchmake the buyer's request and tickets. We may examine properties of P using the following queries:

$B_T(P)$ testing satisfiability

$D_{cv(PR)\in Dep}(P)$ searching tickets whose price varies with selection

$S_{MS="1stSun"}(P)$ making decision that "return after the 1st Sunday"

$C_{|AD|>1}(C_{|PR|>1}(P))$ searching tickets that price and date have corelation

5.2 Comparison

Now we discuss comparing tickets by total-order and partial-order comparisons. Firstly, let us consider total-order comparison. The attribute Advance Purchase

Table 3. Constraint Relation: FlightList (Part)

AL	PR	AP	AD	AW	AT	MS	Constraint
AW	pr_0	21 days	ad_0	d	10:00-12:00	ms_0	$pr_0 = \{\text{"339"}\mid\text{"384"}\mid\text{"453"}\}$ $\wedge(ad_0 \neq \{\text{"01/11/22"}\mid\text{"01/11/23"}$ $\mid\text{"01/12/23"}\ldots\text{"01/12/31"}\}$ $\rightarrow ms_0 = \text{"1st Sun"})$ $\wedge(ad_0 = \{\text{"01/11/22"}\mid\text{"01/11/23"}$ $\mid\text{"01/12/23"}\ldots\text{"01/12/31"}\}$ $\rightarrow ms_0 = \text{"No Restriction"})$
AA	pr_1	ap_1	ad_1	aw_1	at_1	1st Sun	$pr_1 = \{\text{"339"}\mid\text{"453"}\mid\text{"536"}\}$ $\wedge pr_1 = \{\text{"339"}\mid\text{"453"}\}$ $\rightarrow (ap_1 = \text{"21 days"} \wedge$ $at_1 = \text{"6:30AM-12:30AM"})$ $\wedge pr_1 = \text{"339"} \rightarrow aw_1 = \{\text{"Tue"}\mid\text{"Wed"}\}$ $\wedge pr_1 = \text{"536"}$ $\rightarrow (ap_1 = \text{"14 days"}$ $\wedge aw_1 = \{\text{"Mon"}\mid\text{"Tue"}\mid\text{"Wed"}\mid\text{"Thu"}\}$ $\wedge \neg ad_1 = \{\text{"01/11/21"}\mid\text{"01/11/26"}\})$
ATA	pr_2	ap_2	ad_2	aw_2	d	1 day	$pr_2 = \{\text{"225"}\mid\text{"271"}\mid\text{"316"}\mid\text{"340"}$ $\mid\text{"384"}\mid\text{"407"}\mid\text{"498"}\}$ $\wedge pr_2 = \{\text{"225"}\mid\text{"316"}\}$ $\rightarrow aw_2 = \{\text{"Tue"}\mid\text{"Wed"}\mid\text{"Sat"}\}$ $\wedge pr_2 = \text{"340"} \rightarrow ap_2 = \text{"3 days"}$

Table 4. Constraint Relation of Buyer's Wish: Wish

Price	Date	Condition
pr	dt	$(dt = \text{"2/14"} \vee dt = \text{"2/15"}) \wedge$ $(pr = \text{"398"} \vee pr = \text{"453"})$

(AP) has an obvious total order such like 21 days is more restrictive than 14days. We intend to sort the tickets by AP to find the least restrictive one. However, some tickets may have several options for AP because a certain selection rule is imposed on those tickets. We use the query $C_{|AP|=1}(P)$ to find tickets such that options on AP are reduced to a singleton set by the buyer's request Wish. Now we can sort the result by AP and obtain the answer.

As for partial-order comparison, let us assume that we would like to compare tickets by Available Day of the Week (AW). Here a ticket t_1 is more restrictive than another ticket t_2 if t_1's available days are contained by t_2's available days, as P is the comparison type of AW in Table 2. The set of available days is defined by a selection rule. Now this partial-order comparison is formulated as $t_1 \subseteq_{AW} t_2$, as we defined in Section 3. To evaluate the comparison, we perform the following: (1) Let t_1 be a ticket and let Q be a constraint relation of a singleton tuple such that the tuple represents t_1. For each tuple in P and Q, rename the variable on AW to a common variable v_{AW}. Also rename variables of Q appropriately so that Q's variables are isolated from P's variables except v_{AW}. Now we take the difference $P - Q$, and the result consists of tickets s_1 such that $t_1 \subseteq_{v_{AW}} s_1$ holds, thus the partial-order comparison is done.

We implemented a prototype of this airline ticket searching system as an web application. It works with the DCA query processing engine we have developed. The queries shown in the previous section can be evaluated on this system.

6   Conclusion

In this paper, incentive rules on commercial goods were considered and techniques for searching and comparing those rules were investigated. We have categorized incentive rules into several classes, and discussed methods to query and compare those rules using the dynamic constraint algebra. We took an example of online airline tickets, and it is shown that our model can deal with various complicated restrictions.

References

1. M. Bichler and H. Werthner, "A Classification Framework of Multidimensional, Multi-Unit Procurement Auctions", *Proceedings of the DEXA Workshop on Negotiations in Electronic Markets*, Greenwich, UK, September 4-8, 2000.
2. H. Boley, S. Tabet and G. Wagner, "Design Rationale of RuleML" *A Markup Language for Semantic Web Rules, Semantic Web Working Symposium*, July/August 2001, Stanford, 2001.
3. H. Boley, "The Rule Markup Language: RDF-XML Data Model, XML Schema Hierarchy, and XSL transformations", *INAP2001*, Tokyo, October 2001.
4. B. N. Grosof, Y. Labrou and H. Y. Chan, "A Declarative Approach to Business Rules in Contracts: Courteous Logic Programs in XML", *E-COMMERCE 99*, Denver, Colorado,1999.
5. IBM Common Rules, http://alphaworks.ibm.com.
6. M. Iwaihara, "Supporting Dynamic Constraints for Commerce Negotiations," *2nd Int. Workshop in Advanced Issues of E-Commerce and Web-Information Systems* (WECWIS), IEEE Press, pp. 12–20, June 2000.
7. M. Iwaihara, "Matching and Deriving Dynamic Constraints for E-Commerce Negotiations," *Proc. Workshop on Technologies for E-Services*, Cairo, Sep. 2000.
8. D. Konopnicki, L. Leiba, O. Shmueli, and Y. Sagiv, "A Formal Yet Practical Approach to Electronic Commerce," *Proc. CoopIS*, pp.197-208, 1999.
9. G. Kuper, L. Libkin, J. Paredaens (eds.), *"Constraint Databases,"* Springer-Verlag, 2000.
10. D. M. Reeves, M. P. Wellman, and B. N. Grosof, "Automated Negotiation from Declarative Contact Descriptions," *Proc. AGENTS'01*, ACM Press, 2001.

XML Query Processing Using Signature and DTD[*]

Sangwon Park[1], Yoonra Choi[2], and Hyoung-Joo Kim[3]

[1] Department of Digital Contents, Sejong Cyber University, Seoul, Korea
swpark@cybersejong.ac.kr
[2] Korea Computer Communications, Ltd., Seoul, Korea
yulla@unisql.com
[3] School of Computer Science and Engineering, Seoul National University, Seoul,
Korea
hjk@oopsla.snu.ac.kr

Abstract. Having emerged as a standard web language, XML has become the core of e-business solution. XML is a semistructured data that is represented as graph, which is a distinctive feature compared to other data dealt with existing database. And query is represented as regular path expression, which is evaluated by traversing each node of the graph. In XML document with DTD, the DTD may be able to provide many valuable hints on query optimization, because it has information on the structure of the document. Using signature and information from DTD, we can minimize the traverse of nodes and quickly execute the XML query of regular path expression fast.

1 Introduction

One of the most attractive technologies in the 21st century would be XML. Various kinds of standards have been established, and much more data will be represented by XML. XML is very similar to semistructured data[1,2] which is based on the OEM model.

The query on semistructured data often contains regular path expression which requires much more flexible query processing than the ones for relational or object oriented databases for retrieving irregular and sometimes unknown structure. Several indexing methods for semistructured data are proposed[6,8, 9].

The signature method has been proposed to process queries[3,5,11,14]. This method reduces the search space according to result value from bit operations of hash values. When an XML data is stored in object repositories and each node is stored as an object, the signature method can be used, which decreases the number of fetching nodes during query processing[10]. However this method has a problem that the signature bits can be saturated when the number of sub elements or the depth of the tree is increased. And at the same time, there

---

[*] This work was supported by the Brain Korea 21 Project.

K. Bauknecht, A M. Tjoa, G. Quirchmayr (Eds.): EC-Web 2002, LNCS 2455, pp. 162–171, 2002.
© Springer-Verlag Berlin Heidelberg 2002

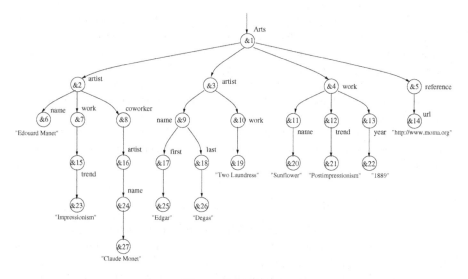

Fig. 1. DOM graph

has been studies on query processing using DTD information which has the structural hints as to an XML document[13].

In this paper we propose to improve the performance of query processing using both signature and DTD which are helpful to reduce the search space. To do this, we first find all possible paths suitable for the given query in DTD declaration and merge them into one query graph. Whenever visiting each node in DOM, we compare between the signature of a node in the data graph and the query graph. It reduces the search space and minimize the number of fetching node in object repositories.

The remainder of this paper is organized as follows: Section 2 presents related works. Section 3 briefly explains what a signature is. The sequential steps of query optimization using signature and DTD are given in Section 4 and 5. And Section 6 discuss the experimental results. Finally, conclusions and future works are presented in Section 7.

2   Related Work

The query on XML often contains regular path expressions. This means the expression of a query contains wild cards like *, $, and so on. DataGuide[6] can decrease query processing time by the path index which gives a dynamic outline of the structure of semistructured data. But this is only applicable to the query with single regular expression and not applicable to the query with complex regular expression having various ones. The 2-Index[9] overcomes the weak point of previous work, but the size of indexes may be the square of the data nodes. T-Index partially solved the problems in 2-Index, but still could not overcome the problem where indexes can not cover all possible paths.

The query processing techniques using signature also have been largely studied [3,5,14,10]. In relational database, the signature technique is used to select matched tuples by select condition[3]. The signature is used in object-oriented database to reduce page I/O when evaluate the path expression[14]. However, regular path expressions can not be processed by these methods.

Lore[7] and eXcelon[4] are the representative databases that deal with semistructured data or XML. These keep the structure of graph for atypical data and store the nodes of the graph as objects. As the query is processed by visiting nodes of a tree, the reduction of the node fetching is the key point for query optimization.

3   Preview on Signature

XML data can be depicted as a tree such as Figure 1. If each node in this graph is stored as an object in object repository, the objects have to be visited when evaluating regular path expression.

The method of generating a signature is the similar to the one of [5] where a signature is built from hash values of element labels. Each node of DOM tree is stored as an object with a signature. The signature of each node is hash value from label of the matching element. An upper node contains signature information of the lower nodes and the signature is generated by bit-wise ORing of the signatures of lower nodes. Let the hash value of a node n_i be H_j, the signature be S_i, and the child node of n_i be n_j. On this assumption, it is true that $S_i = H_i \vee (\bigvee_j S_j)$. For example, the signature value of node &9 in Figure 1 is the result of bit-wise ORing of the signatures of nodes &17, &18, and the hash values to names of the nodes.

An example for traversing nodes of DOM tree using signature is as follows. For node &2 in Figure 1, the bit-wise AND of signatures results in like

$$H_{\text{``coworker''}} \wedge S_{\&2} \equiv H_{\text{``coworker''}}$$

So it is possible that the node with label of coworker exists in the sub-tree of node &2. But in the case of node &4, the result is

$$H_{\text{``coworker''}} \wedge S_{\&4} \neq H_{\text{``coworker''}}$$

In this case, we can be sure that there is no node having the label, coworker, in the sub-tree, and thus we need not visit the child nodes of &4 [10].

4   Building DOM Based on Signature

As we have seen in Section 3, we traverse the sub-tree of a node only when the value of bit-wise AND of signature of the visited node and hash value of the required element is equal to the hash value. Otherwise, the sub-tree are not visited, which would reduce the search space and eventually speed up query processing.

```
<!ELEMENT Arts (artist+,work+)>
<!ELEMENT artist (name,work,coworker?>
<!ATTLIST artist name CDATA \#IMPLIED>
<!ELEMENT work (#PCDATA | name | trend | year)*>
<!ELEMENT reference (url)>
<!ATTLIST reference url CDATA #IMPLIED>
<!ELEMENT coworker (artist)>
<!ELEMENT name (#PCDATA | (first, last))>
<!ELEMENT trend (#PCDATA)>
<!ELEMENT year (#PCDATA)>
<!ELEMENT first (#PCDATA)>
<!ELEMENT last (#PCDATA)>
```

Fig. 2. DTD

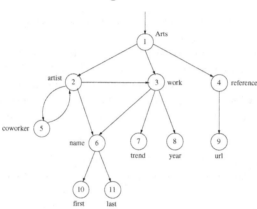

Fig. 3. DTD graph

However, if there is more elements or if the sub-tree is deeper, it is more likely that all bits of signature are set to '1'. We call thus saturation. If saturation occurs in node n_i, the equation $H_l \wedge S_i \equiv H_l$ is true even if the label l does not exist in the sub-tree of node n_i. This problem can be solved by extracting only indeterminate elements.

4.1 Extraction of Indeterminate Elements

Unlike [10], this paper does not obtain hash values from all elements. Figure 2 is DTD of the Figure 1. The DTD can be depicted as Figure 3. Following the definition in DTD, each element can be separated into either determinate or indeterminate one. It can be judged by the definition of sub-element of an element. There is a quantity indicator attached to the sub-element such as '?', '*', or '+'. The mark '?' or '*' means that this element may not appear in the XML document. While '+' means that this element must appear in the XML

Table 1. Hash values of the labels

Arts	00000000	first	11000110	artist	00000000	last	11011000
work	00000000	trend	11111100	reference	00000000	year	10001111
coworker	11001110	url	00000000	name	11000110		

Table 2. Signatures of each Node

&1	11111111	&2	11111110	&3	11111110	&4	11111111	&5	00000000
&6	11000110	&7	11111110	&8	11001110	&9	11011110	&10	00000000
&11	11000110	&12	11111100	&13	10001111	&14	00000000	&15	11111100
&16	11001110	&17	11000110	&18	11011000	&24	11000110		

document once or more time. The former is an indeterminate element, while the latter is called a determinate one.

And a sequence connector of sub-elements may be ',' or '|'. The connector ',' means that the elements will be enumerated in order. On the other hand, '|' means that only one of the elements connected by '|' may appear but it can not be known in advance which one will appear in the actual XML document. Therefore, the elements connected by ',' are determinate, while the ones connected by '|' are indeterminate.

Definition 1 *The element with quantity indicator is '?' or '*' and the elements connected by '|' are defined as indeterminate. All the other elements are defined as determinate.*

4.2   Generating DOM Based on Signature

It is assumed that each node in DOM tree is stored as an object with a signature. The signature of each node is evaluated by bit-wise ORing from hash values and signatures of child nodes. The process for calculating the signature of a node follows Algorithm 1.

5   Query Optimization Using a Query Graph

5.1   Generating Query Graph

We extract all paths satisfying the given query in advance, which means that we are filtering the sequences of labels to visit. We visit only the nodes on the paths which limit the scope of search. This section will explain how all paths for the given query is extracted.

Example 1 *The NFA of regular path expression* Arts.*.name *is as follows. This is generated by the rules defined in [10].*

Algorithm 1 MakeSignature(node)

1: s ← 0
2: **if** node is an Element or Attribute node **then**
3:    **for** each ChildNode of node **do**
4:       s ← s ∨ MakeSignature(ChildNode) /* bit-wise ORing */
5:       **if** node is indeterminate **then**
6:          s ← s ∨ hash value of node
7:       **end if**
8:    **end for**
9: **end if**
10: node.signature ← s

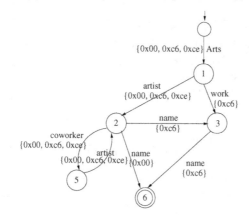

Fig. 4. Query Graph

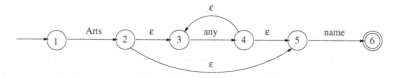

We transform the regular path expression into NFA. Example 1 shows the NFA of a regular path expression. Then we traverse the DOM graph such as Figure 3 to get a query graph. Figure 4 is the query graph of the query in Example 1. The labels of the query graph is different from the DTD graph. The label of a node is attached to in-coming edges. The signature of the query graph is made by propagating the hash value of the indeterminate label from final node to the start node. The detailed algorithm is described in [12].

5.2 Query Optimization Using a Query Graph

The signature of each node in the DOM tells which labels exist in the sub-tree. And the signature list in the query graph represents the summary of required labels satisfying the given query. Especially in the case of signature list, only indeterminate elements are considered. By comparing the label and the signature of the node in DOM and the edge in query graph, we determine whether to traverse the sub-tree of the node or not. If the labels are not the same or even if the signature of the node of DOM is not matched with any others in the signature list of the edge in query graph, we will not traverse the sub-tree. Algorithm 2 is the scan operator which returns the nodes satisfying the query in DOM tree.

The function ForwardLabel() first compares the labels between the DOM and the query graph. If they are the same, then it compares the signatures between them. This means that we reduce the search space by filtering the nodes through the query paths first and comparing the signatures next.

Algorithm 2 next()

```
 1: /* states: state set of QueryGraph */
 2: node ← next node by DFS from DOM
 3: while node is not NULL do
 4:    forwardLabel(states,node)
 5:    if existFinal(states) then
 6:       return node
 7:    end if
 8:    if isReject(states) then
 9:       node ← next node by DFS from DOM
10:    end if
11: end while
```

Example 2 *If the nodes in the DOM of Figure 1 have the signatures of Table 2, the node fetching process for query of Example 1 using query graph is as follows.*

First the node &1 is read, then the state set S={2}. As the nodes are visited in the DFS order, first child &2 is read and S={3}. Again the first child &6 is read and S={4}, where query graph arrives the final state. So the node &6 is returned. The state transition occurs only when the label and the signature of the node is equal to those of the edge of query graph.

The sibling of node &6 is node &7, where S={5} and the label to appear in the query graph is name*. But not even if child of &7 do not have the label* name *at all, therefore we do not traverse the sub-tree of &7. Instead &8, the sibling node of &7, is read. By doing this repeatedly, the nodes &6, &24, &9 and &11 are returned in sequence as a result.*

6 Experimental Results

In this section, we will analyze the experimental results of two methods of query optimization, i.e.,the one using signatures only[10] and the other, proposed in this paper, using signature and DTD together. As can be seen from the comparison

Table 3. Characteristics of the XML Files

	No. of Nodes	File Size
Shakespeare	537,621	7.5 Mbytes
Bibliography	19,854	247 Kbytes
The Book of Mormon	142,751	6.7 Mbytes

Table 4. Queries Used in the Experiment

Q1	Shakespeare	PLAY//STAGEDIR
Q2	Shakespeare	//SPEECH//STAGEDIR
Q3	The Book of Mormon	tstmt//p
Q4	The Book of Mormon	//sura/epigraph
Q5	Bibliography	bibliography//'in.*'/year
Q6	Bibliography	//misc

results of the number of node fetching and the number of page I/O, the latter method shows the better efficiency than the first.

6.1 Conditions of Experiment

The programs are coded by JAVA, and the data used in this experiment are Shakespeare, The Book of Mormon, and Michael Lay's bibliography. Six queries are used and are described in Table 4. The first queries for each document retrieve the nodes which are located on the specific path. And the second queries retrieve the nodes located at arbitrary positions of DOM tree. The signature technique for query optimization of [10] is targeted to compare with the technique of this paper.

6.2 Performance Evaluation

In Figure 5, the vertical axis represents the number of node fetching and the horizontal axis represents the size of signature. A zero sized signature means the method not using signature.

In Figure 5 (a), the number of fetching nodes has decreased to 1/40. In the case of Q3 at Figure 5 (b), the number of fetching nodes has decreased 1/10 and 1/7 times for 0 and 1 byte of signature, respectively, and 1/1660 for two or more bytes. And for Q4, the number of fetching nodes decreased to 1/10 times as small as the one of [10] for zero size signature, and the number of fetching nodes converges for one more bytes of signature. Even in (c), the number of fetching nodes decreased to half in Q5 and decreased from half to less converging point in Q6.

As we have seen from the results in Figure 5, the query optimization using both signature and DTD greatly decreases the number of fetching nodes. Especially the number of fetching nodes is dramatically dropped for one or two bytes

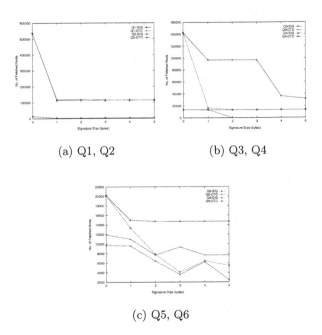

(a) Q1, Q2   (b) Q3, Q4

(c) Q5, Q6

Fig. 5. The number of fetching nodes

of signature, and maintained for more bytes of signature. This is a very strong point that the performance of less bytes signature is equivalent to larger ones, because we are able to decrease the bytes of signature.

The results show that the performance improvement of query optimization is better for the graph of long depth, but is less for the graph of wide breath. This is related to the fact that the deeper the graph, the greater the probability of signature saturation to occur. Bibliography is the data with the structure of slight depth and wide breath. Considering the results of Q3 and Q4, the difference in the number of fetching nodes fetching between the method of [10] and the one proposed in this paper is less than the difference in Q1 and Q2 for Shakespeare.

And as in Q3, if the regular path expression like '//' is not contained in the path expression of query, the number of fetching nodes largely decreases. This is because the query path in DTD is determined uniquely.

7   Conclusion

In the previous sections, we have proposed the technique of XML query optimization using both signature and DTD. By processing the regular path expression with query graph, the numbers of fetching nodes. largely decreased. Especially it shows greater efficiency improvement with even smaller size of signature than the one of [10]. This eventually means that the small size of storage for a node is needed.

Contrary to the efficiency improvement in the selection query, the insertion and deletion queries cause propagation overheads to change signatures of parent nodes. In the latter case, the cost usually exceeds the one of selection query. But most queries on XML document are selections, therefore this paper do not consider the modification queries. The process of changing the signatures of each node in DOM is like the algorithm in [10].

The DTD given by XML v1.0 is insufficient in the respect of providing the accurate and comprehensive information on the structure of XML document. XML schema is the definition format that can overcome such defects in DTD. Thus, the performance of query optimization may be improved by using XML schema and research on it should be considered as future work.

References

1. Serge Abiteboul. Querying Semistructured Data. *International Conference on Database Theory*, January 1997.
2. P. Buneman. Semistructured Data. *ACM SIGACT-SIGMOD-SIGART Symposium on Principles of Database Systems*, May 1997.
3. Walter W. Chang and Hans J. Schek. A Signature Access Method for the Starburst Database System. *VLDB*, 1989.
4. eXcelon. An XML Data Server For Building Enterprise Web Applications. *http://www.odi.com/products/white_papers.html*, 1999.
5. Chris Faloutsos. Signature files: Design and Performance Comparison of Some Signature Extraction Methods. *SIGMOD*, 1985.
6. Roy Goldman and Jennifer Widom. DataGuides: Enabling Query Formulation and Optimization in Semistructured Databases. *VLDB*, 1997.
7. Jason McHugh, Serge Abiteboul, Roy Goldman, Dallan Quass, and Jennifer Widom. Lore: A Database Management System for Semistructured Data. *SIGMOD Record*, 26(3), 9 1997.
8. Jason McHugh and Jennifer Widom. Query Optimization for XML. *VLDB*, 1999.
9. Tova Milo and Dan Suciu. Index Structures for Path Expressions. *ICDT*, 1999.
10. Sangwon Park and Hyoung-Joo Kim. A New Query Processing Technique for XML Based on Signature. *7th International Conference on DASFAA*, pages 22–29, April 2001.
11. R. Sacks-Davis, A. Kent, and K. Ramamohanarao. Multikey Access Methods Based on Superimposed Coding Techniques. *TODS*, 12(4), 1984.
12. Sangwon Park and Yoonra Choi and Hyoung-Joo Kim. XML Query Optimization using Signature and DTD. *Technical report http://swpark.pe.kr/publication.html*, November 2001.
13. Tae-Sun Chung and Hyoung-Joo Kim. Extracting Indexing Information from XML DTDs. *Information Processing Letters*, 81(2), 2002.
14. Hwan-Seung Yong, Sukho Lee, and Hyoung-Joo Kim. Applying Signatures for Forward Traversal Query Processing in Object-Oriented Databases. *ICDE*, 1994.

Modelling and Predicting Web Page Accesses Using Burrell's Model

Devanshu Dhyani, Sourav S. Bhowmick, and Wee Keong Ng

School of Computer Engineering, Nanyang Technological University,
Singapore 639798
{assourav, awkng}@ntu.edu.sg

Abstract. The significance of modeling and measuring various attributes of the Web in part or as a whole is undeniable. In this paper, we consider the application of patterns in browsing behavior of users for predicting access to Web documents. We proposed two models for addressing our specification of the access prediction problem. The first lays out a preliminary statistical approach using observed distributions of interaccess times of individual documents in the collection. To overcome its deficiencies, we adapted a stochastic model for library circulations, i.e., *Burrell's model*, that accounts for differences in mean access rates of Web documents. We verified the assumptions of this model with experiments performed on a server log of accesses recorded over a six month period. Our results show that the model is reasonably accurate in predicting Web page access probabilities based on the history of accesses.

1 Introduction

The importance of measuring attributes of known objects in precise quantitative terms has for long been recognized as crucial for enhancing our understanding of our environment. In this paper, we focus on characterizing the usage of Web resources from the perspective of modeling and predicting Web page accesses. We begin by relating Web page access modeling to prediction for efficient information retrieval on the WWW and consider a preliminary statistical approach that relies on the distribution of interaccess times. The deficiencies are addressed by adapting a more refined stochastic model due to Burrell [1,2,3] to the context of Web page accesses. We discuss in detail results of experiments for verifying and applying Burrell's model for access prediction.

Let us first elucidate the general access prediction problem. Our basic premise is that page accesses should be predicted based on universally available information on past accesses such as server access logs. Given a document repository and history of past accesses, we would like to know which documents are more likely to be accessed within a certain interval and how frequently they are expected to be accessed. The information used for prediction, typically found in server logs comprises the time and URL of an HTTP request. The identity of the client is necessary only if access prediction is personalized for the client. From this information about past accesses, several predictor variables can be determined,

K. Bauknecht, A M. Tjoa, G. Quirchmayr (Eds.): EC-Web 2002, LNCS 2455, pp. 172–181, 2002.
© Springer-Verlag Berlin Heidelberg 2002

for example, the frequency of accesses within a time interval and inter-access times.

2   Statistical Prediction

An obvious prediction is the time until the next expected access to a document, say A. The duration can be derived from a distribution of time intervals between successive accesses. This kind of statistical prediction relates a predictor variable or a set of predictor variables to access probability for a large sample assumed to be representative of the entire population. Future accesses to a document can then be predicted from the probability distribution using current measurements of its predictor variable(s). A variant of this approach is to use separate distributions for individual documents measured from past accesses.

Let us illustrate the above approach for temporal prediction using interaccess time. Suppose $f(t)$ is the access density function denoting the probability that a document is accessed at time t after its last access or its *interaccess time probability density*. Intuitively, the probability that a document is accessed depends on the time since its last access and duration into the future we are predicting. At any arbitrary point in time, the probability that a document A is accessed at a time T from now is given by $\Pr\{A \text{ is accessed at } T\} = f(\delta + T)$ where δ is the *age* or the time since the last access to the document. The function $f(t)$ has a cumulative distribution $F(t) = \sum_{t'=0}^{\infty} f(t')$ which denotes the probability that a document will be accessed *within* time t from now. Since $f(t)$ is a probability density, $F(\infty) = 1$, meaning that the document will certainly be accessed sometime in the future. If $f(t)$ is represented as a continuous distribution, the instantaneous probability when $\delta, T \to 0$ is zero, which makes short term or immediate prediction difficult. To find the discrete density $f(t)$ from the access logs, we calculate the proportion of document accesses that occur t time units after the preceding access for t ranging from zero to infinity. This approach assumes that all documents have identical interaccess time distributions, that is, all accesses are treated the same, irrespective of the documents they involve and that the distributions are free from periodic changes in access patterns (such as weekends when interaccess times are longer.) The implication of the first assumption is that the prediction is not conditioned on frequency of past accesses since all documents in the observed repository are assumed equally likely to be accessed giving rise to identical frequency distributions.

Since frequency distributions are more likely to vary between documents than not, it is clear that the above assumptions make this analysis suitable only on a per-document basis. However, the approach still holds, notwithstanding that the distribution $F(t)$ is now specific to a particular document. To predict the probability of access within time T from now, for a particular document A, we may use A's distribution function $F_A(t)$ to obtain $F_A(\delta + T)$ where δ is the age at the current time. If the interaccess time distributions are similar but not identical, we could condition these distributions on the parameters and find distributions of these parameters across the documents.

Our use of a single predictor, the interaccess time, obtained from the age δ and prediction interval T does not imply that the technique is univariate. The use of multiple predictors, such as the frequency of accesses in a given previous interval can easily be accommodated into a multidimensional plot of access probability. The method becomes complicated when several dimensions are involved. To alleviate this, we may derive a combined metric from the predictor variables, transforming the problem back to univariate prediction. However, this requires empirical determination of correlation between predictors and subsequently a combination function.

Given the statistical principle, one might naturally be led to ask how the distribution $F(t)$ (or its variant $F_A(t)$) can be used for actionable prediction. Recall that $F(t)$ is a cumulative probability distribution. For a given document age, it tells us the probability that a document is accessed within a certain interval of time. If a single probability distribution is used, this probability is an indicator of overall document usage with respect to time interval. If we use individual distributions $F_A(t)$, it can be used to compare the relative usage of documents. The expected time to next access, $\overline{T}$ is given by the mean of the distribution: $E[T] = \sum_{t=0}^{\infty} t \cdot f(t)$. The expected time $\overline{T}$ before the next access to a document, if it is known for all documents, can be used as a criteria for populating server side caches.

The temporal approach discussed above bases prediction on interaccess times. Equally, we may use a frequency based alternative for predicting access. A *frequency distribution* denotes the probability of a certain number of accesses to a document or a sample of documents over a *fixed* time interval. Using an analogous method to that discussed earlier, we can answer the following for prediction over the next time interval: (1) What is the probability that exactly N documents will be accessed? (2) What is the probability that N or more documents will be accessed? (3) How many documents are expected to be accessed?

This approach has the same drawbacks as discussed previously—it does not account for periodic changes in access rates, rather it aggregates them into a single distribution and accesses to all documents are treated the same. Finally, both temporal and frequency prediction may be combined to ascertain probabilities of a certain number of accesses during a given time period in the future.

3   Burrell's Stochastic Model

The temporal and frequency-based approaches for statistical access prediction aggregate access statistics—interaccess times and frequency of access—into a single distribution. By treating all document accesses identically, they do not distinguish documents that are more frequently accessed than others. Our experiments on server access logs collected over a six month period[1] show that Web documents have highly varying average frequency of access ranging from several hundred to just a few. This observation confirms the intuition that aggregated

---

[1] Center for Advanced Information Systems Web server, April to October 2000.

statistical distributions are not ideal for predicting document access in the Web environment. Adopting interaccess or frequency distributions for individual documents alleviates this problem, but makes the solution impractical due to the overhead in computing and storing distributions for all documents on the server.

To address the problem of differential access rates, we investigate a stochastic model for library loans originally introduced by Burrell [1,2,3]. Burrell's model accounts for the fact that some items are borrowed more often than others and explains the observed geometric distribution of circulation frequencies. We present the model in a generic context below.

Let us consider a static (not growing) collection of items over a fixed period of time, long enough to even out cyclic variations in accesses. The distribution of accesses, known as the *frequency of circulation distribution* (or FOC distribution) is observed to be *geometric*. That is, if the random variable X denotes the number of accesses to a randomly chosen item, then the probability of x accesses is given by

$$\Pr\{X = x\} = (1 - p)^{x-1}p \tag{1}$$

for $x = 1, 2, \ldots$ and where $0 < p < 1$. Acknowledging the differences in access patterns of individual items, we term the average number of times an item is accessed in a unit time as its *desirability* λ. Burrell makes the following assumptions regarding FOC and desirability distributions:

- Given an item with desirability λ, the number of times it is accessed is a *Poisson process* of rate λ. Thus if we denote with Λ the desirability of a randomly chosen item and by X the number of accesses to it in a unit period of time, the probability conditioned on Λ that this item is accessed x times in a unit time period is given by

$$\Pr\{X = x | \Lambda = \lambda\} = \frac{e^{-\lambda}\lambda^x}{x!} \tag{2}$$

for $x = 0, 1, 2, \ldots$
- Accordingly, in order for the overall distribution of X to be geometric, the distribution of desirabilities must be *negative exponential*. That is,

$$\Pr\{\Lambda \leqslant \lambda\} = 1 - e^{-\alpha\lambda} \tag{3}$$

for $\lambda \geqslant 0$.

The desirability distribution of Equation 3 is a cumulative distribution. The continuous exponential density function obtained by differentiation is $\alpha e^{-\alpha\lambda}$. The overall FOC is then defined in terms of the two densities using the law of total probability as follows[2]:

$$\Pr\{X = x\} = \int_0^\infty \frac{e^{-\lambda}\lambda^x}{x!}\lambda e^{-\alpha\lambda}dx = \left(\frac{1}{1+\alpha}\right)^{x-1}\left(1 - \frac{1}{1+\alpha}\right)$$

---

[2] The overall distribution is actually derived by convolving the generating functions of the desirability and conditional FOC distributions.

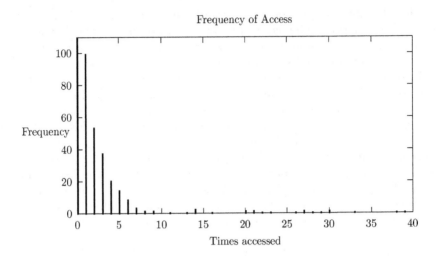

Fig. 1. Frequency of access histogram for approximately 900 pages in the CAIS Web server observed over one week.

Comparing with Equation 1, we see that the above is equivalent to a geometric distribution as observed, with $p = \alpha/(1+\alpha)$. Burrell's model has been generalized in [3] to account for the negative binomial distribution of loan frequencies by modeling the desirability as a gamma distribution. This model, known as the gamma mixture of Poisson processes has been widely applied in other contexts such as analyzing accident data, industrial sampling, and absenteeism data.

Burrell's model also accounts for items that have been implicitly out of circulation, (equivalent to "dead" Web pages.) Estimation of usage such as the expected number of items loaned out x times during a period and the probability that an item will not circulate during the period are discussed further in [4]. Finally, Burrell incorporates *ageing* whereby the desirability of an item decays exponentially with time according to the relationship: $\lambda(t) = \lambda e^{-\beta t}$; $t > 0$ and $\beta > 0$. The resulting distribution of loan frequencies is found to be negative binomial.

A limitation of Burrell's model is that it does not accommodate cyclic variations in access rate. Desirabilities computed over too short an interval may not be reflective of the longer term access patterns. Consequently, it can only be used to explain access patterns for durations long enough to iron out such variations.

3.1   Verification of Burrell's Model

We noted earlier that Web page access rates show high variance. Could this suggest a geometric distribution for *frequency of access* or FOA as addressed by Burrell's model? Figure 1 shows a histogram of access frequencies for a collection of over 900 pages observed over one week. The distribution is approximately geometric, confirming an earlier observation by Pitkow and Pirolli [6].

We briefly discuss some of the issues related to analysis of server log data. Server logs record each HTTP request explicitly received by the server. For the purpose of studying document access frequencies, only two fields are of relevance, namely the URL of the page requested and the time of the request. Server logs do not record repeat accesses to pages because these are served instead by browser caches residing on the client machine[3]. If the time dimension in this analysis is made less granular, the effect of this missing data is mitigated due to the periodic cleaning of client-side caches. Personalized access prediction which requires client identification must in addition devise ways of uniquely identifying users behind proxies and firewalls.

For the purpose of our experiments, we used server logs containing over 50,300 records of accesses over six months from April to October 2000. We considered only requests to HTML documents as valid accesses, discarding image and script accesses since these are either not consciously requested by the user or present a different URL to the server each time. Requests originating from the same domain as the server were also removed since these are more likely to represent internal development activity than authentic user visits. After the cleaning phase, the combined log contained nearly 38,200 entries. An important parameter in log analysis is the size of time window over which statistics are aggregated. Each window acts as one time unit in modeling. To even out the influence of cyclical variations such as those over weekends in access rates, we chose weekly time windows. The final preprocessing step is to organize the log as a matrix, *Log* defined as Log_{ij} = number of accesses to page j in week i.

From Figure 1, it is clear that the FOA distribution is similar to the FOC distribution of Burrell's model for library loans. However, the application of this model to FOA is not justified until its assumptions outlined by Equations 2 and 3 are deemed reasonable for Web page accesses. We conducted further experiments on the processed Web logs to plot the distribution of desirabilities or mean number of accesses to documents per unit time period, in this case one week. For a page j, the desirability is given by $\sum_i^{|i|} Log_{ij}/|i|$. Figure 2 shows the distribution of desirabilities computed over the six month period. It resembles the highly concentrated negative exponential distribution of Equation 3.

Given the similarity of the FOA and desirability distributions to their equivalents in Burrell's model, it is reasonable to expect the access frequency conditioned on desirability to be a Poisson process. Before proceeding to measure this distribution we examine two important properties of Poisson processes in modeling Web page accesses. Let us model the sequence of accesses to a Web page repository as a *counting process*, i.e., a set of random variables $\{N(t), t > 0\}$ where $N(t)$ counts the number of accesses that have occurred at or up to t. (1) *Stationarity*: In a stationary counting process, the probability of a certain number of events is the same for any two intervals of equal length. Our choice of one week as the unit time period satisfies this condition, since it is safe to assume that there is little variation in access trends in between weeks (though accesses certainly vary within a week.) Web page accesses can therefore be con-

---

[3] This problem is detailed in [5] along with possible solutions.

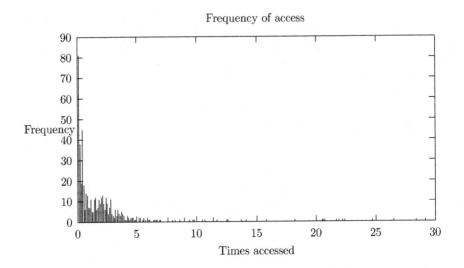

Fig. 2. Frequency histogram for desirabilities of 918 documents in the CAIS Web server over 27 weeks.

sidered a stationary process. (2) *Independent increments*: A counting process is said to have independent increments if the occurrence of a certain number of events in an interval is independent of the number of events in previous intervals. Because previous accesses to Web pages do not in any way affect current or future accesses, it is reasonable to classify the process as having independent increments.

The Poisson process allows us to calculate the probability of x accesses in any period of length t (i.e., t weeks)

$$\Pr\{X(t) = x\} = \frac{(\lambda t)^x e^{-\lambda t}}{x!} \tag{4}$$

where λt is the expected number of accesses in t weeks. This implies that $E[X(t)]$ need not be determined separately. The only unknown parameter is average accesses in one time unit or λ. This result is used for access prediction in the next section.

Measuring the conditional distribution of access frequency poses a challenge. Although the access frequency is a discrete random variable (denoted by X in the previous section), the desirability is necessarily continuous. To plot the distribution $\Pr\{X = x | \Lambda = \lambda\}$, desirability measurements must be discretized. Figure 3 shows the corresponding histogram for the conditional distribution $\Pr\{X = x | \Lambda = 2\}$ with desirability discretized in the range [1.5, 2.5] (having a mean of $\lambda = 2$.) The conditional distribution compares well with the Poisson function having an average arrival rate of 2. The empirical verification of Figure 3 becomes the basis for applying Burrell's model to Web document accesses and predicting access.

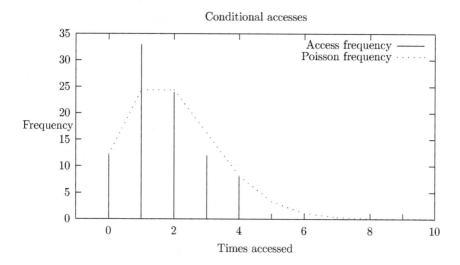

Fig. 3. Histogram of access frequency of documents with mean accesses in [1.5, 2.5] (i.e., desirability = 2) observed over eight weeks. The distribution resembles the Poisson function with mean $\lambda = 2$.

The observation that the accesses to a set of documents having the same desirability are Poisson distributed has an interesting consequence. The Poisson process has the property that the time interval between successive events has an *exponential density*. We noted in the previous section that statistical prediction using individual interaccess time distributions for documents is impractical. However, having shown that Web page access for a group of documents having similar desirability is a Poisson process, we could categorize documents according to their desirabilities and maintain a single distribution per category. Knowing that the density is exponential, we may fit an analytical form to the observed distributions to further reduce the amount of data required for prediction.

3.2 Poisson Prediction of Web Page Accesses

If the conditional distribution $f_{X|\Lambda}(x|\lambda)$ is known to be a Poisson process as in Equation 4, we can use it to predict accesses to a document from the observed mean accesses. That is, given that a document has been accessed on an average λ times over a unit time interval the probability of x accesses to it over t units of time can be found as $f_X(x,t) = \frac{e^{-\lambda t}(\lambda t)^x}{x!}$.

This method only requires knowledge of a document's desirability to make access predictions anytime into the future, say t units later. The simplest predicted quantity—expected number of accesses over time t is given by $E[f_X(x,t)] = \sum_{x=0}^{\infty} x \cdot f_X(x,t) = \lambda t$ by the stationarity property. Recall that the desirability λ is simply the mean number of accesses in a unit time period or $E[f_X(x,1)]$. This quantity can be estimated from a sample of past accesses to a document. In our experiments we found that computing λ over eight weeks gives a good

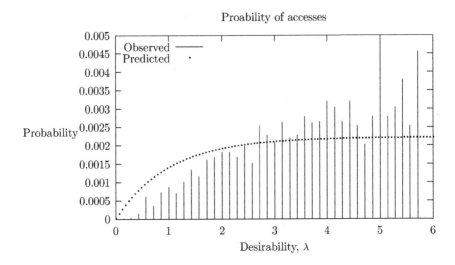

Fig. 4. Histogram of *a-posteriori* access probability versus desirability compared with the predicted access probability as a function of desirability, $\Pr\{$a document with desirability λ is accessed once or more$\} = 1 - e^{-\lambda}$ using the Poisson model. The observation interval for computing desirability was eight weeks.

estimate of a document's desirability. Another predictive measure, the probability of one or more access within time t or the cumulative FOA distribution can be determined as follows: $\Pr\{X > 0\} = \sum_{x=1}^{\infty} f_X(x,t) = 1 - \Pr\{X = 0\} = 1 - e^{-\lambda t}$ using Equation 4.

The results of the above prediction for $t = 1$ for desirability computed over eight weeks are compared with the actual access probabilities determined *a-posteriori* from the processed access log, *Log* in Figure 4.

Modeling Web page accesses as a Poisson process helps us predict future accesses to particular items given their desirabilities calculated from past usage. Burrell's model can also aid in making access predictions about the *entire* repository. If we denote by $P_r(T)$ the proportion of pages accessed r times during a period T and by $1 - \beta$ the proportion of dead pages, then $P_0(T) = (1 - \beta) + \beta p$ and $P_r(T) = \beta p (1 - p)^r$.

The values P_r are indicators of usage in the future and can be determined using estimates of β and p. Suppose $f_r(T)$ is the number of pages that have been accessed r times during the period T. Then the maximum likelihood estimators of β and p are given by $\hat{p} = \frac{N - f_0(T)}{\sum r f_r(T)}$ and $\hat{\beta} = \frac{N - f_0(T)}{N(1 - \hat{p})}$.

4   Related Work

In this section, we discuss some of the recent research in modeling and predicting Web page accesses. Sarukkai [8] has applied a variation of Markov chains to predict user accesses based on the sequence of previously followed links. Consider a stochastic matrix P whose elements represent page transition probabilities and a sequence of vectors, one for each step in the link history of a user, denoted $I^1, I^2, \ldots I^{t-1}$. The ℓth element in vector I^k is set to 1 if the user visits page ℓ at time k, otherwise it is set to 0. For appropriate values of constants $a_1, a_2, \ldots, a_k$, the state probability vector S^t for predicting the next link is determined as follows: $S_j^t = \sum_{k=1}^{n} a_k I^{t-k} P^k$. The next page to be accessed is predicted as the one with the highest state probability in the vector S^t. The same approach can be used to generate tours by successively predicting links of a path. Recker and Pitkow [7] have used the human memory model to predict document accesses in a multimedia repository based on the frequency and recency of past document accesses.

5   Conclusions

In this paper we considered the application of patterns in browsing behavior of users for predicting access to Web documents. We proposed two models for addressing our specification of the access prediction problem. The first lays out a preliminary statistical approach using observed distributions of interaccess times of individual documents in the collection. To overcome its deficiencies, we adapted a stochastic model for library circulations that accounts for differences in mean access rates of Web documents. We verified the assumptions of this model with experiments performed on a server log of accesses recorded over a six month period. Our results show that the model is reasonably accurate in predicting Web page access probabilities based on the history of accesses.

References

1. Q. BURRELL. A Simple Stochastic Model for Library Loans. *Journal of Documentation*, Vol. 36, No. 2, June 1980, pp. 115-132.
2. Q. BURRELL. The 80/20 Rule: Library Lore or Statistical Law. *Journal of Documentation*, Vol. 41, No. 1, March 1985, pp. 24-39.
3. Q. BURRELL. A Note on Ageing in a Library Circulation Model. *Journal of Documentation* Vol. 41, No. 2, June 1985, pp. 100-115.
4. L. EGGHE, R. ROUSSEAU. Introduction to Informetrics. *Elsevier Science Publishers*, 1990.
5. R. FULLER, J. GRAAFF. Measuring User Motivation from Server Log Files. In *Designing for the Web: Empirical Studies*, Microsoft Usability Group, Redmond (WA), October 1996.
6. J. PITKOW, P. PIROLLI. Life, Death and Lawfulness on the Electronic Frontier. *Proceedings of the ACM SIGCHI Conference on Human Factors in Computing*, Atlanta, GA, March 1997.
7. M. RECKER, J. PITKOW. Predicting Document Access in Large Multimedia Repositories. *ACM Transactions on Computer-Human Interaction*, Vol. 3, No. 4. December 1996. pp. 352-375.
8. R. SARUKKAI. Link Prediction and Path Analysis Using Markov Chains. *Proceedings of the Ninth World Wide Web Conference*, Amsterdam, Netherlands, May 2000.

Metamodelling Platforms

Invited Paper

Dimitris Karagiannis and Harald Kühn

University of Vienna, Department Knowledge Engineering, Brünnerstr. 72,
A-1210 Vienna, Austria
{dk, hkuehn}@dke.univie.ac.at

Abstract

The elements of an enterprise are managed more and more model-based. The state-of-the-art in the area of modelling of organisations is based on fixed metamodels. Product models are created by using product modelling environments, process models are created in business process modelling tools and organisational models are realised in personnel management tools. Web service models link these business models to information technology. They are created by using standardised languages and common ontologies. Information technology is modelled in tools supporting notions such as workflow or object-orientation. The models of the company's strategy, goals and the appropriate measurements are described and monitored by using tools supporting management concepts such as Balanced Scorecard.

Major requirements to an enterprise modelling platform are flexibility and adaptability. These are fulfilled by environments providing flexible metamodelling capabilities. The main characteristic of such environments is that the formalism of modelling - the metamodel - can be freely defined. This raises research issues on how to design, manage, distribute and use such metamodels on a syntactic as well as on a semantic level and how to integrate, run and maintain a metamodelling platform in a corporation's environment.

Platforms based on metamodelling concepts should support the following topics:
1. Engineering the business models & their web services
2. Designing and realizing the corresponding information technology
3. Evaluating the used corporation resources and assets

This paper presents a framework for metamodelling platforms and gives some answers to the research issues stated above. As part of the framework flexible metamodel integration mechanisms, using meta-metamodels (meta^2-models) and semantical mapping, are discussed. Additionally, a system architecture and the building blocks of a corporate metamodelling platform are described. Finally, best practices from three EU funded projects - REFINE, ADVISOR, and PROMOTE - all realised with industrial partners, are presented.

The full version of the paper can be downloaded from
http://www.dke.univie.ac.at/mmp

K. Bauknecht, A M. Tjoa, G. Quirchmayr (Eds.): EC-Web 2002, LNCS 2455, p. 182, 2002.
© Springer-Verlag Berlin Heidelberg 2002

Homogeneous EDI between Heterogeneous Web-Based Tourism Information Systems

Wolfram Wöß, Anton Dunzendorfer

Institute for Applied Knowledge Processing (FAW)
Johannes Kepler University Linz, Austria
{wwoess, adunzendorfer}@faw.uni-linz.ac.at

Abstract. During the last years the tourism industry realized the potential of Web-based tourism information systems (TIS) to increase the competitiveness by providing individual and specialized information about tourism objects. This leaded to a broad spectrum of tourism information systems distributed over various Web sites. But the described situation is not really satisfying for the users of such systems, the tourists, which required flexible and easy-to-use search functionalities.

To fulfill the tourists request for an extensive data collection on the one hand and to provide adequate search functionalities on the other hand, it is inevitable to make accumulated data from different sources accessible. The integration of distributed data sources has great impact on the quality of tourism information systems and follows the trend not to implement further systems, but to extend and improve existing systems. Beside comprehensive integration of tourism data, for tourists simultaneous availability and access to distributed tourism information systems supported by a generic and universally valid client application is desirable.

In this paper an adapter concept is introduced which allows uniform and homogenous data interchange between a Web-based client application and several distributed heterogeneous tourism information systems. Moreover, data interchange between different TIS server applications is supported. The key advantage of this concept is that both the client adapter and the server adapter are designed as add-on modules and therefore their installation causes only low adaptation effort concerning existing applications.

Keywords. tourism information systems (TIS), electronic data interchange (EDI), information integration, eTourism, E-Commerce.

1 Introduction

During the last years the introduction of <u>W</u>orld <u>W</u>ide <u>W</u>eb (WWW) based applications has been very successful especially in the field of tourism electronic commerce and still the turnovers are increasing rapidly. Until now, many Web-based tourism information and reservation systems have been developed. To fulfill the tourists request for an extensive data collection on the one hand and to provide adequate search functionalities on the other hand, it is inevitable to make accumulated data from different sources accessible. There are a number of approaches that have

K. Bauknecht, A M. Tjoa, G. Quirchmayr (Eds.): EC-Web 2002, LNCS 2455, pp. 183–192, 2002.

been investigated so far to realize data access to heterogeneous data sources, for example, IRODB [1], XML-KM [2] or InTouriSME [3]. A further approach is the reference model RMSIG [4], [5], which enables uniform access to and interaction between components of an electronic market based on different specific models.

To establish a communication line between the client and the server existing solutions use standardized messages based on application depending guidelines. Updates of such messages entail the adaptation of each connected application which processes the affected message(s). This is a main reason, why standards which are based on structured messages require a long-term specification process. Especially for applications in eTourism which are characterized by frequent updates and extensions, this inflexibility is not appropriate.

In general, data access to heterogeneous tourism information systems (TIS) is possible in a twofold way: Firstly, as business-to-consumer (B2C) communication between a potential tourist and a tourism information system. Secondly, as business-to-business (B2B) communication between various tourism information systems [6].

To enable uniform data access to heterogeneous TIS in the field of B2C and especially in the field of B2B several problems have to be considered [6], [7]. The main problem is the establishment of *adequate* data interchange facilities between heterogeneous TIS server applications as well as between client and server applications.

The approach presented in this paper primarily focuses B2C electronic data interchange (EDI) [8]. The underlying adapter concept allows uniform and homogenous data interchange between a Web-based client application and several distributed heterogeneous TIS. Moreover, EDI between different TIS server applications is supported.

The paper is organized as follows: Section 2 gives an overview of the TIS-QL approach which enables data access to heterogeneous TIS based on a standardized interface. After the introduction of the client/server adapter concept in Section 3, Section 4 describes the implemented client adapter prototype. Finally, Section 5 concludes and gives an outlook on future work.

2   The TIS-QL Approach

In a previous contribution TIS-QL (tourism information system query language), a uniform interface for data access and data interchange between heterogeneous tourism information systems was introduced [9]. TIS-QL supports the architecture illustrated in Figure 1.

In contrast to existing EDI solutions TIS-QL is a *query language* which is designed for tourism information systems. A primary goal of TIS-QL is not to provide a further communication and message standard, but to enable flexible specified queries with the purpose to exchange data between a client and a server.

For a correct usage of TIS-QL it is not necessary to consider a structural order of attributes. It is sufficient to specify a valid query statement depending on the language rules and the underlying general data model for tourism information systems [10]. The syntax of TIS-QL is similar to the standard query language (SQL) [11] of relational database systems. Tourism information systems are treated as database systems for tourism data, regardless whether the underlying database is managed by a file system or a relational database system.

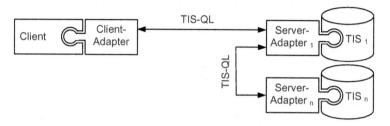

Fig. 1. TIS-QL communication between client/server adapter and server/server adapter

TIS-QL supports interchange of two kinds of information:

- plain tourism data, e.g. hotels, sightseeing, sports facilities, camping sites and
- common (meta) information about tourism information systems, e.g. national languages or currency information.

Meta information is important for both B2C and B2B communication. For example, in the case of B2C communication a user needs information about the national languages which are supported by a TIS or which attributes are used to describe a special tourism object, e.g. a camping site. In the case of B2B communication data interchange is only useful and possible, if both systems support a subset of equal national languages or a subset of equal attributes of camping sites. To establish such a TIS-QL based connection a client and a server adapter are required. In the following section, the client/server adapter concept is introduced.

3 The Client-Server Adapter Concept

The client/server adapter architecture consists of two components, a *client adapter* at the client side and a *server adapter* which extends a TIS server. These components on the one hand allow uniform communication and data interchange between a consumer (tourist) and a TIS (B2C) and on the other hand uniform communication between various TIS (B2B). Both adapters are used as interfaces to client or server applications respectively.

3.1 The Client Adapter

The client adapter is responsible for the availability of a uniform user interface presented to a user. For this, the client adapter initiates the communication process, temporarily stores the query results and transfers this result to the encapsulated client application (see Figure 2). Updates of the communication specification only affect the client adapter – the client application itself remains unchanged.

For a tourist using the client adapter offers the possibility to communicate with those TIS which support the adapter concept. In this context, a key advantage is that users no longer have to cope with differences in information presentation and interaction with TI systems, because tourists have access to various TIS via a generic and uniform user interface provided by the client adapter. Hence, users need not to be familiar with the individual functionality of each TIS.

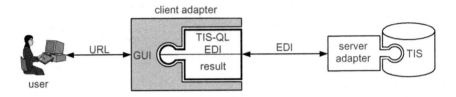

Fig. 2. Components of the client adapter

There are several possibilities for the activation and implementation of the client adapter, which each are based on actual Internet technologies: Plug-in, Java applet [12], Java servlet [12], [13], [14], JavaServer pages [12], [15] and ".jar"-files.

The realization of the client adapter as plug-in is a proper approach, since in this case it operates as autonomous application. In the first step, the client adapter plug-in is requested from a Web server (Figure 3, A). Afterwards, the client application (e.g., Web browser) receives the file (plug-in) which works as an extension of the client (Figure 3, B). In the last step, the client activates and starts the client adapter with the purpose to establish a connection with tourism information systems (Figure 3, C).

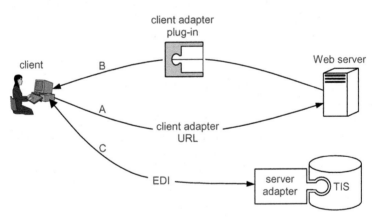

Fig. 3. Client adapter realized as plug-in

The client adapter concept offers two important advantages concerning the search functionalities of the system.

- Firstly, a tourist easily gains an overview about kind and type of information a tourism information system offers. This aggregated view about languages, currencies, tourism objects, describing attributes, etc., helps a tourist to decide, if a particular TIS fulfills his personal needs.

- Secondly, a tourist achieves the possibility to reach different and heterogeneous TIS by using a homogeneous GUI (graphical user interface).

The architecture of the client adapter is illustrated in Figure 4. To provide the necessary functions, two modules are established. The TIS-QL EDI module is responsible for data interchange functions and the result module temporarily stores and transforms the data stream into the requested format. In the first step, the TIS-QL EDI module receives a text string representing the TIS-QL statement which is transmitted to the server adapter. After the server adapter has processed the TIS-QL statement, it returns the DB (database) output which corresponding to the original TIS-QL statement to the result module of the client adapter. The result module is divided into two components which transform the DB output either in an XML (eXtensible Markup Language) or HTML (HyperText Markup Language) DB output stream.

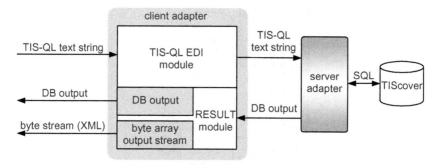

Fig. 4. Architecture of the client adapter

To enable uniform communication beside a client adapter also a server adapter is required. Concept and functionality of the sever adapter are described in the following section.

3.2 The Server Adapter

Analogous to the client adapter, the server adapter transforms data of the uniform TIS-QL interface into a form which corresponds to the data structures of the TIS database [10]. Hence, a server adapter has to be implemented for a specific TIS individually. The TIS itself is independent from changes of the B2B or B2C communication specification, because it remains encapsulated, since the sever adapter is designed as advanced data interface (see Figure 5). The main task of the server adapter is to transform the TIS-QL communication and the resulting data flow into a form which is appropriate for the database or file system of the TIS.

Fig. 5. Communication between client adapter and server adapter

The server adapter provides the following functions:

- Transformation of a TIS-QL statement into a TIS appropriate DB statement (for B2C and B2B communication)
- Adaptation of TIS specific characteristics in order to use them with TIS-QL (for B2C and B2B communication)
- Generation and transmission of the result files (for B2C and B2B communication)
- Communication with other tourism information systems by simulating a client adapter (for B2B communication, Figure 6)

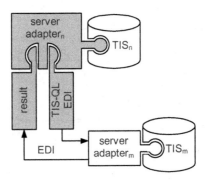

Fig. 6. Server adapter as "client adapter" for B2B communication

The general architecture of the server adapter is illustrated in Figure 7. After the server adapter is initialized in the first step, general information is polled from a tourism information system (e.g. the official Austrian destination information and booking system TIScover [16], [17]). This is necessary to receive data for the system info statements of TIS-QL. Methods which belong to the *update block* are responsible to update the *storage pool* using the results of SQL statements which are executed within the TIS. For example, the method *update language* fetches all existing national languages and the method *update object type* fetches all existing object types of a TIS. The results of the *update block* methods are stored within the storage pool in all those languages, which are provided by the TIS ①.

If the server adapter receives a TIS-QL statement from the client adapter, first, this statement is processed by the *client thread*, which establishes the connection to the client adapter. The next actions depend on the type of the TIS-QL statement. If the TIS-QL statement is a system info statement, then the system information is fetched from the *storage pool* and returned to the client adapter ②. In the case that a TIS-QL "select" statement is received it is passed through to the *select block*. After a syntax check, the methods of the *select block* generate the corresponding and equivalent SQL statements of the TIS, also including data out of the *storage pool* ③.

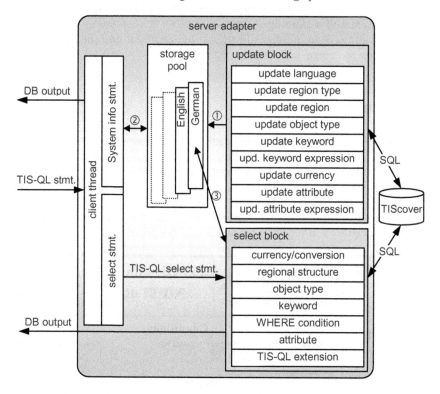

Fig. 7. Architecture of the server adapter

The methods of the *select block* provide the following functionality:

- Currency/conversion: generates the SQL statements which are necessary to fetch data about currency conversion from a TIS.
- Regional structure: generates SQL statements to fetch the structure of regions from a TIS.
- Object type: generates SQL statements to fetch the object types of a region.
- Keyword: generates SQL statements to fetch various keywords of object types.
- WHERE condition: generates SQL statements which correspond to the WHERE-clause of a TIS-QL statement.
- Attribute: generates SQL statements which correspond to the SELECT-clause attributes of the TIS-QL statement.
- TIS-QL extension: allows to extend the existing server adapter with new methods to cope with future TIS-QL requirements.

After all methods are executed and the TIS-QL statement is processed completely, the query result (DB output) is returned from the *select block* to the client adapter.

One key advantage of the introduced server adapter architecture is that the system information is *temporarily* stored within the server adapter. Therefore only TIS-QL "select" statements or updates of internal data require further database access, thus making the system well performing.

In the following section, the functionality of the graphical user interface (GUI) of the client adapter prototype is introduced.

4   The Client Adapter Prototype

The generic version of the client adapter starts with the presentation of a selection list containing all those tourism information systems which are supported by the client/server adapter communication system. After the user has selected a TIS, the connection is established and the main window of the client adapter is presented (Figure 8). The implemented client adapter prototype is confined to enable data access to the tourism information system TIScover. First of all, the main window allows the user to specify a query and finally, it presents the query results.

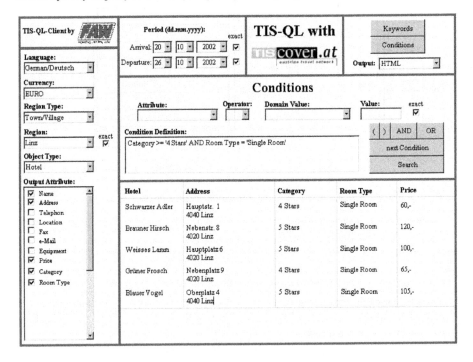

Fig. 8. The client adapter user interface

In Figure 8 the following criteria are selected:

- Language: German
- Currency: Euro

- Region type: Town/Village
- Region: Linz
- Object type: Hotel
- Condition definition: category $\geq$ 4 stars, room type = single room
- Period: 20th– 26th October 2001

Subsequently, due to the described selection every information is presented in German in combination with Euro prices. The selected output attributes are hotel name, address, price, category and room type. The selected output format is HTML. The user starts the query process by clicking on the *search* button. The result set is presented within the frame at the right bottom of the window. The attribute order depends on the selection order of the output attributes.

The total implementation effort for client and server adapter is approximately 5 person-month.

5 Conclusions

Data access to different heterogeneous data sources is an important competition factor for the participants of electronic markets. Especially in the field of tourism information systems, the tourists request for an extensive data collection and adequate search functionalities more and more increases the necessity of co-operations between tourism information systems. Hence, data access to heterogeneous tourism information systems is required in the field of B2C as well as B2B to be able to provide accumulated data of different sources (TIS).

In order to support both communication types the presented approach is based on a uniform client/server and server/server communication using TIS-QL and the introduced adapter concept. The client adapter as add-on for client applications realizes two functions: uniform communication at the client side and a generic and uniform GUI for tourism information systems. The server adapter extends a specific TIS, thus, enabling data access to the TIS database by processing TIS-QL statements and returning uniform result sets to the client (adapter). In order to evaluate the client and server adapter concept and to have a detailed look on performance and usability features, prototypes for the Austrian tourism information system TIScover were implemented.

In most cases existing standards for uniform communication use predefined messages for data interchange. Updates of such messages entail the adaptation of each connected application which processes the affected message(s). Especially for applications in eTourism which are characterized by frequent updates and extensions, this inflexibility is not appropriate. This is in contrast to the discussed approach which offers high flexibility in combination with a uniform communication and which can easily be adapted to existing systems. A further advantage is that the client adapter establishes a generic and uniform graphical user interface to search for and to present data of heterogeneous TIS by using TIS-QL.

Further work will be the development of a mediator between client adapter and server adapter in order to offer the possibility to send only *one* request and to get and collect the results of multiple alternative tourism information systems at the same time.

References

1. Gardarin G., Gannouni S., Finance B., Fankhauser P., Klas W., Pastre D., Legoff R., Ramfos A.: IRO–DB – A Distributed System Federating Object and Relational Databases, In: Bukhres O. and Elmargarmid A.K. (eds.), Object–Oriented Multidatabase Systems, Prentice Hall (1994)
2. Gardarin G., Huck G., Bezares J. L., Muñoz J. M., Pühretmair F., Busse R., Muñoz J. L., Iglesias J., Niño M.: General Architecture Specification, Project: XML–KM, XML–based Mediator for Knowledge Extraction and Brokering, EU–Project IST 12030, Deliverable D11 V2.3, e–XMLmedia, GMD, IBERMATICA, SITESA (2001)
3. Antich A., Merino M.: MDS structure inside CAP Database, Deliverable of InTouriSME – Building an Internet–based Tourism Constituency for SMEs in the Less Favored Regions of Europe, EU–Project 21349, Deliverable D.5.1.2.5.2 V2.0 (1999)
4. Höpken W.: Modeling of an Electronic Tourism Market, Proc. Information and Communication Technologies in Tourism (ENTER) 1999, Innsbruck, Springer Computer Science (1999)
5. Höpken W.: Reference Model Of An Electronic Tourism Market, Proc. Information and Communication Technologies in Tourism (ENTER) 2000, Barcelona, Springer Computer Science (2000)
6. Wöß W., Dunzendorfer A.: Configurable EDI for Heterogeneous Tourism Information Systems Based on XML, Proc. Information and Communication Technologies in Tourism (ENTER) 2001, Montreal, Springer Computer Science (2001)
7. Dunzendorfer A., Küng J., Wagner R.: Data Access to Heterogeneous Tourism Information Systems, Proc. Information and Communication Technologies in Tourism (ENTER) 1998, Istanbul, Springer Computer Science (1998)
8. Schmoll, Thomas: Handelsverkehr elektronisch, weltweit: Nachrichtenaustausch mit EDI/EDIFACT. Markt & Technik Verlag, München (1994)
9. Küng J., Dunzendorfer A., Wagner R.: TIS-QL – A Unified Query Language for Tourism Information Systems. Journal of Information Technology & Tourism (ITT), Applications, Methodologies, Techniques, Werthner H. (Ed.), Vol. 1., Inaugural Volume, Cognizant Communication Corp., New York Sydney Tokyo, ISSN 1098-3058, USA (1998), pp. 73-82
10. Küng J., Dunzendorfer A., Wagner R.: A General Datamodel for Tourism Information Systems, Proc. Information and Communication Technologies in Tourism (ENTER) 1999, Innsbruck, Springer Computer Science (1999)
11. Date C.J., Darwen H.: A Guide to the SQL Standard, Third Edition Addison Wesley ISBN 0–201–55822–X (1994)
12. SUN Microsystems: http://java.sun.com/docs/books/tutorial/getStarted/intro/index.html; Lesson: The Java Technology Phenomenon (February 2002)
13. Moss K.: Java Servlets 2nd edition, McGraw–Hill, New York (1999)
14. SUN Microsystems: http://java.sun.com/products/servlet/, Java Servlet Technology (February 2002)
15. SUN Microsystems: http://java.sun.com/products/jsp/, JavaServer Pages Technology (February 2002)
16. Pröll, B., Retschitzegger, W., Wagner, R: TIScover – A Tourism Information System Based on Extranet and Intranet Technology. Proc. of the 4th Americas Conference on Information Systems (AIS 1998), Baltimore, Maryland (1998)
17. TIS Innsbruck, FAW Hagenberg: Homepage of TIScover, http://www.tiscover.com (2000)

A Model for XML Schema Integration

Kalpdrum Passi[1], Louise Lane[1], Sanjay Madria[2], Bipin C. Sakamuri[2],
Mukesh Mohania[3], and Sourav Bhowmick[4]

[1] Dept. of Math. & Computer Science, Laurentian University, Sudbury ON P3E2C6, Canada
kpassi@cs.laurentian.ca
[2] Dept. of Computer Science, University of Missouri-Rolla, Rolla, MO 65401, USA
madrias@umr.edu
[3] IBM India Research Lab, Block No. 1, IITD, New Delhi – 110016, India
mkmohania@in.ibm.com
[4] School of Computer Engineering, Nanyang Technological University, Singapore
assourav@ntu.edu.sg

Abstract. We define an object-oriented data model called XSDM (XML
Schema Data Model) and present a graphical representation of XML Schema
integration. The three layers included are, namely, *pre-integration*, *comparison*
and *integration*. During *pre-integration*, the schema present in XML Schema
notation is read and is converted into the XSDM notation. During the
comparison phase of integration, correspondences as well as conflicts between
elements are identified. During the *integration* phase, conflict resolution,
restructuring and merging of the initial schemas take place to obtain the global
schema.

1 Introduction

XML documents are self-describing, and provide a platform independent means to
describe data and therefore, can transport data from one platform to another [5]. XML
documents can be both created and used by applications. The valid content, allowed
structure, and metadata properties of XML documents are described by their related
schema(s) [17]. An XML document is said to be *valid* if it conforms to its related
schema. A schema also gives additional semantic meaning to the data it assigns to
different tags. The schema is provided independently of the data it describes. Any
given data set may rely on multiple schemas for validation. Any given schema may
itself refer to multiple schemas.

The availability of large amounts of heterogeneous distributed web data
necessitates the integration of XML data from multiple XML sources for many
reasons. Each organization or application creates its own document structure
according to specific requirements. These documents/data may need to be integrated
or restructured in order to efficiently share the data with other applications.
Interoperability between applications can be achieved through an integration system,
which automates the access to heterogeneous schema sources and provide a uniform
access to the underlying schemas.

Throughout the rest of the paper we shall use the *example* of the integration of
GSE data of Air Canada and Canadian Airlines [8]. Fig. 1 shows sample XML

---

[1] Partially supported by NSERC grant 228127-01 and an internal LURF grant.

K. Bauknecht, A M. Tjoa, G. Quirchmayr (Eds.): EC-Web 2002, LNCS 2455, pp. 193–202, 2002.

schemas in XSDM notation pertaining to GSE for Air Canada and Canadian Airlines. The idea is to create a global schema to achieve interoperability among the existing XML documents mapping the local schemas to a single global view.

2   Related Work

The problem of schema integration of heterogeneous and federated databases has been addressed widely. Several approaches to schema integration are described in [2,6,7,11,13,15]. A global schema eliminates data model differences, and is created by integrating local schemas. The creation of a global schema also helps to eliminate duplication, avoid problems of multiple updates and thus minimize inconsistencies.

Most schema integration approaches decompose integration into a multi-layered architecture like the one followed in this paper constituting *pre-integration*, *comparison* and *integration* [2,9]. There have been some recent systems [1,3,14,18] that integrate data from multiple sources. Most of these systems provide a set of mediated/global schema(s). Some systems like *Garlic* [16] use wrappers to describe the data from different sources in its repositories and provide a mechanism for a middleware engine to retrieve the data. The *Garlic* system also builds global schema from the individual repositories. The *comparison* and *restructuring* phase of integration is handled in some systems through human interaction using a graphical user interface as in Clio [10,20] and in others semi-automatically through machine learning techniques such as in *Tukwila* data integration system [19]. The *Tukwila* integration system reformulates the user query into a query over the data sources, which are mainly, XML documents corresponding to DTD schemas and relational data. XML integration in YAT system [6] is considered as a query mechanism on the local documents and algebra has been defined to query local documents for integration.

3   Schema Integration Model

3.1   Requirements of Integrated Global Schema

Schema integration should be both *extensible* and *scalable* [9]. It should be easy to add or remove sources of data (i.e. schemas), to manage large numbers of schemas, and to adjust the resulting global schema. With the XML Schema integration approach described here, multiple schemas can be integrated at one time. Any global integrated schema must meet the following three criteria: *completeness*, *minimality*, and *understandability* [2]. In order to meet the first, *completeness*, all the elements in the initial schemas should be in the merged schema. The merged schema can be used to validate any of the XML instance documents that were previously validated by one of the initial schema specifications. To satisfy the second criterion, *minimality*, each unique element should be defined only once in the schema. Finally, to comply with the third criterion, *understandability*, in the case of XML Schema integration, the global schema must be formulated in a referenced style, rather than an inline style (nested definitions) [17], for ease of reading and assessment.

3.2   XML Schema Integration Architecture and Methodology

Our approach to XML Schema integration involves an initial *pre-integration* step. Then, for each element, *comparison* and *merging* occurs. In the final step, the merged schemas are transformed into a human readable global XML Schema document. During *pre-integration*, element, attribute and data type definitions are extracted through parsing of the actual schema document. Schema is read and converted into the XSDM notation and an analysis of the schemas occurs [2].

During the *comparison* stage of integration, correspondences as well as conflicts between elements are identified and resolved. This can be done either by using the semantic learning or through user interaction. *Naming conflicts, datatype conflicts & scale differences*, and *structural conflicts* can occur during XML Schema Integration.

In the *integration* phase, the elements and attributes of the schemas are merged. The resultant integrated schema in XSDM notation is then transformed into XML Schema notation.

3.3   XML Schema Data Model (XSDM)

The XML Schema structures [17] are both syntactic and partially semantic in nature. Syntactically, they contain the structure and type of the data they are used to describe. Semantically, their structures, constraints, and namespaces allow partial inference of the meaning of the data that they describe.

We adapt the essentially flat text-based semantic schema document into an object-oriented model of nodes, data types, namespaces and operations that can be transformed back into a flat text-based XML Schema document.

We define four structures for use in the XML Schema integration process – *Node Object, Child Object, Datatype Object* and *Attribute Object*.

A *Node Object* represents an element, which may be either non-terminal or terminal in nature. Each Node represents another set of structures that define the Node – Name, Namespace, Nodetype, Attribute, Datatype, Substitution Group Name and ChildList. Nodetype can have six types: *terminal, sequence, choice, all, any* or *empty*.

A *Child Object* represents an element, which as part of a ChildList, defines the structure of a Node. Each Child has structures that define the Child – Name, Namespace, Childtype, Max Occurrence, Min Occurrence.

Datatype Object represents data types of the terminal nodes. Attributes may have an associated datatype. A *Datatype Object* has structures that define the datatype – Name, Variety, Kind, and Constraining Facets.

An *Attribute Object* represents attributes that may be associated with a non-terminal or terminal element. Each Attribute has the structures that define an attribute – Name, Namespace, Form, Use, Datatype, and Value.

3.4   Graphical Representation of XML Schemas

XML Schemas can be represented graphically as a modified directed graph where each element should appear only once and elements are modeled according to their relationship with their children if they are non-terminal nodes. In a completely integrated schema, the children of any two elements with the same name are identical in nature.

The following rules are defined as a means to model the graphical representation of XML Schema structures and are depicted in Fig. 1.

The name of a given *Node* or *Child* as defined in XSDM is contained within a rectangle.

A unique element no is assigned to all the elements present in the schema and the element number is shown in the left bottom corner of the top rectangle.

In cases where the element is a child of another element, the minimum and maximum numbers of times it may appear are indicated. The number in the right hand bottom corner of the rectangle indicates the minimum times that the element may occur. The number in the right hand top corner indicates the maximum number of times that the element may occur. The infinity symbol in the right hand top corner indicates that the maxOccurs is unbounded.

If present, the namespace prefix [17] associated with an element may be recorded in the top left-hand corner of the rectangle.

The symbol in the bottom most rectangle indicates the structure [17] of the element. The symbol 'S' represents a *sequence*; a 'C' represents a *choice*; an 'A' represents an *all*. A capital "E" represents a terminal element that is defined as *empty*. A capital "T" represents a terminal element that contains data (i.e. not empty). A capital "N" represents an *any*. The presence of "-m" beside the symbol indicates that the element may have mixed content.

The element that appears at the top of the tree is referred to as the *root element*. Each schema, whether it is a DTD or XML Schema, may have only one root element.

Arrows connect a given element to its child(ren). In cases where an element is defined in terms of a *sequence*, the sequence is denoted in the adjacent flower braces present after 'S'.

4   Issues in Integration of Schemas

4.1   Conflict Resolution during Integration of Elements/Attributes

During the *comparison* stage of integration, correspondences as well as conflicts between elements are identified. There are four *semantic relationships* defined in [2]. The schematic representations can be viewed as *identical, equivalent, compatible* or *incompatible*. We identify six types of semantic relationships, which apply to XML Schema elements – *identical, equal, equivalent, subset, unique*, and *incompatible*. Elements that have the same name and the same namespace are *identical*. Each namespace is unique. Each element name within a given namespace is unique. Therefore, two elements with the same name and namespace must be the same element. Elements that have the same name, different namespaces and the same definitions are *equal*. Elements that have different names but the same definitions are *equivalent*. Elements with the same name, different namespaces, and the condition that the children of one element exist as a direct child group of the second element that is defined in terms of an *all* or *choice* satisfy the *subset* semantic relationship. Elements that have different names and definitions that are not equivalent to the definition of any other element across all the local schemas are considered to be *unique*. Elements with the same name, different namespaces and definitions that do not satisfy the subset semantic relationship are seen as *incompatible*.

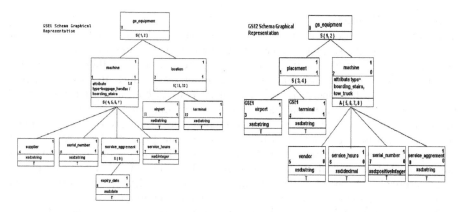

Fig. 1. Graphical representation of the sample XML Schemas

Naming conflicts, data type conflicts & scale difference and structural conflicts that can occur during the XML schema integration are defined below.

A. Naming Conflicts

Synonym Naming Conflict: Synonym XML Schema elements have different names but the same definitions. Synonym naming conflict corresponds to the *equivalent* semantic relationship. For the non-terminal elements that are *equivalent*, synonym naming conflict can be resolved in the global schema through the use of a substitution group. Terminal elements are defined in terms of their data types and can also be *equivalent*. However, for resolving synonym conflict among terminal elements that are semantically equivalent requires semantic learning or human interaction.

Homonym Naming Conflict: Homonym XML Schema elements have the same name but different definitions. Homonym naming conflict corresponds to *subset* and *incompatible* semantic relationships. *Incompatibility* can occur in non-terminal elements due to various combinations of *sequence, choice, all, any* or *empty* characterizations of the elements. Homonym naming conflicts are overcome for the non-terminal elements in the global schema (Fig. 2) through the *choice* and *all* mechanisms inherent to XML Schema structures [17]. For the terminal elements, homonym conflict becomes data type conflict and is discussed below.

B. Datatype Conflicts & Scale Differences

Two terminal elements or attributes may have the same name but have different data types. The conflict may be of a *scale difference* or because of *disjoint data types* among the terminal elements. To resolve such conflicts, data types are expanded through the use of constraint facet redefinition [4] (i.e. adjustment of scale), or through union of disjoint data types only so far as necessary to satisfy boundary conditions. In the case of the GSE schemas (Fig. 1), in the schema GSE1, the element *service_hours* is defined as having an *integer* datatype.

C. Structural Conflicts

Type Conflicts: A given element in one schema may be modeled as a terminal element, while in the second schema it might be modeled as a non-terminal element. We suggest two possible solutions for resolving the structural conflict and argue for our preference of one solution over the other. According to XML Schema recommendation [17], one cannot define an element as both a non-terminal and a terminal. As well, each element may be defined only once in a given namespace. In the first solution we add the element from both the local schemas to the global schema, so that the element that is modeled as a terminal element has a reference to its original namespace, thereby distinguishing it from the element that is modeled as a non-terminal element. In the second solution, we define that global element should be a non-terminal with mixed content, its datatype being the datatype of terminal local element and the children of the non-terminal local element optional.

A well-formed XML Schema, by definition, is *minimal* and *complete*. There is only one root element. All other elements present in the schema are related to the root element as either direct or indirect children. Each element has a unique name. Each element is defined only once. Transformations that occur to align the initial schemas are accomplished using *restructuring* (renaming, substitution groups and subsetting) in the global schema.

During schema *merging*, initial schemas are superimposed onto each other to result in the merged global schema. The merged schema is *complete* and *minimal*. The global schema is rearranged to ensure the highest level of minimality and understandability [2].

4.2   XML Schema Integration Rules and Strategies

We employ XSDM for the integration process. Essentially, two Schemas represented as trees are merged together. The merging of trees representing XML Schemas is achieved by merging the nodes. We define rules and strategies for merging of different types of nodes in the local XML Schemas into nodes representing global Schema. Here we present only some of the more common rules due to lack of space.

A. Integrating Terminal Elements

The new element receives the same name as the initial elements' name and the global namespace. The integrated definition is determined according to the following cases. The attributes of the two initial elements are integrated and assigned to the global integrated element.

(i) An element with the same name as the terminal element in the second schema is defined in terms of an EMPTY: The data type of the new terminal in the global Schema is that of the non-Empty element in one of the schemas. Any attributes defined as part of the Empty element in one of the schemas, are included in the global Schema but are defined as *optional* to retain the validity of both the initial schemas.

(ii) An element with the same name as the terminal element in the second Schema is defined in terms of an ANY: The terminal element in the global Schema is defined as

an ANY. Validation will occur but a strategy needs to be developed to retain the initial non-any terminal's definition.

(iii) Neither Terminal is defined in terms of an EMPTY or ANY : The terminal elements to be merged may have compatible or incompatible data types. We consider simple data types and the simple data types that are derived by restriction from other simple data types, as described in [4]. Complex data types can be built from these simple data types. The rules of merging for these cases are described below.

Compatible Data types: Compatible data types are closely related; for example, a decimal and integer. The less constraining of the two data types, in this case the decimal is assigned as the integrated terminal's datatype. Scale adjustment is used to merge the two terminal elements, as is shown for the element *service_hours* in the global schema GSEM (Fig. 2).

Incompatible Data types: Incompatible data types are not closely related; for example a Boolean and CDATA. The integrated terminal is assigned a datatype which is a union of the two initial data types, complete with all their originally stated constraints. The element *serial_number* in the global schema GSEM (Fig. 2) is constructed by taking the union of the data types string and positive Integer.

B. Merging Non-terminal Elements

Knowing how to properly merge non-terminal elements is key to being able to validate all existing instances of the schemas that are being integrated. The attributes of the initial non-terminals are integrated after integrating the non-terminal elements. The merged attributes become the attribute structure for the global non-terminal. We discuss three cases for integrating the non-terminal elements.

(i) Elements are equal: The integrated element has the same definition of the initial elements.

(ii) Elements are equivalent: The integrated element is assigned the name and definition of one of the initial elements. It is also assigned a substitution group [4] that indicates the name of the second element. The non-terminal element "location" (Schema GSE1) and "placement" (Schema GSE2) are equivalent (see Fig. 2). The conflict is resolved through Substiution Group in the global schema GSEM, which keeps a record of equivalent names for the same element

(iii) Elements satisfy the subset relationship, are different or incompatible: Non-terminal elements that have the same name but exist in different namespaces must be merged in the global schema. We identify twelve distinct non-terminal combinations that satisfy this case and we define the rules for integrating such element nodes. Not all apply to integrating DTD non-terminal elements. Since an *all* is not defined in a DTD, the defined rules are not applicable in the integration of DTD non-terminal elements for the combinations having an *all* as one of the element nodes.

*(a) Elements A and B are both defined in terms of a **sequence** of child groups*: The merged element will be a *choice* of the two sequences A and B. Moh et al. [12] chose to use a Longest Common Sequence approach (LCS) to integrate two elements defined in terms of sequences of children. Such an integration strategy introduces a high level of possibility that XML documents, formed after the integrated schema is described, contain structures, which are invalid according to all the initial schemas. Our solution to integrating two non-terminal elements defined as sequences ensures that the integrated schema structures remain valid according to the initial schemas. The merged Schema from GSE1 and GSE2 for

the nodes 'gs_equipment' represented as a *choice* between the two incompatible sequences is shown in Fig. 2.

(b)   Element A is defined in terms of a **sequence** and Element B is defined in terms of a **choice**: The merged element will be a choice of sequence (element A) and choice group (element B).

(c)   *Element A is defined in terms of a **sequence** and Element B is defined in terms of an **all***: The merged element will be *choice* of *sequence* (element A) and *all* (element B).

(d)   *Elements A and B are both defined in terms of a **choice** of child groups*: The merged element will be a *choice* of unique *choice* groups (element A and element B).

(e)   *Element A is defined in terms of a **choice** and Element B is defined in terms of an **all***: The merged element will be a *choice* of a *choice* group (element A) and an *all* (element B).

(f)   *Elements A and B are both defined in terms of an **all***: The merged element will be an *all* of unique *all* elements (element A and element B).

(g)   *Element A is defined in terms of a **sequence** and Element B is defined in terms of a **choice** of which one of its **choice** groups is the **sequence** which defines Element A*: This is a special case of rule (b). The merged element will be the element B, which is a *choice* of child groups and it will acquire a global namespace. The reverse case, where element A is defined in terms of a *choice* group and element B is defined as a *sequence*, and the *sequence* is a *choice* group of element A is merged in a similar manner.

(h)   *Element A is defined in terms of an **all** and Element B is defined in terms of a **choice** of which one of its **choice** groups is the **all** which defines Element A*: This is a special case of rule (e). The merged element will be the element B, which is a *choice* of its child groups and it will acquire the global namespace. The reverse case is handled similarly.

(i)   *Element A is defined in terms of a **sequence** of elements which occur a maximum of 1 times and Element B is defined in terms of an **all***: This is a special case of policy (c). The merged element will be an *all* of unique *all* (element B) and *sequence* elements (element A). The merged Schema from GSE1 and GSE2 for the nodes representing 'machine' as a *sequence* in GSE1 and as an *all* in GSE2 is shown in Fig. 2.

(j)   *Element A is a non-Any and non-Empty element and Element B is an EMPTY element*: The definition of the original non-empty non-terminal is encapsulated in a *placeholder* child group which has a minOccurs = 0 and maxOccurs = 1. This allows the non-terminal to be either empty or have its original non-empty definition without introducing a new layer of nesting of elements in the instance documents. If present, attributes are integrated and assigned to the new integrated element.

(k)   *Element A is non-Empty element and Element B is an ANY*: The new element must be defined as an **ANY**. If present, attributes are integrated and assigned to the new integrated element.

(l)   *Element A is an ANY element and Element B is an EMPTY element*: The new element must be defined as an **ANY**. If present, attributes are integrated and assigned to the new integrated element.

The global schema GSEM is obtained Fig. 2 after applying the rules of integration explained in this paper on the local schemas GSE1 and GSE2 for the airline example.

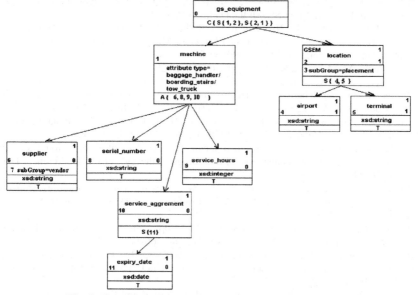

Fig. 2. Graphical representation of the global schema GSEM

5   Conclusions and Future Work

Traditional integration strategies and their application to XML Schema integration have been discussed. We have defined a graphical XML Schema representation model. The XML documents may not have an associated XML Schema as it is not mandatory for such documents to have a schema file attached to it. It would be interesting to extract the XML Schema from such documents and integrate the XML data from these local XML Schemas and the integrated document to be validated through the global schema. We are currently working on XML Schema querying using the integrated schema, based on the data model and integration strategies developed herein.

References

1. Adali, S., Candan, K., Papakonstantinou, Y., Subramanian, V.S.: Query Caching and Optimization in Distributed Mediator Systems. In: Proc. ACM SIGMOD. 25(2). Montreal Canada (June 1996) 137-148
2. Batini, C., Lenzerini, M., Navathe, S.B.: A Comparative Analysis of Methodologies for Database Schema Integration. ACM Computing Surveys, Vol. 18, No. 4 (December 1986)
3. Bontempo,C.: DataJoiner for AIX. IBM Corporation (1995)
4. Biron, P.V., Malhotra, A. (eds.): XML Schema Part 2: Data types. W3C Recommendation. (2 May 30, 2002) http://www.w3.org/TR/xmlschema-2/

5.   Bray, T., Paoli, J., Sperberg-McQueen, C.M.: Extensible Markup Language (XML) 1.0 – W3C Recommendation. (10 February 1998) http://www.w3.org/TR/REC-xml.html
6.   Chritophides, V., Cluet, S., Simon, J.: On Wrapping Query Languages and Efficient XML Integration. In: Proc. ACM SIGMOD. Dallas, Texas (2000)
7.   Haas, L.H., Miller, R.J., Niswanger, B., Roth, M.T., Schwarz, P.M., Wimmers, E.L.: Transforming Heterogeneous Data with Database Middleware: Beyond Integration. IEEE Data Engineering Bulletin, 22(1) (1999) 31-36
8.   Lamprecht, M.: Air Canada's IT Integration. (April 2001) http://www.gsetoday.com/issues_by_month/articles/090346.html
9.   Miller, R.J.: Using Schematically Heterogeneous Structures. Proc. of the ACM SIGMOD. Intl. Conf. on the Management of Data. 27(2), Seattle USA (June 1998) 189-200
10. Miller, R.J., Hernandez, M.A., Haas, L., Yan, L., Ho, C.T.H., Fagin, R., Popa, L.: The Clio Project: Managing Heterogeneity. SIGMOD Record. 30(1) (March 2001)
11. Miller, R. J., Ioannidis, Y.E., Ramakrishnan, R.: The Use of Information Capacity in Schema Integration and Translation. Proceedings of the 19th VLDB Conference. Dublin, Ireland (1993)
12. Moh, Chuang-Hue, Lim, E., Wee-Keong Ng.: Re-engineering Structures from Web Documents. Proceedings of the Fifth ACM Conference on Digital Libraries. San Antonio USA (June 2-7, 2000)
13. Parent, C., Spaccapietra, S.: Issues and Approaches of Database Integration. Communications of the ACM. Vol. 41, No. 5 (1998) 166-178
14. Papakonstantinou, Y., Garcia-Molina, H., Widom, J.: Object Exchange Across heterogeneous Information Sources. Proc. IEEE Conf. on Data Engineering. Taipei, Taiwan (1995) 251-260
15. Ram, S., Ramesh, V.: Schema Integration: Past, Present and Future. In: Elmagarmid, A., Rusinkiewicz, M., Sheth, A. (eds.): Management of Heterogeneous and Autonomous Database Systems. Morgan-Kaufmann, San Mateo CA (1998)
16. Roth, M.T., Schwarz, P.: Don't Scrap it, Wrap it! A Wrapper Architecture for Legacy Data Sources. In: Proc. of the Intl. Conf. of Very Large Databases (VLDB). Athens, Greece (August 1997) 266-275
17. Thompson, H.S., Beech, D., Maloney, M., Mendelsohn, N. (eds.): XML Schema Part 1: Structures – W3C Recommendation. (2 May 2001) http://www.w3.org/TR/xmlschema-1/
18. Tomasic, A., Rascid, L., Valduriez, P.: Scaling Heterogeneous Databases and the DESIGN of DISCO. In: Proc. ICDCS. (1996)
19. Tukwila Data Integration System, http://data.ca.washington.edu/integration/tukwila/index.htm
20. Yan, L., Miller, R.J., Haas, L.M., Fagin, R.: Data-Driven Understanding and Refinement of Schema Mappings. ACM SIGMOD. (May 2001).

XML-Based Distributed Access Control System*

Javier López, Antonio Maña, and Mariemma I. Yagüe

Computer Science Department
University of Málaga. Spain.
{jlm, amg, yague}@lcc.uma.es

Abstract. The use of attribute certificates and the concept of mobile policies have been proposed to overcome some of the limitations of the role based access control (RBAC) paradigm and to implement security requirements such as the "originator controlled" (ORCON) policy. Mobile policies are attached to the data that they control and enforced by their execution in trusted servers. In this paper we extend this idea to allow the execution of the policies in untrusted systems. Our extension allows policies to be bound to the data but not attached to. Through this modification security administrators are able to change policies dynamically and transparently. Additionally, we introduce X-ACS, an XML-based language designed to express policies in a simple and unambiguous way overcoming the limitations of other approaches. Important features of X-ACS are that it can be used by processors with limited capabilities such as smart cards while allowing the automated validation of policies.

1 Introduction

Despite of the popularization of distributed systems in most computing disciplines, systems for access control to information still rely on centralized security administration. Centralized control has important disadvantages [1] and does not facilitate the deployment of originator retained control mechanisms.

On the other hand, solutions proposed for distributed access control do not provide the flexibility and manageability required. An interesting approach based on the concept of mobile policies [2] has been proposed to solve some of the limitations of RBAC [3]. This system introduces the remote execution of the access control policies, addressing a solution for some of the problems of centralized access control, but requires that access control policies are executed in trusted computers (data servers in this case) which, in practice, represents just a small improvement over the single server model. Once access to a data object is granted, this data is sent to the client computer where it has no protection. Furthermore, because data and policy are compiled in a package, a change in the policy that controls a data object requires that the data-policy package is recompiled and distributed to all trusted servers.

In this paper we present ACDACS (Attribute Certificate Distributed Access Control System). ACDACS extends the mobile policy concept by allowing the

---

* Work partially supported by the E.U. through project IST 2001-32446

K. Bauknecht, A. M. Tjoa, G. Quirchmayr (Eds.): EC-Web 2002, LNCS 2455, pp. 203–213, 2002.

execution of mobile policies in untrusted systems and enabling that policies are linked to the data object but not integrated with it. Therefore, policies can be dynamically changed in a transparent manner. We also introduce X-ACS, an XML-based authorization language designed to support a wide range of authorization scenarios in a simple and unambiguous way. X-ACS can be used by processors with limited capabilities such as smart cards and facilitates policy validation.

The rest of the paper is organized as follows. Section 2 presents the motivations. Section 3 summarizes some related work. Section 4 describes the ACDACS system. Finally, section 5 summarizes the conclusions and presents ongoing and future work.

2   Motivation

In distributed computing environments, such as extranets or research networks that comprise several institutions, the access policy applicable to each resource (data object, service, etc.) must be defined by the owner of the resource. The access control system must guarantee that the policy is enforced before access is granted to the resource. Moreover, there are many different situations where it is desirable that the owner of each resource is able to retain the control over it and to change the access policy dynamically and transparently. In these systems traditional centralized access control mechanisms do not provide the necessary functionality and flexibility. The need of a central authority and repository is not always acceptable by the institutions sharing the network. Furthermore, centralized systems are unable to provide means to guarantee that originators retain control over their information.

Several access control models have been introduced to fit different access control scenarios and requirements. Some schemes have also tried to integrate different models into a unified framework [4]. These approaches represent significant advances over traditional single-policy systems but, unfortunately, are still constrained by the underlying models and do not provide the necessary flexibility.

Role based access control is commonly accepted as the most appropriate paradigm for the implementation of access control in complex scenarios. RBAC can be considered a mature and flexible technology. Numerous authors have discussed its access properties and have presented different languages and systems based on this paradigm [5][6].

The main problem with RBAC is that the mechanisms are built on three predefined concepts: "user", "role" and "group". The definition of roles and the grouping of users can facilitate management, specially in corporation information systems, because roles and groups fit naturally in the organizational structures of the companies. However, when applied to some new and more general access control scenarios, these concepts are somewhat artificial.

We believe that a more general approach is needed in order to be used in these new environments. For example, in the referred situations, groups are an artificial substitute for a more general tool: the attribute. In fact, the definition of groups is usually based on the values of some specific attributes (employer, position, ...). Some attributes are even built into most of the access control models. This is the case of the user element; the identity is just one of the most useful attributes, but it is not necessary in all scenarios and, therefore, it should not be a built-in component of a general model.

In actual access control models, the structure of groups is defined by the security administrator and is usually static. Although the grouping of users can suffice in many different situations, it is not flexible enough to cope with the requirements of more dynamic systems where the structure of groups can not be anticipated by the administrators of the access control system. In these scenarios new resources are incorporated to the system continuously and each resource may possibly need a different group structure and access control policy. Furthermore, the policy for a given resource may change frequently.

Our work is focused on the solution of the originator retained control issue providing fair distributed access control management and enforcement. The basic goal is to be able to express, validate and enforce access control policies without assuming the trust in the rest of the computers of the network. Finally, because the creation and maintenance of access control policies is a difficult and error prone activity, we have developed a language to express those policies and validate them to find contradictions or ambiguities.

3   Related Work

Access control is one of the most mature disciplines in computer security. Nevertheless, new models and functionalities in access control systems are required to fullfil the needs of new Internet applications. An interesting system for policy-based management of networks and distributed systems is presented in [7]. The separation of the policy specification from the access control implementation has been proposed in [8]. This separation follows the "network-centric" approach of Röscheisen and Winograd [9] and allows the policy to be modified dynamically, without changing its underlying implementation [10]. Other access control languages have been developed in the security community to support different access control approaches. Jajodia et al. present in [11] a logical language which allows users to specify the policy according to what access control decisions are to be made as well as the authorizations.

Several proposals have been introduced for access control to distributed heterogeneous resources from multiple sources. The Akenti Project [1] proposes an access control system designed to address the issues raised in allowing restricted access to distributed resources controlled by multiple stakeholders. The requirement for the stakeholders to trust the rest of the servers in the network, the assumption of the existence of a supporting identity PKI (public key infrastructure) and some security vulnerabilities related to the existence of positive and negative use-conditions are the main drawbacks of the Akenti system.

The PERMIS Project [12] objective is to set up an integrated infrastructure to solve identification and authorization problems. The PERMIS group has examined various policy languages – such as Ponder [7] – concluding that XML is the most appropriate candidate for a policy specification language. Because the PERMIS system is based on the RBAC model it shares its limitations. Also the requirement of a supporting PKI is hard to fulfil and it is not necessary in many authorization scenarios.

Since its inception, XML has been used for defining specific vocabularies to represent different human endeavor. In our context, the eXtensible rights Markup Language (XrML) [13] and eXtensible Access Control Markup Language (XACML) [14] are two proposals for standard XML extensions for digital rights management and access control. While XrML can be considered a mature specification, its complexity makes it not appropriate for our application scenarios where simplicity is essential. XACML is a very recent (still in the development process) and promising competitor in the field of access control languages. Both, XACML and our X-ACS language are based on XML Schema. The main differences are that X-ACS is designed to be used by processors with limited storage and processing capabilities such as smart cards and oriented to the validation of the policies.

Also based on XML, the Security Assertion Markup Language (SAML) [15] is an assertion language and messaging protocol for describing, requesting and sending authentication and authorization data between security domains. Its basic goal is to promote the interoperability between disparate security systems, providing the framework for secure e-business transactions across company boundaries.

Another interesting work, presented in [16], uses XML to define a fine-grained access control system for XML documents. This approach differs from ours in that it is completely "server-side". Authorizations can be specified at document or instance level (in XML documents), or alternatively at schema level (in DTDs). Authorizations specified in a DTD are applicable to all XML documents that conform to it. Our proposal is based on a higher level language, the XML Schema language which presents an XML syntax and object oriented features. XML Schema can be extended with business rules expressed in Schematron. The expressive power of both languages allows the definition of advanced integrity constraints in a database-like style [17].

4   The ACDACS System

Considering the basic objective of providing means to implement the ORCON policy, the different scenarios considered and the analysis of previous proposals, our main goals for the ACDACS distributed access control system are:

- *Originator retained control.* Originators should be able to retain control over the resources they own even after access is granted to users.
- *Distributed access control management.* Administrators should be able to manage the resources they control regardless of the location of that resource.

- *Distributed access control enforcement.* Access control enforcement mechanisms must be distributed to avoid bottlenecks in request processing.
- *Flexibility.* The system should be applicable in different scenarios.
- *Independence.* The system should not depend on underlying infrastructures or authentication systems.
- *Dynamism.* There should be a fast and secure mechanism to change policies.
- *Ease of management.* The distributed approach should not introduce complexity of management. Supporting tools should be provided.
- *Efficiency.* Access control management and enforcement should be efficient.
- *Security.* The distributed access control mechanism must ensure the same level of security as a centralized one.

4.1   ACDACS System Architecture

The ACDACS system is based on the following idea: the security requirements of the processes related to the transmission and access to information are feasible if we can have a trusted software running in the client computer. Therefore, the creation of mobile software elements that transport the protected content and enforce the access control policies is at the heart of our approach. ACDACS is supported by the SmartProt software protection system [18]. SmartProt partitions the software into functions that are executed by two collaborating processors. One of those processors is a trusted computing device that enforces the correct execution of the functions and avoids that these functions are identified or reverse engineered. We use smart cards as secure coprocessors although special online access servers can also be used as secure coprocessors for this scheme.

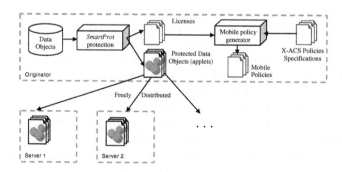

Fig. 1. The ACDACS Architecture

Figure 1 shows the architecture of the system. The unprotected data objects in the originator computer are transformed into PDOs (protected data objects). PDOs are Java applets that protect the data and enforce the access control mechanism. Policies are not included in the PDO. Instead, each PDO is linked

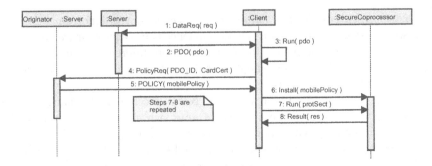

Fig. 2. ACDACS Operation

to the applicable policy by a mobile policy that is produced specifically for the client when requested. PDOs can be freely distributed to untrusted servers.

Figure 2 depicts the dynamic operation of the system. When the client requests some data object from a server it receives the PDO containing it. This PDO runs in the client computer. Before the PDO can execute the protected sections of its code it has to retrieve the corresponding mobile policy (which includes the license that allows the decryption and execution of the protected sections of the PDO). To do this the client sends a request containing the certificate of the public key of the secure coprocessor (the smart card or the access server). In case the PDO is retrieved from its originator, a mobile policy for that PDO is produced. Otherwise the server just forwards this request to the PDO originator.

In scenarios where the number of attributes and attribute certification authorities, known as SOAs (source of authorizations), are high it might be desirable to avoid that clients have to verify all the certificates directly. In this case a temporary authorization mechanism is used to map several attribute certificates from different SOAs to a single temporary authorization. This temporary authorization is a special attribute certificate signed by one SOA which simplifies the verification performed by the PDOs. This solution is especially useful when the client is accessing several PDOs from the same originator.

To allow owners of the information to be able to dynamically change the access control policy we must separate the policy from the PDO. When the PDO is executed it retrieves the policy from the originator and enforces it. The reasons to require the request of the mobile policy at access time and from the originator are that a high degree of flexibility is allowed, and the originator is given more control over the application of the policies. Nevertheless, for efficiency, originators can define certain validity constraints for each policy (based on time, number of accesses, etc. depending on the smart card features). Therefore policies can be cached by clients and used directly while they remain valid. Also the generation of the mobile policy is a reasonably fast process while the generation of PDOs is slower. Furthermore, PDOs are much more stable than policies. Finally, opposed to PDOs, each mobile policy is specific for a smart card (or access server).

Policies are specified using X-ACS and are later translated into a more compact format to be included in the mobile policy. The link between PDO and the corresponding mobile policy is established by cryptographic means. The structure of the mobile policy is defined as follows:

$$MP ::= Policy, Encrypt_{CardPublicKey}(PDOkey, validity, H(Policy))$$

where *Policy* is the compact representation of the X-ACS policy, *CardPublicKey* is the public key of the smart card that will access the PDO, *PDOkey* is the random symmetric key used to encrypt the protected sections of the PDO, *validity* represents the limits of use of the MP and *H* is a collision-resistant one way hash function.

The mobile policy includes the key required by the smart card to decrypt and run the protected sections of the PDO. This key is encrypted for a specific smart card and will only be in the clear inside that card. As the PDO key is only known by the originator it is impossible for dishonest users to alter mobile policies or produce false ones.

We will now describe the main building blocks of ACDACS: (i) an infrastructure for software protection and (ii) a policy specification language and its associated validation mechanisms.

4.2   Software Protection

The ability to protect software that runs in the client computer in order to guarantee that it performs the intended function opens a way to solve the originator retained control problem. Our solution for this problem is based on the protection of the mobile software that we use to convey the information. The mobile software (PDO) contains some protected sections that must be executed by a secure coprocessor.

The SmartProt system includes three actors: the information provider, the card manufacturer and the client (who possess a smart card). The card manufacturer certifies the public keys of the smart cards. SmartProt requires smart cards that have cryptographic capabilities, contain a key pair generated inside the card and ensure that the private key never leave the card. Cards also contain the public key of the card manufacturer and some support software. Particularly, cards contain an interpreter for the protected code sections, a license manager, a runtime manager and, optionally, an electronic purse. Each protected software application runs in a sandbox isolated from others. The contents of the memory used by each application remain between calls to the card.

The process is divided into two main phases: *production* and *authorization*. The first step of the production phase consists in the translation of some specific sections of the original application code by functionally equivalent sections of card-specific code. The translation process also identifies the dependencies between these protected sections, reorganizes the code and introduces fake code to confuse the attacker. These sections are then encrypted with a fresh key using a symmetric cryptosystem. The last step substitutes the original code sections by calls to a function that transmits the respective equivalent protected sections, including code and data, to the card. Some additional support functions are also included. The protected mobile software application generated in the production phase can be distributed and copied freely. In the case of the ACDACS system, the protected application (PDO) is a Java applet responsible for the transport of the information. Therefore, the protected mobile software includes the information to be accessed (which is encrypted), the access control enforcement mechanism and a cryptographic link to the access policy. The production phase is independent of the client card and will be performed just once for each piece of mobile software.

A license (specifically created for the smart card of the user) stating conditions (e.g. validity) is required to run the protected software. In the ACDACS system the license includes the access policy and is called Mobile Policy (MP). In the authorization phase, the new MP is produced linking the policy and the PDO. The MP contains validity constraints that are set by the security administrator according to the volatility of the policies.

MPs can be cached and used in the client computer while they remain valid. Just in the case that no valid MP is available, a new MP has to be requested and produced. The MP is obtained and loaded in the card as part of the PDO. When the MP is received by the client smart card, it is decrypted, verified and stored inside the card until it expires or the user decides to extract it.

Once installed, the MP allows the execution of the protected sections of the PDO. These protected sections do not reside in the cards. Instead, during the execution of the protected program, these sections are transmitted as necessary to the card where they are decrypted using the installed MP and executed. When finished, the card may send back some results. Some other partial results will be kept in the card in order to obtain a better protection against function analysis and other attacks.

The definition of the license (MP) structure permits a high degree of flexibility. Furthermore, licenses can be individually managed because each application has its own key. This is not possible in other software protection proposals where the protected sections of all applications share the same key (usually the protected processor key). In our scheme, because the protected sections are encrypted using a symmetric key kept inside the cards, and therefore known only by the PDO producer, dishonest users can not produce false sections.

4.3   Authorization Language

The XML data model can represent semantic information through descriptive tags. Complemented by related technologies certain types of database-like schemes can also be used [17]. XML Schema presents a rich set of data types, allowing user-defined data types, mechanisms such as inheritance, etc. XML Schema allows us to represent the semantics of the policies. Although some constraints such as, "if the value of <Rights> is Update then the value of <Actions> should be Notify" are not expressible using XML Schema, our Policy Validator application is able to check, among others, this kind of constraints.

X-ACS policies are based on an XML Schema template[1] that facilitates their creation and syntactic validation. X-ACS has been developed taking into account that policies must be evaluated by smart cards. Therefore, other related languages are not well suited for the ACDACS system.

In our language, a policy consists of a set of `access_Rule` elements. Each one of these elements defines all the combinations of attribute certificates that allow the user to gain the access established by the `Rights` attribute. Therefore, it is composed as a series of `attribute_Set` required to gain access and the `Rights` obtained over the data in case access is granted. Each `attribute_Set` defines a particular attribute certificate combination associated with an optional `Action` (that has to be performed before access is granted). Attribute certificates will be used to provide evidence of the possession of each attribute. Therefore, attribute certificates are described stating their name (`attribute_Name`), value (`attribute_Value`) and the signer of the certificate (`SOA_ID`). Optionally, policies include `parameter` elements that are instantiated using the metadata available for the requested object.

Suppose our administrator states the policy shown in figure 3 in order to grant authorization to access the marks of a subject to lecturers and deny it to students. It is possible for lecturers to register as students of courses that they do not teach. In such a case, those lecturers would get access to their own marks.

```
<?xml version="1.0" encoding="UTF-8"?>
<policy xmlns="http://www.uma.es/ecWeb02"
xmlns:xsi= "http://www.w3.org/2001/XMLSchema-instance"
xsi:schemaLocation="http://www.uma.es/ecWeb02 PolicyTemplate.xsd"
policy_Description="GRANT write_access TO marks IF Position='Lecturer'">
  <access_Rules>
    <access_Rule Rights="update">
      <attribute_Set>
        <attribute>
          <attribute_Name>Position</attribute_name>
          <attribute_Value>Lecturer</attribute_value>
          <SOA_ID>LCC_ADM</SOA_ID>
        </attribute>
      </attribute_Set>
    </access_Rule>
  </access_Rules>
</policy>
```

Fig. 3. WrongPolicy.xml

X-ACS policies are verified in several ways. Policies are verified syntactically using an XML Schema validator. Semantic verification is made in an automatic way by the Policy Validator, an XML application based on the DOM API. This validator also allows policies to be verified in the context where they will be applied. Policy context verification is based on the definition of a set of global rules establishing a series of facts about the environment of the system.

---

[1] available as supplementary material

This semantic information allows the detection of possible inconsistencies in the declared policy. Test cases can be defined by the administrator. Parameters are instantiated by the Policy Validator based on metadata expressed in test cases. The X-ACS global rules established about the context enable the detection of semantically incomplete policies. With the aid of the context validation the administrator would have detected the error in the previous example and stated the policy as shown in figure 4.

```xml
<?xml version="1.0" encoding="UTF-8"?>
<policy xmlns="http://www.uma.es/ecWeb02"
xmlns:xsi="http://www.w3.org/2001/XMLSchema-instance"
xsi:schemaLocation="http://www.uma.es/ecWeb02 PolicyTemplate.xsd"
policy_Description="GRANT write_access TO marks (metadata: Subject)
                IF Position='Lecturer' AND Teaches=Subject">
  <parameter>Subject</parameter>
  <access_Rules>
    <access_Rule Rights="update">
      <attribute_Set>
        <attribute>
          <attribute_Name>Position</attribute_name>
          <attribute_Value>Lecturer</attribute_value>
          <SOA_ID>LCC_ADM</SOA_ID>
        </attribute>
        <attribute>
          <attribute_Name>Teaches</attribute_name>
          <attribute_Value>*Subject</attribute_value>
          <SOA_ID>LCC_ADM</SOA_ID>
        </attribute>
      </attribute_Set>
    </access_Rule>
  </access_Rules>
</policy>
```

Fig. 4. RightPolicy.xml

5   Conclusions and Future Work

We have presented the ACDACS distributed access control system to solve the originator retained control problem. We have described the underlying mechanisms that make possible this system: the SmartProt software protection scheme and the X-ACS language and tools. ACDACS is flexible, can be applied regardless of the attribute certification scheme, implements distributed access control management and enforcement mechanisms, does not depend on underlying infrastructures or authentication systems, allows the dynamic modification of policies in a transparent and efficient way and is secure. We have functional implementations of the SmartProt mechanism and the PDO (applet) generator. Regarding X-ACS, we have developed the XML Schema specification and the Policy Validator. Ongoing work is focused on the implementation of some of the components of the system such as the Policy Edition Assistant. We are working on the definition of a generic mechanism to allow access control administrators to gain knowledge about the attributes certified by each SOA. This mechanism allows SOAs to define metadata about the attributes they certify. These metadata are also used by the policy creation and validation tools. We are currently applying the system to other scenarios such as digital libraries.

References

1. Thompson, M., et al.: Certificate-based Access Control for Widely Distributed Resources. In: Proc. of the Eighth USENIX Security Symposium (1999) 215–227
2. Fayad, A., Jajodia, S.: Going Beyond MAC and DAC Using Mobile Policies. In: Proc. of 16th IFIP SEC. Kluwer Academic Publishers (2001)
3. McCollum, C.J., Messing, J.R., Notargiacomo, L.: Beyond the pale of MAC and DAC - Defining new forms of access control. In: Proc. of the IEEE Symposium on Security and Privacy (1990) 190–200
4. Jajodia, S., Samarati, P., Sapino, M.L., Subrahmanian,V.S.: Flexible support for multiple access control policies. ACM Transactions on Database Systems (2000)
5. Osborn, S., Sandhu, R., Munawer,Q.: Configuring Role-Based Access Control to Enforce Mandatory and Discretionary Access Control Policies. In: ACM Transactions on Information and System Security, Vol.3(2) (2000) 85–106
6. Sandhu, R., Ferraiolo, D., Kuhn, R.: The NIST Model for Role-Based Access Control: Towards a Unified Standard. In: Proc. of the 5th ACM Workshop on Role-based Access Control (2000) 47–63
7. Damianou, N., Dulay, N., Lupu, E., Sloman, M.: The Ponder Policy Specification Language. In: Proc. of Policy Worshop (2001)
8. Wedde, H.F., Lischka, M.: Modular Authorization. In: Proc. of the 6th ACM Symposium on Access Control Models and Technologies (SACMAT) (2001)
9. Röscheisen, M., Winograd,T.: A Network-Centric Design for Relationship-based Security and Access Control. In: Journal of Computer Security, Special Issue on Security in the World-Wide Web (1997)
10. Sloman, M.S.: Policy Driven Management for Distributed Systems. Journal of Network and Systems Management, Vol. 2(4) (1994) 333–360
11. Jajodia, S., Samarati, P., Subrahmanian, V.S.: A Logical Language for Expressing Authorizations. In: Proc. of IEEE Symp. on Security and Privacy (1997) 31–42
12. Chadwick, D. W.: An X.509 Role-based Privilege Management Infrastructure. Business Briefing. In: Global Infosecurity (2002) http://www.permis.org/
13. ContentGuard, Inc.: eXtensible Rights Markup Language, XrML 2.0. (2001) http://www.xrml.org
14. Org. for the Advancement of Structured Information Standards.: eXtensible Access Control Markup Language. http://www.oasis-open.org/committees/xacml/
15. Org. for the Advancement of Structured Information Standards.: SAML 1.0 Specification Set (2002) http://www.oasis-open.org/committees/security/
16. Damiani, E., De Capitani di Vimercati, S., Paraboschi, S., Samarati, P.: A fine-grained access control system for XML documents. In: ACM Transactions on Information and System Security (TISSEC), to appear.
17. Yagüe, M.I., Aldana, J.F., Gómez, C.A.: Integrity issues in the Web. In: Doorn, J. and L. Rivero (eds.): Database Integrity: Challenges and Solutions (2002) 293–321
18. Maña, A., Pimentel, E.: An Efficient Software Protection Scheme. In: Proc. of 16th IFIP SEC. Kluwer Academic Publishers (2001)

Transactional Security for a Distributed Reputation Management System*

Dietrich Fahrenholtz and Winfried Lamersdorf

University of Hamburg, Computer Science Department,
Distributed and Information Systems Group
Vogt-Koelln-Strasse 30, 22527 Hamburg, Germany
{fahrenho|lamersd}@informatik.uni-hamburg.de

Abstract. Today, reputation systems such as ebay's prominent "Feedback Forum" are becoming more widespread. In such a system, reputations are formed by aggregating ratings participants give and receive. These reputations, however, are bound to a specific platform preventing participants from taking and showing their hard-earned reputations elsewhere. That makes the reputations less valuable and leaves them vulnerable to manipulation and total loss. In this paper, we propose a viable solution to these issues in which current P2P and PKI technologies are employed to shift ownership and responsibility back to the participants. Our envisioned Reputation Management System, therefore, uses context-dependent feedback gathered in questionnaires and provides security for peer transactions to ensure integrity, confidentiality and privacy.

1 Introduction and Motivation

Every unsecured multi-lateral transaction provides incentives for participants to behave in an unfair, selfish manner. It is the temptation to receive goods or services from others without giving anything in return. This phenomenon of "hit and run" can be mitigated by multiple factors e.g., if participants meet face-to-face, or if they have legal obligations binding them. However, if the sides of a transaction are separated by time and/or space, the party who acts second must be considered trustworthy or provide some form of insurance against fraud. One way of coping with risks of trade is having information of a transaction partner's historical behavior. This information helps us set our expectations when considering future transactions and helps build our trust in a transaction partner.

When it comes to virtual or online communities, the trust problem becomes more acute. There, participants are lacking prospect-related information from their five senses because usually they do not have any direct face-to-face or haptic contact. Theoretical work [18] has shown that communities benefit greatly

---

* This research was made possible, in part, by the kind support of the project unit eSolutions, T-Systems GEI GmbH, Germany. We are especially grateful to Everett Wilson for his support and constructive comments on this paper.

K. Bauknecht, A M. Tjoa, G. Quirchmayr (Eds.): EC-Web 2002, LNCS 2455, pp. 214–223, 2002.

from sharing and aggregating information about members past transactions. The exchange of this kind of reputational information helps a community develop better trust and cooperation. As "reputation is the memory and summary of behavior from past transactions", defined by Lethin [14], we establish in this paper that it can be operationalized in an online Reputation Management System. The application of this definition depends, of course, on the supposition that past behavior is indicative of future behavior.

In the e-Commerce domain, ebay is one of the oldest and most prominent e-auction sites on the Web. ebay manages members' reputations in a centralized fashion with a system called "Feedback Forum". The running total of feedback points is attached visibly to each participant's screen name, so everybody is able to readily check the transaction partner's accumulated "reputation". However efficient and accepted ebay's Feedback Forum is, it lacks the important feature of taking a "reputation" elsewhere on the Web. Furthermore, you never know what will happen to your "reputation" when you are offline or ebay's servers suffer an outage and large amounts of reputation data are lost.

2   Goals and Properties

We feel, every participant who makes use of a reputation system should be entitled to show, give and receive feedback whenever and to/from whomever she wants. Reputation formed by accumulating this feedback should then be the property of the one who was rated. Feedback exchanged between participants is sensitive data, so it needs to be guarded against eavesdropping and tampering. Since feedback should not be stored centrally, we envision a distributed solution where the classical client/server paradigm is significantly weakened. Today's Peer-to-Peer (P2P) technology [16] seems to be the most appropriate to provide basis for such a system.

The basic idea behind a Reputation Management System (RMS) is that past feedback histories guide future trust decisions participants make at the beginning of a transaction. These histories should encourage trustworthy behavior, and deter participation by those who are dishonest or unqualified. Moreover, participants need not be only human beings. It is equally possible that participants can be autonomous software agents [17] rating one another. Accumulated feedback is stored on each participant's computer but looses significance in the course of time as new feedback is sought. In designing our RMS, we set the following requirements the system should attain:

1. RMS services are independent of application domain context.
2. Integrity and confidentiality of participant feedback is secured by cryptographic protocols and algorithms.
3. Users know and comprehend what happens while the RMS processes their requests.
4. The service provider controlling the RMS does not learn any details about participant feedback.

Additionally, we list the following properties our system adheres to:

1. Entities must register with / be authenticated by the RMS.

2. RMS services operate in a distributed fashion. There is, however, a central trans-action control providing third party evidence.
3. Automatic, statistical evaluation of aggregated intra-RMS participant feedback is used as a tool for evaluating trustworthiness. Participants can decide what kind of statistical evaluation they like to run on reputation data.

3   Related Work

Resnick et al. [19] provide a good overview of benefits, threats, challenges to, and about reputation systems in general.

To ensure accountability in Peer-to-Peer systems so that "the tragedy of the commons", i.e., commonly owned resources are depleted until they are ex-hausted, can be averted, authors of [9] outline examples of how this can be accomplished with the aid of micro-payments and reputations in existing P2P systems. A further example is furnished by the authors of [4]. Their Evidence Management Service (EMS) comprises of a central trusted component and set of agents distributed across enterprise PCs. The EMS is designed to store and retrieve digital documents reliably and securely over a long time.

Simulation of reputation and guarding it from unfair or discriminatory be-havior in virtual agent societies can be found in [7,25,22]. Moreover, authors of [15] introduce a Web Service Agent Proxy that facilitates agents' selection of good Web services.

Reputation is always connected with the broader concept trust. There exist different variants of trust and trust relationships between entities.The author of [11] argues to understand and integrate properly the right type of trust into distributed systems. Researchers who published [24,3] define trust in combina-tion with chains of credentials, policies, authorization languages and inference mechanisms. For those researchers, the problem of trust management is strictly a security problem that can be best tackled by cryptography. However, the hu-man dimension of trust is missing which, other authors and we consider quite crucial. A trust-reputation model to reflect real world trust has been devised by authors of [1]. However, their notion of context remains fuzzy and they do not have a refined statistical evaluation mechanism for their recommender trust.

Other trust and reputation management initiatives currently under way are Sun's JXTA sub-project "Poblano" [6] and OpenPrivacy.org's "Sierra" [12]. Both, however, would benefit from a refined conceptual foundation. Quite an in-teresting and unconventional way of reputation management which resists pseu-dospoofing, i.e., more than one pseudonym is linked to and owned by one entity, can be found in [13]. There, trust relationships are represented by a collection of nodes, edges and weights. A trust value of a subject is defined as the graph-theoretical maximum flow of trust from a source to a sink (subject). The system has to have at least one special high-esteemed node as trust source.

Our paper is organized as follows: Section 4 explains the preliminaries and foundations of our work. Then, section 5 shows the architecture of our RMS and explains the necessary protocols. Finally, we provide concluding remarks and give an outlook on future work in section 6.

4   Design Principles

As necessary prerequisites and technological basis for our distributed RMS, we employ two by now well-known technologies, i.e., Peer-to-Peer networking and public-key cryptography (PKC). The former is used because it shifts the power and knowledge from the center (server) to the edge of a network (clients). Thus one gets more flexibility and democracy, but at the same time significant weaknesses notoriously inherent in distributed systems. PKC gives a strong promise to solve those authentication, confidentiality, integrity, and non-repudiation issues. So if PKC is applied appropriately, security is greatly enhanced and trust in the system is fostered.

4.1   Peer-to-Peer Networking

Our Peer-to-Peer network (P2PN) is a group of at least three computers (peers) not necessarily operated by individuals. To communicate with one another, peers use a connection protocol such as TCP/IP and can be temporarily online. Peers running the RMS software operate both as server and client except the portal which serves as a central facilitator to coordinate operations. Participation in this P2PN means, active peers give and share feedback with one another. Peers are looking for other peers offering services. This is supported by a service location protocol. Having found each other but belonging to different P2PNs, peers must use a gateway that cross certifies their reputations. So transferability of reputations accross RMS boundaries is guaranteed. Unfortunately, service location and cross certification cannot be addressed here and will be subject of a future paper.

4.2   Entities and Identifying Pseudonyms

In our RMS, there are basically two entities: *subjects* who wish to transact with one another and the *portal*. Subjects are identified by RMS identifiers. These are necessary for entering the transaction phases. When subjects register with the RMS, they can freely choose a pseudonym [5] not already owned by any other participant. Pseudonyms may be composed of alphanumeric characters except the colon. This is to make RMS identifiers globally unique. So an exemplified RMS identifier would look like <RepNetwork1:bozo> where "RepNetwork1" is the RMS name and "bozo" is the subject's pseudonym. Pseudonymity ensures on the one hand necessary anonymity of subjects, e.g., they cannot easily be identified by their real name, and on the other hand authentication of valid RMS subjects. The portal itself has no RMS identifier because it does not provide any feedback/ratings on subjects' behavior. Subjects, however, identify the portal by its public-key infrastructure certificate.

4.3   Roles and Activities

There are three roles, subjects can take on in our RMS: *rater*, *ratee*, and *mediator*. The task of the first role is to rate the other subject's behavior after the end of the exchange phase in a transaction. The ratee in turn receives the rating and has to accept or complain about the rating. In the course of a transaction, subjects take on both roles. The activity of the third role is to mediate between two subjects who differ seriously in their opinion about a rating. This will happen most likely if a ratee receives a bad rating and is convinced from her point of view that the statement(s) of the rating is/are wrong. A mediator could be any one subject not affiliated with one of the parties. Mediation will be addressed in a future paper.

4.4   Elements of Our Public-Key Infrastructure

Generally speaking, a public-key infrastructure (PKI) contains mechanisms that provide transactional security. PKI security in this context must adhere to four different properties: *integrity, confidentiality, authentication,* and *non-repudiation*. To achieve these properties, there are several means such as *symmetric* and *asymmetric cryptography, digital signatures* and *certificates* (see [23]).

Integrity is the protection of data against unauthorized modification. Once written by raters, the contents of ratings should not be tampered with. We accomplish this by using digital signatures. Moreover, the key pair generating program for RMS subjects is digitally signed by the portal in order to warrant for the program's authenticity and behavior as specified. Thus subjects can rely on the generation of valid public/private key pairs without any backdoor.

Confidentiality is the protection of data against unauthorized access or disclosure. In our RMS, we use standard operating system access control plus PKCS#12 procedures [21] to secure ratings and cryptographic keys. As data transmission encryption, we use the AES/Rijndael cipher with an agreed-upon session key to secure two-party communication. We refrained from using standard TLS [8] because our modified certificates, though similar to those of the X.509 standard, should be compatible with other public-key algorithms besides RSA. Furthermore, current implementations of TLS do not provide necessary feedback of what is happening during communication to inspire trust in RMS subjects.

Authentication is the verification of the identity of a subject and/or the verification of data origin. Subjects in our RMS are identified unambiguously by their RMS identifier as shown above. They authenticate as valid users of the RMS by submitting data appropriate for that authentication protocol step to the portal or other peer subject. We use the X.509 strong three-way authentication protocol (see section 5.1).

Non-repudiation is the combined services of authentication and integrity that is provable to a third party. Digital signatures schemes are mechanisms where only the originator could have produced the signature. However, subjects' private keys can be compromised, e.g. lost or stolen, without their notice. So for them, there is always the possibility to deny a past signature action if they are not obliged to furnish proof of key compromise. We are still investigating this issue.

5   Transaction Phases

A complete transaction in our RMS can be divided into five phases plus a mandatory registration and activation phase. Figure 1 shows a sample setting with two RMS subjects A, B and a mediator who is currently inactive.

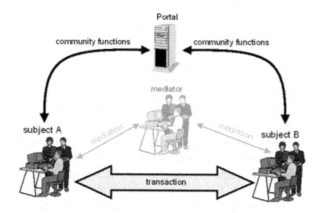

Fig. 1. Interaction relationships between participants of our RMS

① Authentication of RMS subjects
② Service location for a context-specific transaction partner
③ Selection of transaction partner due to its reputation
④ Domain-dependent transaction
⑤ Rating of transaction and partner, rating distribution

In this paper we omit phases ② and ④ due to space constraints.

5.1   Authentication and Registration Phase

Prior to authenticating, RMS subjects are required to register with the RMS portal. They use their TLS-enabled browser to securely access the registration pages to fill in their personal data. After successfully submitting their data, they are asked to download a cryptographically signed program from the portal to generate and register their two public/private key pairs. When the keys have been generated, RMS subjects engage in the X.509 strong three-way authentication protocol [10] with modified key exchange to register their public keys and convince of their authenticity. Notice the generation of two different signature key pairs to avert chosen-text attacks on rating signatures. The portal issues two valid RMS certificates, one for authentication and one for rating purposes, upon subjects entering the activation phase. When RMS subjects need to authenticate each other, the X.509 authentication protocol is used again, so each party is assured of interacting with the party that is mentioned in the certificate body. In the same run, new key generation parameters are transmitted. Hashing those new parameters with subjects' RMS identifiers yields two fresh and unique symmetric session keys. In what follows, we show the three-way case of the X.509 authentication protocol which does not need any more timestamps.

1) $A \longrightarrow B : authcert_A, ratecert_A, d_A, S_{auth_A}(d_A)$ $d_A = (r_A, id_B, P_{auth_B}(r_Z))$
2) $A \longleftarrow B : ratecert_B, d_B, S_{auth_B}(d_B)$ $d_B = (r_B, id_A, P_{auth_A}(r'_Z))$
3) $A \longrightarrow B : r_B, id_B, S_{auth_A}(r_B, id_B)$

$K_{B,A} = H(r_Z, id_B, id_A)$ and $K_{A,B} = H(r'_Z, id_A, id_B)$

Prior to step 1, A needs to obtain B's authentication public key trustworthily, so B's *authcert* can be omitted in step 2. Then A sends to B her certificates $authcert_A, ratecert_A$, data d_A and a signature $S_{auth_A}(d_A)$ obtained by digitally signing d_A with A's authentication private key. Data d_A comprises of the concatenation of a nonce r_A, i.e., a random number generated by some cryptographically secure random number generator, the RMS identifier of B and a random number r_Z encrypted with B's authentication public key. r_Z will be input later to the hash function H to generate B's symmetric session key $K_{B,A}$ (see [2]). The sequence of K's indexes denotes the communications direction. So key $K_{B,A}$ is used by RMS subject B to encrypt messages for RMS subject A. Step 2 is analogous to step 1 but now B sends his data to A. B uses his own random number r'_Z. In this way, we obtain two separate symmetric session keys. So if one of them is compromised, either A's or B's part of the messages transferred and recorded by an eavesdropper till then can be decrypted but not all of the messages. Finally, A sends B's nonce and RMS identifier signed with A's authentication private key to B. This assures integrity and origin of r_B and id_B. The use of nonces (r_A, r_B) guards against replay attacks. So no parts of the protocol can be used in another context or be redirected to other recipients without detecting the fraudulent intention.

During the registration phase both certificates of step 1 are not available and thus left out. So $id_A, P_{auth_A}, P_{rate_A}$ are added to data d_A. At the end of step 3, the portal (B) is convinced that A's two signature public keys are valid so it generates an activation key that is sent by, e.g., regular mail to a real location where A usually resides. When A enters this activation key, the portal sends $authcert_A$ and $ratecert_A$ to A. To foil a man-in-the-middle attack, we use Rivest/Shamir's interlock protocol [20] in the registration phase.

5.2   Transaction Partner Selection Phase

The preceding service location phase yields a list of potential transaction partners. Among these an RMS subject must choose one partner who best fits her wants. This is accomplished by sifting out all inappropriate others according to their context-dependent reputation. A feedback in a reputation is always connected to a particular context, such as selling books, repairing cars, providing expert knowledge, etc., and transaction role such as buyer or seller, for instance. Contexts, however, can be differentiated to the finer or coarser as much as both partners feel necessary. Thus feedback is more to the point. Each rating or feedback can be unambiguously related to a particular, RMS-valid pseudonym by checking its digital signature.

1) $A \longrightarrow B : E_{K_{A,B}}(req\_R'list_{Cxt})$

2) $A \longleftarrow B : E_{K_{B,A}}(\{R'list_{Cxt} \mid R'list_{Cxt'} \mid null\})$

3) $A \longrightarrow T : E_{K_{A,T}}(req\_Count_{B,Cxt})$

4) $A \longleftarrow T : E_{K_{T,A}}(Count_{B,Cxt_{op}}, Count_{B,Cxt_{cl}})$

5) $A \longrightarrow B : E_{K_{A,B}}(\{ok \mid cancel\})$

6) to 10)   same as above but roles and indexes of A and B are swapped.

11) $A \longrightarrow T : E_{K_{A,T}}(gen\_Tickets_{A,B})$

12) $A \longleftarrow T : E_{K_{T,A}}(d_{T,A}, S_{rate_T}(d_{T,A}))$ $d_{T,A} = (id_A, id_B, r_{T,B})$

13) $B \longleftarrow T : E_{K_{T,B}}(d_{T,B}, S_{rate_T}(d_{T,B}))$ $d_{T,B} = (id_A, id_B, r_{T,A})$

14)   context-dependent transaction

$(Q'naire_{Cxt_{X,Y}}, S_{rate_X}(Q'naire_{Cxt_{X,Y}}), id_X, id_Y, r_{T,Y}, S_{rate_T}(id_X, id_Y, r_{T,Y})) \in R'list_{Cxt}$

Throughout this phase, every message is encrypted with the appropriate symmetric encryption key. In step 1, A requests B's aggregated feedback (reputation list) for context Cxt which is either returned by B in step 2 or a list for a more general context Cxt' is sent. If B does not have any reputation at all he returns $null$. After that A requests B's reputation counters for context Cxt or Cxt' from the portal if B's answer was not $null$. $Count_{B,Cxt_{cl}}$ denotes the counter of closed transactions in context Cxt. $Count_{B,Cxt_{op}}$ is the counter of open transactions. Prior to step 5, A checks integrity of the reputation list, i.e., she checks the signature of each questionnaire, checks if id_X, id_Y match the ids in the questionnaire, checks the signature of each portal ticket, and compares the number of ratings in the list with the number of open and closed transactions. Having come to a conclusion, she sends "ok" to B if she wants to engage in a context-dependent transaction or "cancel" otherwise. Steps 6 to 10 are analogous to 1 to 5 but now A and B swap roles. In step 11, A asks the portal to generate transaction tickets for both parties. These security tokens ensure originality and non-replaceabilty of ratings. Steps 12 and 13 show how tickets are composed. First, a ticket attributed to one subject is digitally signed by the portal and sent subsequently to the other subject. Finally, subjects engage in a context-dependent, e.g., e-Commerce transaction in step 14.

5.3 Rating of Transactions and RMS Subjects Phase

When a domain-dependent transaction has come to an end, participants must rate the transaction and each other. In this way both of them build up a reputation. The more ratings a subject receives the more accurate a subsequent statistical evaluation done by any other subject can be.

15) $A \longrightarrow T : req(Q'naire_{Cxt})$ $B \longrightarrow T : req(Q'naire_{Cxt})$

16) $A \longleftarrow T : Q'naire_{Cxt}$ $B \longleftarrow T : Q'naire_{Cxt}$

17) $A \longrightarrow B : E_{K_{A,B}}(Q'naire_{Cxt,B}, S_{rate_A}(Q'naire_{Cxt,B}), r_{T,B})$

18) $A \longleftarrow B : E_{K_{B,A}}(Q'naire_{Cxt,A}, S_{rate_B}(Q'naire_{Cxt,A}), r_{T,A})$

19) $A \longrightarrow T : E_{K_{A,T}}(r_{T,A})$ $B \longrightarrow T : E_{K_{B,T}}(r_{T,B})$

20a) $A \longleftarrow T : E_{K_{T,A}}(\text{"ok"})$ $B \longleftarrow T : E_{K_{T,B}}(\text{"ok"})$

20b) $A \longleftarrow T : E_{K_{T,A}}(\text{"nonce error"})$ $B \longleftarrow T : E_{K_{T,B}}(\text{"nonce error"})$

In step 15, A and B request an empty questionnaire for context Cxt which they receive in step 16. They fill out the questionnaire, i.e., answer questions with respect to the partner and transaction just happened and digitally sign it with their signature private key. After that the questionnaire and the nonce extracted from the portal ticket is sent securely to the transaction partner. When nonces $r_{T,B}$ and $r_{T,A}$ of step 17 and 18 circulate back to the portal, it is clear that both parties have received and added the ratings to their reputation lists. The portal quits each session by sending "ok" or "nonce error" if the nonce generated does not match with the one received. After that, the portal invalidates communication keys $K_{A,T}$, $K_{B,T}$ and A and B are supposed to invalidate $K_{A,B}$, $K_{B,A}$, too. Notice, double actions in steps 15, 16, 19, and 20 need not be executed in parallel. However steps 17 and 18 should be, because the first to receive feedback could be tempted to "tune" his/her rating. A deadlock situation is likely to occur if both parties wait for a rating from the other. A solution might look like this: A encrypts her rating with a symmetric cipher whose key is only known to her at first. After sending this so encrypted rating to B, she waits for B's to arrive. B in turn does the same as A but uses his own key. Finally, the keys are exchanged so both of them can decrypt and inspect the other's rating.

6   Concluding Remarks and Future Work

By introducing current P2P and PKI technology, our RMS offers a more flexible and democratic solution to managing subjects' reputations than other systems. RMS services are not bound to a specific domain, so a reputation earned in one can be transferred to another. Furthermore, intra-RMS subject communication is secured by strong cryptography and ratings are digitally signed to ensure integrity. Transactions must comply with the protocol otherwise participants will not receive any rating. In this way trust is fostered, and participants are encouraged to work with the system. Currently, we are implementing a research prototype of our RMS. There are several problems we think best to tackle in the running system such as "bootstrapping", use transparency and premature transaction termination by subjects. Furthermore, our RMS is presently unable to avert collusion (cooperation of malicious users). An organizational mitigation of this might be, first, to ensure that one pseudonym is linked to exactly one real user, second, to charge a transaction fee which can be spent on an insurance against fraud and, third, to expel misbehaving users for ever from the system. Finally, it will be interesting to see how may disputes will crop up during a number of transactions and how these can be solved by a mediator.

References

1. Abdul-Rahman, A., Hailes, S.: Supporting Trust in Virtual Communities. In: Proceedings of the Hawai'i Int'l. Conf. on System Sciences, Hawaii (2000)
2. Aura, T.: Strategies against Replay Attacks. In: Proceedings of the 10th IEEE Computer Security Foundations Workshop, Rockport, Massachusetts (1997)

3. Blaze, M., Feigenbaum, J., Lacy, J.: Decentralized Trust Management. In: Proc. of the IEEE Symp. on Security and Privacy, IEEE Society Press (1996) 164–173
4. Casassa Mont, M., Tomasi, L., Montanari, R.: An Adaptive System Responsive to Trust Assessment Based on Peer-to-Peer Evidence Replication and Storage. Technical report HPL-2001-133, Hewlett Packard Laboratories (2001)
5. Chaum, D.: Security without Identification: Transaction Systems to Make Big Brother Obsolete. Communications of the ACM **28** (1985) 1030–1040
6. Chen, R., Yeager, W.: Poblano – A Distributed Trust Model for Peer-to-Peer Networks (2001). http://www.jxta.org/project/www/docs/trust.pdf, 02/21/2002.
7. Dellarocas, C.: Immunizing Online Reputation Reporting Systems against Unfair Ratings and Discriminatory Behavior. In: Proceedings of the 2nd ACM Conference on Electronic Commerce, Minneapolis, MN (2000)
8. Dierks, T., Allen, C.: The TLS Protocol Version 1.0 (1999). http://www.rfc-editor.org/rfc/rfc2246.txt, 02/28/2002.
9. Dingledine, R., Freedman, M. J., Molnar, D.: Accountability. In Oram, A. (ed.): Peer-to-Peer. Harnessing the Power of Disruptive Technologies. O'Reilly and Associates, Sebastopol, CA (2001)
10. ITU-T: Public-key and Attribute Certificate Frameworks. Recommendation X.509. (03/2000). http://www.itu.int, 05/17/2002.
11. Josang, A.: The Right Type of Trust for Distributed Systems. In Meadows, C., (ed.): Proc. of New Security Paradigms Workshop, ACM Press (1996) 119–131
12. Labalme, F., Burton, K.: Enhancing the Internet with Reputations (2001). http://www.openprivacy.org/papers/200103-white.html, 02/21/2002.
13. Levien, R.: Advogato's Trust Metric (2000). http://www.advogato.org/trust-metric.html, 02/21/2002.
14. Lethin, R.: Reputation. In Oram A., (ed.): Peer-to-Peer. Harnessing the Power of Disruptive Technologies, O'Reilly and Associates, 2001
15. Maximilien, E. M., Singh, M. P.: Reputation and Endorsement for Web Services. Proceedings of the ACM SIGecom conference **3** (2002) 24–31
16. Oram, A.: Peer-to-Peer. Harnessing the Power of Disruptive Technologies. O'Reilly and Associates, Sebastopol, CA, USA (2001)
17. Padovan, B., Sackmann, S., et al.: A Prototype for an Agent-based Secure Electronic Marketplace Including Reputation Tracking Mechanisms. In: Proc. of the 34th Hawai'i Int'l. Conf. on System Sciences, IEEE Computer Society (2001)
18. Raub, W., Weesie, J.: Reputation and Efficiency in Social Interactions: An Example of Network Effects. American Journal of Sociology **96** (1990) 626–654
19. Resnick, P., Zeckhauser, R., et al.: Reputation Systems. Communications of the ACM **43** (2000) 45–48
20. Rivest, R. L., Shamir, A.: How to Expose an Eavesdropper. Communications of the ACM **27** (1984) 393–395
21. RSA Data Security, Inc.: Pkcs#12 - pers. information exchange syntax std. (1999)
22. Sabater, J., Sierra, C.: Social Regret, a Reputation Model Based on Social Relations. Proceedings of the ACM SIGecom conference **3** (2001) 44–56
23. Schneier, B.: Applied Cryptography: Protocols, Algorithms, and Source Code in C. 2nd edn. John Wiley and Sons, Inc., New York, NY, USA (1996)
24. Winsborough, W., Seamons, K. E., Jones, V. E.: Automated Trust Negotiation. In: DARPA Information Survivability Conference and Exposition, USA (2000)
25. Yu, B., Singh, M. P.: A Social Mechanism of Reputation Management in Electronic Communities. In: Cooperative Information Agents, Boston, MA, USA (2000)

Practical Mobile Digital Signatures*

Antonio Maña and Sonia Matamoros

Computer Science Department
University of Málaga. Spain.
{amg, sonia}@lcc.uma.es

Abstract. There are important details that give legal validity to hand-written signatures: First, the document to be signed is under control of the signatory and it is not possible to substitute or alter it, and second, the tools to produce the signature (the pen and the signatory itself) are also under control of the signatory. These details make possible that handwritten signatures are used in a law court to prove the willingness of the signatory to be bound by the content of the document. Digital signatures require complex calculations that can not be done using mental arithmetic by the signatory. In this case neither document nor tools are under direct control of the signatory but under control of a computer. Consequently, the willingness of the signatory can not be sufficiently demonstrated. Furthermore, to be able to perform digital signatures, we must assume that the user trusts the computer to perform exactly what is intended. This yields digital signatures unusable in scenarios that require mobility. In this paper we present a system to perform digital signatures in environments that require mobility. The system is based on the use of personal digital assistants and smart cards and fulfils the common requirements established in different national laws regarding digital signatures.

1 Introduction and Legal Situation

Many countries have passed laws regulating the use of digital signatures and certificates. Most of these laws include security requirements for both hardware devices and software used in the creation of digital signatures.

The first draft of the digital signature law in Argentina [1] states: "The digital signature technology is not perfect. Hardware devices and software for the creation and verification of digital signatures must be homologated to attest their suitability for the creation and verification of digital signatures with full legal validity...".

The German law distinguishes different requirements and security levels for each one of the components used in the creation of signature keys, visualization of data to be signed and generation and verification of the signatures. This law states: "The competent authority shall publish, in the Federal Gazette, a list of agencies pursuant to § 14 (4) of the Digital Signature Act [2] as well as a list of

---

* Work partially supported by the E.U. through project IST 2001-32446

K. Bauknecht, A M. Tjoa, G. Quirchmayr (Eds.): EC-Web 2002, LNCS 2455, pp. 224–233, 2002.
© Springer-Verlag Berlin Heidelberg 2002

technical components that have received confirmation by such agencies pursuant to (3); the competent authority shall provide this list directly to the certification authorities. Note must be made, for all technical components, of the date until which the confirmation is valid...".

Directive 1999/93/EC of the European Parliament on a "Community framework for electronic signatures" [3] establishes among the requirements for certification service providers that they must "...use trustworthy systems and products which are protected against modification and ensure the technical and cryptographic security of the process supported by them...".

Finally, the Spanish law on digital signatures [4] establishes in its article 3 the security requirements for the digital signature creation devices: "Advanced digital signatures will have for data in electronic form the same legal validity as the handwritten signature for printed data and will be accepted as a proof in a law court ...provided that they are based on a legal digital certificate and produced by a secure signature creation device". Similar requirements are established for the signature verification devices. The law also establishes that "secure signature creation device must guarantee that:

1. the signature-creation-data used for signature generation can practically occur only once, and that their secrecy is reasonably assured;
2. the signature-creation-data used for signature generation cannot, with reasonable assurance, be derived and the signature is protected against forgery using currently available technology;
3. the signature-creation-data used for signature generation can be reliably protected by the legitimate signatory against the use of others.
4. Secure signature-creation devices must not alter the data to be signed or prevent such data from being presented to the signatory prior to the signature process."

Directly related to the topic of this work, we must emphasize the content of article 29 where obligations of the issuer of digital certificates are indicated: "ensure that the signature-creation-data is permanently under the user's control and is not shared with others". This requirement represents, in practice, the impossibility to create digital signatures in computers other than the user's own personal computer.

The issue of mobility in the use of digital signatures has not been sufficiently addressed, although some proposals have appeared in the literature [5] [6]. Currently, digital signatures are created using software or hardware devices that have not been systematically verified. Furthermore, the security of the global computing environment that supports these devices and software has not been considered at all. This situation leads to the impossibility to demonstrate with reasonable assurance the willingness of the signatory when digital signatures are used. Regrettably, many of the digital signature laws establish the presumption of validity of the digital signature when in doubt, which conflicts with the presumption of innocence principle. For this reason, these laws are difficult to put into effect.

As a conclusion it must be emphasized that digital signature laws, and specially European laws, concentrate in the verification of the fact that digital signatures have been created using a certain public key and do not consider the validity of the content and the assurance of the willingness of the signatory to be bound by the content of the signed document [7].

2   Secure Creation of Digital Signatures

A handwritten signature is an intentional human biometric action that proves the willingness of the signatory of a document. The fact that the document to be signed is under control of the signatory and it is not possible to substitute or alter the document without the user noticing it, and also that the tools to produce the signature (the pen and the signatory itself) are also under the signatory's control confer reliability to handwritten signatures and make possible that they are used in a law court to prove the signatory's willingness to be bound by the content of the document. Because digital signatures require complex calculations that are performed by a computer, the willingness of the signatory is difficult to establish.

Asymmetric cryptography [8] provides mathematical algorithms for the computation of digital signatures. The result of these algorithms is a value (the digital signature) that depends on the document that is being signed and also on the key used to sign it. Any change in the document or the key will result in the the signature algorithm producing a different value. These algorithms involve complex mathematical computations but the mechanisms of use are simple. Each user has a key pair consisting in a public key that can be known to the rest of users and a private key that is only known by its owner. Digital signatures are produced using the private key while they can be verified using the corresponding public key.

In digital signatures based on asymmetric cryptography, it is essential that the private key is strongly protected by means of encryption or using tamperproof hardware storage devices. The problem arises when the key is used to produce a digital signature, specially in untrusted computers, because the key must be exposed in the clear in order to be used in the computation of the digital signature value. To solve this problem devices such as smart cards and cryptographic tokens are becoming popular. These devices serve as tamperproof hardware storage and, additionally, have the capability to compute digital signatures and other cryptographic primitives without exposing the private key.

Keeping the private key secured guarantees that only its owner can produce digital signatures with it, but it does not guarantee the willingness of the signatory because the creation of the signature is not under control of the signatory. The digital signature scheme can fail in case control over the private key is lost (e.g. in case it is stored without protection), but it also fails when the digital signature creation element (hardware device or software) signs a different document than the one that the signatory wanted to sign. For this second problem, different approaches have been proposed:

- *Trusted software environment*: The objective in this case is to guarantee that the software used to produce the digital signatures is not forged or altered. To achieve this goal, authenticated (digitally signed) software can be used [9]. An interesting initiative that would guarantee the necessary confidence in the integrity of computing systems is the "Trusted Computing Platform" [10]. The main problems of this approach are the need for a complex infrastructure that, at least on the short term, is not viable and the fact that software must be authenticated at different levels (application, function or even instruction). Moreover, the verification of the software introduces an important overload in the system performance. It must be noted that, in order to be useful, the code authentication mechanism must be applied to all the software and even to the hardware of the computer.
- *External collaboration*: This approach, described in [11], is based on the use of protocols for the creation of digital signatures with the help of a trusted third party that guarantees that the signature is computed on the document desired by the signatory. An important drawback of this system is that the problems related to the establishment of an infrastructure of trusted third parties are at least as complex as those of our original problem. Moreover, users must install specific software to be able to produce the digital signatures (this software has to control directly and exclusively the computer screen), but this software can be forged or substituted by a malicious replica. Consequently, the security of the system is not guaranteed.
- *Hardware signature device*: In this case a secure computing device, such as a cryptographic coprocessor, a mobile phone or a personal digital assistant (PDA) is used. The device must have the capability to compute the signature and also to display the document. Because most of these devices are not tamperproof it is necessary to use a complementary tamperproof device such as a smart card.

3   A Secure Digital Signature Creation Environment

From the analysis of the previous classification we conclude that the most practical and secure approach to build a mobile digital signature creation environment is the one based on a hardware device. There are proposals to use mobile phones as "personal trusted devices" [12] devices carrying a user's PKI credentials and capable of not only signing but also displaying messages that are about to sign. In the same category, PDAs are specially interesting because of their visualization capabilities, rich user interface, programming possibilities and connectivity. Therefore, our system is based on the use of a PDAs.

3.1   System Architecture and Components

An interesting alternative for the deployment of the secure digital signature environment is the use of mobile phones. GSM mobile phones present interesting advantages such as capability to send and receive SMS messages, access to Internet using WAP and the integrated smart card reader (the SIM module is itself a smart card). On the other hand, document visualization and edition capabilities are very limited. For this reason, mobile phones have been used in applications such as electronic ticketing [15] that require the use of digital signatures and other cryptographic operations but do not require complex document edition and visualization.

The decision of using PDAs for our secure digital signature environment is based on the availability of software development tools, their multiple usages and the communication and visualization capabilities. The negative aspects of PDAs are that they are not tamperproof, do not provide cryptographic functions and lack adequate memory protection mechanisms. Our PDA has serial and IrDA ports. We use the serial port to connect the PDA to a smart card reader and also to the PC. Additionally, we use the IrDA port to communicate with other PDAs and with other IrDA-enabled devices.

Our system has been developed on a Palm Vx with PalmOS v.3.5. Although the security issues have not been considered important in previous versions of the PDAs operating systems, this situation is currently changing. For example, there are joint efforts by Palm Computing and Certicom in order to integrate elliptic curve cryptography into PalmOS. At the present time, additional devices must be used to enhance the security of PDAs. Smart cards are the choice for this purpose because they are tamper resistant, have cryptographic capabilities and their memory management is completely secure.

In our scheme, smart cards are responsible for the secure storage of keys and the computation of cryptographic operations. The use of a separate device (the smart card) is justified by the fact that smart cards can be used in different scenarios by different applications. Therefore, the use of smart cards make possible that the same key is used in all applications. Smart cards are also used to authenticate the software loaded on the PDA.

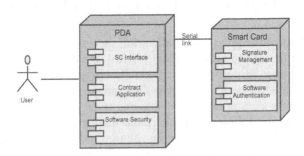

Fig. 1. Deployment Diagram of the Secure Signature Environment

The components of the system are shown in figure 1. The PDA includes components to access the smart card reader (*SCLink*) and to authenticate the software installed in the PDA (*PDASAC*). For the smart card, we have implemented a specific Javacard cardlet that provides functions to perform digital signatures (*Signature Control*) and to support the software authentication component of the PDA (*SCSAC*). The process to produce a digital signature is the following:

- The *PDASAC* component authenticates the software installed in the PDA and displays the document to be signed.
- The user introduces the PIN of the smart card.
- The *PDASAC* component sends the signature request to the smart card using the *SCLink*.
- The *Signature Control* component produces the signature inside the smart card and sends it to the PDA.

The authentication of the software of the PDA is used to avoid that malicious software is introduced in the PDA without the user consent. It does not guarantee that the software in the PDA is not malicious. Users are responsible for the software that is installed with their consent. The reason for this is that there is no code authentication mechanism for PalmOS applications that could be used to guarantee the origin and behaviour of the software produced by third parties.

To be able to authenticate the software the user must produce a "signature" of all the software of the PDA (including the *PDASAC* and the *SCLink* components) and store it inside the smart card. Whenever the software has to be authenticated the *PDASAC* component collaborates with the *SCSAC* component of the smart card to verify this "signature".

3.2 Short-Range Communication Technologies

The proliferation of different electronic commerce solutions based on devices that bring "freedom" or mobility to users such as mobile phones or PDAs has originated the term "mobile commerce". An interesting feature of some of these devices is the capability to communicate with other devices by means of short-range communication technologies such as IrDA (infrared) [13] and Bluetooth (radio) [14]. Currently, IrDA is the most popular one: it is not unusual today that printers, mobile phones, laptops or PDAs have an IrDA port. Bluetooth is a new technology but it is becoming rapidly accepted. Even as they appear to be very different, there's a higher level protocol called OBEX that integrates both of them making possible the development of applications that can use both technologies transparently. The communication using these protocols and channels is restricted by the distance between the devices. This restriction represents an advantage in our system because it simplifies the control of some attacks.

3.3 Contract Signing

Digital signatures are intended to provide authentication, integrity and evidence of the willingness of the signatory. The signing of electronic contracts is used to demonstrate the use of our system.

Contracts are created to attest the conditions that the different actors (parts) involved have established for a transaction. Usually one of the actors will compose the contract, that will be later reviewed by the other parts before signing actually takes place. Sometimes the contract requires modifications that can be introduced by any of the parts involved. In this case the modified contract has to be send to the other parts. Once all parts agree with the content of the contract they sign it and exchange the signatures with the other parts.

Secure Contract Signing Application. Electronic contracting is one of the most interesting applications bring about by the new technologies [16]. Based on advances in the fields of pocket computers, short range communication, smart cards and information security, we have described how to build a secure mobile digital signature environment. Such environment is specially useful for contract signing applications.

The security requirements of the contract signing are critical because the contracts would turn out unuseful in case that it can be demonstrated that the legal requirements are not met by the signature creation environment. For this reason smart cards must be used in our proposal.

Using the secure mobile digital signature environment presented, and given the document edition and interconnection facilities available in pocket computers, the resulting contract signing application allows users to easily and securely create, exchange, review, sign and store contracts in scenarios that demand mobility.

Contract Structure. Because the contract is going to be edited, visualized and stored in a PDA, its definition must be done considering the limitations of the device. First, the amount of memory available is limited and second, although the screen size is large compared to the size of the device, it is small compared to the screen of a desktop computer. Because of the limitations in the amount of information that can be displayed at once, the contract is divided in three main sections:

- *Contract description*: general information about the contract such as the description, the object of the contract and the date.
- *Involved parts*: in this section the identification of the parts involved in the contract will be reflected. There are at least two parts, even though each one can have several representatives.
- *Clauses of the contract*: they specify the terms that both parts establish and agree to be bound by when the contract is signed. The number of clauses is not limited except by the size of the memory available. Clauses can be stored for use in future contracts.

To create a new contract the user specifies all the information relevant to it. Fig. 2 shows different screens that the user has to fill with the contract information. The structure of the user interface follows the structure of the contract described previously.

Fig. 2. Creation of a new contract

Contract Processing. In this section we will review the processes of contract creation and signing. For simplicity the case of a bilateral contract is described. The contract is created by one of the parts it is sent to the other part using some communication medium (IrDA protocol, Bluetooth, a direct cable connection or even Internet). Once both parts have a copy of the contract, any of them can modify the contract. If changes take place, both parts interchange the new versions of the contract. When both parts agree on the content of the contract they proceed to sign it. It is not necessary that both parts meet physically to sign the contract. It is possible that the parts exchange the corresponding signatures of the contract by any other channel.

Because the signature is computed by the smart card, the connection between the PDA and the card reader must be direct and reliable. For this reason we have implemented a specific component (*SCLink*) for the PDA. After both parts sign their copies of the contract, they exchange the signatures. Finally, when the signature of the other part is received, it is verified and stored.

Implementation. The digital signature environment presented has been implemented on a Palm Vx PDA with CodeWarrior 6 for Palm OS. Because of tha lack of support for smart card readers in PalmOS 3.5, the libraries required to connect the PDA to the smart card reader have been developed. This connection implies the total control of the card reader from the PDA.

Software to carry out all the cryptographic processes has also been implemented. This processes imply sending commands to the smart card from the PDA to instruct it to carry out the calculations that produce the cryptographic primitives available in the card.

The card contains software to authenticate the software applications installed in the PDA. In this case the lack of memory protection in the PDA is an advantage for us because it facilitates this process. Any time a new software application is installed in the PDA the user is requested to decide whether to compute a new "signature" on the installed software and or not.

4   Conclusions

The digital signature creation environment proposed combines three interesting issues: mobility, tamperproof hardware devices and software security. In case of digital contracts, users are obliged to use their personal computers for the creation of the signatures, because computation of digital signatures requires the use of their private keys. Therefore, in this situation it is possible to automate those types of contracts that we call intrinsic to Internet because they are originated, managed and refer to Internet objects. But this interpretation of the utility of digital signatures is restrictive and it would be desirable to extend its use to any scenario where the handwritten signature is applicable. The development of secure digital signature environments is necessary to allow their use in situations where the use of personal computers is not possible. If digital signatures could be produced by means of a mobile device, they would replace handwritten ones in most of the situations where handwritten signatures are currently used.

To use digital signatures we must firstly, be able guarantee who is the signer. But, on the other hand, we must also guarantee that the content of the document was not altered by the signature device or software. In order to obtain such objectives it is necessary to use a reliable environment to produce the signature.

In this paper we have presented a secure digital signature creation environment that is based on PDAs and smart cards. Digital signatures produced by this environment fulfils the requirements necessary to guarantee its legal validity. Additionally, this environment can be used to produce digital signatures in scenarios where the use of the existing digital signature environments (based on personal computers) is not possible.

References

1. Dirección Nacional de Coordinación e Integración Tecnológica de Argentina - Subsecretaría de la Gestión Pública: Anteproyecto de Ley de formato digital de los actos jurídicos. Comercio electrónico. http://www.pki.gov.ar/PKIdocs/ley.html
2. Federal Government of Germany: Digital Signature Act of 22 July 1997 (Federal Law Gazette I S. 1870, 1872). http://www.iid.de/iukdg/sigve.html
3. The European Parliament and the Council of the European Union. Directive 1999/93/EC "on a Community framework for electronic signatures". 1999 http://europa.eu.int/comm/internal_market/en/media/sign/Dir99-93-ecEN.pdf
4. Gobierno de España. Real Decreto-Ley 14/1999, de 17 de septiembre, sobre firma electrónica. http://www.sgc.mfom.es/legisla/internet/rdley14_99.htm
5. Freudenthal, M.; Heiberg, S., Willemson, J.: Personal Security Environment on Palm PDA. Perteneciente a: Annual Computer Security Applications Conference, Sheraton New Orleans, Louisiana USA.

6. Daswani, N., Boneh, D.: Experimenting with Electronic Commerce on the PalmPilot. http://www.stanford.edu/~dabo
7. Ang, K. M., Caelli, W. J.: Certificate based PKI and B2B e-commerce: suitable match or not?. Proceedings of the 16th International Conference on Information Security (IFIP/SEC 2001). Kluwer Academic Publishers. (2001)
8. Rivest, R. L., Shamir, A., Adleman, L.: A method for obtaining digital signatures and public key cryptosystems. Communications of the ACM 21(2):120–126. (1978)
9. Davida, G. I., Desmedt, Y., Blaze, M. J.: Defending Systems Against Viruses Through Cryptographic Authentication. Proceedings of IEEE 1989 Symposium on Security and Privacy, pp 312–318. (1989)
10. Spalka, A., Cremers. A.B., Langweg, H.: Protecting the creation of digital signatures with trusted computing platform technology against attacks by Trojan Horse programs. Proceedings of the 16th International Conference on Information Security (IFIP/SEC 2001). Kluwer Academic Publishers. (2001)
11. Helme, A., Mullender, S.J.: What you see is what gets signed. Personal Communication.
12. Minutes from the Ad-hoc PKCS Workshop, April 10, 2001.
    ftp://ftp.rsasecurity.com/pub/pkcs/01conference/minutes.txt
13. IrDa Association. IrDa Standards.
    http://www.irda.org/standards/standards.asp
14. Bluetooth SIG Inc. The Bluetooth Specificdation.
    http://www.bluetooth.com/developer/specification/specification.asp
15. Maña, A., Martinez, J., Matamoros, S., Troya, J.M.: GSM-Ticket: Generic Secure Mobile Ticketing Service. Proceedings of GDC 2001. (2001)
    http://www.lcc.uma.es/publicaciones/LCC803.pdf
16. Yee, B., Tygar, J.D.: Secure Coprocessors in Electronic Commerce Applications. Proceeding of the First USENIX Workshop on Electronic Commerce. (1995)

Secure Client Agent Environment (SCAE) for World Wide Web

Richard Au[1], Ming Yao[1], Mark Looi[1], and Paul Ashley[2]

[1] Information Security Research Centre
Queensland University of Technology
Brisbane, Qld 4001, Australia
{w.au, m.yao, m.looi}@qut.edu.au
[2] IBM Software Group - Tivoli
11400 Burnett Road, Austin, Tx, 78758, USA
pashley@us.ibm.com

Abstract. The agent programming approach can be beneficial for many new applications on the World Wide Web. We propose a novel agent workspace on the client side for hosting Web agents downloaded from different Web servers – the "Secure Client Agent Environment" (SCAE). This user-centred marketplace facilitates collaboration among Web agents, Web servers and the user. In our agent-based framework, domain-based security servers and authorisation tokens are used to complete the trust links between the client and various Web servers dynamically.

1 Introduction

The World Wide Web (Web) forms a global computational resource in the Internet environment. Typically, a user surfs on the Web and visits various Web sites that he is interested in. In most situations, many of these Web sites do not hold any attribute about the user before the sessions. A question of interest is how the user can establish trust relationships with multiple Web sites and interact with the Web applications in a secure and efficient way.

Traditionally, the Web is a distributed hypermedia system adopting the client-server model. The HTTP protocol is directional, stateless, single-stepped and user-centred. This request-respond operation scheme has many advantages, however it also inherits some limitations in Web application development as listed below:

- Synchronous mode – In the Web access protocol, a client application must remain active when accessing a server. The operation of the system is strictly synchronous.
- No collaboration among servers – There is no proper channel for multiple Web applications to work collaboratively to provide a comprehensive service to the client.
- Few environment assumptions – There are few assumptions about the execution environment, available resources etc. on the client's computing platform.

K. Bauknecht, A M. Tjoa, G. Quirchmayr (Eds.): EC-Web 2002, LNCS 2455, pp. 234–243, 2002.
© Springer-Verlag Berlin Heidelberg 2002

- Stateless model – While the Web server has no state, the client has to manage, if needed, all state information between one usage and the next one.

Agent technology can be used to overcome these limitations and extend the functions of Web applications. The term *agent* denotes a hardware or (more usually) software-based computer system that enjoys the following properties: autonomy, social ability, reactivity and pro-activeness [12]. The agent programming approach can be beneficial for many new applications on the Web, such as electronic commerce. However, we argue that the ubiquitous availability of a trusted and secure environment for agent execution is essential for successful usage of the agent paradigm.

Our contribution in this paper is the novel idea of developing a trusted and secure agent workspace on the user side – the so called "Secure Client Agent Environment" (SCAE). The SCAE provides a platform for collaboration among the user, Web agents and Web servers. With the objective of enhancing the functionality and security of Web applications, we propose an agent-based framework consisting of four main components:

- An infrastructure of domain-based security servers for trust distribution;
- Authorisation token for secure delivery of access credentials;
- Client-sided Web agent for enhancing the client/server interactions on the Web;
- SCAE for hosting multiple Web agents on the client side.

2   Some Previous Work

2.1   Domain-Based Trust Distribution

The Internet can be regarded as a dynamic collection of independent administrative domains which may have some form of mutual trust relationship between each other at the organisational business level. Kerberos [9], SESAME[1] and DCE[10] are domain-based security architectures that provide authentication and/or authorisation services using security servers. In addition to the administration of local users, a security server can act as a trusted intermediary between its local users and other external servers. Making use of the relationships among organisational domains, these domain-based servers can be interconnected with one another to form an infrastructure for trust establishment. Some related work is described in [3]. In the E-commerce environment, the business relationships among different companies can be expressed as a "web of trust". After some authentication and authorisation processes, a user acquires a secure trust link with his local security server which then works on behalf of the user to establish trust relationships with other servers within the trust infrastructure.

2.2   One-Shot Authorisation Token for Cross Domain Access

In a traditional user identity-based system, the server (e.g. Web server) collects required information from the user to create a user profile in registration. Before access to protected resources is granted, user authentication must be completed successfully. The process of user registration to remote servers is inconvenient and inefficient in the Web environment. Alternatively, the privilege certification approach allows a user to submit some credentials to request and initiate accesses. Two examples of user credentials are *ticket* in Kerberos and *Privilege Attribute Certificate* (PAC) in SESAME. Following the same line, we have developed the *One-Shot Authorisation Token* by separating authorisation from user authentication [2]. With the trust infrastructure of security servers in position, the user can obtain all the tokens he needs through his local security server, which works on his behalf. In the Web environment, this push approach using One-Shot Authorisation Token enables a user to gain a direct access instantaneously to a Web server in a secure way without user authentication.

3   A New Architecture for Agent-Web Integration

Based on the infrastructure of security servers and One-Shot Authorisation Token, we propose a user-centred model in our agent-based framework for the Web as shown in Figure 1. The client can make an access request to an agent-support Web server by submitting an authorisation token. The Web server, with its security server, gives appropriate access rights according to the information in the token and sends back a Web agent to the client. The client application (working on behalf of the user) manages the download of Web agents into the SCAE, which facilitates secure agent executions as well as interactions among different Web agents.

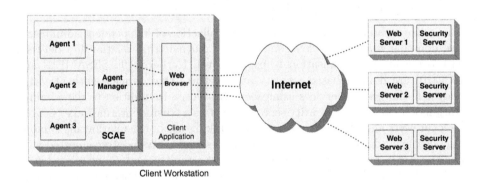

Fig. 1. Architectural overview for the Agent-Web Integration

3.1   Web Server as Agent Provider

In addition to traditional static Web data, applet or other scripts, Web agent can be regarded as an additional data type available to clients on the Web. Agent-support Web servers can be developed to handle the storage and delivery of Web agents. While accessing the Web server, the user will be prompted to download appropriate agents to his workstation whenever necessary.

3.2   Web Agents on Client Platform

Our proposed Web agent can be regarded as one type of single-hop mobile agent because the codes migrate from the server to the client side. A Web agent will stay in the SCAE of the client's computer system in its lifetime until removed after use. The SCAE provides the necessary resources and runtime supports for the execution of agents. With Web agents as the intermediary, the client-server interactions can be extended to be bi-directional, stateful and non-synchronous.

4   Secure Client Agent Environment (SCAE)

Since Web agents act on behalf of their parent servers and they are empowered with authorisation ability, their security in terms of confidentiality, integrity and authenticity is vital [4]. In our architectural design, we propose to develop the SCAE for hosting Web agents. The administrator of a security domain is responsible for setting up the SCAEs of all local users and maintaining their security all the time. Thus there is a direct trust link established between a user's SCAE and the local security server.

4.1   Agent Manager for Central Administration

The agent manager, which is basically a program installed in SCAE, provides the following administrative services in the agent workspace:

- Hosting agents – Arriving Web agents have to be verified, installed and registered.
- Resource configuration – Web agents have to express their resource requirements and collect configuration information.
- Execution management – Web agents may need to access some runtime libraries and services on the platform during execution.
- Communication links – Protected channels are set up for Web agents to communicate with various entities, such as other locally residing agents, the client application.
- Security provider – Privacy and integrity of Web agents with their data have to be guaranteed. Cryptographic methods are used to provide authentication, authorisation and other access control services.

4.2   Platform for Agent Collaboration

Referring to figure 2, when a client accesses different Web servers, Web agents are downloaded and installed in his SCAE. This user-centred workspace serves as a base or marketplace for multiple agents from different domains. Through existing communication channels among various entities, different virtual channels can be established making use of the SCAE:

- Agent-to-Agent channel: On the client platform, multiple agents can interact with one another through the agent manager. These interactions should be authorised by the client. Secure and trusted channels can be built to allow collaboration among agents. As an example, electronic sales from corporate companies may cooperate in the negotiation with the user.
- Cross-domain Agent-to-server channel: An agent from one domain can interact with a Web server of another domain via its agent in the SCAE. Some possible uses are delegation and referral.
- Server-to-Server channel: Through their agents as their representatives, Web servers of different domains can interact in a secure manner. One example is user-authorised bank-to-bank transaction.

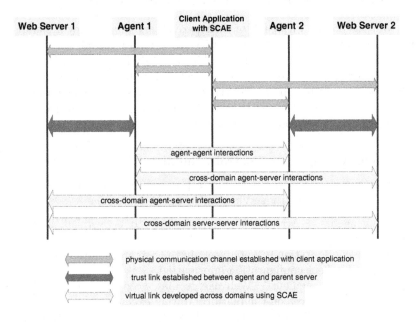

Fig. 2. User-Centred Agent Collaboration

5 Securing Web Agents with SCAE

5.1 Security of SCAE

There are many possible ways to establish a SCAE in a client's computer system. Basically, a self-contained and secure execution platform trusted by the administrator of the security domain is required. A SCAE can be built in a Trusted Computer Base (TCB). Also a tamper-resistant hardware, such as a smart card or iButton[7], can be integrated with the client's computer system to provide flexibility and functionality for building a secure agent environment. Alternatively, software-based technology, such as advanced cryptographic mechanisms, may be used to develop the SCAE on the client platform.

5.2   Configuration of Web Agents

We have identified the following four models for the configuration of Web agents in the client's computer system with a SCAE:

Full Protection Model. The whole agent is installed in the SCAE. The agent manager provides secure communication support for agents and the outside world using cryptographic techniques. The security is high as all data and codes are kept inside the secure environment at all times.

Partial Protection Model. The portion of the agent that needs strong security is installed in SCAE while the other portion is installed on the client's computing platform. These two portions may work co-operatively. The main advantage of this model is that some resources on the client workstation become available to the agents, e.g. CPU computing power, random access memory.

Agent Monitoring Model. The agent is installed and executed on the client's workstation. There is a specialized program installed on the SCAE and it acts as an agent monitor to verify the integrity and possibly confidentiality of the agents and their data. Monitoring mechanisms can be classified into two types, namely detective monitoring (e.g. cryptographic traces[11] and state appraisal[5]) and preventive monitoring (e.g. obfuscation[6]).

Self-Secured Agent Model. The agent is downloaded onto the client's workstation and no secure execution environment is assumed. The agent is capable of protecting itself in order to maintain its trust relationship with the remote server. Many conventional security techniques have focused on "adding" protective mechanisms onto the agents. However, as the nature of an agent is highly self-contained and self-controlled component [8], it is possible that an agent intelligently adopts certain security countermeasures when encountering the attack, based on the pre-defined autonomous processing.

5.3   An Prototype Implementation: Hosting Multiple Agents in SCAE

Following the full protection model, we currently use a Java iButton[7] to facilitate the SCAE in our prototype implementation. It is a personal secure device with its access password protected. The agent manager, in the form of a Java applet, is installed in the iButton and it communicates with the client application through interfaces on the workstation. The client application is developed in Java and it comprises a Web browser. On the server side, the Web server is agent-support with some servlets developed. Various formats of databases are created for storing authorisation token and agent data. Cryptographic methods are used to provide authentication, confidentiality and integrity in the delivery of tokens and agents between the Web server and the client workstation. Public key infrastructure is assumed to be in position.

Referring to figure 3, when a client sends a HTTP request to a URL designating an application on a Web server, he is prompted to submit an authorisation token. After verifying the received token, the servlet on the server side generates a session key and renews the token. Upon the client's request, the servlet retrieves the appropriate agent from the repository and then sends it back in encrypted form along with a signature. On the client side, the agent instance will be installed in the iButton after verification.

In a similar way, more agents from different Web servers can be downloaded into the iButton within its capacity. The agent manager coordinates the agents and can activate one agent at a time in the iButton implementation.

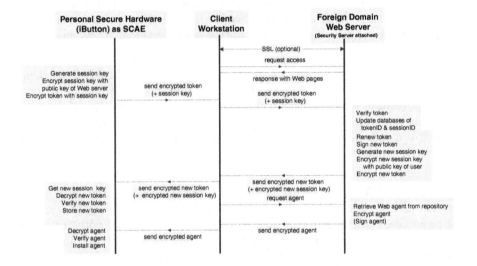

Fig. 3. Downloading and Installation of Web Agent

6   A Demonstrative Application of SCAE: E-sales

In our agent paradigm, the user provides a secure agent workspace on his workstation and invites sales agents from multiple Web shops for a business. These sales agents are trusted and authorised as representatives by their shops. They can work and negotiate with the customer and other agents that may be from partners or opponent shops. It is important that the negotiation is conducted in a secure, trusted and fair environment.

As an example, consider the scenario where Ann tries to organise the air tickets and accommodation for a round-the-world trip. Ann invites many airline companies and hotels via the Web browser to send agents onto her computer platform.

The trusted agent environment in this example, namely SCAE, comprises:

- A number of stationary agents (a *Manager Agent* and some *Agent Brokers*) acting on behalf of Ann that interact with the *Sales Mobile Agents* sent by the suppliers;
- A transaction log that records the transaction between Ann's agents and the *sales agents*;
- A GUI to receive responses from Ann.

When Ann clicks a link on the Web page, it will launch a Java applet acting as a *Manager Agent*. The *Manager Agent* plays the role of an *auctioneer*. An *auctioneer* agent is autonomous in contacting interested parties (namely, *sales agents* representing their owners respectively), negotiating with them to find the best deal and making decisions on its own without user intervention. However, the user does have high-level control of its behaviour.

The communication is composed of a *bulletin board* which is maintained by the *auctioneer* on behalf of Ann, agents' keys (or names), an *auctioneer*, a few *broker agents* which are the clones of *auctioneer*, an access control list, a yellow-page-like directory and the agent's information and messages.

When an agent enters the SCAE (i.e. downloading an agent onto the Secured Client Agent Environment), it has to register as a member. For details of registration see Section 5.3. The *auctioneer* will look at the registered agent's key (or name), and then lead it to an interest group according to the associated category in its local yellow page.

The *auctioneer* firstly announces Ann's preferred travel route and provides a number of route combinations. It starts its negotiation by posting the description of the items to the *bulletin board* (See Figure 4). Then all the invited agents, such as airline agents, hotel agents and car-hiring agents, start to bid. The bidding process is separated by different interest groups.

The *auctioneer* can write item descriptions onto the *bulletin board*, and is able to read the bid information from it. The operations are enabled for specific agents, groups of agents or all agents according to an items' access control list. For example, airline group agents can only access information regarding the airline; whereas multi-services providers' agents, for example a hotel agent that also offers car rental services, can access both hotel information and car rental information. The *auctioneer* also records the purchases in the transaction log.

While the *bulletin board* mainly serves as a means of communication among agents, it can also be used for communication between agents and the host system. For example, in SCAE, an *auctioneer* agent or *broker agents* could be endowed with the higher privileges necessary to gather data and hand out summaries to the visiting agents via the *bulletin board*.

Though a trust relationship is established between the agents and the SCAE, security threats could still exist among agents if there are no secure communication channels between them. We design to implement an *internal security gateway* which will randomly generate a session key based on the identity of the agent. A session key is unique to the agent and is assigned only to the agent who has the corresponding identity. The agent will use this key to encrypt its sensitive data, thus integrity and confidentiality are protected. Here the conventional cryptographic mechanisms can provide sufficient security protection.

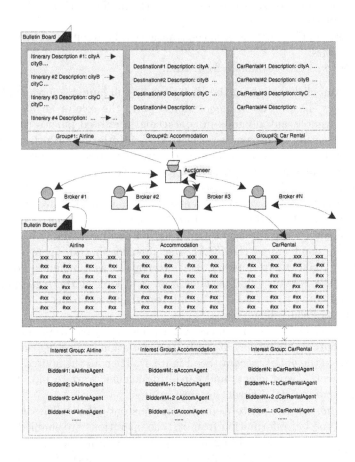

Fig. 4. Communication Among Agents

Finally, there should be a way for agents to communicate with their owners. A simple approach is to let the agent send XML messages (or other forms of messages) back to its owner; this asynchronous method ties nicely with the fact that the owner is probably not on-line all the time, e.g. in a mobile computing environment.

7 Future Work

With the new concept of Web agents on the trusted client platform, two focuses of interest are the security concerns and functionality in the Agent-Web Integration. While new applications using agents in SCAE can be explored, the following areas merit further research:

- Authorisation and access control mechanisms in SCAE;
- Delegation and chaining of Web agents in SCAE;
- Secure interactions among Web servers through their Web agents.

8 Conclusion

We have presented an agent-based framework to enhance the client/server interactions on the Web using the Secure Client Agent Environment (SCAE) as a trusted workspace for agent execution and collaboration.

References

1. Ashley P. & Vandenwauver M. (1999). *Practical Intranet Security : An Overview of the State of the Art and Available Technologies.* Kluwer Academic Publishers.
2. Au R., Looi M. & Ashley P. (2000) *Cross-Domain One-Shot Authorisation Using Smart Cards.* Proceedings of 7th ACM Conference on Computer and Communication Security, pages 220–227.
3. Au R., Looi M. & Ashley P. (2001) *Automated Cross-organisational Trust Establishment on Extranets.* Proceedings of the Workshop on Information Technology for Virtual Enterprises(ITVE' 2001), pages 3–11.
4. Chess D. (1998) *Security Issues in Mobile Code Systems.* Mobile Agent Security, LNCS 1419, Springer, pages 1–14.
5. Farmer W.M. & Guttman J.D. & Swarup V. (1996). *Security for Mobile agents: Authentication and state appraisal.* European Symposium on Research in Computer Security, LNCS 1146, Springer, pages 118–130.
6. Hohl F. (1998). *Time limited blackbox security: Protecting mobile agents from malicious hosts.* Mobile Agents and Security, LNCS 1419, Springer, pages 92–113.
7. iButton Inc. URL: http://www.iButton.com
8. Jonathan B.& David K. & Daniela R. (1998). *Market-based Resource Control for Mobile Agents.* Proceedings of the 2nd International Conference on Autonomous Agents, ACM Press, pages 197–204.
9. Kohl J. & Neuman C. (1993) *The Kerberos Network Authentication Service V5.* RFC1510.
10. Rosenberry, W., Kenney D. and Fisher G. (1992). *Understanding DCE.* O'Reilly & Associates, Inc..
11. Vigna G. *Cryptographic Traces for Mobile Agents.* Mobile Agents and Security, Springer-Verlag, LNCS 1419, Springer, pages 137–153.
12. Wooldridge M. & Jennings N. R. (1995) *Intelligent agents: Theory and practice.* Knowledge Engineering Review, (10):2, pages 115–152.

User Preference Mining through Collaborative Filtering and Content based Filtering in Recommender System

SuJeong Ko, JungHyun Lee

Department of Computer Science & Engineering
Inha University
Yong_hyun dong , Namgu, Inchon, Korea
{sujung@nlsun.inha.ac.kr},{jhlee@inha.ac.kr}

Abstract. Previous studies on implementing both collaborative and content based filtering systems fail to come to a conclusive solution, and in this light, the decreased accuracy of recommendations is notable. This paper shall first address methods on how to minimize the shortcomings of the two respective systems. Then, by comparing the similarity of the resulting user profiles and group profiles, it is possible to increase the accuracy of the user and group preference. To lessen the negative aspects the following must be done. With the case of the multi dimensional aspects of content based filtering, associated word mining should be used to extract relevant features. The data expressed by the mined features are not expressed as a string of data, but as a related word vector. To make up for its faults, content based filtering systems should use Bayesian classification, a system that classifies products by maintaining a knowledge base of related words. Also, to decrease the sparsity of the user-product matrix, the dimensions must be reduced. In order to reduce the dimensions of the columns, it is necessary to use Bayesian classification in tandem with the related-word knowledge base. Finally to reduce the dimensions of the rows the users must be classified into clusters.

1 Introduction

Recommendation systems[7,16,19] originally developed to market products or services to users, recently incorporate a recommendation process based on collaborative filtering techniques. The typical collaborative filtering system represents data as a two-dimensional user-product matrix where the row represents the user, the column represents the list of available products, and the values of the matrix represent the user preference of each product. Collaborative filtering systems use data on the user to predict preference for the product of choice, and are divided largely into model-based and memory-based filtering systems. Collaborative filtering systems based on these models have two great shortcomings[11,13]. First, they overlook the fact that most users do not submit evaluation; because of this oversight the user-product matrix shows great sparsity. For this reason memory-based filtering systems have storage problems and hence prove inefficient when applied on a large scale

K. Bauknecht, A M. Tjoa, G. Quirchmayr (Eds.): EC-Web 2002, LNCS 2455, pp. 244–253, 2002.

where tens of thousands of users and thousands of products represented in the matrix. Next, there is an issue that a product without any previous user evaluation will not be recommended to users. [3,4,5,8,13,15,20] are presented as solutions to the aforementioned problems by using both collaborative and content based filtering methods. LSI[20] and SVD[5] classification are used to decrease the number of dimensions in the matrix to solve the problem of sparsity in collaborative filtering, yet they fail to fix problems with first rater. [3,4,8,11] solve the problems with first rater, yet fail to fix the problem of sparsity. In an attempt to find a solution to both sparsity and first rater problem, method[13] was implemented.

In this paper, Bayesian classification shall be used to classify products to lower the dimensions of the user-product matrix. Also, by implementing a genetic algorithm on the classified products the users can be put into clusters. Then, by feedback on relevance, it is possible to create a profile for new users, hence solving first rater problem. User preference is learned by analyzing both group profile established through collaborative filtering, and the user profiles created by relevance feedback. In order to classify products and to create user profiles the Apriori algorithm is used to mine for related words.

2 Content Based Filtering

This paper uses relevance feedback from the user to solve first rater problem. By the proposed method it is possible to recommend a new user a relevant web document on a product, even if there are no documents about the product in the collaborative filtering system. In this paper Naïve Bayes classifier[12] are used in content based filtering to classify saved web documents in the database. One of the distinctive features of this database is that the index is created from the information mined from web pages. The content based filtering methods use user-focused intelligent information retrieval systems.

2.1 Expression of Document Characteristics

In this paper, to express the characteristics of the documents as either a bag-of-words or a bag-of-associated-words[14], it is a necessary preprocess the document by analyzing its morphology. The system used in the morphological analysis is identical to the user-focused intelligent information retrieval system. The Apriori algorithm [1,2] is used to mine related data from the words extracted from morphological analysis. The associated word mining algorithm, Apriori, is used to find the associative rules of products out of the set of transactions. The mined data, or the set of associated words from each document, are represented as a related-word-vector model. As a result, document $\{d_j\}$ is represented as Equation (1) in the form of a related-word-vector model.

$$\{d_j\}=\{(w_{11}\&w_{12}...\&w_{1(r-1)}=>w_{1r}),(w_{21}\&w_{22}...\&w_{2(r-1)}=>w_{2r}),...,(w_{k1}\&w_{k2}...\&w_{k(r-1)}=>w_{kr}),...,(w_{p1}\&w_{p2}...\&w_{p(p-1)}=>w_{pr})\}_j \quad (j=1,2,...,m)\} \tag{1}$$

In Equation (1), $(w_{11} \& w_{12} ... \& w_{1(r-1)} \& w_{1r})$ represents related words, $\{w_{11}, w_1, w_{1(r-1)}, w_{1r}\}$ the structure of the related words, r the number of words that compose the related words, and m the number of related words that represent the text. The '$\&$' shows that the words on each side are related. For the best results in extracting the related words, the data must have a confidence of over 85 and a support of less than 20[10].

2.2 Creating the user profile

Content based filtering systems create new user profiles by receiving relevance feedback on pages that users access after receiving recommendations to the page. Related words gathered by methods of relevance feedback on pages the user has visited are stored in the user profile. Of the related words stored in the user profile, related words that show a high frequency are given more weight. If WU_a is a user profile with weight given to related words, then WU_a can be expressed as Equation (2).

$$WU_a = \{w_1 \cdot AW_1, w_2 \cdot AW_2, ..., w_t \cdot AW_t\}$$ (2)

In Equation (2), $\{w_1, w_2, ..., w_t\}$ is a weight vector that shows the weight of the related word, and t is the total number of related words within the user profile.

3 Collaborative Filtering

In collaborative filtering, the Naïve Bayes and genetic algorithms are both used to decrease the dimensions of the matrix. Previous clustering algorithms showed problems such as the need to predefine the number of clusters, the high sensitivity to noise in data, and the possibility their resulting data would converge with the region's optimal solution. In this paper, to rid of these problems, clustering is done with genetic algorithms.

3.1 Classifying products

In this paper, the {user-product} matrix used in collaborative filtering recommendations shall be expressed as the matrix $R = \{r_{ij}\}$ ($i=1,2,...,n$ and $j=1,2,...,m$). Matrix R is composed of a set with an m number of "products", a set with an n number of users, and r_{ij}, the value of user u_i 's preference for product d_j. To be more specific, the set of products is expressed as $I = \{d_j\}$ ($j=1,2,...,m$), and the set of users is expressed as $U = \{u_i\}$ ($i=1,2,...,n$). To learn the preferences of user it is necessary to classify the products he or she has rated, and has shows interest in. Interest levels are represented on a scale of $0\sim1.0$ in increments of 0.2, a total of 6 degrees, only when the value is higher than 0.5 is the user classified as showing interest. The product web-documents used are computer related documents gleaned by an http down-loader. The traits of the web documents were gathered by the related word mining described in section 2.1, and product classification was done using the Naïve Bayes algorithm.

3.2 Optimal user clustering

This section will present how to cluster the classified products using the genetic algorithm. To do this, the matrix defined as R, must first be translated to R_1. Matrix $R_1=\{c_{ki}\}(k=1,2...N$ and $i=1,2...n)$ is a {class-user} matrix, where in R_1, class $C=\{class_k\}(\ k=1,2,...,N\ )$ is defined as a set of products divided into classes. The value c_{ki} of matrix R_1 is the number of products classified as $class_k$ the user u_i has evaluated and shown interest in. Using these definitions, Equation (3) must also be defined in order to make out the values of matrix R_1. When the value of r_{ij} in matrix R is that of the product $d_j(0<j\leq m)$, with a value greater than 0.5 and also belonging to class $class_k(0<k\leq N)$, the value of r_{ij} in matrix R is increased accordingly by increments of one.

$$R_1 = \{d_j \in class_k, 0 < j \leq m, 0 < class_k \leq N \big| c_{ki} = c_{ki}+1, R_{r_{ij}} > 0.5\} \qquad (3)$$

In Table 1, the products 18 users reviewed and showed interests in were classified into 10 classes by the Naïve Bayes classifier, and then by applying Equation (3) to the result gives the example matrix R_1.

Table 1. Example of matrix R_1

class	u_1	u_2	u_3	u_4	u_5	u_6	u_7	u_8	U_9	u_{10}	u_{11}	u_{12}	u_{13}	u_{14}	u_{15}	u_{16}	u_{17}	u_{18}
1	3	0	1	1	0	0	0	0	0	0	1	0	1	0	0	0	0	0
2	0	0	2	0	0	0	0	0	0	0	0	2	0	0	1	0	0	1
3	2	0	4	0	1	1	1	2	0	2	0	0	0	0	2	2	1	3
4	2	2	5	4	2	2	3	1	0	1	0	0	0	0	1	1	2	1
5	1	0	1	0	2	0	1	3	0	3	0	0	0	0	3	2	1	2
6	2	3	1	5	3	3	2	1	0	3	0	0	0	0	1	4	3	1
7	3	0	0	0	1	1	1	2	0	0	0	0	0	0	0	0	0	0
8	1	4	1	1	1	1	1	4	0	1	0	0	0	0	1	1	1	1
9	1	1	2	1	2	0	2	1	0	1	0	1	3	3	3	2	2	2
10	1	0	1	0	1	2	0	1	1	0	0	0	0	0	0	0	1	0

The genetic algorithm uses genes, chromosomes, and population to cluster users. The populace evolves by means of initialization, fitness calculation, recomposition, selection, crossovers, and mutation.

Initialization is the phase where each entity expressed. Genetic algorithms do not straightforwardly search for a solution to the given problems, but rather try to solve the problems by encoding multiple solutions into chromosomes and then by subjecting the solutions to evolutionary operators, they choose the most appropriate. Because the solutions to the problem undergo an encoding process into chromosomes, it must be recognized that the encoding process of entities determines the solutions space, the applicable evolutionary operators, as well as the search field created by the evolutionary operators. For these reason, entity expression is critical to efficient searches. Chromosomes in the genetic algorithm are expressed as binary strings, real vectors, and tree structures.

To best express the matrix in Table 1, gene will be expressed in real numbers. The fitness of each of theses chromosomes is calculated to derive the optimal solution. The value c_{ki} of matrix R_1 is converted by Equation (4) to c'_{ki} to increase accuracy and decrease the complexity of the calculations.

$$c'_{ki} = log_2(\sqrt{c_{ki}} + 1) \tag{4}$$

In Equation (4) the logarithmic function and square root are applied to lower the value of c_{ki}, but to prevent c_{ki} from ever having a 0 value, 1 must be added. The value c_{ki} of matrix R_1 is converted by Equation (4) to c'_{ki}, therefore matrix R_1 must be redefined as R_1'. Thus, it can be seen that R_1' is an entity created by the initialization process. The gene is expressed by the element value of c'_{ki} of matrix R_1', the chromosome by each line of matrix R'_1, and the population is represented by the whole of all elements in matrix R'_1.

In the genetic algorithm, each entity is assigned a fitness value by which to compare the performance of the entity with that of others. In this paper, the fitness value shall be calculated to aid the search of classes with a similar distribution to that of the target product class, and also to optimize user clustering. To cluster users, it is necessary to find users with high values of similarity. For this, user similarity is calculated by using the Jaccard method[9]. In the recomposition phase, the value of the object function used to calculate the fitness value must recomposed with a different value. In the selection phase, selection operators use the recomposed fitness values as the basis to choose chromosomes for crossover. In the crossover phase, the crossover operators use crossover rates as the basis to choose chromosomes for crossover. The typical range of crossover rates is between 0.7 and 0.9, in this paper the crossover value of 0.9 is used. In the mutation phase the value of a single bit is changed according to the predesignated probability. Mutation rates are typically set between 0.01 and 0.05, in this paper the mutation rate is set to 0.01. In the evaluation phase, whether or not to continue evolution is decided. Evolution terminates if the average fitness is equal to or greater than the threshold value of fitness, if not evolution continues. In this paper the threshold value of fitness is set to 1, and if the fitness value is less than 1 evolution continues, if equal to or greater than 1, evolution terminates.

Users with chromosomes in the hundredth generation that have gene values equal to or greater than 1, are chosen for a cluster, and those with a value of 0 are discarded. In this manner the first cluster is composed of 7 users. Excluding users of the first cluster the rest of the users repeat the process of initialization, fitness calculation, recomposition, selection, crossovers, mutation, and evaluation. By repeating this process it is possible to classify the users into several clusters. In the end, the genetic algorithm clustered the 18 users of Table 1 into the 4 groups shown in Table 2.

Table 2. User group

group	user
1	user1, user3, user8, user10, user15, user16, user18
2	user2, user4, user5, user17
3	user11, user12, user13, user14
4	user6, user7, user9

In the collaborative filtering recommendation system explained in this paper, groups of similar preferences are matched with user, then the list of products previously purchased by the matched groups are then added to the list of products to be recommended to the user. The similarity between the new user and each group is calculated by first creating the user profile and group profile.

The group profile is created by extracting and gathering the characteristic of its users. The characteristics of the group are expressed as the set of related words extracted from the products that its users have evaluated and shown interest in. In this case, the related word mining explained in section 2.1 is used to extract the characteristics of the products.

4 Learning of User Preference

Fig. 1 depicts a system that uses both collaborative recommendation and content based filtering to learn of user preference.

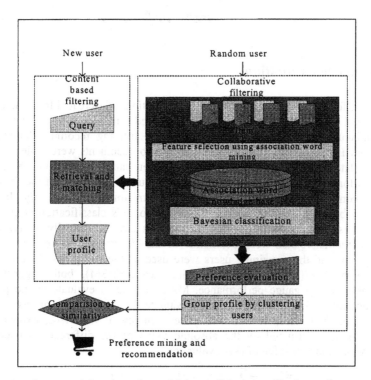

Fig. 1 User preference mining through combining collaborative filtering and content based filtering

In Fig. 1, the user profile is created by using the content based filtering methods in Section 2, so that when a user makes a query, the found products are used to gain relevance feedback. As elaborated in Section 3, collaborative filtering recommendations lower the product dimensions by classifying the products using Bayesian classification, and then by using the genetic algorithm they lower the user dimensions. Preferences of new users can be learned by using both the user profiles created in content based filtering, and the group profiles created through collaborative filtering recommendations. To use both the profile of the new user and the group, user must first be classified into a single group created by the collaborative filtering recommendation. For this, the similarity values between the group profiles and new user profile are calculated, and then the new user is classified into the group with the highest similarity value. In order to calculate the similarity values between the group profile and user profile, vector similarity, a field used in information retrieval, [17,18] is used in this paper. Equation (5) calculates the vector similarities of the new user profiles WU_a with the weight-assigned group profile WC'. In Equation (5), if there are no matching related words in the group with that of the user profile, the related word will be assigned no weight, if there are, weight shall be assigned accordingly as k'_r.

$$s(WC', WU_a) = \frac{\sum_{i=1}^{r} k'_i w_r}{\sqrt{\sum_{i=1}^{r} k_i'^2} \sqrt{\sum_{i=1}^{r} w_r^2}} \qquad (5)$$

5 Performance Evaluation

The database for collaborative filtering recommendations was created from the data of 200 users and 1600 web documents. Users evaluated a minimum of 10 of the 1600 web documents. The database for content based filtering recommendations was created from 1600 web documents. These 1600 web documents were collected from computer related URLs by an http downloader, then hand-classified into 8 areas of computer information. The 8 areas were classified under the labels of the following classes: {Games, Graphics, News and media, Semiconductors, Security, Internet, Electronic publishing, and Hardware}. The basis for this classification comes from search engines such as AltaVista and Yahoo that have statistically analyzed and classified computer related web documents. Of the 200 users, 100 were used as the training group, and the remaining users were used as the test group. In this paper, mean absolute error(MAE) and rank score measure(RSM), both suggested by paper[6] are used to gauge performance. MAE is used to evaluate single product recommendation systems. RSM is used to evaluate the performance of systems that recommend products from ranked lists. The accuracy of the MAE, expressed as Equation (6), is determined by the absolute value of the difference between the predicted value and real value of user evaluation.

$$S_a = \frac{1}{m_a} \sum_{j \in p_a} | p_{a,j} - - v_{a,j} | \qquad (6)$$

In Equation (6), p_{aj} is the predicted preference, v_{aj} the real preference, and m_a the number of products that have been evaluated by the new user. The RSM of a product in a ranked list is determined by user evaluation or user visits. RSM is measured under the premise that the probability of choosing an product lower in the list decreases exponentially. Suppose that each product is put in a decreasing order of value j, based on the weight of user preference. Equation (7) calculates the expected utility of user U_a's RSM on the ranked product list

$$R_a = \sum_j \frac{\max(V_{a,j} - d, 0)}{2^{(j-1)/(\alpha-1)}}$$

(7)

In Equation (7), d is the mid-average value of the product, and α is its halflife. The halflife is the number of products in a list that has a 50/50 chance of either review or visit. In the evaluation phase of this paper the halflife value of 5 shall be used. In Equation (8), the RSM is used to measure the accuracy of predictions about the new user.

$$R = 100 \times \frac{\sum_u R_u}{\sum_u R_u^{max}}$$

(8)

In Equation (8), if the user has evaluated or visited a product that ranks highly in a ranked list, R^{max} is the maximum expected utility of the RSM.

For evaluation, this paper uses the following methods: The proposed collaborative filtering and content based filtering recommendation method(C_G_N), the former memory based methods using the Pearson correlation coefficient(P_Corr), and the recommendation method using only the content based filtering method(Content). Out of the proposed methods only the recommendation method using the content based filtering method(G_N) was used to compare performance by changing the number of clustered users. Also, the proposed method was compared with the previous methods in Section 1 that use both collaborative filtering method and content based filtering method by changing the number of user evaluations on products. The aforementioned previous methods include the Soboroff method that solved the problem of sparsity, the Fab method that solved first rater problem, and the Pazzani method that solved both the sparsity and the first rater problem. Fig. 2 and Fig. 3 show the MAE and RSM of the number of users based on Equation (6) and Equation (8). In Fig. 2 and Fig. 3, as the number of users increases, the performance of the C_G_N, and the P_Corr also increases, whereas the method using content shows no notable change in performance.

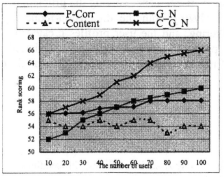
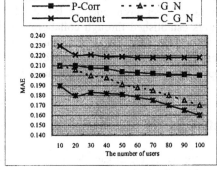

Fig. 2 MAE at varying the number of users Fig. 3 Rank scoring at varying the number of users

In terms of accuracy of prediction, it is evident that method C_G_N, which uses both collaborative filtering methods and content based filtering methods, is more superior to method G_N.

Fig. 4 and Fig. 5 are used to show the MAE and RSM when the number of user's evaluations is increased. In Fig. 4 and Fig. 5 the Soboroff method, which has problems with first rater, shows low performance when there are few evaluations; the other methods outperform the Soboroff method. Although the Pazzani method, which solved both sparsity and the first rater problem, along with the C_G_N show high rates of accuracy, the C_G_N shows the highest accuracy of all methods.

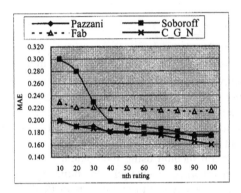 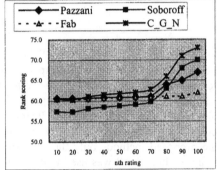

Fig. 4 MAE at nth rating   Fig. 5 Rank scoring at nth rating

6 Conclusion

In this paper, Bayesian classification shall be used to classify products to lower the dimensions of the user-product matrix. Also, by implementing a genetic algorithm on the classified products the users can be put into clusters. Then, by feedback on relevance, it is possible to create a profile for new users, hence solving the problem of first rater. User preference is learned by analyzing both the dimension-reduced-clusters established through collaborative filtering, and the user profiles created by relevance feedback. After comparing the proposed method with content based filtering systems along with collaborative filtering systems, it is apparent that the proposed method shows higher performance.

Reference

[1] R. Agrawal and R. Srikant, "Fast Algorithms for Mining Association Rules," Proceedings of the 20th VLDB Conference, Santiago, Chile, 1994.

[2] R. Agrawal and T. Imielinski and A. Swami, "Mining association rules between sets of items in large databases," In Proceedings of the 1993 ACM SIGMOD Conference, Washington DC, USA, 1993.

[3] M. Balabanovic and Y. Shoham, "Fab: Content-based, collaborative recommendation," Communication of the Association of Computing Machinery, Vol. 40, No. 3, pp. 66-72, 1997.

[4] C. Basu and H. Hirsh and W. W. Cohen, "Recommendation as classification:Using social and content-based information in recommendation," In proceedings of the Fifteenth National Conference on Artificial Intelligence, pp. 714-720, Madison, WI, 1998.

[5] D. Billsus and M. J. Pazzani, "Learning collaborative information filters," In proceedings of the International Conference on Machine Learning, 1998.

[6] John. S. Breese and C. Kadie, "Empirical Analysis of Predictive Algorithms for Collaborative Filtering," Proceedings of the Conference on Uncertainty in Artificial Intelligence, Madison, WI, 1998.

[7] J. Delgado and N. Ishii, "Formal Models for Learning of User Preferences, a Preliminary Report," In Proceedings of International Joint Conference on Artificial Intelligence (IJCAI-99), Stockholm, Sweden, July, 1999.

[8] N. Good, J. B. Schafer and J. A. Konstan, A. Borchers, B. Sarwar, J. Herlocker, and J. Riedl, "Combining collaborative filtering with personal agents for better recommendations," In Proceedings of National Conference on Artificial Intelligence(AAAI-99), pp. 439-446, 1999.

[9] M. Gordon, "Probabilistic and genetic algorithms for document retrieval," Communication of the ACM,31, pp. 1208-1218, 1988.

[10] S. J. Ko and J. H. Lee, "Feature Selection using Association Word Mining for Classification," In Proceedings of the Conference on DEXA2001, LNCS2113, pp. 211-220, 2001.

[11] W. S. Lee, "Collaborative learning for recommender systems," In Proceedings of the Conference on Machine Learning, 1997.

[12] T. Mitchell, *Maching Learning*, McGraw-Hill, pp. 154-200, 1997.

[13] M. J. Pazzani, "A framework for collaborative, content-based and demographic filtering," Artificial Intelligence Review, pp. 393-408, 1999.

[14] M. Pazzani, D. Billsus, *Learning and Revising User Profiles: The Identification of Interesting Web Sites*, Machine Learning, Kluwer Academic Publishers, pp. 313-331, 1997.

[15] D. M. Pennock and E. Horvitz, "Collaborative Filtering by Personality Diagnosis: A Hybrid Memory and Model-Based Approach," Proceedings of the 16th Conference on Uncertainty in Artificial Intelligence, 2000.

[16] R. Raymond and J. Mooney and L. Roy, "Content-Based Book Recommending Using Learning for Text Categorization," Proceedings of the Fifth ACM Conference on Digital Libraries, San Antonio, TX, pp. 195-204, June, 2000.

[17] V. Rijsbergen and C. Joost, *Information Retrieval*, Butterworths, London-second edition, 1979.

[18] G. Salton and M. J. McGill, *Introduction to Modern Information Retrieval*, McGraw-Hill, 1983.

[19] B. M. Sarwar, J. A. Konstan, Al Borchers, J. Herlocker, B. Miller, and J. Riedl, "Using Filtering Agents to Improve Prediction Quality in the GroupLens Research Collaborative Filtering System," Proceedings of the 1998 Conference on Computer Supported Cooperative Work, 1998.

[20] I. Soboroff and C. Nicholas, "Combining content and collaboration in text filtering," In Proceedings of the IJCAI'99 Workshop on Machine Learning in Information filtering, pp. 86-91, 1999.

An Improved Recommendation Algorithm in Collaborative Filtering

Taek-Hun Kim, Young-Suk Ryu, Seok-In Park, and Sung-Bong Yang

Dept. of Computer Science, Yonsei University,
Seoul, 120-749, Korea
{kimthun,ryu,psi93,yang}@mythos.yonsei.ac.kr

Abstract. In Electronic Commerce it is not easy for customers to find
the best suitable goods as more and more information is placed on line.
In order to provide information of high value a customized recommender
system is required. One of the typical information retrieval techniques
for recommendation systems in Electronic Commerce is collaborative filtering which is based on the ratings of other customers who have similar
preferences. However, collaborative filtering may not provide high quality recommendation because it does not consider customer's preferences
on the attributes of an item and the preference is calculated only between a pair of customers. In this paper we present an improved recommendation algorithm for collaborative filtering. The algorithm uses the
K-Means Clustering method to reduce the search space. It then utilizes
a graph approach to the best cluster with respect to a given test customer in selecting the neighbors with higher similarities as well as lower
similarities. The graph approach allows us to exploit the transitivity of
similarities. The algorithm also considers the attributes of each item. In
the experiment the EachMovie dataset of the Digital Equipment Corporation has been used. The experimental results show that our algorithm
provides better recommendation than other methods.

1 Introduction

In Electronic Commerce it is not easy for customers to find the best suitable
goods as more and more information is placed on line. In order to provide
information of high quality a customized recommender system is required. A
customized recommender system can help customers with fast searches for the
best suitable goods by analyzing the customer's preferences. A recommender
system utilizes in general an information filtering technique called collaborative
filtering(CF), even though there are several other techniques such as data mining and pattern recognition. CF is based on the ratings of other customers who
have similar preferences and is widely used for such recommender systems as
Amazon.com and CDNow.com[1][2][3][4][5][7][13].

CF uses the Pearson correlation coefficient for evaluating the similarity between the preferences of a pair of customers, but it assumes that there must
exist some items which have already been evaluated by both. On top of that,

K. Bauknecht, A M. Tjoa, G. Quirchmayr (Eds.): EC-Web 2002, LNCS 2455, pp. 254–261, 2002.
© Springer-Verlag Berlin Heidelberg 2002

the Pearson correlation coefficient is calculated only between a pair of customers, so the prediction accuracy of CF may be degraded[1][2][5]. Another weak point of CF is that it never considers customer's preferences on the attributes of an item.

There have been many researches to overcome these weak points of CF such as the K-Nearest Neighbor method and clustering. They are quite popular techniques for selecting neighbors who have similar preferences for certain items[2][5][7][10]. These techniques then predict customer's preferences about the items through the results of evaluation on the same items by the neighbors. The K-Means Clustering method is one of the clustering techniques and performs well on numeric data sets in general[11][14][15]. These two techniques do improve prediction quality, but they did not overcome the fact that the Pearson correlation coefficient should be calculated only between a pair of customers.

However, we assert that in order to predict customer's preference more accurately, we should consider both high and low similarities of each customer, since a customer who has contradicting similarities may give valuable information in prediction. In this paper we present an improved recommendation algorithm for CF. The algorithm uses the K-Means Clustering method to reduce the search space. It then utilizes a graph approach to the best cluster with respect to a given test customer in selecting the neighbors with higher similarities as well as lower similarities. The graph approach allows us to exploit the transitivity of similarities. The algorithm also considers the attributes of each item.

To compare the performance of various recommendation methods including ours, the EachMovie dataset of the Digital Equipment Corporation has been used[8]. The *EachMovie* dataset consists of 2,811,983 preferences for 1,628 movies rated by 72,916 customers explicitly. The experimental results show that the proposed recommendation algorithm provides better prediction accuracy than other methods.

The rest of this paper is organized as follows. Sect. 2 describes CF, the K-Nearest Neighbor method, and the K-Means Clustering method. Sect. 3 describes our graph mechanism to select neighbors. In Sect. 4, our experimental results are given.

2   Selecting Neighbors in CF

CF recommends items through building the profiles of the customers from preferences for each item[1][3][4]. In CF, preferences are represented generally as numeric values rated by customers. Predicting the preference for a certain item that is new to a given customer(called *the test customer*) is based on the ratings of other customers(called *neighbors*) for the target item. Therefore, it is very important to find similar neighbors to the test customer for better prediction quality[14].

In CF (1) is used to predict customer's preference, where $w_{a,k}$ is the weight of similarity as given in (2), which is the Pearson correlation coefficient[1][2][4][5][12].

$$P_{a,i} = \overline{r_a} + \frac{\sum\limits_{k} \{w_{a,k} \times (r_{k,i} - \overline{r_k})\}}{\sum\limits_{k} |w_{a,k}|}. \tag{1}$$

$$w_{a,k} = \frac{\sum\limits_{j} (r_{a,j} - \overline{r_a})(r_{k,j} - \overline{r_k})}{\sqrt{\sum\limits_{j} (r_{a,j} - \overline{r_a})^2 \sum\limits_{j} (r_{k,j} - \overline{r_k})^2}}. \tag{2}$$

In the above equations $P_{a,i}$ denotes the preference of customer a with respect to item i. $\overline{r_a}$ and $\overline{r_k}$ are the averages of customer a's ratings and customer k's ratings, respectively. $r_{k,i}$ and $r_{k,j}$ are customer k's ratings for items i and j, respectively, and $r_{a,j}$ is customer a's rating for item j.

If customers a and k have a similar rating for an item, $w_{a,k} > 0$. $|w_{a,k}|$ indicates how much customer a tends to agree with customer k on the items that both customers have already rated. If they have opposite ratings for an item, $w_{a,k} < 0$ and $|w_{a,k}|$ indicates how much they tend to disagree on the item that both again have already rated. Hence, if they don't correlate each other, $w_{a,k} = 0$. $w_{a,k}$ can be in between -1 and 1.

Although CF can be regarded as a good choice for recommender systems, there is still much room for improvement in prediction quality. To do so, CF needs refined neighbor selection techniques such as the K-Nearest Neighbor method and the K-Means Clustering method. In the rest of this section we describe the K-Nearest Neighbor method and the K-Means Clustering for selecting neighbors who have similar preferences for certain items.

2.1 The K-Nearest Neighbor Method

The K-Nearest Neighbor method selects the nearest k neighbors who have similar preferences to a given test customer by computing the similarity based on their preferences; it only uses the k neighbors who have higher correlation with the test customer[2].

However, CF suffers from considering all the customers in a given dataset for calculating the preference of the test customer. Thus CF should even consider some customers who may give bad influences on prediction quality. On the other hand, the K-Nearest Neighbor method only accepts the k neighbors with higher correlation with respect to the test customer. It has been shown in several researches that the K-Nearest Neighbor method has better quality of prediction than CF[2][5][7][10].

2.2 The K-Means Clustering Method

The K-Means Clustering method creates k clusters each of which consists of the customers who have similar preferences among themselves[11][14][15]. In this method we first select arbitrarily k customers as the initial center points of the k clusters, respectively. Then each customer is assigned to a cluster in such a way that the distance between the customer and the center of a cluster is minimized. The distance is calculated using the Euclidean distance, that is, a square root of the element-wise square of the difference between the customer and each center point.

Then, for each cluster, we recalculate the mean of the cluster based on the customers who currently belong to the cluster. The mean is now considered as the new center of the cluster. After finding new centers, we compute the distance for each customer as before in order to find to which cluster the customer should belong. Recalculating the means and computing the distances are repeated until a terminating condition is met. The condition is in general how far all the new centers have moved from the previous centers, respectively; if all the new centers moved within a certain distance, we terminate the loop.

3   A Neighbor Selection Method Using a Graph

In this section we describe a new method of obtaining the neighbors of a test customer using a graph. It is based on the fact that the neighbors who have not only high similarity but also low similarity with respect to the test customer may have influence considerably on making prediction. Using a graph approach allows us to overcome the fact that the Pearson correlation coefficient are calculated between only a pair of customers. For example, if we assume the similarity between customers a and b is high and the similarity between customers b and c is high, then the similarity between customers a and c is also considered as high. The same holds for low. That is, we can achieve valuable information for prediction through the transitivity of similarities.

In this graph approach, we treat a dataset as a weighted undirected graph. A vertex in the graph represents each customer and a weighted edge corresponds to the similarity between two endpoints(customers) of the edge. First, we search for a vertex v with the highest similarity with respect to a given test customer u. We then search the neighboring vertices of v who have the similarities either larger than H or smaller than L, where H and L are some threshold values for the Pearson correlation coefficients that can be determined with various experiments. As the threshold values change, the size of the neighbors varies. Hence appropriate threshold values need to be determined through various experiments for better prediction. The search is performed in a breath-first manner. That is, we search all the neighbors of v according to H and L, and then search all the neighbors of each neighbor of v in turn. The search stops when we have enough neighbors for prediction. If a vertex has already chosen as a neighbor, then the vertex is not considered during the search.

Fig. 1 shows how to select the neighbors of v who has the highest similarity with respect to the test customer when depth_count = 2. A solid line indicates that the weight on the edge is larger than H. A dotted line means that the weight of the edge is less than L.

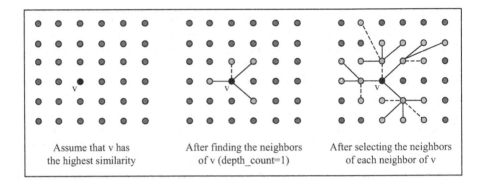

| Assume that v has the highest similarity | After finding the neighbors of v (depth_count=1) | After selecting the neighbors of each neighbor of v |

Fig. 1. An example of searching the neighbors with the graph approach when depth_count = 2

We now describe the proposed recommendation algorithm in detail. In the algorithm, before we apply the graph approach to a given dataset, we want to remove insignificant customers with the K-Means Clustering method. After we obtain k clusters with the K-Means Clustering method, we choose the cluster that holds the customers with higher similarities with respect to the test customer u. We then apply the graph approach only to the chosen cluster(the "*best*" cluster). The following describes the overall algorithm formally. When the algorithm is terminated, the set *Neighbors* is returned as output.

```
1. Create k clusters with the K-Means Clustering method;
2. Find the best cluster C  for a given test customer u;
3. Unmark all the vertices in Cluster C;
4. d=0; // d is for counting the search depth.
5. Find the neighbor v with the highest similarity with respect to u;
6. Mark v;
7. Insert (v,d) into Q;
        // Q holds temporarily the neighbors for a breath-first search.
8. Add v to Neighbors;
9. While (Q is not empty) do
10.   Delete (w,d) from Q;
11.     If (d < depth_count) then
                // depth_count controls the loop-termination
12.       For each unmarked neighbor x of w do
13.           If (the weight similarity between x and w is either
                  greater than H or less than L) then
14.             Mark x;
15.             Insert (x,d+1) to Q;
16.             Add x to Neighbors;
17.           endif
18.        endfor;
19.     endif
20. endwhile;
21. return Neighbors;
```

4   Experimental Results

4.1   Experiment Environment

In order to evaluate the prediction accuracy of the proposed recommendation algorithm, we used the EachMovie dataset of the Digital Equipment Corporation for experiments[8]. The EachMovie dataset consists of 2,811,983 preferences for 1,628 movies rated by 72,916 customers explicitly. The customer preferences are represented as numeric values from 0 to 1.0 at an interval of 0.2, i.e., 0.0, 0.2, 0.4, 0.6, 0.8, and 1.0. In the EachMovie dataset, one of the valuable attributes of an item is the genre of a movie[6]. There are 10 different genres such as action, animation, art-foreign, classic, comedy, drama, family, horror, romance, and thriller.

For the experiment, we retrieved 3,763 customers who rated at least 100 movies among all the customers in the dataset. We have chosen randomly 10 customers out of 3,763 customers as the test customers and the rest customers are the training customers. For each test customer, we chose 5 movies randomly that are actually rated by the test customer as the test movies. The final experimental results are averaged over the results of 5 different test sets. So the total number of experiments is 250.

4.2   Experimental Metrics

One of the statistical prediction accuracy metrics for evaluating recommender systems is the mean absolute error(MAE) which is the mean of the errors of the actual customer ratings against the predicted ratings in individual prediction[2][7][9][10][14]. MAE is computed by (3). In the equation, N is the total number of predictions and ε_i is the error between the predicted rating and the actual rating for item i. The lower MAE is, the more accurate prediction with respect to the numerical ratings of customers we get.

$$| E | = \frac{\sum_{i=0}^{N} | \varepsilon_i |}{N} . \tag{3}$$

4.3   Experimental Results

The proposed recommendation algorithm, we call it *KMGCF*, is compared with four other methods. The first method is the pure collaborative filtering(*PCF*) method used by GroupLens[3][4]. The second method is that collaborative filtering is applied after the K-Nearest Neighbor method selected the neighbors. We call it *KNCF*. The third one is the collaborative filtering method with the K-Means clustering. We denote it as *KMCF*. The last one is the collaborative filtering method only with the graph approach. We call it *GCF*.

The experimental results are shown in Table 1. We determined 100 as the optimal value of k for KNCF and 21 as the optimal value of k for KMGCF through various experiments. Both values of k gave us the smallest MAE values. The number within the parenthesis next to GCF or KMGCF indicates a depth of the search in the graph. In the parameters for GCF and KMGCF, L and H denote that the threshold values for the Pearson correlation coefficients. For example, if L = -0.8 and H = 0.7 means that we'll select a neighbor whose similarity is less than -0.8 or larger than 0.7.

Table 1. Comparison of various methods

Methods	MAE	Parameters
PCF	0.190479	
KNCF	0.189125	$k = 100$
GCF(1)	0.173791	$H = 0.6$
GCF(2)	0.178906	$H = 0.8$
KMCF	0.172146	$k = 21$
KMGCF(1)	0.166095	$k = 21, L = -0.6, H = 0.4$
KMGCF(2)	0.165700	$k = 21, L = -0.8, H = 0.9$
KMGCF(3)	0.167418	$k = 21, L = -1.0, H = 0.7$

The results show that KMGCF outperforms others when depth_count is 2 and the parameters are k=21, L=-0.8, and H=0.9. We found that when depth_count is grater than 2, KMGCF does not provide better results, because as the size of the neighbors gets larger the chances that unnecessary neighbors are included in the neighbors will be higher.

5   Conclusions

It is very crucial for a recommender system to have a capability of making accurate prediction by analyzing and retrieval of customer's preferences. Although collaborative filtering is widely used for recommender systems, some efforts to overcome its drawbacks should be made to improve the prediction quality. Selecting the proper neighbors plays an important role in improving the prediction quality. However, KNCF and KMCF still do have problems for selecting the suitable neighbors.

In this paper, we proposed an improved recommendation algorithm that utilizes a graph along with the K-Means Clustering method. It considers the attributes of each item for customer's preferences and low similarities as well. In the proposed algorithm we could use the transitivity among the customers with the help of the graph approach. The experimental results showed that our algorithm provides the better prediction accuracy than other methods.

Acknowledgements. We thank the Digital Equipment Corporation for permitting us to use the EachMovie dataset.

References

1. Billsus, D., Pazzani, M. J.: Learning Collaborative Information Filters. Proceedings of the ICML. (1998) 46–53
2. Badrul M. Sarwar, George Karypis, Joseph A. Konstan, John T. Riedle: Application of Dimensionality Reduction in Recommender System - A Case Study. Proceedings of the ACM WebKDD 2000 Web Mining for E-Commerce Workshop. (2000)
3. Konstan, J., Miller, B., Maltz, D., Herlocker, J., Gordon, L., and Riedl, J.: GroupLens: Applying Collaborative Filtering to Usenet News. Communications of the ACM, Vol. 40. (1997) 77–87
4. Resnick, P., Iacovou, N., Suchak, M., Bergstrom, P., and Riedl, J.: GroupLens: An Open Architecture for Collaborative Filtering of Netnews. Proceedings of the ACM CSCW94 Conference on Computer Supported Cooperative Work. (1994) 175–186
5. Badrul Sarwar, George Karypis, Joseph Konstan, and John Riedl: Analysis of Recommendation Algorithms for E-Commerce. Proceedings of the ACM E-Commerce 2000 Conference. (2000)
6. Basu, C., Hirsh, H., and Cohen, W.: Recommendation as Classification: Using Social and Content-Based Information in Recommendation. Proceedings of the AAAI. (1998) 714–720
7. Jonathan L. Herlocker, Joseph A. Konstan, Al Borchers, and John Riedl: An Algorithmic Framework for Performing Collaborative Filtering. Proceedings of the 22nd International ACM SIGIR Conference on Research and Development in Information Retrieval. (1999)
8. Steve Glassman: EachMovie Collaborative Filtering Data Set. Compaq Computer Corporation, url: http://research.compaq.com/SRC/eachmovie/. (1997)
9. Good N., Schafer J. B., Konstan J. A., Borchers A., Sarwar B., Herlocker J. L., and Riedl J.: Combining Collaborative Filtering with Personal Agents for Better Recommendations. Proceedings of the AAAI. (1999) 439–446
10. O'Connor M., and Herlocker J.: Clustering Items for Collaborative Filtering. Proceedings of the ACM SIGIR Workshop on Recommender Systems. (1999)
11. Ungar L. H., and Foster D. P.: Clustering Methods for Collaborative Filtering. Proceedings of the AAAI Workshop on Recommendation Systems. (1998)
12. John S. Breese, David Heckerman, and Carl Kadie: Empirical Analysis of Predictive Algorithms for Collaborative Filtering. Proceedings of the Conference on Uncertainty in Artificial Intelligence. (1998) 43–52
13. J. Benschafer, Joseph Konstan and John Riedl: Recommender Systems in E-Commerce. Proceedings of the ACM Conference on Electronic Commerce. (1999)
14. Young-Suk Ryu, Taek-Hun Kim, Ji-Sun Park, Seok-In Park, and Sung-Bong Yang: Using Content Information for Filtering Neighbors in the Collaborative Filtering Framework. Proceedings of the International Conference on Electronic Commerce. (2001)
15. Zheue Huang: Extensions to the k-Means Algorithm for Clustering large Data Sets with Categorical Values. Data Mining and Knowledge Discovery. (1998) 283–304

Series of Dynamic Targeted Recommendations

Natwar Modani, Parul A. Mittal, Amit A. Nanavati, and Biplav Srivastava

IBM India Research Laboratory
Block 1, IIT Delhi, Hauz Khas, New Delhi 110016, India.
{mnatwar,mparul,namit,sbiplav}@in.ibm.com

Abstract. Merchants often use marketing elements such as advertisements, coupons and product recommendations, to attract customers and to convert visitors to buyers. We present a model for making a series of recommendations during a customer session. The model comprises of the customer's probability of accepting a marketing element from a marketing spot and a reward for the marketing element. The probabilities can be estimated from customer history (such as traversals and purchases), while the reward values could be merchant specified. We propose several recommendation strategies for maximising the merchant's reward and analyse their effectiveness. Our experiments indicate that strategies that are dynamic and consider multiple marketing spots simultaneously perform well.

Keywords: E-commerce, recommender systems, targeting.

1   Introduction

For a website that supports electronic commerce, an accurate prediction of a customer's behaviour can be employed towards commercial gain by recommending relevant and profitable marketing elements. The marketing elements ('elements') that a website can recommend include its offerings of products and services, and promotions such as advertisements and coupons. These elements are displayed on certain predetermined web marketing spots ('spots') on the webpages. Commonly used techniques for element recommendation are content based filtering, collaborative filtering and association rules. Content based filtering systems [2] recommend items based on their similarity to what a given person has liked in the past. Collaborative filtering [4] uses customer ratings and preferences to recommend items that *similar* people have liked. Techniques based on association rules [5] compute rules of type $a \Rightarrow b$ based on frequent item sets from past transactional data, to recommend b to a customer who buys a. Lawrence et al [6] use a combination of the above methods by matching products to customers based on the expected appeal of the product and customer purchase history. Such approaches study the recommendation problem in the two-dimensional space of customers and elements. Recently, Adomavicius et al [1] have proposed a multidimensional model that uses various dimensions to enhance customer profiles and make complex recommendations.

K. Bauknecht, A M. Tjoa, G. Quirchmayr (Eds.): EC-Web 2002, LNCS 2455, pp. 262–272, 2002.

Apart from element characteristics and customer behaviour, spot attributes such as location and size are crucial for making relevant recommendations. For example, if a medium-sized spot on the top-right location of a page is more likely to be viewed, then it makes business sense to show a high reward yielding element on that spot. Moreover, it may be worthwhile to consider the *series* of spots that the customer is likely to visit during the remaining session rather than considering the current spot in isolation.

Though some attention has been given to the page characteristics, the authors are not aware of any recommendation system that considers a series of spots (c.f., the taxonomy of recommender systems created by Schafer et al [8]). Tomlin [10] identifies the number of times an advertisement is to be shown to a particular customer cluster during a specified time period, but does not consider the series notion either. A closely related problem is that of predicting the spots that a customer is likely to visit during a session. Information from web-server logs is used to mine customer traversal patterns [3,9]. This knowledge has been applied to customer profiling and recommender systems [7].

We address the problem of making a *series* of recommendations for a given customer session. We present a model that takes into consideration element characteristics, *spot characteristics*, customer traversal patterns and *responses* to recommendations. We propose several recommendation strategies to maximise the merchant's reward, and analyse their effectiveness in various situations. Details can be found in the extended version [11].

The remainder of the paper is organized as follows. Section 2 presents the model. Section 3 describes several element recommendation strategies. Section 4 presents experimental results and analysis. Finally, we conclude with our contributions and possible directions for future work.

2   The Model

Consider an online store that has a set of marketing elements to offer on certain predetermined spots on the website. The reward associated with each element signifies its value to the merchant if the customer 'accepts' (clicks on) the element. A strategy, either apriori or online, defines a mapping from the elements to the spots. A customer may view several spots during a session. The goal is to find a strategy that maximises the merchant's *expected* total reward for a *single customer session*.

The general setting of our problem is unique in the way that: (1) there is a notion of a *series* of recommendations and responses between the website and the customer, and (2) there is a *predictive* aspect in terms of having to guess the next likely move/response of the customer, and offer elements based on such a guess. The customer traversal is probabilistic in nature, as is her interest in the elements. Hence, our model is probabilistic and the goal of strategies is to maximise the *expected* total reward. Two factors have been the primary drivers in choosing the design of the model. The requirements of the various strategies in terms of what they want to compute, and the practical consideration that the model parameters be derivable from the data that is typically available for such applications. We assume that the customer traversal history, customer purchase history, and merchant valuation for each element are available. Although a page may contain several spots, we restrict ourselves to considering only one spot per page. Therefore, 'page', 'spot' and 'location' are used synonymously.

2.1   Parameters of the Model

The model consists of three main components: the probability that the customer accepts an element that is offered on a particular spot (customer preference), the probability that a customer visits a particular page (customer traversal), and the merchant's reward when the customer accepts the element (merchant reward). The model parameters and their update rules are defined for a single customer session.

Customer preference: Let $M = \{m_1, m_2, \ldots, m_r\}$ denote the set of marketing elements and $W = \{w_1, w_2, \ldots, w_s\}$ denote the set of web marketing spots. Let P denote the matrix for a particular customer, where each matrix entry P_{ij} is the probability that the customer (currently on w_j) accepts the element m_i, given that it is offered on w_j. P simultaneously captures the customer's intrinsic interest in the element (I_i), her bias towards the spot (B_j), and the correlation between the element and the content of the page to which the spot belongs (C_{ij}).

The factorisation of P can be expressed in many ways, one of which is

$$P_{ij} = I_i \times B_j \times \frac{(\alpha + C_{ij})}{1 + \alpha} \tag{1}$$

In the above equation, α (≥ 0) is a damping factor used to control the effect of C_{ij} on P_{ij}. If a customer's interests are known, C_{ij} may be insignificant and α can be set to a large value. For example, if we know that Joe is always interested in golf balls, then we can offer him coupons on golf balls even if he is looking at a page on batteries. In cases where the correlation is important, α can be set to a lower value. The values of these individual components are in the range $[0,1]$, so that the corresponding P_{ij} value also lies in $[0,1]$. It seems intuitive that if $I_i = 0$ or $B_j = 0$, then P_{ij} should be 0. We call Equation (1) a *component-based* model for P.

Computing P from real data: From a customer's traversal and purchase history, I_i can be computed as the ratio of the number of times she accepted m_i to the total number of times she was shown m_i. Similarly, B_j is the ratio of the number of times any element was accepted on w_j to the total number of times any element was shown on w_j. The correlation could be specified explicitly by the merchant or computed by representing the elements and spots as feature vectors and calculating the cosine similarity between them. We have presented one possible component-based model for P. As long as the semantics of P are preserved, i.e., "the likelihood of the customer accepting m_i on w_j", any suitable model may be used. As an alternative to the above component-based model, P

could be treated as a *blackbox* and computed directly as the number of times m_i was accepted on w_j, divided by the total number of times m_i was shown on w_j. We conducted two sets of experiments using the component-based model and the blackbox model. The strategies detailed in the next section are independent of the P model.

Updating P: When m_i is shown to the customer on w_j, she may accept it or reject it. P is updated after each customer response as follows:

$$P_{k\ell} = \begin{cases} P'_{k\ell} \text{ if customer rejects } m_i \text{ on } w_j \\ P''_{k\ell} \text{ if customer accepts } m_i \text{ on } w_j \end{cases} \tag{2}$$

where

$$P'_{k\ell} = \begin{cases} P_{k\ell} * \delta_I * \delta_B * \delta_C & k = i, \ell = j \\ P_{k\ell} * \delta_I & k = i, \ell \neq j \\ P_{k\ell} * \delta_B & k \neq i, \ell = j \\ P_{k\ell} & k \neq i, \ell \neq j \end{cases} \tag{3}$$

and

$$P''_{k\ell} = \begin{cases} 0 & k = i \\ min(1, P_{k\ell}/\delta_B) & k \neq i, \ell = j \\ P_{k\ell} & k \neq i, \ell \neq j \end{cases} \tag{4}$$

In the above equations, δ_I is used to update I_i, δ_B for B_j and δ_C for $\frac{(\alpha + C_{ij})}{1+\alpha}$ (all values lie in $[0, 1]$). When a customer rejects m_i on w_j, the measure of her interest in m_i is reduced by a factor δ_I on all spots, her bias towards w_j for all elements is scaled down by a factor δ_B. Her interest in m_i on w_j is reduced further by the factor δ_C. When a customer accepts m_i, the P_{ij} becomes zero (for all j) since it is unlikely that she will accept the same element again. If an element is accepted from a particular spot, then the likelihood of the acceptance of *any* element from that spot increases.

Customer traversal: Given a customer's current location w_c, V_{cd} denotes the probability that she will visit w_d. We assume that customer traversals are Markovian. V_{cd} may be computed as the ratio of the number of paths in which the customer visits w_d after visiting w_c (repeated visits to w_d are ignored) to the total number of paths[1] in which she visits w_c ($V_{cc} = 1$).

Merchant reward: The merchant associates a numeric value R_i with each m_i that signifies the reward when the element is accepted by a customer. For computing these values, the merchant may consider inventory constraints and other vendor contract obligations. Once an element is accepted, the reward from it vanishes[2].

3   Strategies

In this section, we discuss the strategies for selecting an element to offer on a particular spot. Finding an optimal solution for this problem is computation-

---

[1] Given V_{cd} and V_{ce}, the order of visiting d and e cannot be inferred.

[2] Repetition is meaningless for advertisements and product recommendations. In the case of coupons, a customer can select multiple copies while accepting them.

ally infeasible, so we describe various heuristic strategies. The strategies can be broadly classified as static vs. dynamic and single-spot vs. multi-spot. A static strategy precomputes the element-spot mapping and does not change it based on the customer response, whereas a dynamic strategy re-computes the mapping using the updated P and R values. A single-spot strategy uses information about the current spot only, while a multi-spot strategy uses the probabilistic characterisation of a customer's path. To illustrate the strategies, we use the following example.

Example 1: Consider a website with two spots and two elements to offer. The P, R and V matrices are given in Table 1. We assume that the customer's path is $w_1 w_2$, $\delta_I = 0.5$, $\delta_B = 1$ and $\delta_C = 1$.

Table 1. Matrices P, R and V for Example 1.

P_{ij}	w_1	w_2
m_1	0.8	0.9
m_2	0.5	0.1

	R_i
m_1	0.6
m_2	0.7

V_{cd}	w_1	w_2
w_1	1.0	1.0
w_2	0.0	1.0

Consider a strategy T that shows m_1 on w_1. If the customer accepts m_1, it shows m_2 on w_2, otherwise it shows m_1 again on w_2. The expected reward for T can be computed as $P_{11} * P_{22} * (R_1 + R_2) + P_{11} * (1 - P_{22}) * (R_1) + (1 - P_{11}) * \delta_I * P_{12} * R_1 + (1 - P_{11}) * (1 - \delta_I * P_{12}) * 0 = 0.8 * 0.1 * (0.6 + 0.7) + 0.8 * 0.9 * 0.6 + 0.2 * 0.5 * 0.9 * 0.6 + 0.2 * (1 - 0.5 * 0.9) * 0 = 0.59$. Note that updated P and R matrices are used.

Random (R): This strategy randomly picks an element irrespective of the spot characteristic or the customer preference and traversal. In Example 1, this strategy shows either m_1 or m_2 on the two spots, based on a fair coin toss. The expected reward is 0.5854.

Single-spot(SS,SD): This strategy selects the element that maximises the expected reward at each spot. It offers m_{i*} on w_j if $i^* = \text{argmax}_i P_{ij} * R_i$. In Example 1, the static version of this strategy (SS) shows m_1 on both w_1 and w_2. The expected reward is 0.534. The dynamic version (SD) shows m_1 on w_1. If the customer accepts m_1, it shows m_2 on w_2, otherwise it again shows m_1 on w_2. The expected reward is 0.59.

Multi-spot dynamic greedy (MDG): This strategy generates a spot-coupon mapping for all the spots by considering the path on which the expected reward is maximum at each spot. Suppose the customer is on w_c. MDG computes a matrix $Q(c)$ where $Q_{ij}(c) = R_i * P_{ij} * V_{cj}$ represents the expected reward from offering m_i on w_j. Let X be a 0-1 matrix where $X_{ij} = 1$ implies that m_i should be shown on w_j. MDG picks the largest entry $Q_{uv}(c)$ and sets $X_{uv} = 1$. The customer response is *simulated*. The outcome of the simulation is an *accept* with probability P_{uv} and *reject* with probability $(1 - P_{uv})$. $Q(c)$ is updated as follows. If the simulated response is an *accept*, then all the entries in the uth row are set to zero. If it is a *reject*, the uth row is multiplied with δ_I. In either case, since m_u has been assigned to w_v, the vth column is made zero to eliminate it from further consideration. This process is repeated until $Q(c)$ becomes zero, and the entire element-spot mapping is obtained. For the current spot w_c, MDG shows m_g if $X_{gc} = 1$. P and R are modified based on the actual response. This entire process is repeated for every spot the customer visits. In Example 1, MDG shows m_2 on w_1 and m_1 on w_2. The expected reward is 0.89.

Multi-spot optimization (MSO,MDO): This strategy tries to optimise across all the paths probabilistically using an LP formulation. Let $X_{ij}(c)$ denote the optimal probability with which m_i should be shown on w_j when the customer is on w_c. Then the problem can be formulated as:

$$max \ \sum_{ij} V_{cj} * X_{ij}(c) * P_{ij} * R_i \tag{5}$$

$$such \ that \ \sum_{i} X_{ij}(c) \leq 1, \ \forall j \tag{6}$$

$$\sum_{j} X_{ij}(c) \leq K(i, \delta_I), \ \forall i \tag{7}$$

$$and \quad X_{ij}(c) \geq 0, \ \forall i, j \tag{8}$$

Equation (6) encodes the constraint that only one element can be shown at a spot. Equation (8) requires that $X(c)$ be non-negative. Equation (7) controls the number of spots a particular element can be offered on. If δ_I is high, rejection of m_i does not significantly reduce its chance of subsequent acceptance. Therefore K should be an increasing function of δ_I such that when $\delta_I = 0$, K should be 1, and when $\delta_I = 1$, K should be $\geq |W|$. For higher P_{ij}, the chance of m_i being accepted is higher, and it may not be necessary to show it too many times. This means that K should be a decreasing function of P_{ij} such that when $P_{ij} = 1$, K should be 1. The following expression satisfies these conditions:

$$K(i, \delta_I) = \frac{(1 - max_j P_{ij} * \delta_I)}{(1 - \delta_I)} \tag{9}$$

In Example 1, the static version of this strategy MSO shows m_1 on w_1 with probability 0.1, m_2 on w_1 with probability 0.9 and m_1 on w_2 with probability 1. The expected reward is 0.8544. The dynamic version of this strategy, MDO, shows m_1 on w_1 with probability 0.1 and m_2 on w_1 with probability 0.9. If m_1 is shown on w_1 and the customer accepts m_1, then it shows m_2 on w_2, otherwise it shows m_1 on w_2 again. Instead, if m_2 is shown on w_1 then it shows m_1 on w_2. The expected reward is 0.86.

Boosting factor: The reason why SD does not work well for Example 1 is that it fails to recognize the fact that while m_1 is almost equally suited for both the spots, m_2 is more suitable for w_1 than w_2. We introduce a *boosting factor* $b1$ to capture this bias of m_i for w_j:

$$b1_{ij} = \frac{P_{ij}}{\sum_k P_{ik} * V_{jk} / \sum_k V_{jk}} \tag{10}$$

The boosting factor is the ratio of P_{ij} to the mean value of P_{ik} for all spots w_k. If $b1_{ij} > 1$, then m_i is better than average for w_j. We use this factor by replacing P_{ij} by $P_{ij} * b1_{ij}$ for SD and MDG. Another boosting factor $b2$ can be defined to include the effect of the reward, $b2_{ij} = b1_{ij} * R_i$. The boosting variants of the strategies SDb1, SDb2, MDGb1, MDGb2 all offer m_2 on w_1 and m_1 on w_2 in Example 1. The expected reward is 0.89.

3.1   Discussion

All the strategies solve the problem in different ways. SD, SDb1 and SDb2 make a decision for the current spot, whereas MDG and MDO generate a mapping for all the spots. SD uses information about the current spot only, while SDb1, SDb2, MDG and MDO use information about all the spots. MDG and MDO may reserve elements for spots that the customer is likely to visit; SDb1, SDb2 are weakly reserving (or weakly multi-spot) strategies and SD is a non-reserving strategy.

Intuitively, reserving strategies should perform better than SD, which ignores two aspects. First, the current spot w_c may have low B_c value (or equivalently, low $P_{ic}\forall i$) so any element shown on w_c is likely to be rejected. Moreover, if δ_I is small, then the chance of the offered element being accepted from any other spot would also reduce considerably. SD would show the 'best' element on w_c and 'waste' it. Second, suppose there is an element m_i that is almost equally suited for w_c as well as some other spot (say w_l) and another element m_k suitable only for w_c. If $R_i * P_{ic} > R_k * P_{kc}$, SD would show m_i on w_c, but it might be better to show m_k on w_c and reserve m_i for w_l. The loss in expected reward on w_c could be more than compensated for, by a visit to w_l. The first aspect is addressed by MDG and the second is accounted for by the boosting factor. One would then expect MDGb1 and MDGb2 to perform the best, but since MDG guesses a customer path, if the guess is bad (this is more likely for longer paths), even its boosting variants will not perform as well. Although MDO averages on all the paths, it uses only the customer response probabilities, unlike MDG which simulates the customer response.

4   Experiments and Results

We evaluate and compare our strategies based on their performance (measured in terms of the total reward obtained from their recommendations) for different model parameter values. For every spot the customer visits, a strategy recommends an element to the customer. The customer's response is simulated by a loaded coin toss with the probability of customer accepting the recommended m_i on w_j being P_{ij}. If the customer accepts m_i, the reward R_i is added to the reward earned by the strategy. The P and R matrix are updated as described in Section 2.1. We synthetically generated the required inputs P, R, V and the customer paths for both the component-based and blackbox models. We expect to observe the following behaviour:

B1: Dynamic strategies perform better than static strategies.
B2: Multi-spot strategies perform better than single-spot strategies.

B3: The performance improves as the number of elements increases or the path length increases.

B4: MDG's incremental performance decreases as the path length increases.

B5: The boosting variants of SD perform better for small values of α. For large values, their performance is similar.

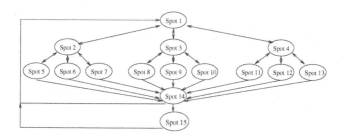

Fig. 1. The sample website used in the component-based P experiment

Generating P: For the component-based model, I, B and C were sampled from a uniform distribution using $\text{Mean}^{good}_{I,B,C}$, $\text{Mean}^{bad}_{I,B,C}$ and $\text{Fraction}^{good}_{I,C}$ where $\text{Mean}^{good}_{B} = x$ implies that B_j for good spots has a mean of x. If w_j has a high (low) B_j it is a *good (bad)* spot and has a higher (lower) P_{ij} assuming other component values are fixed. Suppose each spot can be marked *good* or *bad*. The website structure may impose a particular order of good and bad spots. This Relative Occurrence of (good and bad) Spots in customer traversal is called ROS. For example, if spots 1-13 are good and spots 14-15 are bad in Figure 1, then any traversal on the graph leads to a *goodbad* configuration. For the blackbox model, the P_{ij} values are uniformly distributed random numbers between 0 and 1. The various parameters and values for both the experiments are shown in Table 2.

4.1   Results

For each parameter value combination (case), we computed the reward for a strategy by averaging over 100 customer paths and 5 traversals on each path, i.e., over 500 runs. For a given case, a strategy that yields within 2% of the highest reward is a *candidate* strategy. A case may have multiple candidate strategies. We obtained a *preferred strategy set* that covers the candidate strategies for most of the cases as follows. We defined the strategy preference order as 'R, SS, SD, SDb1, SDb2, MDG, MDGb1, MDGb2, MSO, MDO', based on their simplicity and speed. A case is considered *distinct* for a strategy, if it is not covered by any strategy with a higher preference. Each strategy that contributed at least 5% of the distinct cases was added to the preferred strategy set.

Table 3 summarises the number of cases for which a particular strategy is the candidate strategy and the number of distinct cases covered by every preferred

Table 2. Model parameters and range of values for component-based and blackbox experiments: N – number of elements, S – number of spots, PL – path length, ROS – relative occurrence of states.

Parameter	Values for Component-based P	Values for Blackbox P
N	3, 6, 9, 12, 15	3, 7, 10, 15, 20
S	15	45
PL	≤ 6, ≤ 9, ≥ 9, ≥ 12	≤ 7, ≤ 10, ≥ 10, ≥ 15
δ_I	0, 0.5, 1.0	0, 0.5, 1.0
α	0, 1, 100	N/A
ROS	*allgood, goodbad, mixgoodbad, badgood, allbad*	N/A
$\text{Mean}_{I,B,C}^{good}$	0.9	N/A
$\text{Mean}_{I,B,C}^{bad}$	0.4	N/A
$\text{Fraction}_{I,C}^{good}$	0.5	N/A
R_i	random in $[0,1]$	random in $[0,1]$
# paths	100	100
δ_B	1.0	1.0
δ_C	1.0	1.0

Table 3. Total and distinct cases covered by strategies.

Model	R	SS	SD	SDb1	SDb2	MDG	MDGb1	MDGb2	MSO	MDO
# total cases in component-based P	0	0	317	333	266	456	169	271	7	382
# distinct cases in component-based P	–	–	317	–	–	378	–	118	–	68
# total cases in blackbox P	0	0	23	48	41	11	0	0	5	39
# distinct cases in blackbox P	–	–	23	25	–	6	–	–	4	–

strategy. For each experiment, we built decision trees for each preferred strategy and then merged them using the preference order (Figure 2).

Analysis : B1 is supported by both the decision trees in Figure 2 as a static strategy (MSO) performs better than a dynamic strategy (MDO) only in 4 out of 960 cases. B2 is also reinforced by Figure 2 since MDG, MDO and SDb1 perform better than SD. However, for $\delta_I = 1$, where P_{ij} does not decrease even if the customer rejects the recommended element, SD performs better than MDG while MDO and SDb1 perform as well as SD. The reason is that for short paths, the spot where MDG reserves a good element may not be visited and for long paths MDG may not be able to guess it accurately (see Section 3.1). The fact that ROS appears in the decision tree underscores the importance of considering a series of spots for element recommendation. B3 and B4 are supported by Figure 3. Similar results were observed for all 900 cases. B5 is supported by the component-based P experiment: SDb1 $\geq$ SD in 86% cases for $\alpha = 0, 1$. For $\alpha = 100$, SDb1 = SD in 71% cases and better in 17% cases. Different boosting factors perform better with SD and MDG.

In real life situations, it is expected that the $\delta_I < 1$. This implies that dynamic, multi-spot strategies are preferable (Figure 2). Most existing recommen-

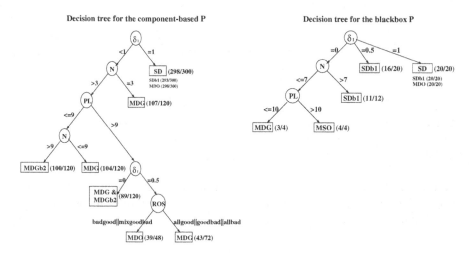

Fig. 2. Decision tree for component-based and blackbox P. The label 'x/y' on each leaf node shows the number of cases where the strategy was the candidate strategy (x) and the total number of cases covered by this leaf node (y).

dation methods are single-spot and static, so MDG, MDO and SDb1 are likely to perform better. MDG and SDb1 are fast enough to be used in practice. To make MDO computationally feasible, the problem can be formulated as a transportation problem, which can be solved [10] an order of magnitude faster than LP solvers. Observe that if ROS can be inferred from P, then the component-based decision tree should be used.

5 Conclusion and Future Work

We considered the problem of making a series of recommendations to a customer during a session. We modelled the customer in terms of her probability of accepting a marketing element from a given marketing spot and her probabilistic traversal pattern. We described several strategies for maximising the merchant's reward and evaluated them empirically on simulated data. All the strategies performed better than recommending a randomly chosen element. Experimental results indicate that dynamic, multi-spot strategies are likely to perform well in practice. We give a rule of thumb for determining an appropriate strategy to use for different model parameter values.

This work can be extended in many directions. The customer model could be enriched by considering factors such as consumption behaviour and frequency of visits, and also extended to capture cross-session behaviour. The model could take element-element and spot-spot interrelations into consideration. The customer response could include actions such as "adding an item to shopping cart" besides *accept/reject*. It would also be interesting to investigate various algorithms for learning P from real data.

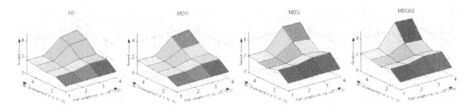

Fig. 3. Performance of SD, MDO, MDG and MDGb2 for component-based P with respect to the number of elements (3, 6, 9, 12, 15) and path length ($\leq 6, \leq 9, \geq 9, \geq 12$), for δ_I = 0, ROS = goodbad and $\alpha = 1$.

Acknowledgements. The authors would like to thank Raghuram Krishnapuram and Ravi Kothari of IBM India Research Lab and anonymous referees for their valuable inputs.

References

1. G. Adomavicius and A. Tuzhilin, "Extending Recommender Systems: A Multidimensional Approach", IJCAI Workshop on Intelligent Techniques for Web Personalization, 2001.
2. C. Basu, H. Hirsh and W. W. Cohen, "Recommendation as classification: Using social and content-based information in recommendation", Proc. of AAAI 1998, pp 714–720.
3. M. Deshpande and G. Karypis, "Selective Markov Models for Predicting Web-Page Access", Univ. of Minnesota Tech. Report 00-056, Oct 2000.
4. J. L. Herlocker, J. A. Konstan, Al Brochers, and J. Riedl, "An algorithmic framework for performing collaborative filtering", Proc. of ACM SIGIR 1999, pp 230–237.
5. J. Hipp, U. Guntzer and G. Nakhaeizadeh, "Algorithms for association rule mining - a general survey and comparison", Proc. of ACM SIGKDD 2000, pp 58–64, Volume2, Issue 1.
6. R. D. Lawrence, G. S. Almasi, V. Kotlyar, M. S. Viveros and S. S. Duri, "Personalization of Supermarket Product Recommendations", RC 21792, IBM Research Report. Also in Special issue of the International Journal of Data Mining and Knowledge Discovery, January 2001.
7. B. Mobasher, H. Dai, T. Luo, Y. Sun and J. Zhu, "Integrating Web Usage and Content Mining for More Effective Personalisation", Proc. of EC-Web, 2000.
8. J. B. Schafer, J.A.Konstan and J. Riedl, "E-commerce recommendation applications", Journal of Data Mining and Knowledge Discovery, 5(1/2), 115–153, 2001.
9. J. Srivastava, R. Cooley, M. Deshpande and P. Tan, "Web Usage Mining: Discovery and Applications of Usage Patterns from Web Data", Proc. of ACM SIGKDD Vol 1, Issue 2, 2000.
10. J. Tomlin, "An Entropy Approach to Unintrusive Targeted Advertising on the Web", Proc. of 9th WWW 2000.
11. Natwar Modani, Parul A. Mittal, Amit A. Nanavati and Biplav Srivastava, "Series of Dynamic Targeted Recommendations: Model and Strategies", IBM Research Report RI 02015, Feb 2002.

A Study of Content Conversion between eBook Standards

Seung-Kyu Ko[1], Won-Sung Sohn[1], Kyong-Ho Lee[2], Soon-Bum Lim[3], and
Yoon-Chul Choy[1]

[1] Department of Computer Science, Yonsei University, South Korea
{pitta, sohnws, ycchoy}@rainbow.yonsei.ac.kr
[2] IT Lab. National Institute of Standards and Technology, USA
lkh@nist.gov
[3] Department of Multimedia Science, Sookmyung Women's University, South Korea
sblim@sookmyung.ac.kr

Abstract. Many countries have established eBook standards adequate
to their environments. In USA, OEB PS is announced for distribution
and display of eBooks, in Japan, JepaX is announced for storage and
exchange, and in Korea, EBKS is made for clear exchange of eBook
contents. These diverse objectives of standards lead to different content
structures, and differences of content structure will cause a problem in
exchanging them. To correctly exchange eBook contents, the content
structure should be considered. So, in this paper, we study content conversion of standard eBooks based on Korean eBook standard, with con-
templating content structures. To convert contents properly, the mapping
relations should be clearly defined. For this, we consider standard's structure and extension mechanisms, and use a path notation and namespaces
for precise description. Moreover, through analysis of each mapping relationships, we classify conversion cases into automatic, semi-automatic,
and manual conversions. Finally we write up conversion scripts and experiment with them.

1 Introduction

An electronic book(eBook) means digital form of a paper book, and it offers the
following advantages [1][5] compared to a paper book.

- Simplification of circulation process.
- Effective communication with multimedia information.
- Various display output suitable to reader's environment.
- Easier management due to storage efficiency and durability.

With these merits, many research centers have predicted that eBook market will
greatly expand. For example, Andersen Consulting has forecasted the eBook
market will be 23 billion dollars in 2005[1], and IDC has estimated it to be
four billion and ten thousand dollars in 2004, only in USA[5]. So, to preoc-
cupy eBook market, many countries have established eBook standards. In USA,

K. Bauknecht, A M. Tjoa, G. Quirchmayr (Eds.): EC-Web 2002, LNCS 2455, pp. 273–283, 2002.
© Springer-Verlag Berlin Heidelberg 2002

OEBF(Open eBook Forum) announced OEB PS(Open eBook Publication Structure Specification)[9] in 1999. In Japan, Jepa(Japanese Electronic Publishing Association) announced JepaX 0.9[8] in 1999. In Korea, the Korean eBook Consortium (EBK: Electronic Book of Korea) sponsored by the Ministry of Culture & Tourism, announced a draft of EBKS(EBK Standard) 1.0[10] in 2001. All these standards are based on XML(eXtensible Markup Language)[15], and objectivities of each standard are distribution or exchange appropriate to their environments. However, when each country defines their own eBook standard, exchanging them will cause the problem of mismatch of content forms. This problem of mismatch is due to the difference of methods for defining the logical structure of a book. Therefore, to exchange eBook conforming each standard, the content has to be converted properly according to its logical structure.

So, in this paper, we study content conversion of standard eBooks based on Korean eBook standard, EBKS. Namely, the conversion methods for EBKS and OEB PS, and EBKS and JepaX are studied. To convert contents properly, the mapping relations should be clearly defined. For this, definition of mapping relations between each standard are based on logical structures. And it made the best use of extension mechanism of each standard, and used a path notation and namespaces for precise description. Moreover, through analysis of each mapping relationship, we classify them into automatic, semi-automatic, and manual conversions. And we write conversion scripts based on XSLT(XSL Transformation)[17] with reference to the proposed mapping table and experimented with them on the eBook content conversion. The remainder of this paper is as follows. In Section 2, we describe eBook content standards. In Section 3 and 4, the conversion of EBKS and OEB PS/JepaX are explained. Finally, we conclude the paper in Section 5.

2   Introduction to eBook Contents Standards

2.1   EBKS

EBKS[10] is established for clear exchange of contents, and it is composed of three parts; content, metadata, and style. For clear exchange of contents, it defines a logical document structure such as shown in Fig. 1(a). The structure of EBKS is made up of "metainfo" and "books". And "books" is composed of "cover", "front", "book", and "back". "books" describes a collection of books, and "book" describes the content of an eBook. "book" is composed of "cover", "front", "body", and "back". The structure of "body" which has the actual content is composed of "part", "chapter", and "section", as shown in Fig. 1(a). EBKS offers the extension mechanism similar to that of SGML[6]. Metadata of EBKS is based on Dublin Core[4] like OEB PS, and does not use qualifiers. For style, XSL-FO(eXtensible Stylesheet Language)[18] is recommended but not specified, so arbitrary style is possible.

2.2   OEB PS

The objectivity of OEB PS[9] is making an eBook success in marketplaces. So, to support existing documents, OEB PS is based on XHTML 1.0[19], which is based on HTML 4.0[14]. OEB PS is composed of OEB document and package, as shown in Fig. 1(b). OEB document is classified into basic document and extended document. Basic document conforms to OEB specification based on XHTML 1.0. Extended document is an XML document, which can describe any document structures. OEB PS defines a package for distribution of publication. Package describes the structure of an OEB publication but not contents itself. It is made up of a *package identifier,* which is a unique identifier that identifies an OEB publication itself; *metadata* based on Dublin Core; a *manifest* expressing files that make up a publication; a *spine* ; *tours* ; and a *guide* that describes extra information such as a table of contents, references, and indexes. OEB PS also defines style information based mostly on CSS1(Cascading Style Sheet)[12], and partially on CSS2[13].

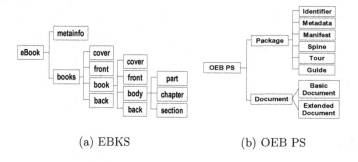

(a) EBKS   (b) OEB PS

Fig. 1. Overviews of EBKS and OEB PS

2.3   JepaX

The JepaX specification[8] has the goal of being used as the means for storing and exchanging contents of eBook. The structure of JepaX is made up of a whole structure, metadata, logical elements, list elements, block elements, inline element, and logical style elements. A whole structure information is composed of "jepainfo" describing extended structure, "bookinfo" describing matatada and constitution of book like "cover", "front", "body" and "back". This structure is shown in Fig. 2. JepaX defines high level structure of book and does not define the structures below "front", "body", and "back". Instead, it defines the constitution of the structure. So, to express the structure, attributes such as "type" or "xtype" of a "div" element are used, as TEI[11] or DocBook[3] does. For example, if lower structure of "body" is "section" and "subsect1", then the structure can be represented as shown in Fig. 2. And it provides an user-defined extension mechanism by offering "xtype", similar to "type" of "div" element. To allow companies to use style appropriate to their needs, style information is not defined.

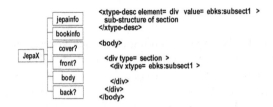

Fig. 2. Overview and an extension example of JepaX

EBKS defines only content and metadata, and style is recommended. Therefore, in this paper, mainly contents and metadata are looked at when conversion.

3   EBKS and OEB PS

Because OEB documents can be extended or basic document, there are two conversion cases. Arbitrary XML documents can be extended documents. So, EBKS document can be an extended document without modification. However, extended document cannot be EBKS document without translation, for EBKS document has a fixed logical structure. Besides, document structure of it can be different depending on publications, so it is difficult to define a consistent conversion scripts from extended document to EBKS. Therefore, when we discuss conversion of EBKS and OEB PS, we consider only basic document of OEB PS.

3.1   EBKS to OEB PS

Contents. Unlike EBKS that defines a logical structure, OEB basic document defines elements related to output. Therefore, when converting EBKS document to OEB document, structural elements of EBKS document should be mapped into output elements of OEB PS. This kind of mapping can be defined in various ways. For example, title of a chapter in EBKS document can be mapped to <H1> or <H3> or <P>. But considering the content structure, the mapping relations can be defined as Table 1. When looking at Table 1, corresponding

Table 1. A mapping table from EBKS to OEB document

EBKS	OEB
ebks	-
ebook	HTML, HEAD, BODY
preface	<H4>Preface</H4>
emph	EM
p	P
artwork, fig	IMG
cover.title	H1
section.title	H4

relation between EBKS and OEB document can be divided into the following six types.

One-to-One This is when an element of EBKS is expressed by exactly one corresponding element. Namely, corresponding semantic and syntax information are equal. Examples are "emph" or "p" of EBKS.

Extension This is when an element of EBKS is expressed by more than one elements in OEB PS. Example is "ebook" of EBKS.

Reduction This is when more than one elements of EBKS are mapped to one element of OEB PS. Examples are "artwork" and "fig".

Omission This is when element of EBKS is ignored in OEB document. "ebks" in Table 1 is not mapped.

Replacement This is when an element of EBKS is mapped not an element but a content of element. "preface" of EBKS is converted to a content of <H4>.

Selection This is when an element of EBKS can be mapped to more than one element. So, for precise mapping, user intervention is needed. "title" of EBKS is a example of this.

Top four of six corresponding relations can be automatically mapped, but "Selection" needs a user intervention. Also, for "Replacement", modification should be allowed depending on the user's needs. When defining mapping table, possibility of elements having different meaning depending on locations should be considered. For example, "title" in Table 1 can be book-title or section-title. Therefore, to express those elements, a path notation must be used, as shown in Table 1.

Metadata. Both OEB PS and EBKS use Dublin Core. And extension mechanism of metadata are almost the same. Therefore, mapping relation of metadata is "One-to-one".

Package. Unlike other two standards, OEB PS has a package mechanism that defines a composition of a publication. In conversion, it is processed as follows. Fist, it is assumed that files in *manifest* of package are combined into a content file using *spine* information. And because there are no methods for describing *package identifier* and *tours* in EBKS, they are not considered. Also only part of *guide* information that can be described in EBKS are considered. These mapping information are shown in Table 2.

Table 2. A mapping table for OEB package

OEB package	EBKS
manifest, spine	combined into one physical file
package identifier, tour	-
guide	index, glossary, ...

To convert EBKS document to OEB document, conversion scripts must be generated with reference to the mapping table. Conversion process is as shown in Fig. 3.

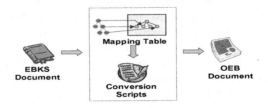

Fig. 3. Conversion process of EBKS to OEB Document

In this paper, we write conversion scripts based on XSLT using the defined mapping table, and they are shown in Fig. 5(a). Figure 4(a) is an original EBKS document and Fig. 4(b) is a converted OEB document. Conversion scripts are processed by Microsoft's XML Parser, MSXML 3.0. Figure 4(b) shows that the conversion resolution, the degree of converted structure information, depends on the degree of mapping table.

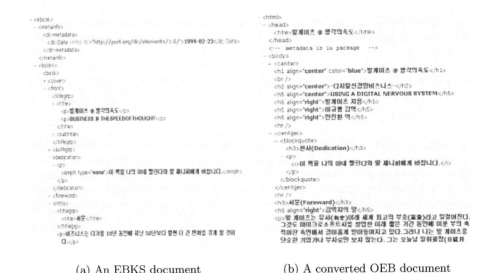

(a) An EBKS document   (b) A converted OEB document

Fig. 4. An EBKS and converted OEB document

3.2   OEB PS to EBKS

Contents. Converting OEB document to EBKS document needs a generation of structure information. But in flat document like OEB PS, structure information cannot be easily extracted, so automatic conversion is not possible. For example, one element may be used for expressing more than one meanings, or it can contain more than one structure components. Therefore, in this case, each part of an actual document has to be converted case by case.

Metadata. Converting metadata is the same as converting EBKS document to OEB document.

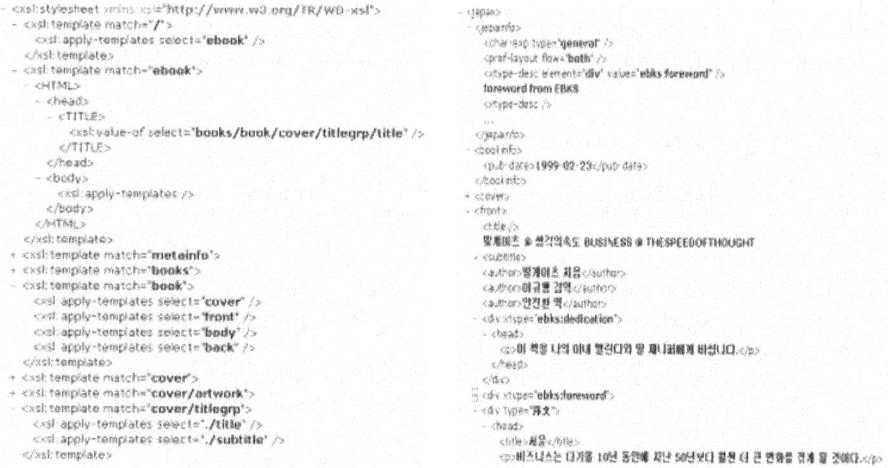

(a) Conversion scripts(EBKS2OEB)   (b) A converted JepaX document

Fig. 5. Conversion scripts from EBKS to OEB PS and a converted JepaX document

4   EBKS and JepaX

Conversion between JepaX document and EBKS document is a conversion between documents with structure. In this conversion, two things should be considered. First is an inconsistency in the range of structural information. In other words, if the ranges of structural information expressed by two documents are equal, the information can be accurately converted, but if they are not equal, some of them are hard to map to corresponding elements. Conversion between EBKS and JepaX come under this case. To manipulate those elements, they need to be mapped to the semantically closest elements or new elements need to be generated. But first method may cause a misinterpretation in a converted document, so it is reasonable to use the second method for consistent interpretation. And since both standards offer extension mechanism, second method can be easily applied. Second is a flexible structure of JepaX. In JepaX, user has to define the logical document structure with "div" element as shown in

Fig. 2. So, structure of a document can vary depending on users. This problem can be solved by defining relations between components of structure in detail in JepaX or describing the originality of each document structure. But, because relations of components of structure should be defined by Jepa, we use a second method. The description of originality is possible using namespace of Web standard. These examples are in Table 3.

4.1   EBKS to JepaX

Contents. Unlike EBKS, JepaX only defines the upper level of a document and lower level is defined by using "div". With this in consideration, mapping table for converting EBKS document to JepaX document is shown in Table 3.

Table 3. A mapping table from EBKS to JepaX document

Classification	EBKS	JepaX
Common Elements	ebks	jepax
	titlegrp	-
	title	(head)title
	vita	div(type="vita")
	emph	em
Exist only in EBKS	subsect1	div(xtype="ebks:subsect1")
	othersect1	div(xtype="ebks:othersect")

In Table 3, corresponding relation between EBKS and JepaX can be classified into the following four types.

One-to-One. Examples are "ebks" and "front" of EBKS.

Extension. Example is a "title" of EBKS.

Omission. EBKS has group elements such as "authorgrp" and "titlegrp" but JepaX does not. This information can be converted using extension mechanism but most of them are not necessary information in JepaX, so they are omitted.

Creation. Elements in EBKS that do not exist in JepaX are expressed by using extension mechanism of JepaX. "subset1" and "othersect" of EBKS do not exist in JepaX, so corresponding elements are created. And the originality of them are expressed by namaspaces.

The four mappings mentioned above can be automatically converted and fixed mapping table can be defined. Normally, since EBKS has more detailed structure than JepaX, "Creation" occurs more frequently than others.

Metadata. EBKS uses Dublin Core for defining metadata but JepaX defines its own nine metadata. Five of them are identical to EBKS and the rest are different. Therefore, for the metadata that cannot be expressed in JepaX, extension mechanism is used as contents do. Table 4 is a mapping table for metadata between JepaX and EBKS.

Table 4. A metadata mapping table from EBKS to JepaX

Classification	EBKS	JepaX
Common Elements	metadata	bookinfo
	dc:identifier	isbn
	dc:title	book-title
	dc:date	pub-date
	dc:publisher	publisher
Exist only in EBKS	dc:subject	div(xtype="dc:subject")
	dc:contributor	div(xtype="dc:contributor")

EBKS document can be converted to JepaX document using the contents and mapping table of metadata described above. To test the conversion process using the defined mapping table, we define conversion scripts based on XSLT. Figure 4(a) is an EBKS source document, and Fig. 5(b) is the converted JepaX document.

4.2   JepaX to EBKS

Contents. JepaX defines document structure as upper structure, logical structure, list, block elements and inline elements. Therefore, for each element, mapping table such as Table 5 can be defined. Looking at Table 5, corresponding relation between JepaX and EBKS can be classified into the following five types.

One-to-One. Examples are "cover" and "front" of JepaX.
Selection. Example is "key" of JepaX.
Extension. Example is "author", a logical element of JepaX.
Omission. Examples is "head", a logical element of JepaX.
Creation. An element that exists in JepaX but does not in EBKS, is expressed by using the extension mechanism of EBKS. "ruby" or "rb" are examples of this.

Three of five mapping relations, "One-to-One", "Extension", and "Omission" are converted automatically, but "Selection" needs user intervention. And, for "Creation", JepaX document should be scanned as a pre-process to determine which structure part of EBKS need to be extended. Mapping relation for "div", an element for defining logical structure of JepaX, can be classified into the following three types.

1. Exist both in JepaX and EBKS
   This is when structure information described by "div" exists both in EBKS and JepaX. "Cover", "vita", "dedication" are some of the examples. "One-to-One" mapping is possible in this case.
2. Exist only in JepaX
   This is when an element defined in JepaX does not exist in EBKS. "Literary property page" and "program_list" are examples of this. "Creation" mapping is possible in this case.
3. User extension in JepaX
   This is similar to "Exist only in JepaX".

Table 5. A mapping table from JepaX to EBKS document

Classification		JepaX	EBKS
Overall		jepax	ebks
Structure		front	front
Logical		title	titlegrp.title
Elements		author	author|(authorgrp.(author|corpauth))
List		ol	list(type="decimal")
Elements		li	item
Block		p	p
Elements		pre	prestr
Inline	Common	em	emph
Elements	Elements	key	keyword|keyphrase
	only in JepaX	ruby, rb	extension
Others		float, res	uri

Metadata. JepaX defines its own nine metadata. Five of them are the same as metadata of EBKS as shown in Table 4 and remains are only in JepaX. So for these metadata, metadata extension mechanism of EBKS should be used which is similar to that of OEB PS.

5   Conclusions and Future Directions

The conversion methods of eBook contents can be classified into *up, down,* and *equal conversion* by structure information, as shown in (Table 6). Converting

Table 6. Classification of conversion methods of eBook standards

Classification	Domain	Conversion scripts	Operation
down	EBKS to OEB PS	standard level	automatic
equal	EBKS and JepaX	structure level	semi-automatic
up	OEB PS to EBKS	document instance level	manual

EBKS document to OEB document is a *down conversion*, which removes structure information. In a *down conversion*, it is possible to map each structure constitution to that of other side, so consistent conversion scripts can be defined and automatic conversion is possible. In an *equal conversion*, like the conversion of EBKS and JepaX, the "Creation" and "Selection" relationship need user interventions. But, because mapping relation can be defined to a document structure, consistent conversion scripts can be defined. But because of manual works, this conversion can be viewed as a semi-automatic conversion. In an *up conversion*, because there is no document structure, conversion scripts are needed for each document instance. So, this conversion process is a manual conversion. In view of XML, a *down conversion* is defining mapping relationships at standard level, an *equal conversion* is defining mapping relationships at DTD(Document Type

Definition)[15] level, and an *up conversion* is defining mapping relationships at DI(Document Instance) level. For exact mapping and consistent interpretation of contents, a path notation and namespaces should be used when defining mapping tables.

In this paper, we studied the conversion of EBKS and other standards centered on text information. But in practice, not only text but also table is considered when converting. Although EBKS uses CALS table, JepaX and OEB PS use HTML table. Therefore, conversion between CALS table and HTML table is needed. Moreover, to make eBook content rich, existing content in a paper book should be converted to eBook forms. We are now studying for this.

References

[1] AAP/Andersen Consulting, http://www.publishers.org/dec2000anderson.ppt. *Ebook Study,* 2000.

[2] Michael Bartlett. E-book market set for explosion – idc study. *Newsbytes,* 2001.

[3] DocBook Technical Committee. *DocBook 2.0.2,* 2001.

[4] Dublin Core Metadata Initiative. *Dublin Core Metadata Element Set, Version 1.1: Reference Description, Internet RFC 2413,* 2001.

[5] Beverly L. Harrison. E-books and the future of reading. *IEEE Computer Graphics and Applications,* 20:32–29, 2000.

[6] International Organization for Standardization. *ISO8879:Information Processing-Text and Office System- Standard Generalized Markup Language(SGML),* 1986.

[7] International Organization for Standardization, Geneva, Switzerland. *Information and Documentation – Electronic Manuscript Preparation and Markup,* 1993.

[8] Japanese Electronic Publishing Association (JEPA). *JepaX 0.9,* 1999.

[9] Open eBook Forum. *Open eBook Publication Structure 1.0,* 1999.

[10] Won-Sung Sohn, Seung-Kyu Ko, Kyong-Ho Lee, Sung-Hyuk Kim, Soon-Bum Lim, and Yoon-Chul Choy. Standardization of ebook documents in korean industry. *Computer Standards & Interface,* 24:45–60, 2002.

[11] Text Encoding Initiative, http://www.tei-c.org/Vault/GL/p4beta.pdf. *Guidelines for Electronic Text Encoding and Interchange,* 1999.

[12] W3C Consortium, http://www.w3.org/TR/REC-CSS1-961217. *Cascading Style Sheets (CSS) level 1,* 1996.

[13] W3C Consortium, http://www.w3.org/TR/1998/REC-CSS2-19980512. *Cascading Style Sheets level 2,* 1996.

[14] W3C Consortium, http://www.w3.org/TR/ REChtml40 -971218. *Hypertext Markup Language (HTML) 4.0,* 1997.

[15] W3C Consortium, http://www.w3c.org/TR/1998/REC-xml-19980210. *Extensible Markup Language (XML) 1.0,* 1998.

[16] W3C Consortium, http://www.w3c.org/TR/xpath. *XML Path Language (XPath) Version 1.0,* 1999.

[17] W3C Consortium, http://www.w3c.org/TR/xslt. *XSL Transformations (XSLT) Version 1.0,* 1999.

[18] W3C Consortium, http://www.w3c.org/TR/xsl/. *Extensible Stylesheet Language (XSL) Version 1.0,* 2000.

[19] W3C Consortium, http://www.w3.org/TR/xhtml1/. *XHTML*

Web-Based System Configuration and Performance Evaluation Using a Knowledge-Based Methodology

Mara Nikolaidou[1] and Dimosthenis Anagnostopoulos[2]

[1] Dept. of Informatics, University of Athens,
Panepistimiopolis, 15771 Athens, Greece
mara@di.uoa.gr

[2] Dept. of Geography, Harokopion University of Athens,
70 El. Venizelou Str, 17671, Athens, Greece
dimosthe@hua.gr

Abstract. Since Internet dominated the world, the World Wide Web platform is used as a type of middleware providing a common platform for Intranet-based and Internet-based application development. Web-based applications have become more complex and demanding, in order to fulfil extended user requirements. In this paper, we propose a systematic approach for the configuration, modification and performance evaluation of web-based systems. Its contribution involves the employment of knowledge-based techniques for the design of web-based systems and the description of problems encountered and the solutions proposed. Emphasis is given on the extendable modelling scheme used to depict web-based application functionality and estimate application requirements from the network infrastructure. Web-based system architectures are designed and evaluated using IDIS environment.

1 Introduction

The enormous success of the Internet is mainly based on the World Wide Web (WWW), built to facilitate access to multimedia documents distributed all over the Internet through a common interface, i.e. a Web Browser. Using a Web Browser is possible to download that part of any application that consists of its user interface from anywhere in the world. Such applications are considered as *web-based applications*, and are built based on the multi-tiered client-server model [1, 2]. The first tier, e.g. the user interface or user service, is implemented using the WWW platform, while the other tiers implement the specific application logic that may be based on different architectures, as discussed in [3]. Thus, WWW platform can be viewed as a type of middleware providing a common platform of Intranet-based and Internet-based application development. Many commercial information systems, such as banking and ordering systems, distant learning environments and workflow management systems, fall in this category. Development of standards, such as CORBA, allowing the interaction between heterogeneous, autonomous applications and of programming languages, such as Java, providing native distributed programming support established a well-defined platform for web-based application

K. Bauknecht, A M. Tjoa, G. Quirchmayr (Eds.): EC-Web 2002, LNCS 2455, pp. 284–293, 2002.

development. A *web-based system* can be described as a set of web-based applications and the underlying infrastructure. Web-based system configuration is based on the successful combination of interacting components spread over the Internet, also facing the internal complexity of these components [4]. The configuration issue is, thus, a multidisciplinary one, imposing examination of a large number of alternative architectural solutions, exploitation of different replication scenarios and estimation of proposed architectures' performance. Complete and accurate description of web-based application functionality is a critical factor in web-based system design. It ensures the accurate estimation of QoS provided by the network infrastructure and the efficient performance evaluation of the overall system.

Simulation tools usually investigate the behaviour of predefined algorithms for the placement of resources and processes, or estimate the performance characteristics of a given network architecture, performing a "what-if" analysis [5, 6, 7]. Such tools do not make suggestions for the design or redesign of the system architecture. When configuring complex systems, experts rely more on experience than on theory-based calculations [8, 9]. Web-based system configuration issues requires dealing with interrelated problems, such as process and file allocation, which are NP-complete. Dealing with such problems requires methods that are more heuristic than algorithmic in nature. Expert system research has often concentrated on the representation and manipulation of heuristic knowledge and its use in *information system design* and *network configuration* problems [10, 11, 12].

In this paper, we describe a systematic approach for the configuration, modification and performance evaluation of web-based systems. Its contribution involves the employment of knowledge-based techniques for the configuration of web-based systems, the description of problems encountered and the solutions proposed. Emphasis is given on the extendable modelling scheme used to depict web-based application functionality and estimate application requirements. Furthermore, one should have the opportunity to evaluate the performance of the proposed solutions and reconfigure the proposed architecture if user requirements are not fulfilled. Web-based systems are configured using the *Intelligent Distributed System Design* tool *(IDIS)* [13].The rest of the paper is organized as follows: In section 2, web-based system configuration issue is discussed and a systematic approach dealing with it is proposed. In section 3, we present a web-based application representation scheme. Conclusions reside in section 4.

2   Configuring Web-Based Systems

Internet technology can be used in conjunction with middleware technology (message-based or object-based) to produce powerful web-based architectures. The configuration of web-based applications is performed based on the multi-tiered client-server model. The Web client, e.g. the first tier, facilitates a standard user interface allowing the user to retrieve information (in the form of HTML pages) or activate applications (through HTML pages). The Web server, e.g. the second tier, process and redirects user requests, gathers results and sends them to the client in the form of HTML documents. Thus, it provides a middleware platform integrating the desired functionality into HTML documents. An easy way to forward requests to other tiers is to activate CGI programs at the web server site. CGIs are portions of executable code written in scripting languages, as PERL and JavaScript. The Web server does not save any context related to a request coming from the browser, thus every request to a CGI program is handled in isolation (stateless server operation). The concept of a *context file* may be used on the server side, in order to temporary store the results of a CGI program before gradually presenting them to the user through the Web client. The weakness of the CGI approach lies on the fact that the program must be restarted on each request. An alternative solution is the provision of a direct interface allowing the connection to an already active external program using shared object technology. The program is permanently loaded into the server memory and associated with a URL used for its activation. An alternative web-based architecture is the one based on *applets*. Web browsers can be used for program execution (intelligent web clients). In this case, an applet may be downloaded from the Web server and be executed on the client machine to activate other tiers. Web-based applications often employ this technique to communicate with other distributed middleware platforms, as CORBA (Common Object Request Broker Architecture). Old-fashioned applications are incorporated with web environment using wrapping techniques.

Hardware used to support web-based applications is usually described in terms of the workstation-server model. Users have their own workstation (diskless or not) for executing client processes. Server processes are executed on dedicated servers. Replication techniques are employed to increase performance and ensure availability.

Web-based systems are viewed as a combination of web-based applications and the underlying network infrastructure. Both can be described in terms of elementary components [14]. The network infrastructure consists of private intranets and Internet connections. Each intranet consists of interconnected local or even wide area networks supporting TCP/IP protocol stack. Network infrastructure configuration requires the following components to be defined: *processing nodes* used for the execution of client and server processes, *storage devices* and *network connections*. For application description, the necessary components are: *processes* (clients, servers), *messages* and *data*. Users are described through *user profiles*. A typical web-based application architecture described in terms of the aforementioned components is depicted in figure 1.

The *Web client* acts as the user interface for application invocation. Users, depicted as user profiles, access applications through HTML pages in the Web client. Processes communicate through exchanging messages based on the request/reply model. As indicated in the figure, when a *get page* request is sent to the *Web server*, the proper functions are initiated and a *HTML file* is retrieved from the *File Server* through a *read* request. Based upon the HTML page content, the Web server may send the *HTML page*, as a reply, back to the client, or initiate a CGI script or an active program to communicate with any *external application server*. The *get page* request is also used to download an *applet* from the *Web server* and communicate with the *external application server*.

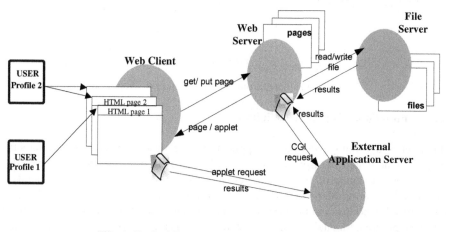

Fig. 1. Typical Web-based Application Architecture

In the following, we propose an integrated approach for web-based system design. System design is performed prior system construction and after user requirement gathering, as indicated in figure 2. It includes web-based application functionality description, process and data allocation to minimize Internet traffic and ensure efficient application operation and network configuration (network topology design). The design phase must facilitate the performance evaluation of the proposed solution prior implementation to ensure reliability. It is important to note the significance of a common modelling scheme for the representation of system entities. This enables the detailed description of user requirements while maintaining simplicity in the description of web applications. System design is accomplished in the following steps (figure 2):

1. Functional topology definition
2. Logical topology definition
3. Physical topology definition
4. Performance evaluation

Functional topology definition corresponds to the systematic description of system requirements. Logical and physical topology definition deal with server and data allocation and network configuration respectively. Both are accomplished using heuristics. Resource allocation and network configuration problem cannot be solved independently [11]. Thus, steps (2) and (3) of the proposed approach are invoked interactively until an acceptable solution is reached, as shown in figure 2. Analytical description of each step is presented in the following. IDIS system provides a semi-automated environment guiding the user throughout the aforementioned steps.

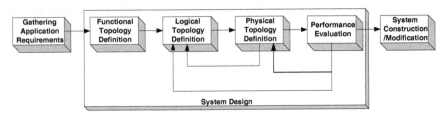

Fig. 2. Web-based Configuration Systematic Approach

2.1   Functional Topology Definition

In functional topology definition, applications are described as sets of interacting processes activated by user profiles. The files used by processes are also specified. There are two kinds of files, data files and code files. Application functionality is described in terms of predetermined, high-level operations (or actions), which are customized to conform to the web-based application architecture presented in figure 1. Operations are ultimately expressed in terms of primitive actions used to estimate application requirements. The desired performance characteristics for each application are also defined. More about the application representation scheme is presented in section 3.

Access points of the web-based system, called *locations*, are also specified. Definition of locations as well as specification of their size is performed with respect to the user's view. At the first level of detail, locations are defined as Internet access points. At next levels of detail, the *location* entity can be refined into more elementary ones, allowing the user to adjust the description of the system according to the application scale. Progressive refinement of location concept enables the progressive solution of resource allocation and network configuration problems.

2.2   Logical Topology Definition

Logical topology definition concerns process and file allocation. Allocation of processes and files is performed aiming at a. minimizing Internet traffic, b. fulfilling application requirements and c. minimizing configuration cost. Minimizing Intranet traffic especially on WAN connections and balancing load is also taken into account. Communication cost function C consists of C_U caused by client access, C_P caused by server access and C_F caused by data access. The optimal allocation solution is reached when $C = \min(C_U + C_P + C_F)$, under conditions ensuring access to all process and data replicas. Different replication scenarios can be applied, while locating processes and data [15]. As proved in [16], minimizing C is considered to be NP-complete problem. For the solution of such problems, heuristic methods are introduced, ensuring that, even if the optimal solution is not reached, one very close to it will be found. A variety of allocation algorithms supporting synchronous and asynchronous replication policies can be applied [17, 18, 19].

Adopting the workstation-server model, $C_U=0$ thus $C = \min(C_U + C_P + C_F)$. Since servers may access shared data, there is dependence between C_P and C_F. Even if the optimal solution is not reached, it is assumed that data are allocated before processes. Since network topology is not predefined during process and data allocation, it should be designed concurrently to ensure the efficient support of the solutions adopted. To achieve the required application performance, locality (i.e. keeping servers and data as close as possible to user) is considered as a basic principle. The most popular algorithm for Web server placement is the one based on the avoidance of unnecessary data transfer between WAN connections with asynchronous data replication support. The algorithm does not support optimal performance solutions, as it only focuses on WAN traffic and searches for a "relative good", cost effective and simple solution. Alternative algorithms supporting different data replication schemes and LAN traffic minimization are also supported [20, 21]. Each supported algorithm has an *Activation_Factor,* indicating activation order. Most simple algorithms are first applied. If the proposed solution does not satisfy application requirements, more complex algorithms are tested resulting in more costly solutions. *Activation_Factor* in each algorithm may be altered during system reconfiguration.

2.3   Physical Topology Definition

At the stage of physical topology definition, the network topology is designed. Network topology design is performed progressively. Since a network must be designed for each location, location refinement leads to a more detailed description of the network architecture. At each level of detail, the network architecture is formed by connections between locations of the specific level. For example, the network supporting the *Building* location is formed by network connections between all the *Floors* belonging to that *Building*. IDIS supports physical topology design by providing alternatives for network topology design and network configuration, but does not indicate commercial solutions.

2.4   Performance Evaluation

To evaluate system performance, a discrete event simulation tool was used [22]. Simulation modeling is widely adopted in the computer network domain for performance evaluation purposes. MODSIM simulation language [23] was used for simulation purposes. Object-oriented modelling and pre-constructed model libraries were employed to ensure efficiency of the simulation process [24]. Using simulation, maximum, average and minimum values of all performance measurements can be estimated. If the system requirements are not satisfied, logical and physical topologies must be redesigned. System performance cannot be partially estimated, e.g. even if only a small part of the overall architecture is altered, the entire system must be simulated again to accurately estimate performance measurements. The completion of the simulation phase is the most time consuming part of the overall design phase. Thus, while redesigning an inefficient architecture, all possible changes will be examined before the simulation process is reactivated.

3   Web-Based Application Representation Scheme

Web-based application functionality is represented using the modelling scheme presented in [22]. Main features of the modelling scheme are modularity, extendibility and wide applicability. It facilitates accuracy in distributed application description using a multi-layer *action* hierarchy. Actions indicate autonomous operations describing a specific service. The main goals of this modelling method are: a. to facilitate the complete description of application functionality in a simple way and b. to ensure the detailed depiction of application requirements. The modelling framework supports multi-tiered client/server models and can be easily extended to support customized applications.

Applications are modelled as sets of interacting processes. The specific *interfaces*, acting as process activation mechanisms must be defined for each process, along with the *operation scenario* that corresponds to the invocation of each interface. Each operation scenario comprises the actions that occur upon process activation. User behaviour is modelled through *user profiles*. Each profile includes user requests resulting in application invocation through the Web platform. Actions are described by qualitative and quantitative parameters, e.g. the processes being involved and the amount of data sent and received. In most cases, the operation scenario is executed sequentially (each action is performed when the previous one has completed). However, there are cases where actions must be performed concurrently. This is supported through specifying groups of actions that have common sequence number. The basic actions used to define operation scenarios are: *processing* indicating data processing, *request* indicating invocation of a server process, *write/read* indicating data storage/retrieval, *transfer* indicating data transfer between processes and *synchronise* indicating replica synchronization.

Actions can be either elementary or of higher layer. In the latter case, they are decomposed into elementary ones. While *processing* is an elementary action, *write* can be expressed through simpler ones, i.e. a *process* and a *request* sent to a *File Server*. All actions can be ultimately expressed through the three elementary ones, *processing*, *network* and *diskIO*, each indicating invocation of the corresponding infrastructure component. Action decomposition is performed through intermediate stages to simplify the overall process and maintain relative data. Action decomposition hierarchy ensures consistency, reduces complexity and enables following a common predefined decomposition mechanism. The most promising feature of this scheme is that the action hierarchy can be further extended to include new actions, placed at the highest layer. Definition of new actions is based on existing ones to ensure consistency during action decomposition.

In order to support Web-based applications, the action hierarchy presented in [22] was extended to include *Web-related actions*. These actions are used to easily describe operation scenarios corresponding to Web server and Web client functionality in the model depicted in figure 1. They include:

- *Get/put page*: indicating retrieving/storing an HTML/XML page
- *Post:* indicating form/field passing on an HTML/XML page
- *Get applet:* indicating applet download
- *Applet:* indicating applet activation
- *CGI*: indicating a cgi program activation
- *Invoke Program:* indicating active program invocation
- *Handle/Retrieve context file*: indicating context file creation or modification/ retrieval of context file data
- *HTTP request/reply*: indicating send request/reply protocol implemented to support HTTP protocol

The first three are usually used to describe Web client functionality, the following three Web server functionality and the last one HTTP protocol functionality. While all others are used for operation scenario description, the last ones are intermediate actions accurately depicting HTTP internal functionality. The functionality of external application servers can be depicted by further extending action hierarchy to support application specific operations. Web related actions hierarchy is depicted in figure 3.

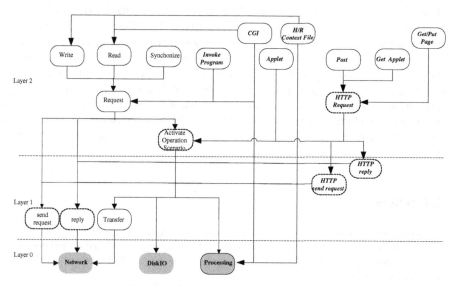

Fig. 3. Action Decomposition Hierarchy

Dotted rectangles represent *intermediate* actions, while gray rectangles represent *elementary* ones. Finally, rectangles with black border represent *application* actions used when defining operation scenarios. Web related actions are indicated using italics. The *request* action is used to depict process invocation and is further decomposed *into send request, activate operation scenario* and *reply actions*. Although not indicated in the figure, the *activate operation scenario* action may result in the invocation of any action included in application description. The *http request* action depicts the request functionality as it is implemented by HTTP protocol and it is used in the decomposition of application actions describing *Web client* functionality. Many application actions, as *read/write* or *get/put page*, actually represent the invocation of the corresponding server interface, and are decomposed into a *request* or *http request* action. This type of actions is supported to simplify the description of operation scenarios, since they are described using less parameters that the corresponding request actions. Furthermore they make server invocation transparent to the user, when describing client operation.

The user may further extend action hierarchy to describe external application functionality. When defining a new action, the user must specify its parameters and the actions used to describe it. During action decomposition, all parameters of the invoked action must be defined. In order to avoid knowledge inconsistency, the user ability to add actions is restricted.

4   Conclusions

Web-based systems provide a standard platform for the development of a wide range of applications. They extend to multiple sites and are characterized by internal complexity. Thus, their configuration is not a trivial task. We proposed a systematic approach for the configuration, modification and performance evaluation of web-based systems. During system design, NP-complete problems, such as resource allocation and network configuration must be solved. The proposed approach employs knowledge-based techniques and heuristics for providing solutions. Simulation is the performance evaluation of the proposed solutions. Emphasis is given on the extendable modelling scheme used to depict web-based application functionality and estimate application requirements. Future work focuses on the support of web-based multimedia and real time applications.

References

1. Serain, D.: Middleware. Springer-Verlag, London, Great Britain (1999)
2. Reeser, R., Hariharan, R.: Analytic Model of Web Servers in Distributed Environments. In: Proceedings of the ACM 2000 International Workshop on Software and Performance. ACM Computer Press (2000)
3. Shedletsky, J., Rofrano, J.: Application Reference Designs for Distributed Systems. IBM System Journal **32**(4) (1993)
4. Coulouris, G.F., Dollimore, J., Kindberg, T.: Distributed Systems - Concepts and Design. 3rd edn. Addison Wesley Publishing Company (2000))
5. Arlitt, M.F., Williamson, C.L.: Internet Web Servers: Workload Characterization and Performance Implications. IEEE/ACM Transactions on Networking **5**(5) (1997)
6. Barford, P., Crovella, M.: A Performance Evaluation of Hyper Text Transfer Protocols. In: Proceedings of the ACM 1999 International Conference on Measurement and Modeling of Computer Systems. ACM Computer Press (1999)
7. Khoroshevsky V. D.: Modelling of Large-scale Distributed Computer Systems. In: Proceedings of IMACS World Congress 1999. IMACS **6** (1999)

8. Juengst, W.E, Heinrich, M.: Using Resource Balancing to Configure Modular Systems. IEEE Intelligent Systems 1(1) (1998)
9. Fleischanderl, G., Friedrich, G.F., et. al.: Configuring Large Systems Using Generative Constraint Satisfaction. IEEE Intelligent Systems 1(1) (1998)
10. Nezlek, G.S., Hemant, K.J., Nazareth, D.L.: An Integrated Approach to Enterprise Computing Architectures. Communications of the ACM 42(11) (1999)
11. Lee, S.J., Wu, C.H.: A Knowledged-based approach to the Local-Area Network Design Problem. Applied Intelligence 4(1) (1994)
12. Dutta, A., Mitra, S.: Integrating Heuristic Knowledge and Optimization Models for Communication-Network Design. IEEE Transactions on Knowledge and Data Engineering 5(12) (1993)
13. Nikolaidou, M., Lelis, D., et. al: A Discipline Approach towards the Design of Distributed Systems. IEE Distributed System Engineering Journal 2(2) (1995)
14. Kramer, J.: Configuration Programming – A Framework for the Development of Distributed Systems. In: Proceedings of the Annual IEEE International Conference on Computer Systems and Software Engineering. IEEE Computer Press (1990)
15. Buretta, M.: Data Replication: Tools and Techniques for Managing Distributed Information. Wiley & Sons Inc., US (1997)
16. Morgan, H.L., Levin, K.D.: Optimal Program and Data Locations in Computer Networks. Communications of ACM 20(5) (1977)
17. Jajodia, S.: Managing Replicated Files in Partitioned Distributed Database Systems. In: Proceedings of IEEE International Conference on Data Engineering. IEEE Computer Press (1987)
18. Awerbuch, B., Bartal, Y., Amos, F.: Competitive Distributed File Allocation. In: Proceedings of ACM Annual Symposium on Theory of Computing. ACM Computer Press (1992)
19. Litoiu, M., Rolia, J.: Object allocation for Distributed Applications with Complex Workloads. In: TOOLS'2000. Lecture Notes on Computer Science, Vol 1786. Springer-Verlag, Berlin Heidelberg New York (2000)
20. Tan, M., Siegel, H.J.: A Stochastic Model for Heterogeneous Computing and Its Application in Data Relocation Scheme Development. IEEE Transactions on Parallel and Distributed Computing 9(11) (1998)
21. Johnson, G., Singh, A.K.: Stable and Fault/tolerant Object Allocation. In: Proceeding of ACM Annual Symposium on Principles on Distributed Computing. ACM Computer Press (2000)
22. Nikolaidou, M., Anagnostopoulos, D.: An Application-Oriented Approach for Distributed System Modeling. In: Proceedings of 21st IEEE International Conference on Distributed Computing Systems. IEEE Computer Press (2001)
23. MODSIM III The Language of Object-Oriented Programming - Reference Manual. CACI Products Company (1999)
24. Anagnostopoulos D.: An Object-Oriented Modeling Methodology for Dynamic Computer Network Simulation. International Journal of Modeling and Simulation 21(4) (2001)

Mapping UML Web Navigation Stereotypes to XML Data Skeletons

Georg Sonneck, Renate Motschnig, and Thomas Mueck

Institute of Computer Science and Business Informatics, University of Vienna,
Austria
Rathaustr. 19/9
A-1010 Vienna, Austria
{sonneck,motschnig,mueck}@ifs.univie.ac.at
http://www.ifs.univie.ac.at

Abstract. Everyone who already experienced "getting lost" in a web
site will agree that navigation support within such sites is a crucial topic
in any but the most trivial web-based system. Modeling navigation links
as special associations between classes in the UML let us arrive at the
conclusion that class diagrams tend to become overloaded with links such
that they are no longer understandable and their function as visual aids
gets lost. Aiming for more transparent high level navigation modeling
within the UML, this paper investigates, in a first step, well-known web
design languages for their approaches to the modeling of navigation.
By comparing Araneus, OOHDM, and RMM, in a subsequent step, we
derive navigation primitives that we suggest to incorporate into the UML
as navigational stereotypes. In a final step for two of these stereotypes
we propose a concrete implementation in XML. These XML skeletons
encode navigation information in a device-independent manner. Thus,
UML static structure diagrams, extended by the navigation stereotypes
introduced in this paper, have the potential to serve as a full-fledged
notation supporting navigation design in web-based systems.

1 Introduction

A particular strength of web-technology is its potential to complement information presented on one page by complementary information according to the
situational information needs of the user or visitor. The basically very support-
ive features of providing rich options for exploring complementary information,
however, tend to be compromised in the case that users loose their way in a
jungle of links with little guidance on how to get back to the starting point or
to some intermediate state of their search.

From conducting web-development projects (for example UniKid [12]) we
experienced that, in general, web-modeling using the UML has several benefits.
This is primarily due to the fact that one standardized and consistent language
can be used for both application- and web-design. Nevertheless, we clearly felt

K. Bauknecht, A M. Tjoa, G. Quirchmayr (Eds.): EC-Web 2002, LNCS 2455, pp. 294–303, 2002.
© Springer-Verlag Berlin Heidelberg 2002

that UML, more precisely both pure UML [13] and UML with web-modeling extensions [5], are deficient in providing the proper constructs for navigation modeling and design. This observation caused us to turn to well-known hypertext- and web-design languages in order to explore their means to support navigation with the goal of finding solutions that could be adapted for their use within UML. In particular, our course has been to investigate the Araneus project [2], RMM [3], and OOHDM [4] for issues of navigation design.

As a result, we found a set of navigational design patterns that are capable of contributing to the solution of our problem in so far, as they provide general, higher level constructs for disciplined linking and corresponding navigation support. Hence, the major contributions of our work are the adaptation of the navigation support primitives, also called navigation patterns, found in the literature for their use with UML and to provide implementation near XML skeletons for these. Our strategy has been to employ UML's extension mechanism of stereotypes in order to enrich UML with higher-level abstractions for navigation modeling. Additionally, for two navigation patterns a concrete implementation in XML is provided by using the XLink [15] and XSLT [16] recommendations of the W3C.

The paper is organized as follows. In the next section we describe the navigation patters we found suitable for their inclusion into the UML and we introduce an example in order to make the subsequent discussion more concrete. Section three then picks index navigation as a representative primitive that is tracked through the various web-design languages we considered in this article. Section four, which is the central one, suggests high-level UML stereotypes to capture the individual navigational patterns and furthermore implements these patterns in XML. Section five discusses the results and points to issues of further research.

2   Survey on Navigation Patterns

In a recent paper by Garzotto et al. [1], several prototypical web navigation patterns are proposed. In the sequel, we give a brief textual overview together with a graphical representation (in Fig. 1) of two of these patterns.

Starting with a simple hyperlink as the core building block for semantically advanced navigation patterns, a few common-sense graph structures can be identified in state of the art web presentations.

Among these advanced patterns we will elaborate on two representatives, i.e., index navigation and guided tour.

2.1   Index Navigation

An index list included into an entry page is used to navigate to particular item pages in a once at a time style. Reverse links enable the web user to return to the entry page after viewing an item page thus providing for a random access pattern via the index list. The underlying link structure is shown in Fig. 1a.

2.2   Guided Tour

Again, starting at an entry page the user is provided with a predefined sequence
of pages ending up at the entry page ("round trip"). The structure is shown in
Fig. 1b.

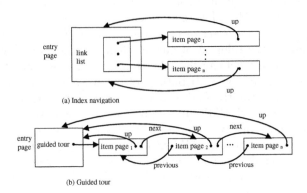

Fig. 1. Navigation Patterns

2.3   Conceptual Model of the Example

Fig. 2 shows the UML static structure diagram, often referred to as class diagram,
of our running example that we will use throughout to make the discussion more
concrete. The example is a fragment of a model of a university institute consisting
of 20 departments as captured in the inception phase of the Unified Process [14].

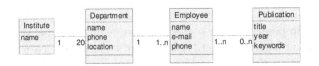

Fig. 2. System architecture

3   Comparison of Web Design Languages

This section aims to compare different approaches to navigation design, namely
Araneus [2], RMM [3], OOHDM [4] and UML [17]. While Araneus views web
application in tight connection with relational database design, RMM (Relationship Management Method) puts emphasis on separating three design issues,
namely content, structure, and the user interface.

OOHDM (Object-Oriented-Hypermedia-Design-Model), being a method for the development of complex hypermedia applications, focuses on individual developmental phases that are arranged to be followed incrementally and iteratively. In OOHDM, conceptual design precedes a separate phase referred to as navigational design whose notation is investigated in our context. For UML a navigation space model and a navigational structure model are proposed in [17], where new constructs representing navigational elements (e.g. a guided tour or an index navigation) are presented. A more complete comparison can be found in [11].

ARANEUS

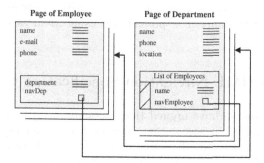

Fig. 3. Index Navigation in ARANEUS

Fig. 3 implements a link from Employee page to Department page and an index navigation from Department page to Employee page. The index navigation is represented by a list of names from employees on the Department page. The names of employees are used as anchors. A navigation to the specified employee is accomplished by clicking on this anchor.

OOHDM

Fig. 4. Index navigation in OOHDM

In OOHDM the diagram of an index navigation is much simpler but it is consequently not so detailed as shown on the right side of Fig. 4. For example the structure of the anchor that will be placed on the Department page is not specified. On the left side of Fig. 4 a corresponding textual description of the objects is presented that is once again more detailed.

RMM

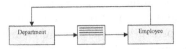

Fig. 5. Index navigation in RMM

The notation used in RMM is particularly simple, as it is shown in Fig. 5. RMM implements an index navigation directly with a new graphical primitive. A specification of the anchor is possible by using M-slices (see [11] for an in depth description).

4   Mapping UML Navigation Specification to XML

In the introduction we have argued that modeling every navigational link between client pages as an association between the classes representing the respective pages leads to class diagrams that are crowded with associations and, in general, are no longer transparent. Therefore higher-level abstractions being capable of hiding some of the links are useful. As will be illustrated below, UML's extension mechanism of stereotypes lends itself very well for introducing higher-level constructs for navigation specification.

In this Section we propose to extend UML by stereotypes that model the navigational patterns reviewed in Section 2. For each pattern, one higher-level relationship stereotype will be introduced and subsequently transformed into XML skeletons. These skeletons use XLink and XSLT to utilize the standardized linking functionality. We present the stereotypes in the context of modeling the university department example introduced in Section 2.3.

4.1   Index Navigation

Fig. 6 shows a new notation for the index navigation pattern in UML. It is modeled as a stereotype called <<index navigation>> on an association relationship between the source - and the target client page. This unidirectional association represents the relationship between one instance of class Department to 1 to n associated instances of class Employee. The unidirectional association from Employee to Department which has the stereotype <<link>> means that an instance of class Employee can navigate to its associated instance of class Department. The information presented on the client pages is specified as attributes of these pages. The attributes file_name and tag_name are class scope attributes because their value must be the same for all instances of the class. They are necessary to generate the XML-skeleton for this pattern.

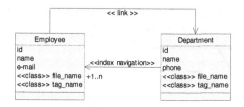

Fig. 6. Index Navigation in UML new notation

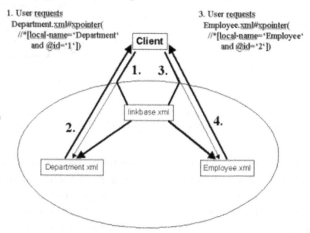

Fig. 7. Request of a resource in Index Navigation

XML Skeleton for Index Navigation

A static XML skeleton can be generated, that corresponds to the index navigation in Fig. 6. The links between resources are modelled using XLink [15]. Fig. 7 demonstrates how a user may request resources belonging to the index navigation of our example. For simplicity the DTDs of Department.xml and Employee.xml are omitted.

A user requests the first department as shown in Fig. 7, step 1. Before transporting the request the linkbase engine works through linkbase.xml and subsequently returns the first department (step 2) with an embedded link list to all associated employees. Using this link list, a navigation to the employee identified by id=2 is possible (step 3 and 4).

Fig. 8 shows the content of Department.xml. Some of the necessary link attributes are specified in the corresponding DTD. Several my_app:department and my_app:ItempageLink elements are nested in the my_app:Departments element. The my_app:Departments element itself represents an extended link, which means, that the xlink:type attribute of this element has the value 'extended'.

Each my_app:Department element has the attributes shown in Fig. 6 and additional linking information. The xlink:label attribute defines an anchor from which an arc starts. The xlink:label of this element is constructed using the

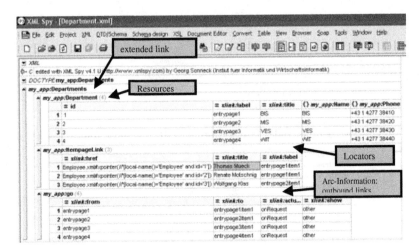

Fig. 8. Content of Department.xml involved in index navigation

keyword *entrypage* plus the id of the corresponding department. The xlink:title attribute has the same value as the name element of the department.

Each my_app:ItempageLink is a locator corresponding to a remote resource (the employee), which the attribute xlink:href identifies. To construct this identifier the file_name and the tag_name of the employees is used. The xlink:title attribute has the same value as the name element of the corresponding employee. The xlink:label attribute is constructed of the corresponding department label plus the keyword *item1*. Each my_app:ItempageLink element of a given department has the same xlink:label. If there existed a second index navigation starting from department the xlink:label of the corresponding my_app:ItempageLink elements would end with *item2*. The xlink:label attribute functions as anchor to which arcs can refer to.

The my_app:go elements specify the arcs between available resources and locators. For each department element a my_app:go element exists, that links the department to all assigned employees. In extended versions the attributes xlink:actuate and xlink:show will not be fixed to specific values.

Fig. 9 shows the content of Employee.xml. The my_app:EntrypageLink allows a navigation from Employee to the corresponding department. This element is a simple link. The attribute xlink:href is an anchor which identifies the remote resource and it is constructed using the file_name and tag_name of the departments plus the specific department id. The xlink:title has the same value as the name element of the department. Other presentation information is declared in the DTD.

4.2   Guided Tour

Fig. 10 shows the guided tour pattern modeled as a new UML constraint. In this example, the Institute functions as the collection center from where a consecutive

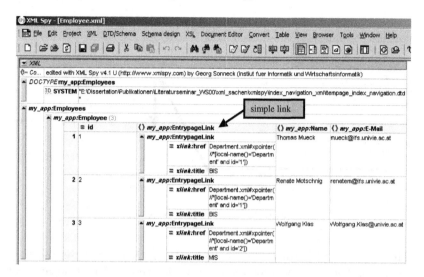

Fig. 9. Content of Employee.xml involved in index navigation

navigation to the Department pages is possible. A unidirectional association with the additional stereotype <<guided tour>> is used to model this navigation pattern. One instance of class Institute is associated to 20 instances of class Department.

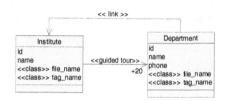

Fig. 10. Guided Tour in UML new notation

As Fig. 11 shows Institute.xml and Department.xml only represent the data of the institute and the departments (as specified in Fig. 10). The following illustrates the steps that occur when a user requests a department in the middle of the guided tour.

- A Client requests the second department by calling:
  Department.xml#xpointer(//*[local-name()='Department' and @id='2'])
- The system checks in linkbase.xml for assigned external linkbases and finds the linkbase Guided_tour.xml for Department.xml (see Fig. 11).
- Guided_tour.xml is the linkbase for Institute.xml and Department.xml. This is done because the linking information has to be modified for each request, which is done by transform_linkbase.xsl, that completes the linking skeleton Guided_tour.xml (see Fig. 12). The ExtLink element is an extended link.

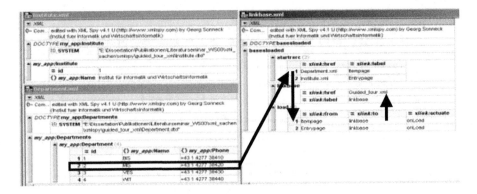

Fig. 11. Guided Tour in XML

This time only locator elements are modelled that are connected by 4 arc elements. The identifiers for the locators institute and first department are known. The reference to the active, next and previous department has to be filled in for each request, because each time a different department could be requested. The modification is indicated by the black rectangle in Fig. 12.

- The final Guided_tour.xml represents the skeleton plus inserted links.
- Department 2 is completed by the link information and is returned.

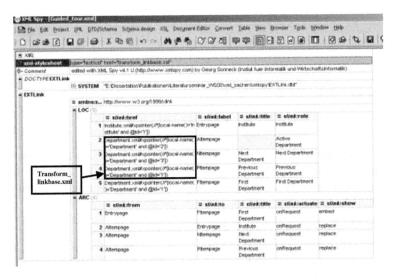

Fig. 12. Content of Guided_tour.xml

5   Conclusions and Further Work

The first part of this paper has been devoted to a comparison of languages for web development with respect to their means to model navigation, where we have observed a tendency towards introducing higher-level constructs in the form of navigational patterns. In this paper we apply the strategy described above to UML by using stereotypes to integrate navigation patterns.

Furthermore we show that the information in UML is sufficient to make a transformation to XML skeletons representing the same navigation patterns.

Further research will deal with the semi-automated generation of web-pages and hence address the transformation between XML and other representation formats. We are also in the process of providing XML skeletons for other navigation patterns (e.g. filtered indexed navigation and indexed guided tour).

References

1. Garzotto, F., Baolini, P., Bolchini, D., Valenti, S.: Modeling by patterns of Web applications, Lecture Notes in Computer Science, Vol. 1727, Springer Verlag, Berlin Heidelberg New York (1999) 203–230
2. Atzeni, P., Mecca, G., Merialdo, P.: Design and Maintenance of Data-Intensive Web Sites, RT-DIA-25-1997
3. Isakowitz, T., Stohr, E. A., Balasubramanian, P.: RMM: A Methodology for structured Hypermedia Design, CACM 38(8), Aug, 1995, 34–44
4. Schwabe, D., Rossi, G.: An Object Oriented Approach to Web-Based Applications Design. TAPOS 4(4): 207–225 (1998)
5. Conallen, J.: Building Web Applications with UML. Addison Wesley Longman, Massachusetts (2000)
6. Schwabe, D., Rossi, G., Barbosa, S.D.J.: Systematic Hypermedia Application Design with OOHDM. In Proc. Hypertex 96, 116–128
7. Atzeni, P., Mecca, G., Merialdo, P.: To Weave the Web. In International Conf. on Very Large Data Bases (VLDB'97), Athens, Greece, August 26–29, 1997, 206–215
8. Baresi, L., Garzotta, F., Paolini, P.: Extending UML for Modeling Web Applications. HICSS 2001
9. Schwabe, D., Simone, D., Barbosa, J.: Navigation Modeling in Hypermedia Applications. IWHD 1995: 34–35
10. Gueell, N., Schwabe, D., Vilain, P.: Modeling Interactions and Navigation in Web Applications. ER Workshops 2000: 115–127
11. Malus, C., Sonneck, G.: Entwurfsmuster und Modellierung von Navigation im Web-Design. Internal Report of the Institute, University of Vienna, 2001
12. Motschnig, R.: Applying the Unified Process for Developing a Medium-Sized Web-Based Application, submitted in 2002
13. Rumbaugh, J., Jacobson, I., Booch, G.: The Unified Modeling Language Reference Manual. Addison Wesley Longman, Massachusetts (1999)
14. Jacobson, I., Booch, G., Rumbaugh, J.: The Unified Software Development Process. Addison Wesley Longman, Massachusetts (1999)
15. W3C: XLink, http://www.w3.org/TR/xlink/, January 2002
16. W3C: XSLT, http://www.w3.org/TR/xslt, January 2002
17. Hennicker, R., Koch, N.: A UML-based Methodology for Hypermedia Design. UML'2000 – The Unified Modeling Language, Springer, October 2000.

KAON – Towards a Large Scale Semantic Web

Erol Bozsak, Marc Ehrig, Siegfried Handschuh, Andreas Hotho, Alexander Maedche,
Boris Motik, Daniel Oberle, Christoph Schmitz, Steffen Staab, Ljiljana Stojanovic,
Nenad Stojanovic, Rudi Studer, Gerd Stumme, York Sure, Julien Tane, Raphael Volz,
and Valentin Zacharias

Forschungszentrum Informatik FZI, 76131 Karlsruhe,
http://www.fzi.de/wim
Institute AIFB, University of Karlsruhe, 76128 Karlsruhe,
http://www.aifb.uni-karlsruhe.de/WBS

Abstract. The Semantic Web will bring structure to the content of Web pages,
being an extension of the current Web, in which information is given a well-defined
meaning. Especially within e-commerce applications, Semantic Web technologies
in the form of ontologies and metadata are becoming increasingly prevalent and
important. This paper introduce KAON - the Karlsruhe Ontology and Semantic
Web Tool Suite. KAON is developed jointly within several EU-funded projects and
specifically designed to provide the ontology and metadata infrastructure needed
for building, using and accessing semantics-driven applications on the Web and
on your desktop.

1 Introduction

The Web in its' current form is an impressive success with a growing number of users
and information sources. Tim Berners-Lee, the inventor of the WWW, coined the vision
of a Semantic Web in which background knowledge on the meaning of Web resources
is stored through the use of machine-processable (meta-)data. The Semantic Web brings
structure to the content of Web pages, being an extension of the current Web, in which
information is given a well-defined meaning. Thus, the Semantic Web will be able
to support automated, electronic services using semantics-based descriptions. These
descriptions are seen as a key factor to finding a way out of the growing problems of
traversing an ever expanding Web. In this sense, ontologies and metadata are becoming
increasingly prevalent and important in a wide range of e-commerce applications.

The technical foundation of the Semantic Web is RDF (Resource Description Framework) which provides a generic core data model. Several software components, such as
parsers, schema and metadata editors, repositories, have already been developed. However, they generally fail to meet the requirements for sophisticated e-Commerce projects.
To support advanced applications much more specialized, comprehensive and intregated
tools are required.

The Karlsruhe Ontology and Semantic Web Tool Suite (KAON) builds on available
resources and provides tools for the engineering, discovery, management, and presentation of ontologies and metadata. It establishes a platform needed to apply Semantic
Web technologies to e-commerce and B2B scenarios. Because of that, important design

K. Bauknecht, A M. Tjoa, G. Quirchmayr (Eds.): EC-Web 2002, LNCS 2455, pp. 304–313, 2002.

goals were robustness and scalability, since these are key quality factors for any enterprise application. In this paper the vision and the current status of KAON are presented. The official KAON community web site[1] also provides up-to-date information about the project and allows downloading the newest version of the software.

The paper is organized as follows: Section 2 introduces the layered architecture and technologies underlying the Semantic Web. Section 3 collects and summarizes requirements for an infrastructure for semantics-based Services and applications. Subsequently we present the formal ontology model behind KAON. This ontology model is implemented within the conceptual architecture section that is presented in section 5. The current status of the actual implementation effort is described briefly in section 6. Before we conclude, we give a short overview on related work and provide an overview on the next steps within KAON.

2   The Semantic Web

The term "Semantic Web" encompasses efforts to build a new WWW architecture that enhances content with formal semantics. This will enable automated agents to reason about Web content, and carry out more intelligent tasks on behalf of the user. "Expressing meaning" is the main task of the Semantic Web. Tim Berners-Lee has conceived a five layer architecture for the Semantic Web which is presented in the followin

XML – The syntax layer. XML allows to markup arbitrary content by means of nested, attributed elements. The names of these elements don't say anything about what the structure means, therefore further means are required for the Semantic Web and the role of XML is reduced to a syntax carrier.

RDF – The data layer. RDF allows the encoding, exchange and reuse of structured metadata. Principally, information is represented by very generic means, i.e. directed partially labeled pseudographs. This graph may be serialized using XML. Contrary to XML, RDF allows to assign global identifiers to resources and allows to refer and extend statements made in other documents. This feature is the main motivation for its use as an data layer.

The ontology layer. The third basic component of the Semantic Web are ontologies. Ontologies describe formal, shared conceptualizations of a particular domain of interest [4]. This description can be used to describe structurally heterogeneous and distributed information sources such as found on the Web.

By defining shared and common domain theories and vocabularies, ontologies help both people and machines to communicate concisely, supporting the exchange of semantics and not only syntax.

The basic building block for ontologies are concepts, which are typically hierarchically organized in a concept hierarchy. These concepts can have properties which establish named relations to other concepts. Several representation languages have been proposed for the specification of ontologies. Section 4 provides a concise description of

---

[1] http://kaon.semanticweb.org

the representation language used within KAON. Since RDF is very generic ontologies can be stored in RDF.

The logic layer The logic layer consists of rules that enable inferences, e.g. to choose courses of action and answer questions.

Current research is mainly focused on the first three layers - which is also the focus of this paper. Our formal ontology model (cf. section 4) includes means to extend the ontology by rules in an arbitrary logic language. This is a first step towards the transition to this fourth layer of the Semantic Web.

The proof layer. A proof layer has been conceived to allow the explanation of given answers generated by automated agents. Naturally, you might want to check the results deduced by your agent, this will require the translation of its internal reasoning mechanisms into some unifying proof representation language.

3   Requirements

While building semantics-based applications within E-Commerce, Knowledge Management, Web Portals, etc. we have gained insight into application features that warrant a success. Based on that experience and in order to enabling reuse across projects, we have decided to build a framework addressing these issues. An extensive requirement gathering process was undertaken to come up with a set of requirements that such framework must fulfill. The following key requirements were identified:

- **Accessability**: A framework should enable loose coupling, allowing access through standard web protocols, as well as close coupling by embedding it into other applications. This should be done by offering sophisticated standard APIs.
- **Consistency:** Consistency of information is a critical requirement of any enterprise system. Each update of a consistent ontology must result in a ontology that is also consistent. In order to achieve that goal, precise rules must be defined for ontology evolution and an evolution service implementing these rules has to be provided. Also, all updates to the ontology must be within transactions assuring the usual properties of atomicity, consistency, isolation and durability (ACID).
- **Concurrency:** It must be possible to access and modify information concurrently. This may be achieved using transactional processing, where objects can be modified at most by one transaction at the time.
- **Durability**: An almost trivial requirement easily accomplished by reusing existing database technology. A sophisticated storage system must offer facilities for replication: for often used ontologies redundant copies must be maintained to address scalability and availability problems.
- **Security**: Guaranteeing information security means protecting information against unauthorized disclosure, transfer, modification, or destruction, whether accidental or intentional. To realize it, any operation should only be accessible to properly authorized agents. Proper identity of the agent must be reliably established, by employing known authentication techniques. Sensitive data must be encrypted for network communication and persistent storage. Finally, means for auditing (logging) of sensitive operations should be present.

- **Reasoning**: Reasoning engines are central components of semantics-based applications. Our tools should have access to those engines which provide the reasoning services required to fulfill a certain task.
- **Mapping**: Often multiple ontologies have to be supported by an ontology system. This support is only complete if means for mapping and mediating between heterogeneous ontologies are provided.
- **Discovery:** We assume that data in the Semantic Web will be distributed. Therefore means for ontology-focused and intelligent discovery of metadata are required. Based on a semantic description of the search target, the system should be able to discover relevant information on the Web.
- **Internationalization:** The framework should allow users to create ontologies and their instances in different languages and should support non-Latin character sets.
- **Formal ontology:** The formal semantics specified by an ontology must be unambiguous and clear.

4 Formal Model for Ontologies

Formal semantics of ontologies are an important requirement for us. The notion and formal semantics of ontologies currently supported by our tools is therefore presented in this section.

Definition 1. *A* core ontology *is a structure*

$$\mathcal{O} := (C, \leq_C, R, \sigma, \leq_R)$$

consisting of (i) two disjoint sets C and R whose elements are called concept identifiers *and* relation identifiers, *resp., (ii) a partial order $\leq_C$ on C, called* concept hierarchy *or* taxonomy, *(iii) a function $\sigma: R \to C^+$ called* signature, *and (iv) a partial order $\leq_R$ on R, called* relation hierarchy, *where $r_1 \leq_R r_2$ implies $|\sigma(r_1)| = |\sigma(r_2)|$ and $\pi_i(\sigma(r_1)) \leq_C \pi_i(\sigma(r_2))$, for each $1 \leq i \leq |\sigma(r_1)|$.*

Often we will call concept identifiers and relation identifiers just *concepts* and *relations*, resp., for sake of simplicity.

Definition 2. *For a relation $r \in R$ with $|\sigma(r)| = 2$, we define its* domain *and its* range *by* $\mathrm{dom}(r) := \pi_1(\sigma(r))$ *and* $\mathrm{range}(r) := \pi_2(\sigma(r))$.

If $c_1 \leq_C c_2$, for $c_1, c_2 \in C$, then c_1 is a subconcept *of c_2, and c_2 is a* superconcept *of c_1. If $r_1 \leq_R r_2$, for $r_1, r_2 \in R$, then r_1 is a* subrelation *of r_2, and r_2 is a* superrelation *of r_1.*

If $c_1 <_C c_2$ and there is no $c_3 \in C$ with $c_1 <_C c_3 <_C c_2$, then c_1 is a direct *subconcept of c_2, and c_2 is a* direct *superconcept of c_1. We note this by $c_1 \prec c_2$. Direct superrelations and direct subrelations are defined analogously.*

Definition 3. *Let $\mathcal{L}$ be a logical language. A $\mathcal{L}$-axiom system for an ontology $\mathcal{O} := (C, \leq_C, R, \sigma, \leq_R)$ is a pair $A := (AI, \alpha)$ where (i) AI is a set whose elements are called* axiom identifiers *and (ii) $\alpha: AI \to \mathcal{L}$ is a mapping. The elements of $A := \alpha(AI)$ are called* axioms.

An ontology with $\mathcal{L}$-axioms is a pair $(\mathcal{O}, A)$ where $\mathcal{O}$ is an ontology and A is a $\mathcal{L}$-axiom system for $\mathcal{O}$.

Definition 4. *An ontology with $\mathcal{L}$-axioms $(\mathcal{O}, A)$ is* consistent, *if $A \cup \{\forall x\colon x \in c_1 \to x \in c_2 \mid c_1 \leq c_2\} \cup \{\forall \boldsymbol{x}\colon \boldsymbol{x} \in r_1 \to \boldsymbol{x} \in r_2 \mid r_1 \leq r_2\}$ is consistent.*

In the sequel, *ontology* stands for either a core ontology or an ontology with $\mathcal{L}$-axioms.

Definition 5. *A* lexicon *for an ontology $\mathcal{O} := (C, \leq_C, R, \sigma, \leq_R)$ is a structure*

$$Lex := (S_C, S_R, \mathit{Ref}_C, \mathit{Ref}_R)$$

consisting of (i) two sets S_C and S_R whose elements are called signs *for concepts and relations, resp., (ii) a relation $\mathit{Ref}_C \subseteq S_C \times C$ called* lexical reference *for concepts, where $(c, c) \in \mathit{Ref}_C$ holds for all $c \in C \cap S_C$, (iii) a relation $\mathit{Ref}_R \subseteq S_R \times R$ called* lexical reference *for relations, where $(r, r) \in \mathit{Ref}_R$ holds for all $r \in R \cap S_R$.*

An ontology with lexicon *is a pair $(\mathcal{O}, Lex)$ where $\mathcal{O}$ is an ontology and Lex is a lexicon for $\mathcal{O}$.*

The requirement of support for internationalization is provided via such a lexicon.

Definition 6. *A* knowledge base *is a structure*

$$KB := (C_{KB}, R_{KB}, I, \iota_C, \iota_R)$$

consisting of (i) two sets C_{KB} and R_{KB}, (ii) a set I whose elements are called instance identifiers *(or* instances *or* objects *for short), (iii) a function $\iota_C\colon C_{KB} \to \mathfrak{P}(I)$ called* concept instantiation, *(iv) a function $\iota_R\colon R_{KB} \to \mathfrak{P}(I^+)$ called* relation instantiation.

Such instances are technically represented in RDF and may be physically located in several documents.

Definition 7. *An* instance lexicon *for a knowledge base $KB := (C_{KB}, R_{KB}, I, \iota_C, \iota_R)$ is a pair $IL := (S_I, R_I)$ consisting of (i) a set S_I whose elements are called* signs *for instances, (ii) a relation $R_I \subseteq S_I \times I$ called* lexical reference *for instances. A* knowledge base with lexicon *is a pair (KB, IL) where KB is a knowledge base and IL is an instance lexicon for KB.*

5   Conceptual Architecture

In this section we introduce the general architecture that is the basis of KAON. We mainly distinguish three layers within our conceptual architecture, namely the data and remote service layer, the middleware layer and the applications and services layer. Figure 1 depicts this layered architecture.

Applications and Service Layer: Application and service clients can be either *(i)* the components of the Java-Application-based OntoMat application framework or *(ii)* applications extending the web-based KAON-PORTAL and web site management framework. All application clients connect with the middleware layer via KAON API, an application programming interface accessing ontology elements. The API realizes the application model by providing a set of object-oriented abstractions of ontology elements. Application clients provide views and controllers for model realized by KAON API.

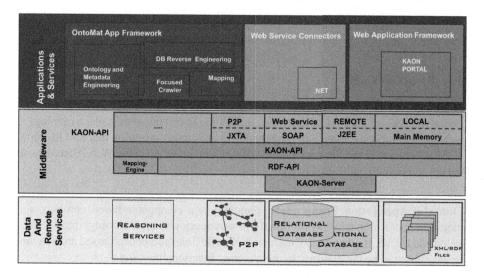

Fig. 1. KAON Architecture

Middleware Layer: The primary role of the middleware layer is to provide an abstraction for ontology access. Its second role is the dynamic instantiation and delegation of requests to the underlying external services layer. The first role is implemented by the KAON API, which isolates clients from different API implementations and provides a unified interface. For example, a transient ontology model is provided by implementing the KAON API on top of RDF files. This implementation may then be used for in-memory processing of ontologies stored in files and stand-alone deployment of tools. KAON RDF Server is a data source specialized in storing RDF data. It allows concurrent modification, supports transactions and persistence. Non-RDF data sources may be accessed using other implementations of the KAON API, thus creating an ontology-compatible view of data not in a format according to Semantic Web standards.

The dynamic instantiation and delegation of requests to services is out of scope for this paper. The implementation relies on the framework provided by the Java Management Extensions (JMX).

Data and Remote Service Layer: This layer has several roles. First it offers access to physical data stores such as databases or file systems. Second it groups external services such as reasoning engines, the aforementioned mapping engine etc. and announces availability to the middleware layer.

6 Implementation of the Conceptual Architecture – The KAON Tool Family

This section explains how the conceptual architecture has been implemented describing its current status and underlying technologies. We mainly distinguish between tools which are intended to be directly used by users (*frontend tools*) and tools which are intended to be used within other applications (*backend tools*).

6.1   FrontEnd Tools

KAON PORTAL. KAON PORTAL is an ontology-based web portal generator. The underlying idea of the KAON PORTAL application is that based on a given ontology, a web application is automatically generated. It is important to mention that KAON Portal is capable to automatically provide metadata-driven services on the Web. Therefore all data is additionally published in RDF.

OntoMat Application Framework. OntoMat is a component-based ontology and metadata application framework. Initially it was developed as an ontology-based annotation and HTML markup tool. On account of its flexible, component-based architecture it was chosen to be the platform to realize other functionalities, e.g.:

– It includes a multi-lingual Ontology Engineering and Evolution Environment (OntoMat-SOEP) that allows the manual development and maintenance of ontologies.
– It provides means for database reverse engineering via OntoMat-REVERSE, a tool and approach that allows mapping JDBC-compliant relational databases onto ontologies [6].
– The OntoMat-SILVA tool implements a comprehensive methodology for ontology mapping and mediation consisting of means for normalization heterogeneous ontologies, detecting similarities, providing graphical means for specifying associations and semantic bridges between two ontologies.
– The OntoMat-Catyrpel tool which provides user-support for the ontology-focused discovery of RDF-based metadata in the Web.

It is important to mention that due to the flexible and component-based approach each component is able to communicate with all other components realized using OntoMat.

6.2   Backend Tools — KAON API and Server

Backend tools provide the middleware layer and offer access to external services. Due to lack of space we will restrict our attention to the two focal components in this layer, namely the KAON API and KAON Server.

KAON API. KAON API is the focal point of the middelware layer. It provides objects representing various pieces of an ontology, such as Concept, Relation, Attribute or Instance, objects for creating and applying changes to ontology entities as well as objects providing query facilities. KAON API itself doesn't realize persistence, concurrency or security. Rather, it relies on lower layers to provide these features.

The Observable design pattern is used for notifications about model changes, thus achieving low coupling between model and associated views. All changes to application model, whether local or remote, are propagated to registered listeners allowing them to display model updates immediately as they happen. Java Messaging Service (JMS) is used to propagate change notifications in distributed environment. The API is entirely based on interfaces, allowing users to choose the appropriate implementation, depending on the needs.

To provide ontology-compliant access to data stored in existing systems, such as relational or XML databases, special mapping implementations may be used. These implementations must align the respective data sources to ontologies. The conversion is dynamic - all modifications to the ontology and all queries are transformed and propagated to the underlying data source.

The KAON API is responsible for providing consistency of the underlying ontology. All access to the API is performed through a dedicated evolution strategy whose purpose is to define and implement a set of change rules. For example, when a concept is removed from an ontology, it must be decided what to do with its subconcepts - they may be deleted, attached to the parent of the deleted concept or attached to ontology's root concept. Several evolution strategies have been implemented for each of these policies, allowing the user to choose the appropriate one when the ontology is instantiated. Finally, in order to improve performance, KAON API allows using a pluggable caching scheme. In that way many costly requests to KAON SERVER may be avoided and the overall application performance increased.

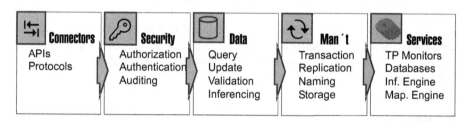

Fig. 2. KAON Server - Modules and Request Processing

KAON SERVER. KAON SERVER is responsible for providing a persistent, transactional and secure RDF repository accessible by multiple users are the same time. It is realized within J2EE framework, technically it is therefore a component hosted by EJB application servers. The conceptual architecture of the system follows a Layers architectural pattern, as presented in Figure 2.

Connectors layer. Several APIs are provided to connect to KAON SERVER: An RDF API is used for accessing RDF data, a querying API is used for RDF querying and inferencing. Additionally a special remote implementation of the KAON API is provided. Since KAON SERVER is realized within J2EE framework, the SERVER is accessible to non-Java clients using the CORBA-IIOP protocol.

Security layer makes server operations available to the client only if the caller is properly authenticated and authorized to access them. Authentication and authorization are implemented using the Java Authentication and Authorization Service (JAAS) allowing easy integration to any existing (corporate) security services. In a nutshell, JAAS provides role-based autorization and authentication. Users are mapped into abstract roles, and a set of privileges is determined for each role.

Data access layer. This layer allows management of RDF model elements, inferencing and querying. Queries are supported using RDF-QEL query language designed in the Edutella project [5]. KAON SERVER does not implement inference itself but interfaces to other systems. The integration with these systems is seamless - the users of KAON Server do not distinguish between inferred and ground facts.

Management layer encapsulates all "basic" services such commonly found in information systems. The transaction management system is responsible for ensuring the commonly known ACID transaction properties. The replication service must ensure all external systems work with the same data sets (e.g. inference engine must be kept in synchrony with the persistent storage). By interplaying with the naming service, the replication service can also manage duplicate RDF models to enhance scalability and availability. The naming service maps model identifiers (as presented by URIs) to persistent identifiers (URNs) and keeps information about the location of the information. Finally, system configuration modules are realized in this layer.

External services are systems and services external to KAON Server. Databases are used for persisting RDF model data. Inference engines are reused to offer reasoning capabilities. Transaction Processing Monitors ensure transactional integrity if data is replicated to external systems.

7   Resume

With the upswing and proliferation of ontologies and metadata, the need for comprehensive managing infrastructure has been recognized recently. A comprehensive overview and state-of-the-art survey on ontology library systems with respect to the dimensions management, adaptation and standardization has been provided by [2]. Whereas these ontology library systems mainly focus on ontology storage and reuse, our approach provides a RDF-based framework including ontology management for semantics-driven applications. Comparing to available RDF data stores[2] our approach is the only available RDF data store dealing with replication. An approach that comes close to our open-source framework is the commercial system, ontology builder and server, proposed in [1]. Nevertheless, in contrast to this system, our approach is completely based on RDF and is therefore Semantic Web conform. Additionally we provide access to existing relational data sources via OntoMat-REVERSE. In this paper we have introduced KAON, the Karlsruhe Ontology and Semantic Web Tool Suite. We have gathered requirements for large scale semantic web systems and presented a formal ontology model that can

---

[2] See http://www.w3.org/2001/05/rdf-ds/DataStore lists existing RDF data stores.

be mapped to several logic languages and may be extended with further axioms stated in these logic languages. Thereby we have established a first step towards the fourth layer of the Semantic Web. We have presented a conceptual architecture that allows to realize the established requirements and presented the first steps taken by us towards implementation of this architecture. The tools mentioned within the paper are freely available via the web at http://kaon.semanticweb.org/.

In the future we will focus on making existing corporate data sources available to ontology-based applications. We are also working on extensions of the formal ontology model to provide a more expressive core language. We are also working on a query language for ontologies which will offer view-support.

Additionally we will further extend the accessibility of the system towards peer-to-peer systems enabling a new level of knowledge interchange and ontology-based communication.

References

1. Aseem Das, Wei Wu, and Deborah McGuinness. Industrial strength ontology management. In *Proceedings of the First Semantic Semantic Web Working Symposium, SWWS-01, Stanford, USA, August 2001*, 2001.
2. Ying Ding and Dieter Fensel. Ontology library systems — they key to successful ontology re-use. In *Proceedings of the First Semantic Semantic Web Working Symposium, SWWS-01, Stanford, USA, August 2001*, 2001.
3. Erich Gamma, Richard Helm, Ralph Johnson, and John Vlisside. *Design Patterns*. Addison-Wesley, 1995.
4. T. R. Gruber. A translation approach to portable ontology specifications. *Knowledge Acquisition*, 6(2):199–221, 1993.
5. Wolfgang Nejdl, Boris Wolf, Changtao Qu, Stefan Decker, Michael Sintek, Ambjoern Naeve, Mikael Nilsson, Matthias Palmer, and Tore Risch. Edutella: A p2p networking infrastructure based on rdf. In *In Proceedings of the 11th World Wide Web Conference — WWW-11, Hawaii, USA, 2002*, 2002.
6. L. Stojanovic, N. Stojanovic, and R. Volz. Migrating data-intensive Web Sites into the Semantic Web. In *to appear in: Proceedings of the ACM Symposium on Applied Computing SAC-02, Madrid, 2002*, 2002.

Privacy Protection through Unlinkability of Customer Activities in Business Processes Using Mobile Agents[*]

Matthias Enzmann, Thomas Kunz, and Markus Schneider

Fraunhofergesellschaft, Institute for Secure Telecooperation, D-64293 Darmstadt, Germany
`firstname.lastname@sit.fraunhofer.de`

Abstract. Web technologies provide several means to infringe user privacy. This is especially true when customers with the intent to buy tangible goods submit their orders containing their real identity and physical address. Then in practice, the vendor can link this information with all information gathered about the customer beforehand, e.g., observation data on him while browsing through the product catalog. In this paper, we present a solution based on mobile agents that can be used to prevent the vendor from directly linking information gathered about the customer while searching with identifying information that is contained in the order. The system allows to introduce an agent delay at the agent base station which can increase the cardinality of the group of candidates to be linked to a product, and thereby to decrease the linking probability.

1 Introduction

Privacy threats and problems in the context of electronic commerce are extensively discussed in literature since the discovery of the economical importance of the Internet. In academic work done so far, solutions were mostly proposed for those cases in which the trade objects are restricted to intangible goods, e.g., see [2,11]. These intangible goods —such as electronic documents, image, music, or video files— can be delivered via communication networks. There, all phases of a typical business process consisting of *search*, *order*, *pay*, and *deliver* can be performed electronically. As a consequence, technical means developed so far for communication networks can be used to protect a customer's privacy, e.g., anonymity networks [8,9,12].

When dealing with tangible goods —e.g., books, CDs—, these techniques can also be used. In the *search* phase, when the buyer browses through the product catalog, anonymity networks can be used to prevent re-identification and to protect the buyer against some threats, e.g., prize discrimination. But unfortunately, these techniques cannot be used to prevent *linkability* between the phases which allows the vendor to learn much more about the buyer than necessary. In practice, in order to receive a tangible good a buyer has to reveal his identity and address to the vendor for reasons of delivery. It is not realistic to assume that either all buyers get their ordered goods in a *poste restante* manner where the identity of a buyer can remain hidden, or that an additional third party receives the package on behalf of the buyer in order to hide his identity. Thus, the vendor

---

[*] This work was partly supported by the German Ministry of Education and Research, projects *NSI* and *HORN*, and by the European Commission, project *OPELIX*.

K. Bauknecht, A. M. Tjoa, G. Quirchmayr (Eds.): EC-Web 2002, LNCS 2455, pp. 314–323, 2002.

learns at least who is buying what. But presently, the vendor can learn much more. Since the vendor can link the data given to him during the *order* phase to the buyer's activities during the *search* phase, the vendor gets much deeper insight into the buyer's interests than necessary. This situation can be compared to physical world scenarios, where one is being completely observed while leafing through a catalog before filling out the order form.

The vendor's ability to link these two phases may be achieved by using IP addresses, cookies, and dynamic URLs that allow the concept of sessions in HTTP communication. In general, there are possibilities for the buyer to avoid linking by himself, but unfortunately, these solutions are not very convenient. Therefore, it is not very likely that these solutions will be used in practice.

The goal of this work is to present a convenient and secure solution that prevents the vendor from linking data collected during the *search* phase with data collected in the *order* phase of the same business process. In this work, we propose the usage of a mobile agent system to solve the problems described above. The main idea of our solution is as follows. Instead of filling a virtual trolley during the *search* phase with some desired goods, the customer inserts this order information into a mobile agent. Then, after having selected all desired goods —maybe even a list of goods that have to be bought at distinct shops— the buyer sends the agent to a central mobile agent base station from where it starts its journey. Since the base station provider does not get any information about the *search* phase, he cannot exploit this information for himself nor pass it to others. After all orders have been delivered the agent returns to its base station confirming to the user that it fulfilled its job properly. Thus, there is no possibility for the vendor to link the order information with the *search* phase via technical parameters like IP addresses, cookie information, or dynamic URLs. In order to prevent the vendor from linking via product identifiers some rules regarding their encoding have to be followed. What remains for the vendor is just a linking probability that depends on the number of customers that viewed a specific product during a relevant period. The solution provides some additional useful features. The buyer has the possibility to define a certain delay between the transfer of the agent and the start time of the agent's journey. Thus, there is the possibility to increase the cardinality of the group of potential candidates to be associated to a product, and thereby, he can reduce the linking probability for the vendor. Another advantage of our solution results from the functionality that is given by a mobile agent. Due to its capability to actively make decisions with regard to results that were created on its journey, it is possible to define orders depending on previous executions of ordering.

2 Tracking Users

The vendor's ability for linking activities of the buyers is based on the technical solution to track them in HTTP communication. Here, *tracking* means the re-identification of a user subsequently sending requests to a server. We can distinguish between the re-identification of users in distinct sessions and the re-identification of users within one session. In general, tracking users can be achieved in different ways.

IP addresses. The first means to link the phases is given by IP addresses. One possibility to cope with this problem from the customer's perspective is to disconnect in order to conduct the *order* phase with a new IP address given from his provider after connecting again —a rather inconvenient solution. Another option for the buyer to solve the problem could be the use of an anonymity network based on mixes [8,12] in order to hide his own IP address from the vendor. But if all requests are routed via the same sequence of mixes the probability for correct linking on the vendor side can be very high. They can be correlated by the IP address of the last mix in the chain. Another possibility for the buyer to hide his own IP address could be the use of the *crowds* approach where routes of subsequent messages can be different with high probability [9]. But all these anonymization countermeasures can be circumvented if a vendor uses cookies or dynamically generates URLs that allow session binding.

Cookies. Another means to track the buyer and to link the phases is given by cookies [6]. As a countermeasure, a buyer may refuse cookies. But for shopping applications, they are often required. In a more laborious way, the buyer could first browse through the product catalog, then delete his cookies, and afterwards come back to the desired products and fill them in the virtual trolley without any further detours. Beside the inconvenience of this countermeasure, the vendor can still track the buyer with the method presented below.

Dynamic URLs. Dynamic URLs allow the introduction of sessions in HTTP communication. There, references contained in a web page are unique in a sense that distinct requesters of the same web resource can be distinguished via these references. This allows a web server to track a customer. A countermeasure for this would be to shut down the browser after the *search* phase and restart it in order to go directly to the *order* phase.

Of course, a customer can also be tracked by combinations of these methods. The previous consideration shows that there are only inconvenient solutions for the buyer to avoid undesired linking. As long as customers do not prevent the vendor from tracking them the vendor is able to record profiles. Such profiles can be understood as a sequence of requests for resources —like web pages— that can be associated to one session and thereby to one customer by the means described above. Finally, the vendor's database contains a variety of profiles $prof_1, prof_2, \ldots$ that could be exploited afterwards. When a customer clicks on products $p_1, \ldots, p_\nu$ while browsing through the catalog, then $prof_i = (p_1, \ldots, p_\nu)$ can be created.

3   Privacy and Threats

Privacy can be understood as the interest of individuals or the moral or legal right —that depends on the legal framework varying all over the world— that allows an individual to have control over information about oneself by granting, limiting, or denying others access to this information. In today's web practice, we can realize a lack of privacy enhancing technologies [3]. It can be assumed that this lack of adequate privacy enhancing technologies is an additional barrier for the diffusion of e-commerce applications [4]. Thus, there is a need to change the present situation by the introduction of new technical solutions that allow to avoid or to reduce the invasion of privacy. Privacy infringement is usually understood as the unauthorized collection, disclosure, or use of personal information for some other purposes beyond the business process in which these data were collected. Then, they can be used for many purposes: direct marketing, spamming, prize discrimination, or selling it to other parties not involved in the business process.

In practice, a customer that decides to buy a tangible good electronically usually has to reveal his identity and address to the vendor for delivery. Thus, a vendor clearly learns who is buying what. We do not intend to introduce new parties that receive the shipped goods on behalf of the buyer in order to hide the buyer's identity completely from the vendor. We do not think that this approach is realistic because of considerable overhead costs. Furthermore, the building of an infrastructure consisting of such providers — maybe worldwide— with required physical presence would take some time. Thus, in contrast to other approaches that claim to achieve full protection but are not used in practice, we propose a solution in which the vendor gets aware which customer is buying which product.

4   Mobile Agents

Mobile agents are autonomous programs, which, following a route, migrate through a network of sites to accomplish tasks on behalf of their owners. The owner of an agent can instruct it to visit many hosts in a network, and thereby execute some desired tasks. After having carried out all instructions the agent returns to its base station and delivers the results it collected during its journey to its owner. One of the advantages for using mobile agents technology is that interaction cost is remarkably reduced since after leaving its owner the agent migrates from one host to the next autonomously. Thus, during this period the owner is not required to maintain his online connection. In the past years, lots of work has been done in the area of mobile agent systems, e.g., Aglets [7].

In the following, we will not focus on a specific mobile agent system. We will consider mobile agents in a rather abstract way. This means that exclusively those components of mobile agents will be considered which are of special relevance for the solution presented in this paper. In our level of abstraction a mobile agent a consists of the following components: $a = (bc, r, d, \delta)$. There, the component bc denotes the *binary code* of the agent to be executed. Furthermore, r describes the mobile agent's *route* as an $(n+1)$-tuple (with $n \geq 1$) consisting of host addresses $ad(s_i)$ that have to be visited on the agent's journey: $r = (ad(s_1), \ldots, ad(s_n), ad(bs))$. This route is given by the agent owner. The agent starts its journey at a base station bs where it returns to when it has visited the stations contained in the route. Since the first migration is $bs \rightarrow s_1$ the first route entry is given by $ad(s_1)$. The component d denotes the *data* given by the agent owner. This data will be used as input for the computations at the hosts $s_1, \ldots, s_n$ on the agent's journey. Thus, we can think of it as $d = (d_1, \ldots, d_n)$ where d_i means the input data for s_i with $1 \leq i \leq n$. The data obtained as an output of the computations are contained in δ. Similarly, we have here $\delta = (\delta_1, \ldots, \delta_n)$.

5   Adaptation of Agent Components

In the following, we will adapt the previously introduced components of a mobile agent according to the requirements of our solution. Thereby, the main protection goal we have in mind is *privacy*. Additionally, we also focus on *data origin authentication* that includes *data integrity* of the mobile agent, and *non-repudiation*.

In order to do this, we introduce some expressions. Let $E_{e_i}(d_i)$ denote a ciphertext obtained via an asymmetric algorithm E, e.g., *RSA* [10], for the encryption of the data d_i by using s_i's public key e_i. Furthermore, $Sig_x(y_1, \ldots y_\nu)$ denotes a digital signature of party x on some contents $y_1, \ldots y_\nu$. This allows us to introduce an element $\tilde{d}$ consisting of encrypted input data for $s_1, \ldots, s_n$ and a signature of the agent owner b —which will be the buyer: $\tilde{d} = (E_{e_1}(d_1), \ldots, E_{e_n}(d_n), Sig_b(E_{e_1}(d_1), \ldots, E_{e_n}(d_n), bc))$.

Furthermore, we protect the agent route in a similar way as it was done in [13] by an onion-like encryption concept. In each layer of the onion structure we have a host address and a signature by the agent owner b on this address combined with other agent components.

$$
\begin{aligned}
\tilde{r} = \Bigg(& \big(ad(s_1), Sig_b(ad(s_1), bc, \tilde{d}), \\
& E_{e_1}\big(ad(s_2), Sig_b(ad(s_2), bc, \tilde{d}), \\
& \quad E_{e_2}\big(ad(s_3), Sig_b(ad(s_3), bc, \tilde{d}), \\
& \qquad \ddots \\
& \qquad E_{e_{n-1}}\big(ad(s_n), Sig_b(ad(s_n), bc, \tilde{d}) \big) \ldots \big) \Big), \\
& ad(bs) \Bigg)
\end{aligned}
\tag{1}
$$

The principle of how to deal with $\tilde{r}$ is as follows. The base station learns through the first entry of $\tilde{r}$ where to dispatch the agent. Before the agent is sent to s_1, bs deletes this entry from $\tilde{r}$. When s_1 receives the agent with the new $\tilde{r}$, then it decrypts the ciphertext contained in $\tilde{r}$ and obtains the successor address $ad(s_2)$, a signature, and a further ciphertext. Before sending the agent to s_2, the address and the signature are deleted from $\tilde{r}$. This procedure will be repeated until the agent arrives at s_{n-1}. Here the last decryption is necessary, i.e., s_{n-1} gets the last address $ad(s_n)$ and signature contained in the onion. After deletion of these parameters from $\tilde{r}$, the agent is sent to bs as defined by the last entry $ad(bs)$. The idea of the route protection is that visited hosts do not learn to which hosts the agent migrates to except its predecessor and successor. If the agent owner has the interest that visited hosts do not get information about other hosts contained in the route, he can introduce some dummy hosts in the route that just forward the agent. If this is also not desired, then the agent owner can send multiple agents where these agents migrate to exclusively one host.

The signatures contained in $\tilde{r}$ and $\tilde{d}$ are for reasons of data integrity. They allow that modifications can be detected. The signatures depend on several agent components that prevent attackers from the exchange of components taken from different agents belonging to the same agent owner b. After having produced the computation results δ_i at host s_i, they will be signed by s_i. Thus, we define $\tilde{\delta}_i = E_b(\delta_i, Sig_{s_i}(\delta_i, bc, \tilde{d}))$. At the end of the journey, the agent contains all computation results, i.e., $\tilde{\delta} = (\tilde{\delta}_1, \ldots, \tilde{\delta}_n)$.

Initially, portions $\tilde{\delta}_i$ are empty. In the following, we assume that an agent consists of components $\tilde{a} = (bc, \tilde{r}, \tilde{d}, \tilde{\delta})$.

6   Achieving Privacy via Agents

In this section, we show how to prevent a vendor from linking gathered information obtained by tracking a buyer during the search phase with his real identity when he submits an order. Furthermore, we give some more requirements that have to be fulfilled in order to avoid linking via product IDs. In 6.1, we show how to deliver an order where the shopping tour contains only one vendor visit. In 6.2, we point out how to decrease the linking probability. Routes containing several vendors are discussed in 6.3.

6.1   Order Delivery via Agents

For simplicity, we assume that a buyer b decides to buy at just one vendor, say s_1. While searching through s_1's catalog, b has a look at various products, and finally decides to buy a subset $p_1, \ldots, p_k$ of these products. During this time, s_1 can track b's activities storing them as a new profile, say $prof_i$, belonging to one identity but he is unable to map these to b's identity. Then, b creates the order information including identifiers of these products, his name and address, to be contained in d_1. Furthermore, b should have the possibility to arrange the product identifiers in an arbitrary sequence not matching the order in which he selected these products. This is necessary since the sequence of product identifiers to be obtained later in the order cannot be correlated with the click sequence contained in $prof_i$ —provided that there are other profiles stored in s_1's database produced by other customers also viewing $p_1, \ldots, p_k$ in one session beside some other products. After b has created d_1, he creates $d = E_{e_1}(d_1, Sig_b(E_{e_1}(d_1), bc))$ and $\tilde{r} = (ad(s_1), ad(bs))$, and finally $\tilde{a} = (bc, \tilde{r}, \tilde{d}, \tilde{\delta})$, with $\tilde{\delta} = \emptyset$.

In a next step, b will transfer $\tilde{a}$ to bs and instruct bs to dispatch $\tilde{a}$. Now, $\tilde{a}$ can migrate to s_1 and deliver its data d_1. Since d_1 is encrypted asymmetrically, it can only be opened by s_1, i.e., bs does not learn which products were ordered by b. Furthermore, s_1 can check by verifying the signature if the order was undeniably created by b and if it was modified. When the data contained in the agent does not seem to be corrupted, s_1 creates the output δ_1 and $\tilde{\delta}_1 = E_b(\delta_1, Sig_{s_1}(\delta_1, bc, \tilde{d}))$ to be handed over to the agent. E.g., such a computation output could be s_1's confirmation of having received the order and a declaration of carrying it out immediately. For integrity reasons, all outputs should be signed by the vendor. Afterwards, the agent is sent to bs according to the last route entry $ad(bs)$. There, $\tilde{a}$ waits for b until he connects the next time to bs.

Following this approach, the vendor cannot use IP addresses, cookies, or dynamic URLs for linking the received order to *search* phase activities. In order to get a deeper insight into b's interests, s_1 can try to link the profile data $prof_1, prof_2, \ldots$ with the data obtained from the agent to find out b's real profile $Profile(b)$. But this means for him to carry out a random experiment. Since b has ordered $p_1, \ldots, p_k$, the vendor searches in his database for profiles that include $p_1, \ldots, p_k$ and that have been recorded in a relevant time interval. Certainly, the order does not belong to a profile that has been recorded one year ago. If we assume that s_1 finds $\mu \geq 1$ profiles $prof_1, \ldots, prof_\mu$ containing

$p_1, \ldots, p_k$, then for s_1 the probability for correct linking of a stored profile to b is given by $P(Profile(b) = prof_i) = \frac{1}{\mu}$, provided that there is no other hidden information that makes linking easier. The probability depends on the number μ of profile candidates. Obviously, μ decreases monotonically when k increases, i.e., including a higher number of products in the order can increase the linking probability.

An unfair vendor could try to offer such a privacy protecting service based on mobile agents, but could try to link the *search* and *order* activities via leaking product IDs. E.g., this could be achieved by product IDs consisting of a static part referring uniquely to the product and a dynamic part referring to the session. In such a case, the linking probability for the vendor would be $P(Profile(b) = prof_i) = 1$. In order to prevent such attacks, product IDs must be verifiable by the buyer in a sense that information hiding becomes obvious. E.g., this could be achieved by some natural language coding of product IDs. In such a scheme, the set of potential candidates for product IDs is rather small, e.g., for a music CD the product ID could be *(artist name, title)* instead of some ID *B0000262WI*. In such a natural language scheme, a customer can detect with high probability if there is some hidden information.

6.2 Decreasing Probability for Linking

In the following, we will show how a buyer can decrease the linking probability. Since this probability depends on the number μ of candidates it is the goal to increase μ. A solution would be to motivate a large community to visit the vendor's catalog. But this is not realistic. We propose that the base station should provide a service for the buyer to define a delay between receiving the agent from the buyer and dispatching it, finally. Since this delay time is unknown to the vendor, he does not know whether to link the order with some profiles stored in the past minutes or hours, or even some days. In order to have the correct profile with high probablity in the set of candidates, the time interval considered by the vendor should be large. But then, μ can be assumed to be larger. Of course this depends on the specific statistics of the vendor's web site. The dispatching time can be specified by the buyer by instructing the base station not to release the agent before a delay Δt, or not before a time *MM:dd:hh:mm*.

6.3 Routes with Several Shops

So far, we have considered only cases in which a mobile agent exclusively visits one vendor for delivering some order information. Shopping tours with several vendors can be advantageous, e.g., in cases when an order for vendor s_i should only be delivered if products at s_j, to be visited before, are available. Furthermore, this possibility reduces the number of mobile agents migrating through the network. Concerning the order information transfered by the agent, there arise no privacy problems since this information can only be opened by the desired vendor because of asymmetric encryption.

One could argue that with longer routes vendors learn which other hosts have to be visited on the shopping tour which gives some further insight into the buyers behaviour or interests. But this threat can be tackled with the route protection scheme presented in expression (1). With this solution, a vendor only learns about his predecessor and successor in the shopping tour. If a buyer does not like that a vendor gets aware of other

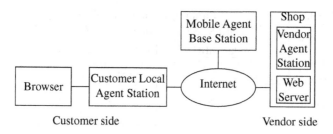

Fig. 1. Architecture view

shops that could be predecessor or successor then the buyer could create the agent route $\tilde{r}$ with intermediate bs. This increases the number of migration steps on the agent's journey but allows the buyer to enhance his privacy.

In the case of dependent agent computations —e.g., when order delivery at s_i depends on computation results at s_j— results have to be communicated from one vendor to another. If one is immediately following the other then the exchange of the required results can be done directly —provided that the buyer is willing to reveal these shopping tour stations to the vendors. If the buyer decides to hide the vendor identity from other vendors by agent exchange via bs, then the results can be encrypted for bs which decrypts and re-encrypts them for the vendor that requires these results. By applying such concepts, it can be achieved that a vendor will not get aware of what b is ordering at other vendors as far as the vendors are not colluding and exchange their trading information.

7   Architecture

In the following, we will shortly sketch the architecture of our solution. Figure 1 depicts the basic components which are required in our system. The customer uses a simple web browser and the *Customer Local Agent Station* (CLAS) which is a specific component of our solution. The vendor runs a usual web server and a *Vendor Agent Station* (VAS). Additionally, there is the *Mobile Agent Base Station* (MABS) which is provided by a third party that offers mobile agent services to customers.

The customer is running two applications: a browser and a CLAS. The CLAS component is independent of a specific vendor. The CLAS software is provided by a party that is trusted to not have embedded a Trojan horse in it. The CLAS comprises several functionalities: (1) a client-side proxy, (2) a *Product Selector* (PS) from which products can be put into a trolley-like agent, (3) a *Mobile Agent Generation* (MAG) component like an agent workbench, and (4) a client to use the services of the MABS.

When the customer browses through the vendor catalog all requests are first sent to the CLAS (message 1) which forwards them to the vendor system (message 2). The corresponding vendor response is received by the CLAS (message 3). Message 3 consists of a part destined to the CLAS and another part destined to the browser. After having extracted his own part, the CLAS forwards the remaining message part to the browser (message 4). The browser message part consists of a normal web page content, e.g., displaying products with some additional information. The CLAS message part consists

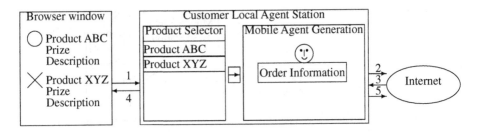

Fig. 2. CLAS and browser interaction

of the product identifiers for the same products which are displayed at the same time by the browser. These identifiers are displayed by the PS subcomponent. In contrast to normal scenarios, when the customer decides to buy a product, he does not put it in some virtual trolley by clicking in the browser window. The browser window is just used to get product information and to navigate through the catalog. Instead, he takes the product ID from the PS and transfers it to the MAG. On this agent workbench, the customer composes the agent in an appropriate manner. After having finished the shopping tour, the buyer transfers the agent to the MABS (message 5). Then, he can also give some additional instructions, such as agent release delay. When the agent comes back to the MABS after its journey, the MABS can inform the buyer that it returned and can be picked up.

On the vendor side, the solution requires a *Vendor Agent Station* beside usual vendor infrastructure. Furthermore, the vendor has to provide messages that consist of a CLAS part and a browser part.

By using the CLAS for selecting the product to be ordered in the proposed way, we can be sure that no hidden channel to the vendor is established. Hidden channels could be possible when a buyer selects a product directly from a browser. Such a hidden channel would increase the linking probability by reducing the set of candidates to those parties that really selected the corresponding products. But our solution deals with a set of candidates containing parties that only viewed or decided to buy the product.

8   Related Work

Other work done in the area of privacy protection also focusing on the prevention of exploiting server log files can be found in anonymity literature, e.g., see [8,9,12]. There typically, the goal is on *sender anonymity*, *receiver anonymity*, and *unlinkability of sender and receiver*, while we are considering unlinkability of subsequent messages exchanged between a customer and a web server. Since we are dealing with applications in which the buyer reveals his identity in some phase of the business relationship, we require this unlinkability of messages exchanged in distinct phases. Most of the work done so far (e.g., [2,11]), that deals with online selling and privacy, focuses exclusively on the trade of intangible goods where anonymity networks can be used without any problems. There, no real identity and physical address have to be revealed. Other work dealing with privacy protection concerning gathering information on customer activities in business processes was presented in [1,5]. There, they deal with privacy protection in customization and targeting.

9 Conclusion

We have presented a solution which allows a buyer of tangible goods to enhance his privacy. Our solution applies mobile agents in order to prevent a vendor from linking information gathered in the *search* and *order* phase of the whole business process. For the vendor, the linking of these activities is a random experiment. The success probability of this experiment depends on the number of customers that have viewed the corresponding products. Our solution allows the introduction of an agent delay time which has an advantageous effect on the linking probability. Furthermore, we have considered the case of shopping tours.

References

1. Robert M. Arlein, Ben Jai, Markus Jakobsson, Fabian Monrose, Michael K. Reiter. Privacy-preserving global customization (extended abstract). In *Proceedings of the 2nd ACM conference on Electronic Commerce (EC'00)*, October 2000.
2. Feng Bao,Robert Deng. Privacy protection for transactions of digital goods. In *Information and Communications Security (ICICS 2001)*, LNCS 2229. Springer Verlag, November 2001.
3. Roger Clarke. Internet privacy concerns confirm the case for intervention. *Communications of the ACM*, 42(2), February 1999.
4. Donna L. Hoffman, Thomas P. Novak, Marcos Peralta. Building consumer trust online. *Communications of the ACM*, 42(4), April 1999.
5. Ari Juels. Targeted advertising ... and privacy too. In *Progress in Cryptology — CT-RSA 2001, RSA Conference 2001, Proceedings*, LNCS 2020. Springer Verlag, 2001.
6. D. Kristol, L. Montulli. HTTP State Management Mechanism. RFC 2109, February 1997.
7. Danny B. Lange, Mitsuru Oshima. *Programming and Deploying Java Mobile Agents with Aglets*. Addison-Wesley, 1998.
8. Michael G. Reed, Paul F. Syverson, David M. Goldschlag. Proxies for anonymous routing. In *Proceedings of 12th Annual Computer Security Applications Conference (ACSAC'96)*. IEEE Press, December 1996.
9. Michael K. Reiter, Aviel D. Rubin. Crowds: Anonymity for web transactions. *ACM Transactions on Information and System Security*, 1(1), 1998.
10. Ron L. Rivest, Adi Shamir, Leonard M. Adleman. A method for obtaining digital signatures and public-key cryptosystems. *Communications of the ACM*, 21(2), February 1978.
11. Stuart G. Stubblebine, Paul F. Syverson, David M. Goldschlag. Unlinkable serial transactions: Protocols and applications. *ACM Transactions on Information and System Security*, 2(4), 1999.
12. Paul F. Syverson, Michael G. Reed, David M. Goldschlag. Private web browsing. *Journal of Computer Security — Special Issue on Web Security*, 5(3), 1997.
13. Dirk Westhoff, Markus Schneider, Claus Unger, Firoz Kaderali. Protecting a mobile agent's route against collusions. In *Selected Areas in Cryptography, 6th Annual International Workshop (SAC'99)*, LNCS 1758. Springer Verlag, 2000.

Secure Electronic Copyright Distribution with Public Key Based Traitor Tracing

Hyung-Woo Lee[1], Sung-Min Lee[2], and Im-Yeong Lee[3]

[1] Div. of Information & Communication Engineering, Cheonan University,
Chungnam, Korea, 330-704
hwlee@cheonan.ac.kr
http://infocom.cheonan.ac.kr/~hwlee/index.html
[2] Div. of Computer Science & Engineering, Korea University, Seoul, Korea, 136-701
smlee@netlab.korea.ac.kr
[3] Div. of Information Technology Engineering, Soonchunhyang University,
Chungnam, Korea, 336-745
imylee@sch.ac.kr

Abstract. In order for the Internet-based digital products to be widely accepted, secure copyright distribution mechanism must be provided with advanced traitor tracing mechanism. We present new software copyright protection and electronic license distribution model based on public key scheme. In this model, digital contents can be distributed over a broadcast channel in a encrypted form and the authorized user can decrypt it, which can be traced back with proposed public key tracing mechanism. Proposed model provides efficiency since merchant server can issue electronic licenses in advance by preprocessing. It also provides secure and efficient software live-update mechanism based on traitor tracing scheme.[1]

1 Introduction

It is important that the common users can use publicly verifiable copyright proving mechanism over a strongly reliable medium such as public key based traitor tracing schemes. Digital contents can be distributed over a broadcast channel with a encrypted form and only the authorized users are able to decrypt these encrypted contents. A critical issue on digital copyright mechanism is to make provision for settling possible dispute over provided digital services, especially in the cast that the illegal or abnormal usage in the middle of a session.

In this study, we propose advanced digital copyright protection scheme based on the secure authentication and public key traitor tracing scheme, which is modified from the existing copyright protection systems. We proposed new electronic software distribution and copyright protection model based on traitor tracing scheme. When a user executes software, authentication is transparently

[1] This work is supported in part by the Ministry of Information & Communication of KOREA ("Support Project of University Information Technology Research Center" supervised by KIPA)

K. Bauknecht, A M. Tjoa, G. Quirchmayr (Eds.): EC-Web 2002, LNCS 2455, pp. 324–332, 2002.
© Springer-Verlag Berlin Heidelberg 2002

processed. The proposed model is efficient since a merchant can generate electronic license and personal keys in advance. We showed two precise models based on optimum traitor tracing scheme and public key traitor tracing scheme respectively. It is secure unless a buyer distributes her electronic copyright and personal key to unauthorized users. Even if software is copied and redistributed illegally, a merchant can trace back to its original owner once the electronic license and personal key are found.

The rest of the paper is organized as follows. In section 2 and 3, we introduce an overall process for tracing the traitor. In Section 4, we present public key based *TTS* protocol and analysis its usefulness. In Section 5, we compare the proposed scheme with the existing digital copyright protection schemes. And in Section 6 we conclude our works with future works.

2   Traitor Tracing

We concentrate on preventing traitors from distributing the *keys* that enable the decryption of the encrypted content. Consider a ciphertext that may be decrypted by a large set of parties, but each and every party is assigned a different *personal key* for decrypting the ciphertext. If the key used in a pirate decoder will be discovered, it will be linked to a personal key of a traitor and this traitor will be identified. Clearly, a possible solution is to encrypt the data separately under different personal keys with "copyright verified software".

A traceability scheme[5] is a broadcast encryption scheme such that a data supplier T can trace malicious authorized users(*traitors*) who gave a decryption key to an unauthorized user(*pirate*). In digital contents based applications should only be available to authorized users. To prevent unauthorized users from accessing these digital contents, the data supplier will encrypt data and provide only the authorized users with personal keys to decrypt it. However, some unauthorized users may obtain some decryption keys from a group of one or more authorized users. Then the pirate users can decrypt data that they are not entitled to. To prevent this tracing traitor algorithms are proposed by using the k-resilient traceability schemes which reveal at least one traitor when a pirate decoder is confiscated if there are at most k traitors.

An optimum traitor tracing scheme[8] is a multiple-use traceability scheme. And these scheme use similar mathematics to threshold cryptosystem, (k,n)-one-time scheme. This scheme requires one personal decryption key, $O(k)$ many encryption keys and $O(k)$ many ciphertexts. And this scheme is proven to be secure in the sense that (1) it satisfies secrecy requirement against outside enemies if and only if *ElGamal* cryptosystem is secure and (2) it can trace traitors if and only if the discrete log problem is hard. And this scheme shows two practical asymmetric traitor tracing schemes with agents or with an arbiter. The first is a multiple-use asymmetric scheme. The second is a one-time use asymmetric scheme with an arbiter which is unconditionally secure.

A public key traitor tracing encryption scheme[10] is a public key encryption system in which there is a unique encryption key and multiple decryption keys. The scheme is made up of four components: Key generation, Encryption, Decryption and Tracing. Key generation algorithm takes an input a security parameter s and a number l of private keys to generate. It outputs a public encryption key e and a list of private decryption keys $d_1, \ldots, d_l$. A decryption key can be used to decrypt a ciphertext created using the encryption key. The encryption algorithm takes a public encryption key e and a message M and outputs a ciphertext C. The decryption algorithm takes a ciphertext C and any of the decryption keys d_i and outputs the message M. This is an 'open' scheme in the sense that only the short decryption keys are secret while the decryption method can be public. In the tracing procedure, suppose a pirate gets hold of k decryption keys $d_1, \ldots, d_k$. Using the k keys he creates a pirate decryption box or decryption software DS. The tracing algorithm is said to be 'black box' if its only use of DS is as an oracle to query on various inputs. Existing public key tracing algorithm relies on the *representation problem*.

3   Electronic Copyright Distribution

We present an efficient software copyright protection model based on TTS. There are several software copyright protection schemes. But they still have some disadvantages with regard to security and cost. Especially, some of these schemes are based on public key cryptography (PKC) which uses customer's public key to generate an electronic license. This makes the schemes inefficient since a merchant can't issue electronic licenses by preprocessing. In order to address this problem we propose a TTS-based model without authentication agent. We first present overall framework of TTS-based protection model. We then describe Copyright and key issuing procedures. Finally we propose secure software installation and illegal copying protection scheme based on TTS.

3.1   Overall Framework

We can construct a overall framework of the proposed model for electronic software distribution. The proposed model is based on electronic software distribution (ESD) concept. So a user can download software free but she cannot install and execute the software without an authentic *e-Copyright* and her *e-Copyright* decryption key. Three types of principals are involved in our TTS-based protocol: producer, merchant server, and buyer.

- Step 1 : Copyright holder(producer) pre-generates *e-Copyright* and key used in electronic copyright distribution process.
- Step 2 : Original copyright holder generate(produce) watermarked software $f_W(S)$ and send it to the merchant.
- Step 3 : Buyer(customer) contact with merchant and request to download electronic software after electronic payment process.
- Step 4 : Merchant send personal decryption key to buyer for installing *e-Copyrighted* software on his computer.

The function of merchant server consists of three modules such as producer input processing, customer input processing, and electronic Copyright issuing. Each software producer embeds a watermark W into a software S such that: W can be reliably located and extracted from S even after S has been subjected to code transformations such as translation, optimization and obfuscation. After completing software watermarking, she registers the watermarked software and its information including *product-ID*, corporation, and so on, in a merchant server via web. When a copyright theft is occurred, the producer's copyright mark W can be extracted from the software. A merchant server issues an electronic Copyright and generates *e-Copyright* decryption key for each buyer then sends them to the buyer via secure channel. These electronic Copyright and key generation can be done by pre-processing procedures. A buyer selects a software that she wants to buy, and registers her information including her name, email address, and so forth after completing payment process. Then the buyer receives an electronic Copyright and her *e-Copyright* decryption key.

3.2   Electronic Copyright and Key Issuing

This scheme is also designed based on a user Copyright and a traitor tracing scheme. In our model, a merchant server can issue electronic Copyrights encryption and decryption keys in advance. A merchant server generates one *e-Copyright* encryption key (E_{eC}) and corresponding *e-Copyright* decryption key (D_{eC}^i) for personal user i. A merchant server then issues electronic Copyright using E_{eC}. It encrypts a serial number with E_{eC}. The issued electronic Copyright is following form: *e-Copyright*= $\{SerialNumber\}_{E_{eC}}$. When a customer wants to buy a software, a merchant server stores the buyer's information including her id i, her codeword in its database for copyright violator detection. It then sends an electronic Copyright and an D_{eC}^i for i'th user. When a pirate electronic Copyright decryption key is found, the original owner of the key can be traced since a merchant server keeps user-key mapping table.

3.3   Secure Installation

When a buyer completes her software payment process, she receives an electronic Copyright and D_{eC}^i from a merchant server via secure email. She then puts the electronic Copyright and D_{eC}^i in her storage for reference of authentication process to check whether a user is authorized or not. Whenever an installation program is executed, it first loads electronic Copyright and electronic Copyright decryption key from user's storage for authentication. It then decrypts $\{e\text{-}Copyright\}_{D_{eC}^i}$ to get a serial number. This computation is possible only when a user i has authentic D_{eC}^i. If the extracted serial number is valid, it continues installation otherwise it is aborted. This method is secure unless a buyer publishes her D_{eC}^i. Even if the key is distributed to unauthorized users, a merchant can trace the copyright violator.

4   Public Key Traitor Tracing

Now we propose two concrete models for software copyright protection based on optimum traitor tracing scheme and public key traitor tracing scheme respectively.

4.1   Applying Optimum Traitor Tracing

It is important to provide trace mechanism of the copyright violator when an unauthorized copy is found. To address this problem, we use optimum traitor tracing scheme (OTT). We first present e-$Copyright$ generation and electronic software distribution protocol. We then present software installation scheme based on OTT.

(1) e-$Copyright$ Generation & Distribution Procedures. The personal key and electronic Copyright generation procedures are as follows. Merchant server initializes system parameters for electronic Copyright encryption key generation. It first chooses a random polynomial $f(x) = a_0 + a_1 x + \cdots + a_k x^k$ over Z_q and computes $y_0 = g^{a_0}, y_1 = g^{a_1}, \cdots, y_k = g^{a_k}$, where p is a prime power, q is a prime such that $q | p - 1$, $q \geq n + 1$, and g is a qth root of unity over $GF(p)$. We assume all the buyers agree on p, q and g. The merchant server makes $E_{eC} = \{p, g, y_0, \cdots, y_k\}$ as an electronic Copyright encryption key. When an authorized buyer tells the merchant server he/she wants to buy a software, the merchant server first issues a serial number (this process can be done by preprocessing procedures), SN, and computes an e-$Copyright$ as e-$Copyright(k_s, r) = (g^r, SN \cdot y_0{}^r, y_1{}^r, \cdots, y_k{}^r)$, where r is a random number. It also generates a unique member id i that identifies the new authorized buyer and a personal electronic Copyright decryption key (D_{eC}^i), $f(i)$, to the party and sends them to the new buyer via secure channel. The merchant server store the buyer information including member id i, and her personal key $f(i)$ in its database for copyright violator detection.

When a pirate personal key is confiscated, the original owner of the key can be traced. Namely if pirate key e_p contains $(i, f(i))$ for some i, then merchant server decides that user i is a copyright violator. This threat of detection will deter users from releasing unauthorized copies.

(2) OTT-based Installation. When a buyer executes an installation program, the program (install shield) first loads electronic Copyright and buyer's personal key. It computes serial number SN from e-$Copyright$ using her personal D_{eC}^i. Namely it computes the following expression $\{SN \cdot y_0{}^r \times (y_1{}^r)^i \times \cdots \times (y_k{}^r)^{i^k}\} / (g^r)^{f(i)}$ to get a serial number, SN. If the extracted SN is valid, it continues installation otherwise it is aborted.

4.2 Applying Public Key Traitor Tracing

In Public Key Traitor Tracing Scheme ($PKTT$), there is one public encryption key, but many private decryption keys. Previous approaches were combinational with probabilistic tracing, and could be either public key or symmetric-key. $PKTT$ is algebraic with deterministic tracing, and is inherently public key. In addition, previous approaches incur an overhead that is proportional to the logarithm of the size of the population of honest users. $PKTT$ eliminates this problem. Furthermore, secret keys in this scheme are very short. Each private key is just the discrete log of a single element of a finite field (as small as 160 bits in practice). The size of an encrypted message is just $2k + 1$ elements of the finite field. The work required to encrypt is about $2k + 1$ exponentiations. Decryption takes far less than $2k + 1$ exponentiations. During decryption, only the final exponentiation uses the private key, which can be helpful when the secret is stored on a weak computational device. Therefore, $PKTT$ can be efficiently applicable to software protection model.

(1) Electronic Copyright and Key Issuing Procedures. In our model, a merchant server can issue electronic Copyrights and *e-Copyright* decryption keys in advance. Let s be a security parameter and k be the maximal coalition size. The public key traitor tracing scheme defends against any collusion of at most k parties[4]. It makes use of a certain linear space tracing code Γ which is a collection of l codewords in Z^{2k}. The set $\Gamma = \{\gamma^{(1)}, \cdots, \gamma^{(l)}\}$ is fixed and publicly known. A merchant server generates one public key and l corresponding private keys. We'll call electronic Copyright encryption key (E_{eC}) and electronic Copyright decryption key (D^i_{eC}) instead of public key and private key respectively since a merchant server never publishes its public key in our model.

In order to generate E_{eC}, a merchant server chooses a random $r_i \in Z_q$ and computes $h_i = g^{r_i}$ where $g \in G_q$ is a generator of G_q and $i = 1, \cdots, 2k$. The E_{eC} is $< y, h_1, \ldots, h_{2k} >$, where $y = \prod_{i=1}^{2k} h_i{}^{a_i}$ for random $\alpha_1, \ldots, \alpha_{2k} \in Z_q$. It then generates i'th electronic Copyright decryption key D^i_{eC} which is derived from the i'th codeword $\gamma^{(i)} = \{\gamma_1, \ldots, \gamma_{2k}\} \in \Gamma$. An electronic Copyright decryption key for i'th buyer is following form: $D^i_{eC} = (\sum_{j=1}^{2k} r_j \alpha_j)(\sum_{j=1}^{2k} r_j \gamma_j)(mod q)$.

A merchant server then issues electronic Copyright using E_{eC}. To encrypt a serial number SN in G_q do the following: It first chooses a random element $a \in Z_q$ and computes $SN \cdot y^a$. The issued electronic Copyright is following form: *e-Copyright* $= < SN \cdot y^a, h_1^a, \ldots, h_{2k}^a >$.

When a customer wants to buy a software, a merchant server stores the buyer's information including her id i, her codeword in its database for copyright violator detection. It then sends an electronic Copyright and an D^i_{eC} for i'th user. When a pirate electronic Copyright decryption key is found, the original owner of the key can be traced since a merchant server keeps user-key mapping table.

(2) PKTT-based Installation Procedures. When a buyer completes her/his software payment process, she/he receives an electronic Copyright and D^i_{eC} from a merchant server via secure channel. She/He then puts the electronic Copyright and D_{eC}^i in her storage for reference of authentication process to check whether a user is authorized or not.

When an installation program is executed, it first loads electronic Copyright and electronic Copyright decryption key from user's storage for authentication. It then computes $\prod_{j=1}^{2k} H_j^{\gamma_j}$ from the electronic Copyright. Here $\gamma^{(i)} = \{\gamma_1, \ldots, \gamma_{2k}\} \in \Gamma$ is the codeword from which D_{eC}^i is derived. The cost of this computation is far less than $2k + 1$ exponentiations thanks to simultaneous multiple exponentiation. It also computes $(\prod_{j=1}^{2k} H_j^{\gamma_j})^{D_{eC}^i}$ using the buyer's electronic Copyright decryption key, D_{eC}^i. Finally it computes the following expression $C/(\prod_{j=1}^{2k} H_j^{\gamma_j})^{D_{eC}^i}$ to get a serial number, SN. This computation is possible only when a user i has authentic D_{eC}^i.

If the extracted SN is valid, it continues installation otherwise it is aborted. This method is secure unless a buyer publishes her D_{eC}^i. Even if the key is distributed to unauthorized users, a merchant can trace the copyright violator. This scheme is sound since any electronic Copyright decryption key D_{eC}^i correctly decrypts electronic Copyright. Given an electronic Copyright e-Copyright $=< SN \cdot y^a, h_1^a, \ldots, h_{2k}^a >$, decryption yields $SN \cdot y^a/U^{D_{eC}^i}$ where $U = \prod_{j=1}^{2k} (h_j^a)^{\gamma_j}$

Proof verification works

$$
\begin{aligned}
C/U^{D_{eC}^i} &= C/(g^{\sum_{j=1}^{2k} a r_j \gamma_j})^{D_{eC}^i} = C/(g^{\sum_{j=1}^{2k} r_j \gamma_j})^{a \cdot D_{eC}^i} \\
&= C/(g^{\sum_{j=1}^{2k} r_j \gamma_j \cdot \sum_{j=1}^{2k} \alpha_j/\gamma_j})^a = C/(g^{\sum_{j=1}^{2k} r_j \alpha_j})^a \\
&= C/(\prod_{j=1}^{2k} h_j^{\alpha_j})^a = C/y^a \\
&= SN \cdot y^a/y^a = SN
\end{aligned}
\tag{1}
$$

5   Comparison with Previous Approaches

Several approaches for software copyright protection were proposed. However, these methods still have disadvantages. A merchant sells software on a per-usage basis. This approach based on function hiding technique ensures that only Copyrighted users are able to obtain the cleartext output of the program since users never gain access to the application itself but rather connect to the developer's site to run the program remotely. But it requires network connection and merchant server's computations whenever a user executes the software. It also cannot be applicable to general-purpose software but only special-purpose software such as equation computation.

A merchant could protect her code through encryption. This method requires most of cost since the speed of encryption/decryption of entire code through encryption. This only works if the entire decryption/execution process takes place in hardware. It is not scalable since it needs special hardware.

A copyright protection is based on public key cryptography. It requires a number of exponential computations. It also should install a client program called authentication agent for authentication. It may not be secure when a user replaces agent by a faked authentication agent. In addition, a merchant can issue an electronic Copyright only when a user wants to buy software, since she needs buyers' public key. Namely it is impossible to generate electronic Copyrights in advance. So electronic Copyright issuing process is inefficient.

The proposed approach is fully software based and does not rely on tamper resistant hardware. Also it encrypts only partial codes such as a serial number and main executable file instead of entire code. It is applicable to every type of software models and the cost for protection is not expensive.

Our model has one electronic Copyright encryption key and many electronic Copyright decryption keys since it is based on public key traitor tracing scheme. So a merchant can pre-process to issue electronic Copyrights without buyer's public key. A merchant allocates D_{eC}^i generated in advance to buyer i only when a buyer wants to buy software. This electronic Copyright decryption key is just a single element of a finite field and can be as short as 160 bits to achieve 2^{60} security[4,7]. So it is efficient and practical. It also provides an illegal copying protection mechanism after software installation.

6   Conclusions

Today there are diverse efforts for enhancing electronic software distribution and software copyright protection technologies. However existing models still have several problems with regard to security and efficiency. Most of existing methods leave the software vulnerable to unauthorized use and redistribution by customers once the product has been unlocked. In this paper we proposed several enhanced software protection and electronic software distribution models.

Our model provides efficiency since merchant server can issue electronic Copyrights in advance by preprocessing. It also provides secure and efficient software live-update mechanism based on traitor tracing scheme. Only authorized customers can update their software since data transferred are encrypted with key. The proposed model considers post installation security using electronic Copyright. When a user executes software, authentication is transparently processed since multi-thread mechanism is used.

We proposed new electronic software distribution and copyright protection model based on traitor tracing scheme. Our model guarantees the right of both producer and merchant since it uses traitor tracing scheme. It also considers post-installation security using electronic Copyright and personal electronic Copyright decryption key. When a user executes software, authentication is transparently processed since a multi-thread mechanism is used. The proposed model is efficient since a merchant can generate electronic Copyright and personal keys in advance.

We showed two concrete models based on optimum traitor tracing scheme and public key traitor tracing scheme respectively. It is secure unless a buyer distributes her electronic Copyright and personal key to unauthorized users. Even if software is copied and redistributed illegally, a merchant can trace back to its original owner once the electronic Copyright and personal key are found.

References

1. A. Fiat and A. Shamir: How to Prove Yourself : Practical Solutions to Identification and Signature problems, Advances in Cryptology-CRYPTO '86, LNCS Proceedings, Springer-Verlag, pp.186-194, 1987.
2. A. Fiat and A. Shamir: Unforgeable Proofs of Identity, Proceedings of Securicom '87 , Paris, pp.147-153, 1987.
3. A. W. Roscoe, M. H. Goldsmith: The Perfect 'spy' for model checking cryptoprotocols, In Proceedings of the DIMACS Workshop on Design and Formal Verification of Security Protocols, 1997
4. Alfred J. Menezed, Paul C. van Oorschot, Scott A. Vanstone (ed.): Handbook of Applied Cryptography, CRC Press, 1996.
5. B. Chor, A. Fiat and M. Naor: Tracing Traitors, Advances in Cryptology-CRYPTO'94, LNCS Proceedings, Springer-Verlag, pp.257-262, 1995.
6. B. Pfitzmann: Trials of Traced Traitors, Information Hiding, First International Workshop, LNCS Proceedings, Springer-Verlag, pp.49-64, 1996.
7. B. Pfitzmann, M. Waidner: Asymmetric Fingerprinting for Larger Collusions, IBM Research Report, 1996.
8. T. ElGamal: A Public Key Cryptosystem and a Signature Scheme based on Discrete Logarithm, IEEE Transactions on Information Theory, Vol. IT-30, No. 4, pp.469–472, 1985.
9. D. Boneh, M. Franklin: An Efficient Public Key Traitor Tracing Scheme, Advances in Cryptology-CRYPTO '99, LNCS Proceedings, Springer-Verlag, pp.338-353, 1999.
10. D. Boneh, J. Shaw: Collusion-Secure Fingerprinting for Digital Data, Advances in Cryptology-CRYPTO '95, LNCS Proceedings, Springer-Verlag, pp.452-465, 1995.
11. B. Schneier: Applied Cryptography, Second Edition, Wiley, 1996.
12. W. Diffie, M. Hellman: New Directions in Cryptography, IEEE Transactions on Information Theory, Vol. IT-22, No. 6, pp.472–492, 1976.
13. K. Kurosawa, Y. Desmedt: Optimun Traitor Tracing and Asymmetric Schemes, Advances in Cryptology-EUROCRYPT '98, LNCS Proceedings, Springer-Verlag, 1999.
14. M. Rabin: How to Exchange Secrets by Oblivious Transfer, Technical Reports TR-81, Harvard Aiken Computation Laboratory, 1981.

Watermark Embedding Mechanism Using Modulus-based for Intellectual Property Protection on Image Data

Shiuh-Jeng Wang[1] and Kai-Sheng Yang[2]

[1]Department of Information Management Central Police University
Taoyuan, Taiwan 333, sjwang@sun4.cpu.edu.tw

[2]Computer Crime Squad, Criminal Investigation Bureau, National Police Administration,

Ministry of the Interior, Taiwan, yccs@email.cib.gov.tw

Abstract. In this paper, an intellectual property protection mechanism realized on a watermarking scheme is proposed. The embedding technique we adopted in this paper is based on the modular operation. The modulus is a threshold value which determines how the binary pattern of watermark to be embedded into an image. In order to conduct a better fidelity of the image with the embedded watermark against the perception of human vision system, the random bit-string transformed from the watermark is done first. Then there are two classifications required to perform for the random bit pattern 0/1 during the embedding procedure. Afterwards, we issue several frequent image processing tests, such as JPEG compression, diverse filtering treatments, resampling and requantization, etc., to promote our remarkable result. Comparing to the previous literature in [12] as observed from the experiments, not only the advantages emphasized in [12] are remained, but also the original image is not necessary to check again so as to extract the embedded watermark. Therefore, the scheme explored in this paper is more efficient than the previous scheme, and it is feasible to cope with the protection of intellectual property on the digital image recognition.

Keywords: Intellectual property protection, watermark embedding, JPEG compression

Introduction

With the rapid progress of electronic technology in conjunction with computer network in the new information century, there were plenty of digital products made and applied for the benefit in our lives. Accompanying the in-progress information technology era, to duplicate a digital material has become simple and easy. Furthermore, these duplicates could be extensively delivered to anywhere around the word via network links. That is to say, the intellectual property of an original material is capable of being pirated easily for personal profit if there isn't an adequate way to protect the ownership. To cope with the anxious demand, a hot issue about how to guarantee the copyright on licit material against the possible threats, such as tempering, masquerading and occupation, etc. is widely explored in recent years.

Watermarking is a technique that hides the representative information of digital kind into a host image. It is used to aim at the purpose of proclaiming the ownership of a host image. It is indispensable to claim that watermark is insensitive for human eyes when it is embedded into the image. The examples for watermark application could be seen on the most digital multimedia process, such as of text, video, image, and audio broadcast system,

Bauknecht, A M. Tjoa, G. Quirchmayr (Eds.): EC-Web 2002, LNCS 2455, pp. 333–342, 2002.

etc. Usually, an effective watermarking technique should content with some typical requirements, including transparency, universality, robustness and security consideration.

Over the past years, there are many literatures proposed in the discussions of watermarking [1, 8, 9, 12, 21]. To realize the techniques on embedding watermark into a host image, there are two categories developed, as the spatial-domain manner [1, 2, 12, 15, 17, 19, 20] and the frequency-domain manner [3, 4, 8, 11, 14, 16, 18, 21]. The former manner is to directly modify/adjust the distributed pixels (regions) to complete the embedding work. The later one is to transform the host image by using the frequency-oriented mechanism, such as DCT-based, wavelet-based, etc. The watermark is then incorporated into the coefficients conducted from those frequency transformation approaches. Another standpoint on classifying the study of watermarking systems is dependent on whether the original image is necessary or not in the course of watermark extraction process. We call such catalog as the non-oblivious watermarking and oblivious watermarking [5, 6, 13]. Owing to the host image is no longer required in developing oblivious watermarking system, it is thus widely applied to the issue of intellectual property on the digital image recognition. The reason is that the storage occupation for the host image is released during the extraction of watermark. It is available to directly retrieve the exact watermark only using the secret seed and without the assistance of the original image.

Review the spatial-domain manner. Basically, it is simpler to efficiently achieve the information hiding on image data. In particular, the least significant bit (LSB for short) or LSB-like later is the most commonly used skill to compass the end. In general, the least 1-4 bits of a pixel in a host image could be selected to embed the information under the acceptance of human vision system. Another branch study on spatial-domain is the patchwork [1]. This approach is oriented by the statistics of the randomized pixels. By the luminance control of the correlated pixels, increase/decrease the intensities of the neighboring pixels, the bit information is thus embedded into the host image in place.

In this paper, an intellectual property with the watermark embedding is proposed using the LSB-like skill in the spatial-domain explorations. The technique we adopted is a modular operation. In our paper, we further perform several frequent images processing, such as JPEG compression, diverse filtering treatment and resampling and requantization, etc. to promote our results.

The rest of our paper is organized as follows. In Section 2, we depict our scheme using the modulus-based mechanism. The empirical experiments and performance analysis are given in Section 3. In Section 4, we conclude our scheme.

2   Our Watermarking Scheme Using Modulus-based Mechanism

The embedded area shown in the host image to accommodate the bit pattern hiding is due to the block-oriented technique. First of all, we define the basic images utilization in our process as follows. A host image, O, which is used to embed the logo of watermark of size $M_o \times N_o$, with gray-level, where M_o is the length and N_o is the width of an image to be distributed, respectively. The watermark W is a binary (write/black) image of size $M_w \times N_w$, where M_w and N_w are less than M_o and N_o, respectively. That is to say, W is composed of binary pattern with 0/1. We further give the detailed formation with O and W to get familiar with our embedding procedure as follows. $O=\{ O(i, j)| \ 0 < i < M_o, \ 0 < j < N_o \}$, where $O(i, j) \in \{0, \ldots\ldots, (2^L-1)\}$ is the intensity of pixel (i, j) and L is the bit-length of each pixel $W=\{ w(i, j), 0 < i < M_w, \ 0 < j < N_w \}$, where $w(i, j) \in \{0,1\}$ is the intensity of pixel (i, j) Owing to the bit pattern hiding is subject to block-oriented approach, we therefore divide the host image with numerous non-overlapping blocks, where each block is of size $r \times c$. As a result, there are $\frac{Mo}{r} \times \frac{No}{c}$ blocks in total to constitute the host image. Here, we set $O_B = \{ O_B(i) \mid 0 \le i \le \frac{Mo}{r} \times \frac{No}{c} - 1 \}$, a set of non-overlapping blocks in O, where a block i of $O_B(i) = \{b(x, y) \mid 0 \le x \le (r-1), 0 \le y \le (c-1)\}$. Subsequently, these blocks are randomly employed to embed the watermark. Followings are the detailed three phases to go through our scheme: Pre-process phase, watermark embedding phase and watermark extraction phase.

Phase I: [Pre-process for mixing the input binary pattern]

In general, in order to reinforce the protection of embedding watermark, the watermark is first encrypted before being mapped onto the host image. The activated cipher is usually one-key system used, such as DES-like system. The reason is that the bit-string length of the output pattern is same as the input bit-length. Afterwards, we launch a permutation function with the encrypted pattern so as to uniformly distribute the binary pattern of 0's and 1's. The procedure is then listed as follows:

Input: A watermark W, an one-key system OKS, and a permutation function PF
Output: A uniform bit-string of distributing 0's and 1's
Step 1:   Line a bit sequence from W in light of the rule of left-to-right and top-to-down. Set BSW = the lined bit-string of W.
Step 2:   Assign BSW as the input of the DES-like system. Then perform the encryption operation as $W_E = OKS_{ek}(BSW)$, where ek is the encryption key.
Step 3:   Reshuffle W_E with the permutation function PF devoted to uniformly distribute of bits 0's and 1's in W_E, i.e. $W_b = PF(W_E)$, where $W_b(i) \in \{0,1\}$ denotes the ith bit in the new bit-string.

■

Phase II: [Watermark embedding]

In this stage, the bit $W_b(i)$ is ready to be embedded into the host image. Due to our strategy is a block-oriented approach, each non-overlapping block $O_B(i)$ in O is thus a basic unit to be inserted a bit of $W_b(i)$. Firstly, we enumerate the order of bit-string $W_b(i)$ starting 0 to ($M_w \times N_w - 1$) from left-to-right. Secondly, the blocks $O_B(i)$'s are then enumerated starting 0 to ($\frac{Mo}{r} \times \frac{No}{c} - 1$) from left-to-right and top-to-down. Thirdly, a pseudo-random number generator with the seed S_B is required to generate a random number with the ordered blocks in the range of [0, $\frac{Mo}{c} \times \frac{No}{c} - 1$], so that the $W_b(i)$ is inserted in turn the randomly selected block. Meanwhile, there are two parameters t and n, chosen beforehand to incorporate the modular operation in the bit embedding computation. The detailed embedding watermark procedure is logically itemized as follows:

Input: The host image O, the bit-string W_b, the seed S_B and two parameters t and n
Output : A watermarked image
Step 1:   Divide O into several non-overlapping blocks, each block is of size $r \times c$.
Step 2:   Select a workable block, $O_B(i)$, in O by the random generation of the seed S_B.
Step 3:   Compute the mean intensity, g_{mean} for the selected $O_B(i)$ of containing $r \times c$ pixels as the form:

$$g_{mean} = \frac{1}{r \times c} \sum_{x=0}^{r-1} \sum_{y=0}^{c-1} b(x, y), \tag{1}$$

where $b(x, y)$ denotes the intensity of pixel on the x row and y column in $O_B(i)$.
Step 4:   Set the threshold value T and compute the range value $g_{remainder}$ as the following

forms:

$$T = t * 2^n \tag{2}$$

and

$$g_{remainder} = g_{mean} \bmod T, \tag{3}$$

where t and n are adaptively chosen to capture a better *PSNR* measurement.

Step 5: Compute two pointers g_{q0} and g_{q1} and set a value of variation δ according to the following two classifications:

- Classification one: the gain assignment of g_{q0}
  1. If $0 \leq g_{remainder} < \frac{T}{4}$, gain $g_{q0} = (- g_{remainder}) + \frac{T}{4}$ and set $\delta=1$.
  2. If $g_{remainder} = \frac{T}{4}$, gain $g_{q0} = (g_{remainder})$ and set $\delta=0$.
  3. If $\frac{T}{4} < g_{remainder} \leq \frac{T}{2}$, gain $g_{q0} = (- g_{remainder}) + \frac{T}{4}$ and set $\delta=-1$.
  4. If $\frac{T}{2} < g_{remainder} < \frac{3T}{4}$, gain $g_{q0} = (- g_{remainder}) + \frac{T}{4}$ and set $\delta=1$,
  5. If $g_{remainder} = \frac{3T}{4}$, gain $g_{q0} = (- g_{remainder}) + \frac{T}{4}$ and set $\delta=-2$,

  or $g_{q0} = T + (-g_{remainder}) + \frac{T}{4}$ and set $\delta=2$.
  6. If $\frac{3T}{4} < g_{remainder} \leq T - 1$, gain $g_{q0} = T + (-g_{remainder}) + \frac{T}{4}$ and set $\delta=2$.

- Classification two: the gain assignment of g_{q1}
  1. If $0 < g_{remainder} < \frac{T}{4}$, gain $g_{q1} = (- g_{remainder}) - T + \frac{3T}{4}$ and $\delta=-2$.
  2. If $g_{remainder} = 0$, gain $g_{q1} = (- g_{remainder}) - T + \frac{3T}{4}$ and $\delta=-1$.
  3. If $g_{remainder} = \frac{T}{4}$, gain $g_{q1} = (- g_{remainder}) - T + \frac{3T}{4}$ and $\delta=-2$,

  or $g_{q1} = (-g_{remainder}) + \frac{3T}{4}$ and $\delta= 2$.
  4. If $\frac{T}{4} < g_{remainder} < \frac{T}{2}$, gain $g_{q1} = (- g_{remainder}) + \frac{3T}{4}$ and $\delta=2$.
  5. If $\frac{T}{2} \leq g_{remainder} < \frac{3T}{4}$, gain $g_{q1} = (- g_{remainder}) + \frac{3T}{4}$ and $\delta=1$.
  6. If $\frac{3T}{4} < g_{remainder} \leq T - 1$, gain $g_{q1} = (- g_{remainder}) + \frac{3T}{4}$ and $\delta=-1$.

Step 6: Embed the bit 0/1 of $W_b(i)$ into the block $O_B(i)$ according to the bit sequence of W_b by performing the following cases.

Case I: $W_b(i) = 0$:

If $(x < \frac{r}{2}$ and $y < \frac{c}{2})$ or $(x \geq \frac{r}{2}$ and $y \geq \frac{c}{2})$, gain $b(x,y)' = b(x,y) + g_{q0} + \delta'$,
Otherwise, gain $b(x,y)' = b(x,y) + g_{q0} - \delta'$.

Case II: $W_b(i) = 1$:

If $(x < \frac{r}{2}$ and $y < \frac{c}{2})$ or $(x \geq \frac{r}{2}$ and $y \geq \frac{c}{2})$, gain $b(x,y)' = b(x,y) + g_{q1} + \delta'$,
Otherwise, gain $b(x,y)' = b(x,y) + g_{q1} - \delta'$.

In the two cases, $b(x,y)'$ denotes the new intensity of pixel on the x row and y column in $O_B(i)$, and g_{q0} / g_{q1} is determined by previous steps (from step 1 to step 5) and δ' is a dynamic value in the interval of $\frac{-2}{\delta}, \frac{+2}{\delta}$.

■

In our embedding procedure, we take the Fig. 2 and Fig. 3: (b) into account as the host image and the embedded watermark to evaluate the fidelities of the test images, respectively. The variation of *PSNR* for evaluating the distortion ratio with the choices of parameters, t and n, is listed in Table 1. Examining the Table 1, T denotes the modular threshold value operated by $t * 2^n$. The best quality on image display is resulted on $T=3$, since *PSNR*=46.25. It could be seen that he quality on image display will gradually degrade when either the parameter n or t is increasing, as observed from Table 1. Nevertheless, the evaluation of *PSNR*=30.09 at $T=27$ is still remained based on the human vision system. In other words, it is the lowest bound at $T=27$ to match up the human visual perception, as observed from our experiment. The declining curve showing the relationship between *PSNR* and the modular threshold *T* is illustrated in Fig. 1. As a result, the choice of the modular threshold *T* should become a prominent factor to satisfy the property of high distortion-resistant in embedding the watermark. In particular, the embedded watermark is required to resist the possible image destructions, such as lossy compressions imposed on the watermarked image, hence, the *T* is usually fixed *T=12* or *T=16* to compromise the situation. According to Table 1, there are five pairs of parameter-pair *(t, n)* selected, as (16, 0), (8, 1), (4, 2), (2, 3) and (1, 4), respectively, at the same *T=16* and there are three pairs of *(t, n)* selected, as (12, 0), (6, 1) and (3, 2), respectively, with the same *T=12*. No matter either *T=16* or *T=12* is selected in the embedding procedure, the *PSNRs* are still kept very high. Alternatively, the higher *PSNR=36.68* measured at *T=12* is the option to conduct a robust watermarking scheme in this paper.

Phase III: [Extraction process]

Comparing to the scheme in [12], the key feature of our extraction process is that only the watermarked image and the relevant parameters are required to retrieve the embedded watermark without referring to the host image. As to the work to extract the watermark, however, it is similar to the embedding phase mentioned above, and can be done by the reverse way. Certainly, the seed S_B is needed first to achieve the workable block W'_B during the extraction of watermark. And then a mean intensity g'_{mean} and a range value $g'_{remainder}$ are computed to evaluate the embedded bit pattern, $W'_b(i)$. Afterwards, the inverse permutation function PF^{-1} is launched to recover the original bit-string order, W'_E. Ultimately, the bit-string is decrypted using the previous encryption key, '*ek*', under decryption of the one-key system. As a consequence, the lined bit-string of watermark, *BSW'* is obtained, so that the embedded watermark *W'* is reconstructed and clearly recognized based on the human vision system. The procedure to exactly extract the bit $W'_b(i)$ of embedded watermark is shown as follows: $W'_b(i) = 1$ if $g'_{remainder} > \frac{T}{2}$; otherwise $W'_b(i) = 0$.

■

3 Performance Analyses

3. 1 Empirical experiments

In our experiments, a host image and four logo images of watermark are used as shown in Fig. 2 and Fig. 3, respectively, where the host image is of size 512 × 512 with 256 gray-level and all the watermarks are sizes of 128×128 with binary pattern. There is an approved evaluation function, called peak signal-to-noise ratio (*PSNR* for short), is given to measure the quality of an image. It is basically defined as follows:

$$PSNR = 10*\log_{10}[255^2/MSE], \tag{4}$$

where *MSE* (Mean Square Error) is defined as follows:

$$MSE = \frac{1}{M \times N} \sum_{x=1}^{M} \sum_{y=1}^{N} (P(x,y) - P'(x,y))^2, \tag{5}$$

where $P_{(x,y)}$ and $P'_{(x,y)}$ denote the original and the watermarked image pixel value on the same coordinate point *(x, y)*, respectively. In addition, the normalized cross correlation(*NC* for short) [7] used to measure the similar quantization between two different images is given as:

$$NC = \frac{\sum_x \sum_y W(x,y) * W'(x,y)}{\sum_x \sum_y [W(x,y)]^2} \qquad (6)$$

where $W_{(x,y)}$ and $W'_{(x,y)}$ denote the original and the extracted watermark image pixel value on the same coordinate point (x, y), respectively.

Before inspecting the distortions on imposing the possible images processing, we first show the measurements of *PSNR* and *NC* for the watermarked images in Table 2, where the watermarked images are then shown in Fig. 4: (a)-(d) and the associated watermarks are used in Fig. 3: (a)-(d), respectively. Obviously, the high fidelities of the four watermarked images are gained, as observed from Table 2 showing that the *PSNR* is 36.8 on the average and the averaged *NC*s are all identical to 1. The two measured results clearly explain that the embedded watermarks are imperceptible by human vision system (due to *PSNR* is much greater than 30dB) and each extracted watermark is fully recognizable to human's vision (by *NC*=1).

Subsequently, we conduct a series of frequent operations/attacks, such as filtering treatments, resampling, requantization and compression manners, which are inevitable on image data processing. For simplicity, we use Fig. 3: (b) to be the target watermark against the frequent operations on image processing.

(i). Aspect of filtering test:

There are three filtering tests, such as high-pass filter, low-pass filter, median filter, applied on this manner, where the used filtering mask is adopted of size 3×3. The masked images with the watermark images under the filtering tests are shown in Fig. 5: (a)-(c) and the extracted watermarks are shown in Fig. 5: (a)'-(c)', respectively.

(ii). Aspect of resampling:

In this stage, a 2×2 neighborhood of matrix-pixel is operated to resample the watermarked image. The resulted image and extracted watermark are shown in Fig. 6: (a) and (a)', respectively.

(iii). Aspect of requantization:

The requantization for an image on diverse gray-level display should satisfy with the human vision adaptability, hence the original 256 gray-level is assumed to be degraded to 32 gray-level on the watermarked image in our experiment. The results for requantizing watermarked image and extracted watermark are shown in Fig. 7: (a) and (a)', respectively.

(iv). Aspect of compression manner:

Without loss generality, the most commonly used tool to compress the image is the software of JPEG, which is a version of discrete cosine transformation and subject to a kind of lossy compressions. The optional function of compression ratio, *CR*, manipulated by JPEG is set at *CR*=10.28, *CR*=13.41 and *CR*=16.48, respectively. The results after JPEG compression are shown in Fig. 8: (a)-(c) and (a)'-(c)' for watermarked images and extracted watermarks, respectively.

3. 2 Results

In our experiments, The watermarks shown in Fig. 3:(a)-(d) are first converted into random bit-strings according to the arrangement in the Phase I of our scheme. Then they are embedded into the host image in turn by following the procedure mentioned in the Phase II. The results of watermarked images are shown as Fig. 4:(a)-(d), respectively. And the extracted watermarks are shown in Fig. 4:(a)'-(d)'. Inspecting Table 2, the numeric measurement of quality on watermarked image is indicated by *PSNR* >36.8 on the average, and then the recognition for the extracted watermark is measured by *NC*=1. Accordingly, it has clearly pointed out that the characteristic of transparency is totally satisfied with our proposed scheme. In order to emphasize the efficiency promoted in our scheme, we compare the scheme of Lee et al. in [12] in terms of the various filtering, resampling, requantization and lossy compression with JEPG. The experimental images with watermarked image and the original logo of watermark are shown in Fig. 4: (b) and (b)'.

- Filtering test:

  First, the evaluation of NC with high-pass filtering is 0.9963 in our scheme. Next the evaluation of NC with median filtering is 0.9744 higher than 0.8879 tested in [12]. Lastly, in the test of low-pass filtering, NC=0.9686 is evaluated, which is also higher than 0.9658 of [12]. The resulted figures are shown in Fig. 5.

- Resampling test:

  The result of resampling experiment is inferior to the scheme [12], as observed the comparison that NC =0.8453 in our scheme is less than NC =0.9891 tested in [12]. That is because our scheme is based on the modular operation and oblivious approach so that a few bit patterns of embedded watermark is likely to be extracted from the undefined interval in the extraction phase. While in Lee et al's scheme, the embedded bits are fetched out by the combination of the original host image and watermarked image, so that the losing intensities of pixels within a workable block could be patched back. We show the results in Fig. 6.

- Requantization test:

  The NC evaluation in requantization test is 0.9888 in our scheme, which is certainly greater than 0.9475 in [12], i.e. our performance is better than that of [12] in the image requantization manner. The results are shown in Fig. 8.

- Compression test:

  We use the popular compression tool, JPEG, to test our scheme at various CR=10.28 and 13.41. Thereby, the NC's are measured as 0.9986 and 0.9853, respectively. Furthermore, NC is always identical to 1 when CR is set under 10.28. In such a way, the extracted watermark could be clearly recognized. Consider the higher compression rate at CR=16.48, NC=0.8212 is still acceptable. Comparing to Lee et al.'s scheme, the value of NC is 0.9998 at CR=5.35, and 0.9103 at CR=14.39, respectively. It have been seen that the better quality is achieved in our scheme. The relevant results are shown in Fig. 8.

  Overall the numeric evaluation between our scheme and Lee et al.'s scheme, there is a summary shown in Table 3 to turn out that the results conducted in our scheme is superior to that of Lee et al.'s scheme except for the item of resampleing manner. Nevertheless, our scheme is subject to oblivious watermarking scheme. The removal of host image in our scheme is the most significant achievement when comparing to the non-oblivious scheme, like Lee's et al.'s scheme.

4 Conclusions

In this paper, we have proposed a mechanism using modulus-based to adaptively embed the watermark into a host image with 256 gray-level. The embedded watermark is subject to a binary pattern form, such as binary image, text signature, content of binary representation, etc. In our scheme, a procedure to translate the watermark to a random bit-string is required so as to strengthen the security aspect. Such requirements are compassed with the imposition of a DES-like cipher and a permutation function. For each embedded bit, it is incorporated into a randomly chosen block divided from the host image. A modulo of threshold value T is used to determine the display quality in the course of embedding watermark. A high robustness against the frequent image processing operations, such as JPEG compression, filtering treatments and resampling and requantization, etc. is apparently achieved, as observing from our experiments. The most significant advantage in our scheme is that not only we release the host image required in the watermark extraction phase, but also the higher fidelity is remained under the human vision system. It is believed that no need with the host image in extracting the watermark is superior to the need with the original one in real applications. Accordingly, our proposal is rather suitable for the watermark embedding when aiming at the purpose of intellectual property on image data.

References

[1]   W. Bender, D. Gruhl, N. Morimoto and A. Lu, "Techniques for Data Hiding," IBM Systems Journal, vol. 35, no. 3 &4, pp. 313-336, 1996.

[2]   T. S. Chen, C. C. Chang, and M. S. Hwang, "A Virtual Image Cryptosystem Based upon Vector Quantization," IEEE Trans. on image processing, vol. 7, no. 10, pp.1485-1488, Oct. 1998.

[3]   I. J. Cox, J. Kilian, T. Leighton and T. Shamoon, "Secure Spread Spectrum Watermarking for Multimedia," NECI Technical Report 95-10, NEC Research Institute, Princeton, NJ, 1995.

[4]   J. Fridrich, "Methods for Detecting Changes in Digital Images," IEEE Workshop on Intelligent Signal Processing and Communication Systems, Melbourne, Australia, November 1998.

[5]   J. Fridrich, "Robust Bit Extraction from Images," 1999 IEEE International Conference on Multimedia Computing and Systems. (CMCS 99) Florence, Italy, vol. 2, pp. 536 – 540, June 7-11, 1999.

[6]   A. Herrigel, J. J. K. Ó Ruanaidh, Holger Petersen, S. Pereira and T. Pun, "Secure Copyright Protection Techniques for Digital Images," In David Aucsmith ed., Information Hiding, vol. 1525 of Lecture Notes in Computer Science, pp. 169-190, Springer, Berlin, 1998. (Second International Workshop IH'98, Portland, OR, USA, April 15-17, 1998)

[7]   C. T. Hsu and J. L. Wu, "Hidden Signatures in Images", in Proceedings of International Conference on Image Processing, pp. 223-226, 1996.

[8]   C. T. Hsu and J. L. Wu, "Hidden Digital Watermarks in Images," IEEE Trans. Image Processing, vol. 8, pp. 58-68, 1999.

[9]   N. F. JOHNSON, and S. JAJODIA, "Steganography: Seeing the Unseen," IEEE Computer, pp. 26-34, February 1998.

[10] C. Kotropoulos, and I. Pitas, "Adaptive LMS L-filters for Noise Suppression in Images," IEEE Trans. on Image Processing, vol. 5, no. 12, pp. 1596-1609, December 1996.

[11] C.S. Lu, S.K. Huang, C.J. Sze, and H.Y. M. Liao, "Cocktail Watermarking for Digital Image Protection," to appear in IEEE Trans. on Multimedia, vol. 2, no. 4, December 2000.

[12] C. H. Lee and Y. K. Lee, "An Adaptive Digital Image Watermarking Technique for Copyright Protection," IEEE Transactions on Consumer Electronics vol. 45, no. 4, pp. 1005-1015, November 1999.

[13] C. S. Lu and H. Y. Mark Liao, "Oblivious Watermarking Using generalized Gaussian," 5th Joint Conf. on Information Sciences (JCIS), Vol. II: 3rd Inter. Conf. on Computer Vision, Pattern Recognition and Image Processing , pp. 260-263, Atlantic City, USA, Feb. 28-Mar. 2, 2000.

[14] N. Nikolaidis and I. Pitas, "Copyright Protection of Images Using Robust Digital Signatures," IEEE International Conference on Acoustics, Speech and Signal Processing (ICASSP-96), vol. 4, pp. 2168-2171, May 1996.

[15] R. G. van Schyndel, A. Z. Tirkel and C. F. Osborne, "A Digital Watermark," Proceeding of IEEE International Conference of Image Processing, vol. 2, pp. 86-90 Austin, Texas, November 1994.

[16] M. D. Swanson, B. Zhu, and A. H. Tewfik, "Robust Data Hiding for Images," in Proc. IEEE Digital Signal Processing Workshop, Loen, Norway, pp. 37-40, September 1996.

[17] G. Voyatzis and I. Pitas, "Applications of Toral Automorphisms in Image Watermarking," Proceedings of ICIP'96, vol. 2, pp. 237-240 ,1996.

[18] G. Voyatzis and I. Pitas, "Embedding Robust Logo Watermarks in Digital Images," Proceedings of DSP'97, vol. 1, 213-216, 1997.

[19] G. Voyatzis and I. Pitas, "Chaotic Watermarks for Embedding in the Spatial Digital Image Domain," in Proc. of ICIP '98, Chicago, Illinois, vol. 2, pp. 432-436, October 1998.

[20] G. Voyatzis and I. Pitas, "Digital Image Watermarking Using Mixing Systems," Computer & Graphics, Elsevier, vol. 22, no. 3, pp. 405-416, 1998.

[21] B. Zhu, M. D. Swanson, and A. Tewfik, "Transparent Robust Authentication and Distortion Measurement Technique for mages," preprint, 1997.

Table 1 The comparison table with the relationship between the parameter-pair (t, n) and PSNR

	$n=0$ $2^{n-2}/2^n=1/4$ $2^n(1-2^{-2})/2^n=3/4$		$n=1$ $2^{n-2}/2^n=1/4$ $2^n(1-2^{-2})/2^n=3/4$		$n=2$ $2^{n-2}/2^n=1/4$ $2^n(1-2^{-2})/2^n=3/4$		$n=3$ $2^{n-2}/2^n=2/8$ $2^n(1-2^{-2})/2^n=6/8$		$n=4$ $2^{n-2}/2^n=4/16$ $2^n(1-2^{-2})/2^n=12/16$	
	$T=t*2^n$	PSNR	$T=t*2^n$	PSNR	$T=t*2^n$	PSNR	$T=t*2^n$	PSNR	$T=t*2^n$	PSNR
$t=1$	1	-	2	-	4	45.26	8	39.81	16	34.48
$t=2$	2	-	4	45.26	8	39.81	16	34.48	32	-
$t=3$	3	46.26	6	41.78	12	36.68	24	31.22		
$t=4$	4	45.26	8	39.81	16	34.48	32	-		
$t=5$	5	42.67	10	38.12	20	32.64				
$t=6$	6	41.78	12	36.68	24	31.22				
$t=7$	7	40.40	14	35.55	28	29.76				
$t=8$	8	39.81	16	34.48	32	-				
$t=9$	9	38.74	18	33.53						
$t=10$	10	38.12	20	32.64						
$t=11$	11	37.29	22	31.89						
$t=12$	12	36.68	24	31.22						
$t=13$	13	35.96	26	30.34						
$t=14$	14	35.55	28	29.76						
$t=15$	15	34.98	30	-						
$t=16$	16	34.48								
$t=17$	17	33.91								
$t=18$	18	33.53								
$t=19$	19	33.00								
$t=20$	20	32.64								
$t=21$	21	32.11								
$t=22$	22	31.89								
$t=23$	23	31.62								
$t=24$	24	31.22								
$t=25$	25	31.07								
$t=26$	26	30.34								

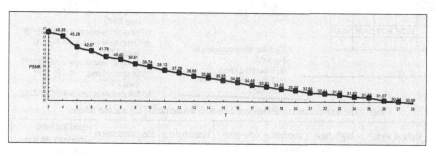

Fig. 1 The declining curve of PSNR relevant to the modular threshold valu

Fig. 2 The host image of size 512×512

(a) (b) (c)

(d)

Fig. 3: (a) - (d) Four recognizable binary watermark image of size 128×128

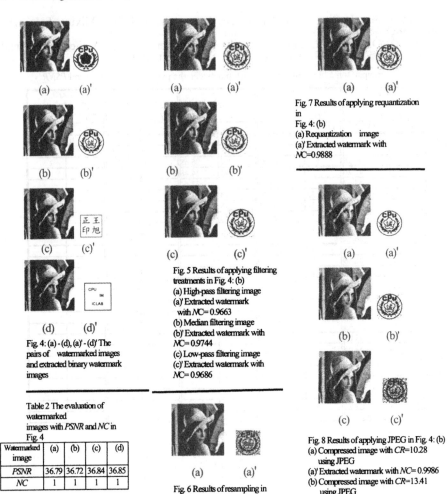

(a)   (a)'

(b)   (b)'

(c)   (c)'

(d)   (d)'

Fig. 4: (a) - (d), (a)' - (d)' The pairs of watermarked images and extracted binary watermark images

Table 2 The evaluation of watermarked images with *PSNR* and *NC* in Fig. 4

Watermarked image	(a)	(b)	(c)	(d)
PSNR	36.79	36.72	36.84	36.85
NC	1	1	1	1

(a)   (a)'

(b)   (b)'

(c)   (c)'

Fig. 5 Results of applying filtering treatments in Fig. 4: (b)
(a) High-pass filtering image
(a)' Extracted watermark with $NC= 0.9663$
(b) Median filtering image
(b)' Extracted watermark with $NC= 0.9744$
(c) Low-pass filtering image
(c)' Extracted watermark with $NC= 0.9686$

(a)   (a)'

Fig. 6 Results of resampling in Fig. 4: (b)
(a) Resampling image
(a)' Extracted watermark with $NC=0.8453$

(a)   (a)'

Fig. 7 Results of applying requantization in Fig. 4: (b)
(a) Requantization image
(a)' Extracted watermark with $NC=0.9888$

(a)   (a)'

(b)   (b)'

(c)   (c)'

Fig. 8 Results of applying JPEG in Fig. 4: (b)
(a) Compressed image with $CR=10.28$ using JPEG
(a)' Extracted watermark with $NC= 0.9986$
(b) Compressed image with $CR=13.41$ using JPEG
(b)' Extracted watermark with $NC= 0.9853$
(c) Compressed image with $CR=16.48$ using JPEG
(c)' Extracted watermark with $NC= 0.8212$

Table 3 The summarized table between Lee et al.'s scheme in [12] and our scheme

Method \ Robust tests	high-pass filtering (NC)	median filtering (NC)	low-pass filtering (NC)	Resampling (NC)	Requantization (NC)	need the host image to retrieve embedded watermark or not
Lee et al.'s scheme	-	0.8879	0.9658	0.9891	0.9475	Yes
Our proposed scheme	0.9663	0.9744	0.9686	0.8453	0.9888	No

A Juridical Validation of a Contract Signing Protocol

Josep Lluís Ferrer-Gomila, Apol·lònia Martínez-Nadal,
Magdalena Payeras-Capellà, and Llorenç Huguet-Rotger

Universitat de les Illes Balears
Carretera de Valldemossa km. 7.5, Palma de Mallorca, 07071, Spain
{dijjfg, dpramn0, mpayeras, dmilhr0}@clust.uib.es

Abstract. Electronic contracting is an essential service to develop electronic commerce. But this service is not very used because merchants and consumers do not trust in contracting by electronic means. For time we already have technical solutions that should allow to give trust to the actors implied in this new scenario. But the lack of international standards and of an appropriate juridical mark, suppose a serious restraint to the contracting by electronic means. Well then, in recent years we can observe some legislative initiatives in the European Union to give full juridical effect to electronic contracting. With these two elements already in course, we believe that a last step will be necessary: to assess the adaptation of the technical solutions regarding the enacted legislation. In this paper, juridical and technical analysis of contract signing protocols is carried out. Besides, we present a modified version of a previous optimistic fair protocol for contract signing.

1 Introduction

The World Wide Web, e-mail, EDI, etc., have proven to be very effective in e-commerce environments (in their multiple alternatives: B2B, B2C, A2C, etc.). Contract signing becomes an essential electronic service, to be used by governments, private companies and consumers. It is clear that it speeds up the commercial transactions, reduces errors, bears (to half term) a saving, etc. But even with all these advantages, potential users (e.g., merchants and consumers) are reluctant to use these new means.

This distrust can be due to a sensation of insecurity in these new contracting means. It is necessary to approach two issues in order to provide security to users. On one hand, we need technical solutions allowing to get the same (or better) level of security that the one obtained in transactions on paper at present. But technical solutions are not enough for security in a broad sense. It is absolutely necessary a juridical mark giving full effect to the electronic contracting, and allowing to eliminate any reticence.

Electronic contract signing is one service offered to users, when they want to obtain a signed copy of a contract from another party. Protocols for contract signing have to provide enough evidence to parties to prove, at the end of the exchange, if the contract is signed and the terms of the contract. We can handle contract signing as a fair

K. Bauknecht, A M. Tjoa, G. Quirchmayr (Eds.): EC-Web 2002, LNCS 2455, pp. 343–352, 2002.
© Springer-Verlag Berlin Heidelberg 2002

exchange of values: the originator has an item (the text of a contract and a non-repudiation of origin token) to be exchanged for a recipient's item (a non-repudiation token bounded to the text of the contract). An exchange is fair if at the end of the exchange, either each player receives the item it expects or neither player receives any additional information about the other's item [2]. Well then, in the technical literature, and even in the market, we already find proposals to solve the problem of electronic contracting.

On the other hand, different international organisms (e.g., UNCITRAL) and different States have enacted or are elaborating laws to give effect to electronic contracts. The European Union enacted the Directive 2000/31/EC, dated 8th of June of 2000, that pointed (see considering 7) that "in order to ensure legal certainty and consumer confidence, this Directive must lay down a clear and general framework to cover certain legal aspects of electronic commerce in the internal market". The different Members States of the European Union, according to first point of article 22, shall bring into force the laws, regulations and administrative provisions necessary to comply with this Directive before 17th of January of 2002. By that time the situation was as follows:

- Luxembourg, Austria and Germany had already law on electronic commerce;
- Finland, France, Denmark, Belgium and Spain had bill or draft bill;
- United Kingdom, Portugal and Italy didn't have bill nor draft bill; and
- Ireland, Sweden, Greece and Holland had not communicated any information to the European Council.

The European Directive, in first point of article 9, establishes that Member States shall ensure that their legal system allows contracts to be concluded by electronic means. Member States shall in particular ensure that the legal requirements applicable to the contractual process neither create obstacles for the use of electronic contracts nor result in such contracts being deprived of legal effectiveness and validity on account of their having been made by electronic means.

Therefore we observe that, a priori, there is no reason for not using electronic means for contracting. But we believe that it is necessary to carry out a last step: to verify if technical solutions are in accordance with legislative initiatives. This is one of the objectives of this paper: to analyse different generic solutions of electronic contract signing, in order to observe their technical and juridical adaptation.

2 Juridical Aspects

From a juridical point of view, there are two specially important issues to be resolved. The first one is the time of contract formation, that is to say, when is an electronic contract considered to be signed? The second issue has to do with the evidence, that is to say, what elements have the contracting parties to be provided in the event of litigation in relation to a signed (or not signed) contract by electronic means?

In different phases of the discussion of the European Directive on electronic commerce, several mechanisms were settled down in relation to the two previous issues (we will not analyse those stages of the discussion of the Directive due to the lack of space, although it is very interesting). In its final writing, and for the sake of getting the consent of the Member States, the proposal was reduced to the minimum. This way, first point of article 11 establishes: "Member States shall ensure, except when otherwise agreed by parties who are not consumers, that in cases where the recipient of the service places his order through technological means, the following principles apply:

- the service provider has to acknowledge the receipt of the recipient's order without undue delay and by electronic means,
- the order and the acknowledgement of receipt are deemed to be received when the parties to whom they are addressed are able to access them."

Regarding this point it is necessary to point out some technical and juridical considerations. In the first place, the Directive doesn't make an explicit pronouncement about the time of contract formation, neither about the evidence mechanisms. In the second place, it introduces an imprecise time issue when it compels to send an acknowledgement of receipt "without undue delay". In the third place, we believe that to consider that an information has been received (the order or the acknowledgement of receipt) when the parties are able to access to them is frankly dangerous (the legislator, probably, was thinking about depositing messages in electronic mailboxes). To end up, and specially important for the content of this paper, the Directive points to a model of electronic contracting in three phases:

- a company carries out an offer by electronic means (a product or a service that it puts for sale)
- a consumer (or another company) carries out an order by electronic means (in relation to the previous offer, that it can be named *acceptance* in juridical terms)
- the first company must send an acknowledgement of receipt of the acceptance that the consumer (or second company) sent.

We have said that the Directive only points to the previous model, and in fact, it doesn't establish explicitly the obligatory nature of the three steps, although it can be deduced from the writing of the first point of article 11. On the other hand, some of the legislation (and bills or draft bills) of the Member States make explicit the obligatory nature of following the three steps: offer, acceptance and acknowledgement of receipt of the acceptance. It is the case of the Spanish bill, the law of Luxembourg, etc.

Nevertheless, these legislation differ in one of the two issues mentioned at the beginning of this section: the time of contract formation. All the legislation of the European Union, according to the Directive, establish the obligatory nature of sending an acknowledgement of receipt. It will be part of the evidence that the consumer (or the second company) will be able to provide as a proof of the signature of the contract. But regarding the time of contract formation, some legislation (for example, Spanish bill) establish that the contract is signed when the consumer (or the second company) sends its acceptance, while other legislation (for example, Luxembourg law) establish that the contract is signed when the consumer (or second company) receives the acknowledgement of receipt (the third step). The first type of legislation doesn't diminish the importance of the acknowledgement of receipt. In fact they establish considerable sanctions for companies that don't send such an acknowledgement of receipt; probably because they observe that the company is leaving the consumer or second company without proof of the contract.

From technical and juridical points of view, we think that solutions based on the three steps model, but considering that the contract is signed when the consumer has received the acknowledgement of receipt, are better, because they provide higher security to the commercial traffic. This way the time of contract formation is linked to the availability of evidences to be used in the event of litigation.

Once we have made an approach to juridical issues of the electronic contracting, in the following section we will carry out a brief analysis of the different types of technical solutions that have been proposed to date.

3 Juridical and Technical Analysis of Contract Signing Protocols

A first kind of solutions (for electronic contract signing) is based on the gradual release of secrets (parties exchange non-repudiation tokens „simultaneously"). This approach [5, 10] achieves fairness by the gradual release of information over many rounds: some knowledge about the non-repudiation evidence is revealed during each round. From a technical point of view, this approach seems to be too cumbersome and inefficient for actual implementation, due to the high communication overhead. Moreover, fairness is based on the assumption of equal computational power. This assumption is unrealistic in practice and undesirable from a theoretical point of view [3]. From a juridical point of view, it's clear that this kind of solutions does not follow the *offer / acceptance / acknowledgement (ACK)* model. On the other hand, to convince a judge, about if a contract was signed or not, would be difficult.

A second kind of solutions are third party protocols (parties exchange items, assisted by a TTP). We can find some fair exchange protocols using a trusted third party [1, 2, 4, 7, 9, 11]. First question a jurist asks is: who can act as a trusted third party? The first answer can be a Public Notary (obviously we mean an Internet server in the name of a Public Notary, with or without human intervention, but with a Public Notary in charge of the proper working of the system). But, it is well known that Public Notaries, as a high qualified professionals, establish high fees for their intervention in paper world (and probably they will do the same in the electronic world). So we have to wonder if other entities (for example, Internet Service Providers, or *ad hoc* entities) can assume the role of trusted third party. We think so, but with one condition: TTP's intervention has to be verifiable. It's to say that if the TTP tries to cheat (when it has to intervene) then contracting parties will be able to prove the fraud in courts.

Contract signing protocols with TTP differ in the degree of the TTP's involvement in a protocol run. We classify this kind of protocols into two classes: with active TTPs (a TTP is actively involved in every protocol run) and with subsidiary TTPs or optimistic protocols [1] (a TTP only intervenes in case of exception, not in every protocol run). But solutions with TTP have drawbacks: the trusted third party can become a bottleneck. Besides, a TTP will want to charge for its intervention. Hence, from commercial and technical points of view, one of the goals of designing an efficient contract signing protocol is to reduce TTP's intervention.

So, "optimistic" protocols are specially interesting. Parties will exchange their items, following the sequence of steps specified in the protocol. They hope to receive the expected item from the other party, and this will be the case if the protocol ends successfully. Otherwise, if one party is trying to cheat (or there are communication failures) the other party may contact the TTP to solve the unfair situation. Of course a cheating party can contact the TTP or can conspire with the TTP, and so, good protocols have to foresee these possible situations.

Some formal requirements for fair exchange were stated in [2], and re-formulated in [11]: effectiveness, fairness, timeliness, non-repudiation and verifiability of third party. Two additional properties to be met are efficiency and privacy (this last one is optional for users). Now, from a juridical point of view, we have to add a new requirement: technical solutions must ensure legal fitting. So, we need a protocol for contract signing with three steps: *offer / acceptance / ACK*.

ASW [2] and GJM [8] protocols have, both, three sub-protocols: *exchange*, *abort* and *resolve*. The *exchange* sub-protocols have four steps in both cases. So, none of them follows the agreed model of the European Directive. In next section we adapt a previous solution [6] to observe the legislation.

Finally, we think that solutions have to be secure from a technical point of view, but as simple as possible. Some disputes will be solved in courts, and judges will have to evaluate evidence brought by parties involved in an electronic contract signing. Obviously, judges will have to be assisted by experts, but they (judges) must understand, at the end, conclusions given by those experts.

In next section we present a contract signing protocol with the following characteristics: effective, fair, asynchronous, with verifiable TTP and efficient. This protocol is better than previous solutions at least in three aspects. On one hand, our protocol has less steps than any other solution in the literature. On the other hand, it is easy to understand and so, it can be useful in situations that potentially will arrive to courts. Finally, the solution is adapted to the European Directive on electronic commerce.

4   A Contract Signing Protocol

We will begin describing the proposed protocol, that it is an adapted version of the two-party protocol in [6], where we can find a security analysis.

4.1   Protocol

The originator, *A*(lice), and the recipient, *B*(ob), will exchange messages and non-repudiation evidence directly. Only as a last recourse, in the case they cannot get the expected items from the other party, the TTP (*T*) will be invoked, initiating *cancel* or *finish* sub-protocols. In the following description, we have not included elements to link messages of an exchange, nor operations to achieve confidentiality, in order to simplify the explanation. The notation and elements used in the protocol description are as follows:

Table 1. Notation and elements

notation	
X, Y	concatenation of two messages X and Y
H(X)	a collision-resistant one-way hash function of message X
$Sign_i(X)$	digital signature of principal i on message X
$i \rightarrow j: X$	principal i sends message (or token) X to principal j
elements	
offer	message containing the *offer*
acceptance	message containing the *acceptance*
$h_A = Sign_A(offer)$	signature of A on the *offer*
$h_B = Sign_B(acceptance)$	signature of B on the *acceptance*
$ACK_A = Sign_A(h_B)$	signature of A on h_B; this is an acknowledge-ment that A knows that the contract is signed, and is part of the evidence for B
$ACK_T = Sign_T(h_B)$	signature of the TTP on h_B; this is an equivalent acknowledgement to the one that A should have sent
$h_{AT} = Sign_A[H(offer), h_A]$	this token is an evidence that A has demanded TTP's intervention
$h_{BT} = Sign_B[H(offer), h_A, h_B]$	this token is an evidence that B has demanded TTP's intervention
$h_B' = Sign_T(h_B)$	signature of the TTP on h_B to prove its intervention

The *exchange* sub-protocol is as follows:

  1. A $\rightarrow$ B: offer, h_A
  2. B $\rightarrow$ A: acceptance, h_B
  3. A $\rightarrow$ B: ACK_A

If the protocol run is completed, the originator A will hold non-repudiation (NR) evidence, h_B, and the recipient B will hold non-repudiation evidence, h_A and ACK_A. So the protocol meets the effectiveness requirement. Observe that the protocol follows the model suggested in European legislation: the first company is compelled to send an *acknowledgment* of receipt of the *acceptance*. We have said that some legislation indicate that the contract is concluded when B sends the *acceptance*, while other legislations indicate that the contract is concluded when B receives the *receipt*. We think that it's better the second option because it allows to link the time of contract formation to the achievement of evidence for both parties.

But, what happens if A or B don't finish the execution of the *exchange* sub-protocol? For example, what happens if A does not send the receipt? A can allege that she sent the receipt and that it was lost. Whatever case, if B does not receive the receipt, he will not be able to prove that the contract is concluded (and A will be able to show or not to show evidences she has). To deal with this possible situations we have designed to sub-protocols (*cancel* and *finish*), with TTP's intervention. In order to simplify the sub-protocols descriptions, we assume that the information sent by A or B to the TTP is correct (otherwise the TTP should send an error message).

If B contacts the TTP before A, the TTP will send the NR token, ACK_T, to B:

$2'.\ B \rightarrow T$: $H(\text{offer}), H(\text{acceptance}), h_A, h_B, h_{BT}$

$3'.\ T \rightarrow B$: ACK_T

The TTP will store the NR token, h_B, in order to satisfy future petitions from A. If later A contacts the TTP, the TTP knows that it has *finished* the exchange for B, and it has to send the NR token, h_B, to A, plus a token in order that A can prove TTP's intervention, h_B':

$1'.\ A \rightarrow T$: $H(\text{offer}), h_A, h_{AT}$

$2'.\ T \rightarrow A$: h_B, h_B'

If A contacts the TTP before B, the TTP will send a message to A to *cancel* the transaction:

$1'.\ A \rightarrow T$: $H(\text{offer}), h_A, h_{AT}$

$2'.\ T \rightarrow A$: $Sign_T(\text{„cancelled“}, h_A)$

The TTP will store the exchange state (*cancelled*) in order to satisfy future petitions from B. If later B contacts the TTP, the TTP has *cancelled* the exchange for A, and it has to send a *cancel* message to B:

$2'.\ B \rightarrow T$: $H(\text{offer}), H(\text{acceptance}), h_A, h_B, h_{BT}$

$3'.\ T \rightarrow B$: $Sign_T(\text{„cancelled“}, h_B)$

So, A and B have a fair way to finish the contract signing (concluded or cancelled for both parties), and they always will have enough evidence to be used in case of dispute. As a conclusion, we have achieved fairness and non-repudiation, two fundamental properties to be met from a technical point of view.

Observe that a "conflicting" situation may occur. A can obtain *NR* evidence from B (h_B) and a *cancel* message from T, while B had obtained *NR* evidence from A (h_A, ACK_A). A can do it, for instance, invoking the *cancel* sub-protocol after the end of the *exchange* sub-protocol. It seems that A can affirm that the contract is signed or not signed, depending on her usefulness. But B possesses *NR* evidence that will prove that the contract is signed, and if A tries to use the *cancel* message she will be showing that she is a cheating party. As a conclusion, we repeat again that the protocol is fair and meets the non-repudiation requirement. Besides, observe that we have not established any restriction in regard to time for contacting the TTP, and so it can be proved that the proposed protocol meets the timeliness requirement.

To finish this section, we think that this protocol will be useful for "web based contracting". In accordance with UNCITRAL draft on electronic contracting [20], we think that "the offer of goods or services through automated computer systems allowing the contract to be concluded automatically and without human intervention is presumed to indicate the intention of the offeror to be bound in case of acceptance". A user (e.g., a consumer) will navigate through web pages selecting products. When he has finished, he will push a "*check out*" button, and as a consequence he will receive the *offer*, a web page containing the selected products with final prices (perhaps with discounts and gifts). If the user agree then he will press a button in order to send an *acceptance*, and he will receive a web page as an acknowledgment of *receipt*. The *offer*, *acceptance* and *receipt* are XML documents signed by the sender.

4.2   Verifiability of the Third Party and Confidentiality

We have said that verifiability of the TTP is an important property to be met by proposed protocols, in order to allow that a private company (e.g., an Internet Service Provider) can be a TTP. The presented protocol satisfies this requirement. A TTP's possible misbehavior is: A receives h_B and h_B', while B receives the cancel token. If A uses h_B and h_B' to prove that B has signed the contract, B can use the cancel token to prove the TTP's misbehavior. If A received h_B and then (or before) she cancelled the exchange (and so she did not receive h_B'), and try to use h_B to prove that B received the evidence, and the TTP has the h_{AT} token, it is clear an A's misbehavior.

The other TTP's possible misbehavior is: B receives ACK_T while A receives the *cancel* token. If B uses h_A and ACK_T to prove that A has signed the contract, A can use the *cancel* token to prove the TTP's misbehavior. It should be noted that if B uses h_A and ACK_A to prove that A has signed the contract, A can not use the *cancel* token to prove the TTP's misbehavior, since the TTP did not issue conflicting evidence (it is obvious that A is misbehaving).

Finally, it is possible, and very easy, to conduct a confidential exchange between A and B, even for the TTP (in the case this one has to intervene). This is an important property to be in accordance with European legislation on privacy. If A and/or B want confidentiality then it has to be possible. A and B can exchange a secret key of a symmetric cryptosystem, k, using some key-exchange protocol (for instance encrypting k with the public key of B). Then, they can encrypt the *offer* and the *acceptance* of the *exchange* sub-protocol with that key k only known by them. Now we have to analyze the confidentiality of the exchange for two possible situations:

- the TTP has not intervened in the exchange: observe that only A and B can decrypt the encryption made with key k.
- the TTP has intervened in the exchange: observe that the TTP only needs a hash of the *offer* and/or of the *acceptance* to verify the correctness of the information given by A or B, and so, the TTP can not read the content of the contract, even if it

intercepted the encrypted message (with k) in the communication channel between A and B.

5 Conclusion

We have analyzed proposed solutions for electronic contract signing, from technical and juridical points of view, concluding that it is very important to bind time of contract formation and achievement of evidences related to that contract. We have presented a fair protocol for contract signing, following the model proposed in the European Directive: *offer / acceptance / ACK*. The fairness is guaranteed, provided the existence (and possible involvement) of a trusted third party, that plays a subsidiary role (only intervenes in case of exception). From technical and juridical points of view this role can be assumed by a private company without special or expensive requirements (only verifiability is required, and it is accomplished in our protocol).

References

1. N. Asokan, Matthias Schunter and Michael Waidner: "Optimistic protocols for fair exchange"; Proceedings of 4th ACM Conference on Computer and Communications Security, pages 7-17, Zurich, Switzerland, April 1997.
2. N. Asokan, Victor Shoup and Michael Waidner: "Asynchronous Protocols for Optimistic Fair Exchange"; Proceedings of the IEEE Symposium on Research in Security and Privacy, pages 86-99, Oakland, California, May 1998.
3. Michael Ben-Or, Oded Goldreich, Silvio Micali and Ronald L. Rivest: "A Fair Protocol for Signing Contracts"; IEEE Transactions on Information Theory, Vol. 36, n. 1, pages 40-46, January 1990.
4. Benjamin Cox, J.D. Tygar and Marvin Sirbu: "NetBill security and transaction protocol"; Proceedings of the First USENIX Workshop on Electronic Commerce, pages 77-88, New York, July 1995.
5. Ivan Bjerre Damgard: "Practical and provably secure release of a secret and exchange of signatures"; Advances in Cryptology – Proceedings of Eurocrypt'93, LNCS 765, Springer Verlag, pages 200-217, Lofthus, Norway, May 1993.
6. Josep Lluís Ferrer-Gomila, Magadalena Payeras-Capellà and Llorenç Huguet-Rotger: "Efficient Optimistic N-Party Contract Signing Protocol"; Proceedings of 4th Information Security Conference, ISC 2001, LNCS 2200, Springer Verlag, pages 394-407, Málaga, Spain, October 2001.
7. Josep L. Ferrer, Àngel Rotger and Llorenç Huguet: "Firma electrónica de contratos"; Proceedings of III Reunión Española de Criptología, Barcelona, Spain, 1994.
8. Juan A. Garay, Markus Jakobsson and Philip MacKenzie: "Abuse-Free Optimistic Contract Signing"; Advances in Cryptology – Proceedings of Crypto'99, LNCS 1666, Springer Verlag, pages 449-466, August 1999.
9. Oded Goldreich: "A simple protocol for signing contracts"; Proceedings of a Workshop on the Theory and Application of Cryptographic Techniques, Crypto'83, Plenum Press, pages 133-136, New York, 1984.

10. T. Okamoto and K. Ohta: "How to simultaneously exchange secrets by general assumptions"; Proceedings of IEEE Symposium on Research in Security and Privacy, pages 14-28, Fairfax, Virginia, November 1994.

11. Jianying Zhou, Robert Deng and Feng Bao: "Some Remarks on a Fair Exchange Protocol"; Proceedings of Third International Workshop on Practice and Theory in Public Key Cryptosystems, PKC 2000, LNCS 1751, Springer Verlag, pages 46-57, Melbourne, Victoria, Australia, January 2000.

12. Austria: "Bundesgesetz, mit dem bestimmte rechtliche Aspekte des elektronischen Geschäfts- und Rechtsverkehrs geregelt (E-Commerce-Gesetz – ECG) und das Signaturgesetz sowie die Zivilprozessordnung geändert werden".

13. Belgium: "Projet de loi sur certains aspects juridiques des services de la société de l'information".

14. European Council: "Directive 2000/31/EC of the European Parliament and of the Council of 8 June on certain aspects on information society services, in particular electronic commerce, in the Internal market ('Directive on electronic commerce')"; Official Journal L 178, 17/07/2000, pages 0001-0016.

15. France: "Projet de loi sur la société de l'information".

16. Germany: "Gesetzentwurf über rechtliche Rahmenbedingungen für den elektronischen Geschäftsverkehr – EGG".

17. Luxembourg: "Loi du 14 août relative au commerce électronique".

18. Spain: "Proyecto de ley de servicios de la sociedad de la información y de comercio electrónico".

19. UNCITRAL: "Model Law on Electronic Commerce".

20. UNCITRAL: "Legal aspects of electronic commerce. Electronic contracting: provisions for a draft convention", September 2001.

Designing Business Processes in E-commerce Applications

Hans Albrecht Schmid[1] and Gustavo Rossi[2]

[1] University of Applied Sciences, Konstanz, Germany.
schmidha@fh-konstanz.de
[2] LIFIA-Universidad Nacional de La Plata, Argentina
gustavo@sol.info.unlp.edu.ar

Abstract. Business processes play an important role in E-commerce Web applications as they form an important part of the B2C domain and dominate the B2B domain. However, E-commerce application modeling and design techniques have eluded the special characteristics of business processes by treating them just as a special case of navigation. As a consequence, the resulting E-commerce applications have design and usability problems as well as erroneous results from business process execution. We propose a solution to E-commerce Web application design where business processes are considered first class citizens. In this paper we first demonstrate why modeling business processes is important. After a brief introduction, we extend the Object-Oriented Hypermedia Design Method (OOHDM) with business processes. We show that our approach to E-commerce Web application design involving both hypermedia navigation and business processes is easy and clear and does not cause the listed problems.

1 Introduction

In the last few years, a new generation of Web applications has emerged; they differ from purely navigational applications because they use the Web to support and execute business processes and workflows [7][9]. For example, E-commerce applications for rental and reservation services are formed mainly by business processes; auctions and Web shops combine them with navigation.

However, both the underlying nature of the Web (as a document-centric information base) and the associated design and implementation tools have not evolved to support the new requirements of E-commerce Web applications. Although a business process has characteristics that are quite different from navigation in hypermedia applications, most Web application modeling and design methods like WebML [2] and HDM2000 [1] treat it as a byproduct of a navigation sequence and do not model and design it explicitly. The consequences for the resulting E-commerce applications are design problems as well as usability problems and erroneous results of business process execution.

K. Bauknecht, A M. Tjoa, G. Quirchmayr (Eds.): EC-Web 2002, LNCS 2455, pp. 353–362, 2002.
© Springer-Verlag Berlin Heidelberg 2002

This paper presents our approach to support Web application design that allows modeling both business processes and navigation as first class entities. The structure of the paper is as follows: Section 2 shows why business processes should be considered as first class citizens. Section 3 briefly introduces the Object-Oriented Hypermedia Design Method (OOHDM) [10] for Web applications. In Section 4 we extend OOHDM by introducing business processes and activities and show the resulting benefits.

Although we use OOHDM as a basis for our discussion, the ideas underlying the concepts of processes and activities can be equally applied to other design methods such as WebML [2].

2   Rationale for Representing Business Processes in Web Applications

Most electronic stores (like www.amazon.com) include some business process that users execute as a sequence of steps. A good example is the checkout process. During checkout, a user goes through a predefined sequence of activities: he logs in, confirms the items that he is buying, enters the shipping address, selects the delivery options, select the method of payment, etc. Only after all these steps the process is completed successfully.

Suppose that during the checkout process the pages the user accesses are treated as navigational pages (such as CD or book pages). In our example that means the user navigates from the login page to the confirm items page, and then to the shipping address page, and so on. This may cause severe problems, as we will show. The reason behind them is that the semantic of navigation is quite simple:

*   The state of navigation is only represented with the current node on your screen, enhanced by the browser collecting a set of visited nodes,
*   The user decides freely which node to visit next. That means the designer cannot assume which nodes the user will visit after leaving the current node,
*   The navigation history, i.e. which pages a user has visited cannot be inferred from the current node.

It is possible to simulate a business process by navigation only if the process has a very simple and restricted one-way control flow trough a sequence of pages. In this case, navigation may be guided with some special icons and buttons, which indicate that the user should continue the process, on the bottom of these Web pages. But even in this simple case, problems my come up.

One source of problems is a designer not disallowing navigation during the execution of a business process, since providing a possibility for navigation all time may be desirable e.g. in a Web shop.

First, a user may leave the pages of the checkout process without returning because he may get disoriented, or he may consider the guidance about the next step just as an option like it is in navigation, not knowing that the process should be completed. Second, when exploring other pages after leaving the process, the user may cause an inconsistent state in the checkout process. As an example, suppose that during the checkout process the user wants to see again one of the items he is buying. The user then navigates to the product page and clicks the button to add the product to the shopping cart. Will the product be added to the order again? What happens if the user navigates back to the checkout process, will it be resumed or started newly?

Another source of problems lies in using the back button of a browser in the context of a business process. This is perfectly legal in the context of navigation, since it does not matter how the user changes the current page he is in.

But what is the behavior, and what should it be, if the back button is pressed during a business process? Does going to the previous page undo the action that was done on the last page, as most users may believe? Does the re-entry of data on the previous page update the data entered before? While some may argue that this is an implementation problem, the real problem is that the semantics of navigation are completely different from the semantics of business processes.

A business process [7][8] has the following characteristics:

- It drives the user through its activities. This means it defines the set of activities to be executed, and the control flow among them (like the sequence: login, confirm items, select the shipping address, etc.),

- It has a state that consists of the current activity, including if it is active or suspended, and the previously performed activities (in a simple one-way sequential control flow, these can be implied from the current activity).

As a consequence, the activities already executed (i.e. the history), and the subsequent ones are implicit in the current state. Since the current node on the screen does not contain sufficient state information, a business process has to keep its complete state internally during its execution.

The design of business process should allow describing the set of activities and the control flow that form a business process, and if it can be suspended and resumed. In particular, it must allow specifying if the process should be terminated or suspended (and later resumed) when a user navigates out of a business process. If the process is to be suspended, its state must be stored so it can be retrieved when the process is later resumed. Since a business process defines its component activities, it will guide the user through them after resumption.

The above discussion shows that there is a mismatch between navigation and hypermedia (on which the Web is based), and business processes (which play a crucial role in newer Web applications). Despite this mismatch, mature Web application design methods like OOHDM and WebML neglect business processes, or treat them as byproducts of other design primitives. We solve this problem by introducing business processes and their semantics as first-class citizens of Web applications.

3 The OOHDM Design Approach

This section introduces the Object-Oriented Hypermedia Design Method OOHDM [10] together with a CD Web shop E-commerce example that will help us throughout the rest of the paper. OOHDM comprises four activities, namely conceptual, navigation, and interface design and implementation. We summarize two of them, the conceptual design and navigational design activities, since the other are of minor importance with regard to the introduction of business processes.

Conceptual Design: Creating the Application Model
The OOHDM conceptual schema models the application domain without considering specific use-cases. It uses UML as the base modeling language.
Figure 1 shows a part of the conceptual schema for a CD electronic store with a customer, shopping cart, CD, order and other domain object classes. The business process „checkout" is defined as a method of the class Shopping Cart. When the customer initiates the checkout process, the checkout method (which is called from the ShoppingCart node, see navigation design, section 3) creates an order object with the CDs in the shopping cart. An order will contain a set of items, the shipping address, delivery and payment options, etc. When an order is created, these data are obtained from the user.

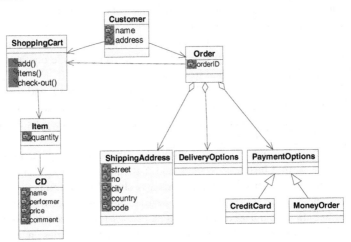

Fig. 1. Class diagram for CD store

Navigation Design: Creating the Navigational Schema
In OOHDM, a Web application is described by a navigational schema as a hypermedia view, which may cover only a subset of the objects and relationships of a conceptual model. The navigational schema contains classes derived from a set of predefined navigational primitives: nodes, links, anchors and access structures, which have the usual semantics of hypermedia applications [10]. Access structures, such as indexes, represent possible ways for starting navigation.
Nodes may contain not only anchors for links, but also behaviors, like „add to shopping cart" in a CD node and „checkout" in the ShoppingCart node (see Figure 2). These methods are triggered from the objects, like buttons, in the graphical interface of a node.

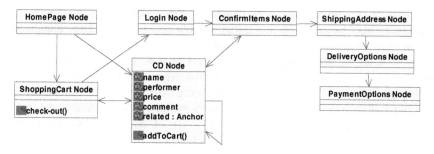

Fig. 2. Navigation Schema for Shopping Use Case

Figure 2 shows on the left the node classes and between them the navigation possibilities as arrows: you may navigate from a customer's HomePage node to a CD node or ShoppingCart node, from the CD node to the ShoppingCart node and vice versa, from a CD to other related CDs by the „related" anchor.

On the top-right, we see the checkout process simulated by a navigation sequence (OOHDM does not use processes as primitives). The Login node is accessed by executing the checkout behavior in the shopping cart (i.e. by pressing the checkout button on its interface). From the Login node, it is only possible to navigate to the ConfirmItems node; from the ConfirmItems Node to the ShippingAddress Node, and so on. Navigation proceeds in sequence, with the only exception is that it is possible to navigate from the Confirm Items node to a CD node and back. The ShoppingCart node and other nodes can be reached from the CD node, with all the consequences described in section 2.

4 Conceptual and Navigational Design of Processes and Activities

Following the OOHDM approach, we introduce in two separate subsections the conceptual definition of business processes and its counterpart in the navigational schema.

4.1 Conceptual Design: Modeling Processes and Activities

To introduce business processes as first class citizens, we partition the conceptual design space in two kinds of objects: entity objects and process objects. Entity objects model permanent entities in the application domain, while process objects model the business processes taking place in that domain. Whether an object should be modeled as an entity or a process is based on different characteristics [7]:

- Entity objects (like customers and orders) have a permanent lifetime and state.

- Process objects do not have a permanent lifetime; their state is temporary. Their instances may be executed in parallel without any problem. They communicate with entity objects sending messages to them.

Figure 3 shows the conceptual schema of the CD store with a design space that is partitioned in entity classes (bottom) and process classes (top). The CheckOut process is composed of several activities like Login Act, ConfirmItems Act, ShippingAddress Act, and DeliveryOptions Act. We consider a business process like Checkout as a parent activity that may consist itself of a set of activities, like Login Act , ConfirmItems Act, etc., following the Composite pattern [4].

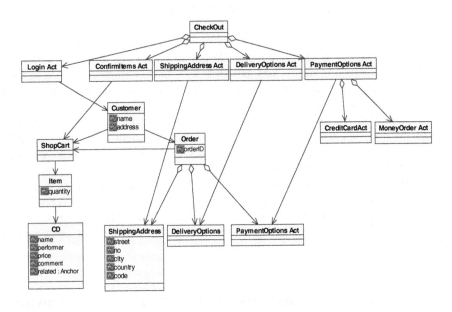

Fig. 3. CD Store with checkout process and activities

A parent activity defines the sequence (the control flow) in which its child activities should be executed, and delegates the work to them. For example, Checkout defines that the activities Login, ConfirmItems, ShippingAddress, Delivery Options, etc. are executed in a strict one-way sequence and invokes them accordingly. Alternatively, CheckOut might define a control flow that gives the user the choice of executing the child activities in any order. The control flow information is not represented in the conceptual schema, since it fits better in the navigational schema.

For a better integration of navigation in business processes, we allow a business process to be suspended and (later) resumed. An activity may finish its processing for several reasons:

- it may terminate if its work is completed,
- it may abort itself since the user cancels the processing,
- it may suspend itself due to a user input like navigation outside of the process.

Each activity has a state, which indicates the current point of control and the current control situation (it may be active or suspended), and other attributes of the activity. A parent activity contains a list of child activities; its state contains information on child activities executed, completed, aborted or suspended. If the control flow among child activities is strictly one-way and sequential, like for checkout, the current child activity is enough as state information. However, checkout with the alternative control flow that gives the user a choice needs additional state information indicating which of the child activities have already been executed.

4.2 Navigational Design: Mapping Processes to Activity Nodes

To model processes and activities, we introduce activity nodes in the navigational schema. We partition the navigational design space in an entity node and an activity node subspace; we map entities from the conceptual schema in navigational nodes (which are nodes as described in navigation design, section 3), and activities in activity nodes.

For example, the navigational schema shown in Figure 4 partitions the navigational design space. On the left, there are the navigational nodes like CD Node, ShoppingCart Node and HomePage Node that were shown in Figure 2. Activity nodes like the LoginAct Node, ShippingAddressAct Node, etc., which map the activities shown in Figure 3, appear on the right. These activity nodes replace the navigational nodes of Figure 2.

Activity Nodes

An activity node represents the output page (HTTP response) and input processing (HTTP request) of an activity; it displays its output and handles its user input. The activity node, or more exactly, its graphical interface contains usually buttons, like *ok*, *commit*, *cancel,* or *next*, which trigger actions related to the input processing of an activity and control the progress of control to a subsequent activity. When an activity allows navigating outside of the process, the associated node contains corresponding anchors for links. From an extended OOHDM point of view, an activity node is a particular node meta-class, which provides an interface for process and activity related behaviors, and another one for navigational links.

An activity node like the LoginAct Node is shown in the navigational schema in the context of the process to which it belongs, which is its parent activity node, in this case CheckOutAct Node. This is indicated by drawing activity nodes within the box of the parent activity node, which may be a process node. Nested process contexts indicate the nesting of composed activities.

Executing Business Processes

When the CheckOut process (see conceptual schema, Figure 3) is started from the navigational ShoppingCart Node by pressing the checkout button, the navigation state is left and the process execution state entered. This is indicated in Figure 4 by an arrow labeled „start" (label not shown in Figure 4) from the ShoppingCart Node to the box of the CheckOutAct Node.

The CheckOut parent activity starts the Login activity (see conceptual schema, Figure 3), which displays its output in the LoginAct Node. After user input, the Login activity receives the user input from the LoginAct Node and processes it. Thus, an activity and its corresponding activity node collaborate closely.

The possible control flow among the activity nodes in a process context is described in a manner that is similar to a UML state diagram (see Figure 4). There is a special initial and final diagram node. Directed edges among activity nodes show the possible flow of control among the activities. In our example, the edges show a one-way sequence from Login over ConfirmItems etc. to PaymentOptions. This contains a nested flow leading from the initial node of the sub-process to its final node, either via CreditCard or via MoneyOrder.

When a business process is terminated, the process execution state is left and the navigation state is entered. In our example CD shop, the application is terminated when checkout is terminated, as Figure 4 shows. But you might as well design the application to enter e.g. the Home Page Node when the check out process is terminated.

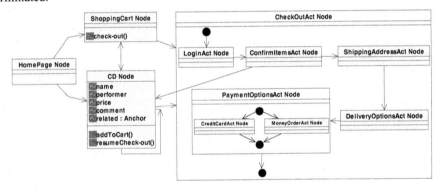

Fig. 4. CD Store navigational schema with activity nodes

Pressing the back button causes the browser to change the displayed activity node, but it does not change the state of the activity. For example, when the back button is pressed during the execution of the ConfirmItems activity, the ConfirmItemsAct Node is left and the LoginAct Node is entered. But the ConfirmItems activity remains active. When the user makes an input to the LoginAct Node, the ConfirmItems activity determines that this is an input not created from its ConfirmItemsAct Node. Thus, it can react in the desired way, one possibility being to tell the user that moving back with the back button was not accepted in a process.

Combining Business Processes with Navigation

You may also suspend a business process to do some navigation, and resume its execution afterwards. The possibility to navigate outside of the process following a link is indicated by an arrow, which goes out from an activity node and leaves the process context box. For example, the arrow from the ConfirmItemsAct Node to the CD Node indicates that you can suspend the CheckOut process and navigate to CDs. When a user follows the link to the CD Node, the ConfirmItemsAct Node suspends the activity, notifies the parent activity CheckOut and returns control to it. CheckOut sets its state to suspended and initiates navigation to the link's target.

The possibility to resume a suspended process is indicated by an arrow labeled „resume" (label not shown in Figure 4) that leads from a navigational node to a business process. For example, the arrow from the CD navigational node to the CheckOutAct Node process context indicates that you can resume the CheckOut process. The arrow does not lead directly to an activity, since the process resumes control as a whole in the state in which it was suspended (i.e. in the corresponding state of the suspended activity). Thus, navigation cannot jump directly to, or within an activity. When the user returns to the CheckOut process, CheckOut knows its suspended state and can resume the suspended activity.

5   Concluding Remarks

Our paper has introduced the modeling and design of business processes in the context of Web applications. Our approach extends OOHDM by introducing process and activity objects in the conceptual design space, and activity nodes and process contexts in the navigation space.

Due to space restrictions, we could not explain navigational contexts defined in OOHDM [10], which may modify the attributes and behavior of a navigational node in a given context. We will show in another paper that navigational contexts may be attached to process contexts to modify the attributes and behavior of a navigational node when accessing it while a process is suspended.

We have shown that considering processes as first class citizens closes the semantic gap between E-commerce business processes and their design notation. In addition, it has important benefits such as:

- Allowing to model and design business processes with a control flow that is more complex than a one-way sequential control flow.
- Solving the usability problems caused by the interplay between navigation and processes, without restricting free navigation.
- Enabling the reuse of activities in different processes. Activities such as customer login or checkout can be reused in the context of different processes, thus improving the quality of design and making implementation more cost-effective.

We have applied the proposed design method to several Web applications in student projects and in cooperation with software houses in real world projects with success. Some of these applications are a customer relation management system for small and medium sized shops and companies, which embodies mainly different business processes, and a cooperative travel agency where users can offer or search for traveling opportunities, which combines different search processes with navigational facilities.

The business processes that are represented in the conceptual schema may be realized and implemented in either an object-oriented or a procedural approach, by putting the state information in the session context of a sevlet.

You may implement a business process directly as a state machine where each state calls for different methods of producing an output page (the response) and reacting on the user input (the request). Alternatively, you may use a state machine framework like Expresso [6]. We have built the WACoF **W**eb **A**pplication **C**omponent Framework [8] with servlet-based parent and child activity components for a seamless development of a business activity and process implementation from the design presented in this paper.

Acknowledgements. Our thanks are due to Alejandra Garrido and Fernando Das Neves who helped to improve the English, to Anabella Cristaldi who helped preparing the paper, to the International Bureau of the BMBF, Germany, for the Bilateral Cooperation with Argentina support, and to the Ministerium fuer Wissenschaft und Kunst, Baden-Wuerttemberg, for its partial support of this project. This project is also partially supported by SeCTIP, Argentina.

References

1. L. Baresi, F. Garzotto, P. Paolini, and S. Valenti: „HDM2000: The HDM Hypertext Design Model Revisited", Tech. Report, Politecnico di Milano, Jan. 2000
2. S. Ceri, P. Fraternali, S. Paraboschi: „Web Modeling Language (WebML): a modeling language for designing Web sites", Proceedings of the 9th. International World Wide Web Conference, Elsevier 2000, pp 137-157
3. J. Conallen: „Building Web Applications with UML", Addison Wesley 2000.
4. E. Gamma, R. Helm. R. Johnson, J. Vlissides: „Design Patterns. Elements of reusable object-oriented software" Addison Wesley 1995.
5. I. Jacobson, M. Christerson, P. Jonsson and G. Overgaard: „Object-Oriented Software Engineering", Prentice-Hall, 1992.
6. P.Pilgrim „Best Practice with Expresso Framework: Using a framework to create a web application", http://www.theserverside.com/resources/articles/Expresso/article.html
7. H.A.Schmid: „Business Entity Components and Business Process Components"; Journal of Object Oriented Programming, Vol.12, No.6, Oct. 99
8. H. Schmid, G. Rossi and F. Falkenstein „Components for the Reuse of Activities in Web Applications", in:OOIS 2001, Proc. 7th. Interntl Conf. on Object-Oriented Information Systems, Springer, London, 2001
9. H. Schmid, A. Cristaldi and G.Jacobson „A Business Process Components Framework", in:OOIS 2001, Proc. 7th. Interntl Conf. on Object-Oriented Information Systems, Springer, London, 2001
10. D. Schwabe, G. Rossi: „An object-oriented approach to web-based application design", Theory and Practice of Object Systems (TAPOS), Special Issue on the Internet, v. 4 No.4, pp.207-225, October, 1998.

A Generic SLA Semantic Model for the Execution Management of e-Business Outsourcing Contracts

Christopher Ward, Melissa J. Buco, Rong N. Chang, and Laura Z. Luan

IBM T.J. Watson Research Center
19 Skyline Drive, Hawthorne, NY 10532, USA
{cw1,mjbuco,rong,luan}@us.ibm.com

Abstract. It is imperative for a competitive e-business outsourcing service provider to manage the execution of its *service level agreement* (SLA) contracts in business terms (e.g., minimizing financial penalties for service-level violations, maximizing service-level measurement based customer satisfaction metrics, etc.). In order to do that, the provider must possess a generic means of capturing and managing the SLA contract data (e.g., quality measurement data sources, service-level evaluation rules, etc.) as well as the relationships between them and internal *service-level management* (SLM) data (e.g., resource management data, system configuration data, etc.). This paper presents the design rationale of a generic SLA semantic model (including a set of semantic elements and relationships) based on an in-depth analysis of nine real e-business outsourcing SLA contracts/templates comprising over 100 service-level guarantees and intents. Our development experience with a state-of-the-art SLA contract execution manager (named SAM) suggests the semantic model is practical and useful.

1 Introduction

Many companies in the world are participating in the Internet-based economy to ensure a prosperous future. It has become increasingly desirable for these companies to outsource the development and/or management of their Internet-based e-business applications/processes due to rapid innovations in Web computing technologies and a serious worldwide shortage of *information technology* (IT) skills. Various e-business outsourcing service providers (e.g., ASP's, ISP's, MSP's, xSP's) are evolving to help these e-business companies to cost-efficiently focus on the growth of their core competency.

A *service level agreement* (SLA) is a legal contract that specifies the minimum expectations and obligations that exist between a service provider and a service customer [1, 2, 3, 4, 5]. An e-business outsourcing SLA contract specifies, among others, the outsourced service functions, service quality measurement criteria, service-level evaluation rules, and ramifications of failing to meet (or indeed exceeding) quality standards (or *service-level targets*, SLTs). An SLT can be stated based upon an objective quantitative measurement of the availability/performance of an IT system (e.g., monthly availability of individual Web server will be no less than 99.7%) or the efficiency/effectiveness of an *operations support service* (OSS) and/or a *business support service* (BSS) process (e.g., no less than 93% of Severity 1 problems are

K. Bauknecht, A M. Tjoa, G. Quirchmayr (Eds.): EC-Web 2002, LNCS 2455, pp. 363–376, 2002.

responded within 30 minutes monthly). The refund policies for service-level violations can be specified relative to the service cost (e.g., credit customer one day of the service cost if the outsourced e-business infrastructure is unavailable more than 15 minutes a day) or in absolute terms (e.g., credit customer two thousand dollars if a monthly average network latency across the provider ISP access links to the ISP's backbone is higher than 95 milliseconds). A sample (abridged) e-business outsourcing SLA contract is provided in Appendix A.

From a provider's viewpoint, offering a few sets of customer-neutral service functions atop a common service delivery infrastructure exploits economy of scale better than pursuing a high degree of customizability of its service functions for every potential customer. However, this customer-neutral approach to establishing SLAs seems effective only for *primitive* e-business outsourcing services (e.g., server co-location services offered by WorldCom/UUNET [6]) so far. The other kinds of e-business SLA contracts (including the ones that incorporate several primitive e-business outsourcing services) normally require *nonstandard* customization of provider's service offerings to accommodate customer's unique data and/or business process management needs. When the number of such nonstandard SLA contracts grows, the difficulty of meeting business-oriented *service-level management* (SLM) objectives increases. One of the most demanding challenges facing an e-business outsourcing service provider today is to manage the execution of its SLA contracts in business terms (e.g., minimizing financial penalties for service-level violations, maximizing service-level measurement based customer satisfaction metrics, etc.).

It is often unappreciated that service-level evaluation related data is a proper subset of the contract-specified data (e.g., SLA refund/reward evaluation algorithms) that is essential for the optimization of business-oriented SLM objectives. We call the set of SLM related contract-specified data the *SLA data*. To give a brief example, a managed storage services contract that offers virtual disk space to a customer with an availability SLT requires the provider to manage the mapping between the virtual disk space and the corresponding real storage resources. The SLA data in this case comprises all data attributes associated with the availability of the virtual disk, including pricing, required capacity, availability SLT, etc. The corresponding set of internal *SLM data* includes the data attributes associated with this mapping (e.g. physical storages server names, allocated capacity, etc.). While the SLM data and the SLA-SLM data relationships must be managed well by the provider, such non-contractual implementation details need not be exposed to the customer.

To the best of our knowledge, there is still no satisfactory means of capturing and managing SLA/SLM data in support of business-oriented SLM objectives. Developing a generic SLA semantic model is clearly an important step toward finding a good means of doing that. Such a model would also provide essential insight into (1) the development of extensible external representations for SLA data and SLA/SLM linkage (e.g. XML representations), (2) the design of physical data models (database schema) for these data, and (3) the creation of an object-oriented programming model as well as API for accessing SLA/SLM data.

Our SLA semantic model was created based upon an in-depth comparative analysis of 9 typical commercial e-business SLA contracts/templates, including, in total, 36 *service-level guarantees* (SLGs) and *83 service-level intents* (SLIs), which are SLGs less penalty clauses for service-level violations. We have also been able to use the model to capture the key (SLM-related) semantics of 10 other e-business-on-demand

SLA contracts/templates and 30 sample ASP SLAs [7] gathered by the Information Technology Association of America (ITAA).

We have been developing an SLA/SLM data manager based upon the SLA semantic model, and making that as an integral component of SAM, a state-of-the-art SLA contract execution manager under development at IBM T.J. Watson Research Center that, among others, (1) enables the provider to deploy an effective means of capturing and managing contractual SLA data as well as non-contractual SLM data; (2) assists service personnel to prioritize the processing of action-demanding quality management alerts according to the provider's business-oriented SLM objectives; and (3) automates the prioritization and execution management of single-/multi-task SLM processes (including assigning SLM tasks to service personnel) as per the provider's business objectives. Our development experience with SAM suggests our SLA semantic model is practical and useful.

The remainder of the paper is organized as follows. Section 2 explores SLA contract components in greater detail. Section 3 illustrates SAM's SLA semantic model, and includes a quick reference table listing the primary semantic elements. The less intuitive relationships are justified against referenced text from the reviewed contracts. Section 4 illustrates a structure diagram of primary semantic elements for the abridged Web Hosting SLA contract in Appendix A. Finally, Section 5 concludes the paper with a summary of our findings and our use of the model in SAM.

2   SLA Contracts for E-business Outsourcing Services

SLA is important to the e-business outsourcing industry for several reasons: (1) SLA legalizes a mutual agreement between two parties on service offering and agreement change management details; (2) SLA codifies how service quality will be objectively measured; and (3) SLA details which remedies are available to both parties for failing to meet or exceeding SLTs. Thus, from a customer's viewpoint, SLA mitigates expensive infrastructure and IT personnel costs, and replaces them with a fee-based service. From a provider's viewpoint, economically managing the execution of SLA contracts is the provider's business.

2.1   Principal Data Elements in an E-business Outsourcing Contract

An e-business outsourcing contract would include, among others:

1. Description of service
2. Functional requirements of the service system
3. Start date and duration of service
4. Pricing and payment terms
5. Terms and conditions for service installation, revisions, and termination
6. Planned service maintenance windows
7. Customer support procedures and response time
8. Problem escalation procedures
9. Acceptance testing criteria, i.e., quality requirements that must be met before the service can be deployed for production use. These criteria could be stated

in terms of, for example, benchmark-based transaction throughput performance, business-oriented synthetic transaction processing performance, failover latency, service usability, service system configurations (e.g. computer main memory size), etc.

Contrasting with the service contracts whose quality of execution cannot be quantitatively measured, e-business SLA contracts include production-time quality standards (a.k.a., SLTs) as the SLA example in Appendix A shows. In order for both customer and provider to objectively determine service-level violations, each service-level specification in an e-business SLA contract must include the components listed below:

1. Location of quality measurement point, which can be in the service system infrastructure (e.g., network access routers, Internet firewall servers, application hosting computers, operating systems, etc.) or in the service system software (e.g., middleware, application servers, browsers, etc.)
2. Service-level monitoring and reporting specifications, including the tools and methodologies that will be used to perform the required service-level monitoring and reporting tasks
3. Workload admission control mechanisms and policies (for performance related service-levels)

Each of these components places unique SLA/SLM data management requirements on provider's SLA execution management system. In particular, we notice that the inclusion of refund policies for non-performing requires a proactive SLA contract execution manager to exploit the relationship between SLA-specified refund evaluation data/algorithms and provider's SLM policies for handling action-demanding quality alerts (because passing through a service-level penalty point could cost the provider an immediate revenue loss). Lack of such SLA/SLM data management capabilities in a provider's SLA execution management system would significantly limit the provider's ability of optimizing its business-oriented SLM objectives.

2.2   A Comparative Semantic Analysis of Real e-Business Outsourcing SLA Contracts/Templates

Table 1 summarizes the nine typical e-business outsourcing SLA contracts/templates we have reviewed in-depth while developing our SLA semantic model. The first column provides a reference name for the contract: three are templates 'Uunet Colo" [6], "Uunet Network" [UunetNS], and "EarthLink" [8]; four are commercial Web hosting contracts "Web Hosting 1-4"[WH1, WH2, WH3, WH4] and two are IT outsourcing contracts "STL" [STL] and "UKERNA" [9]. The second column indicates the type of contract: Colocation, Network Services, eBusiness Hosting, or IT. The third (and forth) column indicates the number of SLGs identified in each contract and the fifth (and sixth) column indicates the number of SLIs. The SLGs and SLIs are further divided into availability and performance categories, respectively.

The first seven SLA contracts/templates include primarily quality assured guarantees, while the last two [STL, UKERNA] comprise many "best effort" intents of achieving SLM objectives. We noticed significant differences between the levels of clarity of SLGs and SLIs in those SLAs. Generally the SLGs provided greater specificity of a few well-understood service-levels (e.g. "Availability" and "Service Outage Reporting Time") while the SLIs were less specific and often addressed more complex quality management issues (e.g. "The volume of traffic itemized into the wrong category shall not exceed 0.5% of the total accounted traffic for that institution" [UKERNA]).

Table 1. Service Level Guarantees and Intents by Contract.

Contract Name	Type	SLGs Avail.	SLGs Perf.	SLIs Avail.	SLIs Perf.	TOTAL
1. UUNET Colo	Network+Colocation	2	4			6
2. UUNET Network	Network	1	3			4
3. EarthLink	Network	1				1
4. Web Hosting 1	eBusiness Hosting	1	1			2
5. Web Hosting 2	eBusiness Hosting	1				1
6. Web Hosting 3	eBusiness Hosting	3	3		1	7
7. Web Hosting 4	eBusiness Hosting	9	7			16
8. STL	IT			10	4	14
9. UKERNA	IT			15	53	68
TOTAL		18	18	25	58	119

The 76 performance service-levels in those SLA contracts/templates can be classified into two groups:

- 36 IT system service-levels, including 15 Network (e.g. Network Latency [UunetColo]), 15 Application (e.g. SQL Response Time [STL]) and 6 Server (e.g. VM Response Time [STL]) service-levels.
- 40 OSS/BSS process service-levels, including 11 Help Desk (e.g. "Severity 1 Problems are to be responded to within 30 minutes" [WH3]), 2 Outage Notification (e.g. "Provider will notify Customer of service outage within 15 minutes" [UunetColo]), 15 Service Responses (e.g. "A response time within five working days to a request for delegation in the target domain from a client institution connecting to JANET" [UKERNA]), 11 Report Timeliness (e.g. "Reports covering total traffic per day and per month shall be made available on the web, in all cases no later than 5 working days after the end of the day or month covered" [UKERNA]) and 1 Maintenance (e.g. "Total maintenance time shall not be more than 0.5% of service time, averaged over the year" [UKERNA]) service-levels.

Our comparative analyis of the SLA contracts/templates yielded several non-trivial observations:

1. The evaluation of a service-level (especially performance service-levels) usually uses a hierarchy of quality measurement threshholds rooted at the SLT (e.g., "99.3% [of Severity 1 problems are resolved] within 30 minutes of the Start Time" [WH3]).

2. A single SLG refund/reward computation may use the evaluation results for several service-levels (e.g. "A Service Level Default occurs when Provider fails to meet a Minimum Service Level during any month of the Term, at any time, or fails to meet an Expected Service Level with a Performance Category on four (4) or more occasions during a calendar twelve (12) month period following the Acceptance Date Plus five (5) months". [WH4]).

3. Due to necessary legal phraseologies, most SLAs include clauses that call for root cause analyses when qualifying availability/performance measurement data (e.g., "This SLA objective specifically does not include failures caused by Customer" [WH2]). These clauses make it impossible to automatically generate correct service-level reports without human intervention.

4. Customer's reaction to abnormal service conditions may affect the outcome of official service-level reports (e.g., "Outages will be counted as Power Unavailability only if Customer opens a trouble ticket with UUNET Customer support within five days of the outage." [UunetColo]).

3   Semantic Elements and Relationship Structure Diagram

A semantic elements and relationship structure diagram that captures the SLA data from the nine reviewed contracts/templates is provided in Figure 1. The semantic model is based on UML [10] and describes the *primary* information flows between the *principal* semantic elements in support of SLA contract execution management. We recognize that other elements and relations will exist to address other SLA life cycle management issues. The relationships are labeled relations with unidirectional cardinality such as "uses" and "includes". To allow easy top-to-bottom reading, some relationships are passive (e.g. "is generated by"). Starting from the top of the diagram, we see the SLA is composed of customer information (customer ID, contact personnel, etc.), the contract duration (start date, end date, termination rules and conditions, etc.), SLA-wide refund/reward data (amount of refund/reward that should apply over the settlement interval after consideration of all SLA-wide terms and conditions, e.g. a refund limit of 15% of service charge regardless of the severity of service-level violations) and provider information (provider ID, contact personnel etc.). As a key, other semantic elements are likewise listed in Table 2, which includes the semantic element description, representative attributes and the "Web Hosting 2" (as detailed in Appendix A) attribute examples.

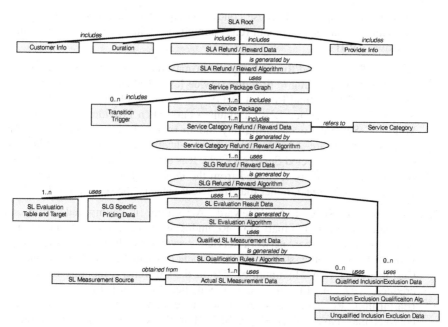

Fig. 1. Primary SLA Semantic Elements & Relationships in UML.

The information flows between the identified key SLA semantic elements, represented in the UML by the solid lines, is an essential component in the structure diagram as it defines the limited set of relationships between the elements. We highlight the more subtle ones:

1. Qualified SL Measurement Data is generated by application of Qualification Rules/Algorithm to the Actual SL Measurement Data, i.e., "raw" service-level measurement data. In computing service availability, for example, the SL Measurement Data includes "Service Up" and "Service Down" times. Qualification rules are extracted from the contract, e.g. "Fault or negligence by the Provider" [WH1]. The qualification rules also take as input "Unqualified Inclusion/Exclusion Data" (such as customer approved downtime and maintenance window start/stop times).[1] Our review of the data models for commercial service-level monitoring tools indicates that this crucial step is often overlooked, leading to the use of unqualified data in the service-level evaluation process or to complex corrections being applied at the service-level evaluation phase. The output from the qualification rules is qualified (i.e. validated) measurement data and qualified inclusion/exclusion data. This latter

---

[1] In some contracts, it is necessary for the inclusion/exclusion data qualification rules to be aware not only of the local site's maintenance window, but also the maintenance windows of others. E.g. "Provider shall perform maintenance in a manner that ensures that one Web Hosting Environment with Geographically Diverse Web Hosting Environments will be fully operational and accessible at all times" [WH3] requires tracking several environments simultaneously.

phase is also important because contracts frequently place restrictions on the excusable downtime per month (e.g. "compliance with scheduled maintenance windows" [WH3]).

2. A single SLG Refund/Reward Algorithm may receive several SL Evaluation Data sets corresponding to different service-level evaluations when computing its output (SLG Refund/Reward Data). An example of this was provided in Section 2.1 ("A Service Level Default occurs when Provider fails to meet a Minimum Service Level during any month of the Term..." [WH4]). In this example, there are two separate service-levels in a "single" guarantee (Minimum and Expected Service Level). It is also important to notice that the service-level default is computed from the *number of occasions the expected service-level is not met*, rather than the actual value of the service-level.

3. The overall SLA Refund/Reward Algorithm is composed from an accumulation of individual SLG Refund/Reward data sets, organized into service categories (e.g. network service, server farm, help desk, etc.) along with SLA-wide policy statements to compute the actual refund/reward due the Customer. E.g., "A Maximum of 25% of the Customer's monthly fee will be credited each month (limit one credit per [network] line per month)." [EarthLink]. Referring to Table 1, we note that a simple network access contract may have only a single SLG [EarthLink], whereas some contracts reviewed have several service categories and many separate service-levels. E.g., UKERNA has 12 service categories and 68 different SLIs. Many of these require tracking of multiple service-levels (e.g. service-levels for "Total Time" and "Prime Time").

4. The SLA semantic model includes a notion of *Service Package Graphs*, composed of Service Packages and Transition Triggers, which reside between the Service Category Refund/Reward Data and the SLA Refund/Reward Algorithm (see Figure 2). They enable to model to capture contractual agreements on how quality standards and SLA refunds/rewards details can change. E.g., "Customer credit for the *first* month of a new order, which meets the [refund] requirements, is 25% of the prorated monthly fee." [EarthLink] or "Customer may add or delete Performance Categories by sending written notice to Provider at least ninety (90) days prior to the date that such new Performance Categories are to be effective" [WH3]. In both these instances, the contract defines rules and procedures for adjusting the algorithms/data and/or service-level measurements used in computing the overall refund/ reward. A Service Package can be considered as a data container for a set of Service Categories under contract-defined circumstances. The transition from one Service Package to another is accomplished by some contract-defined event (e.g. a date, as in five months after the start of the contract, or a new service-level). It is possible that an intermediate Service Package is needed to "tidy" up the service-level computations required during the transition.

4   SLA Semantic Model Validation Using "Web Hosting 2"

The model for the Web hosting contract shown in Appendix A is depicted in Figure 2. The contract was selected for illustrative purposes in this paper; the actual model has been applied to many more complex contracts as briefed in Sections 1 and 2.   It describes a single service category (i.e. service) for a "Web Hosting Environment" with a help desk service function.   The service-level is defined based upon the total number of minutes of qualified downtime in a calendar month. The table in the contract defines an SLT (of four hours or less in a calendar month) and provides refunds for failing to meet this SLT and rewards for exceeding it.   The contract specifies that the SL Measurement Source for all downtime measurement times is provider's help desk trouble ticket system.   Downtime start time is defined as the ticket opening time for customer-initiated tickets or the provider-detected outage begin time recorded in provider-initiated tickets. Downtime end time is defined as the problem resolved time documented in the trouble ticket. Thus the actual SL Measurement Data are time events (when the service system goes up/down). Details of the actual SL Measurement Data (e.g. format of the trouble tickets) and rules/algorithms to qualify the measurement data (e.g. how to identify problems

Table 2. Description for Semantic Elements used in SLA Management Data Model. The description is supplemented with representative values (data attributes) and example data attributes for Appendix A.

Element Name	Description	Key Attributes	Web Hosting 2 Example
SLA Root	Details regarding the overall contract document itself.	Contract ID, Title, Signing Date	N/A
Customer Info	Customer relevant information used in support of the contract. This may include personnel for Change Management, Refund Request, Problem Escalation.	Customer ID (e.g. name etc.), Customer Mgmt Team info	"Customer Name"
Duration	Contract duration including start time, end time and termination conditions.	Start Date, End Date, Termination Rules and Algorithm	None Provided
SLA Refund/Reward Data	Contract-wide refund/reward data, i.e. the amount of refund (or reward) that should be provided to the customer over the settlement interval after consideration of all the SLA-wide terms and conditions.	Settlement Interval, Refund/Reward Amount	Same as SLG since there are no SLA-wide clauses
Provider Info	Provider relevant information used in support of the contract. This may include personnel for Change Management, Problem Reporting and Problem Escalation.	Provider ID (e.g. name etc.)	"Provider Name"
SLA Refund/Reward Algorithm	Combines the refund/reward amounts corresponding to each SLG into a single amount and reviews this against any SLA-wide terms and conditions.	SLG Refund Values, SLA-wide Values, Algorithm	N/A in single SLG Contracts
Service Package Graph	A graph of service packages. Each service package reflects refund/reward data from a set of SLGs under a particular set of circumstances (specified in the contract). The graph shows legal transitions between service packages.	A graph of service packages (vertices) and triggers that transition from one service package to another (edges)	The graph is composed of two packages, one before Jan 1, 1999 and one thereafter. The transition trigger is reaching Jan 1, 1999

Table 2. Continued.

Element Name	Description	Key Attributes	Web Hosting 2 Example
Transition Trigger	The events that cause a change in the service package are called "Transition Triggers".	Time, New Service Agreements	Jan 1, 1999
Service Package	A set of SLG Refund/Reward Data for the service under defined circumstances. Notice that a service package embodies the data from many concurrent SLGs but does not "process it" rather it reflects the state of data attributes below it.	The set of refund reward data for each SLG that is contained in the current package	One service package prior to Jan 1, 1999 and one service package thereafter
Service Category Refund/Reward Data	The refund/reward contribution for a service group over its evaluation interval. This amount, along with any necessary information is all that is needed at the "higher level" to compute the SLA refund.	Refund over the Evaluation Interval	Dollar refund for service category over the month
Service Category	Functional description of the service to be offered. SLG/SLIs are in support of this "service"	Functional Description	Web Hosting Environment
Service Category Refund/Reward Algorithm	Combines refund/reward contributions associated with a particular service group.	Evaluation Interval, Algorithm	Service category includes Availability and Help Desk provisions
SLG Refund/Reward Data	The refund/reward contribution for each SLG over its evaluation interval.	Refund over the Evaluation Interval	Dollar refund amount over the month
SLG Refund/Reward Algorithm	Combines SL Evaluation Result Data with SLG Relevant Pricing Data and the SL Evaluation Table and Data to compute the Refund/Reward for this SLG.	Evaluation Interval, Algorithm	A table is used to document the monthly refunds/rewards based on the number of hours of downtime during the month
SL Evaluation Table and Target	A table of values describing the refund or reward for various levels of service over the evaluation interval. The SL "target" is the table entry to which no refund/reward occurs.	Table of Refund and Reward Values for defined levels of service	Table with two columns "Duration of SLA Downtime" and "Amount of Credit or Premium"
SLG Specific Pricing Data	Pricing data relevant to an individual guarantee, computed from contract.	Interval Fee for Guaranteed Service	Monthly charge
SL Evaluation Result Data	Set of SL evaluation data, i.e. result from applying SL evaluation algorithm.	An average, %, or other value which quantifies the evaluation of the service	The total qualified downtime for the month
SL Evaluation Algorithm	Evaluation of service level based on qualified measurement data.	Algorithm to evaluate a SL. E.g., average of measurements for the interval for percentage of measurements meeting criteria	Total qualified downtime for the month
Qualified SL Measurement Data	The SL data (i.e. measurements directly pertaining to this SLG) after it has been qualified according to the service level clauses in the contract	Measurement data which will be used in calculating SL	Downtime intervals which will be used in calculating the monthly downtime
SL Qualification Rules/Algorithm	An algorithm and set of rules used to examine the SL Measurement data and either include or exclude it from being considered qualified data.	Algorithm and/or rules	Downtime intervals will be excluded based upon contract maintenance provisions, failure of bandwidth connectivity, and external failures
SL Measurement Source	Source of SL measurement data, e.g. system level monitoring systems and trouble ticket systems	Location of Monitoring System, Specification of Measurement data to be extracted	Help Desk trouble ticket system and provider-detected downtime (system not specified)

Table 2. Continued.

Element Name	Description	Key Attributes	Web Hosting 2 Example
Actual SL Measurement Data	The Service Level data (i.e. measurements directly pertaining to this SLG) prior to being qualified according to the service level clauses in the contract. Often obtained from log records from system console monitors and trouble ticket systems	Time Stamped Measurement Data	For Help Desk reported outages, trouble ticket opening and resolve times will be used. For provider-detected outages, first detection and problem resolve times will be used.
Qualified Inclusion/Exclusion Data	Sets of qualified downtime intervals during which service level data may be excused or conditions under which SLG refund/reward may be excused.	Non-SL Measurement Data	Maintenance Schedules
Inclusion/Exclusion Qualification Algorithm	An algorithm and set of rules used to examine non-SL measurement data (e.g. customer refund requests or maintenance) and either include or exclude them from being considered qualified data.	Algorithm and/or rules	N/A
Unqualified Inclusion/Exclusion Data	Sets of unqualified downtime intervals during which service level data may be excused or conditions under which SLG refund/reward may be excused. There are often obtained by examining OSS and BSS data stores.	Non-SL Measurement Data	N/A

associated with provider's loading of the operating system software) are unavailable/unclear as indicated by the white borderlines for the relevant boxes. The contract specifies a maintenance provision, which is considered Inclusion/Exclusion Data. The Qualified SL Measurement Data and the Qualified Inclusion/Exclusion Data are used by the SL Evaluation Algorithm to compute the SL Evaluation Result Data (i.e., total minutes of downtime in a calendar month). These data, along with the SL Evaluation Table and contract pricing data, are used by the SLG Refund/Reward Algorithm to compute the actual refund/reward over the calendar month. The contract further states that rewards in one month may be used to offset refunds in other months. This result becomes the refund/reward for the service category since there is only a single SLG. There are two service packages: one for the "best effort" service level specifications prior to Jan 1, 1999 and the second (with refund/rewards) for the remainder of the term. The transition from one package to the other is date based. Finally, the SLA Refund/Reward Algorithm computes the overall contract-level refund/reward over the yearly settlement interval.

4   Conclusions

It is imperative for a competitive e-business outsourcing service provider to manage the execution of its SLA contracts in business terms. In order to do that, the provider must possess a generic means of capturing and managing SLM-related SLA data and the relationships between them and internal SLM data.

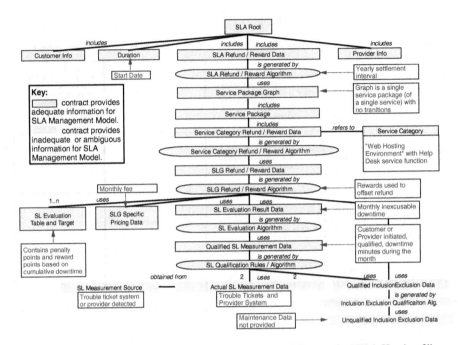

Fig. 2. Semantic Element and Relationship Structure Diagram for "Web Hosting 2".

Since a satisfactory means of accomplishing that is not available yet, we have created a generic SLA semantic model as an important step toward the objective. The model was created based upon an in-depth comparative analysis of nine commercial SLA contracts/templates comprising over 100 service-level components. It has been successfully validated against 40 other e-business outsourcing SLA contracts since then. The identified primary SLA semantic elements and relationships in the model are illustrated in the paper via a quick reference table of the elements and a UML-based annotated structure diagram, which is then applied to the "Web Hosting 2" contract in Appendix A.

We note that our SLA semantic model points to a systematic means of identifying and structuring necessary service-level reporting modules, and a generic means of choosing and integrating necessary SLM modules for time-sensitively processing quality management alerts according to business-oriented SLM objectives. A full appreciation of the model would also provide valuable insight into both the data flows required to support timely business impact assessment of each quality management alert and a common representation framework for the essential elements that comprise the model, such that the elements can be systematically developed to accommodate a wide variety of SLA contract types. We have been developing an SLA/SLM data manager incorporating these aspects as an integral component of our SLA contract execution manager SAM. Our development experience with SAM suggests our SLA semantic model is practical and useful.

References

1. Hiles, A., "The Complete IT Guide to Service Level Agreements - Matching Service Quality to Business Needs", *Rothstein Associates Inc.*, Brookfield, Connecticut, USA, 1999/2000 Edition.
2. Verma, D., "Supporting Service Level Agreements on IP Networks", McMillan Technology Series, 1999.
3. Sturm, R., Morris, W. and Jander, M., "Foundations of Service Level Management", *SAMS*, 2000.
4. ASPIC Best Practices Committee, "A White Paper on Service Level Agreement", *Application Service Provider Industry Consortium*, November 2000.
5. Frey, N., Matlus, R. and Maurer, W., "A Guide to Successful SLA Development and Management", *Gartner Group Research, Strategic Analysis Report*, October 16, 2000.
6. UUNET, "USA Colocation SLA", http://www1.worldcom.com/us/legal/sla/servicessupported/
7. ITAA, "ITAA ASP Service Level Agreement (SLA) Library", Information Technology Association of America, http://www.itaa.org/asp/
8. EarthLink, "Service Agreement", EarthLink, http://www.earthlink.net/biz/broadband/dedicated/agreement/
9. UKERNA, "Service Level Agreement Between JISC and UKERNA". *UKERNA*, April 2001, http://www.jisc-tau.ac.uk/sla/ukerna
10. OMG, "Unified Modeling Language (UML)", *Object Management Group*, http://www.omg.org

Appendix A: An Abridged Web Hosting SLA Contract "Web Hosting 2"

Provider's Service Level Agreement (SLA) standard for Customer's Web Hosting environment is less than four hours per calendar month of downtime, which is an availability of approximately 99.5%. This SLA objective applies to downtime caused by Provider in regard to operation of system software, loading of system software, hardware failure, backup and recovery of files, and connectivity from the server farm to the Internet and from the server farm to the Customer data center. This SLA objective specifically does not include failures caused by Customer, outages associated with contract maintenance provisions, failure of bandwidth connectivity, and external failures outside the Website Hosting Environment.

Availability for the purposes of the SLA objective is based either on Help Desk trouble ticket information or Provider-detected downtime. For problems reported to the Provider Help Desk trouble ticket system, opening of the Help Desk trouble ticket will provide the outage begin time, and the problem resolved time as documented in the Help Desk trouble ticket will provide the end time for that particular outage. For Provider-detected downtime, the outage begin time will be based on the first detection of any outage, and the end time for the outage will be based on the problem resolve time. The amount of downtime in each calendar month will be totaled to determine any failure to meet the SLA objective.

The following table documents the monthly refunds or premiums associated with missing or exceeding the SLA standard for each calendar month.

Duration of SLA Downtime	Amount of Credit or Premium
More than 48 hours in a calendar month	100% credit of monthly charge
More than 36 hours in a calendar month	80% credit of monthly charge
More than 24 hours in a calendar month	60% credit of monthly charge
More than 16 hours in a calendar month	40% credit of monthly charge
More than 8 hours in a calendar month	20% credit of monthly charge
More than 4 hours in a calendar month	10% credit of monthly charge
4 hours or less in a calendar month	None
2 hours or less in a calendar month	10% premium of monthly charge
1 hour or less in a calendar month	20% premium of monthly charge
No downtime in a calendar month	30% premium of monthly charge

In no case shall more than the monthly charge be credited for downtime incurred in a single month.

Credits and premiums will be aggregated and settled on an annual basis. Premiums may be used to offset credits, but will not create an obligation on the part of Customer to pay more than those monthly charges documented in this SOW or subsequent transaction document pertaining to these services. Any payment due from Provider to Customer will be paid by January 31st of the following year.

The credit and premium schedule associated with this Service Level Agreement and described herein will not commence until January 1, 1999; however, Provider will use best efforts to meet the SLA standard.

A Formal and Executable Specification of the Internet Open Trading Protocol

Chun Ouyang, Lars Michael Kristensen*, and Jonathan Billington

Computer Systems Engineering Centre
School of Electrical and Information Engineering
University of South Australia, SA 5095, AUSTRALIA
chun.ouyang@postgrads.unisa.edu.au
{Lars.Kristensen,Jonathan.Billington}@unisa.edu.au

Abstract. The *Internet Open Trading Protocol* (IOTP) is being developed by the Internet Engineering Task Force for electronic commerce (e-commerce) over the Internet. The core of IOTP is a set of trading transactions that reflects the most common trading activities in the real world. We apply the formal method of Coloured Petri Nets (CP-nets) to construct an abstract executable specification of IOTP's trading transaction protocols. The formal semantics of CP-nets allows us to investigate the termination properties of the transactions using state space techniques. This investigation has revealed deficiencies in the termination of IOTP trading transactions, demonstrating the benefit of applying formal methods to the specification and verification of e-commerce protocols.

1 Introduction

The *Internet Open Trading Protocol* (IOTP) [2] focuses on business-to-consumer trading transactions. A main design goal of IOTP is the encapsulation of different payment protocols such as the *Secure Electronic Transaction* (SET) protocol [19] and the *Mondex Value Transfer Protocol* (VTP) [9]. The development of IOTP is in an early stage with research groups and companies working on the first trial implementations of IOTP [5,17] based on the *informal* protocol specification given in RFC 2801 [2]. No complete implementation of IOTP currently exists, and there are still several open research issues concerning IOTP. One of these is to validate and verify the functional correctness of IOTP. Ensuring the correctness of complex e-commerce protocols is a challenging task, and informal methods are in most cases inadequate.

Formal methods [4] have proven to be a powerful tool for investigating the correctness of communication protocols, including e-commerce protocols. The main advantage of using formal methods in protocol engineering is that they result in unambiguous protocol specifications amenable to computer-aided verification. Related work on applying formal methods to the modelling and analysis of e-commerce protocols and trading procedures can be found in [15,20,14,8]. None of them address the formal specification and analysis of IOTP.

---

* Supported by the Danish Natural Science Research Council.

K. Bauknecht, A M. Tjoa, G. Quirchmayr (Eds.): EC-Web 2002, LNCS 2455, pp. 377–387, 2002.

Coloured Petri Nets (CP-nets or CPNs) [6,7] are a formal method for the specification, design, simulation, and verification of concurrent systems. CP-nets are a graphically oriented modelling language capable of expressing concurrency, synchronization, non-determinism, and system concepts at different levels of abstraction. CP-nets are a combination of Petri Nets [16] and the functional programming language Standard ML (SML) [18]. Petri Nets are used to model concurrency, synchronization, and resource sharing, whereas SML is used for modelling data manipulation, and for creating compact and parameterisable models. CP-nets have previously been successfully applied for modelling and analysis of a wide range of communication protocols [1].

In this paper we apply CP-nets and the supporting Design/CPN computer tool [10] to construct an executable specification of the trading transactions that are the core of IOTP. The model is analysed for correctness. Our initial work [12] modelled and analysed just the IOTP Deposit transaction. In [11] we proposed a simplified protocol architecture for IOTP. The contribution of this paper is an improved modelling approach towards developing a formal protocol specification for IOTP, together with a detailed investigation of the termination properties of the trading transactions. Section 2 gives a brief introduction to IOTP using a purchase transaction as an example. Section 3 presents selected parts of the CPN model, and Sect. 4 presents the verification results. Finally, in Sect. 5 we summarize our contribution and discuss future work.

2   The Internet Open Trading Protocol

IOTP [2] defines five *trading transactions*[1]: *Purchase*, *Refund*, *Deposit*, *Withdrawal*, and *Value Exchange*, where the Value Exchange transaction supports the conversion of one currency to another. Below we use the Purchase transaction to illustrate the basic operation of IOTP.

Purchase transaction. Figure 1 shows a possible sequence of messages exchanged between the parties involved in a Purchase transaction. Each column of the message sequence chart corresponds to one of the four[2] IOTP *trading roles*: *Consumer*, *Merchant*, *Payment Handler*, and *Delivery Handler*. The Payment Handler (intuitively a bank) receives money from the Consumer on behalf of the Merchant and the Delivery Handler (intuitively a courier firm) delivers the goods to the Consumer on behalf of the Merchant. IOTP defines three trading phases: *Offer*, *Payment*, and *Delivery*, as shown in Fig. 1.

The first phase is the Trading Protocol Options (TPO) Offer (events 1-4). The Consumer decides to buy goods, and sends an Offer Request for purchasing (event 1) to the Merchant. Upon receiving the Offer Request, the Merchant starts the transaction by offering the Consumer a list of TPO (event 2). This includes the available payment methods and associated payment protocols. The Consumer

---

[1] These are referred to as Payment-related IOTP transactions in [2].

[2] IOTP defines a fifth trading role called Merchant Customer Care Provider, but this trading role is currently not used in any transactions.

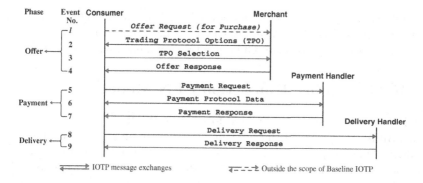

Fig. 1. A possible message flow in a Purchase transaction.

chooses one of the options, and sends it back as a TPO Selection (event 3). The Merchant uses the selection to create and send back an Offer Response (event 4), which contains details of the goods to be purchased together with payment and delivery instructions.

The second phase concerns Payment (events 5-7). After checking the Offer Response, the Consumer sends the Payment Handler a Payment Request (event 5). The Payment Handler checks the Payment Request, and if valid, the payment is conducted using Payment Protocol Data exchanges (event 6) as determined by the encapsulated payment protocol (e.g., SET). The Payment Handler then sends a Payment Response (event 7) containing the payment result (e.g., a receipt).

The third phase is Delivery (events 8-9). After checking the Payment Response, the Consumer sends the Delivery Handler a Delivery Request (event 8). The Delivery Handler schedules the delivery and sends the Consumer a Delivery Response (event 9) containing details of the delivery, and possibly the actual delivery if the goods are electronic (e.g., an e-journal).

Trading exchanges and transactions. We call the three phases Offer, Payment, and Delivery *trading exchanges*[3] which may occur in different variants. For example, event 3 may or may not take place in an Offer exchange, which results in the distinction between a *Brand Dependent Offer* and a *Brand Independent Offer*. The Brand Dependent Offer occurs when the Merchant offers some additional benefit (e.g., price discount) in the Offer Response, *depending* on the specific *payment brand* chosen in the Consumer's TPO Selection. In the Brand Independent Offer, the Offer Response is *independent* of the *payment brand* selected by the Consumer, and the Merchant can send a combined *TPO and Offer Response* message since the Consumer's TPO Selection is not required. IOTP also supports an *Authentication* exchange allowing one trading role (the *Authenticator*) to verify the bona fides of another trading role (the *Authenticatee*). All IOTP trading transactions can be expressed as combinations of these trading exchanges. A Purchase transaction consists of an optional Authentication, an Offer, a Payment, and optionally a Delivery. The Deposit, Withdrawal, and

---

[3] This is defined according to the concept of *document exchanges* given in [2].

Refund transactions start with an optional Authentication followed by an Offer and a Payment. Finally, a Value Exchange transaction starts with an optional Authentication followed by an Offer and two Payment exchanges in sequence.

3   IOTP Trading Transaction CPN Model

A CPN model has been constructed for each of the five IOTP trading transactions. All five CPN models have a similar structure and share a common set of modules. Due to space limitations, we focus on selected parts of the Purchase transaction CPN model, and only informally introduce the concepts of CP-nets [6,7]. The Purchase transaction involves all four trading roles and all types of trading exchanges, and is thus a representative example.

Overview. The *hierarchy page* of Fig. 2 provides an overview of the *pages* (modules) constituting the CPN model. Each node in Fig. 2 represents a page labelled with its *page name* and *page number*. An *arc* between two page nodes indicates that the destination page is a *subpage* (submodule) of the source page.

The Purchase page (top of Fig. 2) provides the most abstract view of a Purchase transaction and has five subpages. Four of these subpages: Consumer, Merchant, PHandler and DHandler correspond to the four trading roles involved in a Purchase transaction, and they specify the Purchase transaction protocol for each of the trading roles. We refer to these pages as *trading role pages*. The last subpage of Purchase is Transport (bottom of Fig. 2). It models the transport medium over which the trading roles communicate, e.g., HTTP. Each subpage of a trading role page specifies a trading exchange used by that trading role. As an example, the page Consumer has six subpages modelling the six different exchanges at the Consumer side. The subpage Authenticatee models an Authentication exchange where the Consumer acts as the Authenticatee. The subpages BrdDepOffer_C and BrdIndepOffer_C specify the Brand Dependent Offer and Brand Independent Offer for the Consumer. The subpages Payment_C and Delivery_C correspond to a Payment and a Delivery, respectively. The subpage PayDelivery_C specifies a Payment with Delivery exchange that supports

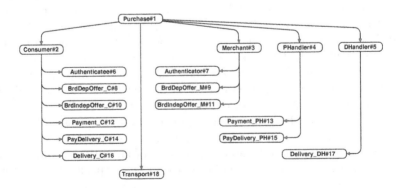

Fig. 2. The hierarchy page of the Purchase transaction CPN model.

combined payment and delivery. Since a trading exchange involves two trading roles, we have modelled each exchange as a pair of subpages - one for each trading role. For example, the subpages PayDelivery_C and PayDelivery_PH represent a Payment with Delivery exchange between the Consumer and Payment Handler.

Transaction Level Modelling. The transaction level is specified by the four trading role pages. We illustrate our approach with the Consumer page, since the Consumer is the only trading role involved in all trading exchanges. The other three trading role pages Merchant, PHandler, and DHandler are similar to the Consumer page. Because of space limitations, we cannot present our exchange level models. Figure 3 depicts the page Consumer that models the Purchase transaction at the Consumer side. It is the subpage corresponding to the Consumer page node in Fig. 2.

The ellipses in Fig. 3 are *places*, used to model message buffers and Consumer states. The places named Send and Receive model message buffers through which the Consumer sends and receives messages from the other trading roles. The two Send places conceptually represent the same place, but have been drawn as two to reduce the number of arc crossings. A similar remark applies to the two Receive places. The remaining six places are used to model the control flow and the internal state of the trading role entity. The state of a CPN model is determined by the distribution of *tokens* on the places of the CPN model. Each place has an associated *colour set* (type) that determines the kind (colour) of tokens that can reside on that place. A state of a CPN model is also called a

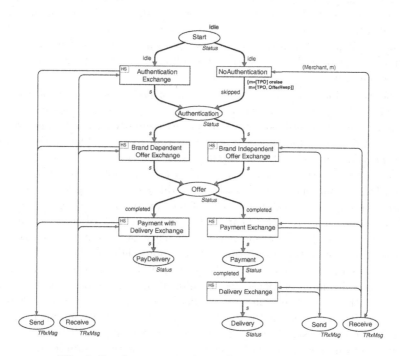

Fig. 3. Purchase transaction – Consumer trading role.

Table 1. Colour sets for modelling trading role states and IOTP messages.

1 color Status = **with** idle | completed | skipped | cancelled | stop;
2 color TradingRole = **with** Consumer | Merchant | PHandler | DHandler;
3 color ProcessState = **with** CompletedOk | Failed;
4 color TradingBlk = **union** AuthReq + AuthResp + AuthStatus: ProcessState + TPO + TPOSelection + OfferResp + PayReq + PayExch + PayResp + DelivReq + DelivResp + Cancel;
5 color IotpMsg = **list** TradingBlk;
6 color TRxMsg = **product** TradingRole * IotpMsg;

marking. The colour set of a place is by convention written below a place. Table 1 lists the definition of the colour sets used in Fig. 3. The colour set Status is an enumeration type containing five values. The value idle is used for modelling the state where the trading role is idle, skipped when the transaction skips an optional trading exchange, completed when a trading exchange is completed, cancelled when the transaction is cancelled, and stop when the transaction has terminated. TradingRole is also an enumeration type with a value for each trading role, and IotpMsg models the set of IOTP messages exchanged between trading roles. The declarations are written in Standard ML [18] and derived from [2].

The rectangles in Fig. 3 are *transitions*, used to model the actions of the Consumer. Transitions with an HS-tag in the upper left corner are *substitution transitions*. A substitution transition represents a compound action, and has an associated subpage which models the compound action in detail. The Consumer page has six substitution transitions corresponding to the six trading exchanges of a Purchase transaction. As an example, the substitution transition Authentication Exchange (upper left) abstractly represents the Authentication exchange at the Consumer side. The details of Authentication are modelled in the subpage Authenticatee (see Fig. 2) which is the subpage associated with the Authentication Exchange substitution transition. The other five substitution transitions abstractly represent the corresponding trading exchanges at the Consumer side in a similar way.

The execution of a CPN model consists of *occurrences* of *enabled* ordinary (i.e., non-substitution) transitions removing tokens from places connected to incoming arcs, and adding tokens to places connected to outgoing arcs. The tokens required on input places for a transition to be enabled are specified by *arc expressions* associated with input arcs of the transition. When an enabled transition occurs, the tokens required for the transition to be enabled are removed from input places, and tokens are added to output places according to the arc expressions on the output arcs of the transition. Page Consumer has one ordinary transition: NoAuthentication. In the initial state of the Consumer (i.e., before execution of the transaction starts) place Start contains the token idle. This is specified by the inscription to the upper right of the Start place. The other places initially contain no tokens. When the transaction starts a token will become available on place Receive indicating an incoming message. If this token has the form (Merchant, m) (indicating a message from the Merchant) and m is either a Trading Protocol Options (TPO) or a combined TPO and Offer Response message, the transition NoAuthentication will be enabled. The requirement on m is expressed by the boolean *guard* expression in square brackets positioned next to the NoAuthentication transition. The occurrence of this transition will remove the idle token from place Start, and add a skipped token to place Authentication modelling that the Purchase transaction starts without an Authentication exchange. If m does not satisfy the above requirement, then transitions on the subpage of Authentication Exchange will be enabled, and their occurrences will correspond to the execution of an Authentication exchange. The output arc of the substitution transition Authentication Exchange is annotated by the variable s of type Status. If the Authentication is successful, a completed token will be bound to s and put into place Authentication. Otherwise a cancelled token will be bound to s and put into place Authentication modelling that the transaction is cancelled. The output arcs from place Start to Authentication Exchange and NoAuthentication therefore model the *choice* of whether or not an Authentication exchange occurs at the beginning of the transaction.

A skipped or a completed token on place Authentication signals that the Offer phase can commence. Here there is a choice between a Brand Dependent Offer and a Brand Independent Offer. Depending on whether the Offer exchange is successful or has been cancelled, a completed or a cancelled token will be put into place Offer. Similarly, there is also a choice between a Payment exchange and a Payment with Delivery exchange. In the course of executing the transaction, tokens will be added and removed from the places Send and Receive, according to the messages being sent and received by the Consumer.

4   Transaction Termination Properties

In this section we apply the state space technique of CP-nets to investigate and formally reason about the termination properties of the Purchase transaction. In state space analysis we compute all reachable states and state changes of the CPN model, and represent these as a directed graph (called a state space). Nodes in the state space represent states (markings), and arcs represent occurrences of transitions. This is essentially model checking [3] of finite-state systems, with the exception that in the Design/CPN tool, *query functions* written in ML are used for investigating properties of the system instead of temporal logic formulae. The full state space of the Purchase transaction CPN model has 116 nodes and 136 arcs, and is generated automatically in less than five seconds on a standard PC.

Inspection of Terminal States. The first step is to determine the possible states in which the Purchase transaction may terminate. A *dead marking* of a CPN model is a marking (state) with no enabled transitions. The set of dead markings therefore represents the terminal states of a Purchase transaction. The CPN model of the Purchase transaction has 12 dead markings. Table 2 lists the corresponding states of each trading role in the 12 dead markings. For each dead marking, the state of each trading role (i.e., idle, wait, cancel, and stop) was obtained from the tokens present on the places modelling the internal states of the trading role. The subscript of a state specifies the trading exchange in question, e.g., Authentication (A), Offer (O), Payment (P), Delivery (D), and

Table 2. Trading role states in the dead markings.

Dead marking	Trading role			
	Consumer	Merchant	Payment Handler	Delivery Handler
106	$stop_P$	$stop_O$	$stop_P$	idle
107	$stop_{PD}$	$stop_O$	$stop_{PD}$	idle
115	$stop_D$	$stop_O$	$stop_P$	$stop_D$
23	$cancelled_A$	$cancelled_A$	idle	idle
35	$cancelled_O$	$cancelled_O$	idle	idle
70	$cancelled_P$	$stop_O$	$cancelled_{PD}$	idle
76	$cancelled_{PD}$	$stop_O$	$cancelled_P$	idle
101	$wait_P$	$stop_O$	$stop_{vPD}$	idle
104	$wait_{PD}$	$stop_O$	$stop_P$	idle
72	$cancelled_P$	$stop_O$	$cancelled_P$	idle
74	$cancelled_{PD}$	$stop_O$	$cancelled_{PD}$	idle
116	$cancelled_D$	$stop_O$	$stop_P$	$cancelled_D$

Payment with Delivery (PD). The state wait is used where the trading role is waiting to receive a message *within* a trading exchange. No subscript is used for idle as it represents the idle state of a trading role before execution of the transaction starts. In the following, marking n is written as M_n.

M_{106}, M_{107} and M_{115} represent the three possible successful terminations of a Purchase transaction. In M_{106} and M_{107}, the Purchase transaction is completed at the end of a Payment or a Payment with Delivery exchange, respectively. The Delivery Handler is therefore never active and is in state idle at the end of the transaction. In M_{115}, the Purchase transaction is completed with a Delivery exchange after the Payment, and all trading roles terminate in state stop. M_{23} and M_{35} are expected and correspond to the transaction being cancelled during an Authentication or an Offer exchange between the Consumer and the Merchant.

Problem 1: Lack of Synchronization between Consumer and Payment Handler. The 4 *undesired* terminal states, represented by M_{70}, M_{76}, M_{101}, and M_{104}, show that the Consumer and the Payment Handler execute different trading exchanges, when they should be executing the same exchange. For example, the path in the state space leading to M_{70} reveals that the Consumer is executing a Payment exchange, while the Payment Handler is executing a Payment with Delivery exchange. Similar lack of synchronization is revealed by the paths leading to M_{76}, M_{101} and M_{104}. M_{101} and M_{104} also reveal an *unspecified reception*, where the Consumer is still in state wait since it cannot process the message sent from the Payment Handler that is executing a different exchange.

The reason for this lack of synchronization is that IOTP does not specify how the Payment Handler is notified about which of the trading exchanges (a Payment or a Payment with Delivery) is to be executed. According to [2], a Payment or Payment with Delivery exchange is initiated by the Consumer sending a Payment Request message to the Payment Handler. This message however does not specify whether a Payment or a Payment with Delivery is to take place. Upon receiving such a message, the Payment Handler thus cannot tell whether a Payment or a Payment with Delivery is initiated by the Consumer. The result is the lack of synchronization in IOTP when executing either a Payment or a Payment with Delivery exchange between Consumer and Payment Handler.

One solution to this problem is to define a message that would be sent from the Merchant to notify the Payment Handler which exchange is to occur. This requires server-to-server communication, which is beyond the scope of the current version of IOTP (version 1.0) [2]. Another solution is to add a *Delivery Component* into the Payment Request message sent from the Consumer to the Payment Handler. The Delivery component is defined [2] in the Offer Response message. It contains the information about the delivery to be made, and has an attribute named *DelivAndPayResp* indicating whether or not a Payment with Delivery exchange is to occur. This solution is within the scope of IOTP version 1.0, and we have modified the original CPN model to reflect this solution. The full state space of the modified CPN model has 88 nodes and 104 arcs. In this CPN model the 4 undesired terminal states are not present, and only the other 8 dead markings remain. Hence this lack of synchronization no longer occurs. We can also show that the Purchase transaction will *eventually* terminate in one of these 8 dead markings, demonstrating the absence of livelock.

Problem 2: Inconsistent Terminal States. The transaction can also be cancelled during a Payment or a Payment with Delivery exchange, as indicated by M_{72} and M_{74}, respectively. M_{116} represents the state where the transaction is cancelled during a Delivery exchange. These three dead markings exhibit deficiencies related to cancellation of a Purchase transaction. As indicated by M_{72} and M_{74}, the Merchant is not informed when a cancellation occurs between the Consumer and the Payment Handler during a Payment or a Payment with Delivery exchange (the Merchant is still in the stop state). In this case, the Merchant may purchase goods from the manufacturer but unexpectedly cannot sell these goods to the Consumer, resulting in an inventory problem. Similarly in M_{116}, neither the Merchant nor the Payment Handler is notified of a cancellation between the Consumer and the Delivery Handler during a Delivery exchange. In this case, the Consumer will not receive the goods that have been paid for, and may not be able to receive a refund. A possible solution is to inform the Merchant and Payment Handler about the final outcome of the transaction, i.e., whether the transaction is successfully completed or has been cancelled. We plan to model and analyse this solution in the future.

5   Conclusions

We have presented a hierarchical CPN model of the IOTP trading transactions based on RFC 2801 [2]. The analysis has revealed deficiencies in the Purchase transaction procedure in terms of 1) lack of synchronization of a Payment exchange and a Payment with Delivery exchange by Consumer and Payment Handler, and 2) inconsistent states of the trading roles upon termination in the case of cancellation. The former problem is specific to a Purchase transaction, whereas the second problem is also present in other IOTP trading transactions. In the former case we have proposed a solution, modified the CPN model accordingly and proved it to be correct. This demonstrates that the CPN model can be used to effectively evaluate modifications to IOTP transactions.

In the current model of IOTP trading transactions, we have made some simplifying assumptions, which are primarily related to IOTP error handling. For example, we have only investigated the situation where all IOTP messages are well-formed. Besides error handling, *arbitrary* cancellation during a transaction has not yet been taken into consideration. As part of future work we plan to include error handling and arbitrary cancellation into our CPN model. IOTP requires improvement due to the identified deficiencies related to cancellation (Problem 2). Investigating additional properties such as atomicity, fairness, and non-repudiation of IOTP transactions is also part of future work.

In parallel with the development of the *protocol* specification presented in this paper, we have also proposed a formal *service* specification for IOTP using CP-nets [13]. A challenging part of future work is to investigate whether the CPN protocol specification of IOTP presented in this paper formally conforms to, i.e., is a faithful refinement of, the CPN service specification for IOTP.

References

1. J. Billington, M. Diaz, and G. Rozenberg, editors. *Application of Petri Nets to Communication Networks: Advances in Petri Nets*, Volume 1605, *Lecture Notes in Computer Science*, Springer-Verlag, Berlin, 1999.
2. D. Burdett. *Internet Open Trading Protocol IOTP Version 1.0.* IETF Trade Working Group, April 2000. Available via: http://www.ietf.org/rfc/rfc2801.txt.
3. E. Clarke, O. Grumberg, and D. Peled. *Model Checking.* The MIT Press, 1999.
4. E. M. Clarke and J.M Wing. Formal Methods: State of the Art and Future Directions. *ACM Computing Surveys*, 28(4):626–643, December 1996.
5. JOTP Open Trading Protocol Toolkit For Java. URL: http://www.livebiz.com/.
6. K. Jensen. *Coloured Petri Nets. Basic Concepts, Analysis Methods and Practical Use. Vol 1-3.* Monographs in Theoretical Computer Science. Springer-Verlag, 1997.
7. L.M. Kristensen, S. Christensen, and K. Jensen. The Practitioner's Guide to Coloured Petri Nets. *International Journal on Software Tools for Technology Transfer*, 2(2):98–132, 1998. Springer-Verlag.
8. R.M. Lee. Documentary Petri Nets: A Modelling Representation for Electronic Trade Procedure. In *Business Process Management*, Volume 1806, *Lecture Notes in Computer Science*, pages 259–375. Springer-Verlag, 2000.
9. Mondex. URL: http://www.mondexusa.com/html/content/technolo/technolo.htm.
10. Design/CPN Online. URL: http://www.daimi.au.dk/designCPN/.
11. C. Ouyang, L.M. Kristensen, and J. Billington. An Improved Architectural Specification of the Internet Open Trading Protocol. In *Proceedings of 3rd Workshop and Tutorial on Practical Use of Coloured Petri Nets and the CPN Tools (CPN'01)*, pages 119–137. DAIMI PB-554, University of Aarhus, ISSN 0105-8517, 2001.
12. C. Ouyang, L.M. Kristensen, and J. Billington. Towards Modelling and Analysis of the Internet Open Trading Protocol Transactions using Coloured Petri Nets. In *Proc of 11th Annual International Symposium of the International Council on System Engineering (INCOSE)*, 2001. CD-ROM 6.7.3.

13. C. Ouyang, L.M. Kristensen, and J. Billington. A Formal Service Specification of the Internet Open Trading Protocol. In *Proceedings of 23rd International Conference on Application and Theory of Petri Nets*, Volume 2360, *Lecture Notes in Computer Science*, Springer-Verlag, 2002. To appear.

14. M. Papa, O. Bremer, J. Hale, and S. Shenoi. Formal Analysis of E-commerce Protocols. In *Proceedings of 5th. International Symposium on Autonomous Decentralized Systems*, pages 19–28. IEEE Computer Society, 2001.

15. I. Ray and I. Ray. Failure Analysis of an E-commerce Protocol using Model Checking. In *Proceedings of 2nd International Workshop on Advanced Issues of E-Commerce and Web-Based Information Systems*, pages 176–183. IEEE Computer Society, 2000.

16. W. Reisig and G. Rozenberg, editors. *Lectures on Petri Nets: Advances in Petri Nets. Volume I: Basic Models*, Volume 1491, *Lecture Notes in Computer Science*, Springer-Verlag, Berlin, 1998.

17. Hitachi SMILEs.
    URL: http://www.hitachi.co.jp/Div/nfs/whats_new/smiles.html.

18. J. D. Ullman. *Elements of ML Programming*. Prentice-Hall, 1998.

19. Visa and MasterCard. *SET Secure Electronic Transaction Specification. Version 1.0. Vol 1-3*, May 1997. URL: http://www.setco.org/set_specifications.html.

20. P. Yolum and M. P. Singh. Commitment-based enhancement of e-commerce protocols. In *Proceedings of IEEE 9th International Workshops on Enabling Technologies: Infrastructure for Collaborative Enterprises*, pages 278–283, 2000.

Using EMV Cards to Protect E-commerce Transactions

Vorapranee Khu-Smith and Chris J. Mitchell

Information Security Group, Royal Holloway, University of London,
Egham, Surrey, TW20 0EX, United Kingdom
{V.Khu-Smith, C.Mitchell}@rhul.ac.uk

Abstract. A growing number of payment transactions are now being made over the Internet. Although transactions are typically made over a secure channel provided using SSL or TLS, there remain some security risks. Meanwhile, EMV-compliant IC cards are being introduced to reduce fraud for conventional debit/credit transactions. In this paper, we propose a way of using EMV IC cards for secure remote payments, such as those made via the Internet, with the goal of providing protection against some of these residual risks. The scheme described in this paper is based on the EMV 2000 Integrated Circuit Card Specification for Payment Systems, which is first outlined. Threats to, and advantages and disadvantages of, the scheme are also examined.

Keywords: EMV cards; e-commerce security; payment protocol

1 Introduction

The Internet is now widely used for electronic commerce. Consumers typically make a payment with a debit/credit card and SSL/TLS is used to protect the transaction details against eavesdroppers. Although SSL/TLS has become a de facto standard means to secure an electronic transaction made over the Internet, it only provides security for the communications link between the consumer PC and the merchant server. As a result, there are a number of security risks in such use of SSL/TLS, as pointed out in [6]. One of these is the lack of client authentication and the associated lack of client non-repudiation. Even though SSL/TLS offers client-side authentication, it is optional and often bypassed. Consequently, it is not easy to verify if the client is the legitimate cardholder and there is no way to determine if the client actually has the card. A malicious user, who may have obtained a card number by some means, can then use it to make payments over the Internet at the expense of the legitimate cardholder.

Meanwhile, for transactions taking place at the Point of Sale (POS), a variety of frauds are possible against debit/credit card transactions. In recent years this has led the major card brands to develop an industry standard means of employing IC cards to replace the existing magnetic stripe cards, with a view to both reducing fraud and reducing the costs associated with online transaction authorisation at the POS. This collaboration between Europay, MasterCard

K. Bauknecht, A M. Tjoa, G. Quirchmayr (Eds.): EC-Web 2002, LNCS 2455, pp. 388–399, 2002.

and Visa resulted in the EMV card/terminal specifications, the latest version of which are known as EMV 2000 [1,2,3,4]. The EMV specifications standardise interactions between a debit/credit IC card and a terminal.

In an annex to Book 3 of EMV 2000 [3], the use of an EMV card and the Secure Electronic Transaction (SET) protocol [5] to conduct an e-commerce transaction is defined. However, SET (which provides security for an entire e-commerce transaction) has not been adopted to any significant extent—indeed, it is not clear if it will ever become widely used. Although the integration of EMV and SET removes some of the issues with SET, notably it simplifies user registration, there still remain large obstacles to its adoption.

As a result, in this paper we consider an alternative way in which the growing use of EMV IC cards can be used to enhance the security of e-commerce transactions. The goal is to design a scheme whereby EMV cards can be used to enhance e-commerce transaction security, and hence reduce fraud, whilst imposing minimal overheads on the involved parties. The paper begins with an overview of the EMV payment system. We subsequently propose the use of EMV cards for Internet electronic transaction processing. Threats to the proposed scheme are then analysed, and its advantages and disadvantages are considered.

2   An Overview of EMV

In a debit/credit card payment system, there are four major parties, namely a client, a merchant, an acquiring bank and a card issuing bank. A client, i.e. the cardholder, makes a payment using a card issued by the card issuing bank (issuer) for something purchased from a merchant. The acquiring bank (acquirer) is the financial institution with which a merchant has a contractual arrangement for receiving (acquiring) card payments. The payment model is shown in Figure 1.

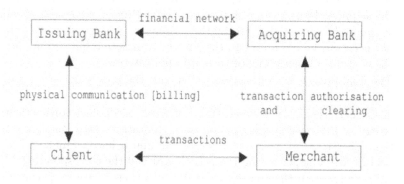

Fig. 1. Debit/credit card payment system model

The debit/credit card payment system is the model underlying the EMV system defined in EMV 2000 [1,2,3,4]. The EMV transaction process involves the following steps. Note that the order of the steps is not completely fixed; for example, cardholder verification can precede data authentication.

1. When the IC card is inserted, the terminal reads application data from the card and performs Terminal Risk Management. Terminal Risk Management provides positive issuer authorisation for high-value transactions and ensures that transactions initiated from IC cards go online periodically to prevent threats that might be undetectable in an offline environment.
2. The Data Authentication process enables the terminal to verify the authenticity of the card. There are two options for Data Authentication, namely Static and Dynamic Data Authentication. Not all EMV cards are capable of performing Dynamic Data Authentication.
3. After successful Data Authentication, the Process Restrictions are performed to determine the compatibility of the terminal and IC card applications.
4. Cardholder authenticity is verified by PIN entry. The PIN verification process can be either online to the issuer or offline to the card.
5. After successful Cardholder Authentication, the terminal performs Terminal Action Analysis, which is the first decision on whether the transaction should be approved offline, declined offline, or an online authorisation performed.
6. The IC card then performs Card Risk Management to protect the card issuer against fraud or excessive credit risk. Details of card risk management algorithms are specific to the issuer and are not specified by EMV.
7. The IC card performs Card Action Analysis to decide whether the transaction will be processed offline, or will need online authorisation. If the decision is offline processing, the transaction is processed immediately. If the transaction is to be processed online, Online Processing will be performed to ensure that the issuer can review and authorise or reject transactions that are outside acceptable limits of risk defined by the issuer, the payment system, or the acquirer. Issuers can also perform Script Processing, enabling command scripts to be sent to the card by the terminal to perform functions that may not necessarily be relevant to the current transaction but are important for the continued functioning of the card application.
8. The final process is Completion which ends the processing of a transaction.

In essence, the EMV scheme supports both cardholder authentication by PIN entry and IC card authentication through Static or Dynamic Data Authentication. Therefore, an unscrupulous user will find it hard to make a fraudulent transaction without possessing the actual card and the corresponding PIN.

We next focus on the security-related interactions between IC card and terminal. This is of particular interest here, since in the scheme proposed below the user PC plays the role of the merchant terminal and interacts with a merchant server across the Internet. The merchant server communicates with the acquirer, e.g. using the same interface as is currently used for merchant terminal-acquirer communications. An acquirer and an issuer typically communicate via a brand-specific network, which is outside the scope of this paper.

2.1   Card Authentication

The EMV specifications allow card authentication to be either offline or online. The decision regarding whether to perform online authentication can be made by the IC card or the terminal at the time of the transaction.

Static data authentication (SDA). SDA involves the terminal verifying the integrity of static data signed by the card issuer and stored in the IC card. In this case the card does not need its own signature key pair.

SDA is supported by a two-level key management hierarchy. The top-level certification authority (CA) is the card scheme, e.g. Visa or Mastercard. This CA certifies the issuer public keys. The static data is signed using the appropriate issuer private key and stored in the card, along with the CA-signed certificate for the issuer public key. A terminal with a trusted copy of the CA public key can then verify the issuer public key certificate and hence can verify the signature on the static data, thereby verifying the IC card.

Dynamic data authentication (DDA). Like SDA, DDA is based on digital signatures, although in DDA the card has its own key pair. The terminal sends an Internal Authentication Command (IAC), including an unpredictable number, to the card. The card then digitally signs the IAC data. The terminal verifies the signature to authenticate the dynamic data and hence the card.

DDA is supported by a three-level key management hierarchy. The first and second level CAs are the card scheme and issuer respectively, and the card public key is certified by its issuer. In order to verify the signed data, the terminal needs to contain the top-level CA public key to verify the issuer public key certificate. The issuer public key is then used to verify the IC card public key certificate. The terminal can then verify the card signature.

2.2   Cardholder Verification

The cardholder is verified using a PIN. The EMV Specifications require every EMV card to possess a method to limit the number of unsuccessful PIN tries.

PIN verification may occur offline to the IC card, or online to the card issuer (or a third party acting for the card issuer). For offline verification the PIN may be encrypted between the PIN pad and the IC card. A key pair assigned especially for PIN encryption or the key pair used in DDA can be used for encryption. In either case, the card public key is first retrieved by the PIN pad or a secure terminal component. The IC card also sends a random number to be concatenated with the entered PIN. The result is encrypted and sent back to the card. The card then decrypts the ciphertext, checks the random number and verifies whether the recovered PIN matches the one stored in the card.

2.3   Application Cryptograms

Transaction message integrity and origin authentication are guaranteed by the use of Application Cryptograms (ACs), generated by the IC card and issuer using shared-secret-based Message Authentication Codes (MACs). There are four types of ACs, namely Transaction Certificates (TCs), Application Authentication Cryptograms (AACs), Authorisation Request Cryptogram (ARQCs) and Authorisation Response Cryptograms (ARPCs). If the transaction is approved offline, the card generates a TC. If the transaction is declined offline, then an AAC is generated. If the transaction needs to be approved online, the card generates an ARQC which will be sent to the issuer. The issuer then responses with an ARPC. As in the offline case, if the transaction is approved by the issuer, the card computes a TC; otherwise, an AAC is computed.

As mentioned above, ACs are cryptographically protected using a MAC. The issuer and card share a long term secret key MK_{AC} known as the card AC master key. This master key is used to generate an AC session key (SK_{AC}) which is used to compute the AC MACs. The session key SK_{AC} is computed as a function of MK_{AC} and diversification data R; the value R must be different for each session key generation to prevent replay attacks. Note also that, to avoid the issuer having to store the master key MK_{AC} for every card, each such master key is derived from an issuer master key MK_I. This key derivation takes as input the Primary Account Number (PAN) and the PAN sequence number.

3   Using EMV Cards for E-commerce Transactions

We now describe how an EMV-compliant IC card can be used to conduct remote transactions. The system architecture is described, as are the transaction processing procedures and how security services are provided.

3.1   System Architecture

The e-commerce payment system we describe employs five main components: an EMV card, an IC card reader, the Cardholder System, the Merchant Server, and the Acquirer. We now examine each of these system components.

EMV card and IC card reader. The tasks of the EMV card are the same as those given in the EMV Specifications. The card is assumed to be a completely 'standard' DDA-capable EMV card — indeed, the scheme is designed so that existing EMV cards can be used to support e-commerce security without any modification. The EMV card interacts with a combination of system components, i.e. the card reader, the Cardholder System and the Merchant Server, just as it does with a merchant POS terminal.

The IC card reader, which can include a PIN pad, is required for interactions between the cardholder and the card, and between the card and the Cardholder System. Physical requirements for this device are similar to those in [1].

Cardholder System. The Cardholder System is the combination of hardware and software required to interact with the cardholder, the IC card, and the Merchant Server. The Cardholder System is assumed here to be a combination of a user PC and special purpose software which could, for example, be either a small program distributed with the IC card by the issuer or, to make system installation maximally transparent, a Web browser applet. The source of cardholder system software is not an issue we address here but it might be the card issuer, the card brand, or an associated party. The Cardholder System is jointly responsible, along with the IC card reader and the Merchant Server, for performing the tasks of the terminal defined in the EMV specification.

Merchant Server and Acquirer. The Merchant Server is the component that interacts with the Cardholder System to support electronic payments. The Merchant Server also interacts with the Acquirer. As specified above, the Merchant Server, the Cardholder System and the IC card reader collectively fulfill the role of the EMV merchant terminal. The Acquirer interacts with the issuer via the financial network to support transaction authorisation. To support SDA and DDA, the Merchant Server needs a trusted copy of the CA public key to enable it to verify issuer public key certificates.

3.2   Transaction Processing Procedures

In this section, we describe the processes necessary to complete a payment transaction. The protocol for using an EMV card for an e-commerce transaction is also described. The decision about which purchase to make are outside the scope of this paper — we simply assume that the cardholder and the merchant wish to perform a specified transaction.

The transaction flow is shown in Figure 2. In the protocol description, $X\|Y$ denotes the concatenation of data items X and Y. Other terms are defined as they arise in the text below.

Card authentication and process restriction. A transaction begins after the cardholder has decided to make a purchase. The Merchant Server and the EMV card first perform SDA (step 1 in Figure 2). In this process, the Merchant first verifies the issuer public key certificate using its copy of the CA public key. The issuer signature on the Static Authentication Data (SAD), sent by the IC card, is then verified. Data communicated between the Merchant Server and the card are sent and received via the Cardholder System.

After successful SDA, the Merchant Server generates a random number, which is sent in the IAC, and constructs the purchase information (PI), which may contain a description of goods, the price, the date, and transaction id. The Merchant Server then sends $IAC\|PI$ to the Cardholder System (step 2).

Upon receipt of the above message, the Cardholder System displays the purchase information to the cardholder and checks for the presence of an EMV card. It then forwards the IAC to the card (step 3). The IC card computes the signature $S_{IC}(DAD)$ and sends it to the Cardholder System along with the IC card's public key certificate Cert$_{IC}$ (step 4), where DAD is the Dynamic Authentication Data containing the random number sent in the IAC. In step 5, the Cardholder System sends $S_{IC}(DAD)\|$Cert$_{IC}$, to the Merchant Server. Since the issuer public key is used and verified in the SDA process, the Merchant Server now only needs to verify the card certificate and then the signature $S_{IC}(DAD)$.

After successful card authentication, Process Restriction (step 6) is performed. Data Authentication and Process Restriction take place between Mer-

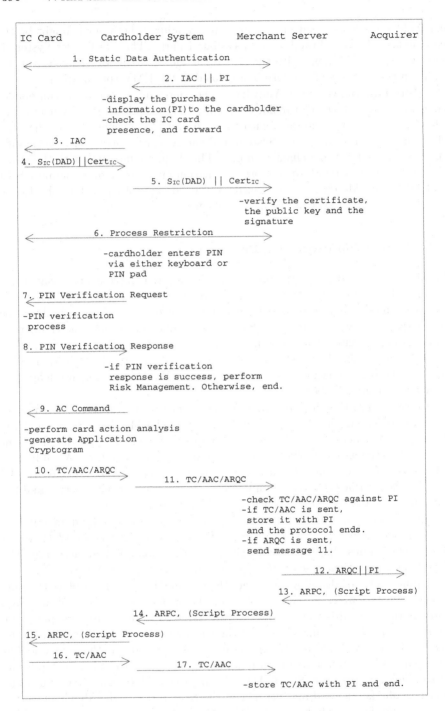

Fig. 2. Transaction flow for remote EMV

chant Server and card, and the Cardholder System simply forwards messages. Note that these processes remain unchanged from the EMV specification.

Cardholder verification. The Cardholder System next requests the cardholder to enter the PIN; PIN verification can take place online or offline. To perform offline verification, the Cardholder System sends a PIN Verification Request message to the IC card (step 7). The PIN does not need to be encrypted, since the environment is under cardholder control. On receipt of the PIN Verification Request, the EMV card returns a PIN Verification Response message (step 8) which indicates whether PIN verification is successful. If so, the Cardholder System performs Terminal Risk Management; otherwise, the protocol ends.

Terminal risk management and action analysis. After successful cardholder verification, the Cardholder System performs Terminal Risk Management and Terminal Action Analysis. These two processes are as in the EMV specification. The Cardholder System then generates and sends an AC Command to the EMV card (step 9).

Card action analysis. The IC card first performs its own risk management and then executes the Card Action Analysis to determine whether the transaction is to be approved offline, rejected offline, or processed online. In step 10, an AC will be generated by the IC card and sent to the Cardholder System. The Cardholder System in turn forwards it to the Merchant Server (step 11) where the AC will be checked against the *PI*.

Offline approval. If the transaction is approved offline, the card generates and sends the TC to the Cardholder System, from where it is forwarded to the Merchant Server (steps 10/11). The TC will be held with the *PI* and acts analogously to the receipt in a conventional payment system. The Merchant Server can later send a batch of TCs, with the corresponding *PI*s, to the Acquirer. The issuer will verify the MAC in the TC and compare the information in the TC with that in the *PI*. If they match, the payment is accepted and processed.

Offline decline. If the transaction is declined offline, the IC card generates an AAC which is sent to the Cardholder System where it will be forwarded to the Merchant Server (steps 10/11). The merchant can store the AAC with the *PI* for card management purposes, and the transaction now ends.

Online processing. If the IC card decides that online authorisation is needed, it generates an ARQC which is forwarded to the Merchant Server via the Cardholder System (steps 10/11). The Merchant Server then sends the ARQC with the *PI* to the Acquirer and thence to the issuer (step 12). The issuer responds to the ARQC with an ARPC (step 13). The Script Processing may also now be performed by the issuer, to send command scripts to the IC card (steps 14/15). The transaction will be accepted or declined according to the ARPC. If it is accepted, the IC card generates a TC (step 16) and the process previously described under offline approval is performed. Similarly, if the transaction is declined, the IC card generates an AAC (step 16). The TC or AAC is then forwarded to the Merchant Server (step 17) and the transaction processing ends.

3.3 Security Services

We now describe how the desired security services are provided.

Authentication. Cardholder and IC card authentication are provided in the same way as in 'standard' EMV. Cardholder authentication is based on knowledge of a PIN. IC card authentication uses SDA and DDA. Merchant Server authentication, however, is not provided in the protocol.

Confidentiality and integrity. Although the entered PIN is not encrypted, its confidentiality and integrity are protected since it never leaves the environment over which the cardholder has control. AC integrity is guaranteed by the use of MACs, as in the EMV specifications. Nevertheless, AC confidentiality is not provided by the protocol. Unlike in a conventional EMV environment, it is transmitted over an unprotected link, i.e. the Internet. Therefore, it is possible for an eavesdropper to learn the card details contained in the ACs.

Non-repudiation. A measure of Cardholder non-repudiation is provided by the TC. The existence of a valid TC provides evidence that the cardholder authentication process has taken place, and hence the cardholder has consented to the transaction by entering his/her PIN. By contrast, merchant non-repudiation is not provided, although the value of such a service is unclear.

4 Threat Analysis

In the protocol, there are five locations where the transaction data is at risk. These are the Cardholder System, the card reader, the link between the two, the Internet link between Cardholder System and Merchant Server, and the Merchant Server. Threats to the Merchant Server-Acquirer link are outside the scope of this paper, since such threats apply equally to conventional use of an EMV card, and we only consider here threats introduced by 'remote EMV'. Also, since physical access to the Cardholder System, the card reader, and their link is limited to the cardholder, the cardholder is the only threat to them.

Therefore we divide our threat analysis into three parts, namely threats to the cardholder environment, threats on the Internet link, and threats at the Merchant Server. In each case, the possible types of transaction data which may be at risk are considered, along with the entities who may pose a threat. There are six types of transaction data that need to be examined, namely the Static Authentication Data (SAD), PI, IAC, $S_{IC}(DAD)$, PIN, and four ACs. Note, however, that integrity threats to $S_{IC}(DAD)$ and the four ACs are minimal since they are cryptographically protected using 'standard' EMV techniques. We thus focus most of our attention on the SAD, PI, IAC, and PIN.

Threats at the cardholder system. We refer to the combination of Cardholder System, card reader, and link between the two, as the cardholder environment. The SAD, PI, IAC, $S_{IC}(DAD)$, PIN, and four ACs pass through this environment. However, cardholder threats to the SAD, IAC, $S_{IC}(DAD)$, and PIN are not serious since the cardholder has the card and knows the PIN.

A malicious cardholder can modify the PI to make the Cardholder System send a smaller transaction value to the card than specified by the Merchant

Server. However, the fraud will be detected as soon as the AC arrives at the Merchant Server. As a result, modifying the PI yields little to the cardholder. More seriously, because the Merchant Server does not have the MAC key necessary to verify the ACs, the Merchant Server cannot determine if the ACs received are authentic. Modifying the ARQC and the ARPC will yield no gain since they are sent online to the issuer, and altering the AAC is also unattractive for the cardholder because it yields nothing financially. However, an unscrupulous cardholder can modify or replace an offline-approved TC sent from the IC card, thereby causing the payment capture to fail at a later stage.

However, this risk also exists in the conventional EMV environment. Special equipment could be used to interfere with the communications between the POS terminal and the IC card. As in our scheme, the equipment could replace or modify the TC so that the MAC becomes invalid. A possible way to address this threat is to delay DDA until the TC is generated, and then include the TC in the DAD signed by the card. The Merchant Server can verify the card public key and signature, using the issuer public key, thereby guaranteeing the authenticity of the TC. Including the TC in the DAD should not be a problem in the future, since such a process is supported by the latest version of the EMV specifications (see Section 6.6 of [2]).

Threats to the Internet link. The transaction data at risk on the Internet link are the SAD, IAC, PI, and the four ACs. The main threat here is a third party eavesdropper (passive or active). From a third party point of view, modifying the four types of transaction data is possible but also detectable, and there is little possibility for financial gain. The only benefit may be to deny service, a threat that always exists when using a public network.

A threat does arise from the way SAD is authenticated. Only the issuer signature on the static data is verified. Therefore, it is possible for an attacker to replay the SAD and pass the SDA process. Nevertheless, if DDA is performed, the attacker will not be able to generate a valid $S_{IC}(DAD)$ and hence cannot complete the transaction process.

Reading the four Cryptograms can provide an attacker with the card/account details. However, if the proposed protocol is in use, an EMV card and the corresponding PIN are required to complete a transaction. As a result, knowing only the account/card number is not so useful. If confidentiality of the ACs is a concern, a way to reduce the threat is to employ a secure channel such as TLS or HTTPS to protect the Internet link. This is a cheap, user-transparent and simple solution, since the technology is already widely available (and widely used). Use of TLS can also provide other security services such as additional integrity checks and Merchant Server authentication.

Threats at the Merchant Server. The transaction data available at the Merchant Server are the SAD, IAC, PI, and the ACs. The Merchant Server is either the legitimate recipient or the generator of the four types of data. There is thus no serious threat to data confidentiality. There is also no obvious financial gain for the merchant from breaching data integrity. The ARQC and the ARPC will be sent online to the Issuer, and the TC and the PI will also be checked by the issuer. If any modification is detected, the payment capture or authorisation process will fail. It is also clear that there is no point in modifying the SAD or the IAC since doing so will simply interrupt the transaction process.

5   Advantages and Disadvantages

Using EMV cards to make a remote payment may compromise certain EMV security elements. A POS system has the advantage of face-to-face interactions as well as use of a tamper-resistant POS terminal. By contrast, Internet transactions involve no face-to-face interactions, and the terminal, here a combination of card reader, Cardholder System and Merchant Server, is clearly not tamper-resistant. Indeed, certain data which would be sent via internal communications in an EMV POS terminal, are sent via the Internet in the proposed scheme.

The proposed protocol enhances the security of existing Internet payment methods, typically relying on SSL/TLS for transaction security. There are known security risks with such an approach, including lack of cardholder authentication [6]. Our scheme provides cardholder authentication by using EMV PIN verification. The PIN is also associated with the IC card such that without the correct PIN the card will not work and hence no transaction can be made.

A major advantage of the scheme is that it uses existing technologies. This include the EMV PKI established by the card brands and the issuers, and the EMV cards themselves. Moreover, the scheme reduces the online authorisation overhead because the IC card can make some decisions offline. Using an IC card remotely does requires special software (e.g. an applet) to be installed in the cardholder PC. An IC card reader is also needed. Nevertheless, use of the proposed scheme is 'light' compared to the SET initialisation process.

The protocol does rely on Cardholder System integrity, since the Cardholder System could be modified by a malicious cardholder to send a bogus TC or by an unscrupulous merchant to display different payment information to the cardholder from that sent to the IC card. Another weakness of the proposed protocol may be that confidentiality of the card details is not provided; the Cryptograms are transmitted over the Internet and hence may be intercepted. However, as described above, a secure channel can be used in combination with the protocol to protect the transaction data en route.

6   Conclusions and Directions for Future Research

In this paper, we have proposed a way to use an EMV-compliant IC card for e-commerce transactions. In the scheme, a user card reader and PC (the Cardholder System) together with the Merchant Server collectively take the role of the EMV Merchant Terminal. Most of the transaction procedures are similar to those in the EMV specification. Although some of the EMV security requirements are compromised, the proposed scheme can be seen as a step towards enhancing the existing SSL/TLS enabled electronic transaction processing.

The most closely related work is probably the scheme described in an annex of [3]. This scheme combines SET with EMV-compliant IC cards to conduct Internet transactions. However, as discussed in the Introduction, there remain serious obstacles to the use of SET.

GeldKarte [7] is an electronic cash card developed by the German banking industry. GeldKarte applications have also been extended to Internet uses, allowing the cardholder to use the value in the card to buy things from the Internet as well as to enhance the security of Internet transactions. However GeldKarte is clearly different from the proposed protocol since it is an electronic cash scheme.

To reduce the trust required in the Cardholder System, and prevent any attacks by malicious cardholders, a trusted card reader with a simple user interface such as a PIN pad and small display could be used. It is interesting to consider to what degree the risks of a remote EMV transaction could be reduced by using such a trusted card reader, and this is a possible topic for future research. How payment schemes might best be designed to use such a trusted card reader is also a possible future research topic. Finally, a further possible research area relates to mobile-commerce (m-commerce). It would be interesting to see how the proposed protocol could enhance the security of m-commerce by using a mobile phone as both the IC card reader and the Cardholder System.

References

1. EMV. *EMV 2000 Integrated Circuit Card Specification for Payment Systems Version 4.0 — Book 1: Application Independent IC Card to Terminal Interface Requirements*. EMVCo, 2000.
2. EMV. *EMV 2000 Integrated Circuit Card Specification for Payment Systems Version 4.0 — Book 2: Security and Key Management*. EMVCo, 2000.
3. EMV. *EMV 2000 Integrated Circuit Card Specification for Payment Systems Version 4.0 — Book 3: Application Specification*. EMVCo, 2000.
4. EMV. *EMV 2000 Integrated Circuit Card Specification for Payment Systems Version 4.0 — Book 4: CardHolder, Attendant, and Acquirer Interface Requirements*. EMVCo, 2000.
5. SETCo. *Secure Electronic Transaction Specification — Books 1–4*. SETCo, 1997.
6. L. D. Stein. *Web Security: A step-by-step reference guide*. Addison Wesley, 1999.
7. R. Keller, G. Zavagli, J. Hartmann, F. Williams. *Mobile Electronic Commerce: Research investigation into loading and paymnet functionality in wireless wallets*. available at http://citeseer.nj.nec.com/cs, 1998.

Standardized Payment Procedures as Key Enabling Factor for Mobile Commerce

Nina Kreyer[1], Key Pousttchi[2], and Klaus Turowski[2]

[1] University of Augsburg, Chair of Business Information Systems (Wirtschaftsinformatik I), Universitaetsstrasse 16, 86135 Augsburg, Germany, phone: +49 (821) 598-4138, fax: -4225, nina.kreyer@wiwi.uni-augsburg.de
[2] University of Augsburg, Chair of Business Information Systems (Wirtschaftsinformatik II), Universitaetsstrasse 16, 86135 Augsburg, Germany, phone: +49 (821) 598-4431, fax: -4432, {key.pousttchi, klaus.turowski}@wiwi.uni-augsburg.de

Abstract. Companies are not going to invest into the development of innovative applications or services unless these can be charged for appropriately. Thus, the existence of standardized and widely accepted mobile payment procedures is crucial for successful business-to-customer mobile commerce. In this paper we reflect on the acceptance of mobile payment and examine the characteristics of current mobile payment procedures. The outcomes of the paper are a categorization of current mobile payment procedures with *strategic, participation* and *operational* criteria and, based on these results, the derivation of the five mobile payment standard types *prepaid, mobile money, conventional settlement, premium rate number* and *dual-card.* Finally, a prospect is given to possible further development of mobile payment procedures in the direction of an integrative universal mobile payment system (UMPS).

Keywords: Mobile payment, electronic payment, mobile commerce, mobile added values, universal mobile payment system, UMPS

1 Introduction

The ever growing number of mobile phone users as target group represents an enormous potential for mobile commerce (MC) as a new level of electronic commerce (EC). So far, mobile applications are mostly still the transformation of conventional Internet applications or EC business models on mobile devices. But in order to be successful (and thus gain profits) in a MC setting, this is not sufficient. Added values are necessary.

For purposes of this paper, we define EC as any kind of business transaction, in the course of which transaction partners employ electronic means of communication, may it be for initiation, arrangement or realization of performance (cf. [2]). We define MC as a subset of these, on condition that at least one side uses mobile communication techniques.

Typical mobile added values originate from ubiquity, context-sensitivity, identifying functions or command and control functions of MC applications (cf. [10] and the extension introduced in [17]). To realize their potential, a new technical infrastructure is needed, e.g. allowing "always-on" functionality through package-oriented data transmission. While the forthcoming availability of GPRS (Generalized Packet Radio Service) and UMTS (Universal Mobile Telecommunications System) in

K. Bauknecht, A M. Tjoa, G. Quirchmayr (Eds.): EC-Web 2002, LNCS 2455, pp. 400–409, 2002.
© Springer-Verlag Berlin Heidelberg 2002

Europe will solve this shortcoming, another major problem still remains unsolved: the availability of adequate payment procedures. Since companies are not going to invest into the development of innovative applications or services unless these can be charged for appropriately, the existence of standardized and widely accepted mobile payment (MP) procedures is crucial.

This is especially true for business-to-customer (B2C) MC, for which reason we focus on B2C MP in this paper. The customer-to-customer (C2C) variant itself may perhaps not be a good deal for the payment provider. But as it provides an added value for the customer and thus, an incentive for usage and spreading of a MP procedure, C2C MP is to be examined along with B2C MP. For special target groups, C2C MP could be the main reason to use a MP procedure, e.g. for young people with high affinity to technology, but without own income.

We define MP as a subset of MC, which deals with the completion of payment. We focus therein not on technical issues or the clearing process, but on the payment interface to the customer. As is shown later, MP is crucial for, but not limited to MC scenarios. On the contrary, usability of a MP procedure in scenarios other than MC is relevant for its acceptance.

After a reflection on the issue of acceptance, characteristics of MP procedures are identified, classified and MP standard types are derived. Based on these results, major shortcomings of existing solutions are explained and opportunities for their improvement are shown.

Whenever we talk in this paper about a general payment method such as credit card usage, electronic payment or MP, we refer to the term *payment systems*. Whenever we talk about concrete solutions such as Paybox, Paysafecard or Sonera Mobile Pay, we refer to the term *payment procedures*.

2 Acceptance of MP

2.1 General Acceptance

The examination of the development of payment procedures in the past shows that the key to acceptance is in the hands of customers (cf. [9], [16]).

In the course of a study on mobile banking, Speedfacts Online Research interviewed about 16.500 Internet users about their payment preferences if away. On the issue of general acceptance, about two third stated that they will surely or can imagine paying with their mobile phone; more than half stated that they will surely or can imagine making money transfers with their mobile phone. The most significant acceptance was ascertained with persons already using electronic banking (cf. [19]). On the issue of the preferred payment method if away, the mobile phone would already be preferred by about a quarter of the interviewees for micropayments (less than 2.50 €), a third for macropayments from 2.50 € up to 50 €, a fifth for macropayments from 50 € up to 250 € and anyhow by 13% for amounts over 250€. In the segment between 12.50 € and 50 € paying by mobile phone would be the most preferred method.

These numbers cannot implicitly be extrapolated on the whole target group of mobile device users, because the average Internet user may tend to show more affinity to technology than the average user of a mobile device (who often just uses phone functionality). Nevertheless it can be concluded a tendency showing that general preconditions for an acceptance of MP by the customer are good. But the decisive factor for a market breakthrough is the acceptance and actual usage of concrete MP procedures.

This consideration allows us to identify a major failure risk in the transformation of general MP acceptance into this concrete acceptance and usage.

2.2 Acceptance of Individual Payment Procedures

If, as we concluded in chapter 2.1, the key is in the hands of customers and a general acceptance of MP can be stated at least in a significant part of the target group, this leads us to the question on determinants influencing the acceptance of a single MP procedure by the customer. Furthermore, other participants (above all, merchants) will only be able to follow customer preferences up to a defined point, where disadvantages overweigh significantly the advantages.

It is already much said about this issue of acceptance (cf. e.g. [18], [8], [1]). In our point of view most of the arguments can be subsumed to the categories

- *cost* (which includes direct transaction cost and fixed cost of usage as well as cost for technical infrastructure on the part of the customer, e.g. a new mobile phone perhaps necessary, and the merchant, e.g. the integration of the payment solution in his existing IT infrastructure),

- *security* (which includes not only integrity, authorization, authentication, confidentiality and non-repudiation of transactions, but also the issue of subjective security from the viewpoint of the customer),

- *convenience* (which includes e.g. ease and comfort of use as well as the attainment of concrete benefits through the use).

For the latter, it is important that a procedure is not limited to MC scenarios, but can be used in as many as possible other settings, too. Briefly: It should be possible to use the procedure whenever, wherever and for whatever kind of payment the user wants to.

2.3 Relevant M-payment Scenarios

Brokat calls the different payment settings "r-world", "e-world" and "m-world" (cf. [8]). We will distinguish them a little more precisely and, for the reasons mentioned in chapter 1, add the C2C scenario.

This leads us to four general scenarios for the usage of MP: the *mobile commerce scenario*, the *electronic commerce scenario*, the *stationary merchant scenario* and the *customer-to-customer scenario* (cf. table 1). We also note that in different settings MP also is competing to different other payment systems. In this connection, we already treated a comparison with competing systems for the stationary merchant scenario in chapter 2.1 and furthermore noted the high influence of the amount level on this competition.

Table 1. Relevant MP scenarios

Scenario	Description/Example	Competing payment
mobile commerce scenario	new applications and services, e.g. context-sensitive information	- - -
electronic commerce scenario	all kinds of B2C EC excluding MC, e.g. purchase of goods or content via the Internet	offline debit-/credit card e-payment
stationary merchant scenario	classical "face-to-face" commerce, e.g. purchase in a supermarket, usage of a ticket machine, taxi	cash debit-/credit card
customer-to-customer scenario	money transfers between individuals, e.g. pocket-money for children, settling debts for small amounts	(cash) (offline)

The distinction of these scenarios is not only important for the examination of different payment procedures and the derivation of standard types in chapters 3 and 4, but also for a strategy of market entry and its conclusions on the construction of payment procedures. For a brief look on these issues, cf. [9].

We claimed in chapter 1, that MP is thus crucial for, but not limited to MC scenarios. We will see later, that in any payment scenario there is at least some MP procedure that makes sense and that there are several MP procedures usable in more than one payment scenario.

Before we use these payment scenarios, it is useful to give a short reflection on the relevance of the usability in each of the payment scenarios for the diffusion process of the procedure.

- *Mobile commerce scenario.* As we stated above, MP allows unfolding MC's potential. But as MC itself represents only low revenue rates up to now, it is questionable if customers accept a MP procedure just to possibly use it sometimes in a MC setting. The dilemma could arise that nobody uses a MP procedure because it is limited to MC and nobody uses MC because there is no widely accepted MP procedure.

- *Electronic commerce scenario.* In opposite to MC, EC already represents a good revenue potential today. But the payment problem remains still unsolved and most transactions are paid through offline methods such as money transfer after delivery, debit procedures or credit card (cf. e.g. [18], [23]), with obvious disadvantages. On the other hand, we saw that the acceptance potential for MP among Internet users is already high (cf. chapter 2.1) and that this target group could be very interesting for MC.

- *Stationary merchant scenario.* As we illustrated in chapter 2.1, there also is a good acceptance potential for MP as new mean of payment in this scenario, especially for low to medium macropayments (2.50€ to 50€). The revenue potential is definitely the highest of the four scenarios. But it remains uncertain not only if the average mobile phone user is the right target group for a pioneer application like MP, but also if it will be possible to convince traditional merchants of a payment procedure without a significant number of people already using it, thus, demanding him to accept it.

- *Customer-to-customer scenario.* The opportunity to transfer money from customer to customer represents mostly an incentive for usage and spreading of a MP procedure. Although for special target groups, C2C MP may be the main reason to use a MP procedure; this is unlikely for the average user (cf. chapter 1).

3 Typical Characteristics of MP Procedures

In order to distinguish different types of MP solutions – and thus unambiguously identify any given payment procedure - the characterization of significant differences in MP systems is crucial. Besides analyzing if a MP procedure works within a certain payment scenario (cf. chapter 2.3) it is also necessary to decide whether it can be used to cost-efficiently settle micro-, macro- or picopayments (cf. [6], [22]). Since within most MP procedures a variety of different stakeholders, such as merchants, telecommunication providers (telcos), banks or financial service providers (e.g. credit card companies), specialized intermediaries and old economy companies are joined, their roles and objectives have to be analyzed. Telcos may e.g. operate the technical infrastructure and be involved in the payment process as well, e.g. when they offer billing services or operate a MP procedure (cf. [20]). Since the customer will finally decide about the establishment of payment procedures (cf. chapter 2.1, [9], [16]), customer specific topics, such as the need for a pre-registration or the technology required to use a MP procedure, have to be examined. While most current MP procedures are based on simple message exchange via short-messaging-services (SMS) or the wireless application protocol (WAP), some MP procedures require dual-slot or dual –chip-phones. Some MP procedures even require the installation of special software tools, e.g. to create digital coins. The MP procedures themselves are either token or account-based. Within token-based procedures virtual cash, representing (fractions of) "real" money, is exchanged whereas account-based procedures settle payments via the customers settlement-account. The payments are either deducted via prepaid, instant-paid or post-paid methods and may be settled via various payment methods such as prepaid-cards, digital wallets, direct debiting, offline payments, credit cards or phone bills. For a more detailed analysis of the instances mentioned above cf. [9]. According to these results the main characteristics of MP procedures and their instances can be combined. In table 2 we do this following the morphological method (cf. [24]).

Table 2. Morphological box of MP characteristics and instances

characteristic		instances					
Strategic	payment scenarios	MC	EC	Stationary merchant		C2C	
	payment heights	picopayments		micropayments		macropayments	
Participants	involved parties	customer	merchant	telco	bank/FSP	spec. intermediary	old econom y
	receiver of customer data	merchant	telco		bank/FSP	spec. intermediary	none
	pre-registration needed?	yes			no		
Operational	technology required	SMS		WAP	dual-slot/dual-card phone	special payment software	
	basis of payment	account-based			token-based		
	payment frequency	pay per time unit		pay per product unit		subscription	
	deduction time	prepaid		instant-paid		post-paid	
	method for settlement	smart cards/ prepaid cards	electronic cash/ digital wallet	direct debiting	offline payment	credit card	tele-phone bill

4   Derivation of MP Standard Types

4.1   General Remarks

As we have shown in chapter 3, a broad variety of characteristics is necessary to classify a MP procedure. The examination of current MP procedures (cf. e.g. [6], [9]) shows that neither these and their properties are evenly distributed within the scheme, nor typical patterns are existing which are valid over all of the relevant characteristics. Therefore, we cannot decompose the box in clusters and have to state the absence of accurately definable disjoint types. Anyhow, we can identify single instances of the shown characteristics as respectively constituent for a significant group of MP procedures. These groups *prepaid*, *mobile money*, *premium rate number*, *conventional settlement* and *dual-card* represent different concepts, but are not totally disjoint. Any of the current MP procedures can be ranked in (at least) one of the groups. We term these groups as *standard types of MP procedures* or *MP standard types*.

4.2 The Prepaid Standard Type

The *prepaid standard type* is defined by the instance *prepaid* of the characteristic *deduction time*.

Typical use are micro- and lower macropayments in the EC and MC scenario. Prepaid procedures are either based on pre-registration and a rechargeable account or on a prepaid card which contains a code number and is bought in a store. Up to now, the latter is the only possibility to realize the instance *none* for *receiver of customer data*, thus, to realize anonymous payment.

Because of the inherent budget restriction and prove of solvency, prepaid procedures are particularly suitable for minors or young people without own income.

So far, no prepaid-card system has evolved within MC payment procedures. However, this seems to be a question of marketing because the use of these procedures is principally already possible. A reason may be the low revenue rates in the MC scenario up to now.

Samples for the *prepaid standard type* are Paysafecard (cf. [15]), MicroMoney (cf. [11]) and Mobilix (cf. [12]).

4.3 The Mobile Money Standard Type

The *mobile money standard type* is defined by the instance *token-based* of the characteristic *basis of payment*.

This type, using digital coins or wallets, can be considered as a subtype of prepaid procedures, but represents an own weighty concept and principally can exist outside of this superordinate group (and perhaps will do so for future MP procedures). For this reason, we adequate it with the other groups as a separate standard type.

After various attempts to place token-based electronic payment procedures have failed (such as eCash supported by Deutsche Bank in Germany), the development in this domain has slowed down. Up to now, no MP procedure of this standard type is in use.

For future applications, mobile money could be especially interesting for the stationary merchant scenario, where payment with digital coins from a mobile device could e.g. be carried out via Bluetooth at the point of sale in a store, at a vending machine or in a taxi.

A sample for the *mobile money standard type* is FairCash (cf. [7]), which is still in a development state.

4.4 The Premium Rate Number Standard Type

The *premium rate number standard type* is defined by the instance *telephone bill* of the characteristic *method for settlement*.

This type covers the call of premium rate numbers for obtaining a code via voice interface as well as premium rate SMS and the settlement of specially labeled data packets for value added services.

The type is characterized through the dominant role of the telecommunication provider. A settlement over the already existing billing relationship is especially interesting for the MC scenario. While this is univocally true for value added services, it can be problematic for other services or for physical goods, since in a number of countries legal restrictions prohibit the settlement of services others than telecommunication-related ones via the telephone bill (requirement of a bank license).

For mobile phone subscribers using prepaid cards, the premium rate number type coincidences with the prepaid type.

The *premium rate number standard type* is carried out by nearly any telecommunication provider. A particular sample for a MP procedure based on this is Sonera Mobile Pay (cf. [6], [3]), an interesting example for the settlement of value added services provides i-mode (cf. [5], [3]).

4.5 The Conventional Settlement Standard Type

The *conventional settlement standard type* is defined by the instance *direct debiting* and/or *credit card* of the characteristic *method for settlement.*

This type covers any procedure which is just using an interface on a mobile device to access a conventional mean of payment such as direct debiting or credit card. The interface can be based either on voice or on a data transmission solution.

The type is characterized through the dominant role of a specialized intermediary. But since it is based on conventional settlement, it is in truth bank/FSP-centered. Thus, the relations between the specialized intermediaries and the banks/FSP merit closer examination in the future.

Samples for the *conventional settlement standard type* are Paybox (cf. [13], [4]), the former Payitmobile (cf. [6]), Street Cash (cf. [21]) and PayPal (cf. [14]).

4.6 The Dual-Card Standard Type

The *dual-card standard type* is defined by the instance *dual-slot/dual-card phone* of the characteristic *technology required.*

This type, using either dual-slot or dual-SIM technology for security or other issues, can presently be considered as a subtype of conventional settlement procedures. But like the *mobile money standard type* in chapter 4.3, it represents an own weighty concept and principally can exist out of conventional settlement, wherefore we adequate it with the other groups as a separate standard type.

In addition to using the chip of the user's standard credit card to carry out a MP procedure with a dual-slot phone, another particularly interesting concept could be the use of dual-card in combination with digital coins and conventional settlement, which could potentially allow for an innovative procedure to generate digital coins on a mobile device for instantaneous disposal, where the generation of the coin uses an online debit procedure with the customer's bank.

Dual-card/dual-slot solutions are playing also an important role in current developments in the field of mobile banking (especially for mobile signatures).

Present samples for the *dual-card standard type* are Iti Achat and EMPS (cf. [3]).

5 Conclusions and Perspectives

In this paper we reflected on the acceptance of MP and examined the characteristics of current MP procedures.

As the outcome of the paper we presented a scheme with strategic, participation and operational criteria which allows us to unambiguously identify and characterize any given MP procedure and, based on these results, introduced the MP standard types prepaid, mobile money, premium rate number, conventional settlement and dual-card.

In chapter 2.1, we characterized the starting conditions for MP as good and identified the decisive point in the transformation of this general interest of users into their everyday usage of concrete MP procedures.

We did not find an "ideal" procedure type who fits all needs and do not believe that we will see one in the future. A possible solution, however, would be MP procedures which aggregate two or more of the standard types, making it possible for the customer to use their advantages without giving up too much convenience. On the other hand, widely accepted standardization in the field of MP procedures' interfaces would be hard to accomplish and is not in sight.

A more global approach could be the development of an integrative universal mobile payment system (UMPS) based on an abstraction layer above the procedure level. This UMPS would have to be user-centered and allow to use any given payment procedure on any given mobile device and network with any given merchant and financial service provider interface.

A respective solution would allow maintaining the variety of existing MP procedures and the variety of mobile devices. At the same time, customers as well as merchants could be relieved of the need to occupy themselves with the payment problem for mobile solutions.

References

[1] Cheong, Y.C.; Tan, C.-L.: *Payments in Mobile Commerce.* Singapore, 2001
[2] ECOM: *Electronic Commerce – An Introduction.* Source:
     http://ecom.fov .uni-mb.si/center/ [1998, 05-15].
[3] EPSO: *ePSO Inventory DataBase.* Source:
     w.jrc.es/cfapp/invent/list.cfm [2002, 06-05].
[4] Henkel, J.: *Mobile Payment.* In: Silberer, G.; Wohlfahrt, J.; Wilhelm, T. (Hrsg.): *Mobile Commerce.* Wiesbaden, 2002.
[5] I-mode: Information available at: http://www.nttdocomo.com [2002, 06-01].
[6] Kieser, M.: *Mobile Payment – Vergleich elektronischer Zahlungssysteme.* In: Meier, A.: Mobile Commerce. Heidelberg, 2001.
[7] Kreft, H.: The FairCash System. München, 2002.
[8] Kruppa, S.: *Mobile Payment. Beyond the M-Commerce Hype.* Stuttgart, 2002.
[9] Kreyer, N.; Pousttchi, K.; Turowski, K: *Characteristics of Mobile Payment Procedures.* In: *Proceedings of the ISMIS 2002 Workshop on M-Services,* Lyon 2002.
[10] Kuhlen, R.: *Informationsmarkt: Chancen und Risiken der Kommerzialisierung von Wissen.* 2. Aufl., Konstanz, 1996.
[11] MicroMoney: Information available at: www.detecardservice.de/de /micromoney [2002, 06-01].

[12] Mobilix: Information available at:
www.pbs.dk/english/nyheder/nyheder /mobilixpress.htm [2002, 06-01].

[13] Paybox.net AG: Information available at: www.paybox.de [2002, 02-12].

[14] PayPal: Information available at: www.paypal.com [2002, 02-14].

[15] Paysafecard: Information available at: www.paysafecard.de [2002, 02-12].

[16] Pousttchi, K.; Selk, B.; Turowski, K.: *Akzeptanzkriterien für mobile Bezahlverfahren*. In: *Tagungsband zur MKWI 2002 Teilkonferenz* **Mobile und Collaborative Business**, Nürnberg, 2002.

[17] Pousttchi, K.; Selk, B.; Turowski, K.: *Enabling Mobile Commerce through Mass Customization*. Augsburg, 2002.

[18] Robben, M.: *ePayment: Alte Besen kehren noch am besten*. Available:
http://ecin.de/zahlungssysteme/epayment, 2001.

[19] Speedfacts Online Research GmbH: *mBanking – The Future of Personal Financial Transaction?* Frankfurt, 2001.

[20] Stone, A.: Working *Towards Universal Payment Solutions*. Available:
www.mcommercetimes.de [2002, 02-22].

[21] Street Cash. Information available at: www.streetcash.de [2002, 02-14].

[22] Sutherland, E.: *Minipayments Start Adding Up for Carriers*. Available:
www.mcommercetimes.de [2001, 12-04].

[23] Wiegmann, D.: *Vielfalt an Bezahlsystemen bremst E-Commerce*. dpa 2002, 03-07.

[24] Zwicky, F.: *Entdecken, Erfinden, Forschen im Morphologischen Weltbild*. München, 1966.

Some Thoughts on Research Perspectives in E-business

A Min Tjoa[1] and Gerald Quirchmayr[2,3]

[1]Vienna University of Technology
[2]University of Vienna
[3]University of South Australia

Abstract. Research perspectives in the field are still very bright, in spite of the burst of the dot.com bubble approximately a year ago. Systems grounded in solid research and providing a mature technology are starting to dominate a field that was once plagued by immature approaches. This contribution tries to give an overview of what the challenges and opportunities for research will be in this environment.

1. After the dot.com Bubble Has Burst

The initial phase of electronic commerce was characterized by an incredible boom and by a hype that substituted solid work and business planning. Technology also was very immature and led to several problems, such as frequent breaches of security. What had to come, came about a year a go – the burst of the dot.com bubble and a reorientation towards traditional solid and methodologically sound information technology. The first products representing this very positive development are secure payment standards, such as SET, and robust server technology, such as IBM's e-servers. Software is also getting more and more mature, i.e. security holes are plugged and systems are becoming more stable. Researchers can now look forward to investigating the hard and interesting questions which do admittedly request a lot of time and resources. This development is only possible because of industry and users realizing that without the solution of the underlying conceptual problems, there will never be a sound e-business environment.

2. On the Way to Amore Mature Field

The turnaround starting from research some years ago is now also strongly developing in the IT industry. The gold rush is over and the stability and soundness of systems do again shape the market. IBM's WebSphere Application Server is perhaps the most significant success story of the last few months. A solid software package sitting on top of a robust and solid hardware infrastructure, combined with highly advanced accompanying services is again becoming the number one on the market. The best news however is that IBM is not the only company gaining back a large market share with quality products. Be it SAP, SUN, Oracle, Microsoft, or others:

K. Bauknecht, A M. Tjoa, G. Quirchmayr (Eds.): EC-Web 2002, LNCS 2455, pp. 410–411, 2002.
© Springer-Verlag Berlin Heidelberg 2002

quality products are in high demand again. There are clear signs of the field becoming mature. Quality products are one, very solid research is another, the almost complete disappearance of quick and dirty hacks is perhaps the most significant one.

3.   New Research Areas Emerging in the EC-Web Conference

EC-Web [1], [2] has always been at the forefront of research and industry since it was first held in 2000 at the University of Greenwich. This year some sessions have entered new research areas, new ideas are presented, some of them quite revolutionary. All presentations have in common that they start from a solid theoretical foundation and try to advance applications through new models and new theoretical concepts. Papers presented on architectures, applications, foundations, such as query processing and data integration, security solutions and emerging standards, business models and new ideas for e-payment show how advanced the field has become.

New areas emerging on the horizon, such as wireless network technology and new models for mobile communications, will offer a new challenge for researchers in the fields of electronic business and web-based technologies. Integration issues will become more and more demanding, from the technological as well as from the organizational perspective. Real world problems will again provide ample research topics, this time however with more realistic constraints: financial resources are not unlimited and the infrastructure built over the past years has to be made use of. Ideas and products will only be considered as valuable if they can contribute to revenue under these restrictions. The challenges and the number of research questions which have to be addressed are therefore greater than before. Stability, robustness, security, integration, user interface design and mobility are only some of the most promising areas that need to be looked into.

4.   Conclusion

The fields of electronic business and web-based technologies have changed dramatically. The economic crises caused by the burst of the dot.com bubble slowly turns into a sound environment in which quality, security, reliability and stability of systems are becoming the focus of development. It is undoubtedly research that has to take the lead in developing sound approaches that lead to systems meeting these requirements.

References

1.   Kurt Bauknecht, Sanjay Kumar Madria, Günther Pernul (Eds.): Electronic Commerce and Web Technologies, Second International Conference, EC-Web 2001 Munich, Proceedings. Lecture Notes in Computer Science. 2115 Springer 2001
2.   Kurt Bauknecht, Sanjay Kumar Madria, Günther Pernul: Electronic Commerce and Web Technologies, First International Conference, EC-Web 2000, London, Proceedings. Springer 2000

Author Index

Lecture Notes in Computer Science

For information about Vols. 1–2358
please contact your bookseller or Springer-Verlag